Handbook of Research ~~on~~ Business and Entrepreneurship

Edited by

Elizabeth Chell

Professor of Entrepreneurial Behaviour, Small Business Research Centre, Kingston Business School, Kingston University, UK; Research Consultant

Mine Karataş-Özkan

Professor in Strategy and Entrepreneurship, University of Southampton, UK

Edward Elgar
Cheltenham, UK • Northampton, MA, USA

Published by
Edward Elgar Publishing Limited
The Lypiatts
15 Lansdown Road
Cheltenham
Glos GL50 2JA
UK

Edward Elgar Publishing, Inc.
William Pratt House
9 Dewey Court
Northampton
Massachusetts 01060
USA

A catalogue record for this book
is available from the British Library

Library of Congress Control Number: 2013949792

This book is available electronically in the ElgarOnline.com
Business Subject Collection, E-ISBN 978 1 84980 924 5

ISBN 978 1 84980 923 8 (cased)

Typeset by Servis Filmsetting Ltd, Stockport, Cheshire
Printed and bound in Great Britain by T.J. International Ltd, Padstow

Contents

Figures

Tables

Contributors

Anderson, Alastair is Professor of Entrepreneurship and Director of the Centre for Entrepreneurship, Aberdeen Business School, at the Robert Gordon University, UK. His research interests include the social aspects of entrepreneurship, including social constructions of entrepreneurship, networking and social capital.

Barrett, Rowena is Professor of Human Resource Management and Head of the School of Management at Edith Cowan University, Perth, Australia. Her research centres on understanding the organisation and management of people in smaller firms.

Bird, Barbara is Professor of Management at Kogod School of Business, American University, Washington DC, USA. She is a senior editor for *Entrepreneurship Theory and Practice* and past Chair and past Historian of the Division of the Academy of Management. Her research focuses on entrepreneurs' cognition and behaviour.

Broad, Jean was a researcher employed by the University of Sheffield, UK when the original study was carried out. She worked previously with Dr Richard Thorpe at Leeds University Business School and at both institutions she focused on entrepreneurship, networking and innovation.

Byrne, Janice is an Assistant Professor of Organisational Behaviour and Human Resources at IESEG School of Management, France. Her research focuses mainly on entrepreneurship, gender and management training and development. She received her doctorate in Management from EMLYON Business School in May 2012.

Casson, Mark is Professor of Economics and Director of the Centre for Institutional Performance, University of Reading, UK. His recent publications include *The Entrepreneur in History: From Medieval Merchant to Modern Business Leader* (2013); and he was joint editor of *The History of Entrepreneurship: Innovation and Risk-taking 1200–2000* (both with Catherine Casson).

Chalmers, Dominic is Lecturer at the Hunter Centre for Entrepreneurship, Strathclyde Business School, UK. His research interests include social innovation, adsorptive capacity and the micro-foundations of innovative capabilities.

Chell, Elizabeth is Professor of Entrepreneurial Behaviour, in the Small Business Research Centre, Kingston Business School, Kingston University, UK and Research Consultant. Elizabeth retired from Southampton University where she was the director of the Institute for Entrepreneurship. Over her career she has researched many aspects of entrepreneurship in a number of industrial settings, including the entrepreneurial personality, social constructionism and entrepreneurial behaviour, gender, networking and social entrepreneurship. She first pursued the issue of paradigm framing of methodologies and the interpretivist approach to the critical incident method in the mid-1990s.

De Bruin, Anne is founding Director of the New Zealand Social Innovation and Entrepreneurship Research Centre, and Professor of Economics, in the School of Economics and Finance, Massey University, New Zealand. Her current research interests include entrepreneurship with a focus on social, creative and women's entrepreneurship, sustainable employment and regional development. She received a 2009 Fulbright New Zealand Senior Scholar Award to research entrepreneurship.

Della Giusta, Marina is Associate Professor of Economics and Head of Department of Economics, University of Reading, UK. Her research in behavioural economics focuses on conformism in social norms, values and personality and how these affect decision-making in relation to both engagement within the paid labour market and the provision of unpaid care work for children and the elderly within families. Recent work has focused on behaviour change in the context of green choices. She has also researched aspects of well being; particularly why men and women experience differences in life satisfaction, and happiness in couples. She has also researched attitudes to risk and gender.

Discua Cruz, Allan is a Lecturer of Entrepreneurship and member of the Centre for Family Business at the Institute for Entrepreneurship and Enterprise Development in the Lancaster University Management School, UK. His current research focuses on family entrepreneurial teams, entrepreneurial dynamics of families in business and entrepreneurship in developing economies in Latin America. Allan is also a visiting professor in Honduras where he contributes to national research initiatives in entrepreneurship and family business.

Fayolle, Alain, PhD, is a Professor of Entrepreneurship at EM Lyon Business School, France, where he founded and became Director of the Entrepreneurship Research Centre. His research interests cover a range of topics in the field of entrepreneurship, including principally: education and training; also corporate entrepreneurship, new venture creation process, family entrepreneurship, and opportunity and necessity entrepreneurship.

Forson, Cynthia is Head of Department of Management, Leadership and Organisation at the Hertfordshire Business School, the University of Hertfordshire, UK. Her research focuses on equality and diversity in the labour market and organisations and in particular the experience of ethnic minority women. She has published work in top journals on gender, ethnicity, class and migrant status and their intersectional influence in the lives and careers of ethnic minority people. Her work has been funded by the Equality and Human Rights Commission, the BBC, and the Royal Academy of Engineers.

Garnsey, Elizabeth is Reader in Innovation Studies, Emeritus, at the Centre for Technology Management, University of Cambridge, UK. Her current research is on university spin-outs in advanced materials, bio-pharmaceuticals and environmental innovations and effects of their growth and setbacks on local high technology clusters. Her interests include resource-based and evolutionary theory and their integration with complexity theory. Her papers have appeared in a range of top peer-reviewed journals.

Gartner, William B. is Professor of Entrepreneurship and the Art of Innovation at the Copenhagen Business School, Denmark and Visiting Professor of Entrepreneurship at

California Lutheran University, USA. He is 2005 winner of the Swedish Entrepreneurship Foundation Global Award for outstanding contributions to entrepreneurship and small business research.

Gherardi, Silvia is full Professor of Sociology of Work and Organization at the University of Trento, Italy, where she is responsible for the Research Unit on Communication, Organizational Learning and Aesthetics (RUCOLA, www.unitn.it/rucola). In 2005 she was named Doctor Honoris Causa by Roskilde University (DK), and in 2007 was appointed as Egos Honorary Member. Her research activities focus on workplace learning and knowing. Her theoretical background is in qualitative sociology, organizational symbolism, and feminist studies.

Gu, Xin, PhD, is a research fellow in the School of Culture and Communication, Faculty of Arts, University of Melbourne, Australia. Her research has spanned creative entrepreneurship, cultural economy and cultural policy in post-industrial cities. She has worked with local governments in UK and China in developing policy to support entrepreneurship in the cultural sector.

Hanke, Ralph is an Assistant Professor of Entrepreneurship at Missouri University of Science & Technology, USA. He received a PhD in Business Administration from Pennsylvania State University and has been an active member of the USASBE since 1999. His research interests include team creativity, entrepreneurial pedagogy, intra-team conflict and philosophy of organising. He has published in several top journals and in 2005 received the Best Paper Award at the Academy of Management Meeting for a paper outlining problem-based learning in the entrepreneurship classroom. He serves as Vice-chair for the Entrepreneurship Pedagogy and Teaching Group.

Holt, Robin is Professor of Organisation and Management at Liverpool University Management School, Liverpool, UK. He has worked in departments of politics and philosophy, as well as business and management, at a number of UK universities, including Southampton, Bath, Manchester Metropolitan and Leeds. His research has focused on the meanings associated with words like: value, production, good, work and wealth, and he currently researches ethics, in entrepreneurial activity and strategic practices.

Howells, Jeremy is Dean of the Faculty of Business and Law at the University of Southampton, UK. He was previously the Eddie Davis Chair of Entrepreneurship and Innovation and Executive Director at the Manchester Institute of Innovation Research (MIoIR) at the University of Manchester. He is a prolific writer and researcher in the field of innovation.

Howorth, Carole is Professor of Entrepreneurship and Family Business at Bradford University School of Management, Bradford, UK. Carole researches entrepreneurship, particularly as it relates to family businesses and social contexts of entrepreneurship and the need to balance competing objectives of family, community and business. Most recent publications have been on portfolio entrepreneurship, entrepreneurial teams, family businesses, social entrepreneurs, stewardship, trust and governance.

Jack, Sarah is Professor of Entrepreneurship at the Institute for Entrepreneurship and Enterprise Development (IEED), Lancaster University Management School (LUMS),

UK. Her research interests include the social aspects of entrepreneurship, especially social networks and social capital.

Jackson, Jacqueline is the Director of Lancaster University, UK's LEAD programme, a highly effective leadership development programme specifically designed for SMEs. Working within the Institute for Entrepreneurship and Enterprise Development (IEED), her research considers leadership and leadership identity within the context of the family business. She previously owned and operated a fourth-generation family business and acted as Vice Chairman of a retail group representing over 1300 SME operators. She now combines a wealth of practical experience with the rigours of academic research.

Jones, Oswald is Professor and Head of the Organisation and Management Group at the University of Liverpool Management School, UK and co-editor-in-chief of the *International Journal of Management Reviews*. He has published widely on the topics of entrepreneurial learning and the management of smaller firms. Current research interests concern the resourcing of start-up businesses and the nature of dynamic capabilities in family-owned firms.

Karataş-Özkan, Mine is Professor in Strategy and Entrepreneurship at the University of Southampton, UK. Her work focuses on social and diversity dimensions of entrepreneurship with an emphasis on international and sectoral perspectives. She has published her research in leading academic journals including the *British Journal of Management*, *Entrepreneurship and Regional Development* and the *International Journal of Management Reviews*.

Kerrin, Máire is a director of the Work psychology group and Visiting Lecturer at City University, London, UK. She previously worked as a senior Consultant with the Institute of Employment Studies and has held a number of academic posts, including Senior Lecturer in Organisational Psychology, at City University and Nottingham University Business School, UK.

Lévesque, Moren is a Professor and the Certified General Accountants of Ontario Chair in International Entrepreneurship at the Schulich School of Business, York University, Toronto, Canada. Her research applies the methodologies of analytical and quantitative disciplines to the study of decision-making in new business formation. Moren is a senior editor at *Production and Operations Management* and department editor for *Technology & Innovation Management at the IEEE Transactions on Engineering Management*.

Lubik, Sarah is a Lecturer in Entrepreneurship and Innovation at the Beedie School of Business, Simon Fraser University, Canada. Her research focuses on university spin-outs, incubation, innovation ecosystems and the commercialization of advanced technologies. She is also a certified business coach and the marketing director of a high-tech start-up. Her work has been published in a number of top journals, including *Technovation*, *R&D Management*, and the *Journal of Manufacturing Technology Management*.

Macpherson, Allan is an Associate Professor of Management at University of Wisconsin – La Crosse, USA. He has published a range of articles investigating the evolution of business knowledge and learning from crises in entrepreneurship. His current research projects focus on learning, dynamic capabilities and growth in new businesses and barriers to learning during and after crisis events within UK and US fire services.

McKeever, Edward is Research Fellow at the Institute for Entrepreneurship and Enterprise Development (IEED), Lancaster University Management School (LUMS), UK. After a career in small business and economic development Ed McKeever undertook a PhD in the role of networks and social capital in entrepreneurship. From his anthropological background he is particularly interested in how entrepreneurs engage socially with their surroundings.

Mayson, Susan is in the Department of Management, Monash University, Australia. Dr Mayson's research focuses on human resource management and employment relations in small and medium-sized firms. She co-edited the *International Handbook of Entrepreneurship and HRM* with Professor Rowena Barrett in 2008. She is currently researching SMEs' responses to regulation, in particular, work health and safety regulation.

Minniti, Maria is Professor and Bantle Chair of Entrepreneurship and Public Policy at the Whitman School of Management of Syracuse University and holds a PhD in Economics from New York University, USA. She is field editor of economics for the *Journal of Business Venturing* and associate editor for the *Small Business Economics Journal*. She is currently working on the relationship between institutions and entrepreneurship.

Özbilgin, Mustafa is Professor in Organisational Behaviour at Brunel University, London, UK and serves as co-chair of Diversity Management at the Université Paris Dauphine, France and is a visiting Professor of Management at Koc, University of Istanbul, Turkey. His work is on equality, diversity and discrimination at work from comparative and international perspectives.

Ozturk, Mustafa Bilgehan is Senior Lecturer in Management, Middlesex University Business School, UK. His research interests include equality, diversity and inclusion issues at work, qualitative methods in business research and gender and entrepreneurship.

Patterson, Fiona is Professor and Principal Researcher at the University of Cambridge, UK, Department of Psychology and Visiting Professor of Social Sciences for the Interdisciplinary Centre for Creativity in Professorial Practice at City University, London, UK. She is founding Director of the Work Psychology Group, a research-led occupational psychology consultancy.

Perrotta, Manuela is a lecturer in the School of Business and Management, Queen Mary University, London, UK. Her research falls between Organisation Studies and Science and Technology. Her main research interests concern the relations among learning, work and innovation in organisations.

Pittaway, Luke is Professor of Entrepreneurship, Ohio University, USA where he is Director of the Center for Entrepreneurship. He was previously William A. Freeman Distinguished Chair in Free Enterprise, Georgia Southern University where he was also the Director of the Center for Entrepreneurial Learning and Leadership. In this role he led the development of entrepreneurship education within the College of Business, across the university and for local entrepreneurs. He also holds a part-time Chair in

Entrepreneurship at Swansea University, UK. His research expertise is in entrepreneurship education and learning and he has published in leading journals on these subjects.

Rauch, Andreas is Professor of Entrepreneurship and Regional Enterprises at the Leuphana University of Luneburg, Germany and Senior Lecturer at Exeter Business School, UK. His research focuses on psychological approaches to entrepreneurship. He is an appointed editor of *Entrepreneurship: Theory and Practice* and on the review board of the *Journal of Business Venturing*.

Schjoedt, Leon earned a PhD from the University of Colorado at Boulder and is an associate Professor of Management at Judd Leighton School of Business and Economics, Indiana University South Bend, Indiana, USA. His research focuses on entrepreneurial behaviour: the intersection of entrepreneurship and organisational behaviour.

Shaw, Eleanor is Professor of Entrepreneurship and Principal Investigator, the Centre for Charitable Giving & Philanthropy, the Hunter Centre for Entrepreneurship, Strathclyde Business School, UK. Her research in diversity includes social entrepreneurship, entrepreneurial philanthropy, and women's entrepreneurship. She is a research affiliate of the New Zealand Social Innovation and Entrepreneurship Research Centre.

Spence, Laura J. is Professor of Business Ethics and Director of the Centre for Research into Sustainability at Royal Holloway University, London, UK. She specialises in research on small business social responsibility and ethics. She is an editor of the *Journal of Business Ethics* and has co-edited several books including *Ethics in SMEs: A Global Commentary* and *Corporate Social Responsibility: Readings and Cases in a Global Context* (2nd edn). She has also published articles in a variety of top journals.

Tatli, Ahu is a Senior Lecturer in the School of Business and Management, Queen Mary University of London, UK. The focus of her research is equality and diversity at work. Her empirical research explores the strategies of key equality actors, the intersectionality of disadvantage and privilege in organisational settings, diversity management, agency and change in organisations, and inequality in recruitment and employment. She has published widely in top peer-reviewed journals and edited collections, and practitioner and policy outlets.

Toutain, Olivier is a permanent faculty member in the Management and Entrepreneurship department at ESC Dijon Burgogne, France. He successfully completed his PhD entitled 'Experiential learning and meta-cognition in Entrepreneurship Education' at the University of Lyon 3 in 2010. He is a research associate and active member of EMLYON's Entrepreneurship Research Centre and has over ten years' experience of teaching and training entrepreneurship at various institutions and levels across France.

Yavuz, Cagla is a Doctoral Researcher at the University of Southampton, UK. Her research focus is on institutional entrepreneurship in higher education.

1. Introduction to the handbook
Elizabeth Chell and Mine Karataş-Özkan

Entrepreneurship is a relatively young field; arguably, it is progressing through ado-lescence, struggling with issues of its identity, with how it is perceived and valued. This may be a contentious statement, but relative to other social sciences, for example, economics, entrepreneurship is perhaps ill-defined and still developing its theoretical base which has yet to be stoutly tested through sound empirical research. The Academy of Management views entrepreneurship as a division not a discipline and likewise the British Academy of Management categorises it as an area of special interest; this despite the scope of entrepreneurship. Entrepreneurship has only two four-star-rated journals in which scholars may publish their work; the alternative is to publish in lower-rated journals in the field or in journals from the mainstream disciplines. Hence, this series of handbooks published by Edward Elgar is potentially a significant milestone; a marker which may help scholars reflect on how far the subject has come, and where further inter-disciplinary research may be usefully carried out to help solidify the knowledge base that is entrepreneurship.

Scholarship in entrepreneurship has grown significantly since the mid-1990s. Over the years we have witnessed disputed territory of how it is defined, its disciplinary bases, the language in which it is couched, the unit of analysis upon which researchers should focus their attention, and a tussle over paradigmatic approaches. Despite interesting and original contributions from across the globe, the field of entrepreneurship has been dom-inated by Anglo-American perspectives and hence academic production in associated journals. This volume deliberately highlights all these issues on which we as researchers may reflect and learn, and advance the field by questioning prevailing, indeed dominant, assumptions, historically internalised research practices and perspectives with a focus on inclusivity and rigour in scientific endeavour, and its impact on society and economy. Although there is considerable new work produced and published in the area, we should never forget that as scholars we aim to stand on the shoulders of other great thinkers so that we can see further. As Alvarez and Barney (2013) have pointed out in a recent paper, for entrepreneurship to stand as a unique subject domain, it needs to generate theories that delineate things in other disciplines in ways that scholars in those disciplines have not done previously. This entails a more reflexive approach and theorising from an empirical evidence base.

This series of *Handbooks in Entrepreneurship* produced by Edward Elgar facilitates an important task in scholarship, that of reviewing, reflecting upon and presenting the state of the art of our subject. Entrepreneurship is potentially vast, multi-faceted and complex, so much so that we can each only claim expert knowledge in a narrow segment. However, we do need to be able to see the bigger picture and in doing so the possible connections between the various parts that help draw them together into a coherent whole. To this end, this *Handbook* commences with two thought-provoking chapters, raises issues of theoretical framing, moves on to highlight the importance of paradigm choice, methodology and method, considers different disciplinary approaches to entrepreneurship and small business, and raises different questions about entrepreneurship education and learning before moving on to consider the application of entrepreneurship research in different sectors.

We think of the entrepreneurship scholar as being multi-skilled, having not only the breadth of knowledge of the discipline, but the research tools to delve deeper into its subject matter, ask the relevant questions and design research that is methodologically sound in respect of the chosen lines of enquiry. Many of our chapters raise issues that are pursued in greater depth by other authors in this volume; we have therefore made considerable effort to cross-reference chapters to enable you the reader to work your way through not only your specialism but additional chapters that should broaden your purview and deepen your understanding of the subject.

In this slightly lengthier introduction than might be expected we want to highlight some of the key issues raised by authors so that you may use this introduction as more than a roadmap, but a guide and a taster to the discoveries that you will make. In this regard we have attempted a logical sequencing of the chapters but, as is the case with any handbook, the reader may dip into any of the chapters that intrigue you, or will inform your on-going research, in whatever order suits you. We commence with theoretical framing, but especially those tantalising chapters that should get you thinking from whatever direction you approach the discipline! Building on the theoretical framing section, we continue with presenting the chapters on methodologies, paradigms and methods. We then present a range of disciplinary approaches to entrepreneurship including behavioural, sociological and psychological approaches. We have chosen to present two chapters on entrepreneurship education and learning, which exemplifies the intersectionality of behavioural and sociological approaches as a sub-domain of entrepreneurship. Our final section puts forward five chapters that demonstrate applications of entrepreneurship research with a view to moving the field forward.

PART I   THEORETICAL FRAMING

Chapter 2, William B. Gartner: Notes Towards a Theory of Entrepreneurial Possibility

Entrepreneurs operate in a future that is uncertain, where judgements are needed and decisions difficult to make on the back of information that may not be readily available, expensive to collect or at best incomplete. In such a context entrepreneurs should not have fixed ideas, rather they should arguably be flexible in their quest to pursue entrepreneurial opportunities. But here is the problem which Gartner highlights and explores: much of decision theory and entrepreneurial decision-making is based on probability theory. However, in situations where changes and future outcomes are unknown a probability distribution cannot be attached to outcomes (Knight, 1921). This surely takes one into the realm of possibility and as some have argued it is in the realm of the possible with which entrepreneurs deal (e.g. Shackle, 1972; 1979). In his chapter, Gartner plays with the concepts of the probable and the possible and gives us a different sense of what the thought processes and mind of an entrepreneur might be like. But Gartner does more than that, he attacks the deterministic positivistic approaches of the statistician for whom probability holds the key to prediction of likely events. Statisticians focus our minds on particularities such as the higher probability that entrepreneurs are, for example, male, of a certain age range and ethnicity. However, as Gartner points out there are plenty of counterexamples—outliers—of the statistical profiles of entrepreneurs. Statistical profiles tell us what *is*; not what *might be* or what *might become*. This type of thinking opens up our minds to practical and policy issues of how one might increase entrepreneurial activity amongst groups of individuals for whom rates of entrepreneurship have been historically low. Gartner concludes by acknowledging that he is still developing his ideas on the possible and calls for more research in this fascinating area, using stories which act as models for the possible.

Chapter 3, Mark Casson and Marina Della Giusta: Buzzwords in Business and Management Studies

There are times in the development of a discipline when it is appropriate to ask deeper questions about the shape, state and trends that demarcate its direction and evolution. As Casson and Della Giusta note there are some trends that are unhelpful; one such is 'conceptual redundancy'. Conceptual redundancy or the excessive use of 'buzzwords' can only work if certain conditions hold, the authors argue. These are that academics who innovate by developing new concepts will only do so if there are incentives to drive the process. The incentive is the enhancement of their reputation. This is accompanied by a weak elite that do not profess to understand their discipline and allow this tendency to flourish. Peers who either like to innovate or to imitate disseminate the buzzwords and a wealth of new terms is created that are essentially vacuous; vacuous because they are either ill-defined or not defined at all.

Two different things are going on here, which it is important to recognise for research purposes. First is the unnecessary proliferation (essentially of synonyms) of redundant terminology, which the authors refer to as 'duplication' and second, the refinement of conceptual terms through detailed, often qualitative, research. The former has the feel of the 'Emperor's new clothes'; a 'band wagon' on which academicians enthusiastically leap, thus exacerbating the problem. For some research purposes, especially where quantitative research or economic analysis is concerned, a clear, simple definition is a prerequisite to analysis (see also Minniti and Lévesque, Chapter 9 in this volume). For other purposes, that is, building theory and gaining a nuanced understanding of context and behaviour, qualitative research methods are appropriate (see especially Chell, Chapter 7 in this volume). However the latter method should also build on prior work; position new knowledge relative to extant knowledge; and refrain from proliferating redundant terms.

Casson and Della Giusta illustrate this with reference to the (over)use of the term 'strategy'. They argue, somewhat controversially, that 'strategy has succeeded purely because it is a buzzword not an important conceptual innovation'. A key point that they make is that strategy research has tended to focus on successful firms that have survived rather than firms that have failed and become extinct thus potentially biasing views of strategic issues of the business as a whole. The authors go on to critique Porter's work on strategy, in particular as presenting the monopolist as being a competitive force for good. The term 'strategy' may be used if it is given a carefully defined meaning rather than the loose usage that it has fallen into. The definition may be generic or specific; the former, the choice amongst alternative courses of action, the latter, a strategic decision that commits resources for a future course of action that usually involves sunk costs and is in that sense irreversible. Given clear and tight definitions rigorous analysis can proceed and for quantitative research purposes based on formal models.

The terms 'entrepreneur' and 'entrepreneurship' could be considered to be buzzwords. In the UK, 1971, in a 'Committee of Enquiry on Small Firms' was set up under the chairmanship of John Bolton. No University business schools included 'Entrepreneurship' as one of their offerings; now most do. There is a small rump of scholars who see 'small businesses' as an interesting area of study and a 'laboratory' for understanding theory, practice and policy of small business behaviour. Now anyone who sets up a business, be it a small shop on the High Street, a social enterprise or a nursery is designated an entrepreneur. Once we talked about the 'petite bourgeoisie', 'small business owner-managers', 'the self-employed', 'caretakers' and 'professional managers' of enterprises; we differentiated and looked at the context and the motivations of founders, successors to, or people who bought into or inherited an enterprise (c.f. Chell et al., 1991 for further references). Howorth et al. (Chapter 18 in this volume) offer a typology of family business (owners). Arguably it is only by retaining this rich nuanced contextual data that we can build meaningful theory about the foundations, entrepreneurial processes, outcomes and so forth that we wish to understand. The important point however is that where for example, entrepreneurship is being used in different senses as a function (innovation), role (e.g. owner-manager), personality (e.g. imaginative) or behaviour (e.g. proactive) then adopting different definitions or no definition at all only adds to the confusion (Casson, 2010; Casson & Della Guista in this volume). If we are to build the discipline then we should not use the richness of the English language and its proliferation of synonyms (with slight nuances of different meaning) as a means of enhancing our reputation or giving a positive 'spin' to the discipline, rather we should take definitions of terms as our starting point. Where we are genuinely exploring new territory using qualitative methods, there is no reason not to define terms. While we may have built a new conceptual framework; we should reflect and make explicit what those concepts mean, how we are defining them, and what theoretical import they hold.

Chapter 4, Cynthia Forson, Mustafa Özbilgin, Mustafa Bilgehan Ozturk and Ahu Tatli: Multi-level Approaches to Entrepreneurship and Small Business Research – Transcending Dichotomies with Bourdieu

Forson et al. argue that the field of entrepreneurship and small business is complex, interdisciplinary and would be best served by multi-level investigations that transcend separate framing levels and dichotomies. Indeed, small business owner-managers, entrepreneurs, their businesses, their behaviours and the various outcomes of their activities are heterogeneous and can be said to operate at different social levels: individual (micro), firm (meso) and societal, institutional (macro) (Karataş-Özkan and Chell, 2010). The implicit question they answer is what conceptual framework is available to deal with the multiple forces of structure and agency in entrepreneurship and small business. They suggest Bourdieu's sociological framework that captures the field (both wider and narrower context), *habitus* (strategies, practices and dispositions of agency) and capitals (the resources, including where appropriate the intellectual capital, cognitive maps and frameworks, experience and profile of the agents themselves). This they term an integrative framework which crosses the artificial boundaries created by research silos (quantitative versus qualitative methods and methodologies, disciplines and preferred methods). Bourdieu's framing reminds us that entrepreneurship and small business is couched in social, political and economic relationships that exert multiple influences on the behaviours of individuals, firms and industries and the wider socio-political economy. Such framing gives a common language to facilitate understanding entrepreneurial and small business phenomena which transcends cultural and national boundaries aiding the growth and development of entrepreneurship and small business as a field; and contributing both to the further development of grounded policy and practice.

Chapter 5, Mine Karataş-Özkan, Cagla Yavuz and Jeremy Howells: Theorising Entrepreneurship: An Institutional Theory Perspective

Karataş-Özkan and her colleagues succinctly review the literature on institutional theory from social, political and economic perspectives. They explain how this works as a process through regulative, cognitive and normative forces. By taking an institutional perspective they emphasise the multiple levels and complexity of institutional environments in which enterprises operate within transitional economies, where gender and ethnicity are salient issues, and where emerging markets provide institutional voids for the recognition of entrepreneurial opportunities. They highlight the importance of the term 'institutional entrepreneur' to challenge the concept of 'opportunistic entrepreneur' and give weight to the agency of entrepreneurs in shifting institutions, and fields that change socially and politically institutionalised practices.

Furthermore they highlight the importance of the different strategies employed by entrepreneurs locally and nationally. This is particularly evident in social enterprises and here they forge a link with de Bruin et al.'s chapter in this *Handbook*. The discussion of 'entrepreneurial strategies' makes an interesting counterpoint with Casson and Della Guista's chapter. From a methodological viewpoint Karataş-Özkan et al.'s chapter raises implicitly the unit of analysis that researchers should consider when planning their work. They argue that through institutional theory the unit of analysis may be the organisation, a group within or an individual agent. Furthermore in referencing Bourdieu's work, they suggest the importance of an institution's capital in its exercise of power. It is this power and domination of the institutional environment that influences the actions and entrepreneurial processes of enterprises. Again there is a connection made on this occasion to Forson et al.'s chapter which explicates Bourdieu's framework further. As these authors conclude, there is more work to be done that aims to explain entrepreneurship from within the multi-layered complexity of the field or context in which entrepreneurs seek to make their livelihood. Understanding how this works at an individual country-level and then launching further comparative, cross-country studies would be informative to the discipline as a whole.

PART II   METHODOLOGIES, PARADIGMS AND METHODS

Chapter 6, Luke Pittaway, Robin Holt and Jean Broad: Synthesising Knowledge in Entrepreneurship Research – The Role of Systematic Literature Reviews

Carrying out research in any discipline in a way that builds and enables the development of theory requires a depth of knowledge and understanding of the state of the art of the subject; to know what is currently known, what we do not yet know and more specifically what the right questions we should be addressing are. Pittaway et al.'s chapter on the use of 'systematic literature reviews' (SLRs) addresses this crucial issue. The chapter opens with a brief discussion of the nature of enquiry pointing to two aspects of reflection on the development of any discipline: (a) philosophical reflections; and (b) the development of research methodologies that encourage systematic reflection on empirical evidence, synthesising research findings and making sense of them holistically, that is, across the discipline. The authors then make a case for the adoption of the systematic literature review to facilitate the development of evidence-based policy and practice as well as theoretical foundations of the discipline. They compare the use of meta-analysis suggesting that the latter technique is less relevant in management research. This provides an interesting point of comparison with Rauch's chapter in which he adopts the latter technique to reveal the strengths of research on the entrepreneurial personality (see below).

Having made a case for the adoption of SLRs the authors usefully go on to explain lucidly how the research team may go about conducting such a review. This emphasises the reflective nature of the process commencing as it does with 'identifying the need for the review'. It essentially includes framing the research question, developing a protocol and applying relevance assessment criteria. Carrying out the citation and literature search is likely to throw up a very large number of citations which need to be screened and whittled down to a manageable number. The smaller number of citations is then appraised using content analysis and thematic coding. The identification of themes is particularly useful where a team of researchers is carrying out the work. Finally the results are synthesised and reported.

Researchers have long argued about the fragmentation of the discipline of entrepreneurship; that it is interdisciplinary but researchers sit principally in their own 'silo' (compare Forson et al., Chapter 4 in this volume). One important advantage of the SLR is that it draws findings from across disciplinary boundaries and aids building an evidence base. Other advantages are that it is a transparent procedure and structure which is reported explicitly. While these are important advantages the method also has some disadvantages which the authors recount. Of these, the fact that it is a 'scientific method' and sits within the positivist paradigm would not be lost on many qualitative researchers. A discussion of the philosophical underpinnings of positivism and anti-positivism can be found in the ensuing chapter where I introduce the two approaches to using the critical incident technique.

Chapter 7, Elizabeth Chell: The Critical Incident Technique: Philosophical Underpinnings, Method and Application to a Case of Small Business Failure

Several of the chapters in this *Handbook* indicate the importance of a qualitative methods approach to exploring further the conceptual framework the authors concerned are expounding. This may be in part due to the need to develop theory, but also authors have pointed to the complexity of entrepreneurial activity, processes and outcomes and the need to capture such detail through thick descriptions and analytic methods. Qualitative methods are difficult to execute well and their philosophical underpinnings vary. Chell's chapter on the critical incident technique traces the history and development of this particular qualitative method, namely the critical incident techniquer (CIT) interview, the philosophical assumptions of functionalism that were made by its originator Flanagan (1954) and those of an interpretivist perspective developed by Chell in her earlier work (Chell, 1998; 2004; Chell and Baines, 1998; 2000). Chell examines critical reviews of the method, taking points of contrast and exposing any weaknesses and how they have been dealt with. Researchers have expressed concern about the credibility and trustworthiness of qualitative methods in general and attempts have been made to address this issue (see Seale, 1999; Patton, 2002; Hammersley, 2007). Chell discusses these issues and provides a way through, touching on philosophical issues such as the nature of truth, the form of life that is entrepreneurship and its social connectedness and the nature of insight and generalisation. In alignment with many other chapters in this *Handbook*, Chell stresses the use of CIT in exploring entrepreneurial issues within context as it allows for understanding the perspectives, frames of reference, experiences of participants (entrepreneurs or small business owner-managers) and views on matters of critical importance to them.

Chell then moves on to the practical application of CIT particularly within an interpretivist framework and illustrates using a case study of a failed small business. She argues as have others of the need for more research on business failure. Importantly Chell discusses the case study technique and the practical aspects of performing a CIT interview. She raises the importance of reflexivity, the use of language during the interview and afterwards when coding and analysing transcripts. One example of the significance of the choice of language in asking questions around critical incidents was provided by Karataş-Özkan and Chell (2010) in their study on nascent entrepreneurship and learning whereby they demonstrate, for example, the importance of aligning with the language of the participants and making the inquiry accessible to them by using terminology such as 'significant occurrences' rather than critical incidents, which may have connotations for the interviewees. A further important aspect is gaining access to significant others as well as any documentary evidence. This is a particular challenge for the researcher but will ensure that what happened, when, and the significant part that events and other players exercised on outcomes is well understood.

Chapter 8, Sylvia Gherardi and Manuela Perrotta: Gender, Ethnicity and Social Entrepreneurship: Qualitative Approaches to the Study of Entrepreneuring

Gherardi and Perrotta demonstrate what the original contributions of qualitative research grounded in non-positivist research paradigms are, echoing with the recent broader debate in the field of entrepreneurship (see Anderson et al., 2014). They initially address the problem for qualitative research methodologies in gaining acceptance and legitimacy in a research world where positivist approaches based on the scientific method are still favoured. Reflecting on Calás et al (2009), Gherardi and Perrotta remind readers of the importance of questioning the biases and limitations of dominant research by revealing the value of marginal practices to the broader research community. The authors skilfully review the issues as a prelude to considering how gender and ethnicity issues in entrepreneurship and social entrepreneurship might be addressed through rigorously conducted qualitative research. A crucial matter is that traditional approaches tend to reproduce the normative model of functionalism and market capitalism and pay scant attention to processual and contextual dynamics. This is a theme that is echoed in other chapters (e.g. Chell; Forson et al.; Karataş-Özkan et al.; and McKeever et al.) where the importance of understanding context is underscored.

Gherardi and Perrotta argue for the importance of critical reflection to create space for qualitative, non-positivist research methods that enable analysis from a feminist empiricist perspective. In this regard the authors provide an incisive overview of qualitative methods; the importance of understanding narrative, different perspectives on the stories told, and the symbolic framing and cultural meaning of stories that entrepreneurs use to legitimate their new ventures to others. Legitimacy building becomes a key theme and has echoes of Bourdieu's conceptual framework outlined in Forson et al. in this volume (see also Karataş-Özkan and Chell, 2013). Turning to gender and entrepreneuring, Gherardi and Perrotta point to the emancipatory assumptions that feminist theory brings which is apposite in a field emphasising social (and economic) change and power relations. The authors review some very interesting studies that show how gender and entrepreneurship are culturally produced and reproduced in situated social practices. In this regard they draw out the preponderant influence of masculinity in public situations and market activities and how this delimits female entrepreneurs' discourse and behaviour. They go further to delineate how hegemonic entrepreneurial practices are not only interconnected with gender, but also ethnicity, religion and geographic context. These unarguably are complex issues which require the depth of analysis, the richness of data, and the critical interpretation of multiple layers of discourse and perspectives which robust qualitative approaches can furnish. While some work has been undertaken to address such an agenda, carefully reviewed by the authors, many challenges remain, not least of which are the methodological considerations of 'doing such research': through reflexivity understanding the flexibility of human interactions, the ambiguity of interpretations and the ability to generate new knowledge that aids theory development and further research on entrepreneurship.

Chapter 9, Maria Minniti and Moren Lévesque: Mathematics and Entrepreneurship Research

Mathematics has a founding place in the history of thought over the millennia and so it is, Minniti and Lévesque argue, fundamental to the scientific enquiry into the nature of entrepreneurship, small business behaviour and outcomes. Since the Enlightenment and the birth of modern thought of David Hume and philosophers such as Rousseau, alluded to by the authors, and the development of mathematical reasoning in economics in the late nineteenth and early twentieth centuries; mathematics has provided the basis for logical thought, parsimony of argument and model development in the social sciences. It is with this backcloth that the authors make a case for the continued and extensive use of mathematics in research in this field. The case is well made, in a way that is accessible to non-mathematicians and entrepreneurship researchers who have not embraced quantitative approaches to researching their subject. The authors explain the various advantages of adopting mathematics including the systematic rules that assure consistency; the ability to generalise from the findings; the simplicity of mathematical models that allow the researcher to identify the relationships between input variables and outcomes; the efficiency with which hypotheses may be tested and verified; and the robustness of the model, including objectivity, validity and independence of the variables. Here it is worth noting some comparisons with the chapters of Casson and Della Giusta and Rauch. Having established what the properties of mathematical models are the authors then show their application to entrepreneurship theory. They round off the chapter by identifying some exemplary areas of mathematics for elucidation in respect of their application to entrepreneurship research problems. In this endeavour the authors give the reader a greater appreciation of the use of mathematical models in entrepreneurship research. They give us an insight into the way of thinking and the mathematically based approach. Of course that is not to say that all research problems can be reduced to mathematical forms of enquiry; all research depends on what questions are being asked and what is the best way for the researcher to answer the particular question and solve the research problematic. In this regard Andreas Rauch, in the next chapter, asks an age-old question of 'who is an entrepreneur' and how might such a question be best answered.

Chapter 10, Andreas Rauch: Predictions of Entrepreneurial Behavior: A Personality Approach

The idea of an 'entrepreneurial personality' and the ability of traits to predict entrepreneurial behaviour has been an area fraught with criticism and a scepticism bordering on disbelief for many decades (e.g. Gartner, 1988; Chell et al, 1991; Chell, 2008). Indeed I think it would be true to say that most sociologically-oriented academics have dismissed the idea that personality traits may play any part in explaining entrepreneurial behaviour and outcomes such as business success, founding or other measures of entrepreneurial performance. Rauch's review of the state of the art, however, suggests that we should not be too hasty. He demonstrates that advances in personality theory and relatively new tools, in particular meta-analysis, are able to show modest effects of trait on behavioural and performance outcomes. Important, he argues, is the identification of specific traits that may be related theoretically to tasks and outcomes. Also traits should be considered as part of a model that includes mediating (e.g. goals and plans mediate the effects of achievement motivation) and moderating variables that demonstrate the contingent nature of traits (Chell, 1985). Developing such models is still in its infancy and shows there is a considerable amount of work to be carried out. Careful consideration of Rauch's step-by-step explanation should be a prerequisite for that further work in this area. This chapter is one of three key chapters that specifically examine aspects of psychology and entrepreneurship. Readers who have enjoyed Rauch's chapter will also be interested in that of Fiona Patterson and Máire Kerrin (Chapter 11) and Barbara Bird and her colleagues (Chapter 12), both of which apply our understanding of psychological principles in the context of entrepreneurial behaviour and outcomes. Other chapters which cross-cut some of Rauch's themes are Pittaway et al. (Chapter 6) which alludes to the role of meta-analysis in systematic reviews and Minniti and Lévesque (Chapter 9) who highlight the role of mathematics in research.

PART III   DISCIPLINARY APPROACHES TO ENTREPRENEURSHIP

Chapter 11, Fiona Patterson and Máire Kerrin: Characteristics and Behaviours Associated with Innovative People in Small- and Medium-sized Enterprises

Patterson and Kerrin argue that understanding the innovative characteristics of their employees will aid the SME to be more competitive. A crucial problem is how this might be delivered when there is so little agreement about what innovation is; when innovative work is influenced at individual, group and organisational levels; and how it relates to entrepreneurship and small business behaviour. They put forward a detailed and relatively comprehensive model of the organisational resources that are believed to impact innovation, focusing particularly on employee behaviour and leadership performance. This provides a refreshing examination of innovation within SMEs that highlights the considerable scope for further research which views the owner-manager as a leader who has the task of marshalling resources with a view to delivering creative and innovative outcomes of the enterprise. Underlying this is the understanding that there are multiple factors at different levels operating on the working environment of the firm; that a thorough understanding of leadership role, style and behaviour is a prerequisite of effective innovative practice; and that management should align their HR interventions, selection and retention of employees, working environment and skills training development to develop increased innovation outcomes. This chapter should excite the interest of readers of Mayson and Barrett (Chapter 14) who focus on the organisational aspects of human resources and also that of Andreas Rauch (Chapter 10) which approaches the problem of entrepreneurial behaviour from a psychologist's perspective and emphasises the need for model building. Casson and Della Giusta (Chapter 3) and Minniti and Lévesque (Chapter 9) also highlight the need for model building where a quantitative approach is being proposed.

Chapter 12, Barbara Bird, Leon Schjoedt and Ralph Hanke: Behavior of Entrepreneurs – Existing Research and Future Directions

Barbara Bird's work is in a lengthy tradition seeking to understand what it is that entrepreneurs do that distinguishes them from others, including managers and leaders. In this chapter she and her colleagues review the state-of-the-art literature on entrepreneurs' behaviour and relate the work to current constructs, such as cognition, motivation and decision-making. The purpose for both practical and research purposes is to be able to understand, predict and control behaviour of entrepreneurs, as individuals as well as in groups or teams. This is especially important in research design; distinguishing terms such as behaviour (input), performance (an outcome), ability, skills and competences, which are also inputs but differentiated from behaviours, and processes, such as planning. As in the case of Rauch's chapter, Bird et al. emphasise the need to build a model, and in particular, to develop good measures of identified behaviours and other variables. In reviewing the literature on model building, they identify a number of key issues that future research should address, including measurement issues, such as construct validity, the lack of longitudinal research designs, the use of self-report and the threat to validity, the lack of consistency in conceptualisation and measurement leading to low levels of reliability and validity. Readers should also find reading Casson and Della Giusta (Chapter 3) and Minniti and Lévesque (Chapter 9) to be of interest. Importantly the authors here point out that research should be designed to facilitate outcome predictions otherwise what is the point? Finally Bird and colleagues identify selling behaviour as a much neglected aspect of entrepreneurs' behaviour and rightly urge further empirical work not only on the behaviour of entrepreneurs but also, and specifically, their selling behaviour which they correctly emphasise has been a much under-researched topic despite its centrality to what an entrepreneur does.

Chapter 13, Edward McKeever, Alastair Anderson and Sarah Jack: Social Embeddedness in Entrepreneurship Research: The Importance of Context and Community

McKeever, Anderson and Jack provide an informative state-of-the-art review of the historical underpinnings and current developments in the concept of social embedding in entrepreneurship. The roots of the social embeddedness concept can be traced back to sociologists such as Karl Marx, Herbert Spencer, Max Weber, Ferdinand Tönnies, and Emile Durkheim, who all contributed to illuminating the importance of structures in sociology. Marx offered the earliest and the most comprehensive account of social structure, by relating political, cultural, and religious life to the mode of production (an underlying economic structure). Initially the concept of social embeddedness lacked theoretical rigour but the seeds of the idea of the influence of social structure on the functioning of exchange relationships took hold, not only from the input of sociologists but also from social psychologists and anthropologists. Names like Weber, Simmel, Polanyi, Lewin, Festinger, Levi-Strauss, Giddens and Granovetter were just some of the giants of the various disciplines upon whose shoulders later theorists stood.

From a research perspective, criticisms of the construct are important to identify. For example, Uzzi (1997) identified the problem of attempting to combine specific economic propositions with broad statements about how social ties influence entrepreneurial actions. This led to the emergence of key research themes: structural contexts, processes and performance implications. It should be noted also that this work, at the turn of the twenty-first century, drew upon contemporary philosophical debates about the nature of structure and the ontological status of entrepreneurial processes of opportunity-seeking or discovery depending upon which side of the debate one seated oneself (outlined in Chell, 2008). These debates were further enriched by a consideration of multi-level theorising in entrepreneurship (see Karataş-Özkan and Chell, 2010; Karataş-Özkan, 2011) and the writings of theorists such as Bourdieu who maintained a practical import to their work (Özbilgin and Tatli, 2005). In this regard reading Forson et al. (Chapter 4) is to be recommended.

Research stimulated by Jack and Anderson (2002) suggested that embedding is a bilateral process whereby mutuality, credibility, knowledge and experience are accumulated in a specific social space. This development in thinking highlights the relational dynamics but not the impetus that energises action. Here we believe further theoretical and empirical work that draws on Bourdieu's framework including his notion of power would make an interesting and unique contribution. However, McKeever et al. suggest that informal social contexts provide a 'moral framework which largely determines what types of behaviours are socially appropriate'—a strand of further research that readers might consider in relation to Spence (Chapter 20).

McKeever and his colleagues also point out the importance of unpacking the notion of social embeddedness within different types of structures, such as family, ethnicity, social class and gender, all of which have both facilitating and constraining aspects. A further area ripe for research which McKeever and his colleagues identify is that of the constraining influences of embeddedness. We sometimes paint too shiny a gloss on our constructs emphasising the positive aspects and overlooking the negative. This deficiency we should urgently address. It may not go as far as sampling cases of enterprise failure (see Chell, Chapter 7) but as the authors suggest, research that examines the unforeseen exit of a crucial member of staff, institutional forces that affect the market(s) in which the enterprise is embedded, 'over embeddedness' that may stifle economic action and result in sub-optimal performances should be encouraged.

The stage of our understanding of embeddedness and the amount of further research that should be done to enrich and deepen our knowledge of the phenomenon suggest the need for qualitative, theory-building research that may include multi-level perspectives. One such level might be the family and in this regard the work of Howorth and her colleagues (see Chapter 18) offers interesting detailed perspectives. In this way it will be possible to go beyond describing what is the case and ask the all-important why and how?

Chapter 14, Susan Mayson and Rowena Barrett: Human Resource Management and Entrepreneurship: Building Theory at the Intersection

Mayson and Barrett's chapter addresses a timely research problem, which is to demonstrate the intersectionality between fields of HRM and entrepreneurship. In responding to the call for putting the HRM in the picture for small, growing and entrepreneurial firms, the authors highlight the importance of entrepreneurial context along the dimension of how HRM contributes to organisational performance (readers might like to compare Patterson and Kerrin's approach, see Chapter 11 in this volume). They illustrate the application of a range of theoretical lenses in exploring the HRM in entrepreneurial contexts, such as resource-based view, social exchange theory and institutional theory.

The authors have worked tirelessly to encourage the development of research at the interface between entrepreneurship and HRM, but claim that the majority of the contribution comes from 'one side of the ledger', that of HRM, and that entrepreneurship scholars appear to be rather uninterested in exploring this interface. Nonetheless they have uncovered a sufficiency of papers covering specific aspects of this interface, viz: the performance link between HRM, firm performance and entrepreneurial processes; the development of Human Capital (HC) with a view to understanding better the influence of entrepreneurial behaviour within SMEs; the impact of formality and informality in SMEs and entrepreneurial firms and the effects of structure or lack of structure on growth, productivity and performance; the impact of single HRM practices such as training and skills development on small firm performance. Such an agenda should excite entrepreneurship scholars especially as there are many lacunae for further research. Interestingly Mayson and Barrett separate out research which has focused on the employers from that which has focused on the employees' perspective. More multiple perspectives research in entrepreneurship should be encouraged in this post-modern age as it helps gives richness and depth to the data. In the current climate, however, developing a model of context, actions and outcomes—where context may include HRM systems (or lack of them), actions include strategic and tactical decisions, including HRM practices such as recruitment and training, and outcomes, such as productivity, growth, profitability—is what is needed to advance research in this area. Of course other methods may be adopted such as detailed case studies especially where depth of understanding and theory-building is needed.

Mayson and Barrett have thus pointed up a rich seam of potential for a considerable amount of further work which should be both fascinating and worthwhile. In this regard, they argue for moving beyond the level of theorising whereby there is an acknowledgement that small and entrepreneurial firms present a unique context for managing human resources. Due to overemphasis by entrepreneurship scholars on the opportunity creation process, an important part of the equation, which is garnering human resources, is often neglected, particularly in the context of sustainability and growth of an entrepreneurial venture. Echoing with this recognition, Mayson and Barrett remind us of the significance of HRM to explore entrepreneurial dynamism.

PART IV ENTREPRENEURSHIP, EDUCATION AND LEARNING

Chapter 15, Janice Byrne, Alain Fayolle and Olivier Toutain: Entrepreneurship Education: What We Know and What We Need to Know

Byrne and her colleagues offer a critical review of research and practice on entrepreneurship education (EE) in their chapter. They point out that entrepreneurship education as a subject domain suffers from a lack of clear theorising and organising taxonomies. They challenge ontological assumptions of entrepreneurship research by raising the questions of what, who, why and how to teach, as well as for which results? This scrutiny leads them to deal with definitional and conceptual debates surrounding entrepreneurship education, followed by context and audience. In addition to raising some uncomfortable questions about what entrepreneurship educators are doing, how they are doing it, and with what aims and objectives, this reflexive state-of-the-art chapter on entrepreneurship education offers a review of the literature clustered by five interrelated themes: state of play (the scope, evolution and institutionalisation of the field of entrepreneurship education); specific audiences and their needs; measurement and evaluation; entrepreneurial learning; and teaching methodology and mediums.

This chapter is very timely given the rapid expansion in EE during this century. Arguably entrepreneurship is not only a contact sport but rather in respect of education it has characteristics of, say, learning to play the piano: (a) start with theory (the scales) and playing small pieces; (b) practise and gain experience; (c) test oneself; and (d) move on to more complex and challenging pieces. No one can be said to play the piano until they have mastered all such aspects. While one might think the same argument applies in EE, many educators apparently either teach from a theoretical perspective, or in practical skills (e.g. business planning) training. Indeed the authors suggest that there has in recent years been a move away from teaching about entrepreneurship (i.e. theory) to teaching for entrepreneurship (i.e. instilling personal and social skills, attributes and behaviours).

There are a number of reasons why it is still important to combine theory and practice. First, the educator should ask: Who is the intended audience? This means understanding socio-economic context especially for marginalised groups, the particular challenges that they face, and the implications for their relationality and skills set in order to meet those challenges. As many have argued in the past (Chell, 1985; Jack and Anderson, 2002) context and situation have implications for behaviour. This theme is taken up in several of the chapters in this *Handbook* from various disciplinary and topical perspectives.

The above suggests that entrepreneurship educators should reflect further on the content and design of their courses. A more comprehensive typology is required to capture the diversity of material that is the basis for entrepreneurship teaching. The dissemination of good practice is crucial to this but, the authors argue, is impeded by the fact that entrepreneurship educators are not publishing in mainstream entrepreneurship journals. The authors back up this contention by reviewing five leading entrepreneurship journals and two high-impact education reviews. They classify what they found according to the above-mentioned five themes. Many of the articles addressed more than one of these themes.

The authors identify a number of noteworthy issues for entrepreneurship educators: (a) the need for more complex taxonomies to account for the complexity of entrepreneurship educational offerings; (b) an imperative to integrate EE with concepts and models from the field of education; (c) a requirement to provide a clear and precise definition of entrepreneurship on which a non-ambiguous definition of EE may be based; and (d) an observation of a distinct absence of philosophical underpinnings to the teaching of entrepreneurship, surprising perhaps, given European philosophical traditions and, furthermore, a tendency to pursue functionalism, thus potentially linking what is known and may be taught to performance outcomes at individual and enterprise levels. Some outstanding questions include: how does the construction of entrepreneurial actions and behaviour and in particular the construction of opportunities affect EE? Should relational aspects of entrepreneurial learning be further developed and nurtured? How might EE courses be designed around how entrepreneurs think and act? How do entrepreneurship educators address the many issues of learning from failure and handling emotional aspects of entrepreneuring? These authors are not the only researchers to raise such issues (see in particular Chell, Chapter 7). However further research is urgently needed to evaluate the effectiveness of EE programmes and to assess the pedagogical transferability of experiential and relational entrepreneurial learning. Apart from an excellent review and state-of-the-art overview, Byrne and her co-authors suggest the need to create a virtuous circle aimed at sharing knowledge and including all stakeholders in EE to improve the design of courses, inform policy, support research and aid and develop educational good practice across the globe. The authors advocate a collaborative partnership between these stakeholders, i.e. researchers, educators, mentors, policy-makers and learners themselves in order to render the research and practice of EE with legitimacy and effectiveness.

Chapter 16, Oswald Jones and Allan Macpherson: Research Perspectives on Learning in Small Firms

Through their state-of-the-art review of the literature of the past 30 years, Jones and Macpherson demonstrate the changes that have taken place in understanding how small firms develop by means of a process of collective, social learning and why this is so difficult to link causally to firm performance. However the authors maintain that there is convincing evidence of links between better performing firms and effective learning. This they argue is a consequence of the more sophisticated approach to training in leadership skills and business management. Furthermore they maintain that the integration of learning theory with small firm development initiatives has supported this progress. The authors offer a range of learning perspectives in their chapter and propose a framework that links individual (cognitive and behavioural) learning and social learning. This link is useful particularly in the context of the shift from a focus on individual know-how to owner-managers as part of a learning community.

Learning entrepreneurial competencies is wider than focusing on individual learning of owner-managers and this has implications for design and delivery of entrepreneurship education and training. There is no simple recipe for the management of the small firm; delivering on key management skills through training was not sufficient; it had to be more flexible and problem-oriented. Further development of the notion of entrepreneurial competencies showed that such competences enable owner-managers to develop organisational capabilities which are appropriate to the environment in which the firm is operating. But this did not resolve the problem of a purported learning-performance linkage; what it did was place emphasis on the need to encompass the firm's environment in any theorising.

Such understanding of the complexities of small firm learning led to the development in research about 'critical learning events' based on the phenomenological approach to the critical incident technique (see Chell, Chapter 7). This experiential approach focused on how managers learn from day-to-day experience and includes their emotional responses to their individual learning encounter (Cope, 2003). It concerns learning by doing, lived experience and reflection on opportunities, hence problem-based action learning and critical reflection skills were thought to be crucial. This moved the research into current thinking about the social context of learning (Karataş-Özkan, 2011). The gap between individual and organisational learning needed to be addressed and this was done by introducing institutional theory. Neither individuals, nor groups nor firms learn in isolation from the institutional environment in which they are operating and embedded. Through such porosity small firm players negotiate and embed new practices within the firm.

Jones and Macpherson illustrate the application of current learning theory through the LEAD programme offered to owner-managers in 2010 and 2011 provided by Liverpool and Lancaster Universities in the UK. A key part of the programme is the reflection and sharing of experiences by participants to promote genuine social learning. Delegates are also encouraged to think about the context of their business and what they are trying to achieve. To complete the picture these authors link six key research findings to policy and practice. This forms the basis of collective learning and a plethora of aspects of social and institutionally-based learning opportunities evident in new practices integrated and sustained within the firm. This gives a sense of the need to constantly refresh and renew rather than a static picture of small firm learning. Only then presumably will the link between organisational learning and performance be evident.

PART V   APPLICATIONS OF ENTREPRENEURSHIP RESEARCH

Chapter 17, Sarah Lubik and Elizabeth Garnsey: Entrepreneurial Innovation in Science-based Firms: The Need for an Ecosystem Perspective

How does any firm get started? Scholars of entrepreneurship and small business have been asking this question for decades, producing models, theoretical and practical ideas, and an evidence-based upon which policy makers can make their decisions. New technology small businesses, and in particular those emanating from the university sector as spin-outs are, the authors argue, a specific subset. An ecosystem's perspective places the firm as the unit of analysis within its environment and seeks to explore the resource endowments available to it; viewing the internal resource environment against the business and policy environment in which the nascent firm may struggle to emerge and survive. The authors take a broader view of the environment to include policy development, market, partners and the national innovation system as key influences on the survival and success of such germinal science-based ventures. Lubik and Garnsey trace the recent history of the development of science-based policy for university spin-outs in the UK, which was particularly evident in the first decade of the twenty-first century. They examine the business models which link technology developments to the realisation of scientific value. In order to achieve their core objectives, science-based ventures need to gain access to considerable resources and this, the authors claim, is often a major stumbling block. Indeed more research is needed to examine under what circumstances novel business models are effective or ineffective. To achieve this they believe qualitative research on a case-by-case basis would provide the richness of data required to get a full grasp of the issues. Further research is also needed to examine the fledgling firm's marketing strategy, which should be a narrow niche, allowing for the development of specific technologies for specific markets. These firms need to pursue a frugal design strategy and be wise to possible risks of partnerships and alliances. In particular there is surely further research that could be carried out here to examine partners who explore opportunities and those that exploit them. Indeed perhaps there is a case for investigating cases where there is a consortium of different types of partner where the nascent firm is embedded in a network of valuable relationships in comparison with those with a narrower, say, 'fortress' mentality? In essence Lubik and Garnsey make a case for science-based firms building a supportive ecosystem which is primarily focused on investment, where the resources invested are not only funds but management, business and strategic expertise.

They conclude with a useful policy perspective on the issue of how science-based innovation can become an important plank in the UK's (but presumably any country's) growth strategy. The authors also include an invaluable table listing areas for further research in theory, methodology, policy and practice.

Chapter 18, Carole Howorth, Jacqueline Jackson and Allan Discua Cruz: Entrepreneurship in Family Businesses

Howorth and her co-authors have provided a state-of-the-art review of research in family businesses in respect of entrepreneurship theory, practice and policy. Initially they search for a definition which has eluded many researchers given the heterogeneity of the family business and settle on one which might usefully be embraced by future scholars. They go on to highlight important debating points in this field and provide an insight into key theoretical, empirical and methodological issues, exploring some of the myths and invalid assumptions which they argue plague research on family businesses. Such themes are redolent of Casson and Della Giusta (Chapter 3) and of Gherardi and Perrotta (Chapter 8) in the sense of being rigorous in carrying out research.

Due to the preponderance of family businesses, it is much more difficult for researchers to make generalisations, to understand the various contexts in which they operate and the nature and influence of family dynamics. This is both a fascination and frustration of the subject matter! These authors show just how central entrepreneurship is to family businesses but also point to gaps in research such as the need for further work on entrepreneurial succession; the impact of family dynamics on the entrepreneurial process; and incorporation of family business into mainstream management fields. The authors also address various methodological issues for family business researchers and so reading this and the chapters in this *Handbook* that deal with both qualitative and quantitative methods would be appropriate. Research in this field also raises the issue of multiple levels which Forson and colleagues (Chapter 4) address from a Bourdieuan perspective. Certainly there are some outstanding issues such as culture that may be dealt with in this way; considering issues of power and domination in the management of the family firm as well as day-to-day family dynamics, leadership and the exercise of entrepreneurialism and innovation. Howorth et al.'s chapter gives a solid research basis from which further work should emanate. For example, as Howorth and her co-authors argue, research should explore emerging areas and questions with reference to relevant conceptual platforms that draw upon complementary theories, rather than reliance on a single theoretical perspective. This supports the thread of the discussion in the theoretical framing section of the *Handbook*.

Chapter 19, Xin Gu: Developing Entrepreneur Networks in the Creative Industries – A Case Study of Independent Designer Fashion in Manchester

Xin Gu's chapter picks up a number of themes that have interlaced themselves throughout this *Handbook*; notably, qualitative research methods; social networking; and the embeddedness of small firms, and also touches on the impact of local institutions on small firm behaviour (see Chell, Chapter 7, McKeever et al. Chapter 13 and Karataş-Özkan and her colleagues, Chapter 5). Gu is concerned to develop a depth of understanding of social networking in the creative industries and in particular fashion design, based in Manchester, UK—a centre with deep historical roots in the textile and clothing industry. Her main focus is on the relationship aspects of social networks, how this enables the development of a culture and identity for fashion designers and their small enterprises and how culture tends to override business issues. The fragmentation of the industry in the Manchester region, where almost 70 per cent of fashion designers are self-employed, suggests two issues: a lack of power and influence by the many; and a question of what constitutes entrepreneurial behaviour in this sector. If it is creativity, what does this imply for definitions of entrepreneurs and the self-employed in other sectors?

Gu brings out the embedded nature of small firms in this socially networked sector, where friendship and community form the links in the network, blurring the edges between formal (business) and informal friendship relations. She shows how different 'doing business' is in the fashion design sector and from the outside looking in, how support and policy-making agencies viewed the industry as 'flaky' comprising by and large lifestyle cottage businesses. Gu argues that these creative entrepreneurs do not reject the idea of business success but want it on their own terms. What was aesthetically pleasing was fundamental to their brand-building strategy and overrode other considerations. High quality and craft skill was not only crucial to the product but also to the entrepreneur's sense of identity. Further, it is that uncertainty that pervades all small business but in particular creative business that Gu argues is the main reason for relationship building through affective bonding. Not only does this present a network of like-minded people but it is also built on the principles of trust and reputation.

In line with several other authors in this *Handbook*, Gu demonstrates how context matters, showing for example from a policy perspective how the newly formed Manchester Fashion Network met the fashion designer's need for a non-standard business network built on personal relationships, for facilitation rather than direction. Moreover the industrial context in which the fashion designers felt relatively powerless also suggests a crossover with Forson et al. (Chapter 4) and, in particular, the work of Bourdieu.

Chapter 20, Laura J. Spence: Business Ethics and Social Responsibility in Small Firms

Departing from the premise that business is a social and moral terrain (Jackall, 1988), Laura Spence provides a state-of-the-art review of ethical issues researched in respect of small business and entrepreneurship. She then usefully discusses current understanding of ethics and social responsibility in the small business. However there are many ethical theories which Spence then presents and usefully nominates just two ethics frameworks—moral proximity and social care—through which she explains their essence and application in small firms. This review has the advantages of being integrative—integrating large disparate bodies of literature—and focused on how particular ethics frameworks show particular relevance to known attributes of small firms, such as family business, relationship-orientation and social embeddedness (note potential research links with Howorth et al. (Chapter 18) and McKeever et al. (Chapter 13)). As Spence claims, it breaks down silos—an objective of several authors in this *Handbook*—and offers two theoretical avenues for future SME, ethics and social responsibility research thus facilitating the all-important accumulation of knowledge in this developing field. Furthermore, Spence identifies an important research gap which is related to the theorisation process in this area. She calls for going beyond the empirical description of social and ethical issues in small firms and moving towards explaining the phenomena observed. She raises issues about the dominance of empirical research conducted in developed country contexts, mainly in Europe. She highlights the importance of informal economy and the implications for ethics research, challenging very fundamental assumptions about what is ethical. In presenting future research directions, she also cites the family firm as an interesting context and as an under-researched area from an ethics perspective. This is a fertile area to apply ethics of care and moral proximity lenses as she has discussed in her chapter. Her discussion implies not only these research directions but also policy and practice consequences. She argues that large firm decentralisation resulting in emulation of a small firm context has implications for ethics and creates challenges for business leaders and managers. In alignment with the corporate social responsibility paradigm and related trends, her chapter also highlights the importance of a nuanced and context-sensitive (large versus small firm context) approach to policy-making.

Chapter 21, Anne de Bruin, Eleanor Shaw and Dominic Chalmers: Social Entrepreneurship: Looking Back, Moving Ahead

De Bruin and colleagues offer an interesting read on social entrepreneurship (SE) by examining the phenomenon in the complex milieu of political and socio-economic developments across the globe. They argue that heterogeneous geo-political and socio-cultural contexts underpin the development of the SE phenomenon. This implies that the drivers for SE are highly context-dependent. SE has its origins in the politics of liberal conservatism away from state involvement in solving social problems. However, the seeds of social entrepreneurship were sown in the nineteenth and twentieth centuries through the philanthropy of wealthy industrialists. In this vein the authors trace the historical roots of SE, outlining the change in socio-economic conditions and the rejection of Keynesian economics which influenced successive governments into finding non-statist solutions to welfare and public service problems. The authors critique the 'Big Society' discourse created by the recent Coalition Government in the UK, by raising the issue of shrinking the state through drastic cuts in government budgets and social enterprise being 'misused' as a substitute for the provision of public and social services.

This political view was not confined to the UK but is apparent in both developed and emerging economies, notably China. The Global Economic Crisis of 2008 has merely acted to heighten the problem, revealing large swathes of world poverty and vast differences in lifestyle between the wealthy and the very poor. Whilst this scenario is well documented the question is can social entrepreneurship provide solutions? Is SE a sufficiently robust paradigm? Can it provide socially innovative solutions to the world's most intractable social problems? De Bruin and her colleagues explore the literature on social entrepreneurs and social entrepreneurship in search of solutions. As ever in entrepreneurship, the lack of a unifying definition poses problems for those who want to move forward. The language of 'opportunity' that has typified research in entrepreneurship more broadly suggests an individualistic endeavour whereas for social entrepreneurs the driving force is the social need. This implies that SE involves the innovative, socially-oriented development of opportunities for social value creation. How should researchers frame their work into social enterprise? De Bruin et al. suggest a resource-based perspective driven by social innovation, though acknowledging the contentious nature of the definition of 'social innovation'. Perhaps we have to come to terms with the notion that all innovations and inventions can be used for good or ill? The research question, however, is: Is it possible to solve this dark side of social innovation, for example, where micro-finance initiatives can be implemented in an exploitative manner? The issue of 'conflicts of interest' perhaps should be just as much an integral part of theorising social entrepreneurship as of capitalism itself? Traditional approaches (viz. neo-liberal economic orthodoxy) have failed, leaving space for social innovators to devise creative solutions to market failure. The establishment of social innovation hubs and centres across the world suggests that social innovation is no longer a buzzword but an enduring term.

One important contribution of this chapter is that the authors present social innovation as an evolution of the concept of social entrepreneurship by highlighting the socio-political nature of these phenomena and they encourage interdisciplinary research to address an array of research problems in this sub-domain of entrepreneurship. De Bruin et al. conclude by outlining a rich and diverse research agenda which ties into specific chapters in this volume. For example, such a research agenda should comprise: analysing systems of institutional entrepreneurship and social innovation using an institutional theory approach (c.f. Karataş-Özkan et al., Chapter 5)); analysing social innovation using complexity and resilience theories; using embeddedness and agency theory (cf. McKeever al. (Chapter 13)); adopt a cross-country comparative approach (cf. Chell et al., 2011) and include a comparative study of support environments; examine SE through a relational approach (Hjorth, 2010) in particular focusing on the role of stakeholders; carry out research on under-researched areas such as eco-entrepreneurship; and seek to improve our understanding of the workings of SE through more empirical evidence. Finally these authors suggest that SE researchers have a social responsibility to develop practical and meaningful implications of their work; there is no part in SE for dry theorising for its own sake.

FINAL WORD

Assembling this *Handbook* has been an adventure, and like all adventures it has had its ups and downs, its lows and highs. But having arrived at our destination we are thrilled by the journey and the themes that have emerged and provide links to what superficially appear to be different subject matters. These themes integrate the *Handbook* in a way that is satisfying and we believe will encourage researchers to move beyond the comfort zone of the confines of their particular research topic, and encourage further research that will cross the boundaries of conceptual silos derived from source disciplines.

Given the past decades' explosion of scholarship in entrepreneurship, we are bound to raise the question, when will the Academy of Management and the British Academy of Management begin to recognise that entrepreneurship may be coming of age, and that perhaps it is timely to recognise it as a discipline and not simply an area or field of interest? We can only pose the question; it is for others to debate and take forward.

Finally we hope that all who delve into the pages of this *Handbook* will enjoy reading the chapters as much as we have done. We commend the work of our authors to you and look forward to further research emanating from the advice of our authors and the gaps in the literature that they so skilfully uncover.

REFERENCES

Alvarez, S. A. and Barney, J. B. (2013), 'Epistemology, opportunities and entrepreneurship: comments on Venkataraman et al. (2012) and Shane (2012)', *Academy of Management Review*, 38, 1, 154–66.

Anderson, A., Fayolle, A., Howells, J., Karataş-Özkan, M. and Condor, R. (forthcoming, 2014), 'Understanding entrepreneurship through post-positivistic perspectives', *Journal of Small Business Management*.

Calás, M. B., Smircich, L. and Bourne, K. A. (2009), 'Extending the boundaries: reframing "entrepreneurship as social change" through feminist perspectives', *Academy of Management Review*, 34, 552–69.

Casson, M. (2010), *Entrepreneurship: Theory, Networks, Institutions*. Cheltenham: Edward Elgar.

Chell, E. (1985), 'The entrepreneurial personality: a few ghosts laid to rest?' *International Small Business Journal*, 3, 3, 43–54.

Chell, E. (1998), 'The Critical Incident Technique', in C. Cassell and G. Symon (Eds), *Qualitative Methods and Analysis in Organisational Research*, London: Sage, ch 3.

Chell, E. (2004), 'The Critical Incident Technique' in C. Cassell, G. Symon (Eds) *Essential Guide to Qualitative Methods in Organizational Research*, London: Sage, pp 45–60.

Chell, E, (2008), *The Entrepreneurial Personality: A Social Construction*, London: The Psychology Press/ Routledge.

Chell, E., Haworth, J. M. and Brearley, S. (1991), *The Entrepreneurial Personality: Concepts, Cases and Categories* London & New York: Routledge.

Chell, E. and Baines, S. (1998), 'Does gender affect business 'performance'? A study of micro-businesses in business service in the UK,' *Entrepreneurship & Regional Development*, 10, 117–35.

Chell, E. and Baines, S. (2000), 'Networking, entrepreneurship and micro-business behaviour,' *Entrepreneurship and Regional Development*, 12, 195–215.

Chell, E., Karataş-Özkan, M. and Nicolopoulou, K. (2011), 'Social entrepreneurship: Innovation and cross-cultural aspects', *Entrepreneurship and Regional Development*, 22, 485–94.

Cope, J. (2003), 'Entrepreneurial learning and critical reflection: discontinuous events as triggers for "higher-level" learning', *Management Learning*, 34, 429–50.

Flanagan, J. C. (1954), 'The critical incident technique', *Psychological Bulletin*, 51, 4, 327–58.

Gartner, W.B. (1988), '"Who is an entrepreneur?" Is the wrong question', *Entrepreneurship: Theory & Practice*, (Summer) 47–68).

Hammersley, M. (2007), 'The issue of quality in qualitative research', *International Journal of Research and Method in Education*, 30, 3, 287–305.

Hjorth, D. (2010), 'Ending Essay: Sociality and Economy in Social Entrepreneurship' in Fayolle, A. and Matlay, H. (eds.) *Handbook of Research on Social Entrepreneurship*, Cheltenham: Edward Elgar, pp. 306–17.

HMSO (1971), *Report of the Committee of Inquiry on Small Firms* chaired by John E. Bolton. Cmnd 4811, London; HMSO.

Jack, S. L. and Anderson, A. R. (2002), 'The effects of embeddedness on the entrepreneurial process', *Journal of Business Venturing*, 17, 467–87.

Jackall, R. (1988), *Moral Mazes: The World of Corporate Managers*, New York USA and Oxford: Oxford University Press.

Karataş-Özkan, M. (2011), 'Understanding relational qualities of entrepreneurial learning: towards a multi-layered approach', *Entrepreneurship and Regional Development*, 23, 877–906.

Karataş-Özkan, M. and Chell, E. (2010), *Nascent Entrepreneurship and Learning*, Cheltenham: Edward Elgar.

Karataş-Özkan, M. and Chell, E. (2013), 'Gender inequalities in academic innovation and enterprise: a Bourdieuian analysis.' *British Journal of Management*. DOI: 10.1111/1467-8551.12020.

Knight, F. H. (1921), *Risk, Uncertainty and Profit*, New York: Houghton Mifflin.

Özbilgin, M. and Tatli, A. (2005), 'Book review essay: Understanding Bourdieu's contribution to organization and management studies', *Academy of Management Review*, 30, 855–77.

Patton, M. Q. (2002), *Qualitative Research and Evaluation Methods*, 3rd edition, Thousand Oaks, CA: Sage Publications.

Seale, C. (1999), *The Quality of Qualitative Research*, London: Sage Publications.

Shackle, G. L. S. (1972), *Epistemics and Economics: A Critique of Economic Doctrines*, Cambridge: Cambridge University Press.
Shackle, G. L. S. (1979), *Imagination and the Nature of Choice*, Edinburgh, Scotland: Edinburgh University Press.
Uzzi, B. (1997), Social structure and competition: the paradox of embeddedness, *Administrative Science Quarterly*, 42, 35–67.

PART I

THEORETICAL FRAMING

2. Notes towards a theory of entrepreneurial possibility[1]
William B. Gartner

INTRODUCTION

This chapter serves two purposes. First, it makes some tentative steps towards developing the idea of "possibility" as a fundamental characteristic of entrepreneurship. Second, it offers a reflexive discussion, by way of a series of disjointed "notes," of a history of how and why the idea of "possibility" became an idea the author felt worthy of attention. By offering a narrative on how the idea of "possibility" became possible (to the author), the chapter offers insights into how possibilities are generated and developed.

The "possible" is the potential to become or do. The history of the idea of the "possible" is a bit squirrely, in that, suffice to say, if one begins with Hume (1739/1968: 32) "That whatever the mind clearly conceives, includes the idea of possible existence, or in other words, that nothing we imagine is absolutely impossible," the idea of the "possible" could be thought of as anything that we could conceive (Yablo, 1993). I would not go as far as that. I put the idea of the "possible" as an indeterminate place somewhere between what can be conceived and what is feasible or practical. I define the idea of feasibility or practicability being the ability to actually accomplish the particular potential imagined: The "possible," then, lies somewhere between the conceivable and the feasible. It should be noted that what is feasible or practical, is itself, indeterminate at the moment one sets out to accomplish a particular possibility. I place the idea of possibility as occurring before the recognition/creation of opportunities. I agree with Stevenson & Jarillo's (1990) sense of opportunity as:

> [a] future situation which is deemed desirable and feasible. Thus, opportunity is a relativistic concept; opportunities vary among individuals and for individuals over time, because individuals have different desires and they perceive themselves with different capabilities. Desires vary with current position and future expectations. Capabilities vary depending upon innate skills, training and the competitive environment. Perceptions of both desires and capabilities are only loosely connected to reality (Stevenson & Gumpert, 1985).

From this perspective, possibilities become opportunities when possibilities are perceived as both desirable and feasible. In both cases (possibilities and opportunities) these phenomena are processes occurring over time rather than specific events (Steyaert, 2007). The key point, though, is that possibilities come before opportunities. In other words, there are no opportunities without first having possibilities.

The remainder of this chapter is my attempt to elucidate what the possible is, and, to explore why considering the idea of the possible might have value in entrepreneurship studies.

NARRATING THE POSSIBLE

My interpretation of Selden and Fletcher's (2010) view of the "narrative turn" (Bruner, 1990; Polkinghorne, 1988; Shafer, 1981; Spence, 1984) places my struggle to tell the story of my attempt to develop the idea of possibility within the context of the retrospection of the "grand narrative" (Lyotard, 1984) or "big story:" the autobiographical account, the life history of "what was," the attempt to offer a coherent account of the past (Bruner, 1990; 1993; Georgekopoulou, 2007; Labov, 1972; Polonoff, 1987), and, the "small stories," that is, the real-time stories of the now (Bamberg, 2006; Moissinac & Bamberg, 2005; Georgekopoulou, 2007; Hjorth, 2007) with a sense of "what could be" (Gartner, Bird & Starr, 1992; Hjorth, 2007; Selden and Fletcher, 2010). I would like to tell a story of how I have figured out what possibility is, that I have a "grand narrative" that makes sense, but I do not. I am in the "small stories" of the present, where, frankly the idea of possibility is a muddle:

> So here I am, in the middle way. . .
> Trying to learn to use words, and every attempt
> Is a wholly new start, and a different kind of failure
> Because one has only learnt to get the better of words
> For the thing one no longer has to say, or the way in which
> One is no longer disposed to say it. (Eliot, 1943: 30)

I constantly come back to these lines from T. S. Eliot, because those words express where I begin as a researcher. I am groping for words to make sense of the nature of possibility that I have yet to grasp. It is frustrating and discouraging. I have spent nearly three years trying to get a handhold on the idea of possibility. I feel for the ledge of ideas above me that might pull me forward, yet my purchase slips and I fall, again, backward, further from where I thought I started. "Do not let me hear / of the wisdom of old men, but rather of their folly" (Eliot, 1943: 26). I find no comfort in the idea of research: "go back and look," as a plausible rationale for my failure to move forward with a sense of the possible. I go back and look, over and over and over again. What am I failing to see? Here are notes on the journey, so far.

IMAGINING THE POSSIBLE

Since a conference on "The Toy Story" (Gartner, 2007) held in 2004, I have been drifting towards narrative perspectives as a way to understand aspects of the phenomenon of entrepreneurship. If there was an epiphany of sorts from this event, in terms of its relationship to the idea of possibility, it is expressed in these words:

> The label, "science of the imagination" is suggested as another promise for what entrepreneurship (and specifically, entrepreneurial narrative) might offer as a contribution to scholarship. The narrative of entrepreneurship is the generation of hypotheses about how the world might be: how the future might look and act. The articles in this special issue not only probe how entrepreneurs generate and modify their visions of the future, the scholars in these articles generate and modify alternative visions of the future, as well. (Gartner, 2007: 614).

I sense that imagination plays a large role in the phenomenon of entrepreneurship. The idea of the entrepreneurial imagination has been noticed by other scholars as well (c.f., Buchholz & Rosenthal, 2005; Chia, 1996; Chiles, Bluedorn, & Gupta, 2007; Harper, 1996; Hébert & Link, 1989; Kuhnert, 2001; Sarasvathy, 2002; White, 1976). Yet, how the role of the imagination plays out in the realm of the possible, as well as in all entrepreneurial endeavors as praxis, I am uncertain. Entrepreneurs speculate about the future, they tell stories about what may happen, they act in ways that a possible future may occur (Gartner, Bird & Starr, 1992). They see (imagine) what may come to exist. This is what narrative is. So, I believe that the key to understanding the role of the imagination (and thereby entering into the idea of the possible) will come through narrative approaches.

Yet, the evolution of my views on the use of narrative approaches in entrepreneurship research has been, for me, disjointed (c.f., Gartner, 2008; 2010; 2011). I have been, primarily, a quantitatively oriented scholar, with a qualitative sensibility, but, nonetheless, trained to analyze numbers generated from questionnaires as a fundamental way to explore the phenomenon of entrepreneurship (Gartner, 2008). I feel like a novice in my scholarly attempts to be in the narrative arena. Indeed, in my somewhat scattered efforts to make sense of how narrative methods can be related to entrepreneurship I stumble upon a "Workshop in Narrative Medicine" sponsored by "The Program in Narrative Medicine" at Columbia University in October 2010. I begin to see how narrative approaches might be used in practice, at least in the field of medicine (c.f., Charon & Montello, 2002). This path in the literature of narrative studies and ideas is different from what I see as a foundation for entrepreneurship scholars using narrative approaches (c.f. Hjorth & Steyaert, 2004). I am not sure whether this matters, but I do see my sense of what the field of narrative scholarship in entrepreneurship is different from my path through the narrative literature. I am in the middle way here.

MAKING THE POSSIBLE

I presented a series of lectures, discussions, and experiences at a workshop, "Entrepreneurship as Making" in February 2011 in Kolding, Denmark. The workshop was primarily focused on Saras Sarasvathy expounding on aspects of her ideas about effectuation (Sarasvathy, 2008). My presentations were little amuse-bouches sprinkled among the main courses of her revelations of what effectuation theory is actually about. In one of those sessions I played with this quote: "The crucial test of a story might be the sort of person it shapes" (Hoffmaster, 1994), and the subsequent discussion among the workshop participants about the power of stories to change perceptions about what is possible. An aspect of this discussion centered on the film "The Man Who Planted Trees" (1986) based on a story by Giono (1985). I have an ongoing fondness for this film (Gartner, 1993) as it depicts how the interaction of one individual's intentions and actions over a 50-year time frame led to significant changes in the environmental, social and economic lives of hundreds of people in a particular region in France. The story offers a particular roadmap for creating change. The upshot of the workshop gelled, for me, the idea that stories can be templates for the imagination to contemplate possible future states of existence for ourselves (or others). A story can serve as a guide for us to follow about how a future might occur. When individuals have stories of other individuals becoming entrepreneurs, the idea of becoming an entrepreneur enters the realm of possibility.

During the workshop Saras makes this suggestion: "Have you looked at (Shackle, 1966)?" I find the article online, download it, and, subsequently forget about it among a heap of other electronic documents in my "to-read" folder.

EXTENDING THE LIMITS OF THE POSSIBLE

My next effort towards developing the idea of possibility came in a keynote address for the Danish Entrepreneurship Foundation in Copenhagen, Denmark on April 28, 2011: "Extending the Limits of the Possible." I based my presentation on contrasting what I considered to be a statistical or "probable way" of looking at entrepreneurship versus a "possible way." I contrasted "probable," defined as some degree of 'likely to occur," compared to "possible," defined as "might occur." The probable connotes a sense of likelihood. The probable will vary by degree of certainty from 0 percent to 100 percent. Possible is an either/or occurrence. Something is either possible, or not; It is possible or impossible. There are no shades of grey. While this shift from "probable" to "possible" might seem rather minor, I believe it creates a fundamental change in our understanding of the nature of how and why entrepreneurial situations come into being.

Empirical scholarship on entrepreneurship tends to use what researchers can glean from information collected from the past and present: "what was" and "what is." Based on the knowledge generated from analyses of these events, predictions are offered: "what might be." In other words, if we encounter the pattern of data we just analyzed, again, we would expect to get similar results. Yet, such predictions based on past and current events are, in themselves, limited to the extent that such predictions of the future fail to account for the role of imagination and creativity residing in entrepreneurial choice and action. I fear that our scientific methods of discovery and understanding nudge us towards a more deterministic view of entrepreneurial phenomenon than is actually experienced by the individuals who are engaged in it. Acting (or thinking or doing, etc.) entrepreneurship, inherently, alters the fact patterns of the past and present so that the future, "what might be" is actually less dependent on them. This observation might seem obvious (as will be shown in a later section of this chapter), but I posited, at that moment in my understanding of the possible and entrepreneurship, that such a realization leads to subtle, yet significant changes in entrepreneurship research and practice.

As the basis for a comparison of the differences in viewing entrepreneurship from the perspectives of "probability" and "possibility," I used a research study I champion (Reynolds, Carter, Gartner & Greene, 2004), "The Prevalence of Nascent Entrepreneurs in the United States." I suggested that probability thinking in entrepreneurship may distract us from considering the unique characteristics of specific situations and the subtle leverage points that might enable lower probability situations to be reconsidered as possible, if not achievable, realities. The implications of a theory of the possible is, not that one ignores probability in entrepreneurial situations, rather, a theory of the possible requires one to understand what the probabilities mean in a specific situation, particularly when all entrepreneurial activity comes down to the possibility or impossibility implicit in any situation being an "N of 1" (March, Sproull & Tamuz, 1991). In many respects, at "N of 1," probabilities seem to hardly matter.

First: a rejoinder. I believe the Panel Study of Entrepreneurial Dynamics, PSED I (c.f., Gartner, Shaver, Carter & Reynolds, 2004; Reynolds, et. al., 2004; Reynolds, 2007), its sister, PSED II (c.f., Reynolds & Curtin, 2008), its cousin, the Comprehensive Australian Study of Entrepreneurial Emergence, CAUSEE (Davidsson, Steffens & Gordon, 2011) and the related efforts of the Global Entrepreneurship Monitor – GEM (c.f., Reynolds, 2010) have provided important and critical insights into many of the specific character-istics that comprise the nature of entrepreneurial phenomenon. Indeed, I believe that the insights gained from these studies have yet to be fully integrated into our current thinking about entrepreneurship, and, that current and future research efforts using these data sets are likely to generate even more knowledge about this phenomenon that will significantly impact our theories and understanding about this topic. I do not dis-count the research methods, evidence, or value of the evidence generated from the PSED and subsequent studies. My concern is with the interpretations (my implicit meanings) imbued in this evidence. For example:

What kinds of individuals *are likely* to become entrepreneurs? The broad demographic characteristics of individuals that identified themselves as actively engaged in the busi-ness startup process (Reynolds, et. al., 2004) *are likely to be: men* (Table VI: 274), as that they (at all ages) are twice as likely to be engaged in starting businesses compared to women; *young* (Table VI: 274): after the age of 34, the likelihood of starting businesses for both men and women declines; and have higher levels of *education* (Table VIII: 276): black men with any graduate education are two to three times more likely to engage in startup activities compared to black men with less education and that black and Hispanic men with any graduate education are two times more likely to engage in startup activities compared to white men. Similar differences hold for black women: more levels of education are correlated with higher rates of business startup activity; and higher levels of income (Table VIII: 276).

Since this article was published in 2004, I have used the above findings (and others) to point out that startup activity is highest among those individuals who are employed and well educated, and I have suggested that education is a significant way to increase entre-preneurial activity, particularly among minorities in the United States. And, individuals with low levels of education and without jobs are the least likely of all types of people to engage in startup activities. By implication, using probability thinking I have suggested that individuals without jobs and with low levels of educational attainment should be directed towards employment and schooling: not entrepreneurship (since individuals with those characteristics are less likely to attempt to start businesses).

From my poor perspective of probability thinking, I assume that demographic dif-ferences (in age, gender, ethnicity, education, income, employment) are deterministic: If men are trying to start businesses at rates that are twice as high as women, then, gender must be a factor in determining entrepreneurial activity. If blacks are more likely to try to start businesses than whites, then, ethnicity must be a factor. If those with more educa-tion and with jobs are more likely to try to start businesses, then, these factors must be important for understanding the startup process.

Considering the "possible" provides a disconnection to a probabilistic/ determinis-tic logic. What the statistics in Reynolds et al. (2004) indicate are that the likelihood of anyone attempting to start a business in the United States is, for most groups, rather small. Overall, the likelihood of anyone in the general population engaging in business startup is 6.2 percent. So, while men, overall, engage in startup on average at 8.0 percent and women, on average, engage in startup at 4.5 percent, the likelihood that any one particular person is engaged in business startup is still relatively rare. While gender, age, ethnicity, income, education and other factors certainly drive the likelihood of engaging in entrepreneurship higher (or lower) for certain groups of individuals, these characteristics do not, in and of themselves, prevent any one particular individual from engaging in business startup. Individuals with less education are starting businesses. The unemployed, for example, are starting businesses. So, within the category of the rare event, overall, of individuals engaged in starting businesses, certain factors may influence the likelihood of business startup, but these factors do not determine, specifically, whether a particular individual in a particular situation will actually engage in business startup. I am not saying that demographic (or other) factors are not relevant influences on entrepreneurial activities; rather I question whether I (we) might be treating the likelihood that a factor influences entrepreneurship too deterministically.

This point is probably obvious to you. For example, while, broadly, it might make sense to suggest that individuals should be better educated as one way to increase entrepreneurial activity, this suggestion does not really help or matter to someone who lacks education. While suggesting that "getting a college degree" might improve the odds of engaging in entrepreneurship, in general, it does not matter, specifically.

I think that using the above demographic characteristics might unfairly paint too broad a picture of what factors might truly matter for differentiating between those individuals who decide to engage in business startup compared to others, as well as those individuals who successfully start businesses compared to those who do not. Other characteristics (e.g., risk taking propensity, need for achievement, sociability, aggressiveness, networking, etc.) might be better and more focused characteristics that better explain the likelihood that certain individuals will engage in entrepreneurship and also achieve success at it. This may be so.

The point I am emphasizing is: no matter what characteristic we find that might be correlated to higher (or lower) rates of entrepreneurial activity, we can, with any of these characteristics, find individuals for which that characteristic did not play a role. For example, given the probabilities from the figures presented above, the least likely category of individual to engage in business startup is a Hispanic woman homemaker with less than a high school education. Yet, women who fit that profile do start businesses. The statistics show that. We have cases in the PSED dataset that fit this description. And, this fact, I believe, provides the foundation for the idea of possibility.

In putting together my slides for the Copenhagen presentation I came across this quote in the *New York Times* newspaper:

> (Schwartzel) credited Oosthuizen's win at the 2010 British Open at St. Andrews with helping him win at Augusta National. "To see him win there was just such a big inspiration. . . Just to see him do it made me realize that is possible, and just sort of maybe take it over the barrier of thinking that a major is too big for someone to win" (*New York Times*, 12 April 2011: B12).

One aspect of the possible then is: "If (s)he can do it, so can I."

The Copenhagen presentation ends with a series of stories of individuals who start companies. These individuals are counter examples of the statistical profiles of those individuals who would likely become entrepreneurs described earlier. My intention in offering those stories was to suggest that a statistical profile of entrepreneurship as "what is," in the population, is "merely" a constraint for considering "what it could become." For example, while Hispanic married women with children at home are less likely to start businesses, it is possible to create pathways for these women to actually start businesses at higher rates than other types of individuals. I have been trapped in an assumption that the probabilities reflected in the data of the past and present will determine what will become.

The idea of possibility opens up a realization that just one example of a particular entrepreneurial phenomenon can lead to others. Once there is an instance of a particular way in which entrepreneurial activity has occurred, we have a possible template for increasing this rare occurrence. Just one example of an unemployed Hispanic woman with less than a high school education who starts a business provides a way to consider that other individuals with those characteristics might also be able to achieve similar results. If our implicit (or explicit) agenda is to increase entrepreneurial activity among groups of individuals who have been seen as having low rates of entrepreneurship, then, I believe that we should think about how exceptions (very low probability events) might become the rule.

Rarity, then, from the perspective of possibility, becomes a leverage point. If we can find one instance of entrepreneurial activity occurring in a situation where it should not seem possible (but is), then, why not more?

The value of data sets such as the PSED might be less in finding comparative averages to ferret out significant differences among types, but in finding those rare cases within the generalizable sample of nascent entrepreneurial efforts. How was it possible for such a rare occurrence to come into existence? What might the unique case in the PSED actually tell us about entrepreneurship that the averages in the aggregations in the data do not?

Another way to think about possibility is to consider possibilities as rare occurrences, specifically, that could, in the future, become more common. The possible can be extended. For example, once Roger Bannister achieved running a mile in under four minutes in 1954, this record becomes a goal for others to achieve and better. (The record for running a mile is currently: 3:43.13 minutes set in 1999 by Hicham El Guerrouj.) For achieving world records for running, we do not look to see what the average for all runners is for an event: we look for the outlier(s). And, knowing that men run faster than women does not discount that some women run faster than other women and some men. If we look for insights when studying runners, it would be to explore the processes for how some runners run faster than others. And, we might assume that certain ways to run might be better than others. Whether these running methods work for all runners (at various ages, gender, etc.) could then be explored and compared.

For entrepreneurship, then, outliers in samples should be thoughtfully considered for whether they represent particular exemplars of ways that such rare events might be duplicated. Now, it is not that I have not had such an insight before. I have played with this aphorism for a number of years (Gartner, 1985): There is no average in entrepreneurship. Yet, statistical thinking tends to draw me towards general tendencies (the averages in the phenomenon) rather than to measures of deviations (variation in the phenomenon). The idea of the possible seems to be one way to break free of the thinking of the general tendencies of "what is" determining "what will be."

A written version of the Copenhagen presentation became the initial draft of this chapter. This was sent to the editors of this book for comments. I will summarize the gist of one aspect of their review: "Have you looked at (Shackle, 1966)?"

SHACKLE AND THE POSSIBLE

Chell (2008) offers a very cogent overview of the economist G. L. S. Shackle's work on decision-making under uncertainty and Shackle's insights about the idea of possibility:

> A business person or entrepreneur needs imagination in order to make decisions. "Enterprise" is the choice of course of action, the commitment to resources and the system that is devised in its pursuit. However, at the point, of choice, the future is yet to come and there is a period of "unknowing." In that sense the individual takes a gamble based on their imagination: the imagined sequence of possible events yet to come. At that point, the individual cannot attach a probability to their choice working out; all they can say is that they believe that it will. Thus, those favoured *possibilities* are characterized by an absence of disbelief, with disbelief representing an obstacle to the pursuit of a particular course of action. (p. 39)

Chell (2008) continues with observations Shackle posited that individuals make choices based on desirability and feasibility [albeit in a most sophisticated perspective than that offered in Stevenson & Jarillo's (1990) view of the characteristics of opportunity] and that choices based on possibilities are the products of limited knowledge, an interpretation of what is known, and, speculations about what "might be" given assumptions about particular future actions. There is more to Shackle's work, suffice to say, than what can be offered here, but, my initial reaction to reading Shackle's work was, 1966! I have been actively engaged in research and writing on the phenomenon of entrepreneurship since 1982, and, now in 2012 (30 years later!) I am introduced to Shackle's work? The year 1966 is 16 years earlier than when I began my efforts as a scholar! How is it possible not to notice Shackle's work on entrepreneurship and the imagination before now? How is it possible not to be aware of Shackle's ideas about the nature of possibility and its implication for entrepreneurship before now? The entire odyssey described earlier of my efforts to understand and explore the idea of possibility comes across as a very poor reinvention of Shackle's legacy.

I am in the process of digesting Shackle's writings and working to figure out how his ideas fit into the constellation of other views on the nature of what entrepreneurship is, as well as struggling to position Shackle's ideas of the possible in the context of prior scholarship on this idea (Perlman, 1990). For example, once the idea of the possible is considered as an aspect of future thinking, then, a variety of philosophical viewpoints might also come into play, such as Vaihinger's (1925) philosophy of "as if:" the use of fictions to both organize the present and direct the future. But, there are other philosophical perspectives on the idea of possibility that could be included in the discussion (e.g., Elster, 1978; Loux, 1979; Hawthorn, 1991; Hook, 1945; Gendler & Hawthorne, 2002).

As well as approaches involving mathematical sophistry (e.g., Armstrong, 1989; Dubois, Nguyen, & Prade, 2000; Dubois & Prade, 1988; Zadeh, 2007).

So, I am in the middle way. I see how Shackle's ideas on possibility presage the entire discussion of what opportunities are (Dutton, 1990; Jackson & Dutton, 1988), as well as what entrepreneurship is (Gartner, 1990). But, I do not have a grand narrative that can wrap up this chapter based on Shackle that might provide a coherent sense of what possibilities are, how others have viewed the idea of possibility, and how, exactly, the idea of possibility will likely enrich entrepreneurship and entrepreneurship scholarship. I can only offer a few muddled speculations of what might occur in the future: some possibilities on the idea of the possible.

THE FUTURE OF THE POSSIBLE

First, ironically, the future of the idea of the possible is likely to be best explored through more thorough research of prior scholarship on possibility. The citations I have offered are likely to lead to a large set of core works on possibility from a variety of disciplines, both philosophy and mathematics, and others. While I was able to find additional references in the entrepreneurship area to Shackle's ideas (c.f., Batstone & Pheby, 1996; Harmeling, Sarasvathy & Freeman, 2009) I sense that there is a need for the entrepreneurship field to be more aware of Shackle's work. I may be the last person to know of his ideas. But, I would hazard to guess that Shackle is not as well known as Kirzner (1973; 1979). This should be remedied. But, I believe that Shackle's work, per se, is not the complete answer to an intellectual foundation for the idea of possibility. I sense that an important focus of research in entrepreneurship must now come from scholars who are willing to journey into the territory of philosophy, so as to extend our ontology of entrepreneurship and the idea of possibility beyond the primary discipline of economics.

I believe that an important way to consider the possible in entrepreneurial activities is through the stories that entrepreneurs tell. When entrepreneurs tell their stories, or when we read an entrepreneur's autobiography, or a biography, a significant number of insights are provided about the possible in entrepreneurship:

(1)   the kinds of ideas that become actionable realities;
(2)   the influence of limitations and constraints on shaping the idea towards the real;
(3)   the specific processes for how ideas were transformed into a reality;
(4)   and, by implication, the recognition that these stories show that entrepreneurship is doable: If I can do this, you can too.

I surmise that the study of entrepreneurial narratives will lead towards a serious consideration of exemplars as important models for entrepreneurial activity (Mishler, 1990). Stories are models of possibility. The realm of doing something becomes possible because someone has shown that it is possible: Actors, actions, situations, how constraints are recognized and overcome, and the kinds of outcomes imagined and realized are often described and made graspable. Underlying the idea of the possible, then, in the stories that entrepreneurs tell is a sense that human volition matters (James, 1902; Weick,

1984): If you believe you will make a difference, then you will; if you believe you don't, then you won't.

I suggest that Weick's ideas in "Small Wins" and particularly the quote below reflect an important aspect of what entrepreneurship tends towards and what the idea of possibility opens up:

> One can argue that it is our duty as psychologists to be optimistic. To view optimism as a duty rather than as something tied to unsteady expectations of success is to position oneself in a sufficient variety of places with sufficient confidence that events may be set in motion that provide substance for that hope. (Weick, 1984: 48)

Hope, I believe, is based on the imagination. So, imagination matters because it can set in motion a vision of possible futures upon which action in the present can (hopefully) be fulfilled: Essentially, a play on the idea of entrepreneurs as "dreamers who do" (Pinchot, 1985: ix).[2]

So, there are a number of words, such as: "hope," "imagination," "vision," that require more attention from entrepreneurship scholars. We need to increase our vocabulary of words and ideas that might constellate our sense of entrepreneurship. I feel that the word "opportunity" as a primary construct of entrepreneurship (Shane & Venkataraman, 2000) has limited descriptive and intellectual power to fully portray entrepreneurship. As the quote earlier from Eliot suggests: ". . .one has only learnt to get the better of words / For the thing one no longer has to say, or the way in which / One is no longer disposed to say it." Pursuing possibility may generate a larger language to use in talking about entrepreneurship.

Finally, I reiterate that the possible is future-oriented, and, as such, is prospective rather than retrospective. Our tools for understanding phenomena tend to be retrospective in nature, e.g., if the discussion earlier on probabilistic views of entrepreneurship had any resonance, it should have indicated that the past and present can be analyzed to provide a regression line of what might be, but, in actuality, in terms of the future, the future itself is likely to be on another path.

> There are truth-seekers and truth-makers. On one hand, the pure scientist deems himself to be typically faced with a problem which has one right answer. His business is the map-maker's language, to get a fix on that problem, to take bearings from opposite ends of a base-line and plot them to converge upon the solution, the truth-to-be-found. On the other hand, the poet-architect-adventurer sees before him a landscape inexhaustibly rich in suggestions and materials for making things, for making works of literature or art or technology, for making policies and history itself, or perhaps making the complex, delicate, existential system called a business. . . Problem-solving is the bread and butter of life, and we shall starve without those who can do it. But besides those who can see ahead of them the one right answer, we need those who can see around them a million possibilities. . . (Shackle, 1966: 767)

There is no "one right answer," then, to where research on the idea of possibility will go. Maybe there are footholds, here, that will serve as the basis for further research and effort towards integrating the idea of the possible into the common discourse of entrepreneurship scholarship. Whether the idea of the possible serves as a useful construct for entrepreneurship scholarship remains to be seen. Maybe there is much more to uncover from the past that will prove insightful.

There is only the fight to recover what has been lost
And found and lost again and again: and how under conditions
That seem unpropitious. But perhaps neither gain nor loss.
For us, there is only the trying. . . (Eliot, 1943: 31)

NOTES

1. The initial draft of this chapter was written while the author was on sabbatical as a visiting professor at the ESSEC Business School in France (2011–12). Subsequent drafts were sponsored by the Danish Strategic Research Council and have been carried out within the PACE project (http://www.badm.au.dk/pace) as well as funded through a Batten Fellowship at the Darden School at the University of Virginia during the 2012–13 academic year.
2. Though it appears that individuals have some difficulty with imagining that they have significant potential for change in the future (Quoidbach, Gilbert & Wilson, 2013). How we navigate between our sense of ourselves in the past and what we believe is possible in the future is discontinuous. The images of ourselves then, now, and in the future are not necessarily coherent (Cross & Hazel, 1991; Robinson & Clore, 2002; Ross, 1989; McAdams, 2001).

REFERENCES

Armstrong, D. B. (1989), *A Combinatorial Theory of Possibility*, Cambridge: Cambridge University Press.

Bamberg, M. (2006), 'Stories: Big or small? Why do we care?' *Narrative Inquiry*, **16**, 139–47.

Batstone, S. & Pheby, J. (1996), 'Entrepreneurship and decision making: the contribution of G.L.S. Shackle', *International Journal of Entrepreneurial Behaviour & Research*, **2** (2): 34–51.

Bruner, J. (1990), *Acts of Meaning*, Harvard University Press, Cambridge, MA.

Bruner, J. (2003), 'Self-making narratives.' in: Fivush, R., Haden, C. A. (Eds.), *Autobiographical Memory and the Construction of a Narrative Self*, pp. 209–25, Erlbaum, Mahwah, NJ.

Buchholz, R. A. & Rosenthal, S. B. (2005), 'The spirit of entrepreneurship and the qualities of moral decision making: Toward a unifying framework', *Journal of Business Ethics*, **60** (3): 307–15.

Charon, R. & Montello, M. M. (2002), *Stories Matter: The Role of Narrative in Medical Ethics*, London: Routledge.

Chell, E. (2008), *The Entrepreneurial Personality: A Social Construction (2nd Edition)*, London: Routledge.

Chia, R. (1996), 'Teaching paradigm shifting in management education: university business schools and the entrepreneurial imagination', *Journal of Management Studies*, **33** (4): 409–28.

Chiles, T H, Bluedorn, AC, & Gupta, V. K. (2007), 'Beyond creative destruction and entrepreneurial discovery: a radical Austrian approach to entrepreneurship', *Organization Studies*, **28** (4): 467–93.

Cross, S. & Hazel, M. (1991), 'Possible selves across the life span', *Human Development*, **34** (4): 230–55.

Davidsson, P., Steffens, P. R., & Gordon, S. R. (2011), 'Comprehensive Australian Study of Entrepreneurial Emergence (CAUSEE): design, data collection and descriptive results', in Hindle, K. & Klyver, K. (Eds.) *Handbook of Research on New Venture Creation*, Edward Elgar, Cheltenham, pp. 216–50.

Dubois, D., Nguyen, H. T., & Prade, H. (2000), 'Possibility theory, probability and fuzzy sets: misunderstandings, bridges and gaps', *Fundamentals of Fuzzy Sets*, 1: 343–438.

Dubois, D. & Prade, H. (1988), *Possibility Theory: An Approach to Computerized Processing of Uncertainty*. New York: Plenum Press.

Dutton, J. E. (1990), 'The making of organizational opportunities: An interpretive pathway to organizational change', *Research in Organizational Behavior*, **15**: 195–226.

Eliot, T. S. (1943), *The Four Quartets*, New York: Harcourt Brace & Company.

Elster, J. (1978), *Logic and Society: Contradictions and Possible Worlds*, New York: Wiley.

Gartner, W. B. (1985), 'A framework for describing and classifying the phenomenon of new venture creation', *Academy of Management Review*, **10** (4): 696–706.

Gartner, W. B. (1990), 'What are we talking about when we talk about entrepreneurship?' *Journal of Business Venturing*, **5** (1): 15–28.

Gartner, W. B. (1993), 'Can't see the trees for the forest. A review of the film "The Man Who Planted Trees," directed by Frederick Back', *Journal of Management Education*, **17** (2): 269–74.

Gartner, W. B. (2007), 'Entrepreneurial narrative and a science of the imagination,' *Journal of Business Venturing*, **22** (5): 613–27.

Gartner, W. B. (2008), 'Variations in Entrepreneurship', *Small Business Economics*, **31**: 351–61.

Gartner, W. B. (2010), 'A new path to the waterfall: A narrative on the use of entrepreneurial narrative', *International Journal of Small Business*, **28** (1): 6–19.

Gartner, W. B. (2011), 'When words fail: An entrepreneurship glossolalia', *Entrepreneurship and Regional Development*, **23** (1–2): 9–21.

Gartner, W. B., Bird, B. J. and Starr, J. (1992), 'Acting as if: Differentiating entrepreneurial from organizational behavior', *Entrepreneurship: Theory and Practice*, **16** (3): 13–32.

Gartner, W. B., Shaver, K. G., Carter, N. M. & Reynolds, P. D. (2004), *Handbook of Entrepreneurial Dynamics: The Process of Business Creation*, Thousand Oaks, CA: Sage Publications.

Gendler, T. S. and Hawthorne, J. (Eds.) (2002), *Conceivability and Possibility*, Oxford: Oxford University Press.

Georgekopoulou, A. (2007), *Small Stories, Interaction and Identities*, John Benjamins, Amsterdam/Philadelphia, US.

Giono, J. (1985), *The Man Who Planted Trees*, Chelsea, VT: Chelsea Green.

Harmeling, S. S., Sarasvathy, S. D. & Freeman, R. E. (2009), 'Related Debates in Ethics and Entrepreneurship: Values, Opportunities, and Contingency', *Journal of Business Ethics*, **84** (3): 341–65.

Harper, D. (1996), *Entrepreneurship and the Market Process: An Inquiry into the Growth of Knowledge*, London: Routledge.

Hawthorn, G. (1991), *Plausible Worlds: Possibility and Understanding in History and the Social Sciences*, Cambridge: Cambridge University Press.

Hébert, R. F., & Link, A. N. (1989), 'In search of the meaning of entrepreneurship', *Small Business Economics*, **1** (1): 39–49.

Hjorth, D. (2007), 'Lessons from Iago: Narrating the event in entrepreneurship', *Journal of Business Venturing*, **22** (5): 712–32.

Hjorth, D. and Steyaert, C. (2004), *Narrative and Discursive Approaches in Entrepreneurship*, Cheltenham, UK: Edward Elgar.

Hoffmaster, B. (1994), 'The forms and limits of medical ethics', *Social Science and Medicine*, **39** (9): 1161.

Hook, S. (1945), *The Hero in History: A Study in Limitation and Possibility*, London: Secker and Warburg.

Hume, D. (1739/1968), *Treatise of Human Nature*, Oxford: Clarendon Press.

Jackson, S. E. and Dutton J. E. (1988), 'Discerning threats and opportunities', *Administrative Science Quarterly*, **33**, 370–87.

James, W. (1902), *The Varieties of Religious Experience: A Study in Human Nature*, New York: Longmans, Greene and Company.

Kirzner, I. M. (1973), *Competition and Entrepreneurship*, Chicago: University of Chicago Press.

Kirzner, I. M. (1979), *Perception, Opportunity, and Profit: Studies in the Theory of Entrepreneurship*, Chicago: University of Chicago Press.

Kuhnert, S. (2001), 'An evolutionary theory of collective action: Schumpeterian entrepreneurship for the common good,' *Constitutional Political Economy*, **12** (1): 13–29.

Labov, W. (197), *Language in the Inner City*, Philadelphia: University of Pennsylvania Press.

Loux, M. J. (1979), *The Possible and the Actual: Readings in the Metaphysics of Modality*, Cornell, NY: Cornell University Press.

Lyotard, J.–F. (1984), *The Postmodern Condition: A Report on Knowledge*, University of Manchester Press: Manchester.

March, J. G., Sproull, L. S. and Tamuz, M. (1991), 'Learning from samples of one or fewer', *Organization Science*, **2** (1): 1–13.

McAdams, D. P. (2001), 'The psychology of life stories', *Review of General Psychology*, **5** (2): 100–22.

Mishler, E. G. (1990), 'Validation in inquiry-guided research. The role of exemplars in narrative studies,' *Harvard Education Review*, **60** (4): 415–42.

Moissinac, L. and Bamberg, M. (2005), '"It's weird, I was so mad": Developing discursive identity defenses in conversational "small" stories of adolescent boys', *Texas Speech Communication Journal*, **29** (2): 142–156.

Perlman, M. (1990), 'The fabric of economics and the golden threads of GLS Shackle', in Frowen, S.F. (Eds) *Unknowledge and Choice in Economics: Proceedings of a Conference in Honour of GLS Shackle*, London: Macmillan, pp. 9–19.

Pinchot. G. III (1985), *Intrapreneuring*, New York: Harper & Row.

Polkinghorne, D. (1988), *Narrative Knowing and the Human Sciences*, SUNY Press, Albany.

Quoidbach, J., Gilbert, D. T. & Wilson, T. D. (2013), 'The end of history illusion', *Science*, **339**: 96–8.

Reynolds, P. D. (2007), 'New Firm Creation in the United States: A PSED I Overview', *Foundations and Trends in Entrepreneurship*, **3** (1): 1–150.

Reynolds, P. D. (2010), 'New firm creation: A global assessment of national, contextual, and individual factors', *Foundations and Trends in Entrepreneurship*, **6** (5): 315–496.

Reynolds, P. D., Carter, N. M., Gartner, W. B. & Greene, P. G. (2004). 'The prevalence of nascent entrepreneurs in the United States: Evidence from the Panel Study of Entrepreneurial Dynamics', *Small Business Economics*, 23: 263–84.

Reynolds, P. D. & Curtin, R. T. (2008), 'Business creation in the United States:Panel Study of Entrepreneurial Dynamics II initial assessment', *Foundations and Trends in Entrepreneurship*, **4** (3): 155–307.

Robinson, M. D. & Clore, G. L. (2002), 'Belief and feeling: Evidence for an accessibility model of emotional self-report', *Psychological Bulletin*, **128** (6): 934–960.

Ross, M. (1989), 'Relation of implicit theories to the construction of personal histories', *Psychological Review*, **96** (2): 341–57.

Sarasvathy, S. D. (2002), 'Entrepreneurship as economics with imagination', *Ruffin Series in Business Ethics*, **3**, 95–112.

Sarasvathy, S. D. (2008), *Effectuation: Elements of Entrepreneurial Expertise*,Cheltenham, UK: Edward Elgar.

Schafer, R. (1981), 'Narration in the psychoanalytic dialogue', in Mitchell, W. T. J. (Ed.), *On Narrative*. University of Chicago Press, Chicago.

Selden, P. and Fletcher, D. (2010), '"Practical narrativity" and the "real-time story" of entrepreneurial becoming', in *The Republic of Tea. Entrepreneurial Narrative Theory Ethnomethodology and Reflexivity*, **1** (1): 51–74.

Shackle, G. L. S. (1966), 'Policy, poetry and success', *The Economic Journal*, **76** (December): 755–67.

Shane, S. and Venkataraman, S. (2000), 'The promise of entrepreneurship as a field of research', *Academy of Management Review*, **25**: 217–26.

Spence, D. (1984), *Narrative Truth and Historical Truth: Meaning and Interpretation in Psychoanalysis*. Norton, New York.

Stevenson, H. H. & Gumpert, D. E. (1985), 'The heart of entrepreneurship', *Harvard Business Review*, **85** (2): 85–94.

Stevenson, H. H. and Jarillo, J. C. (1990), 'A paradigm of entrepreneurship: Entrepreneurial management', *Strategic Management Journal*, **11** (Summer): 17–27.

Steyaert, C. (2007), '"Entrepreneuring" as a conceptual attractor? A review of process theories in 20 years of entrepreneurship studies,' *Entrepreneurship & Regional Development*, **19** (6): 453–77.

'The Man Who Planted Trees' [Film] (1986), Societé Radio-Canada/CBS (Producer), & Back, F. (Director). Direct Cinema Limited, Inc. P. O. Box 69799, Los Angeles, CA 90069. (30 Minutes).

Vaihinger, H. (1925), *The Philosophy of "As If:" A System of the Theoretical, Practical and Religious Fictions of Mankind*, (C. K. Ogden, Trans.) New York: Harcourt, Brace and Company.

Weick, K. E. (1984), 'Small wins: Redefining the scale of social problems', *American Psychologist*, **39** (1): 40–9.

White, L. H. (1976), 'Entrepreneurship, imagination and the question of equilibration', *Austrian Economics*, **3**: 87–104.

Yablo, S. (1993), 'Is conceivability a guide to possibility?' *Philosophy and Phenomenological Research*, **53** (1): 1–42.

Zadeh, L. A. (2007), 'Fuzzy sets as a basis for a theory of possibility', *International Journal of Approximate Reasoning*, **45** (1): 82–105.

3. Buzzwords in business and management studies
Mark Casson and Marina Della Giusta

1. INTRODUCTION

This Handbook reviews a large number of concepts and techniques that have been used to analyse small business behaviour. Some have been borrowed from related disciplines, including economics, sociology and psychology, while others have originated within business and management studies itself. Some concepts have well-established intellectual pedigrees, while others are more recent innovations.

Compared to most other social sciences, business and management studies is a relatively new area of professional inquiry, and within this domain small business studies is one of the newest. Given the large number of concepts that are currently employed to analyse small business behaviour, this chapter considers how many of these concepts are likely to survive as building blocks for future research. It argues that there is a significant degree of redundancy in the terminology of small business studies. While a degree of redundancy is typical of language, it is also true that it can generate cognitive overload and hinder learning (Plass et al., 2010) and ultimately damage the development of the discipline itself.

There seem to be many words denoting the same thing, and sometimes no clear definition of the things they are supposed to denote. In the theory of the firm, for example, the success of a firm, in terms of its profitability and growth, is variously imputed to superior capabilities, competencies, entrepreneurship or managerial skills. But is entrepreneurship just a special type of capability, and is competence just another word for skill? Is entrepreneurship just one of many types of capability, or it is it the key capability without which other capabilities (if they exist) are of little value? Furthermore, what exactly is the link between the entrepreneur, considered as an individual, and the firm that they own and control (Casson, 2005)?

There is very little debate on these issues. Some scholars support one view and others another, but the supporters of alternative views rarely seem to engage in meaningful dialogue with one another. Similarly, entrepreneurship is often associated with innovation, risk-taking, business venturing, imagination and creativity. Are all these concepts really different from each other, or are some of them just the same concept by different names? How many genuinely distinctive concepts are required in order to understand business behaviour properly? Judging by the number of concepts in circulation, business and management studies must be an extremely complex discipline, but has it become so complex that it is just confusing. Real-world business behaviour is undoubtedly complex, but if the theory is just as complex as the phenomena it describes then it is any help in actually understanding the phenomena?

While some redundancy is a natural feature of the evolution of language, this chapter argues that the current level of conceptual redundancy in business studies is excessive. The chapter has three main objectives: to analyse the process by which redundancy is generated; to demonstrate that current levels of redundancy are excessive; and to suggest ways by which redundancy can be reduced. The issue of redundancy needs to be addressed, it is claimed, because excessive redundancy creates confusion rather than clarity.

Section 2 introduces a theoretical framework that explains, not the behaviour of firms, but the behaviour of academics seeking to explain the behaviour of firms. An obvious starting point when addressing the behaviour of an academic profession is the set of social networks that the profession employs to develop and diffuse new ideas. Drawing on recent developments in social network theory, the spread of buzzwords is proposed as a major factor generating redundancy. The process of creating and diffusing buzz-words, it is suggested, explains a great deal about the evolution of business studies as a discipline.

The theoretical framework itself is perfectly general, and compatible with existing inter-disciplinary studies on the structure and evolution of language (see a review of papers in psycholinguistics by Christiansen and Kirby, 2003, and also Chater and Christiansen, 2009; in addition, see papers in biology by Greenhill et al., 2010; Pagel, 2009; Ferrer-i-Cancho and Sole, 2001). Its application to business studies is simply a special case. It can be applied to any branch of academia. Using basic behavioural economics principles, the theory proposes that the spread of buzzwords is governed by incentives acting upon individuals seeking to build a reputation in their field through an instantly recognisable (though not necessarily analytically precise) concept. Entrepreneurial individuals innovate new concepts, while imitators, who are seeking to show that they belong to a discourse (particularly once the latter is perceived as promising to become dominant), help their diffusion. Diffusion is therefore driven, not only by the intrinsic properties of the concept (redundancy avoidance, elegance, etc.), but also by the properties of the profession in which it is created.

Although network structure is important, it is incentives that are key. In line with theories of entrepreneurship, the theory emphasises individual rather than collective action, and personal agency rather than social structure. The theory suggests that under certain conditions economic incentives may lead to excessive conceptual innovation. These conditions, it is suggested, have prevailed in business and management studies, and have generated the conceptual redundancy referred to above.

Section 3 applies the theory using a case study. The case study focuses on a single concept: strategy. There are many concepts that could have been selected for a case study, including entrepreneurship, as mentioned above. Strategy was chosen because it is a widely used concept that is regarded by many business academics as fundamental, and its spread is relatively well documented (see Hitt, Ireland, Camp and Sexton, 2001). There are many surveys of the strategy literature and of the various sub-fields that the concept has spawned. The object of this case study is not to review or replicate previous bibliometric work on publications and their citations, but rather to assess how well the theory of buzzwords explains the diffusion of the strategy concept.

The case study shows that the spread of the word 'strategy' has been facilitated by the fact that it can be applied in many different contexts, and therefore appears to be a unifying idea. In practice, it is suggested, strategy has different meanings in different contexts, so that its apparent generality is spurious. The illusion of generality has been maintained because many writers who use the term fail to specify in detail the context in which they use the term. Such spurious generality is characteristic of many buzzwords. Spurious generality undermines logic rigour, rather than reinforcing it, as abstract concepts often claim to do. The harmful effects of excessive reliance on the strategy concept have persisted because of weak intellectual leadership in the profession, it is suggested.

The conclusions, and their implications for the future development of business studies, are summarised in section 4.

2.   A THEORETICAL PERSPECTIVE ON BUZZWORDS AND THEIR DIFFUSION

The Significance of Buzzwords

Most academics, whatever their discipline, would probably agree that their own subject has buzzwords. Taken at face value, buzzwords relate to important aspects of a subject, and are particularly associated with exciting and emergent topic areas. From another perspective, however, they could be indicative of the fads and fashions through which the development of most subjects seems to progress. While they may sometimes relate to novel and important developments, buzzwords can also relate to not-so-novel or not-so-important developments instead. They may lack genuine novelty because they just say the same old thing in a different language – they represent 'old wine in new bottles', in other words. On the other hand, they may be genuinely novel but also genuinely unimportant – an irrelevance or, even worse, a 'red herring'.

Buzzwords appear in both documents and discussion. Referees and research committee members often report that certain buzzwords are regularly repeated in the grant applications that they review. Conference-goers report that buzzwords frequently appear in the titles of conference papers, and in comments and questions addressed to speakers by young and ambitious members of the audience. Buzzwords, it seems, are often used to impress.

Much of the evidence relating to academic buzzwords is anecdotal. This is not due simply to a lack of evidence. For example, there are substantial archives relating to past grant applications, and until recently it was quite common to tape-record discussions at academic conferences for the benefit of rapporteurs who summarised debates on conference issues. Content analysis could readily be applied to such sources in order to determine the frequency with which various words appear. Buzzwords could be identified as frequently occurring words (other than common prepositions, etc.) or as words whose frequency had increased substantially over time.

There is a problem of interpretation, however. The frequency with which a word is used does not, by itself, indicate whether the word is being used through logical necessity or simply because of a desire to impress. Context is needed to address this issue. Context can also indicate whether the use of a redundant word is purely gratuitous, in the sense that no meaning would be lost if the word were left out, or whether it is unnecessary in the sense that it could be replaced by some other commonly used word that has been in circulation for a long time. However, it is much more laborious to analyse context than to simply count the number of times that a word is used.

Context and Definition

The research question addressed in this chapter is why academic buzzwords are so often used in cases where they seem to be either unnecessary or misleading. It is useful to begin with a definition of an academic buzzword. An academic buzzword is defined as a novel and widely adopted label for a concept that features in academic research. This definition is only one of several that could be suggested; it has been selected because it is useful in addressing the following questions:

- Why are academic buzzwords so often used in cases where they seem to be either unnecessary or misleading?
- Are buzzwords simply used to impress?
- If so, is everyone impressed, or just certain people? Does it matter that some people are unimpressed if others are?
- If everyone recognises that buzzwords are used in order to impress, why do people not discount the use of these words and demand that authors and speakers address them in conventional language instead?
- If some people are impressed by buzzwords and others are not, then surely it will be the more gullible people who are impressed. Astute people will not be impressed. But if astute people are influential and gullible people are not then will the strategy not fail, even though some people are impressed?

The use of a buzzword is warranted by its analytical contribution, it is suggested, only when it clarifies distinctions between superficial concepts, develops or improves a theory or paradigm, clarifies the interpretation of evidence, or facilitates inter-disciplinary work. A buzzword does not have to do all of these things, but it should do at least one of them.

The kinds of words included in this study are words that are used to label concepts employed to analyse complex social systems.

- *Typologies* of large social systems typically involve an -ism: socialism, capitalism, individualism, collectivism, etc.
- The *structures and processes* of a system are often described using words ending in -ion: competition, co-operation, specialisation, differentiation, integration, agglomeration, organisation, evolution, etc.
- The *properties* of a system are often described using words ending in -ity: identity, stability, sustainability, creativity, credibility, etc. Modern disciplines are replete with such words: in econometrics, for example, -ity words proliferate; there are desirable properties of a system, such as normality, stationarity and identifiability, and a host of undesirable properties, including endogeneity, multicollinearity, and heteroscedasticity. Anyone who can succeed in adding to the vocabulary of complex systems is guaranteed a glittering academic career; the incentive to coin a new buzzword is considerable.

The Re-labelling of Concepts

There are many pairs of words that mean the same thing. In the context of academic research this implies that the same concept can be labelled in different ways. This duplication provides scope for purely cosmetic innovation, in which one word replaces another while the concept remains the same.

It is unusual, however, for two words to mean exactly the same thing. Words may be similar, but they are rarely identical. This is because most words carry a connotation which is provided by the context in which they originated or in which they are most commonly used. When a novel word replaces another word, therefore, the concept to which it refers may acquire a somewhat different connotation. In the 1970s, for example, the founder of a small business was usually described as self-employed; this terminology emphasised that they were not employed by anyone else, and might suggest to some audiences that no one else was willing to employ them: the small business owner was seen as being a worker who employed themselves. Today such a small business founder would be described as an entrepreneur. This carries the connotation of someone who initiates an innovative project (the formation of their firm) and bears significant risk (of losing the personal capital they have invested in it). The small business owner is therefore seen as more like a successful adventurer than an ordinary worker. The change in terminology partly reflects a different view of small business, driven by wider economic and social changes, but the terminology itself reinforces the change of view (Bechhofer and Elliott, 1971; 1976; Carland, Hoy, Boulton and Carland, 1984; Chell and Hayes, 2000). It is not only small business founders that have benefited from this change; academics who study small business are now perceived to be studying the roots of enterprise and innovation rather than just the survival strategies of people who do not want, or cannot find, a regular job.

Redundancy and connotation between them provide a useful explanation of why scholars may be motivated to introduce new words by replacing existing words. They can gain a reputation as an innovator, and also as someone who has raised the status of their subject by giving it a more positive image with the public.

This does not explain, however, why other scholars in the same profession will wish to take up the new word. Changing vocabulary can be costly, because it involves learning to express oneself in a different way. But where a new word provides a more positive connotation for a subject, other members of a profession may find it useful to embrace the word too. This is particularly true if a profession has acquired a rather negative image that it wishes to live down. In the big-business shake out of the 1970s, for example, personnel departments became extremely unpopular, but they were able to re-invent themselves quite successfully as 'human resources' departments in the 1980s, even though their job was basically the same as before. 'Personnel' was associated with shopfloor conflicts and making people redundant, while 'human resources' was focused on recruitment, training and retention of staff. Increasing the workloads of junior staff became 'empowerment', while laying off senior staff became 'delayering'. In academic research, 'industrial relations' experts reappeared as 'human resource strategy' professors, and 'labour economists' became 'personnel economists' instead.

Conceptual Arbitrage and the Import of Jargon from Other Disciplines

There is, however, another reason why academics may take up a buzzword introduced by others: namely, that the new word establishes a link with a related phenomenon in another field. In the 1950s economists avidly imported jargon from mathematics and statistics because they wished to exploit the concepts to which the jargon referred. 'Equilibrium', 'stability', and 'homotheticity' (constant returns to scale) became extremely fashionable words. Economists of the time were widely criticised for being pseudo-scientific, and even of suffering from 'physics envy', but in the hands of scholars such as Samuelson the novel concepts were put to good use, and their legacy has endured.

The concepts imported into economics in the 1950s were successful because they reflected a logical isomorphism between economic systems and engineering systems. These isomorphisms were particularly strong in respect of linear dynamic systems. The innovation of jargon was therefore associated with the development of a new and profound set of insights that linked economics with an established body of theory about a general class of systems. The new words carried appropriate connotations when they were imported into economics because the logical structures in which they were embedded were the same. Recent examples of useful imports include 'homeostasis' in microeconomic theory, 'gift exchange' in labour economics, and 'altruism' in experimental and behavioural economics.

There are many other examples of the successful transfer of jargon as part of a process of deepening understanding, in which general principles of systems behaviour are discovered to be relevant to fields to which they had not previously been applied. The success of these transfers may wrongly suggest, however, that the transfer of jargon is invariably indicative of an advance in understanding. By exploiting this misunderstanding, astute researchers can gain a reputation as conceptual innovators purely by coining new words, or by taking words from the vocabulary of one discipline and applying them indiscriminately to another.

Following the successful transfer of mathematical methods to economics, it was realised that many mathematical models were too rigid in their structures to accommodate the flexibility that is characteristic of market economies. The structures of economies evolved faster than the assumptions of conventional mathematic models allowed. An obvious – if superficial – response was to turn to biology, which models flexible systems in nature. Furthermore, the fact that theoretical biologists used 'evolutionary' theory suggested a ready set of evolutionary metaphors for models of the economy – an idea reinforced by the fact that economics and evolutionary biology possessed a common intellectual ancestry in the work of Malthus. Unfortunately, however, evolutionary biology did not have an appropriate mathematical model – like physics – but only a set of metaphors and analogies. Where there were exact models, as in evolutionary game theory, they did not fit economic phenomena particularly well. Although 'evolution' has become a buzzword in modern economics, therefore, the question still remains open as to whether it represents a genuine conceptual innovation or just a passing fad.

Economics, like other social sciences, has made many attempts at importing concepts from other disciplines, and indeed few disciplines have been immune. In the 1920s economic theorists, in homage to Einstein, applied the concept of relativity to economics, and in the 1930s business economists experimented with concepts drawn from social psychology. Marxist economists of the 1960s relied heavily on sociological concepts (e.g. class) and political concepts (e.g. power). Most of these applications failed because the buzzwords introduced were merely suggestive of metaphors and analogies. These metaphors and analogies hinted at profound commonalities in the systems studied by the different disciplines, but they have never translated into widely accepted models of the formal mathematical kind that economists prefer. The notion that profound connections do indeed exist still remains, but the logical isomorphisms have never been fully established.

The Proliferation of Buzzwords

If an academic discipline were controlled by a wise and knowledgeable elite, then misguided attempts to import buzzwords from other disciplines would be met by well-informed and closely reasoned objections. Attempts to introduce an entirely new word on the grounds that some new and important concept has just been discovered and needed a name would encounter ruthless criticism. While innovators of new buzzwords may impress the junior members of the profession, or the members who are most naïve, they may lose the patronage of experienced senior people. Experienced members of the governing elite would obstruct any diffusion. Innovative scholars promoting new buzzwords that they could not legitimate would not be acclaimed, but derided. A buzzword innovator would face a serious risk of losing their reputation, rather than enhancing it.

In practice, the opposite situation is often observed. Elites often appear remarkably weak. A simple way of explaining this anomaly is that no one in a profession – including the elite – privately believes that they understand their subject. Their members may feel that they have established their own reputations on the basis of introducing buzzwords themselves. Public criticism and withdrawal of patronage by members of the elite is therefore reserved for those who attack established concepts and the claims that they have made for it, rather than for those who simply propose another word for the same thing.

Members of the elite may privately believe that existing concepts are inadequate for their purpose. In order to address this problem, it may be deemed necessary for the leaders of the profession to encourage innovation in the hope that some of the attempts may prove successful. Since the subject is not well understood, however, it is difficult to know how to discriminate between a successful innovation and an unsuccessful one. Members of the elite could pass arbitrary judgements on innovations as they occur, but denunciations would only carry weight if there were a degree of consensus amongst them. Disagreements may discredit the elite as a whole, as they will appear incompatible with any claim that the elite, as a group, knows best.

If an elite wishes to remain silent, in order to avoid damaging disagreements between themselves, then popularity becomes the obvious criterion by which to determine the success of an innovation. In a world where no one understands very much, popularity itself signifies very little, but it can at least be measured. Furthermore, when no one believes that anyone else knows anything much anyway, popularity may reflect a collective wisdom of the masses, if any such wisdom exists.

Under these circumstances, an individual may acquire a useful reputation simply as someone who is a potential rather than an actual innovator. Unsuccessful innovations are rated more highly than no innovation because successful innovation is recognised as something very difficult to achieve. Successful innovation cannot be achieved without attempted innovation, and so attempted innovation is rewarded to some degree independently of success.

Another implication of a general lack of understanding is that using buzzwords may also be valued highly even though people recognise that a buzzword may quite possibly signify nothing. A person who is quick to adopt a new buzzword signals that they socialise with innovative people, and this may in turn suggest that they are more likely than most to come up with an innovation of their own. 'Dropping names' is a widely recognised way of advertising a person's social contacts, but in an academic environment, dropping buzzwords can be just as effective, because knowing the appropriate buzzwords to drop into conversation can be a signal of knowing the right people too.

Peer Opinion Versus Elite Opinion

Where there is no belief in the value of tradition, or the existence of an accumulated stock of knowledge, the opinions of experienced members may count for little with younger and less experienced members. Furthermore, if the profession is rapidly growing, then the younger and inexperienced members may heavily outnumber the older and more experienced members, and if there are plenty of jobs available then the rationing of jobs by senior members may be only a minor consideration. Under these circumstances, peer opinion may be more important for junior members than the opinions of the elite – peers who are colleagues of similar age and experience who expect, as the rising generation, to become the new elite. In the absence of respect for tradition, the new elite has no need to embrace the ideas of the old elite – they can make up their own systems and beliefs without regard to those of the preceding generation. Under these circumstances, innovators of useless buzzwords have little to fear from reputation loss, because the only people with whom they are likely to lose reputation are people who do not matter much anyway.

Evaluation of Buzzwords

Even if it were true that most professions operate under conditions of very limited understanding, it would still be questionable whether uncritical acceptance of buzzword innovations was an efficient strategy for a profession as a whole. In the absence of any agreed critical standards by which to assess potential conceptual innovations, innovation may come to be regarded as an end in itself, rather than as the necessary means towards a higher end. In pursuit of reputations for innovation, members of the profession may be discouraged from making the effort required to attempt a genuine innovation. They may focus purely on innovating new buzzwords and demonstrating their familiarity with the most recent buzzwords introduced by others. This is a lower cost strategy than attempting a genuine innovation.

A useful way of assessing the seriousness of this problem is to examine some practical case study evidence. The field of business and management studies is a fertile field for case study material. It has been a major growth area for teaching and research in the social sciences in the post-war period. It is a multi-disciplinary area in which inter-disciplinary research has been encouraged. Its leading journals explicitly encourage conceptual innovation. Many of its leading academics have achieved a 'guru' status both in the business community and within the academia profession. Many of the management buzzwords coined in the post-war period have found their way into popular use. The case study below focuses on one of the most important buzzwords in the post-war history of management studies – namely strategy.

3.   A CASE STUDY: 'STRATEGY' AS A BUZZWORD IN BUSINESS STUDIES

The Importance of Strategy to Business Studies

The concept of strategy is widely used in business studies. It has given its name to an entire field of study, to a significant number of sub-fields, and to an associated suite of prestigious academic journals. It has provided a valuable 'meal ticket' for many academics. Indeed, many social scientists publishing in economics, sociology and business history journals might not have had an academic career if it were not for a post in a business school as a strategy professor. By many criteria, strategy is an immensely valuable concept, but the question considered in this case study is whether it actually contributes to conceptual clarity. This case study suggests that strategy has succeeded purely because it is a buzzword and not because it represents an important conceptual innovation.

Strategy, although widely used, is unfortunately rarely defined. Most published definitions of strategy appear in literature reviews, survey articles, handbooks and reference works. Almost all these definitions fudge the conceptual issue by emphasising that strategy is a versatile concept that can be applied in different fields and therefore defies any single definition. Most attempts at definition degenerate into typologies, in which various fields of strategy studies are delineated and labelled. As a result, different sub-fields of strategy are defined with respect to the different contexts in which the concept is applied, but the concept itself remains undefined.

The Emergence of Strategy as an Analytical Concept

Definitions of strategy that address the conceptual issue are mainly found in the early literature. This is quite a common phenomenon where buzzwords are concerned. Scholars who innovate a word often feel obliged to offer a definition, if only a provisional one. As other scholars adopt the word, the original definition may appear too restrictive, or the adopters may simply not care about the original definition. Indeed, if the word that labels the concept is attractive simply because it has other connotations, then it may be advantageous to drop the original definition altogether.

Prior to Porter (1980, 1996), the concept of strategy had strong military connotations. Strategy was usually distinguished from policy, which in military literature was seen as being political in nature. Thus military strategy was often seen as peaceful policy pursued by 'other means'. In a military context a strategist usually faces a clear opponent – the enemy – and the object of strategy is to outmanoeuvre them. In the military literature it is usually assumed that both the strategist and opponent control hierarchical organisations (e.g. armies) in which strategy is set by the leader. Strategy is implemented by middle managers – an 'officer class' – who devise tactics to implement the strategy in the context of specific circumstances that they face. Workers – the 'rank and file' – simply follow orders; they are often referred to as the resources of the organisation.

The application of strategy to business is linked to the evolution of the modern managerial corporation. Early management theorists who invoked the concept of strategy, such as Ansoff, Declerck and Hayes (1976) and Steiner (1979), were concerned with the problems of managing large hierarchical organisations. Strategy speak was a tool by which top managers could communicate with middle managers in order to ensure that the objectives pursued at lower levels of the organisation were compatible with those at the top. The more that middle managers understood about the objectives of senior management, the easier it was to delegate decisions. Delegation in turn made the organisation more responsive to local conditions – especially to moves by local competitors to gain market share. This may explain why strategy has had less influence in small business research than on large business research. Owner-managers of SMEs have less need for formal strategies because they can communicate their objectives face-to-face.

Critics of the strategy concept have claimed that in large organisations discourse about strategy has been used to legitimate the status of senior managers, by implying that they understand strategy better than their subordinates. In a small firm there may be less need for such rhetoric, either because there are fewer levels of management, or because communications are better, or both.

Conceptual Issues: The Relation of Strategy to Entrepreneurship and the Firm

In small business studies the relation between strategy and entrepreneurship is unclear. Does a successful entrepreneur have to have a strategy? If so, is having a strategy a hallmark of an entrepreneur? Indeed, is having a strategy the same thing as being an entrepreneur? Is the theory of entrepreneurship just the theory of strategy by some other name, or conversely, is strategy just the theory of entrepreneurship by another name (Pozen, 2008)?

Then there is the question of strategic interactions between firms. Such interactions can be very complicated, particularly when questions arise about 'who is influencing whom', and 'who is influenced by whom'. Much of the strategy literature discusses these issues from the standpoint of a single firm, rather than from the standpoint of the business system as a whole.

This firm-centred view often appears biased towards pro-active firms which initiate strategies rather than reactive firms that respond to other firms' strategies. It also tends to focus upon successful firms, or at any rate survivors, rather than firms that fail or become extinct through acquisition. In other words, the firm-centred view of strategy can lead to a biased view of strategic issues in business as a whole.

There are two main ways of addressing questions of this type. One is to take the questions at face value and to assume that a careful reading of strategy literature will divulge important insights. The second is to assume that these questions remain meaningless so long as the concept of strategy is undefined. While there are undoubtedly real questions to be asked about the relationship between large firms and small firms, and about the relationship of entrepreneurship to management, it is possible that these issues cannot be illuminated by a discourse that relies on the concept of strategy. These issues may be best resolved by restating the questions without any reference to strategy and then analysing them using plain and simple language instead.

This case study tends to support the second view. It suggests that most arguments expressed in terms of strategy can be expressed equally well without the word, and indeed, can usually be expressed with greater clarity in this way. An examination of the way that the use of the term strategy has evolved suggests that it began as a means of relabelling an unfashionable concept of 'business policy' that was in turn linked to a politically unpopular concept of 'planning'. Although strategy is often presented as a major conceptual innovation in its field, it appears to have created a good deal of confusion, because of the many different ways in which it has come to be used. In the absence of any tradition of formal modelling, there are no unambiguous criteria by which to assess the theoretical contribution of a novel concept in the field of business and management studies. Strategy has acquired and maintained its status as a buzzword even though there is no agreement within the business and management professions as to what the concept actually means.

Porter's Contribution

Porter's research shifted the focus of strategy away from the internal co-ordination of the firm towards the external marketplace. Unlike earlier writers, Porter was less concerned about the communication of strategy to middle managers than with the possibility that the strategy itself could be wrong. Porter started writing at the time of major recession, when Western economies in general – and the US in particular – were facing the full force of Japanese competition. Imports from Asia flooded domestic markets and threatened the viability of large corporations, many of which were obliged to sell off foreign operations in order to fund loss-making domestic activity.

The problem, Porter argued, was that managers did not fully understand the economic logic of the industries in which they were operating. In particular, they did not understand the 'five forces' that governed success, and certainly not the implications of these five forces for their competitive position in their industry. The strength of import competition demonstrated that firms must either cut their costs, or differentiate their products, or preferably both. Otherwise they must give up mass production and concentrate on niche products instead.

The same conclusions could be arrived at using conventional economic theory – indeed, some of Porter's Harvard colleagues – notably Richard Caves (1987) – arrived at similar conclusions at the same time. Porter's five forces, in fact, come straight out of economics textbooks on industrial organisation and market structure. Porter's genius was to adapt the textbook treatment in two important ways.

First, using his value chain concept, he highlighted the multi-stage nature of the production process. Although multi-stage production was well established in the economics literature – notably in the theory of vertical integration – its implications for market structure had not been fully developed.

Secondly, Porter restated the classic theory of monopoly from the standpoint of managers rather than policy-makers. Economists of the time saw themselves as government advisers rather than business consultants, and the economic theory of industrial organisation was therefore expounded from the standpoint of government anti-trust policy rather than business profitability. From the policy perspective competition was 'good' and monopoly was 'bad'. Monopoly provided firms with an incentive to restrict supply and raise price, whereas competition tended to have the opposite effect.

Porter restated the theory from the boardroom perspective. From a firm's point of view, monopoly is good because it yields higher profit. Under competition a firm can only earn a normal profit in the long run – a profit that just compensates for the opportunity cost of the time and money invested in the enterprise. Under monopoly it can earn a super-normal profit. According to economic theory, monopoly profit is appropriated through a redistribution of welfare from consumers to the firm. There is a net loss of welfare as well, associated with the restriction of output arising from the high price. Porter does not emphasise this point.

Monopoly profits can only be sustained in the long run if there a barrier to entry, such as a patent or other 'first mover' advantage held by the firm. In the absence of a barrier to entry, the firm must constantly keep one step ahead of its rivals – in particular imitators who are trying to copy the methods that it uses to achieve its success. Porter restated this argument by saying that a successful firm needs to remain 'competitive'. This meant that the firm had to defend its monopoly profits by maintaining an advantage over its competitors – in other words, it had to create and sustain a 'competitive advantage'.

The rhetoric of competitive advantage allowed Porter to side-step the sensitive issue of monopoly and to describe a successful long-run monopolist as 'competitive'. By implication, the less successful firms that are driven out of the market by the monopolist are 'uncompetitive'. In fact, as Baumol, Panzar and Willig (1982) noted, the uncompetitive firms are the firms that constrain the level of monopoly profit. It is their threat to re-enter the market, or to increase their market share, that forces the monopolist to keep down its price to a 'limit price' sufficient to deter its 'uncompetitive' rivals. If it were not for the uncompetitive competitors, prices would be higher, the redistribution of welfare from customers larger, and the deadweight welfare loss caused by restriction of output would be greater too.

The play on words involved in Porter's presentation of strategy helps to explain the popularity of his concept in business school teaching. Most managers are aware of the need to legitimate business activity in terms of 'wealth creation'; the notion that businesses pursue monopoly profits and seek to suppress competition is unlikely to win popularity with ordinary workers and consumers. On the other hand, the notion that business managers are engaged in a constant struggle to maintain competitive advantage by offering better deals to customers, thereby preserving workers' jobs, is much more attractive.

The Relation of the Strategy Concept to Formal Modelling

Strategy is a useful word if it is embedded in a proper context. The problem with the strategy concept in business and management studies is not the word itself, but the fact that the word is used so loosely. The concept of strategy is also used in economics, but in this context it is used very differently. In economics the concept of strategy is most widely used in industrial organisation theory, where it describes pricing and quantity setting by oligopolistic rivals. More generally, it is used in non-co-operative game theory to identify the options available to the players. In this context, a strategy is simply an element in a choice set; the decision-maker makes a rational choice of strategy based on a ranking of alternative expected outcomes. The advantage of this approach is that the meaning of the strategy is contingent on the assumptions of the model, and because the assumptions are made explicit the meaning of strategy in the context of the model is absolutely clear. There is no possibility of confusing the strategies within the model with unrelated strategies that appear in everyday discourse. This provides the basis for a generic definition of strategy, namely, a strategy is an element in a set of alternative courses of action between which a firm can choose.

Within the context of economic models, the word strategic has another, more specific, connotation. It signifies decisions that are fundamental, in the sense that they have implications for other decisions, which are conditional on the strategic decision. In economics a strategic decision is usually forward-looking and irreversible. It involves the commitment of resources to some specific use from which they cannot later be withdrawn. The costs incurred in procuring the resources become sunk costs once the resources are committed to a specific use. From this perspective, a strategic decision could be defined as a decision that involves an irreversible commitment of resource to a long-term investment that has significant implications for the way that other resources are subsequently used. Economic theory implies that it is most important that strategic decisions are taken correctly, as mistakes will be extremely wasteful. Since different people have access to different information, it is therefore important that the right person is selected to take the decision.

These two definitions of strategy – one generic and the other specific – provide an option for retaining the concept of strategy in the analysis of small business. Both concepts are viable because both can be embodied in a rigorous economic theory of the entrepreneur.

The generic concept implies only that strategy is an object of choice; when used in this way, most of the meaning of the term is provided by the context in which it is used. If the context changes then the meaning changes; deductions and inferences must rely on the logic of the model rather than a play on words.

The specific concept differentiates fundamental decisions from unimportant ones. It resonates quite well with the use of the strategy concept in the organisational literature. The notion that strategy is set at higher levels and communicated to lower levels fits nicely with the notion that higher levels of management take long-term investment decisions and that lower level management take short-term decisions that are conditional on higher level decisions already made. The definition does not, however, assume that strategic decisions have to be taken at higher levels; this is an open question on which hypotheses can be formulated and tested. In other words, the definition can be used to develop a plausible model of organisational structure in which the success of a firm depends on decentralisation, good internal communication, and entrepreneurial ability at the top.

Assessment of the Strategy Concept

Business behaviour is a complex phenomenon, and requires rigorous analysis. Rigorous analysis requires formal models. However plausible a set of propositions may appear, they are no substitute for a formal model. Those who reject formal models need a substitute which appears convincing. The concept of strategy is a very useful substitute; it enables the construction of a plausible discourse which appears to explain the behaviour of firms in terms of the strategies they employ.

Unfortunately the appearance of explanation is largely illusory. Within business and management studies, strategy has become an instrument of description rather than explanation. If more energy had been expended in the past on developing formal models of business strategy, and less on plausible-sounding strategic rhetoric, then the business and management profession would by now have a stock of more plausible and useful formal models. In addition, if the critics of formal models had been more constructive in their criticisms then they could have helped the modellers to improve their models. Instead, most critics of models have tended to repeat the same general arguments against formal models in contexts of different models, and make little attempt to engage with the specific strengths and weaknesses of any particular model. In this hostile intellectual environment, a policy of 'no analysis of strategy without a formal model' could make a substantial contribution to the future development of business studies as a rigorous discipline. In this context the concept of strategy would still have a role, but only as a term that identified specific aspects of decision-making within a formal model.

4. CONCLUSION

This chapter has considered the social mechanisms that lie behind the innovation and diffusion of buzzwords in the social sciences. It has focused on buzzwords that act as labels for concepts used to analyse complex social and economic systems. It has suggested that under certain circumstances the users of buzzwords may receive rewards – in terms of status and reputation within their professional community – merely by revealing a commitment to innovation rather than by demonstrating the proven worth of the innovations that they make.

The circumstances conducive to buzzwords prevail when members of a profession are uncertain about how best to analyse the field of study that they profess to research. Lacking confidence in the understanding afforded by familiar concepts, they believe that their subject will progress mainly through conceptual innovations. They accept that not all these innovations will be useful. Furthermore, they do not have any agreed formal criteria for distinguishing between useful innovations and the useless ones. Thus there are no limits to the proliferation of concepts, and to the proliferation of new words to support them. Furthermore, because they attach little value to their existing body of theory, these professionals are content to re-label existing concepts when they believe that this will make an existing concept more acceptable to some key constituency – e.g. business managers, politicians, the public – that they aim to serve.

Under these conditions, individual members of a profession have a strong incentive to use buzzwords, because they signal to others that they have a capability to innovate. Individuals who have not heard the buzzword before may mistake the adopter of the word for the innovator; if they recognise the word, they may assume that the adopter either knows the innovator, or knows someone who knows the innovator. Individuals who believe themselves to be very knowledgeable may be unimpressed by the use of a buzzword, but if other people do not consider these people to be knowledgeable then they will have little influence, and no harm will be done to the adopter. Provided most people, including influential people, believe that no one really understands the subject very well, then on balance people who matter will still be impressed – and not just those who are gullible.

To maximise their professional reputation, innovators need to secure as many adopters as quickly as possible. Marketing their buzzword becomes a high priority; the greater the use of the word, the higher their status. There is little to be gained by criticising other people's buzzwords, as this only draws attention to them; if anything, the incentive is simply to ignore other people's buzzwords, in the hope that their use will die out as other new words come along. The appropriate strategy is drop your own buzzword into conversation at every opportunity, and to attend as many events as possible (seminars, conferences, etc.) where it can be put to use.

The business and management studies profession affords an instructive case study in this respect. In particular, the concept of strategy, as developed in the post-war period, illustrates many of the features of a buzzword that has been introduced and diffused through mechanisms of this kind. A case study of how the word is used today suggests that the costs to the profession of rewarding buzzword innovation for its own sake have been very high. While it may have successfully advanced the careers of a small group of gurus, conceptual proliferation has not advanced understanding of the subject matter within the profession as a whole. Indeed, it seems to have had the opposite effect. As different members of the profession have attempted to promote themselves as innovative thinkers by consciously deploying buzzwords in their arguments, their arguments have become progressively more confused. When the same word is used by different authors in different contexts where it carries a slightly different meaning, the word itself loses identity. Versatility is achieved only at the expense of vacuousness.

A word that labelled a fundamental concept within a coherent model of a complex system could quite legitimately be used in many different contexts because these different contexts would be logically isomorphic. The model would provide a theoretical context within which the concept could be understood. But where a concept exists in isolation, outside the structure of any formal model, there is no fixed point of reference by which to establish its meaning, and as a result the word that labels the concept loses its meaning too. As a meaningless word it can be added to almost any proposition, for although it is redundant it does not actually change the proposition to which it is applied. This appears to have been the fate of 'strategy' within the business and management studies literature, where it now denotes nothing at all in most of the contexts in which it is used.

The field of small business studies is fortunate in that its reliance on the 'strategy' concept is less than in other fields of management studies, such as organisational behaviour and international business. The term is still used, however, often it seems, in deference to those other fields of the subject. Small business studies has its own problems, however, e.g. in relation to the concept of entrepreneurship. As Casson (2010) notes, entrepreneurship can be defined either in terms of function (e.g. innovation), role (e.g. owner-manager), personality (e.g. imaginative) or behaviour (e.g. pro-active). When different writers define the concept in different ways then confusion develops. When no explicit definition is given, as is often the case, then ambiguity adds to the confusion.

Entrepreneurship has the advantage over strategy, however, in that it refers to a genuine phenomenon, and is a concept that cannot be reduced entirely to some other concept that existed previously. Furthermore, in entrepreneurship studies the type of definition being used by an author can often be inferred from the context in which it is applied and from the nature of the issue being discussed. Unlike strategy, the concept of entrepreneurship has not been so widely used that it has become devoid of meaning, but there remains a danger that this could happen. The continuing success of entrepreneurship studies depends upon restraint in the use of the term entrepreneur, and recourse to an explicit definition whenever the term is used. Using the term selectively and with precision will help entrepreneurship studies to avoid that sad fate of intellectual vacuity that overwhelmed the field of business strategy.

REFERENCES

Ansoff, H. I., R. P. Declerck and R. L. Hayes (eds.) (1976), *From Strategic Planning to Strategic Management*, New York: Wiley.

Baumol, W., J. C. Panzar and R. D.Willig (1982), *Contestable Markets and the Theory of Industry Structure*, San Diego, CA: Harcourt Brace Jovanovich.

Bechhofer, F. and B. Elliott (1971), 'The market situation of small shopkeepers', *Scottish Journal of Political Economy*, **18**(2): 161–80.

Bechhofer, F. and B. Elliott (1976), 'Persistence and change: The petit bourgeoisie in industrial society', *European Journal of Sociology*, **17**(1): 74–99.

Carland, J. W., F. Hoy, W. R. Boulton and J. A. C. Carland (1984), 'Differentiating entrepreneurs from small business owners: A conceptualisation', *Academy of Management Review*, **9**(2): 354–9.

Casson, M. (2005), 'Entrepreneurship and the theory of the firm', *Journal of Economic Behaviour and Organization*, vol 58, 327–48.

Casson, M. (2010), *Entrepreneurship: Theory, Networks, Institutions*, Cheltenham: Edward Elgar.

Caves, R. E. (1987), *American Industry: Structure, Conduct and Performance*, 6th. *Ed.* Englewood Cliffs: Prentice Hall.

Chater, N. and M. H. Christiansen (2009), 'Language acquisition meets language evolution', *Cognitive Science*, 1–27.

Chell, E. and J. Hayes (2000), 'Intuition and entrepreneurial behaviour', *European Journal of Work and Organizational Psychology*, **9**(1): 3143.

Christiansen, M. H. and S. Kirby (2003), 'Language evolution: consensus and controversies', *Trends in Cognitive Science* **7**(7): 300–7.

Ferrer i Cancho, R. and R. V. Sole (2001), 'The small world of human language', *Proceedings of the Royal Society of Biological Sciences*, **268**(1482): 2261–5.

Greenhill, S. J., Q. D. Atkinson, A. Meade and R. D. Gray (2010), 'The shape and tempo of language evolution', *Proceedings of the Royal Society of Biological Sciences*, **277**(1693): 2443–50.

Hitt, M. A., R. D. Ireland, S. M. Camp, and D. L. Sexton (2001), 'Strategic entrepreneurship: Entrepreneurial strategies for wealth creation', *Strategic Management Journal*, **22**(6–7): 479–91.

Knight, F. H. (1921), *Risk Uncertainty and Profit*, Boston: Houghton Mifflin.

Pagel, M. (2009), 'Human language as a culturally transmitted replicator,' *Nature Reviews Genetics*, **10**(6): 405–15.

Plass, J., R. Moreno and R. Brunken (eds) (2010), *Cognitive Load Theory*, Cambridge: Cambridge University Press.

Porter, M. E. (1980), *Competitive Strategy*, New York: Free Press.

Porter, M. E. (1996), 'What is strategy?' *Harvard Business Review*, 74, Nov/Dec: 40–8.

Pozen, D. E. (2008), 'We are all entrepreneurs now', *Wake Forest Law Review*, **43**(1): 283–340.

Steiner, G. (1979), *Strategic Planning: What Every Manager must Know*, New York: Free Press.

4. Multi-level approaches to entrepreneurship and small business research – transcending dichotomies with Bourdieu

Cynthia Forson, Mustafa Özbilgin,
Mustafa Bilgehan Ozturk and Ahu Tatli

OVERVIEW

Entrepreneurship and small business (ESB) research has achieved a level of maturity which now presents a complex mixture in terms of the levels of analysis. As a result of these developments, the research on small business and entrepreneurship has a number of distinct traditions, which somehow remain in silos. In this chapter, we argue that this field of academic endeavour would benefit from a more integrated approach. We first identify the key approaches in ESB research in terms of the levels of analysis. Next, adopting a Bourdieuan perspective, we offer viable strategies for transcending contemporary dichotomies of ESB research, and offer a novel way of approaching multi-level ESB research.

INTRODUCTION

The field of ESB research has received interest and contributions from all disciplines of social sciences and humanities. While the interdisciplinary field of ESB is considered a major source of strength for opening up venues of innovation and creativity in research, it has also brought with it a number of challenges. Growing divergences in the epistemology and ontology of the existing body of ESB research, on the one hand, makes it possible for different approaches to be considered, on the other, it disallows cross-fertilisation of ideas across different perspectives, methods and themes of research. Moreover, mainstream entrepreneurship research still often envisages a typical entrepreneur as *homoeconomicus* stripped largely of affect, intersubjectivity, personal narratives, discursive groundings or intersectional complexities, that is, an economic agent formulated as a demigod, who is continually powered forward by foresight, charisma, analytical prowess and cogency of calculation to control and remake the world in 'his' own image (Ogbor, 2000). We provide Bourdieuan sociology as a way forward, as Bourdieu's work promises to transcend sources and mechanisms of doxic privileging and false dichotomies of science, thereby opening up possibilities for multi-level investigations transcending dichotomous and separate framing of levels.

A highly cited management theorist such as Clegg (1989, 1990), while useful in shedding light on issues of power and discourse, does not provide a complete framework as Bourdieu's body of work does in explicating socially based acts and processes, such as those relating to entrepreneurship. Equally, compared with theories propounded by a comparable social theorist such as Giddens (1984, 1991), Bourdieuan frameworks are uniquely capable of traversing both the qualitative and quantitative domains and displaying empirical and interpretivist sensibilities equally, on the basis of alternating methodologies often within the same project in order to inhabit multiple levels of analysis to secure a more complex and accurate representation of social phenomena (see for instance Bourdieu, 1984). Unlike Giddens, whose works are often non-empirical and concerned with building abstract social theory with latent capacity for application potential, Bourdieu's body of work stands as an active effort at the unification of empirical specificity and theory building, which lends itself to an empirically driven endeavour as entrepreneurship studies which still needs greater theoretical grounding.

We would first like to delve into the frequently noted richness in ESB research that it presents a complex bricolage in terms of the levels of analysis. In the main, research on ESB has followed the consolidated traditions of the disciplines that have engaged in research on the subject. As such psychological approaches to ESB have generally focused on the individual as the unit of analysis whilst sociological research has engaged with the individual in society examining the influence of the social on the individual. However, there has been insufficient dialogue and crossover between these two distinct contributions resulting from the relative scarcity of multi-level studies.

Entrepreneurship is a relative concept and at any particular time some societies and individuals are perceived as more or less entrepreneurial than others, providing a relational dimension to such acts and processes. Yet much of the research on ESB has taken an isolationist view, in terms of place and contextual dimensions of studies, as well as their methodological and theoretical perspectives, where the study of entrepreneurship has come to be viewed by some as an ahistorical endeavour (Landström and Lohrke, 2010). Consequently, there is little agreement or standardisation in terms of definitions and benchmarks by which to measure or indeed study entrepreneurship (Low and Macmillan, 1988 and Chell, 1985). One dominant approach in ESB research is to focus on individual resources and opportunity recognition of the entrepreneurs and small business owners (e.g. Coleman, 2000; Cooper et al., 1994; Dolinsky et al., 1993; Feldman and Bolino, 2000; Robinson and Sexton, 1994). This tradition has the hallmarks of psychological perspectives, which often underplay the role of context in shaping individual choices and chances. Put simply, entrepreneurship is viewed "as a function of the types of people engaged in entrepreneurial activity" (Eckhardt & Shane, 2003, p. 334). In this perspective, achievement motivation, cognitive/rational strength, risk-taking behaviour, systematic recognition of missing links, inspirational leadership, innovative vision, or some combination thereof would emerge as the key facilitators in initiating entrepreneurial action and securing its subsequent success (Begley & Boyd, 1987; Cramer et al., 2002; Hsieh et al., 2007; Johnson, 1990; Miller, 2007). A more finely tuned approach, on the other hand, emphasises the embedded nature of small business ownership and entrepreneurship (see Chell, 1985; Du Gay, 1994; Gartner, 1985 for initial calls to explore contextual and relational of entrepreneurial activity). This second set of studies has moved psychology towards the social and can be traced to a tradition of social psychological research. Owing to this earlier attention to the interplay of individual and social levels of analyses, a growing number of studies explored contextual and institutional influences (Barrett et al., 2001; Bygrave and Minniti, 2000; De Clercq and Voronov, 2009a; Jack &

Anderson, 2002 and Chapter 10 in this volume; Lounsbury and Glynn, 2001; Peterson and Meckler, 2001; Phizacklea and Ram, 1995). This has resulted in an emergent interest in the application of sociological concepts of Bourdieu, a theorist whose main academic project was to reconcile various levels, types and methods of analysis to arrive at a richer relational sense of social life (see Anderson et al., 2010; De Clercq and Voronov, 2009b; Jones, 2008; Karataş-Özkan, 2011). This chapter is an attempt to provide a theoretical framework for such efforts based on the sense that there is a sociological turn of emphasis on structural aspects of ESB dynamics over and above individual level concerns.

Simultaneously, methodological scope of research in small business and entrepreneurship has seen an expansion in recent years. Previously, the research in the field of ESB was dominated by positivist and functional approaches (Pittaway, 2000). The dominant functionalist and positivist approaches have been challenged primarily by scholars from social constructivist paradigms (Bouchikhi, 1993; Chell, 2000; Downing, 2005). Consequently, a methodological heterodoxy has been introduced into the field of ESB research through narrative and ethnographic studies (e.g. Bruni et al., 2004; Karataş-Özkan and Chell, 2010; Nicholson and Anderson, 2005; Steyaert and Katz, 2004). Furthermore, there are renewed calls for a further methodological expansion in the field through the use of a wider set of methodological tools and techniques in order to investigate the realities of ESB in a way to move beyond the orthodoxies of this research field (e.g. Chandler and Lyon, 2001; Chell, 2007; Grant and Perren, 2002).

If we consider both the theoretical and methodological turns above in the field of ESB research, we see a picture that the ESB research is posed to embrace more complexity by allowing layers to be added to its earlier positivist and purist framing of the ESB dynamics. This shift is partly due to different insights generated by the expansion of interest in ESB research in new geographies outside the English-speaking world (Özbilgin and Malach-Pines, 2007). The geographic expansion of the ESB scholarship has challenged the Western theorisation of ESB and appropriateness of the methods used to study it. In particular, recent scholarship has posed a significant challenge to the monolithic framing of entrepreneurial activity as decontextualised, purely economic, universally convergent activity (Steyaert and Katz, 2004). Despite these shifts, the research in ESB remains in silos with insufficient dialogue across its methodological and theoretical borders.

As a result of the expansion in both methodological and theoretical grounds, the research on ESB represents a vibrant field of study. However, we argue that this field of academic endeavour would benefit from a more integrated approach through a multi-level research agenda. Thus far, research involving even mixed-method approaches has often shied away from multi-level analysis due to concerns about the possible compromise of elegance and parsimony of explanation. A multi-level research framework that incorporates the individual, meso and macro dynamics with qualitative and quantitative approaches chosen appropriately to a given level studied in conjunction with other levels would resolve equally concerning reductionist formulations of entrepreneurial processes. For instance, instead of taking individual traits as measured constructs in a quantitative sense alone, it is possible to approach such traits in terms of their social construction by tracing individual meanings through in-depth interview contexts. This can still be accompanied by the quantitative approach to arrive at a fuller picture, which is in turn further supplemented by sectoral, normative and historical drivers that impact upon the individuals, also paying due regard to the interaction of the individual and more macro processes through the cascading of the middle levels of analysis. In this chapter, we first identify the key approaches in terms of the levels of analysis. Next we offer a Bourdieuan approach, which promises viable strategies for multi-level analysis, which can help transcend the entrenched dichotomies of ESB research.

LEVELS OF ANALYSIS IN SMALL BUSINESS AND ENTREPRENEURSHIP RESEARCH

Research in the ESB field is moving from single-level studies to a multi-level understanding of ESB dynamics. However, this emergent shift has found greater welcome in what are called critical entrepreneurship studies, as opposed to a wider recognition in mainstream research. To demonstrate this problem, we first describe research in single-level studies and then explore how multi-level analysis of ESB is treated in the literature. In particular, we explain how ESB research deals with embeddedness and the resultant significance of context in studying small businesses and entrepreneurs.

As stated earlier, micro-individual level of analysis has traditionally been a dominant focus in ESB research. As a result much attention is directed to individual motivations, resources and opportunities of entrepreneurs and small business owners. At the level of the individual, approaches to entrepreneurship research are based on the premise that entrepreneurship stems from enterprising acts by individuals and they highlight the degree of choice demonstrated by entrepreneurs in the entrepreneurial decision (e.g. Feldman and Bolino, 2000) leading to conceptualisations of the business venturing decision in terms of 'push' and 'pull' factors, suggesting that entrepreneurship can be explained in terms of a choice between business ownership and other forms of economic activity. However, such micro-level analysis has been recently criticised for reducing individual choice to intrinsic processes of decision-making, underplaying the significance of contextual factors in shaping individual motivations (Özbilgin and Malach-Pines, 2007; Özbilgin, Küskü and Erdogmus, 2005).

Psychological bases and economic outcomes are most directly connected by McClelland (1965) based on his longitudinal study of achievement motivation where those men with a higher sense of this motive were found to be more likely to engage in entrepreneurial activity. Economists also examine the role of the individual in arbitrage, profiling the entrepreneur as an agent of economic change through their propensities for innovation (Schumpeter, 1996, Drucker, 1985) and risk-taking (Brockhaus, 1980). Similarly, personality approaches focus on the micro-level of analyses, and attempt at determining personal qualities of entrepreneurs, while psychodynamic perspectives (Malach-Pines and Özbilgin, 2010) have attempted to link early socialisation experiences to the personality of the entrepreneur. Such studies identify that successful entrepreneurs have initiative and assertiveness and an ability to see and act on opportunities. Consequently, the entrepreneurial personality is able to take advantage of the availability of resources pursuant to his/her desire to set up a business (Ndofor and Priem, 2005).

Subsequent research into this area, however, has been inconclusive in identifying personality differences between entrepreneurs and non-entrepreneurs (Shurry et al., 2002, Stewart et al., 2003). In addition, the research identified characteristics of the entrepreneurial personality to be fluid, and dynamically changing depending on entrepreneurs' personal relationships and the personality itself (Littunen, 2000). Further, this approach, based on micro-level analyses, clearly places the 'blame' for lack of entrepreneurial ability squarely on the individual, without exploring the relationship of the individual choice with the individual circumstances.

Further problems with this approach are the question of why there are low participation rates among certain groups in studies of ESB in this tradition. Excluded groups include women and racial minorities. This leaves us with a number of questions of gender and ethnicity: while it is not suggested by the dominant scholarship that traits alone explain opportunity recognition, there is a subtext to the literature that is gendered at bottom, with the sense that women lack entrepreneurial characteristics or their psychological characteristics are different from their male counterparts, which is amply showcased by more critical entrepreneurship scholarship (Ahl, 2006; Ogbor, 2000). A study of African-Caribbean communities by Ram and Deakins (1995, cited in Deakins, 1999) suggested factors such as limited opportunities in the inner-city and deprived urban environments may be to blame rather than the psychological make-up of this group. Deakins, 1996 argues that measurements ignore the contextual setting, role of education and learning and demographic influences on personality.

Another trench of studies has focused on the entrepreneur or small business owner and the acquisition of resources for business start-up and/or growth including access to finance (Coleman, 2000; Cooper et al., 1994), education (Dolinsky et al., 1993; Robinson and Sexton, 1994) and information through social networks. Resources available to the would-be entrepreneur include finance, experience, knowledge, skills, a network and a track record. Krueger (1995, cited in Bridge et al., 2009) suggests that it is the interaction between these factors that produces the entrepreneurial response, on the basis of available information when the opportunity comes up and that the attributes and resources are not sufficient without the trigger event but, at the same time, the trigger event is hollow without the presence of these factors.

At the time when the opportunity arises, an entrepreneur needs encouragement and support to make the decision. In other words, attributes and resources should be present when the opportunity arises. In this tradition of studies, we observe that there is a move from single-level (mostly micro-level) analyses of ESB to multi-level (micro and macro level) analyses. However the shift is not unproblematic as the interface of the levels of analyses is left unattended. Studies that pay significant attention to opportunity recognition or base the analysis mainly on attributes and resources fail to draw the full picture, as the variation in decision to engage in entrepreneurship as well as subsequent success may be related to the imbrications of opportunity recognition and attributes and resources which must be studied together in a Bourdieuan multi-level framework.

More recent approaches emphasise the embedded nature of small business ownership and entrepreneurship (see Chell, 1985; Du Gay, 1994; Gartner, 1985 for initial calls to explore context and the relational aspects of entrepreneurial activity). As a result a growing number of studies explored contextual and institutional influences. While acknowledging the fact that personality and genetics influence entrepreneurship this approach broadens the sphere of influence to include the impact of social and cultural variables on entrepreneurship. De Clercq and Voronov (2009a) for example examine the role of education and community status in entrepreneurial conformity and innovation. In fact it has been suggested that it is only through a detailed understanding of the sociological context of the entrepreneur that research on the individual entrepreneur will make further progress (Johnson, 1990). Indeed Jack & Anderson (2002) suggest that recognition and realisation of opportunity are conditioned by the entrepreneur's embeddedness in the social structure (see Chell (2008) for an overview), which in turn generates and fosters entrepreneurial activity among others (Bygrave and Minniti, 2000). The embeddedness approach has emerged as one attempts reconciling macro-contextual and micro-individual level analyses with a view to revealing their interplay. However, the embeddedness approach has a tendency to assume context as fixed, when context is also dynamically changing. While embeddedness brings multi-level analyses in ESB research, it comes with a caveat as many of its examples fail to capture the dynamism in both micro-individual and macro-contextual levels.

Kloosterman et al. (1999) examine the small business owner's embeddedness in varying levels of social structures at the macro and meso levels which create opportunities for them. This mixed-embeddedness concept recognises the significance of cultural links and networks but requires that the wider economic and institutional context be incorporated in any explanation. It places an emphasis on the laws, regulations, institutions and practices which condition the way in which the market operates. The UK literature is awash with examples of ways in which minority businesses are embedded demographically, economically, materially, locally and internationally (Barrett et al., 2001). Barrett et al. (2001) have examined the UK environment and concluded that although cultural factors still create opportunities for many small businesses to survive under harsh conditions, public policy (including legislation and initiatives) has outcomes for minority businesses in Britain, whether so intended or not. Hardill and Raghuram (1998) show how Asian women's businesses are embedded in linkages between their home countries, host countries and other parts of the Asian diaspora. They also show that these linkages are materially embedded and internally differentiated along lines of gender and class. Others have explored the effects of post-colonialism and multiculturalism on the small business milieu, concluding that Birmingham's immigrant businesses, for example, are embedded in the histories of its inhabitants and the city itself, creating a unique 'global city' that enables immigrant businesses to flourish (Pollard et al., 2002).

However Barrett et al. (2001) conclude that embeddedness in laws, regulations, institutions and practices cannot on its own explain the behaviour of minority business owners and their experiences. They argue that although North America and Europe have had different perspectives on immigration policy, the former having a more open policy while the latter closed its doors on immigrants, they have had similar outcomes in terms of the flourishing of minority businesses. In addition they argue that given that Africans and Caribbeans operate within the same policy context as South Asians in Britain, their disparate experiences of self-employment should lead to the conclusion that a combination of the mixed-embeddedness approach and cultural explanations may account for the behaviour of some groups. Further the mixed-embeddedness argument may be overly structural in the sense that it focuses on the external structures that influence the entrepreneur's decision and behaviour without taking into consideration the entrepreneur's own interpretation of these structures and his/her agency in the confrontation and negotiation between him/herself and the structures.

Most of the multi-level analyses in ESB concentrate on the interface between micro- and macro-level analyses. More sophisticated and integrated approaches embrace three levels of analyses. Some integrated approaches have examined the complex interplay between individual, social and environmental factors that impact entrepreneurial behaviour. Cooper (1981) and Dyer Jr. (1994) provide similar comprehensive frameworks for the study of entrepreneurial motivations. Dyer looking at entrepreneurship as a career, analyses the influences on career choice in terms of antecedent influences that include psychological factors (e.g. need for achievement, need for control, tolerance for ambiguity), social factors (e.g. family relationships, family and community support, role models) and economic factors (lack of alternative careers in existing organisations, economic growth/business opportunities and availability of resources). Similarly, Cooper (1981) concentrates on antecedent influences, the incubator organisation and environmental factors.

Other researchers confirm the usefulness of Cooper's and Dyer's approaches with analyses of the impact of culture, role models and family influences (Bygrave and Minniti, 2000), education (Dolinsky et al., 1993), career experiences (Feldman and Bolino, 2000), institutional support (Phizacklea and Ram, 1995), family entrepreneurial tradition (Bygrave and Minniti, 2000), peer influence, social marginality (Phizacklea and Ram, 1995; Kets de Vries, 1977), among others, on the entrepreneurial decision. However, as invaluable as these integrated frameworks are in examining the complexity and interconnectedness of various factors in entrepreneurship, they do not fully capture the underlying structures and social identities that frame individual circumstances, such as ethnicity, gender and class. Complicating this further, Arenius and Minniti (2005) consider such individual circumstances based on GEM surveys and find that perceptual variables and subjective biases such as confidence in one's skills, fear of failure and opportunity perception may vary greatly with possible impact on nascent entrepreneurship. An issue the authors do not consider is that the variation in perceptual indicators, of course, could be endogenous to social construction processes, where certain members of a population are forced to develop less confidence or greater fear, given normative and ideational constraints they face in their environment.

For example, gender can influence educational choices in a manner that may make the essence of one person's decision to become a business owner different from that of another. Gender can also mediate within the same buoyant entrepreneurial environment to give different individuals varied access to finance that will make the decision to become an entrepreneur easier for a man than for a woman. Interestingly, in the United States, Inman (2000) has noted that black women's businesses comprise a larger share of black businesses than white women's businesses do of white firms. Smith (2000) argues that one of the reasons that black women comprise one of the fastest growing groups of new small business owners in the USA is that, in corporate settings, they bear the 'double-yoke' of racism and sexism that spurs them into self-employment. Faced with similar double disadvantages, black women in the UK do not seem to be following suit.

Reynolds (1991) examines three other social contexts that impact individual entrepreneurial behaviour and determines whether a person will pursue entrepreneurship when the opportunity arises. The first of these is the life course stage of the individual, which is also determined by the life event norms of the society in which the individual lives. He identifies entrepreneurship as being an aspect of the life event of initiating a career, which takes place in adulthood in many societies and is affected by level of education and previous career experience.

The second context is the individual's social network and his or her embeddedness within it. The tightness or looseness of this network is irrelevant because both types can have their advantages. Tight groups tend to exhibit a high level of interaction and cohesiveness where strong social pressures give assurance that confidentiality and anonymity will be maintained (Reynolds, 1991). On the other hand involvement in a wide range of casual information networks can be advantageous to entrepreneurs and, it has been suggested, as a prerequisite to starting a successful firm (Birley, 1989). The more successful entrepreneurs are those that have varied sources of information for locating funds, suppliers, facilities and clients.

Industry Life Cycle stage has been proposed to affect the types of entrepreneurs who enter the industry (Romanelli, 1989). Suggesting industry life cycle as a third context, Reynolds (1991) proposes that pioneer entrepreneurs will come from secondary roles in established firms in the industry. For example, car manufacturers came out of the wagon-building industry. Founding during the growth stage of an industry will reflect the fact that there has been a departure from the initial stage and entrepreneurs will come out of central management roles. During the decline and renewal phase, Reynolds reckons that it is those with technical expertise in the industry but who lack management experience that will be founding new firms. He acknowledges though that it is not clear what level of impact the industry life stage has on the decision to become an entrepreneur.

From the foregoing review, it is clear that the entrepreneur is a social agent influenced by a plethora of contextual variables, instead of the simplistic formulation of individual traits. The debate regarding the supremacy of these research approaches, with varied emphasis on different levels of analyses, continues. All contribute significantly in their own way, to enhancing understanding about who an entrepreneur is, what he or she does and why they do it. Even integrated approaches are limited in the understanding of the complexities of entrepreneurship or in the attempt to define it. They neglect to explicitly identify the role of culture and society in the stimulation or stifling of entrepreneurial behaviour. However they shed light on the fact that there is a range of complex factors that shape entrepreneurial activity leading to heterogeneity among entrepreneurs and therefore yet more complex problems in trying to distinguish between types of entrepreneurs and entrepreneurial behaviour.

ESB research at present is vibrant and dynamic not only in terms of conception of levels of analysis but also in terms of the debates around methods and methodologies employed (Davidsson and Wiklund, 2001; Davidsson, 1995). In fact, the treatment of levels of analysis and the challenges associated with multi-level research is reflected in methodological choices in ESB scholarship. In other words, the choice of method is particular to the choice of theoretical frame and paradigmatic approach in the field. Narrative and ethnographic studies (e.g. Bruni et al., 2004; Karataş-Özkan and Chell, 2010; Nicholson and Anderson, 2005; Steyaert and Katz, 2004), which are often based on social constructivism (Bouchikhi, 1993; Chell, 2000; Downing, 2005) exist alongside the traditionally more dominant functionalist and positivist approaches. Yet, recent years brought renewed calls for a further methodological expansion through a use of a wider set of methodological tools and techniques (e.g. Chandler and Lyon, 2001; Chell, 2007; Grant and Perren, 2002).

Despite the availability of a wide repertoire of research methods, which is induced by the interdisciplinary nature of the ESB research, research methods in the field of ESB also suffer from certain limitations, due to dichotomous treatment of these methods. These limitations include: (a) the territory marking behaviour among disciplines, which contribute to the ESB research, privileging particular choice of methods in each discipline. Overcoming the disciplinary silos is not only a theoretical concern in the field of ESB but also a methodological one. (b) Despite a lack of methodological closure in the field, the ESB field is still littered with unresolved and often unwise dichotomies of method, including qualitative versus quantitative methods, inductive versus deductive methods, mainstream versus emergent methods. The dichotomous positioning of methods is visible across all disciplines of ESB and it informs the way research is conducted. In the next section, we provide a Bourdieuian approach as an alternative to resolve the challenges that we identified in the ESB research.

TRANSCENDING DICHOTOMIES WITH BOURDIEU

Bourdieu's body of work can be defined as one big project of developing an alternative to the analytical dualism between structure and agency dominating the social scientific endeavour. Nash (2003: 49) notes:

> Seeking to avoid the polarities of structuralist determinism and phenomenological individualism, Bourdieu attempts to construct a new theory of practice in which the sterile opposition of the old debate (conscious/unconscious, explanation by cause/explanation by reason, mechanical submission to social constraints/rational and strategic calculation, individual/society and so on) can be transcended.

This lifetime endeavour of Bourdieu addresses one of the most significant challenges that contemporary ESB research faces: the limited treatment of levels of analysis, either as autonomous levels or in deterministic relationship with one another. In this section we use four Bourdieuan concepts, i.e. field (social space in which actors are instantiated), habitus (dispositions, attitudes and worldviews located within the individual, but flowing out of social experience), capitals (economic, social, cultural and symbolic resources and competencies differentially available to individuals) and strategies, to demonstrate the value of Bourdieu's sociology to aid multi-level yet relational analysis in ESB research. We have chosen these four concepts to make a case because they constitute the backbone of Bourdieu's (1977, 1984, 1987, 1990, 1998) relational theory of human agency and social life. Therefore, they promise to provide a complex understanding of the ESB phenomenon, beyond simplistic conceptions of deterministic relationships between micro, meso and macro levels.

In the main, Bourdieu's theory can be seen as an endeavour to explain the kinds of varied resources (capitals) that individuals draw on in order to enact their strategies and how their strategies are both negotiated in and shaped by their habitus and the logic of the field, i.e. the social structures, which in turn is altered through enactments of human agency. Bourdieu (1984: 101) illustrates this relationship in the following formula: '*habitus* x capital + field = practice'. Within Bourdieu's framework, field denotes the universe of partly pre-constituted objective historical relations between positions (Bourdieu and Wacquant 1992: 16). Utilising the notion of field in the ESB research is useful for introducing and operationalising the structural forces that are in play at social, institutional and organisational levels. Macro-social and meso-sectoral/organisational fields as the defining principles of the allocation of resources and draw the boundaries of individual agency of small business owners and entrepreneurs. On the other hand, the concept of *habitus* brings the subjective dimension of human agency into the analysis (Grenfell and James, 1998). The *habitus* functions as a bridge between structure and agency. In other words, it is the subjectification and deposition of field in the individual bodies (Bourdieu and Wacquant, 1992). Bourdieu (1977: 72, 95) defines *habitus* as:

> the strategy generating principle enabling agents to cope with unforeseen and ever-changing situations. . . a system of lasting and transposable dispositions which, integrating past experiences, functions at every moment as a matrix of perceptions, appreciations and actions and made possible the achievement of infinitely diversified tasks.

Each field has its own specific habitus which shapes the conduct of individual action through an unspoken and sometimes unconscious agreement, which Bourdieu defines as the 'feel for the game'. The habitus is acquired by individuals through the very act of staying in and playing the game. Individuals are positioned in the field which embeds power relations with respect to the amount of capital at their disposal and employ several strategies to reconfigure the amount of different forms of capital in their portfolio in order to enhance their power position within the field (Bourdieu and Wacquant, 1992: 129). Field, *habitus*, different forms of capital and strategies are used here to elaborate the three layers of social reality in which ESB activity is embedded. These are macro, meso and micro levels respectively. Table 4.1 illustrates an example of how Bourdieu's

Table 4.1   A Bourdieuian multi-level framework for ESB research

Levels	Bourdieuian orienting concepts	Operationalisation
Macro-level (society, culture, political economy)	Macro-field	Social regulation context, industrial relations, legislation, business environment, labour market dynamics, prevailing discourses of legitimacy, structures of resources and constraints
Meso-level (sector and organisation)	Meso-field *Habitus*	Objective structures pertaining to the organisation and sector, sectoral rules and procedures, sectoral patterns of legitimacy and competition entrepreneurial networks which may include associational, professional and organisational linkages, informal codes of conduct, sectoral and organisational history and culture, informal rules of legitimacy
Micro-level (entrepreneurs and small business owners, i.e. ESB agents)	Capital (in social, economic, cultural and symbolic forms) Strategies, dispositions	Educational, financial, cultural, network etc. resources owned by ESB agents Strategies that ESB agents utilise to gain capital and to legitimise their presence in the field Entrepreneurial attributes, biographies and motivations

four concepts, i.e. field, *habitus*, capitals and strategies, can be used as orienting devices in a multi-level ESB research framework.

In Bourdieu's analysis his key concepts such as *habitus*, field, capitals and strategies, work together to generate the social reality as he sets out "not simply to combine, articulate or join agency and structure but, more fundamentally, to dissolve the very distinction between these two seemingly antinomic viewpoints of social analysis' (Wacquant, 1993: 3). Therefore, in utilising Bourdieu's theory in ESB research, we recommend treatment of his theory and concepts as holistic and interconnected rather than in piecemeal fashion. In other words, deeper insights would be gained if Bourdieuan notions are treated in a relational framework rather than focusing on one of his concepts and abstracting it from its relationship to other core concepts. The framework we offer brings together macro, meso and micro levels of ESB under a single roof, and allows explanations of interactions and interrelationships between the levels of individual and society. Accordingly, the framework provides a conceptual model to empirically investigate the multi-level dynamics underlying ESB phenomena, potentially using both qualitative and quantitative methods in the same project.

As we identified earlier, some traditions of ESB research view individuals as atomised and autonomous entities, failing to capture their social, economic, and other relationally configured positions in life. This individualistic tendency creates rather flat, instead of nuanced, pictures of entrepreneurs and individuals in the small business sector. Bourdieu helps us overcome these individualistic tendencies in ESB research showing the interface of routines, cultures and the field of relations and individual choices and chances. ESB agents are depicted here as real individuals in their economic and social setting rather than free-floating practitioners abstracted from their context. They are neither all powerless puppets of the system, nor completely autonomous rational individuals. Instead, as the bearers of capital, they transform and reproduce their organisational and institutional context by employing several strategies. Yet they are bound by the rules, resources and principles of the field within which they are situated. ESB research is not often considered as part of a political economy, which shapes relations of power. For example, entrepreneurial activity is encouraged at a time when social welfare systems are challenged and in contexts where income inequalities are getting deeper. However, such political perspective is often lacking in ESB research, which treats political economy as given and unproblematic. A Bourdieuan approach may help enable ESB researchers to render visible the interplay between individual level entrepreneurial and small business activity and the wider political economy context which may promote or hinder this activity in varied ways and forms.

One challenge in social research, and ESB research is not an exception, is to avoid structural determinism and a static depiction of context and structure. Bourdieu's sociology is also useful in that context as it provides space for accounting for the dynamism of context and structures as it addresses the tension between change and stability. However, Bourdieu also cautions that change in structures is rather slow and routines constitute reproductive systems and as such they are resistant to change. As Özbilgin and Tatli (2005) put forward, *habitus* and field are contested terrains in which actors compete for appropriation of different forms of capital, and that it is this very contested nature which opens up the possibility of continuous reproductive transformation of *habitus* and field, if not an abrupt and radical change of them. Although the notion of *habitus* and field may seem to dictate a rigid and static order over actions of agents at first glance, what is central to Bourdieu's sociological work is to explore the interplay between capitals, strategies, field, and *habitus*, which exist in interdependency and relationality with each other. Notwithstanding the fact that capitals are generated and legitimised by the logic of *habitus* and the field, equally, field and *habitus* owe their existence to the actions of individuals, who strategically deploy different forms of capital at their disposal. Use of the concept of strategies further highlights the non-deterministic dimension of Bourdieu's model. In Bourdieu's framework, several strategies are employed by individuals while they compete for hegemony and ownership of capitals. Nash (2003) notes that the notion of strategy is another area that blurs the boundaries between determinism and non-determinism. It was this power of Bourdieuan model to dissolve false duality between agency and structure, which rendered it valuable and fruitful for overcoming the current challenges of ESB research in terms of use of multi-level approaches.

Methodologically, research that utilises a Bourdieuan framework requires a mindful openness and pluralism because of the necessity of making use of data in various forms in order to unpack dynamics and mechanisms at multiple levels of social reality. As we indicated earlier in the chapter, for instance, there is no obligation to study individual level traits in isolation without considering impact from macro dynamics or cascading effects of the meso level. Equally, it is possible to study individual traits as measured variables in quantitative-based questionnaires accompanied by the analysis of in-depth interview data where individual meanings are derived for traits and interpreted in conjunction with other levels of analysis. Choices of method in the field of ESB suffer from dichotomous fallacies, e.g. the choice between qualitative versus quantitative methods, inductive versus deductive methods. Even when such approaches are reconciled, mixed methods tend to display conformity to discipline and strict tenets of scientific parsimony than the requirements of data and needs for research. Thus, mixed-method research is often still focused on one level of analysis alone. A Bourdieuan turn for pluralism in an epistemological and ontological sense, away from vacant discussions of qualitative versus quantitative, inductive versus deductive, and other false dichotomous debates, can open up room for a wider range of research methods to be used, including visual, ethnographic, participative and even carnal methods. In other words, methodological choices in ESB research need to be governed by the principle of fit for purpose, where the research methods emanate from the field of relations under investigation, crafted to the unique requirements of data.

CONCLUSION

The field of ESB is saturated with contributions from the main disciplines of social sciences and humanities but despite these contributions, the field of ESB does not fully benefit from merits of interdisciplinarity. In this chapter, we explicated the reasons for this as lack of cross-fertilisation between disciplinary silos. We identified a number of challenges in ESB research as an outcome of a lack of interplay among disciplinary perspectives in the field. Some of the challenges outlined are purist treatment of individual levels of analysis; lack of attention to interplay between levels of analyses; deterministic exploration of the interplay between levels without attention to the dynamically changing nature of individual choices and institutional structures; and dichotomous positioning of methods. In order to overcome these limiting tendencies, we provided a Bourdieuan framing for ESB research. We suggested that Bourdieu's sociology can help research in the field of ESB overcome some of its contemporary challenges in a number of ways.

Bourdieuan analysis offers a way to integrate individual, organisational, institutional and social dynamics as interconnected and co-generative. In this chapter, we exemplified the possibilities Bourdieuan sociology opens up for ESB research by using four of his key concepts, i.e. field, *habitus*, capitals and strategies. Therefore, Bourdieu helps solve the deterministic tendency in terms of the duality of agency and structure. This approach calls for exploring agency and structure in interplay rather than as autonomous entities. By situating agentic and structural resources as an integral part of his vision of the social world, Bourdieu stresses the influence of political economy on how certain phenomena may come to be popularised in a particular era. The recent political backing for social entrepreneurship in the UK is a case in point. Bourdieu calls for an understanding of deeper political structures and relations of power that shape the current arrangements of social and economic life. In this approach, which treats ESB issues not as innocuous subjects but also as an important part of the political and economic life, there is more room for engaged scholarship that accounts for and cares about the wider relevance and impact of the topics that we study on the lives of real people. Therefore, we note that there is need for research to explore why and how certain forms of ESB activity are promoted as direct consequences of political choices regarding social welfare and common good in different national settings. Finally, in terms of overcoming methodological dualism, Bourdieuan sociology advocates moving beyond the rigidities of interpretivist and positivist paradigms and calls for openness and sensitivity to the research question in choosing the research method.

REFERENCES

Ahl, H. (2006), 'Why Research on Women Entrepreneurs Needs New Directions', *Entrepreneurship: Theory and Practice*, **30**(5): 595–621.

Anderson, A.R., Dodd, S.D., Jack S. (2010), 'Network Practices and Entrepreneurial Growth', *Scandinavian Journal of Management*, **25**(2): 121–33.

Arenius, P. and Minniti, M. (2005), 'Perceptual Variables and Nascent Entrepreneurship', *Small Business Economics*, **24**(3): 233–47.

Barrett, G.A., Jones, T.P. and McEvoy, D. (2001), 'Socio-Economic and Policy Dimensions of the Mixed Embeddedness of Ethnic Minority Business in Britain', *Journal of Ethnic and Migration Studies*, **27**(2): 241–58.

Begley, T. and Boyd, D. (1987), 'Psychological Characteristics Associated with Performance in Entrepreneurial Firms and Smaller Businesses', *Journal of Business Venturing*, **2**, 79–93.

Birley, S. (1989), 'The Start-Up', in Burns, P. and J. Dewhurst (Eds), *Small Business and Entrepreneurship*, Houndsmills: Macmillan.

Bouchikhi, H. (1993), 'A Constructivist Framework for Understanding Entrepreneurship Performance', *Organization Studies*, **14**(4): 549–70.

Bourdieu, P. (1977), *Outline of Theory of Practice*, Cambridge: Cambridge University Press.

Bourdieu, P. (1984), *Distinction: A Social Critique of the Judgement of Taste*, London: Routledge.

Bourdieu, P. (1987), 'What Makes a Social Class? On the Theoretical and Practical Existence of Groups', *Berkeley Journal of Sociology*, **32**: 1–18.

Bourdieu, P. (1990), *The Logic of Practice*, Stanford: Stanford University Press.

Bourdieu, P. (1998), *Practical Reason: on the Theory of Action.* Cambridge: Polity Press.

Bourdieu, P. and Wacquant, L. (1992), *An Invitation to Reflexive Sociology*, Cambridge: Polity Press.

Bridge, S., O'Neill, K. and Martin, F. (2009), *Understanding Enterprise: Enterprise and Small Business*, Basingstoke: Palgrave Macmillan.

Brockhaus, R.H. (1980), 'Risk-Taking Propensity of Entrepreneurs', *Academy of Management Journal*, **23**(3), 509–20.

Bruni, A., Gherardi, S. and Poggio, B. (2004), 'Doing Gender, Doing Entrepreneurship: An Ethnographic Account of Intertwined Practices', *Gender, Work and Organization*, **11**: 406–29.

Bygrave, W. and Minniti, M. (2000), 'The Social Dynamics of Entrepreneurship', *Entrepreneurship: Theory and Practice*, **24**, 25–36.

Chandler, G. and Lyon, D.W. (2001), 'Issues of Research Design and Construct Measurement in Entrepreneurship Research, The Past Decade', *Entrepreneurship: Theory and Practice*, **25**: 101–13.

Chell, E. (1985), 'The Entrepreneurial Personality: A Few Ghosts Laid to Rest?' *International Small Business Journal*, **3**(3): 43–54.

Chell, E. (2000), 'Towards Researching "the Opportunistic Entrepreneur": A Social Constructionist Approach and Research Agenda', *European Journal of Work and Organisational Psychology*, **9**(1): 63–80.

Chell, E. (2007), 'Social Enterprise and Entrepreneurship: Towards a Convergent Theory of the Entrepreneurial Process', *International Small Business Journal*, **25**(1): 5–26.

Chell, E. (2008), *The Entrepreneurial Personality: A Social Construction*, 2nd ed., London: Routledge.

Clegg, S.R. (1989), *Frameworks of Power*. London: Sage.

Clegg, S.R. (1990), *Modern Organizations: Organization Studies in the Postmodern World*, London: Sage.

Coleman, S. (2000), 'Access to Capital: A Comparison of Men and Women-owned Small Business', *Journal of Small Business Management*, **38**(3): 37–52.

Cooper, A.C. (1981), 'Strategic Management: New Ventures and Small Business', *Long Range Planning*, **14**, 39–45.

Cooper, A.C., Gimeno-Gasco, F.J. and Woo, C.Y. (1994), 'Initial Human and Financial Capital as Predictors of New Venture Performance', *Journal of Business Venturing*, **9**(5): 371–95.

Cramer, J., Hartog, J., Jonker, N. and Van Praag, J. (2002), 'Low risk Aversion Encourages the Choice for Entrepreneurship: An Empirical Test of Altruism', *Journal of Economic Behavior and Organization*, **48**: 29–36.

Davidsson, P. (1995), 'Culture, Structure and Regional Levels of Entrepreneurship', *Entrepreneurship & Regional Development*, **7**(1): 41–62.

Davidsson, P. and Wiklund, J. (2001), 'Levels of Analysis in Entrepreneurship Research: Current Research Practice and Suggestions for the Future', *Entrepreneurship: Theory and Practice*, **25**(4): 81–100.

De Clercq, D. and Voronov, M. (2009a), 'The Role of Cultural and Symbolic Capital in Entrepreneurs' Ability to Meet Expectations about Conformity and Innovation', *Journal of Small Business Management*, **47**: 398–420.

De Clercq, D. and Voronov, M. (2009b), 'Toward a Practice Perspective of Entrepreneurship: Entrepreneurial Legitimacy as Habitus', *International Small Business Journal*, **27**(4): 395–419.

Deakins, D. (1996), *Entrepreneurs and Small Firms*, London: McGraw Hill.

Dolinsky, L., Caputo, R.K., Pasumarty, K. and Quazi, H. (1993), 'The Effects of Education on Business Ownership: A Longitudinal Study of Women', *Entrepreneurship: Theory and Practice*, **18**(1): 43–53.

Downing, S. (2005), 'The Social Construction of Entrepreneurship: Narrative and Dramatic Processes in the Coproduction of Organizations and Identities', *Entrepreneurship: Theory and Practice*, **29**(2): 185–204.

Drucker, P. (1985), *Innovation and Entrepreneurship*, Oxford: Butterworth-Heinemann.

Du Gay, P. (1994), 'Making up Managers: Bureaucracy, Enterprise and the Liberal Art of Separation', *British Journal of Sociology*, **45**(4): 655–74.

Dyer Jr, W.G. (1994), 'Toward a Theory of Entrepreneurial Careers', *Entrepreneurship: Theory and Practice*, **19**: 7–21.

Eckhardt, J. and Shane, S. (2003), 'Opportunities and Entrepreneurship', *Journal of Management*, **29**: 333–49.

Fabian, F. and Ndofor, H.A. (2005), 'The Context of Entrepreneurial Processes: One Size does not Fit All', in Lumpkin, G.T. and Katz, J. (Eds.) *Entrepreneurial Strategic Processes: Advances in Entrepreneurship, Firm Emergence and Growth*. Bingley: Emerald.

Feldman, D.C. and Bolino, M.C. (2000), 'Career Patterns of the Self-employed: Career Motivations', *Journal of Small Business Management*, **38**: 53–67.

Gartner, W.B. (1985), 'A Framework for Describing the Phenomenon of New Venture Creation', *Academy of Management Review*, **10**: 696–706.

Giddens, A. (1984), *The Constitution of Society: Outline of the Theory of Structuration*, Berkeley: University of California Press.

Giddens, A. (1991), *Modernity and Self-Identity: Self and Society in the Late Modern Age*, Palo Alto: Stanford University Press.

Grant, P. and Perren, L.J. (2002), 'Small Businesses and Entrepreneurial Research: Metatheories, Paradigms and Prejudices', *International Small Business Journal*, **20**(2): 185–209.

Grenfell, M. and James, D. (1998), *Bourdieu and Education: Acts of Practical Theory*. London: Falmer Press.

Hardill, I. and Raghuram, P. (1998), 'Diasporic Connections: Women in Case Studies of Asian Business', *Area*, **30**: 255–61.

Hsieh, C., Nickerson, J. and Zenger, T. (2007), 'Opportunity Discovery, Problem Solving and a Theory of the Entrepreneurial Firm', *Journal of Management Studies*, **44**: 1255–77.

Inman, K. (2000) *Women's Resources in Business Start-Up: A Study of Black and White Women Entrepreneurs*, New York: Garland Publishing.

Jack, S.L. and Anderson, A.R. (2002), 'The Effects of Embeddedness on the Entrepreneurial Process', *Journal of Business Venturing*, **17**: 467–87.

Johnson, B. (1990), 'Towards a Multidimensional Model of Entrepreneurship: The Case of Achievement Motivation and the Entrepreneur', *Entrepreneurship: Theory and Practice*, **14**: 39–54.

Jones, S. (2008), 'Learning to Earn: A Bourdieuian Approach to Exploring Women, Enterprise Education and Entrepreneurship', *Annual Postgraduate and Newer Researchers' Conference of the Society for Research into Higher Education* (SRHE).

Karataş-Özkan, M. (2011), 'Understanding Relational Qualities of Entrepreneurial Learning: Towards a Multi-layered Approach', *Entrepreneurship and Regional Development*, **23**: 877–906.

Karataş-Özkan, M. and Chell, E. (2010), *Nascent Entrepreneurship and Learning*, Cheltenham: Edward Elgar.

Kets De Vries, M. (1977), 'The Entrepreneurial Personality: A Person at the Crossroads', *Journal of Management Studies*, **14**: 34–7.

Kloosterman, R., Van Der Leun, J. and Rath, J. (1999), 'Mixed Embeddedness: Informal Economic Activities and Immigrant Businesses in the Netherlands', *International Journal of Urban and Regional Research*, **23**: 252–66.

Landström H. and Lohrke, F. (2010), *Historical Foundations of Entrepreneurial Research*, Cheltenham and New York: Edward Elgar Publishing.

Littunen, H. (2000), 'Entrepreneurship and the Characteristics of the Entrepreneurial Personality: A Person at the Crossroads', *International Journal of Entrepreneurial Behaviour and Research*, **6**: 295–309.

Lounsbury, M. and Glynn, M.A. (2001), 'Cultural Entrepreneurship: Stories, Legitimacy and the Acquisition of Resources', *Strategic Management Journal*, **22**: 545–64.

Low, M.B. & Macmillan, I.C. (1988), 'Entrepreneurship. Past research and future challenges', *Journal of Management*, **14**(2): 139–61.

Malach-Pines, A. and Özbilgin, M. (2010), *Handbook of Research on High Technology Entrepreneurs*, Cheltenham and New York: Edward Elgar Press.

Miller, K. (2007), 'Risk and Rationality in Entrepreneurial Processes', *Strategic Entrepreneurship Journal*, **1**: 57–74.

McClelland, D.C. (1965), 'N Achievement and Entrepreneurship: A Longitudinal Study', *Journal of personality and Social Psychology*, **1**(4): 389–92.

Nash, R. (2003), 'Social Explanation and Socialisation: On Bourdieu and the Structure, Disposition, Practice Scheme', *The Sociological Review*, **51**(1): 43–62.

Ndofor, H.A. and Priem, R. (2005), 'Forms of Entrepreneurial Capital, Venture Strategy and Performance: The Special Case of Minority Entrepreneurs', *Academy of Management Best Paper Proceedings*.

Nicholson, L. and Anderson, A.R. (2005), 'News and Nuances of the Entrepreneurial Myth and Metaphor: Linguistic Games in Entrepreneurial Sense-Making and Sense-Giving', *Entrepreneurship: Theory and Practice*, **29**: 153–72.

Ogbor, J. O. (2000), 'Mythicizing and Reification in Entrepreneurial Discourse: Ideology-critique of Entrepreneurial Studies', *Journal of Management Studies*, **37**(5): 605–35.

Özbilgin M. and Malach-Pines, A. (2007), *Career Choice in Management and Entrepreneurship: a research companion*, Cheltenham and New York: Edward Elgar Press.

Özbilgin M.; Küskü F. and Erdoğmuş, N. (2005), 'Explaining Influences on Career "Choice": The Case of MBA Students', *International Journal of Human Resource Management*, **16**(11): 2000–28.

Özbilgin, M. and Tatli, A. (2005), 'Understanding Bourdieu's Contribution to Management and Organization Studies', *Academy of Management Review*, **30**(4): 855–69.

Peterson, M.F. and Meckler, M.R. (2001), 'Cuban-American Entrepreneurs: Chance, Complexity and Chaos', *Organization Studies*, **22**(1): 31–58.

Phizacklea, A. and Ram, M. (1995), 'Ethnic Entrepreneurship in Comparative Perspective', *International Journal of Entrepreneurial Behaviour and Research*, **1**(1): 48–58.

Pittaway, L.A. (2000), *The social construction of entrepreneurial behaviour*, PhD thesis, University of Newcastle, Newcastle upon Tyne.

Pollard, J., Henry, N. and McEwen, C. (2002), 'Globalization From Below: Birmingham – Postcolonial Workshop of the World', *Area*, **34**: 117–27.

Reynolds, P.D. (1991), 'Sociology and entrepreneurship concepts and contributions', *Entrepreneurship: Theory and Practice*, **16**: 47–67.

Robinson, P.B. and Sexton, E.A. (1994), 'The Effect of Education and Experience on Self-employment Success', *Journal of Business Venturing*, **9**(2): 141–56.

Romanelli, E. (1989), 'Organizational Birth and Population Variety', in Cummings, L. L. and Staw, B.M. (Eds.) *Research in Organizational Behaviour*, Greenwich, CT: JAI Press.

Schumpeter, J.A. (1996), *The Theory of Economic Development*, New Brunswick and London: Transaction.

Shurry, J., Lomax, S. and Vyakarnam, S. (2002), *Household Survey of Entrepreneurship 2001*, London: Small Business Service.

Smith, C.A. (2000), *Market Women: Learning Strategies of Successful Black Women Entrepreneurs in New York State*, Westport, CT: Greenwood Publishing Group.

Stewart, W.H., Carland, J.C., Carland, J.W., Watson, W.E. and Sweo, R. (2003), 'Entrepreneurial Dispositions and Goal Orientations: A Comparative Exploration of United States and Russian Entrepreneurs', *Journal of Small Business Management*, **41**: 27–46.

Steyaert, C. (1998), 'A Qualitative Methodology for Process Studies of Entrepreneurship: Creating Local Knowledge through Stories', *International Studies of Management and Organisation*, **27**(3): 13–33.

Steyaert, C. and Katz, J. (2004), 'Reclaiming the Space of Entrepreneurship in Society: Geographical, Discursive and Social Dimensions', *Entrepreneurship and Regional Development*, **16**: 179–96.

Wacquant, L. (1993), 'On the Tracks of Symbolic Power: Prefatory Notes to Bourdieu's "State Nobility"', *Theory, Culture and Society*, **10**: 1–17.

5. Theorising entrepreneurship: an institutional theory perspective
Mine Karataş-Özkan, Cagla Yavuz and Jeremy Howells

INTRODUCTION

Scholarship in entrepreneurship has taken an institutional turn recently. This is in large part because entrepreneurship scholars have emphasised the need to understand the context of entrepreneurial process. There have been numerous theoretical and empirical attempts to explore entrepreneurship from an institutional theory perspective (see Ruef & Lounsbury, 2007; Thornton, 1999; Sine & David, 2010; Tolbert et al., 2011). Institutional theory allows for understanding the deeper and more resilient aspects of social structures by taking into account the processes by which structures, including rules, norms, and routines, become established as authoritative guidelines for social behaviour (Scott, 1987). Institutional theory has proved to be a useful theoretical foundation for examining a wide array of topics in different domains of organization and management studies (Di Maggio & Powell, 1991). It is traditionally concerned with how various actors and organizations attain and secure their positions and legitimacy by conforming to the rules and norms of the institutional environment (Scott, 2007). As a theoretical lens, it allows for reading of complexities and subtleties involved in the process of entrepreneurship, which is characterised by the contextual embeddedness of entrepreneurs' actions. For the purpose of this Handbook, institutional theory offers a useful framework to study several sub-domains of entrepreneurship by highlighting importance of institutions as facilitating or constraining structures.

Defining the field of entrepreneurship as the scholarly examination of how enterprise ideas are institutionalised by entrepreneurial actors through relational processes in order to create social and economic value (Karataş-Özkan & Chell, 2010), our focus is on the reflexive and embedded nature of the entrepreneurial process. By 'embedded', we refer to socio-economic, political, historical and cultural embeddedness. In this chapter, we seek to demonstrate the value of institutional theory in explaining the complexities of entrepreneurial process as a part of the current trend in entrepreneurship scholarship. In addressing this aim, we first present an overview of institutional theory with its different disciplinary roots and applications to entrepreneurship domain. We then discuss institutional entrepreneurship as a newly emerging domain to show the interface between institutional theory and entrepreneurship. We conclude the chapter by demonstrating transferability of ideas drawn from institutional theory into entrepreneurship field.

INSTITUTIONAL THEORY: DISCIPLINARY PERSPECTIVES AND LINKS TO ENTREPRENEURSHIP

Drawing on different disciplines and schools of thought, institutional theorists have defined institutions from different perspectives. Political scientists and economists imply the importance of negotiated and standardised rules in determining entrepreneurial behaviour and draw attention to the adaptive process of entrepreneurship (e.g. Aidis et al., 2008; Coduras et al., 2009; Veciana & Urbano, 2008; Welter, 2005) with a focus on 'discovery of entrepreneurial opportunities and opportunities for individuals to make a profit' (Bruton et al., 2010: 430). In this vein, the socio-economic and political science perspective is brought to the fore of the debate by North (1990: 3), who has defined institutions as 'any form of constraints that human beings devise to shape human interactions'. He divides institutions into formal and informal institutions. While formal institutions refer to regulative frames including political rules, economic rules, contracts, constitutions, laws and property rights; informal institutions refer to codes of conducts, norms, attitudes and values (Alvarez et al., 2011; North, 1990). From a sociological perspective, in his influential work, Scott (1995; 2001; 2007) defines institutions as social structures made up of cultural-cognitive, normative and regulative components, combined with associated activities and resources, that provide stability and meaning to social life. The main premise of the institutional theory from a sociological perspective is that structures, forms and processes of organizations are shaped in response to changes in the institutional environments in which they are embedded (DiMaggio & Powell, 1983; Meyer & Rowan, 1977; Scott & Meyer, 1983; Zucker, 1977).

Sociological perspectives to institutional theory are characterised by a common understanding of entrepreneurship as an embedded and reflexive process. In this understanding, entrepreneurial opportunities, choices and actions are limited by their institutional environments (e.g. Smallbone et al., 2010; Tolbert et al., 2011). As noted by Bruton et al. (2010), employing different institutional perspectives in entrepreneurship studies might result in different implications, due to the differences in key assumptions of these different disciplinary approaches. Scholars, who studied entrepreneurship through the lens of sociological institutional theory (e.g. Aldrich & Zimmer, 1986; Shapero & Sokol, 1982; Steyaert & Katz, 2004), emphasise the importance of not only regulative frames, but also norms and values of societies, beliefs, and behaviours of individuals in driving entrepreneurial changes. Regulative, normative and cognitive elements form the three pillars of the sociological institutional theory (DiMaggio & Powell, 1993; Scott, 1995; 2005; 2007). They reflect regulatory, social and cognitive influences that promote survival and legitimacy of organizations and organizational practices. The regulative pillar represents 'the rules of the game'; such regulative components usually derive from governmental legislation and industrial agreements and standards (Bruton et al., 2010). The normative pillar refers to taken-for-granted norms and values (Scott, 2007), which determine the way entrepreneurs gain support and legitimacy in enacting entrepreneurial action. While the cognitive pillar is related to the cognitive scripts, schemas and behaviours of individuals, whose evaluation and acceptance of entrepreneurship based on their knowledge and skill is the key focus here. While regulative frames provide the basis for the opportunity field for entrepreneurs; norms, values and individual perceptions play a critical role in recognising entrepreneurial opportunities (Welter & Smallbone, 2008). Overall, an institutional theory perspective is critical in understanding under which conditions entrepreneurship is constrained and facilitated. As such it provides the basis of institutionalised realities and maps legitimised action, which is more critical for new ventures, which need to overcome the 'liability of newness' (Stinchcombe, 1965), rather than established organizations (Bruton & Ahlstrom, 2003; Bruton et al., 2010). Legitimacy and garnering resources are critical in entrepreneurial efforts (Lounsbury & Glynn, 2001). We argue that a sociological view of institutional theory emphasises reflexivity and relationality of the entrepreneurship process.

Applications of institutional theory to sub-domains of entrepreneurship are increasingly evident in the literature. For example, extant studies of international entrepreneurship employ Scott's theory of regulative, normative and cognitive pillars in order to explain national institutional profiles in determining entrepreneurial actions (e.g. Busenitz et al., 2000; Lim et al., 2010; Manolova et al., 2008; Tiessen, 1997). In their study exploring conduciveness of the institutional environment for affecting entrepreneurship in transition economies (Bulgaria, Hungary and Latvia), Manolovo et al. (2008) have reported institutional context-specific factors that impede entrepreneurship in these settings. For example, requisite entrepreneurial knowledge and skill, which is associated with the cognitive pillar, is a major problem in Hungary and Latvia, as traditionally individuals in these societies are not raised and trained in enterprising cultures. Under socialist and communist political and economic regimes, opportunities for building the stock of entrepreneurial knowledge are limited. Hence, entrepreneurial engagement is institutionally constrained. Linked to this, negative social attitudes toward entrepreneurship is another constraint for Hungary, while discontent with legal and regulatory structures, including government policy, is noted as a major hindering factor in Bulgaria. Although laws and regulations in Hungary have been relaxed for enterprise activity, strategic investments to enhance entrepreneurial competencies and raising social awareness for entrepreneurship have not been at adequate levels. Similarly, Smallbone et al. (2010) show that a lack of legislative and regulative frames caused institutional deficiencies and created an opportunity for the emergence of a business service sector in the Ukraine. In a parallel vein, Lim et al.'s (2010) study of 757 firms from eight countries demonstrates that while property rights are important for innovation and value creation and motivate entrepreneurial action, regulatory complexities have adverse impacts on new venture decisions. Shifting the emphasis from the regulative and normative pillars to the cognitive pillar, in their study using secondary data from 32 countries in exploring the moderating effect of informal and formal institutions on individual level resources such as financial, human and social capital in initiating new business activity, Clercq et al. (2011) argue that institutions influence entrepreneurs' social capital and human capital (knowledge, skill and experience), rather than financial capital in starting a new business.

Gender and entrepreneurship is another area to which institutional theory has been applied. These studies show that informal institutions including beliefs, values and attitudes of society play a more critical role in determining entrepreneurial decisions, in particular for female entrepreneurship (e.g. Alvarez et al., 2011; Welter & Smallbone, 2008). Welter and Smallbone (2008) reveal that codes of behaviour and cultural influences, such as attitudes of neighbours, constrain female entrepreneurship in Uzbekistan. Alvarez et al.'s (2011) study, conducted in Spain (2006–09 period), shows that women's entrepreneurship is more closely associated with a supportive environment for entrepreneurship rather than education levels. These examples demonstrate how institutional environments influence the nature and boundaries of entrepreneurship.

Given the emphasis on embeddedness and context, scholars have demonstrated how market characteristics such as emerging (e.g. Marti & Mair, 2009; Tracey & Philips, 2011) and transition economies (e.g. Manolova & Yan, 2002; Smallbone & Welter, 2006; Smallbone et al., 2010; Welter & Smallbone, 2008) influence the nature and characteristics of entrepreneurial process. Emerging markets, which are characterised by weak institutional arrangements and uncertain resource-constraint environments (Ganly & Mair, 2008; Lawrence et al., 2002; Mair & Marti, 2006; Marti & Mair, 2009) create significant opportunities for entrepreneurs and lead them to act as institutional entrepreneurs (Tracey & Philips, 2011; Marti & Mair, 2009). Since these contexts lack mature institutional structures, understanding the nature of informal institutions including values, practices and norms, plays a more critical role in recognising entrepreneurial opportunities. 'Institutional voids' in these environments are recognised as opportunity spaces for entrepreneurs to 'infuse new beliefs, norms and values into social structures' (Marti & Mair, 2009: 4; Rao et al., 2000). These contexts breed 'institutional entrepreneurship', which is a related debate as will be presented in ensuing sections of the chapter.

Understanding cultural norms, values, individual perceptions play a critical role in these environments. Entrepreneurs employ different strategies on the basis of local and national contexts. According to Tracey and Philips (2011), entrepreneurs employ institutional brokering, spanning institutional voids and bridging institutional distance strategies in enacting institutional change in emerging markets. Another example of defining such strategic outlooks is provided by Seelos et al. (2011) in their study of social enterprise organizations (SEOs). They call for the importance of understanding social needs of communities in shaping the strategic orientations of SEOs. The authors define three strategic orientations employed by SEOs in different local contexts: a collective-action orientation to a high degree in close communities, such as Chinese towns in the USA; a market-based orientation in societies where cognitive shifts in society, such as emerging markets, are required for social change; and social-giving orientation in communities with a tradition of philanthropic activity. In Chapter 21 of this Handbook, de Bruin and her colleagues focus on the innovation dimension of social entrepreneurship and they argue how such social entrepreneurship process can offer innovative ways to identify and implement creative solutions to long-standing, complex, and often institutionalised, social problems.

In addition to these applications, one can argue that institutional theory is applicable to exploring entrepreneurial responses of established organizations. Established organizations form divergent strategies, structures and practices in the context of institutional pressures. This can be described as an entrepreneurial response. Earlier institutional theorists assumed that organizations blindly comply with institutional pressures and employ adaptive strategies when experiencing institutional uncertainties. For instance, decoupling as an organizational response strategy has been discussed in the literature (e.g. Boxenbaum & Jonsson, 2008; Fiss & Zajac, 2006; Westphal & Zajac, 1994; 1998). Decoupling refers to symbolically adopting the structures or practices demanded by institutional referents to project a legitimate image (Boxenbaum & Jonsson, 2008). Decoupling is a response strategy, since organizations do not change structurally or strategically in essence.

More recent studies (e.g. Battilana & Dorado, 2010; Binder, 2007; Greenwood et al., 2010; Lounsbury, 2007; Oliver, 1991; Pache & Santos, 2010; 2011) show that organizations are aware of alternative strategic choices, recognise opportunity spaces and develop active organizational responses to institutional pressures. In that sense, hybridization is another strategy. It refers to 'integrating competing logics in unprecedented ways' (Battilana & Dorado, 2010; Bjerregaard & Jonasson, 2013; Pache & Santos, 2011). While hybridization attempts to integrate multiple and often competing institutional logics, strategic isomorphism, as another strategy, refers to selective compliance of organizations with institutional templates in fields exhibiting enduring competing demands (Aurini, 2006; Pache & Santos, 2011). These can be considered as active entrepreneurial strategies, which might differentiate one organization from another. Exploring entrepreneurial responses of large and established firms in transition economies where the harshness and hostility of institutional environments are dominant, Manolova and Yan (2002) argue that organizations show active agency through employing balancing (informal networking), co-optation (surplus extraction), avoidance (short-term orientation) and bargaining with institutional shareholders (bribing of institutional agents) in these environments. Organizations, which develop and execute active strategies in responding to institutional pressures and change the dynamics of the field in which they operate, demonstrate organizational agency, which is a crucial aspect of entrepreneurial organizations. Revisiting the emphasis on reflexivity, their organizational responses and attempts to influence institutional arrangements and change institutions (and fields as the web of institutionalised forces) are shaped by such institutions in a given field.

ENTREPRENEURSHIP AND INSTITUTIONAL CHANGE: INSTITUTIONAL ENTREPRENEURSHIP

More recent studies of entrepreneurship attempt to bridge entrepreneurship and institutional theory and explore entrepreneurs' influence on institutional changes (e.g. Kalantaridis & Fletcher, 2012; Tolbert et al., 2011), bringing about new institutional environments and/or organizational forms. Institutional entrepreneurs are 'actors who leverage resources to create new institutions or transform existing institutions' (Battilana et al., 2009; DiMaggio, 1988; Maguire et al., 2004). Institutional theorists have paid growing attention to institutional entrepreneurship, which allows for agency of organised actors in enacting divergent changes. DiMaggio's (1988) influential article on institutional entrepreneurship (see Battilana et al., 2009 for review) has paved the way for these debates on institutional entrepreneurship.

Institutional entrepreneurs can be organizations (e.g. Garud et al., 2002; Greenwood et al., 2002) or individuals (e.g. Battilana, 2006; Fligstein, 1997; Kisfalvi & Maguire, 2011; Maguire et al., 2004). The resource-allocation process is central for institutional entrepreneurship (DiMaggio, 1988; Hardy & Maguire, 2008). Entrepreneurial motivation and power resources in enacting divergent change vary, based on different conditions. These include market characteristics, such as developed or developing markets (Ganly & Mair, 2008; Marti & Mair, 2009; Tracey & Philips, 2011), field conditions, such as mature (e.g. Greenwood et al., 2002; Lounsbury, 2002) or emerging fields (DiMaggio, 1991; Fazekas, 2009; Garud et al., 2002; Maguire et al, 2004); positioning in a given field, such as centre (Greenwood & Suddaby, 2006) or periphery (Leblebici et al., 1991). Exemplifying established organizations positioning at the centre of the field in mature fields, Greenwood and Suddaby (2006) demonstrate how the 'big five' Canadian elite professional accounting firms introduced a new organizational form, which embraces multi-professional practices rather than serving a single, professional function such as accounting. Their power derives from their structural positioning in a given field, which provided them with access to leading clients.

Turning our attention to those in periphery, powerless entrepreneurs rely mostly on their relation with powerful actors, such as lobbying the labour unions (Holm, 1995; Kalantaridis & Fletcher, 2012) and collaborations with business and government organisations (e.g. Lawrence et al., 1999; 2002; Marti & Mair, 2009). For example, Maria Aparecida Silva Bento (Cida), who is a social entrepreneur fighting racism in work organizations in Brazil, became influential in the Brazilian Government's decision on officially recognising the existence of racial discrimination for the first time through lobbying labour unions. She convinced all three of Brazil's major labour confederations to come together to request an ILO (International Labour Organisation) delegation to investigate and advocate the implementation of the ILO Convention 111, which guarantees equal employment opportunities to all citizens (see Ashoka's website at www. ashoka.org).

Institutional entrepreneurship is a useful lens to explain how actors inside the organizations enact institutional change (see Reay et al., 2006). Their influence on institutional arrangements is associated with their social position (Battilana, 2006) and associated power, social skills (Fligstein, 1997), formal position and organizational affiliation (Maguire et al., 2004) and individual characteristics such as reflexivity (Mutch, 2007), independence and marginality (Kisfalvi &v Maguire, 2011). These are inextricably linked to the accumulation of capital used in exercising power. In this regard, Bourdieu (1986) highlights the importance of capital as an individual-level strategic tool, which is required in securing and maintaining a place in a field. For Bourdieu, power stands at the heart of social life and the struggle for social distinction, in any form it takes, is its fundamental dimension. The successful exercise of power requires legitimation (Swartz, 1997). Explaining power and politics of social relationships form the core of Bourdieu's sociology (Tatli, 2011; Tatli and Özbilgin, 2012). The emphasis is on how individuals and groups go through the process of cultural socialization within competitive status hierarchies; how they engage in social struggles to attain valued resources (i.e. capitals), and how they reproduce social stratifications through these engagements (Swartz, 1997).

In Chapter 4 of this Handbook, Forson and her colleagues offer a comprehensive reading of Bourdieu's theory of social practice and its application to entrepreneurship studies. Therefore, it is not within the scope of the current chapter to further explain his theory. In relation to institutional theory, we wish to emphasize importance of capital as the individual-level dimension and implications of his theory in illuminating power dynamics. The importance of social, cultural, economic and symbolic capital in starting a new business (Clercq & Voronov, 2009; Karataş-Özkan, 2011; Yavuz et al., forthcoming; Tatli et al., forthcoming) and institutions' influence on attaining these resources (e.g. Clercq et al., 2011) have been well-documented in entrepreneurship studies. These individual-level resources attained by entrepreneurs are embedded in their institutional environments, since their meanings and values vary based on the contexts in which they operate (Vaughan, 2008). In parallel to this view, McKeever et al. use the concept of social embeddedness in order to emphasize importance of structural contexts in illuminating the dynamism and complexity of entrepreneurial situations, in Chapter 13 of this Handbook.

Entrepreneurial leadership can be illuminated from an institutional entrepreneurship perspective, bridging the above discussions on organizational strategic responses and the importance of individual agency in affecting institutional change. This forms another stream of institutional theory echoing Selznick's (1957) ideas on leadership and highlighting the importance of organizational leaders in driving institutional change (Kraatz, 2009; Kraatz & Moore, 2002; Oliver, 1992; Greenwood & Hinings, 1996; Hirsh & Lounsbury, 1997; Washington et al., 2008). Pache and Santos (2011) explain the role of leaders in internally representing institutional uncertainties through filtering, interpreting and acting upon competing institutional demands. In their study conducted over 600 private liberal art college leaders across a turbulent 11-year period, Kraatz and Moore (2002) demonstrate how migration of executives (movement of leaders between organizations) with different backgrounds (different skills, understandings, and values) is significant in prompting change in regulative, cognitive, and normative institutional elements, operating both at the level of organization and field. These studies reinforce the importance of a multi-layered examination of entrepreneurship (Karataş-Özkan, 2006; Chell, 2008; Karataş-Özkan & Chell, 2010) including macro (market conditions), meso (organizational positioning in a given field) and individual (role and identity of entrepreneurs) level, as delineated in the previous chapter of this volume by Forson et al. (2013).

CONCLUSIONS AND IMPLICATIONS FOR FUTURE STUDIES

Scholarship in entrepreneurship has taken a more holistic turn lately. Interlocking components of entrepreneurship have been emphasized in recent studies as they offer a comprehensive and critical reading of entrepreneurship explaining subtleties in individual, organizational and field levels. In this chapter, we have attempted to demonstrate the value of institutional theory in explaining entrepreneurship and researching different domains of entrepreneurship, such as social and institutional entrepreneurship, international entrepreneurship, gender and entrepreneurship, and ethnicity and entrepreneurship. Our contribution to knowledge can be explained by demonstrating the applicability of institutional theory with reference to its operationalization in different areas of entrepreneurship.

Reinforcing the need for multi-layered studies, another contribution we make is to bridge the gap between individual agency and institutional responses. There is limited empirical research into the institutional changing potential of entrepreneurs through innovations (Kalantaridis & Fletcher, 2012). Studies examining individual entrepreneurs in respect of institutional changes would contribute to the micro foundations of institutional theory, which is identified as a gap in knowledge (Powell & Colyvas, 2008; Suddaby, 2010). Therefore, further studies that look into these micro-foundations empirically are to be encouraged.

Despite the growing attention, there is a dearth of research exploring the dynamics of entrepreneurship in emerging markets. Institutional theory provides an enabling framework for generating insights into institutional dynamics that facilitate or constrain the nature and boundaries of entrepreneurship (Tracey & Philips, 2011). As stressed in this chapter, resource mobilization process of entrepreneurs (Marti & Mair, 2009) is a relational and reflexive process and they enact institutional change in such emerging market contexts, whereby the interplay of regulative, normative and cognitive pillars takes a different configuration compared with developed economic contexts. This warrants the need for further empirical studies that research the topic in single- or multiple-country settings or across different institutional fields in a given socio-economic and political system.

REFERENCES

Ahlstrom, D. & Bruton, G. D. (2002), 'An institutional perspective on the role of culture in shaping strategic actions by technology-focused entrepreneurial firms in China', *Entrepreneurship: Theory and Practice*, **26**(4), 53–70.

Aidis, R., Estrin, S. & Mickiewicz, T. (2008), 'Institutions and entrepreneurship development in Russia: a comparative perspective', *Journal of Business Venturing*, **23**(1): 656–72.

Aldrich, H. E. and Zimmer, C. (1986), 'Entrepreneurship through social networks', in Sexton, D. L. & Smilor, R. W. (Eds), *The Art and Science of Entrepreneurship*, Ballinger Publishing Co: New York, NY, 3–23.

Alvarez, C., Urbano, D., Coduras, A., & Ruiz-Navarro, J. (2011), 'Environmental conditions and entrepreneurial activity: A regional comparison in Spain', *Journal of Small Business and Enterprise Development*, **18**(1): 120–40.

Aurini, J. (2006), 'Crafting legitimation projects: An institutional analysis of private education businesses', *Sociological Forum*, **21**(1): 83–111.

Battilana, J. (2006), 'Agency and institutions: The enabling role of individuals' social position', *Organization*, **13**: 653–76.

Battilana, J., & Dorado, S. (2010), 'Building sustainable hybrid organizations: The case of commercial microfinance organizations', *Academy of Management Journal*, **53**(8): 1419–40.

Battilana, J., Leca, B., & Boxembaum, E. (2009), 'How actors change institutions: towards a theory of institutional entrepreneurship', in Walsh, J. & A. P. Brief (Eds), *Academy of Management Annals*, (3:65–107), Routledge: Essex, U.K.

Binder, A. (2007), 'For love and money: Organizations' creative responses to multiple environmental logics', *Theory & Society*, **36**: 547–71.

Bjerregaard, T. & Jonasson, C. (2013), 'Organizational responses to contending institutional logics: The moderating effect of group dynamics', *British Journal of Management*, doi: 10.1111/1467-8551.12014

Bourdieu, P. (1986), 'The forms of capital', in Richardson, J. G. (Ed.), *Handbook of Theory and Research for the Sociology of Education*, Greenwood Press: New York, 241–58.

Boxenbaum, E., & Jonsson, S. (2008), 'Isomorphism, diffusion and decoupling', in Greenwood, R., C. Oliver, R. Suddaby, & K. Sahlin-Andresson (Eds.), *The Sage Handbook of Organziational Institutionalism*,. Sage: London, 840.

Bruton, G. D. & Ahlstrom, D. (2003), An institutional view of China's venture capital industry: Explaining the differences between China and the West', *Journal of Business Venturing*, **18**(2), 233–60.

Bruton, G. D., Ahlstrom, D. & Li, H. L. (2010), 'Institutional theory and entrepreneurship: Where are we now and where do we need to move in the future?' *Entrepreneurship: Theory and Practice*, doi: 10.1111/j.1540-6520.2010.00390.x, 421–440.

Busenitz, L. W., Gomez., C., & Spencer, J. W. (2000), 'Country institutional profiles: Unlocking entrepreneurial phenomena', *Academy of Management Journal*, **43**(5): 994–1003.

Chell, E. (2008), *Entrepreneurial Personality: A Social Construction* (2nd ed.), Routledge, London.

Clercq, D., & Voronov, M. (2009), 'The role of cultural and symbolic capital in entrepreneurs' ability to meet expectations about conformity and innovation', *Journal of Small Business Management*, **47**: 398–420.

Clercq, D., Lim, D. S. K. & Oh, C. H. (2011), 'Individual-level resources and new business activity: The contingent role of institutional context', *Entrepreneurship: Theory and Practice*, **37**(2): 303–30.

Coduras, A., Ruiz, J. & Urbano, D. (2009), 'Discriminative model over repeated measures applied to control the evolution of the entrepreneurial environmental factors in the Spanish regions (2006–2008)', Paper presented at the 4th GEM-based Research Workshop, Cadiz, Spain, July.

DiMaggio, P. J. (1988), 'Interest and agency in institutional theory' in Zucker, L. (Ed.), *Institutional Patterns and Culture*, Ballinger Publishing Co; Cambridge, MA, 3–22.

DiMaggio, P. J. (1991), 'Constructing an organizational field as a professional project: US art museums, 1920–1940', in Powell, W. W. & P. J. DiMaggio (Eds.), *The New Institutionalism in Organizational Analysis*, The University of Chicago Press: Chicago, IL, 267–92.

DiMaggio, P. J. & Powell, W. W. (1983), 'The iron cage revisited: Institutional isomorphism and collective rationality in organizational fields', *American Sociology Review*, **48**: 147–60.

DiMaggio, P. J. & Powell, W. W. (1991), 'Introduction', in Powell, W. W. & P. J. DiMaggio (Eds.), *The New Institutionalism in Organizational Analysis*, University of Chicago Press: Chicago, IL, 267–92.

Fazekas, E. (2009), *Institutional entrepreneurship and cross national diffusion: The project of civil society development in Hungary*. Unpublished PhD Thesis, Graduate School of Arts and Science, Columbia University.

Fiss, P. C. & Zajac, E. J. (2006), 'The symbolic management of strategic change: Sense-giving via framing and decoupling', *Academy of Management Journal*, **49**(6): 1173–93.

Fligstein, N. (1997), 'Social skill and institutional theory', *American Behavioral Scientist*, **40**: 397–405.

Ganly, K. & Mair, J. (2008), *Social entrepreneurship in India: A small step approach towards institutional change*. University of Navarra, IESE Business School, Occasional Paper, OP-169-E, Navarra.

Garud, R., Jain, S., & Kumaraswamy, A. (2002), 'Institutional entrepreneurship in the sponsorship of common technological standards: The case of Sun Microsystems and Java', *Academy of Management Journal*, **45**: 196–214.

Greenwood, R. & Hinings, C. R. (1996), 'Understanding radical organizational change: Bringing together the old and the new institutionalism', *Academy of Management Review*, **21**: 1022–54.

Greenwood, R., Suddaby, R. & Hinings, C.R. (2002) 'Theorizing change: The role of professional associations in the transformation of institutionalized fields', *Academy of Management Journal*, **45**(1): 58–80.

Greenwood, R. & Suddaby, R. (2006), 'Institutional entrepreneurship in mature fields: The Big Five accounting firms', *Academy of Management Journal*, **49**: 27–48.

Greenwood, R., Diaz, A.M., Li, S.X. & Lorente, J.C. (2010), 'The multiplicity of institutional logics and the heterogeneity of organizational responses', *Organization Science*, **21**(2): 521–39.

Hardy, C. & Maguire, S. (2008), 'Institutional entrepreneurship', in Greenwood, R., C. Oliver, K. Sahlin–Andersson, & R. Suddaby (Eds.), *The SAGE Handbook of Organizational Institutionalism*, SAGE Publications, 198–217.

Hirsh, P. M. & Lounsbury, M. (1997), 'Ending the family quarrel: Toward a reconciliation of "old" and "new" institutionalism', *American Behavioural Scientist*, **40**: 406–18.

Holm, P. (1995), 'The dynamics of institutionalization: Transformation processes in Norwegian fisheries', *Administrative Science Quarterly*, **40**(3): 398–422.

Kalantaridis, C. & Fletcher, D. (2012), 'Entrepreneurship and institutional change: A research agenda', *Entrepreneurship and Regional Development: An International Journal*, **24**(3–4): 199–214.

Karataş-Özkan, M. (2006), '*The social construction of nascent entrepreneurship: dynamics of business venturing process from an entrepreneurial learning perspective*', Unpublished PhD Thesis, University of Southampton, Southampton.

Karataş-Özkan, M. (2011), 'Understanding relational qualities of entrepreneurial learning: Towards a multilayered approach', *Entrepreneurship & Regional Development: An International Journal*, **23**(9–10):877–906.

Karataş-Özkan M. & Chell, E. (2010), *Nascent Entrepreneurship and Learning*, Edward Elgar: Cheltenham and Northampton.

Kisfalvi, V. & Maguire, S. (2011), 'On the nature of institutional entrepreneurs: Insights from the life of Rachel Carson', *Journal of Management Inquiry*, **20**(2): 152–177.

Kraatz, M. S. (2009), 'Leadership as institutional work: a bridge to the other side', in Lawrence, B. T., Suddaby, R, & Leca, B. (Eds.), *Institutional Work: Actors and Agency in Institutional Studies of Organizations*, Cambridge University Press: Cambridge, 59–91.

Kraatz, M. S. & Moore, J. H. (2002), 'Executive migration and institutional change', *Academy of Management Journal*, **45**: 120–43.

Lawrence, B. T., Hardy, C. & Philips, N. (1999), Collaboration and institutional entrepreneurship: The case of Mere et Enfant (Palestine). Department of Management Working Paper in Operations and Strategy, the University of Melbourne, Australia, June (1): 1–36.

Lawrence, B. T., Hardy, C. & Philips, N. (2002), 'Institutional effects of interorganizational collaboration: The emergence of proto-institutions', *The Academy of Management Journal*, **45**(1): 281–90.

Leblebici, H., Salancik, G.R., Copay, A. & King, T. (1991),' Institutional change and the transformation of inter-organizational fields: An organizational history of the US radio broadcasting industry', *Administrative Science Quarterly*, **36**(3): 333–63.

Lim, D. S. K., Morse, E. A., Mitchell, R. K. & Seawright, K. K. (2010), 'Institutional environment and entrepreneurial cognitions: A comparative business systems perspective', *Entrepreneurship: Theory and Practice*, doi: 10.1111/j.1540-6520.2010.00384.x.

Lounsbury, M. (2002), 'Institutional transformation and status mobility: The professionalization of the field', *Academy of Management Journal*, **45**(1): 255–66.
Lounsbury, M. (2007), 'A tale of two cities: competing logics and practice variation in the professionalizing of mutual funds', *Academy of Management Journal*, 50: 289–307.
Lounsbury, M. & Glynn, M. A. (2001), 'Cultural entrepreneurship: Stories, legitimacy, and the acquisition of resources', *Strategic Management Journal*, **22**(6–7): 545–64.
Maguire, S., Hardy, C. & Lawrence, T. B. (2004), 'Institutional entrepreneurship in emerging fields: HIV/AIDS treatment advocacy in Canada', *Academy of Management Journal*, **47**(5): 657–79.
Mair, J. & Marti, I. (2006), '*Entrepreneurship in and around institutional voids: A case study from Bangladesh*', IESE Business School, University of Navarra, Working Paper No. 636.
Manolova, T. S., Eunni, R. V. & Gyoshev, B. S. (2008), 'Institutional environments for entrepreneurship: Evidence from emerging economies in Eastern Europe', *Entrepreneurship: Theory and Practice*, **32**(1), 203–18.
Manolova, T. S. & Yan, A. (2002), 'Institutional constraints and entrepreneurial responses in a transforming economy: The case of Bulgaria', *International Small Business Journal*, **20**(2), 163–84.
Marti, I. & Mair, J. (2009), 'Bringing change into the lives of the poor: Entrepreneurship outside traditional boundaries', in T. B. Lawrence, R. Suddaby, B. Leca, (Eds.), *Institutional Work: Actors and Agency in Institutional Studies of Organizations*, Cambridge University Press, Cambridge, 92–119.
Meyer, J. W. & Rowan, B. (1977), 'Institutionalized organizations: Formal structure as myth and ceremony', *American Journal of Sociology*, **83**: 340–63.
Mutch, A. (2007), 'Reflexivity and the institutional entrepreneur: A historical exploration', *Organization Studies*, **28**(07): 1123–40.
North, D. C. (1990), *Institutions, Institutional Change and Economic Performance*, Cambridge University Press: Cambridge.
Oliver, C. (1991), 'Strategic response to institutional processes', *The Academy of Management Review*, **16**(1): 145–79.
Oliver, C. (1992), 'The antecedents of deinstitutionalization', *Organization Studies*, **13**(4): 563–88.
Pache, A. C. & Santos, F. (2010), 'When worlds collide: The internal dynamics of organizational responses to conflicting institutional demands', *Academy of Management Review*, **35**(3): 455–76.
Pache, A. C. & Santos, F. (2011), 'Inside the hybrid organization: selective coupling as a response to conflicting institutional logics', *Academy of Management Journal*, doi: 10.5465/ amj.2011.0405.
Powell, W. W. & Colyvas, J. A. (2008), 'The micro-foundations of institutions', in R. Greenwood, C. Oliver, K. Sahlin & R. Suddaby (Eds.) *Handbook of Organizational Institutionalism*, Sage: London, 276–98.
Rao, H., Morrill, C. & Zald, M. (2000), 'Power plays: How social movements and collective action create new organizational forms', in Staw, B. M. & R. I. Sutton (Eds.), *Research in Organizational Behavior*, JAI Press: Greenwich, CT, 239–82.
Reay, T., Golden-Biddle, K. & Germann, K. (2006), 'Legitimizing a new role: Small wins and microprocesses of change', *Academy of Management Journal*, **49**(5), 977–98.
Ruef, M. & Lounsbury, M. (2007), 'Introduction: The sociology of entrepreneurship', in Ruef, M. & M. Lounsbury (ed.) *The Sociology of Entrepreneurship (Research in the Sociology of Organizations, Volume 25)*, Emerald Group Publishing Ltd, 1–29.
Scott, W. R. (1987), *Organizations: Rational, Natural and Open Systems* (2nd Ed.), Prentice-Hall: Englewood Cliffs, NJ.
Scott, W. R. (1995), *Institutions and Organizations*, Sage Publications: Thousand Oaks, CA.
Scott, W. R. (2001), *Institutions and Organizations* (2nd ed.), Sage Publications: Thousand Oaks, CA.
Scott, W. R. (2005), 'Institutional theory: Contributing to a theoretical research program', in K. G. Smith & M. A. Hitt (Eds.), *Great Minds in Management*, Oxford University Press: Oxford, UK. 460–84.
Scott, W. R. (2007), *Institutions and Organizations: Ideas and Interests*, Sage Publications: Thousand Oaks, CA.
Scott, W. R. & Meyer, J. W. (1983), *Organizational Environments: Ritual and Rationality*, Sage: Beverly Hills, CA.
Seelos, C., Mair, J., Battilana, J. & Dacin, M. T. (2011), 'The embeddedness of social entrepreneurship: Understanding variation across local communities', in C. Marquis, M. Lounsbury, R. Greenwood (Eds) *Communities and Organizations (Research in the Sociology of Organizations, Vol 33)*, Emerald Group Publishing Ltd: Bingley, UK 333–63.
Selznick, P. (1957), *Leadership in Administration*, Harper & Row: New York, NY.
Shapero, A. & Sokol, L. (1982), 'The social dimensions of entrepreneurship', in Kent, C. A., D. L. Sexton, & Vesper, K. H. (Eds.) *Encyclopaedia of Entrepreneurship*, Prentice-Hall: Englewood Cliffs, NJ, 72–90.
Sine, W. D. & David R. J. (Eds.) (2010), *Institutions and Entrepreneurship. Research in the Sociology of Work*, vol 21, Emerald Group Publishing Ltd: Bingley, UK.

Smallbone, D. & Welter, F. (2006), 'Conceptualising entrepreneurship in a transition context', *International Journal of Entrepreneurship and Small Business*, 3(2), 190–206.

Smallbone, D., Welter, F., Voytovich, A. & Egorov, I. (2010), 'Government and entrepreneurship in transition economies: the case of small firms in business services in Ukraine', *The Service Industries Journal*, 30(5): 655–70.

Steyaert, C. & Katz, J. (2004), 'Reclaiming the space of entrepreneurship in society: geographical, discursive and social dimensions', *Entrepreneurship & Regional Development*, 16(3): 179–96.

Stinchcombe, A. (1965), 'Social structure and social organization' *The Handbook of Organizations*, 142–93.

Suddaby, R. (2010), 'Challenges for institutional theory', *Journal of Management Inquiry*, 19(1): 14–20.

Swartz, D. (1997), *Culture and Power: The Sociology of Bourdieu*, University of Chicago Press Ltd, London.

Tatli, A. (2011), 'A multi-layered exploration of the diversity management field: diversity discourses, practices and practitioners in the UK', *British Journal of Management*, 22: 238–53.

Tatli, A. & Özbilgin, M. (2012), 'An emic approach to intersectional study of diversity at work: A Bourdieuan framing', *International Journal of Management Reviews*, 14: 180–200.

Tatli, A., Özbilgin, M., Vassilopoulou, J., Forson, C. & Slutskaya, N. (in press), 'A relational perspective for entrepreneurship research', *Journal of Small Business Management*.

Thornton, P. H. (1999), The sociology of entrepreneurship', *Annual Review of Sociology*, 25: 19–46.

Tiessen, J. H. (1997), 'Individualism, collectivism and entrepreneurship: A framework for international comparative research', *Journal of Business Venturing*, 12: 367–84.

Tolbert, P. S., David, R. J. & Sine, W. D. (2011), 'Studying choice and change: The intersection of institutional theory and entrepreneurship', *Organization Science*, 22(5): 1332–44.

Tracey, P. & Philips, N. (2011), 'Entrepreneurship in emerging markets: Strategies for new venture creation in uncertain institutional contexts', *Management International Review*, 51: 23–39.

Vaughan, D. (2008), 'Bourdieu and organizations: The empirical challenge', *Theory & Society*, 37: 65–81.

Veciana, J. M. & Urbano, D. (2008), 'The institutional approach to entrepreneurship research: Introduction', *International Entrepreneurship and Management Journal*, 4(4): 365–79.

Washington, M., Boal, K. & Davis, J. (2008), Institutional leadership: Past, present, and future, in R. Greenwood, C. Oliver, R. Suddaby & K. Sahlin-Andresson (Eds), *The Sage Handbook of Organizational Institutionalism*, London: Sage, 719–33.

Welter, F. (2005), 'Entrepreneurial behaviour in differing environments', in Audretsch, D. B., Grimm, H. & Wessner, C. W. (Eds), *Local Heroes in the Global Village: Globalization and the New Entrepreneurship Policies, International Studies in Entrepreneurship*, Springer: New York, NY, 93–112.

Welter, F. & Smallbone, D. (2008), 'Women's entrepreneurship from an institutional perspective: the case of Uzbekistan', *International Entrepreneurship Management Journal*, 4: 505–20.

Westphal, J. D. & Zajac, E. J. (1994), 'Substance and symbolism in CEOs' long-term incentive plans', *Administrative Science Quarterly*, 39: 367–90.

Westphal, J. D. & Zajac, E. J. (1998), 'The symbolic management of stockholders: Corporate governance reforms and shareholder reactions', *Administrative Science Quarterly*, 43: 127–53.

Yavuz, C., Karataş-Özkan M. & Howells, J. (2014), 'Social responsibility and agency of social entrepreneurs in driving institutional change'. In Karataş-Özkan, M., Nicolopoulou, K. & Özbilgin, M. (Eds) *Corporate Social Responsibility and Human Resource Management (HRM)*, Edward Elgar Publishing: Cheltenham.

Zucker, L. G. (1977), 'The role of institutionalization in cultural persistence', *American Sociology Review*, 42: 726–43.

PART II

METHODOLOGIES, PARADIGMS AND METHODS

6. Synthesising knowledge in entrepreneurship research – the role of systematic literature reviews

Luke Pittaway, Robin Holt and Jean Broad

OVERVIEW

This chapter explains a method new to entrepreneurship inquiry and a recent introduction to management inquiry, the systematic literature review (SLR). It discusses the current status of entrepreneurship research and shows that it has been criticised for being fragmented when drawing evidence from its wide disciplinary base. The chapter argues for greater reflection in entrepreneurship research and the SLR is introduced as one method by which both reflection and integration can be achieved. It progresses by introducing the method using examples from four previous studies and it outlines the basic principles. The conclusions highlight how the method can be of value within the field of entrepreneurship and outline its limitations.

INTRODUCTION

The purpose of this chapter is to introduce SLRs, to explain why the method may be useful within the context of entrepreneurship research and to illustrate how the method has been used within the subject; where it may be useful; and some of the limitations that can be encountered. The chapter begins the discussion by looking at the development of academic inquiry in entrepreneurship. During this part the authors contend that entrepreneurship is a maturing subject and that its multi-disciplinary nature requires methods that enable knowledge to be synthesised in a systematic fashion. The chapter then highlights some of the challenges for entrepreneurship research in the context of management inquiry. The next section shows how the SLR method, which has been enabled by the advance of bibliographical technologies, can be used to address some of the challenges currently faced within entrepreneurship research and it explores how the method is different from narrative approaches. Here, we contend that SLRs have greater transparency: are more objective; clearer and more focused; and, more accessible than traditional narrative reviews (Thorpe et al., 2005). Examples of the use of the method in the subject area are used to illustrate some of the benefits and challenges of SLRs. Finally, the chapter concludes that SLRs can be an effective method for synthesising knowledge in a subject like entrepreneurship where knowledge is becoming increasingly diversified and disconnected, as well as being multi-disciplinary and dynamic.

THE NATURE OF INQUIRY IN ENTREPRENEURSHIP RESEARCH

The nature of the progress of 'inquiry' constitutes a major area of discussion in most academic subjects and the philosophy of science itself constitutes a significant area of academic research. Such debates are most exemplified by the Kuhn (1962) and Popper (1963) debate on the nature of scientific advance. Inquiry in entrepreneurship research has not escaped the ramifications of such epistemological differences even where these are sometimes implicit (Grant and Perren, 2002). Indeed, early studies in economic theory that contributed to the foundations of the subject discussed in great depth the philosophical basis for carrying out research in the subject and there are significant epistemological differences (Pittaway, 2005). Despite this historical basis to the subject entrepreneurship is often considered in contemporary research to be a relatively recent field of study (Davidsson, Low and Wright, 2001; Gartner, 2001; Low, 2001; Gartner, Davidsson, and Zahra, 2006) and during the 1980s the subject was considered to be dominated by exploratory studies lacking empirical strength or theoretical depth (Gartner, 1985; Hornaday and Churchill, 1987; Low and MacMillan, 1988). In the view of many researchers the subject has developed empirically (Bygrave and Hofer, 1991; Hofer and Bygrave, 1992), while perhaps remaining underdeveloped conceptually (Shane and Venkataraman, 2000). The progress of the subject during the 1980s is best highlighted by Bygrave and Hofer (1991, p. 13) when they state:

> At the start of the 1980s, entrepreneurship was, at best, a potentially promising field of scholarly inquiry. However, by the end of that decade, due primarily to impressive advances in its body of empirical knowledge, entrepreneurship could claim to be a legitimate field of academic inquiry in all respects except one: it lacks a substantial theoretical foundation. A major challenge facing entrepreneurship researchers in the 1990s is to develop models and theories built on solid foundations from the social sciences.

During the 1990s entrepreneurship's theoretical foundations did begin to advance (Gartner, 2001) but it has been generally accepted that this enhancement of theory has led to greater fragmentation within the subject, as more researchers have begun to focus on a wider array of subjects (Brazeal and Herbert, 1999; Chandler and Lyon, 2001; Gartner, 2001; Ucbasaran, Westhead and Wright, 2001). This increased fragmentation has led to concern over the future direction of entrepreneurship research with several special issues of leading journals being dedicated to the debate (Davidsson, Low and Wright, 2001; Jennings, Perren and Carter, 2004; Sarasvathy, 2004a). The problem debated is best illustrated by Bull and Willard (1993, p. 184):

> Despite the number of published papers that might be considered related to the theory of entrepreneurship, no generally accepted theory of entrepreneurship has emerged. . .Despite the potential richness and texture that such diverse mix of disciplines brings, a major weakness is that, in many cases, researchers from one discipline have tended to ignore entrepreneurship studies by researchers in other disciplines.

As they highlight here an increasing volume of work, both empirical and conceptual, is being carried out which is broadly conceived to be within the domain of 'entrepreneurship' (Ucbasaran, Westhead and Wright, 2001). This increase in activity has led to an abundance of new theories (Low, 2001), the use of multiple units of analysis (Davidsson and Wiklund, 2001), research from many disciplinary foundations (Gartner, 2001) and 'incompatible' methodologies (Chandler and Lyon, 2001). Given this increase in research volume and the consequent fragmentation it is not surprising that there have been regular calls over the years for reflection; as illustrated by the following quotations which span two decades of research.

> As a body of literature develops, it is useful to stop occasionally, take inventory for the work that has been done, and identify new directions and challenges for the future (Low and MacMillan, 1988, p. 139).

> As the volume of entrepreneurship research continues to grow, it is useful to pause and evaluate existing research methodologies and whether they have kept pace with the development of the entrepreneurship paradigm. Alternatively, one could question whether the methodologies and measurements employed in entrepreneurship research are sufficiently robust to foster paradigmatic growth and maturation (Chandler and Lyon, 2001, p. 101).

Reflection is important, particularly as a field of study develops. Current reflection and debate on the status of entrepreneurship research can be categorised into several types, which illustrate a subject moving away from immaturity (Kuhn, 1962). The first type typifies a 'normal science' perspective whereby 'general theories' are sought to integrate the subject into a conceptual whole (Shane and Venkataraman, 2000). Views here occupy two trajectories: those seeking expansive theories (Shane and Venkataraman, 2000) and those seeking to draw the boundaries around the subject more tightly (Low, 2001). In both views entrepreneurship research involves the representation and analysis of phenomena, such as opportunities and ventures, as they occur in a world under observation. The second type typifies a 'pragmatic science' perspective whereby communities of scholars are encouraged to build research agendas around discrete themes within a general 'political' definition of entrepreneurship in which many perspectives are located (Gartner, 2001; Ucbasaran, Westhead and Wright, 2001). These views remain embedded within the 'scientific' view of knowledge creation. The third type can be described as the 'interpretive' perspective whereby differing philosophical traditions underpin theorising, leading to very different forms of knowledge construction, which are regarded as equally acceptable (Chell and Pittaway, 1998; Grant and Perren, 2002; Gartner and Birley, 2002; Jennings et al., 2005; Pittaway, 2005; Sarason, Dean and Dillard, 2006; Ahl, 2006). Here entrepreneurial judgement is rooted in physical and socially embodied processes (Sarasvathy, 2004b) and entrepreneurial phenomena are recognised less as things to be observed than as complicit with the environments of the research community and its emerging objects of concern.

The current period of reflection would appear to be rather important for the future development of entrepreneurship research (Low, 2001). It can be argued that entrepreneurship research does require a period of reflection, not least to better reflexively engage with the philosophical issues inherent in the current debates. Two aspects of this reflection are proposed here, one of which is the focus of the chapter. First, continued reflection is required on the philosophical debates, as outlined above; secondly, researchers in entrepreneurship need to develop research methodologies that encourage systematic reflections on existing empirical evidence with the aims of: synthesising across approaches; 'making sense' of particular themes through holistic methods (Chandler and Lyon, 2001; Gartner, 2001); and reviewing empirical work to help develop more integrated theoretical frameworks (Bygrave and Hofer, 1991; Shane and Venkataraman, 2000; Ucbasaran, Westhead and Wright, 2001). It is to this second aspect of reflection that this chapter is devoted through the introduction of the SLR. In the following part of the chapter we argue that inquiry in entrepreneurship has reached a point where reflection and synthesis is required and that SLRs provide one method through which such reflection and synthesis can be achieved. In the following part we explain how SLRs can be used in an effective way to facilitate improvements in connectedness of knowledge between different research themes in entrepreneurial inquiry.

THE ROLE OF SYSTEMATIC LITERATURE REVIEWS IN ENTREPRENEURSHIP INQUIRY

Based on the above arguments about entrepreneurial inquiry a summary of the debate on the problems arising from the growth of entrepreneurship research (Bruyat and Julien, 2000; Davidsson, Low and Wright, 2001; Gartner, 2001) might be given as:

(i) There is a lack of consistency in terminology used with little clarity over definitions of phenomena (Gartner, 1985; Brazeal and Herbert, 1999).
(ii) Many research streams are based on a disciplinary basis, which do not always overlap or interact (Gartner, 1985; Bull and Willard, 1993; Brazeal and Herbert, 1999; Gartner, 2001; Low, 2001).
(iii) Research is characterised by a large range of methodologies leading to empirical research that can be atheoretical. Explanations of methodology also sometimes lack detail (Smith, Gannon and Sapienza, 1989; Chandler and Lyon, 2001).
(iv) There is a need to develop more robust theoretical constructs (Bygrave and Hofer, 1991; Shane and Venkataraman, 2000).
(v) There is a requirement for greater inter-relationships between studies conducted at different levels of analysis (Low and MacMillan, 1988; Davidsson and Wiklund, 2001).

These issues have given cause for taking stock; affording researchers the opportunity to begin to frame a disciplinary atmosphere within which they are better able to engage with one another and to foster an interest in their findings among practitioners. Some of these issues have been raised in other disciplines; specifically in the medical field, where there was little awareness, and poor use, of research evidence by both other academics and practitioners (Fox, 2005). Catalysed by evidence-based policy initiatives, medical researchers began to develop protocols to search for research relevant to a specific problem, using rigorous evaluation criteria to ascertain biases that might distort evidence selection from multiple sources, and to integrate the findings using meta-analysis and narrative synthesis (Chalmers, 2003; Fox, 2005).

These concerns have to some extent been recognised by those looking to develop SLR methods within social sciences and in management inquiry in particular (Tranfield, Denyer and Smart, 2003; Denyer and Neely, 2004; Tranfield et al., 2004). Whereas in medicine SLRs partake of statistical summaries of data gathered by studies with similar research questions and using similar methods, such meta-analysis is less relevant to management research because here researchers are often dealing with different research questions among diverging populations and using different methodologies and even epistemological backgrounds (Trinder and Reynolds, 2000; Tranfield, Denyer and Smart, 2003; Pittaway et al., 2004; Tranfield et al., 2004; Denyer and Neely, 2004). Despite the obvious differences between medical research and research in the social sciences, entrepreneurship researchers have attempted to conduct meta-analysis, without a firm understanding of its limitations within the social sciences, or a clear understanding of the role of SLRs in collecting the literature on which a meta-analysis is based (Read, Song and Smit, 2009; Rosenbusch, Brinckmann and Bausch, 2011). For example, in this book Rauch (see Chapter 10) reviews different meta-analyses to consider the value of the personality approach to entrepreneurship but rarely do the reported studies use an SLR to find and select papers they review. These studies in entrepreneurship use the basic principles from the medical field without acknowledging the challenges of applying these to a social science subject. Two specific weaknesses can be noted from the reported studies, first, an assumption of definitional homogeneity across the studies used in the meta-analyses when researchers often operationalise definitions of the 'entrepreneur' differently. Secondly, in these studies there is little acknowledgement that samples vary significantly between studies because of a lack of agreement about 'who' the entrepreneur is. So studies are in some cases 'comparing apples with pears'. Unlike the sciences, social science cannot easily replicate studies and so a true meta-analysis is difficult to carry out well. The use of an SLR alongside other methods of synthesis, rather than a meta-analysis, seems more appropriate to many management researchers who have used this method (Tranfield, Denyer and Smart, 2003; Pittaway et al., 2004; Thorpe et al., 2005). Applied to management inquiry, the emphasis is upon developing systematic methods of narrative integration that review existing studies germane to a research question, rank their relative importance using transparent protocols of evaluation, and summarise their findings in terms of evidence-base, scope, methodology, ambition and implication with clarity and concision. In doing this, the SLR seeks emergent themes and conflicts, assesses both the inherent quality of studies, as well as the relevance of the data and findings to the research question informing the review; and isolates those areas where further contributions might be made. It is because of its abstraction and synthesis that an SLR can broach levels of conceptual and theoretical development unavailable to specific, empirical studies (Tranfield et al, 2004). The assumption is that by gaining perspective on what has been done researchers can attain perspective both on how this activity can be judged as a coherent, disciplinary whole and identify possible future trends. The aim is to make the map as representative of the territory as possible.

To achieve this aim, and warrant the title 'systematic', the review process requires the use of explicit methods. Just as the integrity of academic research of data is attained through careful explication of and adherence to identified methods, so this logic can be extended to cover the search of the literature informing the research; the SLR is a logical extension of good academic practice (Chalmers, Enkin and Keirse, 1993). The principles informing this extension are: transparency; clarity; focus; connection to policy and practice; accessibility; and broad coverage (Thorpe et al., 2005). With a few exceptions systematic literature reviews have not been used within entrepreneurship research[1] and literature reviews have typically been of the narrative form. The narrative form typically uses unrepresentative samples of studies in an unsystematic way, leading some to consider it an unscientific method (Mulrow, 1994; Oakley, 2002). While we believe narrative reviews provide a useful tool, and not all reviews need to be systematic, in order to provide valid accounts of the evidence in a reliable fashion, systematic reviews can play a significant role (Gaffan, Tsaousis and Kemp-Wheeler, 1995). The value of introducing SLRs of studies in entrepreneurship is that they can provide an alternative approach to narrative reviews that often confirm and entrench specific approaches and concerns. SLRs foster analyses of current knowledge that deliberately broaches such specificity; a need for such methods is suggested by Brazeal and Herbert:

> We posit that the next stage of the evolution of the entrepreneurship field may include a more holistic orientation, to include relevant concepts, topics, and selected information the fields of creativity, change and innovation (Brazeal and Herbert, 1999, p. 33).

> . . . the fragmentation of the field of entrepreneurship is at least partially due to the growing need for, but lack of, 'fit' between (a) the increasing amount of data and insights into the entrepreneurial phenomenon and (b) the central requirement for a fundamental mapping of entrepreneurial concepts (Brazeal and Herbert, 1999, p. 41).

Brazeal and Herbert argue that to reflect upon the subject effectively researchers will need the tools to turn disparate knowledge into a holistic picture. This is echoed by Shook, Priem and McGee (2003) who would like to see more integration both conceptually, methodologically and through cross-disciplinary synthesis. Systematic literature reviews within entrepreneurship can start to provide these integrations in the form of maps, based on transparent and repeatable methods. In doing so, such reviews provide the foundation for integrating knowledge across themes and approaches and integrating work that focuses on different units of analysis (Low, 2001). In such integration, however, the review is not so much syncretic, it is not looking to reconcile all existing approaches and findings within a meta-framework of concepts, as syndetic, the researchers propose themes within the studies reviewed that act as means by which studies can be compared to map a terrain in all its distinctiveness as well as commonality (MacPherson and Holt, 2007). So the use of SLRs in entrepreneurship research can be important to the development of the subject because they enable the reduction of fragmentation by providing insights into linkages between studies or by highlighting contradictions in approach. The method provides a basis for drawing and developing thematic frameworks and conceptual maps, which allow for more holistic perspectives to emerge. If carried out effectively it enables synthesis across disciplines where themes are similar, it can accommodate studies with different units of analysis and can enable different methodologies to contribute to understanding on their own merits. To summarise it can be argued that SLRs help:

(i)   Reduce lack of consistency in terminology by forcing reviewers to be explicit about definitions used.
(ii)   Enable overlap between disciplines by applying searches that find relevant studies across disciplines.

(iii)   Conduct literature reviews and evidence-based synthesis of knowledge while being sensitive to different methods.

(iv)   Develop more robust theoretical constructs by basing these on a deep understanding of the existing evidence base.

(v)   Encourage interrelationships between studies by forcing researchers to be more aware of the wider evidence on a particular subject before conducting new empirical studies.

In the next part the authors further develop the argument by introducing a detailed explanation of SLRs showing how they can be developed within entrepreneurship inquiry.

CONDUCTING SYSTEMATIC LITERATURE REVIEWS

Following methods developed within medicine (Chalmers, 2003; Fox, 2005) and in management studies by Tranfield, Denyer and Smart (2003), the authors have themselves undertaken SLRs within the field of entrepreneurship and small firms: looking at the use of business networks in innovation (Pittaway et al., 2004), examining the use of knowledge by SMEs (Thorpe et al, 2005), investigating knowledge and growth in SMEs (MacPherson and Holt, 2007) and reflecting on themes in research on entrepreneurship education (Pittaway and Cope, 2007). Using examples from some of these studies this part of the chapter explains the systematic review method, shows how it can be used within entrepreneurship research and concludes by providing a discussion of its utility and limits. There are a number of identifiable elements to the review process, which tend to exist within all forms of systematic literature review (Tranfield, Denyer and Smart, 2003; Pettigrew and Roberts, 2006). Some approaches identify three major elements (Tranfield, Denyer and Smart, 2003), while others present a number of different stages (Pettigrew and Roberts, 2006). There are some major themes: planning the review; conducting the review; and reporting the review and within these there are some discrete elements (see Figure 6.1). For example, identifying the need for the review; preparing the review protocols; carrying out the citation and literature searches; screening out and selecting studies using criteria; appraising included studies; synthesising results; and dissemination (Tranfield, Denyer and Smart, 2003; Pettigrew and Roberts, 2006).

Stage 1: Identifying the Need for the Review

An SLR begins from the establishment of a rationale and need for a systematic review. An identified need for an SLR may come from many sources. For example, a need to understand 'what works' in a policy context, a need to review assumptions in a field of research or an effort to interpret the knowledge base in order to identify gaps in knowledge and opportunities for empirical study (Pettigrew and Roberts, 2006). In the case of the prior studies highlighted, one was driven by a policy need to understand the role networking played in innovation in order to identify evidence-informed policy interventions (Pittaway et al., 2004), the second and third were designed to inform empirical research (Thorpe et al., 2005), while the fourth was designed to develop thematic and

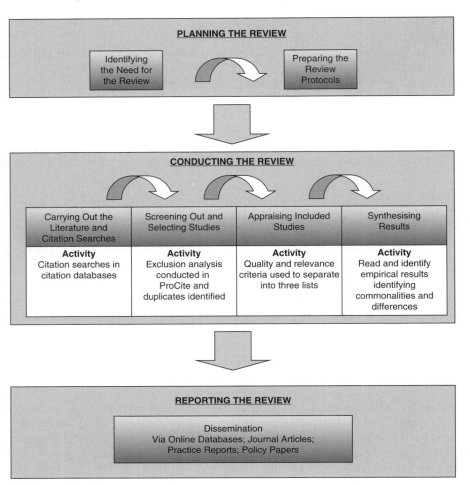

Figure 6.1   The systematic literature review process

citation data for wider use by a research community (Pittaway and Cope, 2007). When conducting this method it is important to ask is a systematic literature review needed? Although narrative reviews do have weaknesses they are less time-consuming and in many cases enough is already known about gaps in knowledge to identify a need for primary research. In the case of the examples used for this chapter there was enough uncertainty, either in policy or research, to support a review and the evidence was spread across many disciplines with little integration of the knowledge base, a situation that occurs in many areas of entrepreneurship research (Low and MacMillan, 1988). An SLR may not be appropriate when: it is not the right research tool to answer the question; where good SLRs have already been carried out, where the question is too vague or too broad; where the question is wrongly focused and not useful to the target community; and where the appropriate resources are not available, for example, citation databases (Pettigrew and Roberts, 2006).

Typically the rationale for an SLR is developed through consultation with a commissioning partner who has either a policy or commercial interest in understanding the current state of knowledge on a particular theme (e.g. effective practices in the management of venture capital). The review team forms a review panel, which is selected to include a number of interested parties for whom the review findings will be of direct interest. This may include other academics who have detailed understanding of the subject and the policy and practitioner community directly affected by the study. The panel remain in place to monitor the process, and provide expert input as to the scope and nature of the findings (Denyer and Neely, 2003). The panel can be important because they provide a narrative check on the systematic aspects of the review via their awareness of the subject (Pittaway and Cope, 2007).

Usually during this stage in the review process the review team need to conduct scoping studies and to carefully frame the question (Clarke and Oxman, 2001). This is important because the framing of the question influences the exclusion and inclusion of studies. For example, in the case of the impact of networking on innovation is the focus on business-to-business networks; supply chain networks; organisational networks or personal networks and what is meant by 'innovation' and what forms of innovation does it include (Pittaway et al., 2004)? In the case of 'entrepreneurship education' which context is the review interested in: secondary education, tertiary education or the education of entrepreneurs outside of formal education (Pittaway and Cope, 2007)? Framing the question involves handling definitional issues associated with the problem, clarifying them and openly reporting what should and should not be included in the review explicitly before the review begins (Wallace et al., 2004). An example of the framing of a review is provided in Table 6.1. One approach to framing the question that has been

Table 6.1   Framing the research question (networking and innovation)

Outline of the review
Explore linkage between networking and innovation using existing citations and research to describe the nature of the relationship.
Explain where the UK stands internationally in terms of business-to-business networking and its contribution to innovation, with particular reference to comparisons between the UK, USA, France, Germany, Japan and Scandinavian countries.
Explore networking activity in the UK within a number of themes:
Explore informal channels of networking leading to innovation, for example: communities of practice; mentoring schemes; knowledge brokerage; and entrepreneurial networks *et cetera*.
Understand how formal institutional mechanisms aimed at promoting business to business networking activity can work, for example: mediated by professional associations; incubators; clusters *et cetera*.
Explore how networking behaviour can be successfully translated into tangible outcomes specifically related to innovation; including a focus on different forms of innovation, such as product and process innovation.
Provide examples of network failure and inertia that prevent the occurrence of innovation within networks and explore why networks fail.

used elsewhere is to frame the question as a series of hypotheses; this can be useful for developing exclusion criteria later and tends to be used where there is an opportunity for meta-analysis of large datasets (Mulrow, 1994).

Scoping studies can be carried out to enable the framing of the question. These can include looking for existing SLRs on the subject; the examination of existing narrative reviews and reference to existing collaborations (e.g. the Cochrane[2] and Campbell[3] Collaborations). One method used by the authors that has proved particularly effective is random sampling of citations using bibliographical software (e.g. Endnote or ProCite), which is designed specifically to explore the types of concepts and keywords that arise from a basic citation search (e.g. 'network' and 'innovation'). Another approach used in one of the studies was to search recognised journals in the field to gain a sample of the literature on which search strings can be based. An outline of the review is then drafted, with a specific focus on how the structure of the review reflects the research questions and interests to which the review is directed. The review is broken into phases, with members of the team identified as 'owning' each task akin to a project plan. The next stage is to develop explicit research protocols.

Stage 2: Preparing the Review Protocol

Conducting the search for relevant studies begins with establishing a protocol framework by which each stage of the review analysis and the reasoning behind it are made clear to the reader (Clarke and Oxman, 2001). The protocol in an SLR is equivalent to descriptions of process and methods in empirical studies and it provides an explicit plan of the proposed work. The first stage in developing the protocol relates back to the description of the project and the rationale for the review question (Pittaway et al, 2004). This is followed by the proposed method, the search parameters and the dissemination strategy. The protocol is a working document and is open to change throughout the duration of the review. While accepting that the protocol is a dynamic document, it is important that all changes are documented and the rationale behind the changes noted because the protocol represents the audit trail of the method employed (Pettigrew and Roberts, 2006). In establishing a clear protocol many of the weaknesses in previous review methods can be avoided (Bruyat and Julian, 2000). For example, the protocol provides a precise definition of the purpose of the review; is explicit about what is to be included and excluded; and clearly defines the key concepts within the review.

The protocol often covers:

(i)   An explanation of the process and methods that will be applied, including a description of and rationale for the review question.
(ii)   Types of data to be searched, such as journal articles or practitioner reports; forms of data, such as text; images; sound, and the timeframe the data covers.
(iii)   Sources of data. Typically these will be online citation indexes, such as ABI Proquest and Web of Science, but can also include web pages, library catalogues, and archives.[4]
(iv)   The identification of keywords and search strings – search strings using Boolean operators for use within online databases are built up from these keywords (see Table 6.2).

Table 6.2   An example of search strings (networking and innovation)

Innovat*AND network*	Innovat*AND network*AND institutional (w) theory OR actor (w) network OR social (w) network	Diffusion AND knowledge AND network*
Innovat*AND network* AND UK	Innovat* AND network* AND incubators OR clusters	Innovat*AND mentors OR knowledge (w) brokers OR communities (w) practice
Innovat* AND network* AND learn* OR collaborat* OR trust OR absorptive (w) capacity	Innovat* AND network* AND ties OR dynamic* OR isomorphism OR knowledge (w) spill*	Innovat* AND collaborat* OR partner*
Network* AND innovat* AND fail*	Network* AND product (w) development OR invent* OR process (w) change	Network* AND innovat* OR effect* OR collapse OR dysfunction OR disintegrate
Other key words for search strings based on 2400 articles in SCI:	*Complexity; embeddedness; entrepreneur*; knowledge; policy; research (w) development; social (w) capital*	*Relation*; co-operation; agglomeration; alliance*; proximity; intermediary; interaction*

(v) Inclusion and exclusion criteria are included in the protocol and are designed to articulate the reasoning behind the types and form of data being considered.

(vi) In some protocols there are rules for refining searches. Where a search string retrieves more than an allotted number of 'finds', which is usually defined by scale and manageability, decisions are taken as to how to refine the search.

(vii) Relevance assessment or quality criteria which are linked to concerns outlined in the review scope. These criteria (see example in Table 6.3) make clear the judgements of those conducting the review subject when they come to analyse studies in detail.

(viii) An outline of descriptive and thematic analysis is given; this is similar to defining and clarifying the method before conducting empirical research.

(ix) Finally, the timescales associated with different aspects of the study are highlighted within the review protocol.

Once the review protocol is drafted it is typically assessed by the review panel and disseminated more widely to gather peer comment before the SLR is carried out. It is not uncommon for the review team to revisit the protocol during different stages of the work and often it is recommended that evaluation sessions with the review panel be embedded into the timescales of the project (Pettigrew and Roberts, 2006).

Stage 3: Conducting the Review

By this point in the process a number of questions will have been asked and answered and these questions should culminate in a clearly defined question for the review, an established review panel or steering group and a review protocol written and peer

Table 6.3   An example of relevance criteria (knowledge in SMEs)

Relevance assessment criteria

Element	Level				
	0- Absence	1- Low	2 – Medium	3 – High	Not applicable
1. Theory robustness	The article does not provide enough information to assess this criterion	Weak development of theoretical insights and limited awareness of prevailing literature	Basic development of theory & use of concepts garnered from existing literature	Good use of theory, including the novel & provocative development of concepts	This element is not relevant to the study
2. Implication for practice	The article does not provide enough information to assess this criterion	Hard to use the concepts and ideas in pragmatic problem solving	The study's findings and observations have potential utility for businesses and policy makers	The utility for practitioners is clear	This element is not relevant to the study
3. Methodology. Data supporting arguments	The article does not provide enough information to assess this criterion	Data incomplete and not related to theory coupled to weak research design	Data broadly related to the arguments, and conveyed through a clear research design	Data strongly supports arguments. Robust research design	This element is not relevant to the study
4. Relevance of three areas: – findings; – theories; – methods	The article does not provide enough information to assess this criterion	Only tangentially relevant; provocative but linked to 'line of flight'	Broadly relevant – perhaps in one of the areas, or applied in different disciplinary field	High level of relevance across findings, methods and theoretical constructs/ concepts	This element is not relevant to the study

assessed. All aspects to this point have been focused on the explicit development of the method for the review. In this stage the 'field work' aspect of the SLR process begins. The conduct of the review should be comprehensive to be classed as 'systematic' (Tranfield et al., 2003); if undertaken correctly the methods applied should provide an efficient and high quality approach for identifying and evaluating literature (Mulrow, 1994).

Table 6.4   An example of citation search records (knowledge in SMEs)

Database: Web of science

Search string	Scope	Date of search	Date range	No of entries	Number of relevant	TOTAL relevant
learn* AND know* AND firm* AND grow*	Title, abstract keyword – rj	05-04-2004	1981-March 04	100	41	**41**
(know* OR learn*) AND (communit* AND practi*)	Title only – rj	05-04-2004	1981-March 04	97	11	**52**
learn* AND know* AND innovat*	Title only -rj	05-04-2004	1981-March 04	17	9	**61**

Carrying out literature and citation searches

The first stage involves searching the wider literature using the methods identified in the protocol and the search strategy should be recorded in detail so that it is possible to replicate the search (Tranfield, Denyer and Smart, 2003). Typically a good SLR involves searches of multiple citation databases and will draw on sources other than journal articles, such as book chapters, conference proceedings and policy reports. The output from these searches should be both a comprehensive record of the searches themselves and a full listing of citations on which the review will be based, which is usually managed in bibliographical software. For example Table 6.4 shows a record of searches in one citation database (Web of Science) listing the search string used, the number of studies retrieved, with those considered potentially relevant when applying the inclusion and exclusion criteria. Table 6.4, however, only records outputs from three search strings in one database in the knowledge in SMEs study. There were many search strings used and three citation databases searched: ABI ProQuest (1715 documents, 597 relevant); Web of Science (1898 documents, 544 relevant); Science Direct (1437 documents, 603 relevant). The end result of the initial search is usually a comprehensive citation list in a bibliographical reference manager, which provides a map of the subject. In the studies used as examples in this paper the initial output varied from 500 to 2000 citations.

Screening out and selecting studies

Even during the initial searches the inclusion and exclusion criteria must be applied to select citations for download[5] to a bibliographical database. Even when these criteria have been applied thoroughly it is not unusual to have a large citation list. At this stage it is then necessary to screen studies in more depth to assess whether they truly meet the criteria for inclusion. In each of the SLR examples used in this chapter the titles, keywords and abstracts of the citations were then downloaded into ProCite. Downloading citations enables the researchers to identify and eliminate any duplicates[6] and conduct further filtering using the searches, and more detailed reading of abstracts. For example, in the knowledge in SMEs study there were 1744 citations at this stage, 373 duplicates were found, 12 anonymous authors were excluded, 14 book reviews were excluded, and 396 citations were excluded, using the exclusion criteria, leaving 941 citations. That number of studies is still too many to allow full application of the relevance criteria, so further filtration was undertaken using keyword analysis and the application of exclusion criteria to abstracts, which left 462 studies.

Final screening of studies is carried out by the application of the relevance criteria. In the networking and innovation study these were split into A, B and C lists, in the knowledge and SMEs study and growth study they were separated into 'less relevant'; 'partially relevant'; and, 'relevant', while in the entrepreneurship education study impact criteria from journals and other sources were used as a proxy for 'quality'. In some respects this is one of the more problematic areas of SLRs; all of the studies are deemed to have some relevance to the question at this stage but a mechanism needs to be employed to enable the review to identify the most important, narrowing the number of papers down to a manageable number. Inevitably, this element depends on the judgement of the researchers and at least in one study these decisions were undertaken by two individuals separately who cross-checked each other's conclusions of the shortlist (Leseure et al., 2004). Once an 'A' or primary list has been identified the full papers need to be assessed.

Appraising included studies
Appraising the studies for information relevant to the research question from the primary studies often involves developing a data extraction form and a table describing each study reviewed. At this point it is common for the remaining full papers to be reviewed using the narrative method but applying systematic methods. In each of the studies used as examples in this chapter a preliminary stage was introduced, which involved a form of inductive content analysis. Each citation (e.g. 209 in knowledge and SMEs and 179 in networking and innovation) was uploaded into NVivo as separate documents. The abstracts were then content analysed and thematically coded for themes around which resulting discussion of the findings could be structured. This analysis enables themes to emerge allowing the review to substantiate the prevailing locations; method; application; and theories to be expressed in terms of density and frequency (see Table 6.5).

This thematic structure has a number of advantages. First, it means each researcher can take responsibility for the analysis of a number of studies within a commonly recognised and agreed set of parameters; enabling the review to be collaborative. Secondly, the thematic structure enables the report structure of the review to be identified inductively from the literature. Thirdly, under each unit of analysis the narrative discussion can be accompanied by tabular summaries of the relevant studies. The approach explained provides one example of how SLRs adopt a formal systematic approach to extracting information (Clarke and Oxman, 2001). In general SLRs use standard templates to appraise studies and are usually assessed regarding methodological soundness. It is often argued that this process helps to eliminate bias and provides a platform for the synthesis of the knowledge base (Tranfield, Denyer and Smart, 2003; Denyer and Neely, 2004). In appraising studies the researcher must be directed to attend to all the key aspects of the study. This aspect is particularly relevant where there are many researchers examining different themes within the SLR structure. As a consequence a systematic approach also involves the use of checklists, scales and templates to formalise the process of appraisal

Table 6.5 An example of thematic coding (entrepreneurship education)

Theme	Character Count	Passages Coded	% of Coded Data
Teaching Entrepreneurship (TE)	51,218	123	35.2
Management Training (MT)	26,713	56	18.4
Enterprising University (EU)	25,502	47	17.6
Student Entrepreneurship (SE)	18,595	37	12.8
Graduate Enterprise (GE)	7,812	16	5.4
Student-Entrepreneur Interactions (SEI)	5,924	16	4.1
Employment of Graduates (EG)	3,694	9	2.5
Doctoral Education (DE)	2,923	6	2.0
Analysis of Policy (AP)	2,946	10	2.0
TOTAL	**145,327**	**320**	**100%**

Theme 1st Level	Theme 2nd Level	Character Count	% of Coded Data
MT	Management Development	11,139	8.5
MT	Business Support	6,495	4.9
MT	Mapping Demand	3,895	3.0
MT	Career Development	859	0.7
MT	Mapping Provision	478	0.4
SE	Factors Affecting Propensity	13,802	10.5
SE	Factors Impacting Capacity	2,108	1.6
SE	Extra-curricula	2,413	1.8
SE	Raising Awareness	215	0.2
SEI	Value for the Student	2,026	1.5
SEI	Value for the Firm	1,890	1.4
SEI	Coaching	181	0.1
EG	Demand for Graduates	2,036	1.6
EG	Graduate Perceptions	696	0.5
EG	Working Conditions	714	0.5
EG	Graduate Careers	158	0.1
TE	Pedagogy	28,173	21.5
TE	Mapping Provision	7,414	5.6
TE	Role of Business Schools	5,408	4.1
TE	Role in the University	4,857	3.7
TE	Impact of Courses	1,828	1.4
TE	Impact of Different Cultures	1,581	1.2
GE	Assessing Success Factors	6,005	4.6
GE	Start-up Support for Graduates	1,171	0.9
DE	Practices	2,031	1.5
DE	Supply of Faculty	142	0.1
AP	*No sub-themes*		
EU	Institutional Policy	13,079	9.9
EU	Commercialisation	5,977	4.5
EU	Outreach Activity	3,671	2.8
EU	Academic Entrepreneurship	1,196	0.9
TOTAL		**131,638**	**100%**

Note: Character count relates to coded data only and differs between first and second levels of coding.

of individual papers to ensure a commonality of treatment across the literature. This ensures that each study is examined systematically and in the same way. While critical analysis is important, it is not an end in itself in an SLR. The study must appraise the validity of studies with regard to their methodology before conclusions can be drawn about the value of the empirical data. In most SLRs it is the empirical output that is the focus. Poor regard for the validity of a method is a serious weakness in a review as work should be excluded if its conclusions are unsound. If not excluded it can have ramifications for the synthesis sought in the next stage of the process.

Synthesizing results

In the synthesis part of the process there are some differences between SLRs in different disciplines. Synthesis typically requires the use of either meta-analysis or narrative or sometimes both. Meta-analysis allows the review to answer the question by calculating a quantitative summary measure using statistical techniques (Chalmers, Hedges and Cooper, 2002) while narrative approaches depend more heavily on description, tabulation and organisation of data (Pettigrew and Roberts, 2006). Tranfield, Denyer and Smart (2003) also point to a number of alternatives to narrative and meta-analysis, including realist synthesis and meta-synthesis (Noblit and Hare, 1988; Sandelowski, Docherty and Emden, 1997). In medical studies it is often meta-analysis which is used and meta-data which is the intended output from an SLR; typically the synthesis is more likely to be narrative with a more transparent structure in SLRs conducted within social sciences. The purpose of the synthesis is to systematically describe, report, tabulate and integrate the results of the studies. Three main steps are often used: organising the description of studies into categories (Britten et al., 2002); analysing the findings within each category; and synthesising the findings across all studies (Pettigrew and Roberts, 2006). Software programmes (such as NVivo); thematic frameworks; conceptual frameworks; models; vote counting; triangulation; and graphical displays of quantitative data are used in different SLRs to achieve this synthesis. One device that is particularly useful is data tables (as presented in Table 6.6) and another used extensively in the studies outlined are thematic maps. The main role of synthesis is to provide a more robust and accessible method of drawing together insights from studies, which is explicit, transparent and to some extent repeatable.

Stage 4: Reporting the Review

The rationale for the SLR and the audience for which it is intended will, to a certain extent, dictate the style of the final output. An effective SLR should make it easier to understand the subject and should enable greater access to the empirical evidence on which it is based. For many SLRs this takes the form of a report or journal articles. With the development of electronic resources researchers may choose to produce an electronic version or database that is accessible to researchers; as was the case in the entrepreneurship education review (see Figure 6.2)[7]. Reporting often includes two elements: a descriptive report of the subject, for example covering information on the citations; the authors; the geographic coverage; the types of empirical studies; and the themes. The second part usually reports: the thematic analysis; the aggregative data or conclusions drawn from the aggregation of the research on particular themes; the identification of

Table 6.6   An example of data tables (networking and innovation)

Author	Data used in the Study	Dates	Location of Study	Summary of Empirical Findings
Ritter and Germünden	Survey of 308 mechanical and electrical engineering companies	2003	Germany	Study focuses on medium sized companies. Data were analysed using LISREL 8 using a polychoric correlation matrix. They show important statistical links between network competence and innovation success. Managing key partners in the network interface is crucial for innovation.
Perez and Sanchez	Postal survey of 58 automotive suppliers	2002	North Eastern Spain	Reasons for suppliers to engage in enterprise networks. Exchange of know-how and access to technologies (93%); Strengthening client-supplier relationships (79%); Use of comparative advantages (80%); Access to new markets (80%); benchmarking (90%). Used bi-variate correlations. Firms cooperating with customers (68%); with suppliers (50%); with Universities and Research Institutes (35%).
Romijn and Albu	Interviews with Small Electronics Firms (17 Software and 16 Electronics firms)	2002	South East of England	Used Spearman correlation coefficients to explore forms of innovation output with key partners in networks. Shows that firms interact with some partners for more radical innovation – suppliers 0.343* and Universities 0.353* while they work with other firms for more incremental forms of innovation – customers 0.437**. (**=0.01 level of significance *=0.05 level of significance).

emerging themes; the identification of key contributions; evidence of disputes in the data; and evidence of common findings. The final version of the review should also include details of the full search, a flow chart tracking the review process, and the descriptive analysis. The review will also include conclusions and recommendations drawn from the knowledge base and targeted at the relevant audience. A fulsome bibliographic detail of all the studies subject to relevance assessment is given in the form of appendices in many SLRs. To allow open access to the findings, SLRs are often put on websites,[8] as

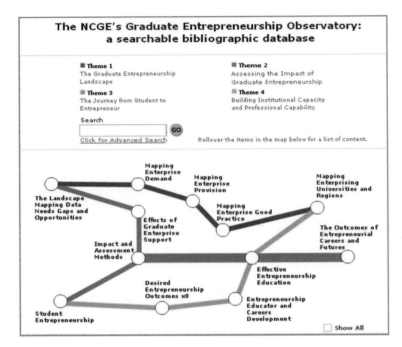

*Figure 6.2   Reporting the review: an example of online output at the National Council
for Graduate Entrepreneurship (entrepreneurship education)*

well as being printed in hard copies and distributed to interested parties. An example of
this is the entrepreneurship education SLR which has provided the foundation for the
National Council for Graduate Entrepreneurship's (NCGE, now National Council of
Entrepreneurship Education) graduate entrepreneurship observatory (see Figure 6.2).

CONCLUSIONS

The previous part of this chapter briefly outlines a rather complex and technical method.
It is the purpose of the conclusion to explain how this method could be more fully
utilised in entrepreneurship research and how it might be able to help address some of
the problems identified in the field. Readers interested in using the method are directed
to the publication by Pettigrew and Roberts (2006) for more information on practical
issues. So the question for this chapter is, how can the SLR method be of value within
entrepreneurship research and what are its limitations? Systematic literature reviews are
shown in this discussion to be highly structured and systematic methods for collecting
large citation datasets and for making sense of a field of inquiry or subject based on
detailed reviews of the empirical evidence. One of the first valuable contributions SLRs
can make to the subject of entrepreneurship is through the careful problem definition
of the review. During this stage particular themes are identified and the review to be
effective must be focused. Lack of consistency in terminology is a recognised problem

in entrepreneurship research (Gartner, 1985) and is best illustrated by the potential for multiple meanings in terms used in the example SLRs. Using the SLR method forces researchers to be both clear in their own mind and explicit with their audience as to the parameters that have guided the literature review. The alternative narrative approach can be criticised for being both overly iterative, emergent and rarely reported explicitly. Within an SLR specific themes emerge inductively from the citation data and the resultant map allows thematic difference between themes in the subject to be identified in a justifiable way.

As SLRs use citation databases and bibliographical software they are able to manage large volumes of citation data and this is something that only recent developments in technology have allowed. This ability to find and manage large volumes of citation information has two implications that are valuable to entrepreneurship research. It provides a method for finding work on common themes across a large number of publications and helps address the problems of the increased volume and fragmentation of research in entrepreneurship (Low and MacMillan, 1988; Brazeal and Herbert, 1999). It does so because it provides an approach for systematically searching multiple sources of information and fragmentation is reduced because the review is specifically designed to be comprehensive and holistic.

SLRs use a range of citation databases and because these databases typically cross many fields when an SLR is conducted in social science, it draws on evidence from multiple disciplines. To some extent SLRs are 'blind' to the disciplinary source, drawing on any citation information that is relevant to the problem definition. This blindness is a valuable commodity as it reduces the chance of partial reviews and partial pictures based on only one discipline. This is valuable in the entrepreneurship domain as it enables reviews to draw holistic pictures of particular issues across the disciplinary foundations of the subject (Gartner, 2001). In drawing together data across disciplines the SLR method can help assist the development of integrated theoretical frameworks and importantly ones based on empirical evidence from multiple disciplines; something that is needed in entrepreneurship research (Bygrave and Hofer, 1991). In addition to these benefits the method, when applied sensitively, can take into account both differences in the unit of analysis and differences in methodology between studies. While it cannot account for different philosophical assumptions it can synthesise evidence based on judgements relevant to the particular methodologies; including data that is considered sound when applying quality judgements relevant to the methodology used. Multiple units of analysis can also be accommodated via thematic structures within reviews enabling links between evidence from different aspects of the subject to be included. The ability of SLRs to synthesise evidence, while incorporating methodological diversity and diversity in the unit of analysis, could assist entrepreneurship research by enabling it to account for these differences while enabling commonalities to be identified (Chandler and Lyon, 2001; Davidsson and Wiklund, 2001).

Despite all of the above the main value of the SLR method is its ability to enable an effective method for reflection in the subject of entrepreneurship (Low, 2001). The method is an improvement on current alternatives in that it is transparent, structured and reported explicitly. This is the most valuable contribution of the method as it provides an effective means to appreciate and incorporate prior empirical research systematically into our formulation of future research. Something that becomes more meaningful as a field becomes more mature or when a field needs to inform policy or practice (Low, 2001).

The above points illustrate that we believe that this method can make an important contribution to research in entrepreneurship. Despite this SLRs are not a panacea, there are some recognised weaknesses and there are critics of the method. It is important, therefore, to outline the limitations. First, as with any method it is only useful if applied in the correct context, for the right reasons and in the right way. If the subject for a review is too broad or ill defined then an SLR may be difficult to apply. An SLR is a relatively rigorous method that is both time-consuming and technically challenging. It would not be sensible to apply it where a narrative review would suffice; where existing reviews have been carried out recently; or, where the resources are limited. Inevitably, like any method it can be applied badly. There are good and bad SLRs with the application depending on the researchers and the speed and rigour with which they conduct it.

Secondly, the SLR method is essentially a 'scientific' method and there are grounds to dispute its value based on philosophical principles. One such criticism is that it is reductionist and accepts generalisation. The reductionist nature of the SLR can be seen in the thematic categories used which reduce complexity into groups. The generalist nature of the SLR can be seen in its attempt to draw common and general conclusions across a field from the evidence when the field of study gains a great deal from its variety and even its contested nature. Such an assumption of the possibility of generality in social science is not accepted by all academics. So researchers must take into consideration their own philosophical stance on the construction of knowledge before using the SLR method.

Thirdly, the SLR method can in some situations reduce the intuitive links between literature and leaps in imagination that can be derived from the narrative method. These intuitive leaps are best demonstrated by the creation of connections between essentially disparate ideas and subjects that have no obvious connection. Intuition is still possible within the boundaries of the problem definition of an SLR but it can stymie potentially interesting 'lines of flight' in confining researchers to those studies 'thrown up' by the search-strings. Moreover, the need to focus the problem definition does restrict the method's usefulness for drawing more creative links between research in very different subjects and in this sense the SLR is an analytical method not an intuitive one.

Finally, there are several technical limitations. The first of these is the need for SLRs to be inclusive across forms of publication. At this point in time this aim is difficult to achieve because comprehensive citation databases exist for journal publications and books but these databases have only limited coverage of book chapters and other sources, such as policy literature. Usually this means that despite being systematic SLRs remain somewhat skewed to research published in journals. Only when more effective citation databases are available for other forms of publication will this weakness be truly addressed. Another technical limitation is the need for researchers to draw up relevance or quality criteria. Such criteria can rarely be objective and tend to follow the prejudices of the researchers to some extent, even where proxies are used, hence the bias of narrative approaches 'creeps back in'. So these criteria need to be viewed critically when analysing papers because they can lead to the exclusion of work that does not fit but is still valuable to the question. The particular restriction here can be the need to seek 'empirical' results that can be 'generalised' and the impact these assumptions can have on what *is valid evidence* and the *extent to which it can be generalised*. For example, such assumptions if applied tightly can lead to the exclusion of ethnographic research even when the research is carried out effectively because it is not recognised as evidence that can be generalised. The implication here is that these criteria represent the researchers' 'taken for granted' assumptions about the validity of different types of knowledge. Although this is a weakness of SLRs one must also recognise that these assumptions occur in narrative reviews. At least in an SLR they are reported somewhat more explicitly and so become the possible subject of discussion within the research community.

What the above benefits and limitations show is that the systematic literature review method is like any other method; it has uses and limitations. We have argued that the timing is right for the SLR method to be used in entrepreneurship research more extensively because it can assist the subject in reflecting on past empirical research and can enable it to make links between approaches achieving greater integration. The limitations presented, however, lead us to suggest that the SLRs are fundamentally about having *a method for conducting literature reviews which is transparent, clear, focused and systematic and which is reported openly*. We do not contend that SLRs should replace narrative reviews, they have their uses but they are more resource intensive and may not be appropriate in every context.

NOTES

1. One of the exceptions in this research was Chandler and Lyon's (2001) review of methodologies in the subject. Also, in terms of its intent, tone and insight, Shook et al.'s (2003) 'review and synthesis' of the literature on venture creation and entrepreneurial intent has systematic elements, without explicitly adopting a systematic review method.
2. The Cochrane Collaboration is a regularly updated evidence-based healthcare database. See http://www.cochrane.org/index.htm for more information.
3. The Campbell Collaboration is an international non-profit organisation that aims to help people make well-informed decisions about the effects of interventions in the social, behavioral and educational arenas. See http://www.campbellcollaboration.org/ for more information.
4. The limitations here are the availability of systematically searchable systems (citation databases) and levels of institutional subscription to these databases.
5. It is technically important that the downloads from citation databases are managed carefully and downloads include abstracts.
6. This must be done both through the duplicate function in ProCite and manually. One of the problems of this method is different formats for citations leading to duplicate citations which are not easily identified.
7. See the National Council of Graduate Entrepreneurship's Graduate Entrepreneurship Observatory http://ncge.com/communities/research/content/get/29
8. For example, the UK's Advanced Institute of Management Research site at: http://www.aimresearch.org/

REFERENCES

Ahl, H. (2006), 'Why research on women entrepreneurs need new directions', *Entrepreneurship: Theory and Practice*, **30**(5), 595–621
Brazeal, D. and Herbert, T. (1999), 'The genesis of entrepreneurship,' *Entrepreneurship: Theory and Practice*, **23**(3), 29–44.
Britten, N., Campbell, R., Pope, C., Donovan, J., Morgan, M., and Pill, R. (2002), 'Evaluating meta-ethnography: a synthesis of qualitative research: a worked example', *Journal of Health Services Research and Policy*, 7, 209–15.
Bruyat, C., and Julien, P. A. (2000), 'Defining the field of research in entrepreneurship,' *Journal of Business Venturing*, 16, 165–80.

Bull, I. and Willard, G. E. (1993), 'Towards a theory of entrepreneurship', *Journal of Business Venturing*, **8**(3), 181–2.

Bygrave, W. D. and Hofer, C. W. (1991), 'Theorizing about entrepreneurship', *Entrepreneurship: Theory and Practice*, **16**(2), 13–22.

Chalmers, I. (2003), 'Trying to do more good than harm: the role of rigorous, transparent and up-to-date evaluations', *Annals of the American Academy of Political and Social Science*, **589**(3), 22–40.

Chalmers, I., Enkin, M. and Keirse, M. (1993), 'Preparing and updating systematic reviews of randomised controlled trials of health care', *Millbank Quarterly*, 71, 411–37.

Chalmers, I., Hedges, L. and Cooper, C. (2002), 'A brief history of research synthesis', *Evaluation and the Health Professions*, 25, 12–37.

Chandler, G. N. and Lyon, D. W. (2001), 'Issues of research design and construct measurement in entrepreneurship research: The past decade', *Entrepreneurship: Theory and Practice*, 25(4), 101–13.

Chell, E. and Pittaway, L. (1998), '*The social construction of entrepreneurship*,' Paper presented at the Institute of Small Business Affairs Conference, Durham, UK, 647–64.

Clarke, M. and Oxman, A. D. (2001), '*Cochrane Reviewers' Handbook 4.1.4*, Oxford, UK: The Cochrane Library.

Davidsson, P., Low, M. B. and Wright, M. (2001), 'Editor's introduction: Low and MacMillan ten years on: achievements and future directions for entrepreneurship research', *Entrepreneurship: Theory and Practice*, **25**(4), 5–15.

Davidsson, P. and Wiklund, J. (2001), 'Levels of analysis in entrepreneurship research: current research practice and suggestions for the future', *Entrepreneurship: Theory and Practice*, **25**(4), 81–100.

Denyer, D. and Neely, A. (2004), 'Introduction to special issue: innovation and productivity performance in the UK', *International Journal of Management Reviews*, 5/6 (3&4), 131–5.

Fox, D. (2005), 'Evidence of evidence-based health policy: the politics of systematic reviews in coverage decisions', *Health Affairs*, **24**(1), 114–22.

Gaffan, E., Tsaousis, I. and Kemp-Wheeler, S. (1995), 'Researcher allegiance and meta-analysis: the case of cognitive therapy for depression,' *Journal of Consulting and Clinical Psychology*, 63, 966–80.

Gartner, W. (1985), 'A framework for describing and classifying the phenomenon of new venture creation', *Academy of Management Review*, **10**(4), 696–706.

Gartner, W. (2001), 'Is there an elephant in entrepreneurship? Blind assumptions in theory development', *Entrepreneurship: Theory and Practice*, **25**(4), 27–39.

Gartner, B. and Birley, S (2002), 'Introduction to the special issue on qualitative methods in entrepreneurship research', *Journal of Business Venturing*, **17**(5), 387–95.

Gartner, W., Davidsson, P. and Zahra, S. A. (2006), 'Are you talking to me? The nature of community in entrepreneurship scholarship', *Entrepreneurship: Theory and Practice*, **30**(3), 321.

Grant, P. and Perren, L. (2002), Small business and entrepreneurial research: meta-theories, paradigms and prejudices', *International Small Business Journal*, **20**(2), 185–211.

Hofer, C. W. and Bygrave, W. D. (1992), 'Researching entrepreneurship', *Entrepreneurship: Theory and Practice*, **16**(3), 91–100.

Hornaday, J. A. and Churchill, N. C. (1987), 'Current trends in entrepreneurial research', in N. C. Churchill, J. A. Hornaday, B. A. Kirchhoff, O. J. Krasner and K. H. Vesper (Eds), *Frontiers of Entrepreneurship Research* (pp. 186–98). Wellesley, Massachusetts: Babson College.

Jennings, P. L., Perren, L. and Carter S. (2005), 'Alternative perspectives of entrepreneurship', *Entrepreneurship: Theory and Practice*, **29**(2), 145–52.

Kuhn, T. S., (1962), 'The structure of scientific revolutions', *International Encyclopaedia of Unified Science*, vol 2, no 2, Chicago: The University of Chicago Press.

Leseure, M. J., Bauer, J., Birdi, K., Neely, A. and Denyer, D. (2004), 'Adoption of promising practices: a systematic review of the evidence', *International Journal of Management Reviews*, 5/6 (3&4), 169–90.

Low, M. B. (2001), 'The adolescence of entrepreneurship research: specification of purpose', *Entrepreneurship: Theory and Practice*, **25**(4), 17–25.

Low, M. B. and MacMillan, I. C. (1988), 'Entrepreneurship: past research and future challenges', *Journal of Management*, **14**(2), 139–61.

MacPherson, A. and Holt, R. (2007), 'Knowledge, learning and small-firm growth: A systematic review of the evidence', *Research Policy*, **36**(1).

Mulrow, C. D. (1994), 'Systematic reviews: rationale for systematic reviews', *British Medical Journal*, 309, 597–9.

Noblit, G. W. and Hare, R. D. (1988), *Meta-ethnography: Synthesizing Qualitative Studies*. London, UK: Sage Publications.

Oakley, A. (2002), 'Social science and evidence-based everything: the case of education', *Education Review*, 54, 277–86.

Petticrew, M. and Roberts, H. (2006), *Systematic Reviews in the Social Sciences: A Practical Guide*. Oxford, UK: Blackwell Publishing.

Pittaway, L. (2005), 'Philosophies in entrepreneurship: a focus on economic theories', *International Journal of Entrepreneurial Behaviour and Research*, **11**(3), 201–21.

Pittaway, L. and Cope, J., (2007), 'Entrepreneurship education – a systematic review of the evidence', *International Small Business Journal*.

Pittaway, L., Robertson, M., Munir, K., Denyer, D. and Neely, A. (2004), 'Networking and innovation: a systematic review of the evidence', *International Journal of Management Reviews*, 5/6 (3&4), 137–68.

Popper, K. R. (1963), *'Conjectures and Refutations: The Growth of Scientific Knowledge'*, London, Routledge and Kegan Paul.

Read, S., Song, M. and Smit, W. (2009), 'A meta-analytic review of effectuation and venture performance', *Journal of Business Venturing*, **24**(4), 287–309.

Rosenbusch, N., Brinckmann, J. and Bausch, A. (2011), 'Is innovation always beneficial? A meta-analysis of the relationship between innovation and performance in SMEs', *Journal of Business Venturing*, **26**(4), 441–57.

Sandelowski, M., Docherty, S. and Emden, C. (1997), 'Qualitative metasynthesis: issues and techniques', *Research in Nursing and Health*, **20**(4), 365–71.

Sarason, Y., Dean, T. and Dillard, J. (2006), 'Entrepreneurship as the nexus of individual and opportunity: A structuration view', *Journal of Business Venturing*, **21**(3), 286–305.

Sarasvathy, S. D. (2004a), 'The questions we ask and the questions we care about: reformulating some problems in entrepreneurship research', *Journal of Business Venturing*, **19**(5), 707–17.

Sarasvathy, S. D. (2004b), 'Making it happen: beyond theories of the firm to theories of firm design', *Entrepreneurship: Theory and Practice*, **28**(6), 519–31

Shane, S. and Venkataraman, S. (2000), 'The promise of entrepreneurship as a field of research', *Academy of Management Review*, **25**(1), 217–26.

Shook, C., Priem, R., McGee, J. (2003), 'Venture creation and the enterprising individual', *Journal of Management*, **29**(3), 379–99.

Smith, K. G., Gannon, M. and Sapienza H. (1989), 'Selecting strategy measures for entrepreneurial research: trade-offs and guidelines', *Entrepreneurship: Theory and Practice*, **14**(1), 39–49.

Thorpe, R., Holt, R., Macpherson, A. and Pittaway, L. (2005), 'Knowledge within small and medium sized firms: a systematic review of the evidence', *International Journal of Management Reviews*, **7**(4), 257–81.

Tranfield, D., Denyer, D. and Smart, P. (2003), 'Towards a methodology for developing evidence-informed management knowledge by means of systematic review', *British Journal of Management*, 14, 207–22.

Tranfield, D., Denyer, D., Marcos, J., Burr, M. (2004), 'Co-producing management knowledge', *Management Decision*, **42**(3/4), 375–86.

Trinder, L. and Reynolds, S. (2000), *Evidence-Based Practice: A Critical Appraisal*. Oxford, UK: Blackwell Science.

Ucbasaran, D., Westhead, P. and Wright, M. (2001), 'The focus of entrepreneurial research: contextual and process issues', *Entrepreneurship: Theory and Practice*, **25**(2), 57–80.

Wallace, A., Croucher, K., Quilgars, D. and Baldwin, S. (2004), 'Meeting the challenges: developing systematic reviewing in social policy', *Policy and Politics*, 32, 455–70.

7. The Critical Incident Technique: philosophical underpinnings, method and application to a case of small business failure
Elizabeth Chell

INTRODUCTION

The Critical Incident Technique (CIT) was first used in a scientific study over half a century ago (Flanagan, 1954). The significance of this time span is that then the assumption of a functionalist or positivist approach to social science investigations was largely unquestioned. It was the dominant paradigm in the social sciences as it was in the natural sciences (Burrell and Morgan, 1979; Pittaway, 2000). In 1998 I began to consider how CIT might be utilised from an interpretivist perspective (Chell, 1998; 2004). This means that there are two main variants of the CIT—positivist and anti-positivist. The CIT is thus a very flexible method which may be used in task analysis in specific occupations to identify those factors that lead to successful or unsuccessful performances; or, more broadly as an exploratory tool to develop a depth of understanding of the context and actions of a subject in the face of what they perceive to be critical incidents that affect outcomes of success or failure. The use and further development of the CIT method has been carried out in small business and entrepreneurship research, management, marketing and the service sector (Gremler, 2004; Chell and Pittaway, 1998). Reviews have focused on the CIT's trustworthiness as a method (Butterfield et al., 2005), its practical value, and its ability to explore issues and build theory from the respondents' perspective (Gremler, 2004).

This chapter comprises several sections: initially I shall explore the background to the CIT, including background assumptions; I consider issues relevant to the choice of CIT as a method of investigation; next I present a detailed breakdown of the method, giving practical tips for the interviewer; and finally I discuss some key analytical issues.

BACKGROUND TO CIT

Following Flanagan (1954), researchers used CIT in occupational settings, and it was here that the validity and reliability of the method was initially established (Andersson and Nilsson, 1964; Ronan and Latham, 1974). Butterfield et al. (2005) have since carried out further work and discussed and elaborated on the method's reliability in some detail. Much of the research has focused on managerial and employee performance and the identification of intangible factors that might affect it (McClelland, 1976; 1987; Spencer, 1983). The use of CIT within an interpretivist or social constructionist paradigm emerged in the early 1990s (Chell et al., 1991; Chell and Adam, 1994a; 1994b; Chell and Pittaway, 1998; Pittaway and Chell, 1999; Wheelock and Chell, 1996). Additionally it has been used to identify the context of emotionally laden critical events (Chell and Baines, 1998), from which experiential learning takes place (Cope and Watts, 2000). A potential problem raised by Butterfield et al. (2005) is that of researchers attempting to reinvent the CIT by a slight modification of its name; the work of Cope and Watts is one such example where they use the term 'critical episodes' rather than 'incidents'. Proliferation of terminology is, they argue, unhelpful to the kind of scientific endeavour that Flanagan was about. The later work of Cope (2005a; 2005b) shows that the main objective is to theorise about entrepreneurial learning and that the critical event or experience is a stimulus to higher level learning and reflection on, in particular, emotionally charged, critical, negative events. This is one example of how the notion of the critical affects entrepreneurial behaviour. This stream of research was undoubtedly given impetus by the seminal work of John Flanagan.

Flanagan's Development of the CIT

Flanagan defined the CIT as:

> [A] set of procedures for collecting direct observations of human behaviour in such a way as to facilitate their potential usefulness in solving practical problems and developing broad psychological principles. . .By an incident is meant any specifiable human activity that is sufficiently complete in itself to permit inferences and predictions to be made about the person performing the act. To be critical the incident must occur in a situation where the purpose or intent of the act seems fairly clear to the observer and where its consequences are sufficiently definite to leave little doubt concerning its effects (Flanagan, 1954: 327).

The studies reviewed by Flanagan (1954) assumed that reality was tangible, the occupational group was identifiable and the situations could be defined and classified. Observations were deemed to be factually correct if a number of independent expert observers made the same judgement. Thus fundamental to the method is the ability to classify the critical incidents. Ideally it is desirable to observe a comprehensive set of incidents from which a classification system is derived. This presents the analyst with objective criteria for application to a fresh study. As the classification has been arrived at inductively it can never be assumed to be fully comprehensive. The outcome of Flanagan's research on pilots' capability to fly combat missions was a set of descriptive categories—'critical requirements'—of effective combat leadership. By the use of expert observers whose independent judgements were compared, the essentially subjective nature of this process was converted into an objective set of criteria, which could be rigorously applied to further groups.

The 'behavioural event interview' (BEI) developed by David McClelland and colleagues was derived from the Flanagan critical incident method. But, a crucial difference was the move from observation of behaviour to verbal recall in interview. The initial study concerned the performance of diplomats. It was already known that verbal fluency and cultural knowledge did not predict their performance and so the objective was to develop a means whereby the less tangible aspects of behaviour, specifically 'soft' skills and competencies, could be identified. The interviewees were asked to identify the most critical incidents they had encountered in their job and to describe them in considerable detail. The interview transcripts were content-analysed to identify behaviours and characteristics that distinguished superior from average job performance. Cross-validation tests were also used. The outcome of this work was the development of a Job Competence Assessment procedure to identify 'soft skills' which predict performance in more than 50 professions (Spencer, 1983).

Phenomenological Approaches to the Development of the CIT

In the 1990s, the CIT was developed within a qualitative, social constructionist (Chell et al., 1991) or grounded theory (Curran et al., 1993) framework. For example, Chell et al. (1991) sought to distinguish behavioural differences between business owners of small- to medium-sized enterprises (SMEs) across a range of business sectors. The specified activity was business development. The interviewee identified critical incidents that affected development. Thus the *outcome* was the nature of business development (assessed in terms of growth indicators) whilst the inputs were behaviours carried out by the owner-manager in relation to the incidents they identified. The research focused on the perspective of the respondent. Research questions included: what incidents in the opinion of the business owner shaped behavioural and business outcomes; and how did they handle those incidents? Content analysis attempted to answer the further question whether the behaviours by which they handled the events could be construed as evidence of entrepreneurship?

A study that focused upon inter-regional comparisons in locations in the north-east and south-east of England was carried out, the aims and objectives being to examine the interaction between business and household and the implications for each (Wheelock and Chell, 1996). Micro-business owners could select 'domestic' incidents if they wished in order to explain business development activity or inactivity. Some of this work is reported in Chell and Baines (1998). This study adopted an interpretive approach and the CIT method was based on Chell's alternative view of CIT. This warranted a new definition:

> The critical interview technique is a qualitative interview procedure, which facilitates the investigation of significant occurrences (events, incidents, processes or issues), identified by the respondent, the way they are managed, and the outcomes in terms of perceived effects. The objective is to gain an understanding of the incident from the perspective of the individual taking into account cognitive, affective and behavioural elements (Chell, 1998; 2004).

Pittaway's study of the social construction of entrepreneurial behaviour (Pittaway, 2000) applied the CIT to a study of restaurateurs and café owners in Newcastle (UK). The data were analysed and profiles of entrepreneurial behaviours from two 'benchmark' cases were used for purposes of interpretation of the sample (Chell and Pittaway, 1998; Pittaway and Chell, 1999). The method yielded a rich dataset.

Later work includes that of Cope and Watts (2000) who explore the learning process of entrepreneurs in relation to the parallel processes of personal and business development. They discuss the impact of critical incidents on the developmental history of the business. They show that the entrepreneurs often face prolonged and traumatic critical periods or episodes that are emotionally laden. Further, they demonstrate that the incidents result in higher levels of learning, and conclude that entrepreneurs need support to interpret critical incidents as learning experiences. Cope (2005a; 2005b) also develops the view of critical incident methodology as a phenomenological form of inquiry that is consistent with my own work in this regard (Chell, 1998; 2004). However, while I have emphasised the spatial and contextual nature of the method, Cope emphasises its temporal nature. In other words, there is a temporal aspect to understanding (and learning about and from) a critical incident whose impact may be experienced in a transformative way over an indeterminate period. During this period, critical events may be experienced which are likely to constitute emotionally charged events that result in higher levels of learning (see Chell, 1998; 2004 and ensuing pages for an account of a case that fits these criteria).

The CIT Applied in the Service Sector

Gremler (2004) provides a review of the CIT in service research, identifying a number of key advantages: it is explorative and theory-building; it is a flexible method that enables the researcher to study phenomena where it is not possible to specify all variables a priori; through this method it is possible to generate an accurate record of events; to obtain a rich dataset of first-hand experience from the respondent's perspective, which can lead to sound management applications; and in the service sector the CIT may be used to assess customer perceptions thus yielding practical applications. His review highlights research in the service sector which showed how the CIT produces nuanced datasets, for example, Keaveney (1995) investigated why customers switch providers and showed that switching was not simply a matter of feeling dissatisfied, rather, customers could be satisfied but still switch for reasons of convenience, competition, involuntary switching and/or pricing.

Gremler's (2004) review of 141 studies raises a number of issues. It revealed that in nearly 95 per cent of cases of the service contexts the offering was found to be intangible; that there were issues of sampling, in particular of number of respondents and usable critical incidents; reliability, especially interjudge reliability; objectivity, systematisation assessed through specifity, overall purpose and triangulation. Among Gremler's recommendations is the need to focus more on context, to collect data from different perspectives, i.e. respondents, collect physical evidence where appropriate, and to seek to understand just how critical the critical incident is to the business. Furthermore, he suggests that an interpretive approach could be used more widely as an explorative tool to develop theory.

Butterfield et al. (2005) support the view that the CIT is flexible and may be used within either a positivist or post-modern paradigm. However, Butterfield et al.'s main concern was to examine the credibility and trustworthiness of the method given its shift away from Flanagan's direct observation techniques to self-report, from task analysis to exploration of psychological feelings, affect and beliefs, from the concrete to the intangible. They put forward nine credibility checks which may be used where the critical incident data primarily concerns psychological constructs. This appears to reaffirm the place of CIT within a positivism framework, consistent with Flanagan's original tenets for the method. However, they also suggest that this extension to the method is consistent with an exploratory approach where theory-building is the objective (see Table 7.1 below).

Table 7.1   Flanagan's functionalist tenets in respect of the Critical Incident Technique

1. Although a qualitative method it assumes *the tenets of the scientific method*
2. Hence, the researcher's job was to *observe* behaviour of the subject and classify it objectively
3. The *reality and context* in which the subject performs their task is *concrete*
4. The *objective* is to discern effective and ineffective work-related behaviours in specified contexts
5. The focus on context is *narrow and well-defined*
6. The data is analysed independently by at least two researchers who cross-check to obtain a measure of *reliability*
7. The research measures *typical* performance and *proficiency* in performance
8. The researcher seeks *measured outcomes* of effective performance i.e. ability to do the job at hand
9. Outcomes may include: job redesign, revised operating procedures, equipment design
10. And for behaviours, outcomes include changes to motivation, leadership and attitudes.

Summary

In almost 60 years the CIT has been developed from a fundamentally psychological tool used in occupational settings to identify criteria of success using direct observation to a subject-centred, qualitative, interview method of a sociological complexion where the subject seeks to recall critical incidents that affect future outcomes, and where both incidents and outcomes were adjudged to be critical. Other developments include those of Cope (2005a; 2005b) who conceives of the process as one of a number of incidents occurring over a span of time which he refers to as an episode, the impact of which is primarily that of learning. Further work by Gremler (2004) focuses on the method, its merits in exploring phenomena, in particular in the service sector and building theory. Whereas Butterfield and his colleagues (2005) working in counselling psychology are particularly concerned with the credibility and trustworthiness of the method. In reviewing the developments in CIT they note the increased use of self-report rather than direct observation. Their work brings us back to Flanagan's original tenets though they appear to want to retain the interpretative approach.

While such reviews are helpful in crystallising research carried out using the CIT, when researchers initially consider its adoption they should reflect on their own assumptions and the paradigm within which they believe they are working. To some degree Hopkinson and Hogarth-Scott (2001) by exploring how we as researchers deal with stories do just this. They believe that the CIT deals with stories as factual report, whereas our work deals with the CIT as a means of generating a narrative from an interpretivist or social constructionist perspective. In the next section we will explore the assumptions underlying positivist, interpretivist—hermeneutics and social constructionist— paradigms that the researcher should consider in pursuing their investigative work using an appropriate variant of the CIT.

ASSUMPTIONS MADE

Scientific Method

Research is intended to discover new knowledge and understanding of phenomena whether they are physical or social. The physical sciences use the scientific method and through experimentation, inductive reasoning and sustained testing what is known with a probability of its likely occurrence is arrived at. The physical world is assumed by the scientist to be 'out there', that is external to the human mind and observable in a detached and unbiased way. The scientist thus records clinically his or her observations and experiments by changing the conditions under which the phenomenon is observed; fresh observations are then recorded. To the scientist phenomena are real, i.e. tangible, not theoretical constructs, but an entity: this is their ontological status. Even in particle physics and astronomy sophisticated experiments have been constructed to demonstrate the existence (even though they are not directly observable by the human eye) of phenomena. Hence through systematic investigation scientists reveal knowledge and demonstrate what the case is. Truth is probable not absolute and knowledge is external, public and checkable.

Functionalism

In the social sciences Functionalism or Positivism makes the assumptions of the scientist. It assumes the same ontology that social objects are tangible and that they enjoy an external existence (outside the mind of the observer). Knowledge can be revealed through a systematic approach. Flanagan (1954) made just such assumptions and adopted a scientific approach when he was tasked with discovering the reasons for pilot failure during training. The behaviours associated with flying were specifiable; the criteria of what constitutes effective or ineffective performance could be identified, and observers could be given explicit criteria for judging or evaluating observed behaviours as reaching the requisite standard. Observations were deemed to be factual and objective if a number of independent observers made the same judgement.

An example of one study was of combat leadership. Veterans were asked to make observations of specific (extreme[1]) incidents of effective or ineffective behaviour in accomplishing a mission. This was a large-scale study and resulted in several thousand incidents describing officers' actions. The outcome of the research was a set of descriptive categories—'critical requirements'—of effective combat leadership. By the use of expert observers whose independent judgements were compared, the essential subjective nature of this process was converted into an objective set of criteria that could be rigorously applied to further groups.

Just as the dominance of the functionalist paradigm was exposed and questioned by sociologists (ibid.), so too has it been questioned by other social researchers (Harré, R, 1979; 1986; Shotter, 1993). Functionalism as with science seeks consensus, whereas discourse often reveals dissension (Deetz, 1996) about ambiguous or ephemeral phenomena. This anti-positivist stance takes on many forms from extreme phenomenology, including solipsism, social constructionism and hermeneutics.

Interpretivist Approaches

These alternative interpretivist approaches make totally different assumptions about the nature of reality, how we come to know and understand ourselves and the world, and what methodology is appropriate. Such theoretical perspectives point to the intangible nature of social phenomena, for example of percepts, ideas and mental states, the use of language, and the social construction of relationships. Knowledge and truth are relative and contextually grounded, and formulated from the integration of various perspectives and consequent interpretations. Many social constructionists assume that such phenomena are unique to individuals and based on subjective experience. As such insights may be gleaned from sensitive analysis of individual cases but the scientific outcomes of generalisation are not possible. However, other interpretivists combine phenomenological assumptions with realist methodologies.

Dilthey (as explained in Burrell and Morgan, 1979: 236 *et seq*) was concerned with how conscious thought is externalised as cultural artefacts which take on an objective character. He was concerned with their meaning and significance and importantly that words in a sentence could only be understood in terms of their total context. Phenomenological sociology and hermeneutics are more concerned with the role of language as a medium of practical social activity; the importance of meaning in context. Following Wittgenstein (1978) communication is that of indexing thoughts and actions (nominalism) and reflexivity in which we each carry out meta-analyses as practical sociologists seeking meaning and understanding of everyday actions. Wittgenstein went further in arguing that what represents reality depends on social rules underlying what he termed 'forms of life'.

Hence, it is assumed that while the social phenomena are internal to the conscious mind, and as such ephemeral, subjective and unique to the individual, the fact that they are contextually embedded, articulated through language and their behavioural consequences observable, they can be externalised and objectified such that generalisation *to theory* can be made (Yin, 1984).

Table 7.2 summarises the assumptions made by three approaches: positivism, and anti-positivism, viz. interpretivism, instances of which are hermeneutics and social constructionism. It is clear that the assumptions have implications for the investigator, how they conduct the research, and the relationship between researcher and subject. Outcomes are also viewed differently; in particular the nature of truth, the ability to establish knowledge and whether it is possible to generalise the results to a similar or like class.

THE CHOICE OF CIT

As a researcher a fundamental issue is which method to select in order to research an issue, event or subject appropriately. Hence the question whether CIT would be an appropriate choice is apposite. CIT is a qualitative method but there are other methods which some would argue are simpler to administer, so what criteria should be considered in one's decision?

CIT enables the researcher to probe linkages between an event or situation, an action, behaviour or decision, its consequences and the incumbent's attitude, feelings and beliefs

Table 7.2   Contrasting assumptions of three research approaches

Dimension	Positivism	Interpretivism: hermeneutics	Interpretivism: social constructionism
Ontology	Concrete, tangible	Ambiguous; reality is the product of individual consciousness	Intangible, ephemeral. Subjective experience unique; extreme form veers toward solipsism
Objective-subjective	The unit of analysis is treated as object; the assumption is that criteria may be applied that have universal agreement. Values neutrality	Has at its heart the subjective interpretation of the world from the perspective of the subject. However cultural artefacts, institutions & religions etc are objectified in the minds of the perceivers	Subjective interpretation of the world from the perspective of the subject
Status of researcher	Elite/expert; detached observer; privileged; superior representation of reality	Do not see themselves as scientific investigators but as skilled inquirers whose primary aim is to understand meaning and significance of the subject's situation	A skilled inquirer whose primary aim is to glean a depth of empathic understanding of the subject and gain insights into the particular case
Status of respondent	Source of data the process of which is controlled to eliminate bias, ambiguity & misunderstanding. Actions are determined	Respondents have free will and create their own situation; their actions are not determined, but emerge through their chosen course of action and are limited by structural elements of the context	Respondents are unique, with free will; create their own world and determine their own fate
Reliability of data	Data should be subject to tests of consistency as reliability & trustworthiness of data is paramount	Feeding back results of textual analysis to the subject, seeking to probe any inconsistencies and obtaining narratives from more than one subject are ways of establishing credibility of the data	Gaining a depth of understanding may be enhanced through immersion; observing and talking to other subjects; generating questions through reflexivity and feedback

Table 7.2   (continued)

Dimension	Positivism	Interpretivism: hermeneutics	Interpretivism: social constructionism
Truth	Truth is the outcome of analytical testing and scrutiny carried out in an objective and detached fashion	Truth emerges from the consistency and coherence with which a narrative hangs together; is meaningful in relation to a particular form of life. As such interpretation emerges from the context	Truth emerges from the consistency and coherence with which a narrative hangs together and interpretation from the context
Generalisability	Generalisation of results to a class is the object; as is the ability to test theory	May be able to generalise to theory given sufficient cases and detailed content analysis	Impossibility of generalising from one case. The insights may raise questions about other ways of viewing the world and dealing with it
Essentialism	Categorisation & data reduction tends toward essentialism, i.e. that necessary ingredient that is a differentiator	Values the subjects' interpretation of their world, which defies reduction to general higher order statements	The opposite; data are tentative and emergent
Type of knowledge	Objective, general, robust theory-led, theory confirming, rational, scientific	Subjective, particular, local; exploratory, theory building	An emergent discourse that tends towards dissension (with the status quo) and critical reflection on what subject views as is or is not part of their world

that propelled him or her to take such actions in order to manage (or not) the situation or event.

Alternative Methods to CIT

Would the unstructured or semi-structured interview or participant observation be just as, or more, effective? In some circumstances undoubtedly they may well be. Practical considerations may come into play, but the key issue that the researcher should bear in mind is the aims and objectives that they are trying to achieve. Should they not have the resources to fulfil their aims and objectives, should they consider modifying their aims and selecting the appropriate method based on the revisions? Let us, therefore, assume that resources are not an issue; what therefore are the pros and cons to be considered?

An unstructured approach may well be appropriate in qualitative research where the researcher needs to scope the problem as a preliminary to developing a more tightly designed, data-collection tool that collects relevant data to the research problematic and takes account of a wide range of issues. The CIT may also be used in this way where subjects have relevant experience to share. Flanagan's research is a case in point. Other examples may be drawn from the hospitality industry (Pittaway and Chell, 1999).

The use of a semi-structured interview schedule implies that the researcher already has scoped the research problematic and has a firm idea of the research questions to be addressed. Some open-ended questions are used selectively to explore broader issues that may help provide reasons or explanation for particular views. Where the researcher is not so confident of the nature, scope and criticality of any broader issues, the CIT would be an appropriate choice.

Both the unstructured interview and participant observation have in common with the interpretivist version of CIT the ability to get closer to the subject (Bryman, 1989). This may be important in qualitative research that aims to understand the subject's perspective, which is fundamental to research within a phenomenological paradigm. Participant observation[2], however, has a number of disadvantages. Covert participant observation raises ethical issues (for example of deception), it focuses upon the 'here and now' and it presents difficulties in recording observations immediately thus relying on the researcher's recall or ability to make surreptitious notes.

Some Advantages of CIT

CIT is overt in that the subject is aware of being interviewed and what issues are being discussed. The interviewee will have given consent to the interview and can refuse to answer a question should s/he object to it. This clearly is not the case where the participant observer is undercover. In CIT the interviewer should give assurances of confidentiality and anonymity before commencing the CIT and observe ethical guidelines. This has the added benefit usually of relaxing the interviewee who is then able to recount their story.

A disadvantage is that CIT accounts are retrospective; the fact that the incidents are 'critical' means that subjects usually have good recall. A skilled interviewer should be able to probe for nuances, consistency of statements and develop a relationship of trust such that an honest account (as perceived by the subject) is presented. Unlike the unstructured interview there is a focus, which enables the researcher to probe aptly and the interviewee to 'hook' their accounts. As is the case with participant observation, CIT is context-rich, but unlike participant observation the context is developed entirely from the subject's perspective. Some things can be checked. It is therefore possible to use other documentary evidence as a means of triangulation to check factual statements, and if possible to interview at least one other person in order to get multiple perspectives on the issues in question. Also where the CIT is used across multiple sites the researcher can look for evidence of commonalities in themes, that is, 'incidents' that suggest a generally perceived problem.

A further advantage of CIT is that it enables the researcher to relate context, tactic or strategy for handling the situation, and outcomes, including unforeseen consequences. In an organisational context, a variety of ways of dealing with a critical incident, event, situation or problem, may suggest the absence of training; a consistent way of dealing with a problem by a number of employees in the same organisation with a poor outcome may suggest a faulty organisational policy. Hence the CIT enables the researcher to build a picture of tactics adopted to handle difficult or problematic situations and enables them to glean first-hand evidence of the relationship between context and outcome.

In the next section, I explain how the CIT may be applied where the subject matter is intangible and the research paradigm phenomenological.

THE ADOPTION OF CIT METHOD TO THE INTANGIBLE SUBJECT

As explained above, interpretivism makes totally different assumptions about the nature of reality, how we come to know and understand ourselves and the world, and what methodology is appropriate. Such theoretical perspectives point to the intangible nature of social phenomena, for example of percepts, ideas and mental states, the use of language, and the social construction of relationships. Knowledge and truth are relative and contextually grounded, and formulated from the integration of various perspectives and consequent interpretations. Many social constructionists assume that such phenomena are unique to individuals and based on subjective experience (see Table 7.2 above). As such insights may be gleaned from sensitive analysis of individual cases but the scientific outcomes of generalisation are not possible. Hermeneutists combine phenomenological assumptions with realist methodologies in that they assume the objectification of institutional and cultural artefacts. Institutions operate through socially understood rules which create forms of life and socially acceptable or unacceptable behaviours. This creates an objectified social order. Power imbalances in society also act to subjugate different social groups and alternate meanings to their experience. CIT interviews aim to elucidate the form of life of particular social groups, the rules and meaning that are revealed through their engagement in life and those contextually situated incidents or events that expose behaviour and its consequences.

For example, the nature of opportunity in entrepreneurship is much researched; indeed there are two broad schools of thought (Chell, forthcoming). On the one hand, Shane (2000) argues that opportunities are objective phenomena that exist 'out there', whereas others argue the opportunity is a creation of the human mind, where the perceiver (in this case the entrepreneur) perceives a situation about which s/he has certain knowledge, attitude and beliefs; and toward which s/he is differentially motivated, based on his/her judgement whether what is perceived *is* indeed an opportunity. Hermeneutics would argue that opportunity qua idea is a product of human consciousness whereas the context in which that idea is embedded may be objectified in the mind of the entrepreneur who perceives institutional hurdles as obstacles to be overcome and, say, financial backers as institutional supporters to be embraced. Such assumptions give a subtlety to the method by which interviewers are handled and critical incidents exposed.

I will tease out the aspects of such entrepreneurial phenomena and how they might be researched using the CIT.

DETAILED BREAKDOWN OF THE CIT METHOD

Elements of what might be termed a complex social issue, event, or situation may be thought to be tangible but it is the perceptual and judgemental basis of entrepreneurial decision-making about the phenomenon that places the object of the study in the non-positivist camp. For example, two people might be taken to view a derelict piece of land; one sees its potential for development, the other, at best, an area to be grassed over by the council or hidden from view. In other words people respond differently to different situations; even when presented with an identical view they construe it differently.

Research Design

Adoption of the CIT within the phenomenological paradigm particularly lends itself to a detailed case study method, where one or more people may be interviewed in depth using CIT. The aim is to understand the mental processes—the thoughts, feelings and machinations—of the person when faced with a particular incident or set of incidents. The procedure is akin to that of an unstructured interview but focused on capturing the thought processes, the frame of reference and the feelings evoked about the incident, all of which have meaning for the respondent. In the CIT the interviewee is required to identify and describe in detail the incident(s) which they have named, how they responded, and bring into play information that has a bearing on how they chose to handle the incidents, what decisions they made at the time and what the consequences of those decisions were for them, relevant others (possibly including family) and the business.

Unlike Flanagan, I define the CIT as:

> . . . a qualitative interview procedure which facilitates the investigation of significant occurrences (events, incidents, processes or issues), identified by the respondent, the way they are managed, and the outcomes in terms of perceived effects. The objective is to gain an understanding of the incident from the perspective of the individual, taking into account cognitive, affective and behavioural elements (Chell, 2004: 48).

This is best illuminated by the use of a case study. Below I explain the nature of the case study and the preparatory steps to utilising the CIT. I then go on to explain further the interview procedure, aspects of the process and key aspects that the interviewer should bear in mind as they conduct the CIT interview. This is followed by discussion of various analytical issues and then illustrated by the presentation of a brief case study. Beyond this I raise ethical issues as being an important consideration when embarking on this type of research. And finally, as regards analysis the difficult issue of generalisation. I conclude the chapter with some general remarks about the ability of the CIT to enable the researcher to focus on different forms of life, to create thick descriptions of what happens, and to thereby build and ground theory. And lastly I discuss the issue of reliability of this particular qualitative research method.

The Case Study Technique

Phenomenologists vary considerably (Burrell and Morgan, 1979; Deetz, 1996; Gergen, 1999; see also Chell, 2008: 175–209). However what appears to unite them is the assumed 'objectivity' of the scientific approach to understanding social phenomena; so-called 'facts' cannot be rinsed clean of social interpretation, reflection and judgement. The investigator is not the detached social scientific observer, but, as it were, a collaborator in the co-production of knowledge in the research process. Hence whether the research design combines a single or multiple cases, the aforementioned principle applies.

The case study is an approach or strategy to carrying out research and is preferred when answers to questions of 'how' and 'when' are sought, when the investigator has little control over events and when the focus is on contemporary phenomena. Case studies comprise detailed investigations, often with data collected over a period of time (in contrast to the one-off 'snapshot' survey) with a view to providing an analysis of the context and processes under study. The phenomenon is not isolated from the context (as in, for instance, laboratory research) but is of interest precisely because of its relation to the context (Hartley, 1994). Multiple data sources may be used in case study research, but in this chapter we will focus solely on the CIT as a means of data gathering.

The CIT Method

Preparatory design work

This is fundamental to any research and comprises the careful formulation of the research aims and objectives; in other words the investigator reflecting on what s/he is trying to achieve by means of the research, the case study and use of the CIT. Without using significant terms that may influence the subject, the investigator should formulate the aims in terms that are meaningful but do not contain leading terms. For example, the aim may be to (a) examine the processes by which the entrepreneur identifies and develops ideas to aid business growth; (b) discuss any events or issues that the respondent identifies which aid or impede said processes. Putting the research problematic in such words avoids the use of terms like 'opportunity', 'prior experience', 'knowledge', 'feelings', 'attitude' and so forth. Respondents then use their own words and the skilled interviewer will probe to help develop a depth of understanding of the processes and the subject's way of going about developing the business.

Introducing CIT in the field

Introducing CIT occurs once the researcher has identified a suitable case, written and/ or telephoned in order to gain access to a face-to-face meeting. This initial meeting is used to gain further access, explain succinctly the nature of the research aims, the value of the critical incident interview, the purposes and possible benefits of the research to the incumbent, especially where there may be practical and possibly policy implications. It is expedient to raise issues of confidentiality at this juncture and to give assurances as necessary. This type of interview often gives the respondent 'time out' to reflect upon a number of key issues and events. For this reason it is often viewed by the respondent as more like a conversation and enjoyed. Thus establishing a rapport of trust and confidence is important. Conducting the interview where the respondent is uncomfortable or tense can happen. Under such circumstances the interviewer should draw on all her/his skill to handle the respondent's feelings before commencing.

In some instances the respondent may not be able to identify any critical incidents. This may be puzzling; as it seems difficult to comprehend that nothing of substance appears to have been happening. Clearly there is an ethical issue in respect of how the interviewer then handles the interview. The interview should not be 'forced'; although it may be more difficult for the interviewer to explore the apparent non-events and lengthy periods of absence of incident with the interviewee in a way that yields useful information.

Alternatively as some have written numerous incidents may be reported (Gremler, 2003; Butterfield et al., 2004). The researcher should take a view concerning the sampling of incidents. Do they want (after Flanagan) to sample extreme incidents which may be shown to impact behaviour; or should they attempt to be as comprehensive as possible noting even minor incidents. The interpretivist would tend to argue that the subject/respondent should determine which incidents are identified and discussed. Whereas to attempt completeness smacks of positivism. Flanagan, as a psychologist, would see nothing wrong in seeking out extreme cases because this in psychological terms would be where the impact would most likely be felt.

Reflexivity

Reflexivity is an important tool that the researcher should encompass as part of the process. This takes a number of forms: the investigator: (a) may reflect back to the respondent what they think the respondent has told them and adjust their understanding as necessary; (b) may reflect on what has been said in combination with probing to gain greater depth of understanding; (c) should compile notes immediately after the meeting on reflections about what has been seen and heard, and reflect on his/her own assumptions and position in respect of the various issues raised; and (d) s/he should reflect on whether his/her own position may be influencing the interview.

All this should be borne in mind during the course of the data collection process during each meeting.

Focusing the theme

The interviewer must focus the respondent's attention and be able to explain succinctly what s/he wants them to consider in relation to the CIT and context of the topic being discussed. The interviewer must also be ready for a respondent who denies that 'anything has happened'. One ploy is to simply get the interviewee to talk about the business and how it has developed over the past few years (depending on its longevity). Then the interviewee should be encouraged to talk about where they intend to take the business over the foreseeable future (this may be defined subsequently). The interviewee should then be asked to consider what has happened in the past which may affect the entrepreneur's future plans.

At this juncture the researcher should reflect back to the entrepreneur their understanding of what they have been told about what has happened and how it is likely to influence future decisions. Having checked their understanding and probably expanded on it, they should try to isolate particular events and get the entrepreneur to discuss them in greater depth. They should probe who else was involved, what actions they took and understand the consequences (as seen by the entrepreneur) of such actions and decisions.

Controlling the interview

During the interview the entrepreneur will be telling his or her story, with the researcher actively engaged in steering the respondent to discuss in greater depth those critical incidents that have been identified. It is important that the researcher prevents the interview descending into a loose, unfocused and rambling account. This is achieved by the use of generic probes. For example, the interviewer should typically seek answers to the following questions:

- *What* happened next?
- *Why* did it happen?
- *How* did it happen?
- *With whom?*
- *What* did the parties concerned feel?
- *What* were the consequences—immediately and longer term?
- *How* did you cope?
- *What* tactics did you use?
- *What* do you feel you learnt from the incident?
- *Would* you do anything differently?
- *How* does this affect your plans going forward?

Such generic probes are translated into specific questions, which relate to the context, language and rapport established during the interview. For example, some interjections by the interviewer may seek *clarification*: 'And he came in as a partner?' They help control the flow of the interview and keep the interviewer alert. They also give breathing space to the respondent to gather their thoughts. In critical incidents with high emotive content the interview could become a monologue—an outpouring. This is not desirable as the interview may ramble and lose focus. Whilst understanding the interviewee's feelings is important, it is also important for the researcher to gain a genuine understanding of the nuances of the situation that evoked such strong feelings—what did it mean to the entrepreneur and important others (family, employees, friends and so forth)? Thus the interviewer should *seek further information* until satisfied that they do understand. Crucially, however, the interviewer should not dominate the discussion or interrogate the respondent; a balance must be struck.

Concluding the interview

Closing the interview and taking care of ethical issues is likely to arise naturally, although where a detailed case study is desired the researcher should be aiming to arrange further interviews. The interviewer should thank the entrepreneur for their time and energy in giving an interesting account of the incidents identified. S/he must leave the impression that the interview was valuable and that any revelations will be treated in the strictest confidence. Such issues should be addressed before the researcher departs. S/he should then explain what s/he would like to happen next. The data will be analysed. S/he would like to return to feedback and discuss the findings further and/or s/he would like to interview other members of the team/family/such relevant others as are identified during the interview. The entrepreneur may be reluctant to allow the researcher to interview subordinates and the ease with which such an agreement is reached will in large part depend on the degree of trust and the rapport established thus far. As the researcher has offered confidentiality then nothing the entrepreneur has said during the interview can be fed back to a subsequent interviewee; the researcher should reassure the entrepreneur of this and explain what themes will be discussed. The researcher will jeopardise the whole research enterprise should s/he breach that trust.

Analysing the data

An analysis is likely to be based on a grounded approach. Grounded theory assumes that the researcher abandons preconceptions, reflects on the assumptions s/he may be making about aspects of the topic and subject, and interrogates the data critically to elicit the subject's meaning. Grounded theory aims to build theory; as such an explanatory framework is built through the conceptualisation of the data. Thus there emerge categories of behaviour, context and strategies adopted for dealing with it. The evidence of patterns of categorical behaviours builds up within a transcribed interview and also across the body of transcripts (where multiple CI interviews have taken place) to enable theory to be developed. Only after the accumulation of a considerable body of material can theory move from the substantive to the level of formal theory. An extant conceptual framework, on the other hand, suggests a set of preconceived categories—a coding frame—for which evidence may be sought in the data. Such a framework may not only be tested but also extended using the CIT methodology.

In general, the unit of analysis using CIT is the critical incident recounted by the individual, the group or team, but the CIT allows the focus to shift, for example to the organisation, the industrial sector or the location. The CIT within a case study allows for multiple levels of analysis and assumes the presence of a considerable number of variables.

A research project has aims and objectives from which central themes are deduced. For example if the central theme is *business development* then the coding technique works by first identifying the central idea, in this case business development. This forms the core category. The link between the core category and its subcategories is by means of relational concepts: the context in which the action took place, the strategies or tactics adopted for dealing with the phenomenon, and the outcomes of the action. The conditions that obtain may be, for example, the need to establish a client base, or to firm up relations with suppliers or to strengthen the top management team. The next step is to identify what strategy or tactic the interviewee adopted in order to achieve the particular outcome. Furthermore, the researcher should consider and have pursued this in interview, any unintended consequences and what they meant to the incumbent.

Various tactics may be adopted by the entrepreneur in the pursuit of business growth/development: for example, the identification of new opportunities, the recruitment of new staff, thus expanding the skills set of the business or taking on a new business partner prepared to invest in business expansion. In the hospitality industry, the entrepreneur may decide to experiment with new dishes, offer an early bird menu, or hire a new chef with a view to offering better quality cuisine. Whatever the industry, whatever the strategy, the CIT enables the researcher to examine how the new development was handled and what the outcome was.

To examine how the newly introduced strategy was handled means identifying *what events took place*. For example, the critical event is *setting up a business partnership*. Further analysis seeks to identify what the properties of this event were. For example, the quality of the relationship, the individual's performance, the change brought about in business fortunes and so forth. But how much detail is needed? The answer to this question will clearly depend on the aims and objectives of the project. Where further detail is required the *dimensions of properties* are identified. Thus a relationship may be categorised as *close* or *distant, sad or miserable, firm or fickle*, and so on; the individual's performance *as effective or ineffective, persistent, insightful* or whatever; the business performance *as declining, expanding, flat-lining*, and so on. Thus the subcategories may code at a considerable level of detail.

Discussion

Analytical issues
In 1998 and 2004 I wrote about a case in which an entrepreneur and owner of three small businesses founded a new micro-business in the service sector, which failed and brought down his other businesses. This was a rare recorded case of business failure. The critical incidents which our hapless entrepreneur ('Bernard') identified were: the problems associated with bringing in a business partner; an attempted renegotiation of the leasehold on a property; the fraudulent behaviour of staff; and the asset stripping and loss of the business at the hands of a dishonest solicitor. The case which involved an interview with Bernard's wife and examined the consequences for the family as well as the business fallout, involved in the account considerable affect, and a mix of information and beliefs. The CIT captured well the extent of the businessman's commercial and familial problems which even semi-structured interviews would have had difficulty realising.

Complex cases such as these pose problems for the interviewer in so far as conducting critical incident interviews demands alertness, skilled probing, sensitivity and empathy. It helps to be able to return after the first interview has been transcribed and read to identify issues that should be resolved, developed or clarified further by the respondent. Often there is a need to disentangle events; some may overlap contemporaneously, and there is always the problematic issue of recall. Patience and good-quality access is needed to piece together a picture of events that resonates with any documentary evidence and separate accounts of significant others. In the case referred to, we did not have access to the solicitor, the landlord, the business partner or any of the staff, although there were some indisputable facts of the case; the business had failed, and the entrepreneur and his family were left with very little.

As research analysing such cases we are looking for a kind of truth; does what we have been told ring true? As Gergen (1999: 35) argues, telling the truth is entering into a specific form of game.

> Within the game of chess, it is either true or not that I have exercised a manoeuvre that has resulted in 'checkmate'. Hence, 'truth' assumes the implicit rules of what counts as a proper description in the context of a game or 'form of life'. Telling the truth is like performing a specific game; we describe, explain and theorise about what may have happened, usually in narrative form. But our descriptions are circumscribed within the context, the form of life (Chell, 2008: 191).

Bernard's and his wife's accounts of the demise of their businesses rang true, but of course it would have been helpful to have had the business partner's account of what was perceived as his mismanagement, incompetence and fraudulent behaviour. However that proved not to be possible. It is a dilemma for any researcher conducting a case study; how many sources of corroborative and/or independent evidence and accounts of the incident can they acquire. Documentary evidence would also help, especially in the case of fraud, financial irregularities and staff failings. Each element; financial accounting, legal niceties, the contract with the landlord, and so forth—has its own rules of procedure, which in each form of life may be conformed to or abused. The narrative told by Bernard and his wife strongly suggested abuse, both in the details of the tale but also the consequences which were only too apparent. Could we have elicited more independent information in this case? Probably not. . . What we do claim is that the CIT enabled us to deliver and analyse quite detailed accounts of this particular business failure which held up to scrutiny. Moreover the CIT delivered in an efficient and effective way; comprising two lengthy CI interviews.

The issue of taking on a new business partner is not unusual in small business, nor is it unusual for business partnerships to dissolve in acrimony. In the case, the dissolution of the partnership took two years. As with a marriage, severing the ties may be difficult and it is during this period of separation that the real damage is done. The business partner ('Bill'), we were told, did not fit in (he was not a member of the family, could this have been an issue?), became aggressive and is alleged to have become involved in fraud. We were given sufficient detail to feel confident about its detrimental effect. Both spouses appeared to have been taken in by Bill, believing him to be a useful addition to the team who would give a growth spurt to at least one of the businesses. This rationale is not unusual either; small especially micro-businesses need to expand their skills set. What we do not know is how Bernard handled Bill, or indeed if he was frozen out of this close-knit family team (Chell and Baines, 1998).

The incident over the leasehold and the 'crooked landlord' appeared to be sheer bad luck. But was it? Bernard's eight year-old daughter who was present but not being interviewed as such, had said, 'Daddy why do you deal with these people?' and he commented, '. . .you make your own work. . .' In other words, people create their own luck; they can create a situation that increases the probability of a particular outcome by the choices they make. In this case by associating with people who tended towards dishonesty the likelihood of one of them 'doing him' was thereby increased. As a consequence of this glimmer of self-insight Bernard changed his lifestyle, his business activity and his friends. Treating the case as a socio-economic unit that involved family and looking at the CIs in the round enabled us as researchers to gain a depth of understanding of the issues and their individual and collective impact. We can only speculate whether, without the perceptive question of his daughter and the obvious impact on the family, Bernard would have changed his modus operandi. The upshot was that he set up a much smaller operation, which relied less on other people and rather more on new technology. He and his wife increased their leisure and time spent at home as a family.

Interpretivism
It is undoubtedly the case that some research problems will lend themselves to research using Flanagan's methodology. However, where the research problem is multi-layered,

where the events and issues cannot be anticipated by the researcher, and in particular where the researcher feels strongly that in any account the subject's perspective should predominate, then adopting the CIT method within an interpretivist paradigm would be an appropriate methodological choice, yielding nuanced data and detailed case study.

The researcher may reflect on what has been said and in doing so consider his own position on various issues but this is done to enrich understanding not to impose the researcher's point of view. The critical incidents cannot be anticipated and as the case revealed they may be negative, hinder growth or even undermine the firm's continued existence. While the interviewees may well have reflected long and hard on incidents that have affected their fortunes and those of the business, the retelling of the events, taking into consideration the questions and reflections of the researcher provides another lens through which to view their experiences. Using skilled interviewers a greater depth of discussion is achieved, with subjects appreciating the confidential but nonetheless revelatory nature of what becomes a fluid conversation.

The choice of what incidents to recount is entirely under the control of the subject; all that the researcher is doing is attempting to ensure that there is thorough coverage of the issues. But are interviewees likely to be so compliant? Will they tell the truth? If the researcher is unsure that the strands of the interview hang together as a coherent story then the only recourse is to collect other data either from other personnel involved, or documentary evidence. The researcher also should acknowledge the potential problem of recall. This may present an opportunity to seek further evidence; a legitimate pretext which the interviewee may accept. But of course such access requires careful negotiation and cannot be assumed. This is part of the skill of dealing with each subject as an individual, and, as it were, tuning into their 'wavelength'.

The CIT enables the issues to be viewed in context and is a rich source of information from the perspective of the incumbent, their conscious reflections, their frame of reference, feelings, attitudes and views on matters of critical importance to them. In the case, Bernard recounted how they were cheated of their firm and what it felt like. Both he and his wife were able to put the incident in perspective, as they contemplated the 'knock-on effects' and how stressful the experience had been. The information revealed using CIT enables a fine-grained analysis and detailed explanation of the behaviour of the incumbent and the outcomes of behavioural and managerial processes. While other methods may also enable the researcher to achieve this, the advantage of the CIT is the perceived linkage between context, action and outcomes that is more readily teased out because the technique is focused on the incident, which is explicated in relation to what happened, why it happened, how it was handled and what the consequences were. This not only feeds into the experience of the entrepreneur, but has potential as a learning event. Combined with an action research approach the research can facilitate feedback and learning. However the experience of Bernard and his family was so poignant that learning took place without the intervention of the research team.

Ethical issues are likely to be prevalent when the CIT is adopted. Subjectivity and personal interpretation of matters of crucial importance to individuals increases the likelihood of ethical considerations. There are confidentiality issues that should be respected as interviewees may name other people and/or their businesses, other organisations or institutions, that may constitute slander, or in some cases hint at criminal activity. In such cases a strict code of ethics and a procedure for handling tape-recordings and transcripts is essential in order to protect all parties and the integrity of the research process.

Generalisation is not possible from single cases nor is the assumptions of the phenomenological paradigm consistent with statistical generalisation. Within this broad genre is the interpretive approach which enables the researcher to generalise to theory (Yin, 1994: 31), i.e. 'analytic generalization'. Analytic generalisation assumes the performative role of language; it enables the person to gain an understanding of what is happening around them, the behavioural patterns and routines, and reflexively their own behaviour. Such patterns arise from an assumed social order and objectification of institutional and cultural practices. Language enables the person to communicate meaning within the context of a situation, for which there are rules. Wittgenstein (1978) used the term, 'game' and 'form of life' to indicate typical modes of living, for which there are rules or as the psychologist would have it social norms. Forms of life include institutions such as marriage, the family; business behaviour, such as doing deals; accounting practices and financial undertakings, including malfeasance; and so forth.

The CIT enables the researcher to focus on particular forms of life that have an impact on the subject in question (in our case business development or specifically failure). By examining multiple cases, using grounded theory for analytical purposes, patterns of behaviour may well emerge. From this the researcher aims to build theory (Strauss and Corbin, 1990).

Reliability

The CIT interview is not easy to conduct well. It requires a skilled and mature researcher who can manage the respondent, directing the interview to achieve clarity of understanding and who can handle the expression of emotion, including distress. Of course not all respondents will reveal negative incidents and here the interviewer must be able to probe sensitively and not be carried away by the wave of success which the respondent may be putting across. In other words the interviewer must under all circumstances try to establish a rapport of trust, honest and open exchange. In the case study cited, the interviewer probed with relevant questions, first to ensure her understanding, and secondly to ensure that the account did not become a monologue. Thus the interaction between interviewer and interviewee can help control the pace, add light relief and steer the interview so that it remains focused. Further, the interviewer should reflect upon their role as interviewer, the style adopted and the way the interview was conducted. Additionally they should reflect on their assumptions, especially when tempted to be judgemental. When engaged in a programme of action research, they should reflect back their thoughts in respect of the analysis by way of feedback and further engagement of the subject concerned.

An added difficulty of conducting the interview well is that of attempting to ensure that either all or all relevant critical incidents have been captured. This begs the question as to whether the researcher needs to capture all incidents and that 'relevant' is viewed to be from the respondent's perspective. Indeed, as has been pointed out, some interviewees do not appear to be able to identify a single incident. Should this arise, the interviewer needs to deal with it skilfully and ethically. Clearly in an inductive situation, whether all incidents have or have not been identified cannot be 'proved'. Techniques such as using a diagram to facilitate recollection of the chronology of the events should help assure this part of the process. Critics evaluating this method might argue that it is difficult to test for reliability (compare, Andersson and Nilsson, 1964). Andersson and Nilsson do so from within a positivist paradigm. This is also true of Butterfield et al. (2005), who take a pragmatic view believing that criteria should be applied to test the robustness of the method and demonstrate the trustworthiness of the data.

There are several things that can be done to improve reliability within an interpretivist framework. The use of two interviewers where resources permit is helpful: (a) because it facilitates completeness of coverage, such as probing different angles; (b) gives each interviewer time to reflect during the interview; and (c) gives greater opportunity to check understanding and enable the subject to clarify, explain or elaborate as appropriate. Further, the possibility of conducting more than one interview with the subject should always be considered. Time, budget and access are likely constraints. The key issue is whether additional interviews are likely to improve reliability (through the ability to check what has previously been said, develop a strand of thought and go over sequences of events by way of clarification). Consideration should be given to conducting further CIs with relevant others. The difficulty as always is gaining access especially where permission from the respondent (entrepreneur and boss) is required, for example to access other members of the firm or indeed family. Crucially the point is that one is not trying to find a single truth but to understand the respondent's perspectives and actions. When it comes to data coding; reliability can be improved by two researchers independently coding the interview transcript. Not only does this give the researchers further opportunity to reflect on the interviewee's account of the critical incidents, their interpretation of the subject's perspective, the extent of their agreement especially with regard to the categorisation of interview data and CIs. They should then feedback tentative interpretations to the subject for their affirmation or otherwise; in particular to ensure that they keep faith with the subject's language, expression and meaning. Reliability, therefore, is built into a quality interview process in which there is coherence. It may be thought desirable to triangulate findings with other sources of data, as discussed in Yin's case study method.

CONCLUDING REMARKS

The creation of management knowledge has relied upon the scientific method and positivist paradigm for the greater part of the twentieth century. Phenomenology was considered to be an approach associated with esoteric areas of sociology or cultural anthropological enquiry (Burrell and Morgan, 1979). Now management researchers recognise the need to identify and explain processes, which go on within organisations. There is no textbook answer to what is a dynamic process and real life is messy; the people immersed in those situations and circumstances are trying to make sense of them (Weick, 1995). Their accounts are partial; but partial or not, biased or not, such accounts constitute *their* reality, and arguably, it is the way they view the world which shapes their future actions. How, if those closest to the events have only a partial view which they may not have clearly articulated, can we as researchers hope to collect valid data by use of extensive survey techniques? How can we hope to gain a genuine understanding of the persons involved in an organisational drama if we do not know anything of the context, situation or circumstances in which it was to unfold? The case of Bernard illustrates graphically this point. Had we not known about his previous business undertakings, the bad practices verging on criminality of significant other players that led to the circumstances surrounding the business's unfortunate demise, we would not be able to understand him, his subsequent decisions and his present business activity.

Some critics have been known to question the integrity of qualitative researchers: 'how do we know they haven't made it up?' Such criticism—we might regard as despicable and unworthy, but still it requires an answer—misses the point; the point is that the qualitative researcher can only present an interpretation of the events recounted to them, but whose truth shines out from the coherence of the nuanced narrative and the insights gleaned. The value of this approach is that it yields genuine insights into processes, incidents and events that shape behaviour, and as a coherent account which is independently checkable it has face validity. Furthermore the integrity of the research is maintained by either permitting public access or disseminating sufficiently widely so enabling wider debate and critical appraisal.

Finally, within an interpretivist framework, the CIT permits a degree of replication and generalisation. While the individual firm's circumstances may be unique, the type of incident, the context, strategy and outcomes as a pattern of related activities may in general terms be apparent in other businesses. Moreover, what is said about them is also constrained according to the rules of the form of life. The relationship between context and actions is *contingent*. This contrasts with the nature of those relations within positivism where they are assumed to be *causal*. CIT enables the development of case-based theory grounded in actual and critical events that shape future actions. The insights gathered and the conclusions drawn not only facilitate the development of theory but also policy. In combination with the application of grounded theory (Strauss and Corbin, 1990), CIT is capable of extending our theoretical understanding and our ability to explain organisational as well as entrepreneurial behaviour.

NOTES

1. Flanagan tended to focus on those incidents that led to success or failure. This is an important methodological issue of sampling. Should one sample those incidents that 'cause' extreme behaviours or should one sample as comprehensive a set of incidents as possible?
2. Note the contrast with Flanagan's non-participant observatory method, using expert observers to identify and classify critical incidents.

REFERENCES

Andersson, B.E. and Nilsson, S.G. (1964), 'Studies in the reliability and validity of the critical incident technique', *Journal of Applied Psychology*, 48, 1: 398–403.
Bryman, A. (1989), *Research Methods and Organisation Studies*, London and New York: Routledge.
Burrell, G. and Morgan, G. (1979), *Sociological paradigms and Organisational Analysis*, London: Heinemann.
Butterfield, L.D., Borgen, W.A., Amundsen, N.E., Maglio, A.T. (2005), 'Fifty Years of the CIT: 1954–2004 and beyond', *Qualitative Research*, 5, 4: 475–97.
Chell, E. (1998), 'The Critical Incident Technique', in G. Symon and C. Cassell (Eds.) *Qualitative Methods and Analysis in Organisational Research—A Practical Guide*, London: Sage, pp. 51–72.
Chell, E. (2004), 'The Critical Incident Technique', in C. Cassell and G. Symon (Eds.) *Qualitative Methods in Organisation Studies*, London: Sage, pp. 45–60.

Chell, E. (2008), *The Entrepreneurial Personality: A Social Construction* 2nd Ed., London and New York: Routledge.

Chell, E. (forthcoming), 'The Critical Incident Technique and the entrepreneurial process', in H. Neergaard and C. Leitch (Eds.), *Handbook of Qualitative Research Techniques and Analysis in Entrepreneurship*. Cheltenham: Edward Elgar (in press).

Chell, E. and Adam, E. (1994a), 'Exploring the cultural orientation of entrepreneurship: conceptual and methodological issues', *Discussion paper 94–7*, School of Business and Management, University of Newcastle, UK.

Chell, E. and Adam, E. (1994b), 'Researching culture and entrepreneurship: a qualitative approach', *Discussion paper 94–9*, School of Business and Management, University of Newcastle.

Chell, E. and Adam, E. (1995), 'Entrepreneurship and culture in New Zealand', *Discussion paper 95–8*, Department of Management Studies, Newcastle upon Tyne, UK: University of Newcastle.

Chell, E. and Allman, K. (2003), 'Mapping the motivations and intentions of technology-oriented entrepreneurs', *R&D Management*, 33, 2: 117–34.

Chell, E. and Baines, S. (1998), 'Does gender affect business 'performance'? A study of micro-businesses in business service in the UK', *Entrepreneurship & Regional Development*, 10: 117–35.

Chell, E., Haworth, J.M. and Brearley, S. (1991), *The Entrepreneurial Personality: Concepts, Cases and Categories*, London and New York: Routledge.

Chell, E. and Pittaway, L. (1998), 'A study of entrepreneurship in the restaurant and cafe industry: exploratory work using the critical incident technique as a methodology', *International Journal of Hospitality Management*, 17, 1: 23–32.

Cope, J. (2005a), 'Toward a dynamic learning perspective of Entrepreneurship', *Entrepreneurship: Theory and Practice*, July, 373–97.

Cope, J. (2005b), 'Researching entrepreneurship through phenomenological inquiry: Philosophical and methodological issues', *International Journal of Small Business*, 23, 2: 163–89.

Cope, J. and Watts, G. (2000), 'Learning by doing: an exploration of experience, critical incidents and reflection in entrepreneurial learning', *International Journal of Entrepreneurial Behaviour and Research*, 6, 3: 104–24.

Curran, J., Jarvis, R., Blackburn, R.A. and Black, S. (1993), 'Networks and small firms: constructs, methodological strategies and some findings', *International Journal of Small Business*, 11, 2: 13–25.

Deetz, S. (1996), 'Describing differences in approaches to organisation science: re-thinking Burrell and Morgan and their legacy', *Organisation Science*, 7: 191–207.

Flanagan, J.C. (1954), 'The critical incident technique', *Psychological Bulletin*, 15: 327–58.

Gergen, K.J. (1999), *An Invitation to Social Constructionism*. London: Sage.

Gremler, D.D. (2004), 'The CIT in Service Research', *Journal of Service Research*, 7, 1: 65–89.

Harré, R. (1979), *Social Being: A Theory for Social Psychology*. Oxford: Blackwell.

Harré, R. (1986), 'An outline of the social constructionist point of view. In R. Harré (Ed.). *The Social Construction of Motions*. Oxford: Blackwell.

Hartley, J. (1994), 'Case study research', in C. Cassell and G. Symon (Eds.) *Qualitative Methods in Organisation Studies*, London: Sage, pp. 323–33.

Haworth, J.M., Brearley, S., and Chell, E. (1991), 'A typology of business owners and their firms using neural networks', *Entrepreneurship and Regional Development*, 33, 3: 221–35.

Hopkinson, G.C. and Hogarth-Scott, S. (2001), '"What happened was. . ." Broadening the agenda of storied research', *Journal of Marketing Management*, 17, 1: 27–47.

Keaveney, S. M. (1995), 'Customer switching behaviour in service industries: an exploratory study', *Journal of Marketing*, 59 (April): 71–82.

McClelland, D.C. (1976), *A Guide to Competency Assessment*. Boston: McBer Books.

McClelland, D.C. (1987), 'Characteristics of successful entrepreneurs', *Journal of Creative Behavior*, 21, 3: 219–33.

Morgan, G. and Smircich, L. (1980), 'The case for qualitative research', *Academy of Management Review*, 5, 4: 491–500.

Pittaway, L.A. (2000), *The Social Construction of Entrepreneurial Behaviour*, Doctoral Thesis; Newcastle University, Faculty of Law, Environment and Social Sciences.

Pittaway, L.A. and Chell, E. (1999), 'Entrepreneurship in the service sector life cycle', *Proceedings of the Eighth annual CHME Hospitality Research Conference* vol 1 (April 7–9): 203–19, University of Surrey, UK.

Ronan, W.W. and Latham, G.P. (1974), 'The reliability and validity of the critical incident technique', *Studies in Personnel Psychology*, 6, 1: 53–64.

Sarason, Y, Dean, T. and Dillard, J.F. (2006), 'Entrepreneurship as the nexus of individual and opportunity: a structuration view', *Journal of Business Venturing*, 21, 3: 286–305.

Schultz, M. and Hatch, M.J. (1996), 'Living with multiple paradigms: the case of paradigm interplay in organisational culture studies', *Academy of Management Review*, 21, 2: 529–57.

Shane, S. (2000), 'Prior knowledge and the discovery of opportunities', *Organisation Science*, 11, 4: 448–69.

Shotter, J. (1993), *Conversational Realities*, London, Thousand Oaks, CA, New Delhi: Sage.

Spencer, L.M. (1983), *Soft Skill Competencies*. Edinburgh: Scottish Council for Research in Education.

Strauss, A. and Corbin, J. (1990), *Basics of Qualitative Research: Grounded Theory Procedures and Techniques*. Thousand Oaks, C.A.: Sage.

Weick, K. (1995), *Sense-making in Organizations*, Thousand Oaks, CA: Sage.

Wheelock, J. and Chell, E. (1996), *The Business-owner-managed Family Unit: An Inter-Regional Comparison of Behavioural Dynamics*. Ref. No. R000234402, London: Economic and Social Research Council.

Wittgenstein, L. (1978), *Philosophical Investigations*, Oxford: Blackwell.

Yin, R.K. (1994), *Case Study Research*, 2nd Ed., Thousand Oaks, California: Sage.

Yin, R.K. (2003), *Applications of Case Study Research*, 2nd Ed., Thousand Oaks, London and New Delhi: Sage.

8. Gender, ethnicity and social entrepreneurship: qualitative approaches to the study of entrepreneuring[1]

Silvia Gherardi and Manuela Perrotta

INTRODUCTION

The literature on the topic of entrepreneurship and small business has diversified and developed constantly since its first formulations. In the past 30 years, moreover, an independent field of studies has developed especially in the area of economics and business studies (Busenitz et al. 2003).

While it can be argued that economic theory has still not furnished a thoroughgoing definition of entrepreneurial activity (Bull and Willard 1993), one may nevertheless note that what we know about entrepreneurship derives mainly from the early and classic studies of the twentieth century. This concerns Schumpeterian theories (Schumpeter 1934), the theories on 'enterprise creation' of Collins and Moore (1964), and Knight's theory of risk (1921). According to these authors, the distinctive feature of entrepreneurial activity is a capacity for innovation. This, however, is regarded as being essentially a quality intrinsic to persons, rather than simultaneously a set of practices, so that some theoreticians have been explicit in criticizing the underlying Darwinian and heroic model of entrepreneurship.

However, in recent years the debate has been enriched by new perspectives and has assumed a central role in other fields, organization studies for example. The past ten years, in fact, have seen a flourishing of approaches and perspectives 'alternative' and innovative with respect to the dominant paradigm. A first example is represented by the anthologies in the *New Movements of Entrepreneurship* series (Steyaert and Hjorth 2003; 2006; Hjorth and Steyaert 2004; 2009a), which present some of the more innovative qualitative research studies on entrepreneurship. A second example is the special issue on *Alternative Perspectives on Entrepreneurship Research* (Jennings et al. 2005) published in *Entrepreneurship: Theory and Practice*, which identifies and promotes three research paradigms alternative to the functionalist one identified by Burrell and Morgan (2003): interpretative, radical humanist, and radical structuralist. Finally, the recent special issue on *Critical Perspectives in Entrepreneurship Research* published in *Organization* (Tedmanson et al. 2012) demonstrates the increasing critical interest in a revision of the concept of entrepreneurship and methodologies for its study.

Despite the larger number of studies conducted from other perspectives, however, the bulk of entrepreneurship research is still functionalist (Chell and Pittaway 1998; Grant and Perren 2002; Jennings et al. 2005), characterized by an objectivist perspective, and rooted in regulation. Entrepreneurial activity is largely viewed as "a positive economic activity" (Calás et al. 2009, p. 552), and "the more the entrepreneurs the merrier" (see Weiskopf and Steyaert 2009). Moreover, entrepreneurship research concentrates on "the study of sources of opportunities; the processes of discovery, evaluation, and exploitation of opportunities; and the set of individuals who discover, evaluate, and exploit them" (Shane and Venkataraman 2000, p. 218). This view, which is widespread in the Western economic debate, conceives the entrepreneur as a pure decision-maker possessing superior 'alertness', although this capacity is not always backed with personal economic resources. This pure entrepreneur, in fact, earns profits by "discovering" and seizing objectively existing but previously unperceived opportunities to arbitrage price discrepancies between a bundle of complementary inputs and the output that it yields (Salerno 2008).

Although other authors have pointed out that "limiting entrepreneurship to the specific domain of opportunity may be shortsighted" (Busenitz et al. 2003, p. 297), the mainstream discourse on entrepreneurship is characterized by a predominantly economic interpretation of the phenomenon. This interpretation is also characterized by an implicit vision of the entrepreneurial reality as objectively existent, and therefore as a tangible phenomenon that can be measured, foreseen, and encouraged (Chell and Pittaway 1998; Pittaway 2005).

According to Gartner and Birley (2002), studies on entrepreneurship have undergone a long process of normalization – especially in the field of economics and business schools – which has made some definitions, methodologies and research problems more legitimate than others (see also Grant and Perren 2002). Principles like causality, generalization, foresight, and statistical significance have become the only "scientific and rigorous" option to describe the "reality" of the entrepreneurial phenomenon in objective and true manner. Hjorth and Steyaert (2009b) maintain that this crystallization occurred during the 1990s, the golden years of studies on entrepreneurship, which saw an endeavour to develop the bases for the establishment of entrepreneurship as an accepted (and acceptable) discipline at business schools. An emblematic example of this development in studies on entrepreneurship is the search for statistically valid measures of the characteristics of the actors and contextual factors that enable definition of what constitutes entrepreneurship, what behaviours are successful and what are not, and even what policies are "right" and what are "wrong".

The traditional approaches to entrepreneurship thus tend to reproduce a specific normative economic model (that of market capitalism) which takes it for granted that development of this model will be beneficial to the system as a whole (Calás et al. 2009). *Homo economicus* is a rational actor driven by self-interest. However, the organizing principle underlying the approach is that the overriding objective should be the efficiency of the system.

However, the ontological and epistemological assumptions at the basis of such research have almost never been explicitly discussed, even though they influence both the research process and its results. The discourse – the words that we use to define entrepreneurship – sets the boundaries of how we think about and study it. It theoretically marks out the field of entrepreneurship and identifies its distinctive characteristics, legitimating only some research methods and teaching topics (Busenitz et al. 2003; Edelman et al. 2008; Shane and Venkataraman 2000).

In their attempt to identify an allegedly universal form of market-based entrepreneurship, the dominant theoretical perspectives pay scant attention to the contextual dynamics in which entrepreneurial activity acquires meaning for specific people, in specific places, and for contextual reasons which may differ from those normatively presumed by the mainstream literature.

A crucial consequence of the supremacy of approaches of this kind is the exclusion – empirical, practical and political – of numerous actors (for example, women, immigrants, or people in the emerging economies) from the category of entrepreneur identified in the stereotype of the male, white, and Western innovator.

To remedy these shortcomings, recent critical, ethical and political perspectives on entrepreneurship have encouraged reflection on the heterogeneous and problematic nature of entrepreneurship (Ogbor 2000; Armstrong 2005; Steyaert and Hjorth 2006; Hjorth and Steyaert 2009a; Essers 2009; Jones and Spicer 2009; Calás et al. 2009).

Some of these studies attempt to exemplify a processual ontology of entrepreneurship, to direct attention to societal movements and how entrepreneurship motivates people, "and, finally, to position entrepreneurship beyond its narrow business location by connecting social and discursive, political and aesthetic forces" (Hjorth and Steyaert 2009c, p. 221). Moreover, they criticize the essentialism inherent in many key concepts of the mainstream approaches: entrepreneurial personality, entrepreneur, entrepreneurship, opportunity (Weiskopf and Steyaert 2009). Counterposed to these notions is an ontology of becoming and movement, whose focus is no longer on the discovery of opportunities but on the creative process: the attention therefore moves from the entrepreneur to entrepreneuring (Steyaert 2007).

Three principal indications emerge from this literature for the development of critical reflection and to bring this discussion into the mainstream of entrepreneurship scholarship:

1. explore the reflexive aspects of research practices, rendering explicit what type of knowledge is produced, how it can be used and for what purposes, and introduce ethical criteria for evaluation of the knowledge produced (Calás et al. 2009);
2. shift the focus of research from the single individual that undertakes economic initiatives to the phenomenon of entrepreneurship as a process (Steyaert 2007);
3. welcome "new" qualitative/interpretative methodological approaches (Steyaert 1997; Gartner and Birley 2002) which take account of the processual and situated dimension of entrepreneurship and mainly employ a social constructionist approach (Chell 2000; Lindgren and Packendorff 2009).

Starting from these considerations, the aim of this chapter is to analyse the entrepreneurial literature on qualitative and non-positivist research methods from a feminist empiricist perspective. Feminist theorizing is predicated on the assumptions that gender relations are fundamental in the structuring of society and that a critical and reflexive lens makes it possible to question how gender relations are "done' and may be "done" differently. A reframing from positivist epistemology to feminist empiricism stresses the plurality of notions of objectivity, considering that all forms of knowledge advance the interests of some and not others (Harding 2004; Calás et al. 2009; Gherardi 2011).

In the chapter, we shall introduce what can be considered a "qualitative approach" by examining what different studies have produced in terms of contributions to the field, and by identifying their research implications. For the sake of brevity, we shall concentrate on three areas of research particularly rich with examples of the potential of these approaches: gender, gender and ethnicity, and social entrepreneurship. Our aim is to stress how qualitative methodology in entrepreneurship studies has taken a reflexive and critical stance that acknowledges the active role of the researchers in framing and reframing the field through their epistemic practices.

THE SPREAD OF QUALITATIVE APPROACHES IN ENTREPRENEURIAL RESEARCH

In the past decade, studies characterized by qualitative approaches to small business and entrepreneurship have proliferated, not only in the "core" community of entrepreneurship studies but in other areas as well.

This tendency was already present in 2002, when Gartner and Birley edited a special issue on 'Qualitative methods in entrepreneurship research' for the *Journal of Business Venturing*. The aim of the authors was to celebrate the use of qualitative methodologies which enabled the investigation of substantial aspects little explored by the mainstream literature: "many of the important questions in entrepreneurship can only be asked through qualitative methods and approaches" (p. 387). According to Gartner and Birley, although quantitative studies were institutionalized in the field of entrepreneurship research, "there is something missing here" (p. 388).

Despite this stance, qualitative studies in this field are often still marginal to the quantitative mainstream. On the one hand, as several surveys of the literature have shown, the majority (more than 80 per cent) of studies are characterized by a quantitative (Chandler and Lyon 2001) and positivist approach (McDonald et al. 2004). On the other hand, notwithstanding invitations to extend the repertoire of research designs, analytic techniques, and more interpretative approaches to understanding the phenomenon of entrepreneurship (Bygrave 1989; Aldrich 1992; Davidsson and Wiklund 2001), these are still viewed with suspicion by the reference community of these studies (economics and business schools). The difficulties encountered by qualitative research on entrepreneurship, more widespread and well-established in North America than in Europe, and the lack of recognition by a large part of mainstream studies of the significant contributions that qualitative research can make, have been synthesized as follows by Gartner (2007, p. 617):

> the "problem" of qualitative researchers publishing their work in North American based academic journals; the issues of validity and reliability in case research that quantitative-oriented journal reviewers seemed to have with manuscripts that didn't have numbers; and the general lack of knowledge and interest of most North American scholars in the history and philosophy of the science embedded in qualitative entrepreneurship scholarship.

An example of this suspicion, and of the attempts to gain approval and positive evaluation by many authors using qualitative approaches, is provided by the introduction to the recent *Handbook of Qualitative Research Methods in Entrepreneurship*, edited by Neergaard and Ulhøi (2007), in which one reads: "This handbook can be perceived as a response to the trend and critique directed at the entrepreneurship field for producing (i) predominantly descriptive research and (ii) qualitative research of doubtful standard" (p. 2).

The opposition between qualitative and quantitative methodologies, and deductive and inductive methods, which has provoked long and heated discussion on the presumed lack of rigour of the latter, and the need to establish quality criteria with regard to qualitative research in various areas (Seale 1999; Tracey 2010), has been resumed with renewed vigour in the debate on entrepreneurship.

According to some, the introduction of criteria for the evaluation of excellence in qualitative research would demonstrate the greater complexity of qualitative methodology. In qualitative research, in fact, it is not possible to identify counterparts to criteria such as validity, reliability, generalizability, and objectivity in quantitative research (Winter 2000). Nevertheless, Tracey (2010) maintains that there are good reasons to seek "universal" criteria with which to evaluate qualitative research: (i) to be appreciated and understood by a variety of audiences, including grant agencies, governmental officials, and media contacts; and (ii) to promote dialogue among qualitative researchers who draw on different paradigms.

Tracey accordingly proposes eight principal characteristics of high-quality, qualitative methodological research: (a) a worthy topic, (b) rich rigour, (c) sincerity, (d) credibility, (e) resonance, (f) significant contribution, (g) ethics, and (h) meaningful coherence.

It is not our purpose here to demonstrate the "correctness" of qualitative methodologies (Czarniawska 2011). Instead, our objective is to evidence what might be the original contributions ensuing from qualitative research and interpretative methods. It is interesting to note, however, that in recent years invitations to consider qualitative research as a valid instrument for the analysis of entrepreneurship have begun to appear in the mainstream literature (Piperopoulos 2010).

Consideration of the broader debate shows that numerous conceptual proposals have developed around methodologies of qualitative non-positivist research.

Besides the more "classic" ethnographic studies (of which examples will be provided below), one of the strands that has achieved most success in the recent qualitative literature rotates around the narrative approach – as shown, for example, by the collected volume edited by Hjorth and Steyaert (2004), *Narrative and Discursive Approaches in Entrepreneurship* and the special issue edited by Gartner (2007) on 'Entrepreneurial narrative and a science of the imagination', published in the *Journal of Business Venturing*.

To quote Gartner (2007, p.613): "a simple definition of narrative approaches is: an analysis of the stories that people tell". As the same author specifies in the same article, however, "while it might be appropriate to surmise that narrative approaches might challenge us to collect more stories, I now believe that the issue is not a 'story deficit' but a deficit in how entrepreneurship stories are told" (p. 624). In order to show the existence of a variety of narrative approaches offering a multitude of insights, the special issue included six articles which analysed just one story told by an entrepreneur from different perspectives. What differentiates narrative approaches and narrative methodologies from the simple analysis of stories is that these approaches are reflexive: "in the process of analyzing other people's stories, we, as researchers, are also looking into the mirror of our own stories of how and why our research is conducted" (Gartner 2007, p.613).

To exemplify this difference, we present two studies on the relationship between the construction of legitimacy through "stories" and the acquisition of resources. Legitimacy, in fact, is a central problem in entrepreneurship studies: in order to provide legitimacy, accounts about a company's activities "must mesh both with the larger belief systems and with the experienced reality of the audience's daily life" (Suchman 1995, p. 582). However, using apparently similar qualitative methodologies (storytelling) – but making reference to different epistemological and ontological conceptions – produces very different research results and knowledge.

The first example is the study by Lounsbury and Glynn (2001). By examining entrepreneurship in the symbolic and cultural frame of meaning, these authors have explored the relationship between entrepreneurial stories (focusing on media stories or company advertisements) and wealth creation. The study highlights what Lounsbury and Glynn call a process of cultural entrepreneurship: "stories function to identify and legitimate new ventures, thus mediating between extant stocks of entrepreneurial resources and subsequent capital acquisition and wealth creation" (p. 546). The authors show that entrepreneurs must learn how to tell stories about their stock of capital in order to identify and legitimate their new ventures; in turn, these stories enable the acquisition of new capital and, ultimately, the generation of wealth. In other words, entrepreneurs need to learn how to become skilled cultural operators who can develop stories about who they are and how their resources or ideas will yield future benefits for consumers and society. The criteria on which to construct an entrepreneurial story that gives legitimacy and access to resources must respect societal norms about what is appropriate and efforts to create unique identities that may differentiate and lend competitive advantage.

Lounsbury and Glynn believe that more grounded study using an ethnographic approach could yield more significant results than analysis of the "public" stories that appear in the media and in advertising, which may condition the results of the research. But despite its qualitative approach, this study is a typical example of a positivist approach, which assumes that entrepreneurship has a realist ontological status. According to Lounsbury and Glynn:

> researchers interested in cultural entrepreneurship must be cautious of the potential correlation between observed stories and entrepreneurial resources. For instance, the more successful or visible a particular venture is, the more it will become the object of media attention. Similarly, the more resources a company has, the more it will be able to develop elaborate and visible marketing campaigns, including advertisements (p. 560).

The second study considered (O'Connor 2004) is instead based on a narrative approach and adopts the perspective of intertextuality. This study positions the entrepreneur in an overarching storyline of legitimacy building accomplished through dialogue. According to O'Connor, in fact, "entrepreneurs operated in a world of long-standing conversations. To achieve legitimacy, their conversations must engage with these pre-existing, ongoing, and encompassing conversations" (p. 105). In particular, this study examines the narratives of an entrepreneurial team pursuing acceptance and legitimacy over a critical 12-month period at the initiative stage, in a high-technology innovation business.

In this case the principal data-collection method was participant observation, while the stories were analysed using Burke's pentad, which focuses on five key dimensions: act, agent, agency, scene, and purpose. From the methodological point of view, particular attention is paid to gathering stories in natural settings as people do their jobs, and more subtly, at the interpretative level, to a recursive contextualization process in which the researcher locates a specific story as interrelating with others.

The main contribution of this research is to reformulate legitimacy building as a highly observable, social and linguistic activity, thereby making the practice of legitimacy building easier to study empirically. By showing the chaotic nature of legitimacy building, moreover, the study contributes to it as a social and linguistic practice conducted in a dynamic, experimental, and improvisational way. By using an interpretative frame which considers the emerging nature of entrepreneurial behaviour (Gartner et al., 1992), this study belongs among the interpretative approaches that view entrepreneurship as a process in continuous evolution.

The third study we will present (Karataş-Özkan 2011) is underpinned by social constructionism, a specific strand of interpretivism. This study focuses on narratives of young student-entrepreneurs' legitimacy building and how they gained agency through entrepreneurial activity. Working from a social constructionist premise of business venturing and standpoint of studying nascent entrepreneurs' learning processes, the study explores relational processes of entrepreneurial learning at multiple levels of new venture creation.

The research is concerned with a single case account of business venturing as experienced by a venture team of five nascent entrepreneurs, and data were collected primarily through participant observation and in-depth interviews. This in-depth exploration of entrepreneurial learning processes illustrates how processes of entrepreneurial learning include learning to legitimize the business, perform certain discourses while omitting others, and use and exert influence. The study points out that nascent entrepreneurs create their symbolic capital as they develop a sense of ownership, achievement, and legitimacy of their new venture. Moreover, learning to legitimize the business is a part of learning to cope with the liabilities of newness. The main contribution of the study, as the same author seems to claim, is that it "captures the lived experience of nascent entrepreneurs and offers some insights into a complex and multi-faceted phenomenon of entrepreneurial learning at the interface of micro-individual and meso-relational layers" (p. 902).

Having explained the differing nature of positivist and non-positivist approaches in qualitative methodologies, we now turn – as anticipated – to three specific strands of research: gender, gender and ethnicity, and social entrepreneurship. These have been selected because of the importance of some particular studies described below and chosen for their explanatory capacity and the disruptive nature of the knowledge produced.

The examples provided can be located within the body of analysis which rotates around the concept of "entrepreneuring" as a process which can be studied without focusing on economic or managerial logics, but as part of society and fundamentally as a process of social change (Hjorth and Steyaert 2004; Steyaert and Katz 2004; Steyaert and Hjorth 2006; Steyaert 2007; Jones and Spicer 2009). These emancipationist assumptions are also adopted, in fact, by feminist theorizing (Calás et al. 2009).

Although these studies differ in various respects and represent the methodological and analytical richness of the tradition of qualitative studies, they have in common an emphasis on studying entrepreneurship as an activity and a focus on ongoing and context-specific social practices and on the relationships that are created through them. Paying attention to the "how" of entrepreneurial processes and to the reflexive aspects of research, they emphasize "both what entrepreneurs do while entrepreneuring and, as important, what researchers can do when observing and portraying entrepreneurs' actions" (Calás et al. 2009, p. 561).

Finally, the three strands selected represent the different ways in which marginal entrepreneurial practices coexist with dominant practices and how these practices can reproduce social conditions of domination and subordination or potential emancipation. One objective of the three research strands considered, in fact, is to obtain a more complete picture of a world made up of power relations. This means that analyses must start from the position of non-dominant participants and their understanding of themselves in relation to the dominant ones. This is also because, as Calás et al. argue (2009, p. 562), "it is incumbent on the critical researcher to correct the biases of dominant research by revealing to the broader research community the value of apparently marginal practices".

GENDER AND ENTREPRENEURING: UNMASKING INVISIBLE MASCULINITY

Our survey of the contributions made by qualitative/interpretative approaches starts with the literature on gender and entrepreneurship, which has developed considerably in recent years (Ahl 2004, 2006; Bruni et al. 2004a; 2004b; 2005; Calás et al. 2007; 2009) with the purpose of evidencing the difference between study of women entrepreneurs and study of the relation between gender and entrepreneurship as intertwined practices.

The assumption of these studies is that the representations of the world communicated by language, and particularly by the discourse used to represent and codify what is meant by "knowledge", produce what they claim to represent. For example, Ahl (2006) has analysed 80 articles in the mainstream literature to show that the presupposition of a difference of sex in women entrepreneurs (although not founded on "scientific" bases) strongly influences power relations between men and women. Adopting a feminist poststructuralist analytical approach, including analytical tools from deconstruction, Ahl shows how this literature – by reproducing a gender-based polarization – risks reproducing the subordination of women.

Bruni et al. (2004b), making explicit reference to Foucault's governmentality, have proposed the neologism "entrepreneur-mentality" to highlight how an entrepreneurial discourse is mobilized as a system of thinking about women entrepreneurs which is able to make some form of that activity thinkable and practicable: who can be an entrepreneur, what entrepreneurship is, what or who is managed by that form of governance of economic relations? Discourses on women entrepreneurs are linguistic practices that create truth effects. Social studies on women entrepreneurs tend to reproduce an androcentric entrepreneur-mentality that makes hegemonic masculinity invisible.

In another study Bruni et al. (2005) illustrate the difference (and the consequences of the failure to differentiate) between studying women entrepreneurs and the assumption of a gender perspective inspired by a postmodern philosophy. They emphasize that one of the effects of gendered research on "women entrepreneurs" has been the construction of pigeonholes or labels used to classify highly diverse experiences assumed to be internally homogeneous because they pertain to a category ("woman") conceived, interpreted, and represented as "the Other". In the former case, the focus is on the differences between women entrepreneurs and the scientific standard of entrepreneurship represented as "gender-neutral" in that masculinity has been made invisible. In the latter case, the difference is framed within a system of relations. Studying gender means studying the social processes which categorize persons within a binary system, attributing to them features of masculinity or femininity, and constructing symbolic systems which are defined by difference but which are only meaningful within the reciprocal relation.

Turning to study of women entrepreneurs and of gender as a social practice, the research objective is no longer to understand why women are not "as good as men", but rather to focus on how gender and entrepreneurship are both culturally produced and reproduced in situated social practices. Several approaches have explored the gendered nature of entrepreneurship, looking at its actual "doing" and showing its production and reproduction in terms of gender relations. A central role in this process has been performed by the new wave of qualitative studies that empirically explore how the relationship between gender and entrepreneurship is performed and situationally enacted. According to this literature, one of the main reasons for choosing a qualitative approach is its appropriateness to analysing the processual nature of gendering and entrepreneuring (Bruni et al., 2005).

For example, Bruni et al. (2004a), by means of ethnographic study of two sisters running a welding firm and the editorial office of a gay and lesbian magazine, describe what the authors call an anti-heroic story. They argue that gender and entrepreneurship are discursively performed by constantly shuttling between different and dichotomous symbolic spaces. Gender and entrepreneurship are constructed through the dual presence that characterizes and situates the action of the male and female entrepreneurs studied. These men and women, in fact, regardless of their sexuality, adapted their gender performance to the situation and to the people, with whom they interacted, constantly redefining what kind of gender relations were possible and appropriate. Among the possible alternatives, the one most practised was the hegemonic masculinity (Connell 1995), because in public situations tied to market activities both males and females opted for a discursive position that conformed to the dominant discourse of a heterosexual masculinity. Moreover, gender and entrepreneurship construction negates the crossing of symbolic boundaries, thus sanctioning separation and making masculinity and heterosexuality the invisible standards of entrepreneurship. When actors behave in breach of the "ceremonial' aspects of doing gender and doing business, or when critical situations arise and order must be re-established, activating "the correct gender score" (i.e. adhering to the invisible masculinity of entrepreneurial discourse) constitutes an efficacious remedial practice.

To sum up, the contribution from this area of study reframes "doing gender" and "doing business" as the symbolic spaces of intertwined practices: home and business merge, and it is difficult to draw a clear demarcation line between public space and private space.

ETHNIC AND INDIGENOUS ENTREPRENEURING: UNMASKING GENDER AND ETHNICITY

Ethnic and indigenous entrepreneurship as a social phenomenon has long fascinated many social scientists and stimulated considerable research and debate (Portes et al.

2002; Essers and Benschop 2007; 2009; Bruton et al. 2008; Banerjee and Tedmanson 2010). In the past 30 years, many concepts and theories on ethnic and indigenous entrepreneurship have been developed, challenged, and revised to provide a fuller account of the phenomenon. Even if these studies often pertain to traditions and strands of inquiry that deal with ethnic minorities and indigenous entrepreneurs, they show that these categories of entrepreneurs often rely on cultural networks of shared language, family relationships, and the accumulation and exchange of communal social capital. Numerous studies have deconstructed hegemonic entrepreneurial standpoints (Chakrabarty 2000) and revealed other dimensions interconnected with gender, such as ethnicity, religion, and geographic context.

The first study considered in this section is one by Essers and Benschop (2007) which discusses how female entrepreneurs of Moroccan and Turkish origin in the Netherlands construct their ethnic, gender and entrepreneurial identities in relation to their Muslim identity. In this regard, it should be emphasized that "the term 'ethnic' group is always constructed relationally as it only makes sense in the context of the ethnicization of another population and involves a process of differentiation" (Anthias 2001, p. 629). Ethnicization, therefore, like other marginalization phenomena, refers to the formation of social boundaries intended to differentiate between (presumed) ethnic-cultural or religious heritages. On the basis of this interpretation, Essers and Benschop use the intersectionality of social categories of exclusion such as gender and ethnicity within entrepreneurial contexts to analyse how they are simultaneously involved in the construction of entrepreneurial identity.

In another of their works, Essers and Benschop (2009) study how Islamic identification intermeshes with gendered and ethnicized practices and experiences of inclusion and exclusion in entrepreneurial activities. Analysis of 20 life stories of migrant women and ethnic-minority entrepreneurs shows how these businesswomen give meaning to their multiple identities. On the one hand, gender – specifically femininity – and ethnicity are used as symbolic markers to illustrate the tensions between Western and Islamic norms and values; on the other, Essers and Benschop seek to understand how woman entrepreneurs adhere to or eschew possible constraints or even use them to their advantage.

Exploring four narratives, the authors show how the women interviewed performed creative boundary work at these hitherto under-researched intersections. Islam was employed as a boundary to let religious norms and values prevail over cultural ones and to make space for individualism, honour, and entrepreneurship. Moreover, different individual religious identities were crafted to stretch the boundaries of what was allowed for female entrepreneurs in order to resist traditional, dogmatic interpretations of Islam. The women studied did this by claiming the right to decide for themselves which religious rules applied to their working lives and which rules – in their eyes dogmatic – could be disregarded.

On considering the contribution of Essers and Benschop's study to the literature on entrepreneurship, it emerges that there is more than inequality and exclusion when the social categories of gender, ethnicity and Islam intersect. Analysis of the lived practices of a hitherto marginalized and understudied group of entrepreneurs demonstrates what kind of power processes emerge in the workplace at the crossroads among gender, ethnicity and religion. These female entrepreneurs gained agency and legitimacy at the intersection of gender, ethnicity and religion.

In opposition to the orientalist discourse that suggests the incompatibility of Islam and entrepreneurial identities, this area of study clearly shows that Islamic identification is compatible with gender, entrepreneurial, and ethnic identities, even though this sometimes requires creative identity work. As also shown by other studies (Shane and Venkataraman 2000), in fact, entrepreneurial identities can even be strengthened by using religion to identify innovative, new market niches. Finally, the study of these Muslim women's completion of entrepreneurship makes a situated contribution to the revision of the archetype of the white, male, individualistic, Calvinist entrepreneur.

The second study discussed here (Banerjee and Tedmanson 2010) belongs among post-colonial studies on native entrepreneurship and reports the results of two research projects exploring opportunities for indigenous enterprise development in remote locations in Northern and Central Australia.

The article discusses the barriers to economic development faced by indigenous communities in remote regions, arguing that many of these barriers are the material effect of discursive practices of "whiteness" in the political economy. The theme of the intersection of race and colonialism – little considered by the mainstream literature on entrepreneurship – is analysed in terms of "regimes of representation" and "regimes of governance" in the indigenous political economy of Australia. The analysis of a series of focus groups and in-depth interviews with indigenous community leaders, traditional owners, government officials, land council officials and other stakeholders describes how whiteness is deeply rooted in regimes of indigenous representation and governance. Whiteness emerged as a key discursive and material practice that is a source of structural advantage for the dominant culture, which assumes that its own cultural practices are normative. These assumptions inform much indigenous policy in Australia, and they have the effect of either negating or exploiting local knowledge systems.

Contrary to the classic discourse on entrepreneurship which obscures or annuls the power differentials created by whiteness, Banerjee and Tedmanson's study (2010) shows that the "taken for granted" assumption of the normativity of non-indigenous cultures produces and reproduces "white" privilege as both epistemological and ontological dominance. As the authors claim, the discourse of whiteness was a source of structural advantage for the dominant culture. One of the main contributions of this study, therefore, is to illustrate how:

> understanding whiteness through a framework of power relations allows us to see how particular Indigenous economic development and governance arrangements are racially constructed, as well as the role of capitalist modes of production in sustaining existing relations between Indigenous people and institutions and organizations that govern their everyday life (p. 159–60).

Moreover, this research has implications for organizations that operate at the interfaces of state, market and Indigenous political economy. What became evident using the authors' lens is the need for governance models involving greater Indigenous participation at policy levels, such as Indigenous organizations with the power to make decisions about their economic, cultural and social life.

SOCIAL ENTREPRENEURING: NOT ONLY GENDER BUT ALSO SOCIAL CHANGE

Studies on social entrepreneurship and entrepreneurship as social change have expanded in recent years – as shown, for example, by the collected volume edited by Steyaert and Hjorth (2006) *Entrepreneurship as Social Change*, and by the special issue edited by Steyaert and Katz (2004) entitled 'Reclaiming the space of entrepreneurship in society: Geographical, discursive and social dimensions', published by the journal *Entrepreneurship & Regional Development*, which provoked a minor revolution in the understanding of what constitutes entrepreneurship. Often, in fact, one of the main aims of these studies is to redefine the interpretative categories of entrepreneurship.

The feature shared by these studies is that they consider entrepreneurship to be a societal rather than economic phenomenon (Steyaert and Katz 2004, p. 179). As Nicholls and Young (2008, p. xii) write, the "search for a single definition [of social entrepreneurship] forms a sterile activity"; moreover, "a key part of what makes social entrepreneurship so successful is that it resists isomorphic pressures to conform to set types of action preferring instead to remain fluid and adaptable to fill institutional voids in environmental or social provision". The implicit corollary to these contentions is that various definitions of social entrepreneurship each represent political strategies because they presuppose a selection of what can be considered part of this domain, and censorship of what is to be excluded from it. What certainly unites the various approaches is their openness to innovative framings of entrepreneurship phenomena where interpretations beyond *homo economicus* and technical rationality become possible: "the discourse around social entrepreneurship has moved away from business school-centred accounts that simply applied established neo-liberal economic models and strategic approaches from the commercial world to social problems" (Nicholls and Young 2008, p. xiv).

The practical and political implications of this interpretation of entrepreneurship and social change are rendered explicit in the introduction to the already-cited special issue:

> The question around which we launch this Special Issue is how entrepreneurship is part of how our societies, communities and worlds are created, taking into account, besides economic criteria, social, cultural, political and ecological realities. This implies a study and discussion of how entrepreneurship – and the different forms and practices we can observe – takes part in creating a society we might assess politically and policy-wise based upon multi-dimensional criteria (Steyaert and Katz 2004, p. 179).

The qualitative approaches that adopt this perspective are numerous, and they yield very different results in terms of both the issues addressed and the knowledge produced (Steyaert and Dey 2010). One feature shared by all these studies is the priority that they give to the theme of social change, which is formulated with nuances and aims that differ among authors. In its most common meaning, "social change" refers to the beneficial outcome of associated economic activity: e.g., poverty alleviation (Bornstein 2004; Nicholls 2006), although this can also be understood from other standpoints – for example, from that of feminist theorizing (Calás et al. 2009).

The theme of social change is of especial importance from a social constructionist viewpoint. Entrepreneurship, both as concept and practice, emerges dynamically in social interaction among people: even in cases when one entrepreneur has indeed "singlehandedly" performed the entrepreneurial act, interaction with a social context has still taken place – through upbringing, local culture, inspiration, idea generation, support, resistance, and so forth. Therefore, the entrepreneurial process can be considered a complex web of reciprocal interactions between culturally embedded actors closely connected to each other (Lindgren and Packendorff 2006).

Given the large body of literature, and for the sake of brevity, instead of presenting specific studies that exemplify this strand of analysis, here we illustrate its three principal dimensions – each of which implies a different political choice – as identified by the special issue 'Reclaiming the space of entrepreneurship in society' (Steyaert and Katz 2004), to which we refer for examination of these specific themes:

- the geographical dimension – situated in which are spatial categories in between nations and regions, on the one hand, and neighbourhoods and circles on the other – concerns the power to occupy and reterritorialize the earth;
- the discursive dimension, which focuses on the struggle to enact these geographical spaces of entrepreneurship in a multidimensional sense rather than solely with an economic discourse (for instance, cultural, ecological and civic discourses besides the economic one);
- the social dimension, which focuses on the social process that constitutes entrepreneurship and shifts the focal point from individual entrepreneurs to the everyday processes whereby multiple actors and stakeholders are made visible as related to entrepreneurship.

The authors conclude by arguing that analysis of the geographical, discursive, and social dimension of the space in which entrepreneurship is inscribed makes it possible to explore the question of what spaces, discourses, and stakeholders have been privileged, and what other spaces, discourses and stakeholders can emerge. This is a "political" discussion because it entails stipulating new research agendas for entrepreneurship scholars. At the same time, it is not about academic finesse, but rather about taking care of the societal space in which we would want to inscribe entrepreneurship.

CONCLUSIONS

The aim of this chapter was to examine scholarly work that takes a non-positivist and qualitative approach to studying gender and entrepreneurship with a focus on a feminist empiricist perspective. The foregoing reflection on qualitative methods began with discussion and illustration of the fact that qualitative methods can be employed both within a positivist epistemology and a social constructionism. Having specified that our interest centred on non-positivist qualitative methods, we also explained that the epistemological position assumed referred to feminist empiricism, and therefore to the social construction of both gender and the categories that discursively construct entrepreneurship.

Our purpose has been to inform scholarly debates about disciplinary and methodological trends and key areas of research in entrepreneurship, as well as giving guidance as to where and how further research might be best directed in that domain. We believe this will help future research efforts to draw upon differing feminist analyses to explore the process and practice of entrepreneuring. Moreover, as other authors have pointed out (Ahl and Marlow 2012, p. 558):

> adding to the extant body of research from diverse feminist perspectives will strengthen the critical evaluation of the bounded ontology informing the current entrepreneurial research agenda. With a post-structuralist approach, this entails not merely the identification of limitations of extant approaches, but also critique and change in itself.

The array of non-positivist qualitative studies presented in the previous pages is not an exhaustive review, although it represents some of the most interesting studies in the recent qualitative literature on gender and entrepreneurship. We decided to focus on the three strands of analysis which best represent the state of the art: gender, gender and ethnicity, and social entrepreneurship. We made no attempt to cover everything but selected what in our opinion was worthy of presenting the challenges within entrepreneurial studies. We assumed an explicit feminist lens in order to conduct a critical analysis of how gender and entrepreneurship are studied.

From this epistemological positioning we illustrated two main methodological issues:

- the need for a processual understanding of entrepreneurship. We preferred to use the verb "entrepreneuring" in order to stress the difference with respect to the positivist approach that, in trying to articulate the uniqueness of entrepreneurship as an universal economic phenomenon, assumes a methodological stance that denies the contextual dynamics making these activities important for specific people, in specific locations, and for specific reasons;
- the need for a reflexive positioning of researchers vis-à-vis the object and the subjects of their research. Doing research is to produce knowledge; and it is through these knowledge-producing practices that the phenomenon under study is discursively produced. Therefore questioning the researchers' own assumptions, the interests of those participating in knowledge-production activities, and the value of the knowledge thus produced for society as a whole, become key methodological questions.

Adopting a processual ontology and concentrating on reflexive research processes makes it possible to explore dimensions of the entrepreneurial phenomenon often considered marginal. For example, the topic of gender and entrepreneurship as intertwined social practices enables one to show that the hegemonic discourse on entrepreneurship renders the masculinity of the latter invisible. By means of deconstructionist research techniques and a post-structuralist approach to the analysis of texts, this line of inquiry unmasks the alleged neutrality of the entrepreneurial figure to show that the stereotypical image of the male, Western, white, and Calvinist entrepreneur is the outcome of a discursive construction in which participates the mainstream literature on entrepreneurship that takes masculinity to be the standard for entrepreneurial activity in its entirety.

A second example that destabilizes taken-for-granted categories derives from study of entrepreneuring as a complex set of social activities and processes. It applies the concept of intersectionality (Özbilgin et al. 2011) to illustrate how gender, class, ethnicity, and religion interact in the construction of social categories defining how entrepreneurship is constructed and performed. Finally, a post-colonialist approach also contributes to destabilizing the categories that construct entrepreneurship studies as Western economic phenomena.

A third example, which can be considered the continuation of the previous two, openly raises the issue of social change and knowledge production as emancipationist. Studies on entrepreneurship as social change furnish the most significant methodological recommendation: namely that by exploring the geographical, discursive and social dimension of the space in which entrepreneurship becomes inscribed, it is possible to explore the question of which spaces, discourses and stakeholders have been privileged, and what other spaces, discourses and stakeholders may emerge.

We shall not dwell on the details of specific methodologies, such as ethnography, narrative analysis, or deconstruction; nor on individual techniques (for which the reader is referred to the more detailed discussions conducted in the majority of the works cited). We wish, however, to direct the reader's attention to the active role of the researcher in doing research. Many of the studies cited, in fact, not only contain thorough discussion of the reflexive aspects of doing research but also highlight two key methodological considerations never made explicit in the mainstream literature:

- the flexibility of human exchanges and the ambiguity of interpretations;
- the practices of "doing knowledge" of researchers as integral to theory development and research on entrepreneurship.

NOTE

1. The present article is the outcome of joint and indivisible work by the authors; however if for academic reasons individual authorship is to be assigned, Silvia Gherardi wrote the introduction and the conclusions and Manuela Perrotta wrote the other sections.

REFERENCES

Ahl, H. (2004), *The Scientific Reproduction of Gender Inequality; A Discourse Analysis of Research Texts on Women's Entrepreneurship*, Malmö: Liber AB.
Ahl, H. (2006), 'Why research on women entrepreneurs needs new directions', *Entrepreneurship: Theory and Practice*, **30**, 595–621.
Ahl, H. and S. Marlow (2012), 'Exploring the dynamics of gender, feminism and entrepreneurship: advancing debate to escape a dead end?' *Organization*, **19**(5), 543–62.
Aldrich, H. (1992), 'Methods in our madness? Trends in entrepreneurship research', in Sexton, D.L. and J.D. Kasarda, *The State of the Art of Entrepreneurship*, Boston, MA: PWS–Kent Publishing Company.
Anthias, F. (2001), 'New hybrid ties, old concepts: The limits of "culture"', *Ethnic and Racial Studies*, **24**(4), 619–41.
Armstrong, P. (2005), *Critique of Entrepreneurship: People and Policy*, New York, NY: Palgrave MacMillan.
Banerjee, S.B. and D. Tedmanson (2010), 'Grass burning under our feet: Indigenous enterprise development in a political economy of whiteness', *Management Learning*, **41**(2), 147–65.
Bornstein, D. (2004), *How to Change the World: Social Entrepreneurs and the Power of New Ideas*, Oxford: Oxford University Press.
Bruni, A., S. Gherardi and B. Poggio (2004a), 'Doing gender, doing entrepreneurship: An ethnographic account of intertwined practices', *Gender, Work and Organization*, **11**(4), 406–29.
Bruni, A., S. Gherardi and B. Poggio (2004b), 'Entrepreneur-mentality, gender and the study of women entrepreneurs', *Journal of Organizational Change Management*, **17**, 256–68.

Bruni, A., S. Gherardi and B. Poggio (2005), *Gender and Entrepreneurship. An Ethnographic Approach*, London and New York, N.Y.: Routledge.

Bruton, G., D. Ahlstrom and K. Obloj (2008), 'Entrepreneurship in emerging economies: Where are we today and where should the research go in the future', *Entrepreneurship: Theory & Practice*, **32**(1), 1–14.

Bull, I. and G.E. Willard, G.E. (1993), 'Towards a theory of entrepreneurship', *Journal of Business Venturing*, **8**(3), 183–95.

Burrell, G. and G. Morgan (2003), *Sociological Paradigms and Organisational Analysis*, Aldershot: Ashgate Publishing Limited (12th reprint).

Busenitz, L.W., G.P. III West, D. Shepherd, T. Nelson, G.N Chandler and A. Zacharakis (2003), 'Entrepreneurship research in emergence: Past trends and future directions', *Journal of Management*, **29**, 285–308.

Bygrave, W. (1989), 'The entrepreneurship paradigm (I): A philosophical look at its research Methodologies', *Entrepreneurship: Theory and Practice*, **14**(1): 7–26.

Calás, M.B., L. Smircich and K.A. Bourne (2007), 'Knowing Lisa? Feminist analyses of gender and entrepreneurship,' in Bilimoria, D. and S.K. Piderit (Eds), *Handbook on Women in Business and Management*, Cheltenham UK and Northampton, MA, USA: Edward Elgar, 78–105.

Calás, M.B., L. Smircich and K.A. Bourne (2009), 'Extending the boundaries: reframing "entrepreneurship as social change" through feminist perspectives', *Academy of Management Review*, **34**(3), 552–69.

Chakrabarty, D. (2000), *Provincializing Europe: Postcolonial Thought*, Princeton: Princeton University Press.

Chandler, G.N. and D.W. Lyon (2001), 'Issues of research design and construct measurement in entrepreneurship research: the past decade', *Entrepreneurship: Theory and Practice*, **25**, 101–13.

Chell, E. (2000), 'Towards researching the opportunistic entrepreneur: a social constructionist approach and research agenda', *European Journal of Work and Organisational Psychology*, **9**, 63–80.

Chell, E. and L. Pittaway (1998), 'The social construction of entrepreneurship', Paper presented at the *Institute of Small Business Affairs 21st National Small Firms Policy and Research Conference*, Durham University, 18–20 November.

Collins, O.F. and D.G. Moore (1964), *The Enterprising Man*, East Lansing, MI: Michigan State University Press.

Connell, R.W. (1995), *Masculinities*, London: University of California Press.

Czarniawska, B. (2011), 'How to study gender inequality in organizations?' in Jeanes, E.L., D. Knights and P.Y. Martin (Eds), *Handbook of Gender, Work and Organization*, Chichester, UK: Wiley, 81–108.

Davidsson, P. and J. Wiklund (2001), 'Levels of analysis in entrepreneurship research: Current research practice and suggestions for the future', *Entrepreneurship: Theory and Practice*, **25**, 81–99.

Edelman, L., C. Brush and T. Manolova (2008), 'Entrepreneurship education: correspondence between practices of nascent entrepreneurs and textbook prescriptions for success', *Academy of Management Learning and Education*, **7**(1), 56–70.

Essers, C. (2009), 'Reflections on the narrative approach: dilemmas of power, emotions and social location while constructing life-stories', *Organization*, **16**(2), 163–81.

Essers, C. and Y. Benschop (2007), 'Enterprising Identities: Female entrepreneurs of Moroccan and Turkish origin in the Netherlands', *Organization Studies*, **28**(1), 49–69.

Essers, C. and Y. Benschop (2009), 'Muslim businesswomen doing boundary work: The negotiation of Islam, gender and ethnicity within entrepreneurial contexts', *Human Relations*, **62**(3), 403–23.

Gartner, W.B. (2007), 'Entrepreneurial narrative and a science of the imagination', *Journal of Business Venturing*, **22**(5), 613–27.

Gartner, W., B. Bird and J. Starr (1992), 'Acting as if: differentiating entrepreneurial from organizational behavior', *Entrepreneurship: Theory and Practice*, **16**(3), 13–31.

Gartner, W.B. and S. Birley (2002), 'Introduction to the special issue on qualitative methods in entrepreneurship research', *Journal of Business Venturing*, **17**(5), 387–95.

Gherardi, S. (2011), 'Ways of knowing: Gender as a politics of knowledge?' in Jeanes, E.L., D. Knights and P.Y. Martin (Eds), *Handbook of Gender, Work and Organization*, Chichester, UK: Wiley, 37–49.

Grant, P. and L. Perren (2002), 'Small business and entrepreneurial research. Meta-theories, paradigms and prejudices', *International Small Business Journal*, **20**, 185–211.

Harding, S. (ed.) (2004), *The Feminist Standpoint Reader*, New York: Routledge.

Hjorth, D. and C. Steyaert (Eds) (2004), *Narrative and Discursive Approaches in Entrepreneurship*, Cheltenham, UK and Northampton, MA, USA: Edward Elgar.

Hjorth, D. and C. Steyaert (Eds) (2009a), *The Politics and Aesthetics of Entrepreneurship: A Fourth Movements in Entrepreneurship Book*, Cheltenham UK and Northampton, MA, USA: Edward Elgar.

Hjorth, D.and C. Steyaert (Eds) (2009b), 'Entrepreneurship as disruptive event', in Hjorth, D. and C. Steyaert (Eds) (2009). *The Politics and Aesthetics of Entrepreneurship: A Fourth Movement in Entrepreneurship*. Cheltenham UK and Northampton, MA, USA: Edward Elgar, 1–12.

Hjorth, D. and C. Steyaert (Eds) (2009c), 'Moving entrepreneurship: an Incipiency', in Hjorth, D. and C. Steyaert (Eds) (2009), *The Politics and Aesthetics of Entrepreneurship: A Fourth Movements in Entrepreneurship Book*, Cheltenham UK and Northampton, MA, USA: Edward Elgar, 221–9.

Jennings, P., L. Perren and S. Carter (2005), ''Guest editors' introduction: Alternative perspectives on entrepreneurship research', *Entrepreneurship: Theory and Practice*, **29**(2), 145–52.

Jones, C. and A. Spicer (2009), *Unmasking the Entrepreneur*, Cheltenham, UK and Northampton, MA, USA: Edward Elgar.

Karataş-Özkan, M. (2011), 'Understanding relational qualities of entrepreneurial learning: towards a multi-layered approach', *Entrepreneurship and Regional Development*, **23**(9–10), 877–906.

Knight, F.H. (1921), *Risk, Uncertainty and Profit*, Boston, MA: Houghton Mifflin.

Lindgren, M. and J. Packendorff (2006), 'Entrepreneurship as boundary work: deviating from and belonging to community', in Steyaert, C. and D. Hjorth (Eds) (2006), *Entrepreneurship as Social Change*, Cheltenham UK and Northampton, MA, USA: Edward Elgar, 210–30.

Lindgren, M. and J. Packendorff (2009), 'Social constructionism and entrepreneurship. Basic assumptions and consequences for theory and research', *International Journal of Entrepreneurial Behaviour & Research*, **15**(1), 25–47.

Lounsbury, M. and M.A. Glynn (2001), 'Cultural entrepreneurship: Stories, legitimacy and the acquisition of resources', *Strategic Management Journal*, **22**, 545–64.

McDonald, S., B.C. Gan and A. Anderson (2004), 'Studying entrepreneurship: A review of methods employed in entrepreneurship research 1985–2004', Paper presented at *RENT XVIII*, Copenhagen, Denmark, 25–26 November.

Neergaard, H. and J.P. Ulhøi (Eds) (2007), *Handbook of Qualitative of Research Methods in Entrepreneurship*, Cheltenham UK and Northampton, MA, USA: Edward Elgar.

Nicholls, A. (ed.) (2006), *Social Entrepreneurship: New Models of Sustainable Social Change*, Oxford: Oxford University Press.

Nicholls, A. and R. Young (2008), 'Introduction: The changing landscape of social entrepreneurship', in Nicholls A. (ed.), *Social Entrepreneurship: New Models of Sustainable Social Change*, Oxford: Oxford University Press, Paperback edition vii–xxiii.

O'Connor, E. (2004), 'Storytelling to be real: narrative, legitimacy building and venturing', in Hjorth, D. and C. Steyaert (Eds) (2004). *Narrative and Discursive Approaches in Entrepreneurship*, Cheltenham, UK and Northampton, MA, USA: Edward Elgar, 105–24.

Ogbor, J.O. (2000), 'Mythicizing and reification in entrepreneurial discourse: Ideology-critique of entrepreneurial studies', *Journal of Management Studies*, **37**(5), 605–35.

Özbilgin, M., T.A. Beauregard, A. Tatli, and M.P. Bell (2011), 'Work-life, diversity and intersectionality: A critical review and research agenda', *International Journal of Management Reviews*, **13**, 177–98.

Piperopoulos, P. (2010), 'Qualitative research in SMEs and entrepreneurship: A literature review of case study research', *International Journal of Economics and Business Research*, **2**(6), 494–510.

Pittaway, L. (2005), 'Philosophies in entrepreneurship: a focus on economic theories', *International Journal of Entrepreneurial Behaviour & Research*, **11**(3), 201–21.

Portes, A., W. Haller and L. Guarnizo (2002), 'Transnational entrepreneurs: An alternative form of immigrant economic adaption', *American Sociological Review*, **67**(4), 278–98.

Salerno, J.T. (2008), 'The entrepreneur: Real and imagined', *Quarterly Journal of Austrian Economics*, **11**, 188–207.

Schumpeter, J.A. (1934), *The Theory of Economic Development*, Cambridge: Harvard University Press.

Seale, C. (1999), *The Quality of Qualitative Research*, London: Sage.

Shane, S. and S. Venkataraman (2000), 'The promise of entrepreneurship as a field of research', *Academy of Management Review*, **25**, 217–26.

Steyaert, C. (1997), 'A qualitative methodology for process studies of entrepreneurship: Creating local knowledge through stories', *International Studies of Management and Organization*, **27**(3), 13–33.

Steyaert, C. (2007), ''Entrepreneuring' as a conceptual attractor? A review of process theories in 20 years of entrepreneurship studies', *Entrepreneurship and Regional Development*, **19**(6), 453–77.

Steyaert, C. and P. Dey (2010), 'Nine verbs to keep the social entrepreneurship research agenda ''dangerous''', *Journal of Social Entrepreneurship*, **1**(2), 231–54.

Steyaert, C. and D. Hjorth (Eds) (2003), *New Movements in Entrepreneurship*, Cheltenham, UK and Northampton, MA, USA: Edward Elgar.

Steyaert, C. and D. Hjorth (Eds) (2006), *Entrepreneurship as Social Change*, Cheltenham, UK and Northampton, MA, USA: Edward Elgar.

Steyaert, C. and J. Katz (2004), 'Reclaiming the space of entrepreneurship in society: Geographical, discursive and social dimensions', *Entrepreneurship & Regional Development*, **16**(3), 179–96.

Suchman, M.C. (1995), 'Managing legitimacy: strategic and institutional approaches', *Academy of Management Review*, **20**, 571–610.

Tedmanson, D., C. Essers, K. Verduyn and W. Gartner (2012), 'Critical perspectives in entrepreneurship research', *Organization*, **19**(5) 531–41.
Tracey, S.J. (2010), 'Qualitative quality: Eight "big-tent" criteria for excellent qualitative research', *Qualitative Inquiry*, **16**(10), 837–51.
Weiskopf, R. and C. Steyaert (2009), 'Metamorphoses in entrepreneurship studies: towards affirmative politics of entrepreneuring', in Hjorth, D. and C. Steyaert (Eds) (2009), *The Politics and Aesthetics of Entrepreneurship: A Fourth Movements in Entrepreneurship Book*, Cheltenham UK and Northampton, MA, USA: Edward Elgar, 183–200.
Winter, G. (2000), 'A comparative discussion of the notion of "validity" in qualitative and quantitative research', *The Qualitative Report*, 4(3–4), on-line serial, available at http://www.nova.edu/ssss/QR/QR4-3/winter.html.

9. Mathematics and entrepreneurship research[1]
Maria Minniti and Moren Lévesque

> As a formal model of an economy acquires a mathematical life of its own, it becomes the object of an inexorable process in which rigor, generality, and simplicity are relentlessly pursued.
>
> *(Debreu, 1986, p.1265)*

1. INTRODUCTION

While economics, psychology, political science and some areas of sociology make extensive use of mathematics, organizational and management research rarely does so. This is unfortunate because mathematics can be utilized to describe phenomena, build new theories, and refine existing ones. In this chapter, we discuss why and how mathematics can provide important contributions to the study of entrepreneurship. Indeed, we argue that research in entrepreneurship offers a compelling case for the use of mathematics. Building theory in entrepreneurship is difficult because it often involves a multi-level analysis, where the analysis needs to move between the individual, group, firm or population level (Davidson and Wiklund, 2001; Busenitz et al., 2003; West, 1997). Unlike other methods, mathematics enables researchers to structure relationships between various levels of analysis, and can therefore encourage more theory development in entrepreneurship.

The number and type of research questions in the area of entrepreneurship that can be described mathematically is virtually endless. These include (but are not limited to) identifying thresholds of accumulated knowledge on which the attractiveness of an opportunity is assessed; characterizing how varying environmental conditions affect market entry or entrepreneurial behavior; identifying the relationship between entrepreneurship and economic growth; analyzing the emergence of alternative levels and concentration of entrepreneurial activity in a region; and studying the characteristics of entrepreneurial behavior in families and groups. The number of mathematical methods that can be used to tackle these questions is also considerable. They include (but are not limited to) game theory, complexity theory, Markov decision processes, dynamic programming, and simulation techniques.

Mathematical modeling allows the researcher to formalize assumptions, constraints, relationships, and implied propositions and algorithms. It forces the researcher to be precise about the assumptions that are made and the concepts that are utilized. In doing so, the researcher is also forced to clearly structure the phenomena to be studied and, as a result, the research question(s). In addition to being parsimonious and accurate, mathematical models can also accommodate multiple variables, parameters and functional forms, and can identify definitive tests in ways that other methods do not allow (see, e.g., Lévesque and Minniti, 2011).

The purpose of this chapter is to demonstrate that a mathematical model can be an effective tool for theory development in entrepreneurship research. Specifically, we hope to: 1) help entrepreneurship researchers develop a greater appreciation for mathematical models; and 2) encourage these scholars to equip themselves with the tools necessary for mathematical thinking. Section 2 reviews the widespread use of mathematics in the social sciences and locates entrepreneurship research in this context. Section 3 discusses the features of mathematical thinking and methods that make it particularly useful for entrepreneurship research. Section 4 articulates how and why mathematics provides the tools necessary to the development of complete and consistent theories. Section 5 reviews briefly some branches of mathematics that have been already successfully used in entrepreneurship research, and suggests some areas of entrepreneurship that, in our opinion, could benefit particularly from the use of a mathematical approach. Finally, Section 6 wraps up our argument.

2. ENTREPRENEURSHIP, THE SOCIAL SCIENCES AND MATHEMATICS

Entrepreneurship is a complex and multi-layered phenomenon. Although it is sometimes narrowly identified with the creation of new firms or with self-employment, this is done primarily for empirical and operationalization purposes. Entrepreneurship, however, is a much broader topic. Kirzner (1973; 1979), for example, defines entrepreneurship as the alertness and exploitation of existing opportunities. Shane and Venkataraman (2000) view entrepreneurship as the identification, evaluation, and exploitation of opportunities, and Shane (2012, p.10) describes entrepreneurship as "a process rather than an event or embodiment of a type of person." Finally, Koppl and Minniti (2010) build on Mises' ideas and describe entrepreneurship as a universal characteristic of human action. As a result, much of our understanding of it results from insights rooted in the social sciences applied, among others, to questions of innovation, creativity, organizations and management. In other words, much of entrepreneurship research and its insights rest with the disciplinary groundings and methods of economics, psychology, sociology, and political science among others, and with some of their more applied and specific counterparts such as strategy or organization theory. Within this context, the usefulness of mathematics for the study of entrepreneurship emerges organically from the overwhelming evidence that mathematics has always been a required tool of the social sciences.

What do we mean by mathematics? Several definitions are possible. In this chapter, "mathematics" refers to a method of reasoning and covers the use of mathematical logic and methods. Several historians of the social sciences agree that the late eighteenth century marked the end of the time when social thinkers stopped being primarily concerned with man's place in the universe and his relation to God (Senn, 2000).[2] During this time the idea of *social science*, in other words, the idea that the scientific study of man is possible took hold, and the social sciences began the specialization and differentiation that characterizes them today. Initially, the extent to which early thinkers on social subjects used mathematics varied greatly, and progress in the use of mathematics in social thought was, to some extent, determined by the state of mathematics at the time. Yet, already in 1762, one of the major classics in political science, Rousseau's

(1948[1762]) Social Contract used elementary mathematics to develop an argument that had more influence on political thought and action in the eighteenth century than any other work (Senn, 2000).

Initially, the dominant force driving the use of mathematics in the development of social thought was the desire to provide answers to important macroeconomic issues. Even before Adam Smith, social thinkers had developed an appreciation for numerical information (data) and the statistical and mathematical tools necessary to manipulate them in order to analyze political and economic systems and the effects of alternative policies. At about the same time, one of the great prerequisites of modern science emerged; namely, the consciousness that the critical and systematic building of new knowledge on existing knowledge is a necessary condition for the advancement of science and for the scientific process itself.

Importantly, in the eighteenth and nineteenth centuries, early in the history of the social sciences, because of geographical, logistic and political constraints, researchers kept their distinctive cultural differences, and the emergence of the various disciplines was marked by different approaches. It was only when the use of mathematics became widespread that these differences could be leveraged into a strength. The use of mathematics received further impetus from economics which adopted a mathematical approach early on and became regarded as the "queen of the social sciences". More recently, the use of mathematics has been further encouraged by the advance of computerization which allows researchers to tackle more complex social and economic problems by using mathematical modeling tools. Thus, mathematics became an important reason for the universality of the social sciences. As Senn (2000) argues, mathematics became the lingua franca of social science (and science in general) forcing, among other things, researchers to strive for rigor and coherence. Although it took a long time, thinkers finally arrived at the conclusion that individuals and society could be studied scientifically and, as that realization spread, mathematics emerged as an integral part of the social sciences which, by their very nature, could not exist without it.

Thus, a mathematical approach to entrepreneurship research conforms to the broader requirement of the scientific method. A mathematical approach to developing theory represents relationships mathematically through a model. The implications of the model (called propositions) arise from the logic of solving the mathematical problem. These propositions are not abstract but are direct implications of the assumptions and logic provided through the mathematical formulation. In other words, the model and its implications are the first step of a Popperian scientific process that guides the formulation of hypotheses to be tested.

3.   ADVANTAGES OF MATHEMATICS IN ENTREPRENEURSHIP RESEARCH

Mathematics allows entrepreneurship research to fit and conform to the broader requirements of the scientific method.[3] Several scholars (e.g., Kantorovich, 1989; Dillmann et al., 2000) have provided different, although complementary, lists of the characteristics of mathematics that make its applications to the social sciences desirable. We complement their analysis and identify five features of mathematics that, in our opinion, make it particularly desirable and useful for entrepreneurship research. These features are consistency, generalizability, simplicity, efficiency and robustness.

3.1 Consistency

Mathematics consists of a system in which transformation rules dictate how to derive logical truths from established axioms. In other words, mathematics is an axiomatic system consisting of a set of un-interpreted symbols and transformation rules that indicate how to generate new strings of symbols. These symbols can only be interpreted if a meaning is assigned to them. Mathematical reasoning is a way to use these symbols and their combinations to produce logical deductions; its axioms secure logical consistency in reasoning. Of course, mathematical reasoning is not the only way to achieve logically consistent reasoning. Yet, mathematical reasoning facilitates consistency and allows to control easily for it. Thus, the use of mathematics is useful and helpful, especially in preventing researchers from following the wrong intuition. Take as an example decision-making; when making a decision, an individual may explain the reasons behind that decision using an informal verbal argument. In this case, the reasoning that produced the decision is explained using informal logic. While informal logic is useful and effective, we know it is also subject to biases and errors which are difficult to detect and may lead to sub optimal decisions. By forcing the decision-maker to explain the reasons behind the decision using formal logic (historically called symbolic logic) and established and coherent rules, mathematics ensures that the structure of the argumentation, its relationship of claims, premises, relations of implication, and conclusion, contain no contradictions and inconsistency. In a sense, we can say that mathematics has no bad days. When applied to specific topics, entrepreneurship issues in our case, the real importance of the results can only be judged by the quality of its underlying logic, the adequacy of the process of measurement, the correspondence of reality with its formalization by mathematical operators, and the adequacy of the realism of variables.

3.2 Generalizability

Mathematical models are applicable to a variety of situations and under various conditions because they can accommodate multiple variables, parameters, and functional forms. They are, therefore, generalizable. The function of science, as seen by Braithwaite (1955), is to "establish general laws covering the behaviors of the empirical events or objects with which the science in question is concerned, and thereby to enable us to connect together our knowledge of the separately known events, and to make reliable predictions of events as yet unknown" (p.1). These general laws are more likely to be derived from the use of a methodology that is applicable under various conditions. The achievement of generalizability is, to a large degree, a fundamental goal of mathematics-based entrepreneurship research. Increasing generalizability leads to more significant and robust contributions, although it may also increase the complexity of the analysis. The increased complexity emerging from generalizability stems from the fact that general mathematical models do not require the ad hoc imposition of specific functional forms governing the relationships among variables. In other words, the specific type of relationship existing between the variables emerges endogenously from the model. For instance, in the case of entrepreneurship, an entrepreneur's market entry decision could depend on the quality of her product, which, in turn, could be modeled as $q_t = \sum_{i=1}^{t} X_i$, where Σ is a summation operator and X_i represent potential improvements in product quality from time period $I = 1$ to t. Testable propositions about when the entrepreneur should enter the market could then be derived assuming alternatively that the expected product quality will improve, get worse or stay the same. Of course, researchers have to be aware of the fact that the generality of assumptions does not necessarily accompany empirical relevance in an entrepreneurial context.

3.3   Simplicity

Mathematical models allow relationships and outcomes to be disentangled from a large quantity of information. They can be simple and still be useful for a broad set of applications, as illustrated by the following example borrowed from physics.[4] Newton defined momentum p as the product of mass m and velocity v, that is, $p = mv$. This definition is accurate for both everyday applications and not everyday applications (such as the space shuttle moving objects in space) and has been utilized for several hundred years. Of course, there may be situations where the application of a simple model is at the cost of losing accuracy. If a mathematical model must be complicated because of the complexity of the phenomenon under study, then multiple concrete examples can be offered to guide the reader in interpreting the phenomenon. Extensive numerical or simulation analyses can also be used when appropriate. Mathematics lends itself better than any other method to a *divide-and-conquer* strategy, where a complex problem is divided into multiple parts from which a set solution is identified, and where results are then put together like pieces of a puzzle from which it is then possible to gather the complete picture of a complex problem.

3.4   Efficiency

Mathematics promotes computability and the concordance of means with the problem to be analyzed. In doing so, mathematics makes both theoretical and empirical work technically efficient and cost effective. The formal logic of mathematics lends itself well to empirical verification via hypothesis testing. In other words, from formally logical argument it is possible to derive definitive statements about facts and cause-and-effects relationship. Whether these statements, which we call propositions, are in fact observed in reality can be discovered by verifying them with data, which we call hypothesis testing. There is "no genuine progress in scientific insight through the Baconian method of accumulating empirical facts without hypotheses or anticipation of nature. Without some guiding idea we do not know what facts to gather" (Cohen, 1956, p.148). Mathematics adds structure to the description and analysis of a situation, thereby focusing the researchers' attention on the conditions under which implications of a theory are true. Furthermore, it forces one to be precise about both the assumptions made and the concepts utilized. Mathematics facilitates the articulation of model assumptions, relationships among variables, and testable implications. This is especially useful in situations (common in the entrepreneurial arena) where a hierarchy exists among the various elements of the model (which usually involves movements between various levels of analysis). For example, the study of cognition tells us that entrepreneurial propensity varies across individuals but that across countries, we should expect the distribution of individuals across various levels of entrepreneurial propensity to be similar. Observation, however, tells us that certain countries do have more entrepreneurs than others. Mathematics allows us to build a general model of the relationship between human cognition and entrepreneurship, to link it logically to the aggregate level of entrepreneurship, and to show that country-specific institutions, by altering incentives, cause some countries to emerge as more entrepreneurial than others. It is then possible to isolate the key cause-effect relationships in this model and test them against real world data to see whether the theory holds true.

3.5   Robustness

By making explicit what is hidden implicitly in the premises, mathematics helps identify definitive tests. That is, within the assumptions of the mathematical model, testable hypotheses (propositions) are derived and proofs of these hypotheses are objectively reached. This *objectivity* is an important part of the scientific approach (see Buchler (1955) and Kerlinger (1979) for further discussions of objectivity). New proofs are required when varying assumptions, but these proofs offer the same level of objectivity. A robustness analysis identifies circumstances under which a model's outcomes are invariable to changing assumptions and may have important implications when selecting model parameters for empirical validity. Parameters that are proven independent of outcomes provide control variables, and if these parameters affect outcomes in the empirical analysis, then important new directions for modeling and/or explaining the phenomenon under study can be suggested.

Taken together, the five properties of consistency, generalizability, simplicity, efficiency, and robustness highlight the features that make the use of mathematics necessary in science and, in our opinion, invaluable in entrepreneurship research. This is the case because these features guarantee the objectivity, parsimony, logical coherence and robustness of the research method.

4.   USING MATHEMATICS TO DEVELOP ENTREPRENEURSHIP THEORY

Given the properties just described, one of the main purposes of mathematical modeling is, of course, theory building. A mathematical model begins with a set of assumptions that demarcate the environment being analyzed. Some of these assumptions are structural (i.e., they make the analysis tractable without influencing the environment), while others are substantive (i.e., they define the distinctive features of the environment under study). A mathematical model allows the quick identification and analysis of the *what*, the *how*, the *why*, and taken altogether the *who*, *where*, and *when* of an environment and, therefore, allows for the development of a complete theory (Dubin, 1978; Whetten, 1989).

The variables and parameters that are parts of the explanation of the studied phenomenon constitute the *what*. For example, the profitability of an identified opportunity and the knowledge and resources required to exploit it constitute the variables and parameters used to explain the action of entrepreneurial entry. The functional forms selected to describe the relationships among these variables and concepts, instead, describe *how* the elements of the model are related and whether causal linkages are present. For example, the profitability of an opportunity can be modeled as a function of (being dependent upon) the human capital (knowledge) of the entrepreneur, the physical and financial resources he or she has available, and the state of the economy. Alternative functional forms (e.g., linear, Cobb-Douglas, or exponential) allow the illustration of exactly how such variables interact and contribute to determine the profitability of that opportunity. The structure of the model must also be incentive compatible. That is, the linkages between variables must be logically consistent with *why* the actors would choose particular actions above others. For example, why certain resources are included in the production function would have to be logically sensible and consistent with reality.

In addition, the *who*, *where*, and *when* questions set the boundaries of generalizability, that is, they delimit the assumptions within which the logic of the model developed applies. Some of these assumptions may be straightforwardly justifiable (e.g., level of entrepreneurial experience increases as an entrepreneur spends more time in his or her venture), they may be based on extant literature (e.g., a new venture's likelihood of survival increases over time after a honeymoon period), others may be necessary to construct a model that is tractable or to define sufficiently the distinctive characteristics of the problem under study (of course, wrong assumptions are undesirable – e.g., a probability cannot be negative). For example, a profit maximization problem may be tailored to describe a specific entrepreneur's entry in one particular sector in a predetermined economic condition.

In summary, a mathematical approach to developing theories represents relationships through interdependent functional forms and its implications (propositions) arise from the logic of solving the problem. These propositions are not abstract, but are direct implications of the assumptions and the logic provided through their mathematical formulation. Importantly, outcomes of mathematical models (also referred to as theorems and propositions) can both complement or challenge existing knowledge. Lévesque and Shepherd (2002), for example, utilize such a model to demonstrate a nonlinear relationship between the likelihood of earlier entry and the marginal effect of competitive rivalry on the probability of exit. Scientific knowledge is different than commonsense knowledge. "Science acquires a reach far beyond the limits of our unaided senses" (Feigl, 1953, p.13). A nonlinear relationship may also be missed by empirical analyses because the range of values for the parameter is limited by, among other things, the characteristics (e.g., size) of the firms that are sampled and/or the selected industries. A mathematical model, by contrast, can consider an unrestricted set of numerical values for the parameter (except, perhaps, for a non-negativity condition – e.g., a probability can never be a negative number). Consequently, the set of testable propositions (theories) can be expanded, thanks to the use of a mathematical approach.

Of course, like any other method, the use of mathematics in entrepreneurship research has also some limits. As a result, its use has been the subject of some criticisms, some justified, other unjustified. The more common unjustified criticism on the use of mathematics in entrepreneurship research (and in most social sciences) is whether the construction of mathematical models yields substantial results. For example, the question is sometimes raised whether mathematical models accurately describe entrepreneurial facts or behaviors. Within this context, it is often argued that theoretical formal models either ignore or underrate the complexities characterizing entrepreneurship in the real world. As implicitly demonstrated by our earlier discussion, however, this type of criticism is primarily caused by a lack of mathematical training and by a lack of understanding of what a mathematical model really is and how it works. A different, but related criticism is that mathematics is often reductionist in the sense of trying to explain the nature of complex things by reducing them to simpler or more fundamental things, or to assume that a complex system is nothing but the sum of its parts. Mathematics, of course, is all but reductionist. Recent development in complexity theory (discussed below) and the pervasive use of non-linearity and increasing returns in recent mathematical approaches to social science show the exact contrary. This is not to deny, of course, that the display of mathematical technique for its own sake is useless and should be avoided (Baumol, 1993), and that, like any other method, the usefulness of mathematics in entrepreneurship research hinges on its correct and appropriate use.

A more reasonable and useful category of criticisms accepts the use of mathematics, but is concerned with how the latter is used. Errors of logic, mathematical mistakes, and the kind of mathematics that is appropriate for a given problem are the proper concerns of these kinds of criticisms. This category of criticisms is useful and contributes to improving the quality of mathematical work in the social sciences. Errors are made and need to be identified and corrected. Because of their replicability, mathematical results can be verified and corrected much more easily than those produced with other methods (e.g., reproducing a statistical test can be difficult when the reviewer or researcher does not have access to the raw data). Scientists must be able to use any tools they see fit to tackle their research questions. Their peers will judge the results and, in the long run, accept or reject them.

5. EXEMPLARY BRANCHES OF MATHEMATICS

So far, we have argued that mathematical thinking and the resulting models lend themselves well to entrepreneurship research. Some branches of mathematics, however, are particularly useful for the study of specific aspects of the entrepreneurial process. Examples are game theory, complexity theory, dynamic programming, and multiple criteria decision analysis. In this section we review briefly these branches of mathematics and their characteristics.

5.1 Game Theory

Most decisions should not (and often cannot) be made in isolation. Particularly in business, the reactions of other decision-makers must be taken into consideration to achieve better (more strategic) outcomes. Game theory is a mathematics-based approach that can do just this by explicitly modeling the behavior of others. As Rasmusen (1991) puts it: "[g]ame theory is concerned with the actions of individuals who are conscious that their actions affect each other" (p.21). According to Dixit and Nalebuff (1991), game theory is the science of thinking strategically. Game theoretic modeling thus involves the study of strategic interactions among rational players (that can be individuals, organizations or countries) and where the nature and timing of the game determine whether competition or cooperation prevail among the players.

Saloner (1991) made the case for the use of game theory in strategic management, arguing that the role for game theory (and more generally mathematical modeling) should be metaphorical. That is, the resulting models are not providing algorithms to be calibrated with data and used to predict what actions should be taken (like one might see, e.g., with an inventory model). Instead, by providing an *audit trail* of assumptions (i.e., the logical steps that lie beneath the formal propositions), the possibility of creating novel and surprising insights (with the audit trail allowing to check back to the driving assumptions to explain the surprise), and by building on a common language that allows results to be compared across models, "the model provides well-reasoned arguments by which one can proceed from the assumptions to the conclusions" (p.126). These arguments allow one to identify tradeoffs, which in turn help answer *why*, for instance, a first mover advantage might, or not, result in higher payoffs.

In fact, game theory is one of the branches of mathematics more often applied to the study of organizations and, lately, is being increasingly used in entrepreneurship research. This is perhaps not surprising since the entrepreneurship field, historically, has been populated by researchers with a strategy background and strategists value game theory (Saloner, 1991, Joglekar and Lévesque, forthcoming). For example, Elitzur and Gavious (2003a) examine the relationship between an entrepreneur and a venture capitalist on multiple time periods, enabling them to investigate strategic behavior over time. Elitzur and Gavious (2003b) go further by adding an angel investor to the game in order to study the dynamics in that three-party relationship. They characterize the equilibrium contracts between all parties and observe inefficiencies in the behavior of entrepreneurs and venture capitalists that encourage the free-rider phenomenon. More recently, Fairchild (2011) explored the effects of economic and behavioral characteristics on an entrepreneur's choice between a venture capitalist and a business angel.

The economic literature in industrial organization (e.g., through the *Rand Journal of Economics*) provides a large number of examples in which firms' and individuals' actions are described using game theory. Similarly, from the innovation literature, Harhoff et al. (2003) investigate the decisions of manufactured products' end users to freely reveal the proprietary innovations they develop around these products. A game theory formulation allows them to articulate conditions (e.g., in the presence of complementary capabilities) under which these innovators will benefit from freely revealing their information to others in the supply chain. Adner (2002) is also a classic example of the use of game theory to provide an initial mathematical explanation of the effects of technological disruption.

In general, game theory has allowed scholars to investigate bargaining with entrepreneurs, venture capitalists, angels, and members in the supply chain, using incentive contracts to reduce moral hazard and adverse selection. It has also considered innovation and technology adoption, focusing on timing, investment, first- and second-mover advantages, and learning. In the market entry domain, past research has looked at issues of pricing, scale, product location, as well as spending. Arend (2006), for example, suggested that game theory has shown potential for modeling multi-party relationships (that being competitive as in the Bertrand and Cournot games, cooperative as in coordination games, and zero-sum game or expanding pie) and the location of multi-party relationships (that being internal to a firm as between stakeholders, external to a firm as with financiers, mixed as with business partners, and spatial or temporal). He further maintains that game theory is a promising approach for modeling market failure resulting from information asymmetries in business contracting, externalities such as technology spillovers, and from public goods emerging from nonprofit entrepreneurship.

5.2 Complexity Theory[5]

While game theory is particularly well suited to the study of interdependent decisions, the mathematics of a complex system lend itself remarkably well to analyze how the actions of one entrepreneur (or groups of entrepreneurs) interact with the environment, contribute to shape it and, in return, are influenced by it. Similarly to entrepreneurs, the many independent agents of a complex system interact with each other and with their environment in many different ways. Among other things, the mathematics of complex systems allows entrepreneurship scholars to endogenize ever changing social environments into formal models.

Unfortunately, there is no agreed definition of complexity and of how complexity theory applies to social phenomena.[6] A generally accepted definition is that a dynamical system is complex if it does not tend asymptotically to a fixed point, a cycle, or an explosion (Day, 1994). Although very broad, Day's definition separates clearly complex systems from other types of dynamical patterns such as those studied by catastrophe and chaos theories (Rosser 1999). In fact, while similarities exist among these branches of mathematics, each of them focuses on a different form of nonlinear behavior. Chaotic dynamics, for example, is generated by a deterministic process heavily dependent on its initial conditions and characterized by dramatic unpredictability.[7] Catastrophe dynamics, instead, is based on the existence of a very particular type of discontinuity in the system that causes it to jump from one equilibrium to another.

Unlike chaos or catastrophe, complexity mathematics looks at a class of dynamic systems characterized by nonlinear behaviors in which the elements of the system never quite lock into place, yet never quite dissolve into turbulence. That is, complex systems are both stable enough to store information and ephemeral enough to behave in an unpredictable fashion. Complex systems self-organize in hierarchical layers, react to the environment, and are adaptive and creative. Thus, the dynamics of complexity is characterized by its ability to explore the conditions and properties through which a new order emerges and persists in a dynamic environment; and, specifically, by its ability to illustrate the emergence of structures not directly described by the constraints and forces that control the system and by its ability to explain transition patterns.

Analogously to Hayek's concept of emergent order, complexity describes the formation of a structure as the spontaneous and unplanned outcome of the actions (and interactions) of many heterogeneous agents (Hayek, 1960). This operational definition of complexity is consistent with generally accepted descriptions of the entrepreneurial process (Minniti and Bygrave, 2001). For example, the aggregate level of entrepreneurial activity in a country can be viewed as a complex system and complexity mathematics can be used to study its emergence, its change over time, its stability and reactions in the face of environmental changes such as a financial crisis or a change in policy. In fact, the aggregate level of entrepreneurial activity is a dynamic process based on uncertainty whose behavior changes and adapts as the incentives faced by its components (the entrepreneurs) change. Because entrepreneurs follow incentives, adapt to the environment, and often make mistakes, the overall amount of entrepreneurship in the economy cannot be predicted *ex ante* even if all initial contextual conditions are known. Entrepreneurship is too complicated a phenomenon for that. After all, by definition, entrepreneurs are individuals who deviate from the norm. Because of this unpredictability, aggregate entrepreneurial activity *is* a complex phenomenon and can be studied and better understood through the use of complexity mathematics. A satisfactory model of entrepreneurial behavior will have to describe the emergence of entrepreneurial activity in a community as the outcome of an evolving and adaptive process characterized by deep uncertainty in which heterogeneous agents gain information from each other in a multi-layered variety of actions (Minniti, 2004; 2005).

Entrepreneurship is the result of individual heterogeneity, bounded rationality, and of the incentives generated by the institutional setting. It is also a phenomenon with uncertain outcomes that cause the dynamics of the system to have multiple equilibria. Minniti (2004), for example, argued that a model based on the properties of complex systems describes remarkably well entrepreneurial choice and is very useful in understanding entrepreneurial behavior and the emergence of alternative levels of entrepreneurial activity. Thus, existing research has already shown that the mathematics of complex systems is a promising approach for modeling entrepreneurial behavior, entrepreneurial learning and, in particular, the emergence of aggregate levels of entrepreneurial activity as the result of the interplay between individual actions, information asymmetries, externalities and spillovers such as those emerging from institutions and public goods.

5.3 Dynamic Programming[8]

Many decisions are made over time and the decision made today affects the decision to be made tomorrow. To take such dynamics into consideration, Bellman (1957) developed a tool labeled dynamic programming, which has been used over the years in many fields, including economics and engineering. A dynamic programming formulation includes variables that are divided into two classes, namely control variables and state variables. The control variables, also called decision variables or actions, are to be determined by solving the problem. The state variables, which are affected by the control variables, are defining the dynamics of the decision system from one time period to the next, and are thus associated with a system of state equations.

In a continuous time-setting the movement of the state variables is governed by first order differential equations (these are mathematical equations expressing the rate of change in the state variables), while in a discrete-time case the rate of change in each state variable is a function of the current state (can be a vector of state variables) and decision (can be a vector of control variables). In a deterministic setting, the movement of the state variables is characterized with certainty, while in a stochastic setting this movement is not known with certainty. Hence stochastic dynamic programming models contain random variables (or risks often characterizing the entrepreneurial phenomenon) that typically affect the state variables, and thus the decision variables over time.

A technology-based entrepreneur's market entry decision, for example, is affected not only by product quality but also competition, which could both play the role of state variables when the movement over time of their rate of change rather than that of their absolute value is easier to characterize. More specifically, in a discrete-time setting it could be natural to model the progress in product quality during a period t by a random variable X_t, and hence model product quality at the beginning of period $t+1$ as $q_{t+1} = q_t + X_t$. A similar equation could be developed for competition. In this situation, the control variable – whether or not to enter the market at time t – affects the product-quality state in that if the decision is to enter the market at time t then product quality from time t on would stay at q_t since no more development would be made (i.e., $q_s = q_t$ for any $s \geq t$). State variables thus depend on previous decisions and can be observed during the decision process to guide future decisions.

A dynamic programming formulation also includes an objective function to be maximized or minimized and given initial conditions for the control variables. Kamien and Schwartz (1991) introduce the basic principle of dynamic programming, called the principle of optimality, as follows: "An optimal path has the property that whatever the initial conditions and control values over some initial period, the control (or decision variables) over the remaining period must be optimal for the remaining problem, with the state resulting from the early decisions considered as the initial condition" (p. 259).

Two special types of discrete-time stochastic dynamic programming models offer elegant structured solutions and have been widely used: Markov decision processes and one of their special cases, namely optimal stopping models. Optimal stopping models have been used in the entrepreneurial arena to investigate, for instance, when an entrepreneur should stop gathering information about the attractiveness of a business opportunity and decide to grasp or reject that opportunity (Lévesque and Maillart, 2008), when he or she should stop product development and enter the market with his or her new product (Armstrong and Lévesque, 2002), and when he or she should expedite or delay the exploitation of the business opportunity (Choi et al., 2008).

Of course, such optimal decision-theoretic models assume that the decision-maker is rational. However, decision-makers may violate the requirements of rationality in various ways, as observed in the case of entrepreneurs who may take decisions in a 'non-algorithmic' fashion (Bygrave, 1993) and be overly optimistic (Olson, 1986). There are various bounded-rational models that capture some of these concepts, including Minniti and Bygrave (2001), and Minniti and Lévesque (2008). Standard optimization approaches, such as dynamic programming, can be complemented by the use of chaos theory (system behavior highly dependent on initial conditions and highly unpredictable), catastrophe theory (system jumps from one equilibrium to another), and, as discussed above, complexity theory (system somehow stable yet unpredictable). Moreover, optimization approaches can serve as benchmark for improving decision-making, because they enable us to investigate whether decision-makers "steer" their decisions in the direction predicted by the impact on the optimal solution from a change in key model parameters. The resulting predictions can also be tested with economic experiments, as exemplified recently in Burmeister-Lamp et al. (forthcoming), who investigate the role of risk attitude and regulatory focus (where individuals can be promotion focused, i.e. strive for gains, or prevention focused, i.e., strive to avoid losses) in the context of an entrepreneur's time allocation decisions between a new enterprise and a wage job.

5.4   Multiple Criteria Decision Analysis

Decision-makers (including entrepreneurs and their stakeholders) also need tools to assist them in resolving conflicts between various interests and objectives. Although not a branch of mathematics per se, multiple criteria decision analysis is a mathematically based approach that can fulfill this need. This mathematical-based method takes explicit account of intangible criteria to help decision-makers organize and synthesize information of a complex and conflicting nature. It helps understand tradeoffs (e.g., among economic, social, and environmental perspectives) and hence obtain the relative importance of criteria to be considered in making the decision, rank alternatives, and even eliminate clearly inferior alternatives, which, as articulated by Keeney and Raiffa (1976), promote good decision-making.

Nevertheless, multiple criteria decision analysis does not propose a *best solution*. It focuses on structuring the decision problem in a model that facilitates the evaluation of the consequences from selecting a certain course of actions. Thus, multiple criteria decision analysis can be of considerable help in situations where the criteria exhibit significant levels of conflict or where stakeholders disagree as to the relative importance of criteria.

The process of model building encourages decision-makers to carefully evaluate priorities, engage in systematic rating and critically examine results during sensitivity analysis. Through the identification of the decision-maker's *value* (utility) *function*, multiple criteria decision analysis helps the decision-maker assess his or her relative preferences. In other words, this function attempts to "translate the relationship between a certain evaluation and the satisfaction this evaluation brings to the decision maker" (Beim and Lévesque, 2006, p.267). In addition to scholars using this approach to further their understanding of entrepreneurial decision-making, practicing entrepreneurs can use software based on this decision-making method that is commercially available to help them make and defend/support their decisions.

Although the application of multiple criteria decision analysis in entrepreneurship has been limited, it can lead to productive research and good practice when the decision-maker (e.g., entrepreneur, financier, policy-maker) takes into account multiple criteria that are born from considering multiple perspectives. Beyond the investment decisions of a venture capitalist (see, e.g., the call for decision aids in Shepherd and Zacharakis, 2002) and the decision of which country an entrepreneur should venture into (see, e.g., Beim and Lévesque, 2006), the decision of whether or not to become an entrepreneur (or exit entrepreneurship), selecting a key partner or employee, and selecting a manufacturer or supplier, to name a few, are all important to entrepreneurs, their stakeholders and the success of their new enterprise, and all involve multiple perspectives. Multiple criteria decision analysis can also be used on past decisions to compare and contrast the selection processes performed with and without the aid of such methodology.

6. CONCLUSION

In addition to the applications used as examples in earlier sections of this chapter, the mathematical modeling research in entrepreneurship (which offers additional methods to those reviewed herein) has also looked at issues of business opportunity discovery, such as the impact of formal business networks on entrepreneurs' performance (Parker, 2008), business planning before starting up (Chwolka and Raith, forthcoming), and cooperation between an entrepreneur and a university for technology commercialization (van Burg and van Oorschot, forthcoming). It has also looked at commitment issues, such as career choice and time allocation decisions (e.g., Lévesque and Schade 2005) as well as rapid growth (e.g., Yim, 2008; Lévesque et al., 2012).

Because of its ability to produce generalizable theory and testable hypotheses, mathematical modeling is also very useful in policy applications. One of the important roles played by theory is to provide useful practical insights that can inform best practices and policy. In particular, policy (at all levels of government) shapes the institutional environment in which entrepreneurial decisions are made. Thus, policy is important for entrepreneurship. But what policies are more conducive to productive entrepreneurship? In spite of a significant amount of work on this and related topics, there is still much we do not know about this important relationship (Minniti, 2008). There are plenty of examples of policies that succeed in one place and fail in others, or of policies that end up having results very different from those projected. Mathematical models can help us identify what incentives are more conducive to entrepreneurial behavior and under what precise conditions these incentives are more likely to be effective.

Recent special issues of top-tier management journals on formal approaches to develop management theories also prove the usefulness of mathematics in organizational studies and, more specifically, entrepreneurship research. For example, a 2009 special issue of the *Academy of Management Review* was dedicated to formal approaches (including mathematical modeling), with a leading article on an entrepreneurship topic (Alvarez and Parker, 2009). Furthermore, Joglekar and Lévesque (forthcoming) report that a systematic search of the *Journal of Business Venturing* (a top-tier journal focused on entrepreneurship research) yielded a list of 19 articles that use mathematical modeling in all journal issues (and online forthcoming articles) between 2000 and half of 2011 (omitting empirical articles with advanced econometrics).

Lévesque (2004) maintains that mathematical modeling can generate value in this field, because it is an effective tool for describing phenomena, building new theories, and refining existing ones. Moreover, the use of mathematically-based approaches can help increase the legitimacy of entrepreneurship research as in other more formally refined social science fields. Although a certain set of skills is certainly required to take a mathematical approach to entrepreneurship research, we believe the costs of acquiring such skills are well worth the time if one is serious about taking a scientific approach to the study of entrepreneurship in all its forms.

To conclude, the goal of this chapter was to develop a greater appreciation of mathematical models and the use of stylized theoretical modeling amongst the broader community of entrepreneurship scholars. We discussed why mathematics and, more specifically, mathematical modeling is advantageous to scholarly research and showed that there exists multiple problem-solving situations (or parts thereof) in the area of entrepreneurship that can be adequately described mathematically (e.g., where the dynamic nature of the decision system subject to control and the objective of the decision maker may be expressed mathematically). We have hopefully initiated (or perhaps re-opened) a dialogue on how mathematics can provide important contributions to current theories of management and organizations. We hope others will follow.

NOTES

1. The content of this chapter borrows from previous works by the authors; in particular, Lévesque (2004) and Minniti (2004).
2. Importantly, the motives for the application of mathematics to social subjects were not religious and were, in fact, part of the movement toward the development of a rational and empirical approach to the study of man.
3. Clearly, mathematics is not the only way to achieve this result and other approaches, including verbal logic, are possible.
4. Further details on this example can be found in Resnick and Halliday (1980).
5. This subsection relies heavily on Minniti (2004), where additional details can be found.
6. Waldrop (1992) provides a simple and informative review of the topic broadly defined.
7. The well-known butterfly effect is a typical example of such heavy dependence and unpredictability.
8. This subsection relies heavily on Lévesque (2004), where additional details can be found.

REFERENCES

Adner, R. (2002), 'When are technologies disruptive? A demand-based view of the emergence of competition', *Strategic Management Journal*, 23, 667–88.
Alvarez, S., Parker, S.C. (2009), 'Emerging firms and the allocation of control rights: A Bayesian approach', *Academy of Management Review*, **34**(2), 209–27.
Arend, R. (2006), 'Entrepreneurship and game theory. Presentation at a Professional Development Workshop on *Entrepreneurship and Research Methods*', Academy of Management Meeting, Atlanta, GA.
Armstrong, M.J., Lévesque, M. (2002), 'Timing and quality decisions for entrepreneurial product development', *European Journal of Operational Research*, **141**(1), 88–106.
Arthur, W.B., Durlauf, S., Lane, D.A. (1997), 'Introduction', in *The Economy as an Evolving Complex System II*, W.B. Arthur, S. Durlauf and D.A. Lane (Eds). Addison-Wesley, MA, pp. 1–14.
Baumol, W. (1993), 'Formal entrepreneurship theory in economics: Existence and bounds', *Journal of Business Venturing*, **8**(3), 197–210.
Bellman, R.E. (1957), *Dynamic Programming*, Princeton, NJ: Princeton University Press.
Beim, G., Lévesque, M. (2006), 'Country selection for new business venturing: A multiple criteria decision analysis', *Long Range Planning*, **39**(3), 265–93.
Braithwaite, R. (1955), *Scientific Explanation*. Cambridge, MA: Cambridge University Press.
Buchler, J. (1955), *Philosophical Writings of Peirce*, New York, NY: Dover.
Burmeister-Lamp, K., Lévesque, M., Schade, C. (Forthcoming), 'Wage job or new enterprise? An experimental analysis of time allocation under risk-return tradeoffs', *Journal of Business Venturing*.
Busenitz, L., West, G.P., III, Shepherd, D.A., Nelson, T., Chandler, G.N., and A. Zacharakis (2003), 'Entrepreneurship research in emergence: Past trends and future directions', *Journal of Management*, **29**(3), 285–308.
Bygrave, W.D. (1993), 'Theory building in the entrepreneurship paradigm', *Journal of Business Venturing*, 8, 255–80.
Chwolka, A., Raith, M.G. (Forthcoming), 'The value of business planning before start-up – A decision-theoretic perspective', *Journal of Business Venturing*.
Choi, Y.R., Lévesque, M., Shepherd, D.A. (2008), 'When should entrepreneurs expedite or delay opportunity exploitation?' *Journal of Business Venturing*, **23**(3), 333–55.
Cohen, M. (1956), *A Preface to Logic*. New York, NY: Meridian.
Davidson, P., Wiklund, J. (2001), 'Levels of analysis in entrepreneurship research: Current research practice and suggestions for the future', *Entrepreneurship: Theory and Practice*, **25**(4), 81–99.

Day, R.H. (1994), *Complex Economic Dynamics*, Vol 1, Cambridge, MA: MIT Press.
Debreu, G. (1986), 'Theoretic models: Mathematical form and economic content', *Econometrica*, **54**(6), 1259–70.
Dillmann, R., Eissrich, D., Frambach, H., Herrmann, O. (2000), 'Mathematics in economics: Some remarks', *Journal of Economic Studies*, **27**(4/5), 260–70.
Dixit, A., Nalebuff, B. (1991), *Thinking Strategically: The Competitive Edge in Business, Politics, and Everyday Life*. New York, NY: W.W. Norton & Company.
Dubin, R. (1978), *Theory Development*, New York, NY: Free Press.
Elitzur, R., Gavious, A. (2003a), 'A multi-period game theoretic model of venture capitalists and entrepreneurs', *European Journal of Operational Research*, **144**(2), 440–53.
Elitzur, R., Gavious, A. (2003b), 'Contracting, signaling, and moral hazard: A model of entrepreneurs, 'angels,' and venture capitalists', *Journal of Business Venturing*, **18**(6), 709–25.
Fairchild, R. (2011), 'An entrepreneur's choice of venture capitalist or angel-financing: A behavioral game-theoretic approach', *Journal of Business Venturing*, 26, 359–74.
Feigl, H. (1953), 'The scientific outlook: Naturalism and humanism', in H. Feigl and M. Brodbeck (Eds), *Readings in the Philosophy of Science*. New York, NY: Appleton-Century-Crofts, Inc., pp.8–18.
Harhoff, D., Henkel, J., von Hippel, E. (2003), 'Profiting from voluntary information spillovers: How users benefit by freely revealing their innovations', *Research Policy*, **32**(10), 1753–69.
Hayek, F.A. (1960), *The Constitution of Liberty*. Chicago, IL: The University of Chicago Press.
Hayek, F.A. (1952), *The Sensory Order*. Chicago, IL: The University of Chicago Press.
Holland, J.H., Holyoak, K.J., Nisbett, R.E., Thagard, P.R. (1986), *Induction: Processes of Inference, Learning, and Discovery*. Cambridge, MA.: MIT Press.
Joglekar, N., Lévesque, M. (Forthcoming), 'The role of operations management across the entrepreneurial value chain', *Production and Operations Management*.
Kamien, M.I., Schwartz, N.L. (1991), *Dynamic Optimization: The Calculus of Variations and Optimal Control in Economics and Management* (2nd ed.), Amsterdam, Netherlands: North-Holland.
Kantorovich, L.V. (1989), 'Mathematics in economics: Achievements and difficulties', *American Economic Review*, **79**(6), 18–23.
Keeney, R.L., Raiffa, H. (1976). *Decisions with Multiple Objectives*, New York, NY: John Wiley & Sons.
Kerlinger, F.N. (1979), *Behavioral Research: A Conceptual Approach*. New York, NY: Holt, Rinehart and Winston.
Kirzner, I.M. (1979), *Perception, Opportunity, and Profit: Studies in the Theory of Entrepreneurship*. Chicago, IL: University of Chicago Press.
Kirzner, I.M. (1973), *Competition and Entrepreneurship*, Chicago, IL: University of Chicago Press.
Knight, F. (1921), *Risk, Uncertainty and Profit*, Chicago, IL: University of Chicago Press.
Koppl, R., Minniti, M. (2010), 'Market processes and entrepreneurial studies', in Z. Acs and D. Audretsch (Eds.), *Handbook of Entrepreneurship Research* (2nd Edn), Kluwer Press International, UK.
Lévesque, M. (2004), 'Mathematics, theory and entrepreneurship', *Journal of Business Venturing*, **19**(5), 743–65.
Lévesque, M., Joglekar, N., Davies, J. (2012), 'A comparison of revenue growth at recent-IPO and established firms: Influence of SG&A, R&D and COGS' *Journal of Business Venturing*, 27, 47–61.
Lévesque, M., Maillart, L. (2008), 'Business opportunity assessment with costly, imperfect information', *IEEE Transactions on Engineering Management*, **55**(2), 279–91.
Lévesque, M., Minniti, M. (2011), 'Demographic structure and entrepreneurial activity', *Strategic Entrepreneurship Journal*, 5, 269–84.
Lévesque, M., Schade, C. (2005), 'Intuitive optimizing: Experimental findings on time allocation decisions with newly formed ventures', *Journal of Business Venturing*, **20**(3), 313–42.
Lévesque, M., Shepherd, D.A. (2002), 'A new venture's optimal entry time', *European Journal of Operational Research*, **139**(3), 626–42.
Minniti, M. (2008), 'The role of government on entrepreneurial activity: Productive, unproductive, or destructive?' *Entrepreneurship: Theory and Practice*, **32**(5), 779–90.
Minniti, M. (2004), 'Organization alertness and asymmetric information in a Spin-Glass model', *Journal of Business Venturing*, **19**(5), 637–58.
Minniti, M. (2005), 'Entrepreneurship and network externalities 2005', *Journal of Economic Behavior and Organization*, **57**(1): 1–27.
Minniti, M., Lévesque, M. (2008), 'Recent developments in the economics of entrepreneurship', *Journal of Business Venturing*, **23**(6), 603–12.
Minniti, M., Bygrave, W. (2001), 'A dynamic model of entrepreneurial learning', *Entrepreneurship: Theory and Practice*, **25**(3), 5–16.
Olson, P.D. (1986), 'Entrepreneurs: Opportunistic decision makers', *Journal of Small Business Management*, **24**(3), 29–35.

Parker, S.C. 2008. The economics of formal business networks. *Journal of Business Venturing*, 23, 627–40.
Rasmusen, E. (1991), *Games and Information: An Introduction to Game Theory*. Cambridge, MA: Blackwell.
Resnick, R., Halliday, D. (1980), *Ondes, Optique et Physique Moderne* (trans. Q.-T. Nguyen and D. Martel of *Waves, Optic and Modern Physics*, 1978, New York, NY: John Wiley and Sons), Montréal PQ: Editions du Renouveau Pédagogique.
Rosser, B. (1999), 'On the complexities of complex economic dynamics', *Journal of Economic Perspectives*, **13**(4), 169–92.
Rousseau, J.J. 1948(1762), *The Social Contract and Discourses* (trans. G.D.H. Cole), Everyman's Library, New York, NY: E.P. Dutton & Co.
Saloner, G. (1991), 'Modeling, game theory, and strategic management', *Strategic Management Journal*, 12, 119–36.
Schumpeter, J. (1934), *The Theory of Economic Development*. Cambridge, MA: Harvard Press.
Senn, P. (2000), 'Mathematics and the social sciences at the time of the modern beginnings of the social sciences', *Journal of Economic Studies*, **27**(4/5), 271–92.
Shane, S. (2012), 'Reflections on the 2010 AMR decade award: Delivering on the promise of entrepreneurship as a field of research', *Academy of Management Review* **37**(1), 10–20.
Shane, S., Venkataraman, S. (2000), 'The promise of entrepreneurship as a field of research', *Academy of Management Review*, 25: 217–26.
Shepherd, D.A., Zacharakis, A. (2002), 'Venture capitalists' expertise: A call for research into decision aids and cognitive feedback', *Journal of Business Venturing*, 17, 1–20.
van Burg, E., van Oorschot, K. (Forthcoming), 'Cooperating to commercialize technology: A dynamic model of fairness, experience, and cooperation', *Production and Operations Management*.
Waldrop, M. (1992), *Complexity: The Emerging Science at the Edge of Order and Chaos*. Simon & Schuster, NY.
West, G.P., III. (1997), 'Frameworks for research and theory development in entrepreneurship', in L.N. Dosier and J.B. Keys (Eds.), *Academy of Management best papers proceedings*. Statesboro, GA: Georgia Southern University, pp. 113–117.
Whetten, D.A. (1989), 'What constitutes a theoretical contribution?' *Academy of Management Review*, 14, 490–5.
Yim, H.R. (2008), 'Quality shock vs. market shock: Lessons from recently established rapidly growing U.S. startups', *Journal of Business Venturing*, 23, 141–64.

10. Predictions of entrepreneurial behavior: a personality approach
Andreas Rauch

INTRODUCTION

The personality approach to entrepreneurship intends to show the relationship between personality traits and entrepreneurial behavior such as opportunity recognition, and outcomes such as business creation and business success. Studies in this tradition aimed to identify the most important personality characteristics and, moreover, aimed to understand the conditions under which these traits predict entrepreneurial behavior. Personality theory is one of the classical approaches to explain the activities of enterprising individuals. One reason for this interest is based on early economic theorizing about the role of entrepreneurship in economic growth. For example, Schumpeter (1935) explained economic growth by innovations that destroy equilibrium conditions. The agents of this creative destruction are entrepreneurs that are characterized by innovativeness, foresight, dominance and a desire to create a kingdom (Utsch, Rauch, Rothfuss, & Frese, 1999). Knight (1921) described entrepreneurship as decision-making under uncertainty. McClelland (1961) introduced achievement motivation theory in order to explain economic growth. And even more recent economic theorizing that stressed the role of market disequilibrium and knowledge asymmetries introduced the alertness construct to explain which people recognize business opportunities (Kirzner, 1997). This early interest in personality characteristics was also picked up in numerous books and articles in the popular press describing success stories of entrepreneurs such as Steve Jobs, Richard Branson, or Oprah Winfrey.

Nevertheless, the scientific community has criticized the personality approach heavily during the eighties (Chell, 1985; Brockhaus & Horwitz, 1986; Gartner, 1988). Several issues have stimulated the critique. First, the studies in this area were predominantly descriptive, defying inference about how certain people start a business and become successful entrepreneurs (Low & MacMillan, 1988). Second, entrepreneurs seem to be a highly heterogeneous group of people that cannot be described by an average personality profile. Third, entrepreneurship research has used so many different personality traits that the definition of entrepreneurs based on personality traits is open-ended (Gartner, 1988). Finally, a number or reviews in the eighties concluded that the scientific evidence about the role of personality characteristics is inconclusive (Brockhaus & Horwitz, 1986; Gartner, 1988; Low & MacMillan, 1988). Notably, the critique of the personality approach was based on narrative methods for the review of the literature. While most authors in the field of entrepreneurship asked to stop looking for personality traits of entrepreneurs in the eighties the critique was useful for drawing the attention to deficits in the early studies on entrepreneur's personality (compare reviews by Chell, 2008; Chell, 1985; Rauch & Frese, 2000). As a consequence, subsequent studies relied on more elaborate approaches to study entrepreneurs' personality traits (Baum & Locke, 2004; Frese et al., 2007; Hmieleski & Baron, 2009). Moreover, the emergence and acceptance of quantitative methods for the review of the entrepreneurship literature revealed different conclusions: Personality characteristics affect entrepreneurial behaviors such as business creation, intentions, and business success.

The aim of the present chapter is twofold: First, I will integrate the results of the meta-analyses conducted in the domain of entrepreneurship. This is necessary in order to evaluate the status quo of the personality approach to entrepreneurship. The second aim is to suggest theoretical implications that result from these meta-analyses. Several issues are relevant here: the bandwidth-fidelity dilemma, the process dynamics of personality traits, the role of situational characteristics, level of analysis issues, and personality development. The chapter will suggest a theoretically sound personality approach that can substantially contribute to the domain of entrepreneurship.

PERSONALITY THEORY AND ENTREPRENEURSHIP

Personality traits are enduring dispositions to exhibit a certain kind of response across various situations (Paunonen & Aston, 2001). Personality includes patterns of thought, emotions, and behaviors including the mechanism behind those patterns (Funder, 2001). This definition explicates that it is not sufficient to measure some personality traits to predict an outcome variable, such as having the intention to start a business venture. Rather, personality is a complex construct that requires the assessment of dispositions, mechanisms, and situations.

Personality research has spent intense efforts to categorize the thousands of extant personality traits into a restricted number of factors representing the construct (Eysenck, 1991). The Big Five taxonomy (Costa & McCrae, 1988) is currently the most widely known and accepted personality taxonomy. The Big Five traits were categorized by factor analyzing results of previously published inventories. The model consists of five broad dimensions that are used to describe human personality: conscientiousness (an individual's degree of organization, persistence, hard work, and motivation in the pursuit of goal accomplishment), extraversion (the extent to which people are assertive, dominant, energetic, active, talkative, and enthusiastic), emotional stability (individual differences in adjustment and emotional stability), agreeableness (being trusting, forgiving, caring, altruistic, and gullible), and openness to experience (being intellectually curious and tending to seek new experiences and explore novel ideas). The Big Five traits represent broad and aggregated personality dimensions. Each of the broad factors consists of more specific sub-factors (facets). For example, conscientiousness consists of achievement striving, self-efficacy, dutifulness, discipline, orderliness and cautiousness.

The Big Five model is well validated and has been related to numerous constructs such as career choice and work performance. For example, one key meta-analysis reported that conscientiousness is the personality trait most strongly related to job performance with an average weighted effect size of $r = .22$ (Barrick & Mount, 1991). Several studies tested the validity of such broad trait taxonomies in the domain of entrepreneurship as well (Brandstätter, 1997; Ciaverella, Buchholtz, Riordan, Gatewood, & Stokes, 2004; Wooten & Timmerman, 1999).

However, the use of the Big Five personality taxonomy is not uncontested and, therefore, entrepreneurship research should not study exclusively Big Five traits. First, there is little agreement about the number and organization of lower level personality factors. Second, there are different methods for aggregating personality factors such as, for example, factor analysis and nomological clustering. Factor analytical approaches aggregate personality traits by combining traits based on patterns of similarities. Nomological clustering is based on patterns of relationships with other variables. Such approaches result in different categorizations of traits (Hough, 1992). Since most studies in entrepreneurship are interested in the prediction of entrepreneurial behavior, nomological approaches for aggregating personality traits might be more important as compared to the factor analytically developed Big Five Factors. Third, Big Five traits describe fundamental dimensions of human personality and, therefore, these traits are not specific to entrepreneurship. However, there are alternative conceptualizations of personality traits that might be theoretically more interesting for studying personality traits of entrepreneurs. Some of these conceptualizations focus on sub-factors of Big Five traits, such as need for achievement (McClelland, 1961). Other conceptualizations focus on constructs, such as personal initiative (Crant, 1996; Frese, Krauss, & Friedrich, 2000) that are outside the domain of the Big Five factor model. Finally, the mechanism of how Big Five traits affect entrepreneurial behavior are unknown. Big Five traits are distal to behavior and, therefore, do not directly predict behavior. The effects of such distal constructs on behavior are likely to be facilitated by processes that are more proximal to behavior (Kanfer, 1992). For example, entrepreneurs high in conscientiousness might develop growth intentions which, in turn, affect subsequent company performance.

META-ANALYSIS AS A TOOL FOR EVALUATING THE PERSONALITY APPROACH TO ENTREPRENEURSHIP

The purpose of a meta-analysis is to conduct a review of the literature that is based on statistical analysis (Glass, McGaw, & Smith, 1981). Therefore, a meta-analysis builds on primary studies that preceded the meta-analysis. A meta-analysis can be used to develop and validate theories in a domain and to test the generalizability of research findings (Rauch & Frese, 2006). Specifically, a meta-analysis aggregates the findings of primary studies by combining the effect sizes reported in these studies. The meta-analysis provides a sample size weighted effect size that is often corrected by study artifacts such as measurement error. The weighted effect size is an estimate of the true effect size that is more precise than the individual effect sizes reported in the original studies.

A meta-analysis has certain advantages as compared to narrative methods of the review. First, a meta-analysis shares explicitly stated rules applied for aggregating research findings, which are open to replication and criticism. Second, narrative reviews are easily biased by the limited information-processing capacities of the reviewer. For example, it is difficult for reviewers to consider measurement errors and different sample sizes in narrative reviews. A meta-analysis can statistically control for such problems inherent in primary studies. Third, it allows an estimation of the magnitude of effects. Fourth, a meta-analysis tests for variations in these relationships. A small variation in reported effect sizes indicates that the effects apply in different contexts. A high variation of reported effect sizes indicates that effect sizes may depend on third variables (moderators). Finally, a meta-analysis allows for testing moderator effects that have not been tested in primary studies. In this way, a meta-analysis adds to theory development in a field.

Certainly, a meta-analysis has disadvantages as well. Ultimately it is preceded by other studies and can only quantify evidence for traits that have been addressed in a number of empirical studies. Thereby, the tool is not useful to study individual differences that have only been identified occasionally, such as passion, tenacity (Baum & Locke, 2004) and alertness (Busenitz, 1996). Moreover, it cannot cover theoretical work (Chell, 1985). Finally, while it is possible to meta-analyze qualitative studies (Thorne, 2009), such an analysis has, to my knowledge, not been conducted in entrepreneurship research.

THE EVIDENCE ABOUT THE IMPACT OF PERSONALITY TRAITS IN ENTREPRENEURSHIP

The subsequent sections of this chapter integrate the findings of meta-analyses that have been conducted in the domain of personality traits of entrepreneurs. Table 10.1 provides an overview of the results reported here. Table 10.1 reveals that the effect sizes are in general small to moderate by statistical standards (Cohen, 1977). More importantly, the size of reported relationships varies considerably for specific traits. Therefore, it is useful to look at different conceptualizations of traits and the way they affect entrepreneurial behaviors.

Big Five Personality Traits

Zhao and Seibert (2006) conducted a meta-analysis of 23 studies comparing entrepreneurs with managers. The authors categorized the primary studies under the Big Five factor model. The results of this analysis (Table 10.1) revealed that entrepreneurs differ from managers in conscientiousness (reliability corrected effect size r = .22[1]), neuroticism (r = −.18), openness to experience (r = .18) and agreeableness (r = −.08). Interestingly, the study examined sub-factors of conscientiousness. The results indicated that achievement motivation revealed higher effect sizes (r = .28) as compared to dependability (r = .00). Thus, there is evidence that some sub-factors of the Big Five model have higher predictive validities as compared to the aggregated Big Five factors. Another meta-analysis examined the relationship between Big Five personality traits and venture performance (Zhao, Seibert, & Lumpkin, 2010). The results revealed that conscientiousness (r = .15[2]), openness to experience (r = .15), emotional stability (r = .13) and extraversion (r = .08) were positively related to venture performance. While these meta-analyses stressed the importance of Big Five traits for entrepreneurship, the identified effect sizes are small by statistical standards (Cohen, 1977). Moreover, the effects are smaller than the effect sizes reported for the relationship between Big Five traits and general job performance (Barrick & Mount, 1991).

One problem inherent in these two meta-analyses is that the authors aggregated

Table 10.1   Meta-analysis results on the personality approach to entrepreneurship

Publication	Purpose	Effect size[1]
Zhao & Seibert, 2006	The prediction of business creation:	
	Conscientiousness	.22
	Neuroticism	−.18
	Openness to experience	.18
	Agreeableness	−.08
	Extraversion	.11
Zhao, Seibert & Lumpkin, 2010	The prediction of performance	
	Conscientiousness	.15
	Neuroticism	−.13
	Openness to experience	.15
	Agreeableness	.03
	Extraversion	.08
Rauch & Frese, 2007b	Traits related to entrepreneurship and business creation	.25
	Traits not related to entrepreneurship and business creation	.12
	Traits related to entrepreneurship and performance	.25
	Traits not related to entrepreneurship and performance	.03
Stewart & Roth, 2004	Risk-taking and business creation	.11
Rauch & Frese, 2007b		.10
Rauch & Frese, 2007b	Risk-taking and performance	.10
Collins et al., 2004	Need for achievement and business creation	.17 to .28
Rauch & Frese, 2007b		
Stewart & Roth, 2007		
Zhao & Seibert, 2006		
Collins et al., 2004	Need for achievement and performance	.30
Rauch & Frese, 2007b		.30

Note: [1] converted to r

various traits under the Big Five framework. Thereby, the authors confounded specific traits with broad traits. Moreover, it is likely that some specific traits that have been studied frequently in entrepreneurship research are overrepresented and, thus, biased the results. For example, most studies aggregated under the trait conscientiousness measured achievement motivation – this sub-factor reveals stronger effect sizes than other sub-factors of conscientiousness (Zhao & Seibert, 2006). Other limitations are concerned with the methodological decisions inherent in these analyses. For example, both meta-analyses on Big Five traits tested the significance of effect sizes using the 90 percent confidence interval, while most other meta-analyses in the domain of entrepreneurship used the 95 percent confidence interval as suggested by Lipsey and Wilson (2001) – the latter is a more conservative procedure. Moreover, the authors suggested that a large 80 percent credibility interval indicated the presence of moderator variables without specifying a criterion for a large credibility interval. Therefore, it is not evident that the analyses revealed the presence of moderator effects although such moderators were tested in subsequent analyses.

Personality Traits Related to the Tasks of Entrepreneurs

A number of meta-analyses in the domain of entrepreneurship analyzed personality traits that are theoretically more specifically related to the domain of entrepreneurship. As a matter of fact, one meta-analysis tested whether broad or specific personality traits have higher predictive validities (Rauch & Frese, 2007b). The authors relied on ratings of ten subject-matter experts to categorize traits into two categories: Traits that are related to the task of entrepreneurs and traits that are not related to the task of entrepreneurs. As expected, task specific traits revealed higher effect sizes as compared to traits not related to entrepreneurship with regard to business creation ($r = .25$ and $r = .12$, respectively) and business performance ($r = .25$ and $r = .03$, respectively). In this study, business performance included measures about financial outcomes, accountant based measures, and growth. Thus, personality approaches to entrepreneurship need a theoretical framework for assessing the effects of personality traits. Two traits that are theoretically related to the domain of entrepreneurship received additional meta-analytical support: Risk-taking and need for achievement.

Risk-taking
Risk-taking is a personality trait that is related to the domain of entrepreneurship for several reasons. First, entrepreneurship is concerned with decision making under uncertainty (Knight, 1921). Moreover the concept of uncertainty is a conceptual cornerstone in the theory of entrepreneurship; entrepreneurs are able and motivated to bear this uncertainty (McMullen & Shepherd, 2006). Additionally, the tasks of entrepreneurs include taking risks, since entrepreneurs have a lot of responsibilities and have to deal with unstructured situations. Therefore, entrepreneurship theory is interested in the role of risk-taking. Notably, the literature discussed two competing theories explaining the relationship between risk-taking and entrepreneurial behavior. One approach assumes that entrepreneurs are willing and motivated to take risks and, therefore, should be high in risk-taking propensity (Schumpeter, 1935). A competing proposition assumes that entrepreneurs take moderate risks (McClelland, 1961). The second position assumes a curvilinear relationship between risk-taking and entrepreneurial behavior; this proposition has not been tested in meta-analyses. However, the first proposition received considerable meta-analytical interest; as many as four meta-analyses examined whether entrepreneurs and non-entrepreneurs differ in risk-taking propensity. It seems that the relationship between risk-taking and business creation depends on the assessment of risk-taking: projective measures revealed negative effect sizes, while "objective" measures revealed positive effect sizes (Miner & Raju, 2004; Stewart & Roth, 2001; Stewart & Roth, 2004). Analyzing 18 samples, Stewart and Roth (2004) reported an overall reliability corrected effect size of $r = .11$. Rauch and Frese (2007b) reported a similar effect size of $r = .10$ for the difference between entrepreneurs and non-entrepreneurs. Moreover, Rauch and Frese (2007b) tested the relationship between risk-taking and business performance and reported an effect size of $r = .10$. Thus, risk-taking propensity is significantly and positively related to entrepreneurial behavior; the effect size is as high as, for

example, the relationship between innovation and business performance (Rosenbusch, Brinckmann, & Bausch, 2011) and the relationship between planning and performance (Brinckmann, Grichnik, & Kapsa, 2010). At the same time, the effect sizes for risk-taking propensity are small as compared to the effect sizes reported for other personality traits (compare Table 10.1).

Need for achievement

The interest in achievement motivation theory originates in McClelland's early work proposing a psychological theory of economic growth (McClelland, 1961). The central premise of the theory was that nations with higher levels of achievement motivation show higher levels of entrepreneurial activity and economic growth than nations with low levels of achievement motivation. Despite the fact that this premise was not uncontested (Finison, 1976; Frey, 1984), the theory was transformed from the macro level of analysis to the micro level of analysis. Today, need for achievement is the single most frequently studied personality characteristic in the domain of entrepreneurship research (Chell, 2008; Rauch & Frese, 2007b). Need for achievement is associated with entrepreneurship because entrepreneurs need to perform well at challenging tasks of moderate difficulty, they seek feedback on performance, they take responsibility and try out new ways to accomplish tasks. Accordingly, several meta-analyses reported relatively high effect sizes for the difference between entrepreneurs and non-entrepreneurs on achievement motivation. The effect sizes reported ranged between $r = .17$ and $r = .28$ (Collins, Hanges, & Locke, 2004; Rauch & Frese, 2007b; Stewart & Roth, 2007; Zhao & Seibert, 2006). Importantly, the effects were moderated by third variables. For example, effect sizes were higher for entrepreneurs who were founders of their businesses than for non-founders, indicating that achievement motivation becomes more important with rising demands in initiative and of the environment (Brandstätter, 2011).

Moreover, achievement motivation should also be instrumental for achieving high performance. For example, challenging goals and tasks motivate to accomplish the goals and feedback is necessary to improve one's skills and performance. Therefore, two meta-analyses correlated achievement motivation with firm performance; both analyses found mean effect sized around $r = .30$ (Collins et al., 2004; Rauch & Frese, 2007b). Thus, need for achievement is related to entrepreneurial behavior.

Summary

There are additional personality characteristics that are related to business creation and business performance. There is meta-analytically established evidence for innovativeness, proactive personality, generalized self-efficacy, stress tolerance, need for autonomy, and locus of control (Rauch & Frese, 2007b). Interestingly, generalized self-efficacy was the trait that revealed the highest relationship with performance ($r = .38$).

Thus, various meta-analyses indicated that personality characteristics are valid predictors of entrepreneurial behaviors such as venture creation and business performance. Effect sizes seem to be higher for traits related to the task of entrepreneurship (compare Table 10.1). These findings support the belief that personality traits contribute to our understanding of entrepreneurship and meet many past criticisms of the personality approach. It is important to note that the meta-analyses did not simply replicate each other. They have used different frameworks to classify personality traits, used different conceptualizations of entrepreneurial behavior, and embroiled in an empirical dispute about how data quality and coding affects meta-analytical outcomes about the relationship between risk-taking and performance (Miner & Raju, 2004; Stewart & Roth, 2004). Thereby, the meta-analyses in the domain of entrepreneurs' personality characteristics incrementally contributed to theory building in entrepreneurship research (Frese, Bausch, Schmidt, Rauch, & Kabst, 2012). Another observation is that the effect sizes varied considerably across studies included in the meta-analyses indicating that moderator variables are present. Finally, none of the meta-analyses presented here addressed the mechanisms by which traits affect entrepreneurship behavior. Such mechanisms can be studied by developing a meta-analytical structural equation model as suggested by Viswesvaran and Ones (1995). Such a technique allows the estimation of the causal relationships involving several constructs and, thereby, exceeds that of the bi-variate relationships identified in a traditional meta-analysis.

THEORETICAL ADVANCES IN THE PERSONALITY APPROACH TO ENTREPRENEURSHIP

While meta-analyses can be used to test new hypotheses and theoretical frameworks, the meta-analyses discussed so far only partially cover trends in the domain of entrepreneurship that incorporate more recent developments in personality theory. For some of these trends, the data base is just too small to conduct a meta-analysis. Other issues have been ignored in the meta-analyses discussed. In order to develop a more differentiated picture about the role of a personality approach to entrepreneurship I will next discuss the bandwidth-fidelity dilemma, process approaches, contingency theory, level-of analysis issues, and intervention programs.

The Bandwidth-fidelity Dilemma

The bandwidth-fidelity dilemma concerns the gain or loss of analytical and predictive power when using broad or narrow personality traits (Cronbach & Gleser, 1965). The debate whether it is more useful to use broad or narrow traits is not new in personality psychology (Ones & Viswesvaran, 1996) and this issue is also discussed controversially in the entrepreneurship literature (Rauch & Frese, 2007a). It is important to recognize that broad Big Five traits are aggregated across situations and time points. As a consequence, such traits can only predict broad and aggregated outcome variables (Epstein & O'Brien, 1985). Similarly, more narrow personality traits will predict narrow criteria. Thus, a broad personality trait cannot predict a specific entrepreneurial behavior in a specific situation. As a consequence, the nature of the criterion should dictate the choice of the right personality predictors.

As a matter of fact, the entrepreneurship literature has more recently studied a number of narrow traits that were not included in the meta-analyses discussed. Prominent examples of such narrow traits are passion (Baum & Locke, 2004), proactivity (Crant, 1996), and self-efficacy (Hmieleski & Baron, 2008). Passion is a strong feeling of love and enthusiasm for work and entrepreneurial activities. Passionate entrepreneurs work through barriers and respond to opportunities and challenges with fervor and ardor (Baum & Locke, 2004). Moreover, passion is related to goal setting and entrepreneurial behavior (Cardon, Wincent, Singh, & Drnovsek, 2009) as well as to venture performance (Baum & Locke, 2004). Thus, while passion has not been studied frequently enough in entrepreneurship research to be included in a meta-analysis, it seems to be an important ingredient of entrepreneurial behavior.

Proactivity is another personality characteristic that is not well covered by the Five Factor model. Proactive behavior reflects the propensity to take action and to change the environment (Bateman & Crant, 1993). Proactivity is related to entrepreneurship because proactive behavior is self-starting and it implies overcoming barriers in order to achieve one's goals (Frese, Fay, Hilburger, Leng, & Tag, 1997). Empirically, a number of studies supported the proposition that proactivity is related to business performance (Baum & Locke, 2004; Frese et al., 2007; Glaub, Fischer, Klemm, & Frese, 2012).

Self-efficacy belongs to core self-evaluations. Core self-evaluations are general judgments people make about themselves and their self-worth (Judge, Erez, Bono, & Thoresen, 2002). Core self-evaluations are distinct form Big Five traits and have been shown to be related to different organizational outcomes. Self-efficacy reflects one's confidence in the capabilities to perform various (and often unanticipated) tasks in uncertain situations (Bandura, 1997). Self-efficacy has been related to various entrepreneurial behaviors such as the intention to start a business venture, (Zhao, Seibert, & Hills, 2005), start up behavior (Chen, Greene, & Crick, 1998), and firm performance (Baum & Locke, 2004). Self-efficacy is important for entrepreneurship because it is related to persistence, search for challenges, initiative, active search for information, and long-term performance. Consequently, it is related to business creation and performance (Rauch & Frese, 2007b). Interestingly, self-efficacy can be conceptualized at different levels of specificity. Most studies in entrepreneurship conceptualized self-efficacy either as generalized (Rauch & Frese, 2007a) or as moderately generalized (Chen et al., 1998) but rarely as specific as the belief that one can perform a specific task.

In summary, depending on the criterion used studies should select either broad or narrow personality traits. General criteria such as business owners' self-assessment of his or her performance may well be predicted by broad personality traits. However, if researchers are interested in more specific criteria, such as how to negotiate a specific deal, they should investigate more narrow personality traits in order to achieve a good prediction.

The Process Dynamics of Personality Traits

The process dynamics in personality traits have been discussed with regard to three issues: the causality of effects, the mechanisms through which personality traits affect performance, and the different challenges and tasks during the entrepreneurship process that affect the relative importance of different predictor and criterion variables.

Regarding the causality of effects, most studies do assume that personality affects subsequent entrepreneurship behavior. This argument is based on the relative stability of personality factors. For example, twin studies indicated that about 50 percent of the variance in personality is genetically determined which minimizes the possibility to change personality characteristics (Tellegen, Lykken, Bouchard, Wilcox, Segal, & Rich, 1988). However, this assumption is not uncontested. For example, personality changes over life time indicating that traits are not absolutely stable (Roberts, Walton, & Viechtbauer, 2006). This is even more evident for specific personality traits. Moreover, there is evidence that training interventions increase self-efficacy (Eden & Aviram, 1993), proactivity (Glaub et al., 2012), and achievement motivation (Miron & McClelland, 1979). Therefore, the causality of effects reported in the literature could be reversed: Entrepreneurship behavior affects personality traits. However, the studies that tested causal effects indicated that the causal path goes from personality to entrepreneurial behavior. For example, Baum, Locke, and Smith (2001) showed that specific self-efficacy is related to performance and, most importantly, that this is a causal effect: CEO's self-efficacy affects subsequent performance (Baum & Locke, 2004). Another study indicated that Big Five traits predicted long term survival of business firms (Ciaverella et al., 2004). Clearly, there is a lack of longitudinal studies in entrepreneurship research.

Moreover, personality traits are distal to behavior and, therefore, not directly related to entrepreneurial behavior. Rather, the effect of distal constructs, such as broad Big Five traits, on behavior is transmitted or mediated through more proximal processes (Kanfer, 1992). Thus, entrepreneurship research needs to study a mediator model to explain the effect of personality traits. Mediator models are not new to the domain of entrepreneurship and there are a number of theoretical (Chell, 1985; Rauch & Frese, 2000; Sandberg & Hofer, 1987) and empirical mediator models (Baum & Locke, 2004; Frese et al., 2007) discussed in the literature. What these models usually have in common is the assumption that action related process variables are the mechanisms through which the effects of distal variables are transmitted. Such models explain how entrepreneurs with high levels of achievement motivations become successful, for example, because they develop better goals and action plans to achieve high performance in a given environment. Identifying such mediation processes is also important for developing interventions such as, for example, training programs for entrepreneurs. For example, while it is difficult to train broad Big Five traits, it is possible to train action process characteristics.

Finally, process dynamics also affect the relative importance of different personality variables during the entrepreneurship process. For example, Shane and Venkataraman (2000) defined entrepreneurship as the existence, recognition, and exploitation of opportunities and, thus, as a process that evolves over time. While the recognition of opportunities is predominantly dependent on cognitive processes, the decision to exploit an opportunity is in part driven by personality characteristics, such as risk-taking and self-efficacy. Other process models distinguished between the pre-launch phase, the launch phase, and the post-launch phase (Baron and Markman, 2004). Such models have in common that they assume that entrepreneurs have to accomplish different tasks and challenges during the entrepreneurship process. As a consequence, the relative importance of predictors and criteria changes during the entrepreneurship process (Baron, 2007). For example, one study indicated that extraversion is correlated with intentions in the pre-launch phase, with the amount of capital raised in the launch phase and with personal income in the post-launch phase (Baron and Markman, 2004). While such process models are not well validated in current entrepreneurship research, they point to problems inherent in a static model of entrepreneurship. Thus, entrepreneurship research needs to move beyond static models explaining the impact of personality traits to more dynamic models of the effects of entrepreneurs' personality characteristics on entrepreneurship behavior.

Moderators Affecting the Relationship between Personality Variables and Entrepreneurial Behavior

All meta-analyses that tested for the presence of moderator variables revealed heterogeneous effect sizes indicating that the relationship between personality characteristics and entrepreneurial behavior is dependent on moderator variables. Therefore, it is surprising to see how many studies in the domain of entrepreneurship examined direct relationship between personality characteristics and entrepreneurial behavior. Personality theory would suggest that the relationship between traits and behavior must be studied in a contingency framework (Argyle & Little, 1972; Mischel, 1968). For example, career choice decisions such as starting a business venture depend on the interactions between personality traits and the environment (Holland, 1985). Chell (1985) has argued for such a contingency framework for entrepreneurship as well. Unfortunately, the domain of entrepreneurship lacks a well-validated taxonomy of situational conditions. One categorization distinguishes four contexts: Business context (industry, market), social context (network, household, family), spatial context (geographic location) and institutional context (culture, political, economic context) (Welter, 2011). Other categorizations distinguished between the resource environment, the organizational environment, the task environment, and the macro-environment (Castrogiovanni, 1991). A psychological categorization of the environments is based on situational strength (Mischel, 1968). Strong situations determine behavior and, therefore, do not allow the expression of individual dispositions. In contrast, weak situations allow the expression of dispositions that affect behavior. For example, situations with little and ambiguous information are weaker than situations with more information and less ambiguity. Tasks with low structure and high autonomy are weak and, therefore, allow the expression of individual differences (Hattrup & Jackson, 1996). Notably, all the dimensions mentioned include sub-dimensions of the environment increasing the complexity of studying the effects of personality traits in a contingency framework. This might be one of the reasons that only a few empirical studies investigated interactions between personality traits and environmental conditions.

For example, one moderator that has been tested was culture. However, the meta-analysis by Zhao & Seibert (2006) did not support the proposition that culture affects the relationship between personality traits and career choice. Another study indicated that the relationship between personality traits and business performance was not moderated by culture; however, culture affected how entrepreneurs with high achievement orientations achieve performance. In Germany, a country high in uncertainty avoidance, achievement-oriented entrepreneurs developed detailed business plans in order to achieve performance. In contrast, in the Republic of Ireland, a country low in uncertainty avoidance, achievement-oriented entrepreneurs did not plan in detail in order to achieve performance (Rauch, Frese, & Sonnentag, 2000). Unfortunately, culture is a macro-level construct, which might be too broad to explain the consequences of individual-level behavior. Other studies looked at meso-level constructs of the environment. For example, one study examining different dimensions of the business environment indicated that optimism is positively correlated with venture performance in stable environments (Hmieleski and Baron, 2006). One might speculate whether favorable environments, which provide rich resources, many opportunities and market growth, allow the expression of personality traits and, as a consequence, whether there is a stronger relationship between personality characteristics and performance in favorable environments as compared to unfavorable environments. Given the theoretical arguments in favour of a contingency approach, entrepreneurship research needs more studies looking at interactions between personality and situational conditions. This is all the more important as more proximal personality constructs that are closer to behavior rely more heavily on specific situations. The empirical evidence regarding the interactions between entrepreneurs' personality and situational characteristic is too weak to allow any strong conclusions at present. Future research could contribute to contingency approaches by developing better measures of contexts that are then shown to affect the relationship between personality and behavior.

Multi-level Considerations

While personality characteristics are by definition individual-level constructs, venture performance is a firm-level construct and, moreover, economic wealth is a macro-level construct. A personality approach to entrepreneurship needs to develop arguments in respect of how individual-level personality characteristics affect higher level constructs. It is plausible to assume that personality characteristics are more highly related to individual-level outcomes than to firm-level outcome variables. However, in entrepreneurship many authors assume that in small and in new firms individual-level variables are virtually synonymous with firm-level variables (Hite & Hesterly, 2001). Consequently, the relationships between personality traits and entrepreneurship behavior should be higher in small and new firms as compared to large and established firms. However, the assumption that individual-level variables overlap with firm-level variables in larger and more established firms requires to propose that entrepreneurs with certain personality characteristics make early choices and decisions that affect firm-level variables and performance in the long term. This assumption has been verified to my knowledge only in one study (Baron, Hannan, & Burton, 1999). Most approaches in entrepreneurship research assume that in small and new companies the founder and owner determines judgments and decision-making that have an effect on firm-level variables which, in turn, affect firm-level outcomes (Shane, Locke, & Collins, 2003). This assumption requires developing hypotheses about how individual-level variables affect firm activities, such as planning and innovation.

McMullen and Shepherd (2006) developed a theoretical conceptualization that combines macro-level variables with individual-level behavior. The macro-level variables are the uncertainty that provides opportunities but also threats in the environment. The opportunities in a market become opportunities for those individual entrepreneurs who have the knowledge to reduce the uncertainty and the motivation to bear the uncertainty. We need such theoretical models that explain how individual-level personality characteristics affect firm-level outcomes. Empirically, entrepreneurship research needs to do multi-level research in order to examine, for example, how entrepreneurs' passion inspires the passion of the management team, of the whole firm and of customers and investors of that firm (Shepherd, 2011).

Intervention Programs: Is Personality Management an Issue worth Investing?

As already shown in this chapter, it is one of the myths in the domain of entrepreneurship research that one cannot change personality characteristics in training and intervention programs. In practice, such interventions are not part of entrepreneurship education, which traditionally focuses on providing knowledge about entrepreneurship and skills and tools that (should) help to start and grow new business ventures (Edelman, Manolova, & Brush, 2006). However, ignoring personality-related variables in entrepreneurship education and training implies neglecting one of the most powerful evidence based best practices. In fact, developing entrepreneurial characteristics is probably not more complicated than learning to develop a sophisticated business plan (which is in fact less useful). Of course, a training program would not address broad Big Five traits, which are indeed difficult to modify. Rather, a training program on entrepreneurial personality characteristics would focus on personality characteristics specifically related to the tasks of entrepreneurs. I will briefly describe training interventions that have been done on achievement motivation, proactivity, and self-efficacy.

Achievement motivation trainings have been developed within different formats ranging from week-long workshops to semester-long courses. Achievement motivation training usually forces participants to develop an understanding of the concept of achievement motivation, to achieve an understanding of own characteristics and goals, to practice achievement related activities, to develop the ability to relate achievement motives to own goals, to improve the ability to develop sub-goals and action plans, and to develop the ability to actively monitor progress and to seek feedback on goal accomplishment. Achievement motivation training is effective in underdeveloped economies and increased subsequent firm performance (Miron & McClelland, 1979). Moreover, Hansemark (1998) evaluated a course type of training program that aimed at developing abilities, skills and knowledge about entrepreneurship. The achievement training was only one component of the whole program. Course participants were compared to a control group and did significantly increase their achievement motivation during the course.

Glaub et al. (2012) developed a proactivity training, which was evaluated with a sample of 100 small business owners in Africa using a pre-test, post-test control group design. The three days training consisted of four components. First, the training aimed at developing an action oriented mental model via principles of action. Such models are accomplished by training rules of thumb. The actions principles were developed for each of the different facets of proactive behavior. Second, the principles of action were used for a guided learning-by-doing approach. More specifically, practical exercises exemplified the action principle and allowed learning through acting. Third, external and internal feedback processes were implemented in the training. Finally, transfer was incorporated in the training. The training was very effective; one year after the training, the sales levels of participating business owners increased by 27 percent and the number of employees by 35 percent.

Typical self-efficacy training is probably less complex and time consuming than the two interventions discussed above because it usually aims to achieve more specific training outcomes. Usually participants are confronted with models of successfully performing individuals. After observing these models, participants discuss their observations. Subsequently, participants practice the behavior seen, e.g., by role-playing. Lastly, they receive feedback on the behavior performed. The feedback on the own performance and the mastery experience when performing the behavior are the critical mechanism that make the self-efficacy training effective. While I am not aware about any self-efficacy training in the domain of entrepreneurship, there are many studies in organizational behavior that proved its effectiveness, e.g., on reducing the time of unemployment (Eden & Aviram, 1993).

I think that these examples indicate that personality development is possible, useful, and should be implemented in modern entrepreneurship education and training. An evaluation of the impact of such training interventions requires a two-stage assessment. First, it is useful to measure the immediate impact of entrepreneurship training. In addition, the effects of such interventions evolve over time suggesting that a second assessment should involve a longer time lag (Rauch & Hulsink, 2013).

CONCLUSIONS

The deep skepticism in the academic literature about the personality approach to entrepreneurship motivated me to write this book chapter. A number of recent meta-analyses and developments in the application of the personality approach contributed to my conclusion that this approach is well validated and useful for the domain of entrepreneurship. The review allows drawing several conclusions.

First, personality traits do affect entrepreneurial behavior. The critics of the personality approach to entrepreneurship, which was based on narrative methods for the review was wrong as a number of meta-analyses suggested. As a matter of fact, the effects sizes of specific traits were higher as compared to effect sizes reported for the relationship between business plans and performance (Brinckmann, Grichnik, & Kapsa, 2010) and the relationship between innovation and performance (Rosenbusch, Brinckmann, & Bausch, 2011). Thus, entrepreneurship research should not neglect personality traits but include them in multivariate models explaining venture performance.

Second, the selection of personality characteristics should be based on theoretical considerations (Low & MacMillan, 1988). Descriptive studies will not contribute to understanding how entrepreneurs achieve their goals. For example, an analysis of entrepreneurs' tasks may reveal specific aspects of entrepreneurs' personality that are important for running a business successfully. Accordingly, specific traits that are theoretically related to the tasks of entrepreneurs provide valid estimates for entrepreneurial behavior and business performance (Rauch & Frese, 2007b).

Third, it is probably oversimplified to assume direct effects of entrepreneurs' personality characteristics on entrepreneurial behavior. Rather, the relationship between personality characteristics and entrepreneurial behavior is complex involving mediating and moderating processes. The role of mediators is relatively well known and accepted. For example, the effects of broad personality traits on behavior are mediated by more proximal variables, such as goal setting and action planning (compare Figure 1 by Rauch and Frese, 2000). However, more research is required to identify critical moderator variables. It is in general difficult to identify moderator variables (McClelland & Judd, 1993); in entrepreneurship research, this is additionally complicated by the absence of a decent taxonomy of situational/environmental variables (Welter, 2011). From my point of view, it is a misunderstanding that personality approaches propose an ego-centered framework overemphasizing the role of the entrepreneur. Theoretically, the effects of dispositions depend on environmental conditions, even though many empirical investigations ignored the role of the environment.

Fourth, more research is required to unfold the process dynamics of personality traits. This issue needs to be explored with regard to the causality of effects, changes in personality characteristics, and changing opportunities and threats that require changing decision behavior by the entrepreneur.

Fifth, the effects of personality traits need to be conceptualized in a multivariate and multilevel model of entrepreneurship performance. Such a model needs to include additional individual differences variables as well as other non-personality constructs. Thus, the proponents of the personality approach need to account for non-personality effects and, at the same time, economic models of entrepreneurship need to take individual-level processes into account. Otherwise, their models are miss-specified and potentially spurious correlations may appear and cannot be controlled (Rauch & Frese, 2007a, p. 61).

Sixth, the personality approach to entrepreneurship provides strong practice contributions. Since personality characteristics are valid predictors of entrepreneurial behavior, they can be used for selection purposes by institutions supporting entrepreneurs, such as incubators and investors. Moreover, entrepreneurial personality traits can be modified and, therefore, provide ample opportunities for training and education for entrepreneurs and people interested in starting an entrepreneurial career.

Seventh, many governments support entrepreneurship by focusing on certain industries or innovative business start-ups assuming that these enterprises are most promising agents for economic growth and wealth creation. However, such a focus on innovative businesses is not justified by scientific evidence because personality predictors explain more variance in firm performance as compared to these economic predictors (Frese et al., 2012). Thus, a policy implication of this research is that programs should support individual entrepreneurs.

Taking these considerations into account, personality traits can explain more than just a minor share of entrepreneurial behavior. Thus, in contrast to the conclusions of certain reviews in the eighties, the present chapter provides more ground for optimism with regard to the contributions of personality theory to entrepreneurship.

NOTES

1. The original article relied on d values. For consistency reasons, I converted all d values into r values. r values represent correlations coefficients.
2. I calculated the sample size weighted mean correlation between the different performance measures used by Zhao et al., 2010.

REFERENCES

Argyle, M., & Little, B. R. (1972), 'Do personality traits apply to social behaviour?' *Journal for the Theory of Social Behaviour*, **2**(1), 1–33. doi:10.1111/j.1468-5914.1972.tb00302.x.

Bandura, A. (1997), *Self-efficacy: The Exercise of Control*. New York: Freeman and Co.

Baron, J. N., Hannan, M., & Burton, D. M. (1999), 'Building the iron cage: Determinants of managerial intensity in early years of organizations', *American Sociological Review*, **64**(4), 527–47.

Baron, R. A. (2007), 'Entrepreneurship: A process perspective', in J. R. Baum, M. Frese, & J. Baron (Eds.), *The Psychology of Entrepreneurship*. London: Lawrence Erlbaum Associates.

Baron, R. A., & Markman, G. D. (2004), 'Toward a process view of entrepreneurship: The changing impact of individual-level variables across phases of new firm development', in M. A. Rahim, R. T. Golembiewski, & K. D. McMackenzie (Eds.), *Current Topics in Management* (pp. 44–64). New Brunswick, NY: Transaction Publishers.

Barrick, M. R., & Mount, M. K. (1991), 'The big five personality dimensions and job performance: A meta-analysis', *Personnel Psychology*, **44**(1), 1–26.

Bateman, T. S., & Crant, J. M. (1993), 'The proactive component of organizational behavior: A measure and correlates', *Journal of Organizational Behavior*, **14**(2), 103–18.

Baum, J. R. & Locke, E. A. (2004), 'The relation of entrepreneurial traits, skill, and motivation to subsequent venture growth', *Journal of Applied Psychology*, **89**(4), 587–98.

Baum J. R., Locke, E. A. & Smith, K. G. (2001), 'A multidimensional model of venture performance', *Academy of Management Journal*, **44**(2) 292–303.

Brandstätter, H. (2011), 'Personality aspects of entrepreneurship: A look at five meta-analyses: Special Issue on personality and economics', *Personality and Individual Differences*, **51**(3), 222–30. doi:10.1016/j.paid.2010.07.007.

Brandstätter, H. (1997), 'Becoming an entrepreneur – a question of personality structure?' *Journal of Economic Psychology*, 18, 15777.

Brinckmann, J., Grichnik, D. & Kapsa, D. (2010), 'Should entrepreneurs plan or just storm the castle? A meta-analysis on contextual factors impacting the business planning-performance relationship in small firms', *Journal of Business Venturing*, **24**(1), 24–40.

Brockhaus, R. H., & Horwitz, P. S. (1986), 'The psychology of the entrepreneur', in D. L. Sexton & R. W. Smilor (Eds.), *The Art and Science of Entrepreneurship* (pp. 25–48). Cambridge, MA: Ballinger.

Busenitz, L. W. (1996), 'Research on entrepreneurial alertness', *Journal of Small Business Management*, **34**(4), 35–44.

Cardon, M. S., Wincent J., Singh J. & Drnovsek M. (2009), 'The nature and experience of entrepreneurial passion', *Academy of Management Review*, **34**(3), 511–32.

Castrogiovanni, G. J. (1991), 'Environmental munificence: A theoretical assessment', *Academy of Management Review*, **16**(1), 542–65.

Chen, C. C., Greene, P. G. & Crick, A. (1998), 'Does entrepreneurial self-efficacy distinguish entrepreneurs from managers?' *Journal of Business Venturing*, **13**(4), 295–316.

Chell, E. (1985), 'The entrepreneurial personality: A few ghosts laid to rest?' *International Small Business Journal*, **3**(3), 43–54. doi:10.1177/026624268500300303.

Chell, E. (2008), *The Entrepreneurial Personality: A Social Construction* (2nd ed.), London, U.K: Routledge.

Ciaverella, M. A., Buchholtz, A. K., Riordan, C. M., Gatewood, R. D., & Stokes, G. S. (2004), 'The big five and venture survival: Is there a linkage?' *Journal of Business Venturing*, 19, 465–83.

Cohen, J. (1977), *Statistical Power Analysis for the Behavioral Science*. New York: Academic Press.

Collins, C. J., Hanges, P. J. and Locke, E. E. (2004), 'The relationship of achievement motivation to entrepreneurial behavior: A meta-analysis', *Human Performance*, **17**(1), 95–117.

Costa, P. T. & McCrae, R. R. (1988), 'From catalog to classification: Murray's needs and the five-factor model', *Journal of Personality and Social Psychology*, 55, 258–65.

Crant, J. M. (1996), 'The proactive personality scale as a predictor of entrepreneurial intentions', *Journal of Small Business Management*, **34**(3), 42–9.

Cronbach, L. J. & Gleser, G. (1965), *Psychological Tests and Personnel Decisions* (2nd ed.), Urbana: University of Illinois Press.

Edelman, L., Manolova, T. S. & Brush, C. G. (2006), 'Entrepreneurship education: Correspondence between practices of nascent entrepreneurs and textbook prescriptions for success', *Academy of Management Learning & Education*, pp. 56–70.

Eden, D. & Aviram, A. (1993), 'Self-efficacy training to speed reemployment: Helping people to help themselves', *Journal of Applied Psychology*, **78**, 352–60.

Epstein, S. and O'Brien, E. J. (1985), 'The person-situation debate in historical and current perspective', *Psychological Bulletin*, 98, 513–37.

Eysenck, H. (1991), 'Dimensions of personality: 16: 5 or 3? Criteria for a taxonomic paradigm', *Personality and Individual Differences*, 12, 773–90.

Finison, L. J. (1976), 'The application of McClelland's National Development Model to recent data', *The Journal of Social Psychology*, 98, 55–9.

Frese, M., Bausch, A., Schmidt, P., Rauch, A., & Kabst, R. (2012), 'Evidence-based Entrepreneurship (EBE): Cumulative science, action principles, and bridging the gap between science and practice', *Foundations and Trends in Entrepreneurship*, **8**(1), 1–62.

Frese, M., Fay, D., Hilburger, T., Leng, K., & Tag, A. (1997), 'The concept of personal initiative: Operationalization, reliability and validity in two German samples', *Journal of Organizational and Occupational Psychology*, 70, 139–61.

Frese, M., Krauss, S. I., Keith, N., Escher, S., Grabarkiewicz, R., Luneng, S. T., . . . (2007), 'Business owners' action planning and its relationship to business success in three African countries', *Journal of Applied Psychology*, **92**(6), 1481–98. doi:10.1037/0021-9010.92.6.1481.

Frese, M., Krauss, S. I., & Friedrich, C. (2000), 'Micro-enterprises in Zimbabwe: On the function of socio-demographic factors, psychological strategies, personal initiative, and goal setting for entrepreneurial success', in M. Frese (Ed.) *Success and Failure of Micro-business Owners in Africa. A New Psychological Approach*, Westport, CT: Greenwood, (pp. 103–30).

Frey, R. S. (1984), 'Need for achievement, entrepreneurship, and economic growth: a critique of the McClelland thesis', *The Social Science Journal*, 21, 125–34.

Funder, D. C. (2001), *The Personality Puzzle* (2nd ed.), New York: Norton.

Gartner, W. (1988), '"Who is an entrepreneur?" is the wrong question', *Entrepreneurship: Theory and Practice*, **12**(2), 47–68.

Glass, G. V., McGaw, B. and Smith, M. L. (1981), *Meta-analysis in Social Research*. Beverly Hills, CA: Sage.

Glaub, M., Fischer, S., Klemm, M., & Frese, M. (2012), *A theory-based controlled randomized field intervention: Increasing proactive behavior (personal initiative) in small business owners leads to entrepreneurial success*, Manuscript, University of Giessen.

Hansemark, O. C. (1998), 'The effects of an entrepreneurship programme on Need for Achievement and Locus of Control of reinforcement', *International Journal of Entrepreneurial Behavior and Research*, **4**(1), 28–50.

Hattrup, K., & Jackson, S. E. (1996), *Learning about Individual Differences by Taking Situations Seriously*. San Francisco: Jossey-Bass.

Hite, J. M., & Hesterly, W. S. (2001), 'The evolution of firm networks: from emergence to early growth of the firm', *Strategic Management Journal*, **22**(3), 275–86, doi:10.1002/smj.156.

Hmieleski, K. M. & Baron, R. A. (2009), 'Entrepreneurs' optimism and new venture performance: A social cognitive perspective', *Academy of Management Journal*, **52**(3), 473–88. doi:10.5465/AMJ.2009.41330755.

Hmieleski, K. M. & Baron, R. (2008), 'When does entrepreneurial self-efficacy enhance versus reduce firm performance?' *Strategic Entrepreneurship Journal*, 2, 57–72.

Hmieleski, K. M. & Baron, R. A. (2006), 'Optimism and environmental uncertainty: Implications for entrepreneurial performance', in A. Zacharakis, S. Alvarez, P. Davidsson, J. Fiet, G. George, & et al (Eds.), *Frontiers of Entrepreneurship Research*. Wellesley, MA: Babson College.

Holland, J. L. (1985), *Making Vocational Choices*. Englewood Cliffs, NJ: Prentice Hall.

Hough, L. (1992), 'The 'Big Five' Personality Variables–Construct Confusion: Description versus Prediction', *Human Performance*, **5**(1), 139–55.

Judge, T. A., Erez, A., Bono, J. E., & Thoresen, C. (2002), 'Are measures of self-esteem, neuroticism, locus of control, and generalized self-efficacy indicators of a common core construct?' *Journal of Personality and Social Psychology*, **83**(3), 693–710.

Kanfer, R. (1992), 'Work motivation: New directions in theory and research', in C. L. Cooper & I. T. Robertson (Eds.), *International Review of Industrial and Organizational Psychology* (pp. 1–53). London: John Wiley & Sons, Ltd.

Kirzner, I. M. (1997), 'Entrepreneurial discovery and the competitive market process: An Austrian approach', *Journal of Economic Literature*, **35**(1), 60–85.

Knight, F. H. (1921), *Risk, Uncertainty, and Profit*, New York: Kelly and Millman.

Lipsey, M. W. & Wilson, D. B. (2001), *Practical Meta-analysis*, London: Sage.

Low, M. & MacMillan, B. (1988), 'Entrepreneurship: Past research and future challenges', *Journal of Management*, **14**(2), 139–62.

McClelland, D. (1961), *The Achieving Society*. New York: Free Press.

McClelland, G. and Judd, C. (1993), 'Statistical difficulties of detecting interactions and moderator effects', *Psychological Bulletin*, 114, 376–90.

McMullen, J. S. & Shepherd, D. A. (2006), 'Entrepreneurial action and the role of uncertainty in the theory of the entrepreneur', *Academy of Management Review*, **31**(1), 132–52.

Miner, J. B. & Raju, N. S. (2004), 'Risk propensity differences between managers and entrepreneurs and between low- and high-growth entrepreneurs: A reply in a more conservative vain', *Journal of Applied Psychology*, **89**(1), 3–13.

Miron, D. & McClelland, D. C. (1979), 'The impact of achievement motivation training on small businesses', *California Management Review*, **21**(4), 13–28.

Mischel, W. (1968), *Personality and Assessment*, New York: Wiley.

Ones, D. S. and Viswesvaran, C. (1996), 'Bandwidth-fidelity dilemma in personality measurement for personnel selection', *Journal of Organizational Behavior*, 17, 609–26.

Paunonen, S. V. & Aston, M. C. (2001), 'Big five factors and the prediction of behavior', *Journal of Personality and Social Psychology*, **81**(3), 524–39.

Rauch, A., & Frese, M. (2007a), 'Born to be an entrepreneur: Revisiting the personality approach to entrepreneurship', in J. R. Baum, M. Frese, & J. Baron (Eds.), *The Psychology of Entrepreneurship* (pp. 41–66). London: Lawrence Erlbaum Associates.

Rauch, A., & Frese, M. (2007b), 'Let's put the person back into entrepreneurship research: A meta-analysis of the relationship between business owners' personality traits, business creation and success', *European Journal of Work and Organizational Psychology*, **16**(4), 353–85.

Rauch, A., and Frese, M. (2006), 'Meta-analysis as a tool for developing entrepreneurship research and theory', In J. Wiklund, D. P. Dimov, J. Katz, & D. Shepherd (Eds.), *Advances in Entrepreneurship, Firm Emergence, and Growth* (pp. 29–52). London: Elsevier.

Rauch, A. & Frese, M. (2000), 'Psychological approaches to entrepreneurial success: A general model and an overview of findings', in C. Cooper & I. Robertson (Eds.), *International Review of Industrial and Organizational Psychology* (Vol 3, pp.101–41). New York: John Wiley & Sons, Ltd.

Rauch, A., Frese, M., & Sonnentag, S. (2000), 'Cultural differences in planning/success relationships: A comparison of small enterprises in Ireland, West Germany, and East Germany', *Journal of Small Business Management*, **38**(4), 28–41.

Rauch, A. & Hulsink, W. (2013), '*Putting entrepreneurship education where the intention to act lies: An investigation into the impact of entrepreneurship education on entrepreneurial behavior*'. Manuscript: RSM Erasmus University, Rotterdam.

Roberts, B. W., Walton, K. & Viechtbauer W. (2006), 'Patterns of mean-level change in personality traits across the life course: a meta-analysis of longitudinal studies', *Psychological Bulletin*, **132**(1), 1–25.

Rosenbusch, N., Brinckmann, J. & Bausch, A. (2011), 'Is innovation always beneficial? A meta-analysis of the relationship between innovation and performance in SMEs', *Journal of Business Venturing*, **26**(4), 441–457. doi:10.1016/j.jbusvent.2009.12.002

Sandberg, W. R., & Hofer, C. W. (1987), 'Improving new venture performance: The role of strategy, industry structure, and the entrepreneur', *Journal of Business Venturing*, **2**(1), 5–28.

Schumpeter, J. (1935), *Theorie der wirtschaftlichen Entwicklung (Theory of Economic Growth)*. München: Von Duncker und Humbolt.

Shane, S., Locke, E. A. & Collins, C. J. (2003), 'Entrepreneurial motivation', *Human Resource Planning*, 13, 257–79.

Shane, S., & Venkataraman, S. (2000), The promise of entrepreneurship as a field of research. *Academy of Management Review*, **25**(1), 217–26.

Shepherd, D. A. (2011), Multilevel entrepreneurship research: Opportunities for studying entrepreneurial decision making. *Journal of Management*, **37**(2), 412–20. doi:10.1177/0149206310369940

Stewart, W. H., & Roth, P. L. (2001), Risk propensity differences between entrepreneurs and managers: A meta-analytic review. *Journal of Applied Psychology*, **86**(1), 145–53.

Stewart, W. H. & Roth, P. L. (2004), Data-quality affects meta-analytic conclusions: A response to Miner and Raju (2004) concerning entrepreneurial risk propensity. *Journal of Applied Psychology*, **89**(1), 14–21.

Stewart, W. H. & Roth, P. L. (2007), A meta-analysis of achievement motivation: Differences between entrepreneurs and managers. *Journal of Small Business Management*, **45**(4), 401–21. doi:10.1111/j.1540-627X.2007.00220.x.

Tellegen, A., Lykken, D. T., Bouchard, T. J., Wilcox, K. J., Segal, N. L., & Rich, S. (1988), Personality similarity in twins reared apart and together. *Journal of Personality and Social* Psychology, **54**(6), 1031–9. doi:10.1037/0022-3514.54.6.1031.

Thorne, S. (2009), The role of qualitative research within an evidence-based context: Can metasynthesis be the answer? Clinical Research. *International Journal of Nursing Studies*, **46**(4), 569–75. doi:10.1016/j.ijnurstu.2008.05.001.

Utsch, A., Rauch, A., Rothfuss, R., & Frese, M. (1999), 'Who becomes a small scale entrepreneur in a post-socialistic environment: On the differences between entrepreneurs and managers in East Germany', *Journal of Small Business Management*, **37**(3), 31–42.

Viswesvaran, C., & Ones, D. S. (1995), Theory testing: Combining psychometric meta-analysis and structural equation modeling. *Personnel Psychology*, **48**, 865–85.

Welter, F. (2011), 'Contextualizing entrepreneurship – conceptual challenges and ways forward', *Entrepreneurship: Theory and Practice*, (1), 165–84.

Wooten, K. C. & Timmerman, T. A. (1999), 'The use of personality and the five factor model to predict business ventures: From outplacement to start-up', *Journal of Vocational Behavior*, 54, 82–101.

Zhao, H. S. & Seibert, S. E. (2006), 'The big five personality dimensions and entrepreneurial status: A meta-analytical review', *Journal of Applied Psychology*, **91**(2), 259–71.

Zhao, H. S., Seibert, S. E. & Hills, G. E. (2005), 'The mediating role of self-efficacy in the development of entrepreneurial intentions', *Journal of Applied Psychology*, **90**(6), 1265–72.

Zhao, H., Seibert, S. E., & Lumpkin, G. T. (2010), 'The relationship of personality to entrepreneurial intentions and performance: A meta-analytic review', *Journal of Management*, **39**(2), 381–404.

PART III

DISCIPLINARY APPROACHES TO ENTREPRENEURSHIP

11. Characteristics and behaviours associated with innovative people in small- and medium-sized enterprises

Fiona Patterson and Máire Kerrin

INTRODUCTION

As a result of changes in markets and the competitive strategies of large organisations, there is increasing pressure on small- and medium-sized enterprises (SMEs) to focus on innovation, innovation capabilities and innovation management (McAdam et al., 2004). Shortening product lifecycles and accelerating technological changes have generated a particular innovation imperative, as well as opportunities for SMEs (O'Regan et al., 2005, cited in Hotho & Champion, 2011). Enhancing innovation in SMEs remains at the heart of policy initiatives for stimulating economic development at the local, regional, national and European levels (Jones and Tilley, 2003).

We believe that psychological research on innovation is particularly important, since innovation at work ultimately involves human behaviour. Thus, examining innovation from individual-, group-, and organisational-level applied psychological perspectives may offer a unique perspective on innovation theory and practice. SMEs need to create and sustain conditions relevant to innovation, which broadly relate to facilitating conditions (so that people can innovate) and motivating conditions (so that people are willing to innovate) (Angle, 1989). Moreover, current research evidence indicates that organisations need to understand how to identify the characteristics and behaviours of innovative people and, consequently, how to promote and encourage innovative working within organisations. Although research on human capital is increasingly taking into account social factors, evidence on the psychological determinants of human capital remains a research gap that needs to be filled (Marcati, Guido & Peluso, 2008).

In this chapter, we have identified the people-relevant resources for innovation to occur in organisations (see Figure 11.1). Following a review of the definitions of innovation, the main part of this chapter discusses the roles of employee cognition, personality, motivation, knowledge, behaviour, and mood state, before focusing on psychological characteristics of the owner/leader within SMEs. Practical implications for interventions in small businesses are examined, and future research directions relating to corporate and governmental policy are presented.

DEFINITION OF INNOVATION

Researchers tend to agree that an individual's ability to innovate at work is influenced by several factors: individual-level factors, group-level factors, and organisational-level factors. A key problem within the research literature stems from the inherent difficulty in defining and understanding the phenomenon of innovation and how it can inform practice.

Historically, there has been confusion surrounding the terminology relating to innovation and creativity, particularly in definitions and in criteria for assessment. Although in general terms creativity and innovation may be viewed as overlapping constructs (Axtell et al., 2000; Patterson, 2002), the main distinction between the two constructs is with regard to novelty. Creativity is exclusively concerned with generating new and entirely original ideas. Innovation, however, is a broader concept that also encompasses the application of new ideas to produce something new and useful (in the context of groups, organisations or societies). Innovation is often referred to as a process, because implementing new ideas necessarily involves influencing others (whereas creativity could be achieved in isolation). Employee innovation goes beyond individual creativity as it also concerns the extent to which employees implement and sustain innovations. Further, an innovation could be the application of something familiar in one organisation to another organisation (i.e. imported innovation).

There has been a strong interest in the concept of entrepreneurship within the broader SME literature. The defining features of innovation and entrepreneurship also overlap (Bhupatiraju et al., 2012). Entrepreneurship has been defined as a context-specific social process through which individuals and teams create wealth by bringing together unique packages of resources to exploit marketplace opportunities (Ireland et al., 2001). Generating wealth first requires creating value. Entrepreneurs create value by leveraging innovation to exploit new opportunities and to create new product-market domains (Miles, 2005, cited in Hitt et al., 2011). Shane and Venkataraman (2000) argued that entrepreneurship involves *sources* of opportunities; the *processes* of discovery, evaluation, and exploitation of opportunities; and the set of individuals who discover, evaluate, and exploit opportunities. Thus, development of innovation is a key domain of entrepreneurship (Sirmon & Hitt, 2003), while entrepreneurship may be conceptualised as the 'parent of innovation' (Kerin, 1992).

Consistent with conceptualisations used in both the management and psychology research literatures; in this chapter we adopt the definition of innovation as 'change associated with the creation and adaptation of ideas that are new-to-world, new-to-nation/region, new-to-industry or new-to-firm' (Patterson, Kerrin & Gatto-Roissard, 2009). This definition encompasses both the *processes* individuals use and the *outcomes* that are achieved. It also includes a wide range of innovation types that occur in organisations (e.g. products, process, technological, administrative, incremental, etc.).

EMPLOYEE RESOURCES FOR INNOVATION

Research suggests that a number of individual, work environment and external resources are likely to influence individual innovation within organisations. Figure 11.1 summarises and highlights the general resources related to innovation outcomes. In this chapter, we focus solely on core employee resources, characteristics and behaviours.

The majority of innovation research conducted and published in the psychological research literature over the years has focused on identifying the various traits and

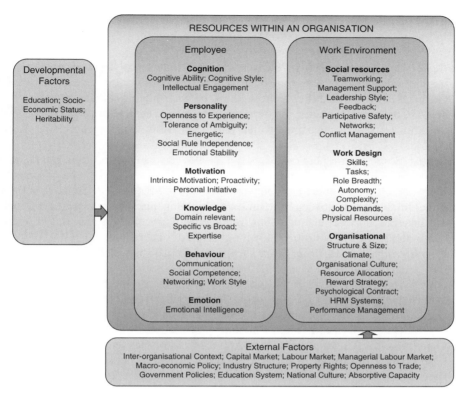

Figure 11.1   Resources within an organisation relating to innovation

personal characteristics that facilitate individual or group innovation. Research shows that innovation involves multiple components at the individual level. In 1999, Sternberg and Lubart proposed an '*investment theory*', suggesting that the propensity to innovate requires a confluence of six distinct resources, including, intellectual abilities, knowledge, styles of thinking, personality, motivation and environment. Other integrative approaches include the '*geneplore*' model and the '*componential*' model. These models reflect the key areas of research at the person-level, whereby previous literature can be classified into associations between innovation and the following constructs: (a) cognitive ability; (b) knowledge; (c) motivation; (d) personality; (e) behavioural abilities; and (f) emotion and mood states.

Research evidence on the relationship between innovation potential and these key individual-level resources is presented in the following sections.

Cognitive Ability

Numerous researchers have explored the association between innovation potential and intelligence. However, the findings are generally inconclusive. Much of the research literature in this area can be classified into four categories, which conceive of innovation as: (i) a subset of general intelligence; (ii) an aspect of genius; (iii) a set of cognitive abilities and mental processes; and, (iv) associated with observer judgements of intelligence. A brief review of these conceptualisations is provided below.

(i) *General intelligence.* Early research claimed that creativity was equivalent to high intelligence (e.g. Spearman, 1923). The best-known researcher in this field is Guilford, who claimed that creative thinking was a mental ability involving divergent production. However, review studies have been critical of the use of divergent thinking tests as a measure of creativity (Barron & Harrington, 1981; Lubart, 2003).

(ii) *Genius.* Some researchers (e.g. Eysenck, 1994) have suggested that genius, as the most obvious manifestation of high intelligence, is closely tied to the propensity to innovate. However, there has been a notable lack of research evidence to support a direct relationship between innovation and intelligence. Many researchers, including Eysenck, have concluded that intelligence is probably a necessary condition (but not a sufficient condition) for innovation to occur.

(iii) *Cognitive abilities.* In 1992, Finke, Ward and Smith suggested a framework called the 'geneplore model'. The model proposes that many creative activities can be described in terms of an initial generation of ideas or solutions, followed by an extensive exploration of those ideas. Individual differences occur due to variations in the use and application of these generative processes, together with the sophistication of an individual's memory and knowledge in the relevant domain. Generative thinking and contextual application are seen as necessary but not sufficient conditions for innovation. More recently, researchers have called for studies that investigate the specific cognitive abilities required for the implementation phase of the innovation process (Mumford, 2003).

(iv) *Observer judgements of intelligence.* Innovative individuals are often perceived and rated by others as more intelligent than less innovative individuals. Historically, the research literature on innovation and intelligence has lacked clarity. Part of the problem has been that intelligence (similar to innovation) is often viewed as a unitary concept. Previous theories of intelligence have tended to over-emphasise cognitive abilities and underestimate the role of knowledge-based intelligence.

Knowledge

Most researchers in this field, regardless of their theoretical approach, have assumed that knowledge is a key variable in both generative thinking and innovation. Immersion in domain-specific knowledge is a prerequisite for innovation, as one must have an accurate sense of a domain (i.e. contextual relevance) before one can hope to change it for the better. However, the research literature highlights the fact that too much expertise in one area may also block innovation within that domain (Sternberg, 1982). There is believed to be an inverted-U-shaped relationship between knowledge and innovation, where too much or too little knowledge inhibits new inventions.

Domain-relevant knowledge reflects how much an individual knows about a given area; the research literature suggests that this knowledge may be broad, and that highly complex or detailed knowledge is not required (Amabile, 1996; Mascitelli, 2000).

Csikszentmihalyi (1988) suggests that an individual who wants to make an innovative contribution must not only work within a system, but must also reproduce that system in his or her mind. Personal mastery and an accurate sense of contextual relevance are also necessary antecedents of innovation. However, like intelligence, domain knowledge is necessary, but not sufficient for innovation to occur.

Motivation

High levels of motivation are believed to be required for innovation to occur and innovators are often viewed as displaying a devotion and total absorption in their work (Eysenck, 1994). In the 1980s, Amabile suggested that innovation comprises three components, including (1) intrinsic task motivation, (2) domain-relevant skills (i.e. expertise), and (3) innovation-relevant process skills (e.g. cognitive skills and work styles conducive to novelty). Amabile's model includes a five-stage description of the innovation process, where the roles of the three components vary at each of the stages. The five stages are: task presentation; preparation; idea generation; idea validation; and outcome assessment. Amabile's model is useful in that it suggests how and where individual skills and motivation affect the progress of the innovation process.

Although theories on innovation and creativity usually refer to intrinsic motivation as one of the most important antecedents of creativity and innovation, few studies have studied the association between intrinsic motivation and innovation empirically. One exception is a study by Shin and Zhou (2003), which reported that a transformational style of leadership promoted employees' intrinsic motivation, which was conducive to creative performance. Similarly, in a laboratory-based study, Sosik et al. (1999) found that a transformational leadership style was conductive to '*flow*', a psychological state characterised by intrinsic motivation, concentration, and enjoyment, which encourages idea generation. These studies provide support for the notion that motivation may be an important mediator between leadership style and creative performance.

Whilst intrinsic motivation is likely to be a prerequisite for innovation (Amabile, 1988; Frese et al., 1999; West, 1987), the role of extrinsic motivators is less clear (Harrison et al., 2006). In exploring environmental influences on motivation, research evidence suggests that constructive evaluation (i.e. being informative and supportive; recognising accomplishment) can enhance innovation. Amabile suggests that intrinsic motivation is particularly important in situations that require novelty, and that extrinsic motivators may be a distraction during the early stages of the innovation process. Later in the innovation process, where persistence and evaluation of ideas is required, synergistic extrinsic motivators may help innovators persist in solving problems. Any extrinsic motivator that enhances an employee's sense of competence without undermining self-determination should enhance motivation and thus increase the propensity for innovation (Eisenberger & Cameron, 1996). Mumford (2003) also suggested that it is possible that intrinsic and extrinsic motivation might serve different functions; intrinsic motivation might be linked to work on a task, while extrinsic motivation might affect choice of task, field, or implementation strategy.

Sauermann and Cohen (2008) recently analysed the impact of individual motivation on organisational innovation and performance. They found that intrinsic and extrinsic motivation affected both individual effort and the overall quality of the innovative endeavours. The study confirmed that extrinsic rewards, such as pay, were not as important in enhancing innovation as certain aspects of intrinsic motivation, such as the desire for intellectual change. These findings have obvious implications for how best to nurture innovation within the workplace. Further research could investigate the part that different aspects of intrinsic motivation play in innovation, such as curiosity, improving feelings of mastery, self-expression potential, and the resolution of conflicts.

Personality

From several decades of research on the association between innovation and personality, a set of characteristics has consistently emerged as being beneficial to innovation. These include being imaginative and inquisitive, having high energy, a high desire for autonomy, social rule independence, and having high self-confidence. The Five Factor Model (FFM) of personality (also known as the Big Five personality traits) has become a near-universal template with which to understand the structure of personality. The FFM dimensions are: (1) Openness to Experience (ideas, aesthetics); (2) Agreeableness (compliance, straightforwardness); (3) Conscientiousness (order, dutifulness, competence); (4) Extroversion (warmth, gregarious, activity); and (5) Neuroticism (anxiety, depression). Given that the FFM is an appropriate model for charting individual differences among adult populations, it provides a useful structure to review the literature exploring associations between personality and innovation. Some researchers (e.g. Rauch & Frese, 2007) argued that 'the predictive validity of Big Five traits should be lower in entrepreneurship research than in research on employees'. In this section, we provide a review of research on innovation and the FFM of personality, which could be applied both to leaders and to employees of SMEs.

(1)   *Openness to Experience.* There is good empirical evidence of a positive association between characteristics associated with innovation and openness to experience (e.g. being imaginative, original, flexible, and unconventional; Feist, 1998). Research suggests that openness enhances an individual's intrinsic motivation towards novelty and, therefore, works in a multiplicative way to produce innovation (King et al., 1996). There are some inconsistencies in the research findings, with recent research suggesting that the relationship between openness to experience and innovation may be moderated by contextual factors (Andrews & Smith, 1996; Burke & Witt, 2002; Baer & Oldham, 2006). However, other research suggests that openness is perhaps the most important personality dimension directly related to propensity for innovation (Patterson, 2002; Batey & Furnham, 2006; Furnham, 1999; Gelade, 1997; Harrison et al., 2006; King et al., 1996; McCrae, 1987; Wolfradt & Pretz, 2001).

(2)   *Agreeableness.* Empirical studies have confirmed a negative association between innovation and agreeableness by showing that innovators tend to have high social rule independence (George & Zhou, 2001; Gelade, 1997; Patterson, 1999). These findings are consistent with Eysenck's emphasis on the potentially negative dispositional characteristics of innovators, where innovators are often outspoken, uninhibited, quarrelsome, and sometimes asocial. Agreeableness is likely to be important in the implementation process of innovation but not for idea generation.

It is logical that the implementation of new ideas is likely to be a group effort, which involves social processes and activities. Such findings have important repercussions for the selection and management of employees.

(3) *Conscientiousness*. The majority of research has demonstrated that lower levels of conscientiousness are associated with innovation (Barron & Harrington, 1981; Gelade, 1997; Harrison et al., 2006; Runco, 2004). Defined by terms such as fastidious, ordered, neat and methodical, research suggests that highly conscientious individuals are more resistant to change at work, and are more likely to comply with current organisational norms. This has important implications for selection and assessment which traditionally places a high value in this area.

(4) *Extroversion*. With regard to the relationship between extroversion and innovation, findings are not clear-cut. The association between extroversion and innovation seems to be context-dependent. Introversion is likely to be related to real-life artistic endeavour, whereas extroversion seems to predict performance measures of creativity and innovation (Patterson, 2002; Batey & Furnham, 2006). Additional research is needed to explore the association between extroversion and innovation in different sectors and domains.

(5) *Neuroticism*. Relatively little research has focused on the relationship between innovation and neuroticism, and there are inconsistencies in results depending on the domain of interest. One explanation for these inconsistencies is likely to be that the association between neuroticism and innovation is domain-dependent. Some research suggests a curvilinear association between emotional stability and performance; too much or too little anxiety is detrimental to innovation, while moderate levels of anxiety may enhance innovative potential. These findings have implications for management practice, particularly at the level of individual departments and projects, and in relation to the role of managers' feedback and support in promoting innovation.

Behavioural Abilities

With few exceptions, the role of discretionary employee behaviours in enhancing innovation has been vastly underestimated. Contemporary research on *proactivity*, including concepts such as personal initiative and *voice behaviour* may also provide valuable insights into our understanding of innovative people (Frese, 2000).

Based on work by Frese and colleagues, the concept of personal initiative (PI) describes a class of behaviours that have been positively linked with innovation and entrepreneurial orientation. PI is defined by three main facets of self-starting, proactivity and persistence (see also Patterson, 2004). Frese and Fay (2001) propose a complex model of distal and proximal factors that influence performance in organisations. In this model, environmental supports (such as support for PI, control at work), knowledge, skills, abilities, and personality-influenced individual orientations (e.g. self-efficacy, handling errors, active coping) influence PI. In this way, PI is conceptualised as a set of active behaviours, and is directly linked to effective performance in organisations.

Research suggests that PI is particularly important in the idea-implementation phase of the innovation process as it involves overcoming barriers and persistence. In a study using path analysis, numerous variables were examined, including individual-level variables (e.g. PI, self-efficacy, interest in innovation), work characteristics (e.g. control, complexity), motives (e.g. reward) and organisational system factors (e.g. supervisor support). Results suggest that being proactive, actively involved in one's work environment, and confident that one is capable of thinking of good ideas were the most important predictors of innovation (Kickul & Gundry, 2002; Parker et al., 2006; Seibert, Kraimer, & Crant, 2001). Organisational factors were also important variables, and the results suggest that innovation is maximised when organisational climates promote an active approach towards work and interpersonal risk-taking. Climates for initiative may improve an organisation's ability to deal with innovation and change, by encouraging self-starting, proactivity and persistence in employees.

Emotions and Mood States

The examination of the complex relationship between emotions, mood states, and innovation is a new but rapidly growing research area. While a wide range of empirical studies have found links between positive mood states and some aspects of innovation (Amabile, Barsade, Mueller & Staw, 2005; Grawitch, Munz, Elliott & Mathis, 2003; Hirt, 1999; Isen, 1993; 1999; Shalley et al., 2004), job dissatisfaction and negative moods and feelings have also been associated with creativity (e.g. Anderson & Pratarelli, 1999; Kaufmann & Vosburg, 1997). Recently, George and Zhou (2002; 2007) found that job dissatisfaction, negative affect, and positive moods were all good predictors of innovation attempts when perceived recognition, support, and rewards for creativity were high. As suggested by Verghaeghen et al. (2005), it is also possible that moods affect creativity indirectly, by means of mood-induced self-reflection. In a recently published meta-analysis, Baas and his colleagues (2008) differentiated between mood states according to their hedonic tone, activation level and focus (prevention versus promotion). They concluded that 'anger and happiness should be cherished, and sadness and relaxation should be frowned upon' (p. 799).

The concept of Emotional Intelligence (EI) has been defined as 'the ability to perceive accurately, appraise and express emotion; the ability to access and/or generate feelings when they facilitate thought; the ability to understand emotion and emotional knowledge; and the ability to regulate emotions to promote emotional and intellectual growth' (Mayer & Salovey, 1997). Research on EI has become very popular in recent years. Some researchers suggest that EI has a positive influence on organisational innovation, both for leaders and individual employees. Specifically, researchers have suggested that employees who show high levels of EI are likely to benefit more from both positive and negative creativity-related feedback (Zhou, 2008). Similarly, leaders' levels of EI are likely to accentuate employees' inclination to engage in the innovation process (Zhou & George, 2003).

IMPLICATIONS FOR LEADERS WITHIN SMES

In this section, we focus on the implications for leaders within SMEs, in terms of their leadership characteristics, roles and style. The concept of organisational ambidexterity is relevant here, particularly given the SME context and leaders' roles in innovation.

Organisational ambidexterity is typically viewed as an organisation's *ability to pursue exploration and exploitation simultaneously*. Exploration is associated with search, experimentation, divergent thinking and variation, whereas exploitation is linked to efficiency, convergent thinking, refinement and improvement. Some researchers claim to have found the key role of leadership in fostering ambidexterity. For example, Gibson and Birkinshaw (2004) found that leaders play a key role in fostering ambidexterity by encouraging a supportive organisational context characterised by discipline, support, stretch, and trust. Jansen and colleagues (2008) analysed the role that senior team attributes (shared team vision, contingency rewards, social integration) and a transformational leadership style play in facilitating ambidexterity. They found that a shared vision, shared values, collective aspiration and goals, and contingency rewards are key influences for organisational ambidexterity. According to Jansen et al., transformational leaders provide the intellectual stimulation required for openly discussing and reconciling conflicting demands within teams. Moreover, Chang and Hughes (2012) indicate that among the top managers of SMEs, the more a top manager's leadership is characterised by risk-taking tolerance and adaptability, the higher the appearance of ambidexterity. We explore some of these leadership characteristics further in the following sections.

Leadership Characteristics

'There is a need to understand the individual traits of the owner-manager in the way in which the business is managed and developed, which in turn affects management behaviour, attitudes to risk (and hence innovation)' (North et al., 2001). The central role of the owner/manager in SMEs is pivotal to the innovation process (Hartman et al., 1994), for example their orientation towards innovation and training (Macpherson et al., 2004; McAdam et al., 2004).

Many researchers have suggested that leaders' behaviours and dispositional characteristics have a profound influence on the innovation process and some have identified leadership as the single most important aspect of organisational innovation (Tierney, 2008). However, there has been relatively little primary research in this area (see Port & Patterson, 2006). Since the early 1980s, several independent studies have identified a range of leadership behaviours that enhance employee innovation. These behaviours include encouragement of risk-taking, an open style of communication, participative and collaborative style, giving autonomy and freedom, support for innovation (verbal and enacted), and providing constructive feedback. Janssen (2005) found that employees are more likely to use their influence to carry out innovative activities when they perceive their supervisors as being supportive of innovation. Research shows that support from managers can come in a variety of forms.

Mumford and colleagues (2002) distinguish three forms of leadership support (idea, work, and social) that enhance employee motivation and innovation. Similarly, Amabile et al. (2004) concluded that instrumental (task- or technically-related) and socio-emotional support promoted employees' creativity. Port and Patterson (2006) also identified managers being optimistic about the future of the organisation as another key factor influencing the propensity for employees to innovate.

Research suggests that the dispositional characteristics associated with employee innovation can be partially transposed to the role of leader, whether the leader is a direct line supervisor or a chief executive of an organisation. There is evidence, for example, that some aspects of cognitive ability, such as general intelligence, adaptive problem-solving skills, and planning ability are important in leading for innovation. Similarly, some have argued that EI is an important prerequisite as it may influence both the ability to provide feedback and the way feedback is perceived. Studies have also provided support for the value of professional and technical knowledge in leading for innovation. Motivation is likely to be a key resource required by leaders to foster innovation but little research has investigated the effects of leaders' motivation on innovation within organisations. One exception is a study by Tierney (1999), which showed that supervisors' intrinsic motivation promoted employee innovation only when the employees were intrinsically motivated themselves. An additional dispositional characteristic linked with the ability to foster innovation is leaders' awareness and sensitivity towards the temporal complexities and cognitive demands that different stages of the innovation process place on employees.

Leadership Roles

The role of leadership is important for the whole process of innovation in SMEs. For instance, Tidd et al. (2004) suggest that leadership has an essential role to develop innovation in organisations. In SMEs, the leadership role is even more important and influential than in larger firms (Hale & Cragg, 1996; cited in McAdam, Moffett, Hazlett and Shevlin, 2010). Voss (1998) suggests that when leadership is dynamic and focused on innovation, then effective and rapid decisions can be made in deploying resources for innovation. Furthermore, Hyland and Beckett (2005) found that innovative leaders were a key driver in effective innovation implementation. The leader's vision and drive must be focused on innovation if it is to be successfully incorporated in the organisation's processes, people and (eventually) its products and performance (Pearce & Ensley, 2004).

Anderson and King (1991) propose a contingency model to understand the role of leadership in relation to four phases of the innovation process: (a) *Initiation*, leader is nurturing, supportive, encouraging ideas, open-minded and non-judgemental; (b) *Discussion*, leader obtains options, evaluates and agrees plans; (c) *Implementation*, leader sells the solution to all stakeholders, designs plans to include stakeholders, and gains commitment plans; and (d) *Routinization*, leader checks effectiveness, modifies and refines. Therefore, the model highlights the notion that leaders need to be flexible in their approach and employ different styles according to the different phases of the innovation process.

Researchers have identified the importance of the leadership role in the progress of innovation in SMEs. In one study of innovation in SMEs, it was stated that 'the owner's innovativeness permeates all variables' (Verbees & Meulenberg, 2004). Similarly, Wilson and Stokes (2006) indicate that the leader's or entrepreneur's role in the SME is central to developing innovation practices. By conducting multiple-case analysis of innovation culture in SMEs, Hyland and Beckett (2005) found that innovative leaders were 'a key driver in effective innovation implementation'. Similarly, the entrepreneur or leader's perception of the importance of innovation was found to affect product innovation and the acceptance of innovation practices (Bhaskaran, 2006). As discussed

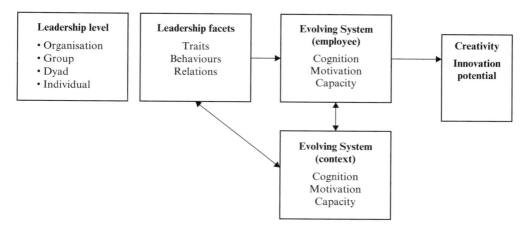

Figure 11.2   A model of leadership for innovation (from Tierney 2008)

earlier, Gibson and Birkinshaw (2004) found that leaders play a key role in fostering ambidexterity, which is supported by recent evidence in the SME sector from Chang and Hughes (2012).

Tierney (2008) describes several aspects of leadership that influence two systems in organisations: the individual and the context. The model, which is reproduced above, highlights the complexity of leadership influences in organisations and the interaction between leadership facets (e.g. traits, behaviours, relations), leadership levels (e.g. organisation, group, dyad, individual), and the cognition, motivation, and capacity of both the individual and the context. Tierney suggests that in order to fully comprehend the association between leadership and innovation within organisations one must consider the complexity of the relationships and the interactions between the aspects included in the model (see Figure 11.2).

Leadership Styles

Recent theories of leadership describe two styles, including a transformational style (inspiring and motivating others to achieve a shared vision) and a transactional style (influencing others through contingent rewards and punishments). The conceptual distinction between the two styles does not prevent managers from showing behaviours related to both styles, and leaders may use a combination of transformational and transactional leadership. Much research has been focused on the link between transformational leadership and innovation. Some researchers argue that a transformational style of leadership is likely to enhance both employee and group innovation and that transformational leaders play a decisive role in motivating employees whilst providing idea, work, and social support.

Researchers have further argued that transformational leadership may be particularly relevant in the context of SMEs (e.g. Matzler, Schwarz, Deutinger & Harms, 2008). Matzler and colleagues argued that due to the dominant role of the owner/manager, and the flatter structure of SMEs, the entrepreneur is often the one who provides both the vision and direction, and he/she is able to communicate the expectations to individual employees personally, and thus would be able to carry out transformational leadership. Furthermore, in the context of SMEs, intrinsic motivation plays a crucial role (McMeekin & Coombs, 1999). Based on the financial resource poverty of SMEs, transformational leadership, which emphasises intrinsic motivation, may be particularly suited in this context. Finally, in response to 'the dynamic environment of the 21st century's global economy' (Hinterhuber & Friedrich, 2002), a high degree of leadership flexibility is needed. A leadership style that is more adaptive and flexible may be more effective given the task context of SMEs. Past research found transformational leadership to affect innovation, specifically an organisation's tendency to innovate (Gumusluoglu & Ilsev, 2009). Moreover, in their study on the relationship between transformational leadership, product innovation and performance in SMEs, Matzler and colleagues found that transformational leadership is particularly appropriate if top management strives to foster innovation in context of SMEs.

When examining the contingent relationships between leader and employee, the quality of the leader-member-exchange (LMX) predicts the propensity for innovation. Leaders naturally develop social relationships with each member of a work group that can be characterised as high quality or low quality. In 1999, Tierney demonstrated that a high quality LMX predicts employee innovation, since employees engaged in more challenging tasks receive more resources and rewards for innovation. In recent studies, job self-efficacy has been shown to be the strongest predictor of creative self-efficacy. This implies that managers need to provide the necessary training and feedback to enhance employee confidence and mastery, in order to enhance employee innovation.

Feedback from Leaders

Research clearly shows that creativity-related feedback has a profound impact on the propensity to innovate. Zhou (2008) provided a framework for examining the theoretical basis behind the value of creativity-based feedback for promoting creativity. The multi-dimensional framework depicts aspects of employee characteristics (i.e. achievement motivation, power motivation) and EI of feedback provider (knowledge, expertise, seniority, status), interacting with feedback content and delivery style (task- versus person-focused; developmental), and affecting several psychological mechanisms, such as intrinsic motivation, the understanding of creativity standards, and the acquisition of creativity related skills and strategies. Findings related to these various aspects of feedback have direct implications for the management of innovation. In an earlier study, Zhou (1998) reported that informational feedback was associated with higher subsequent creativity than feedback delivered in a controlling or punitive manner. A related finding is that employees' level of innovation can benefit from leaders acting as role models for creativity. Research indicates that organisational innovation is influenced by a leader's vision and creative goal-setting. Unfortunately, most studies have focused on only one or two management behaviours, resulting in a lack of integration of results. Further, many investigations have focused solely on either idea generation or implementation of ideas. This is clearly an area that warrants further research.

PRACTICAL ISSUES FOR SMEs

In this section, we translate current research on the innovation process and the employee resources involved, into an analysis of the practical interventions aimed at enhancing employee-based innovation. We review evidence regarding interventions, including strategies towards: human capital policy, culture and climate for innovation, and developing skills for innovation.

Human Capital Policy

Research suggests that firms often adopt ad hoc interventions which are not supported by empirical evidence when faced with the apparently daunting task of fostering employee innovation (Mumford, 2002). Recently, researchers have started to explore the association between various Human Resource (HR) interventions and innovation outcomes. However, with limited sources, it is difficult for SMEs to apply HR interventions to make innovation occur. Nevertheless, we have identified some actions that could be used in the context of SMEs in terms of employee attraction, selection and retention.

A selection process to emphasise the importance of behaviours and skills for innovative working is vital for SMEs to attract innovative employees. Selection criteria for staff should include characteristics and skills that are important for supporting innovative people in firms (e.g. openness to ideas, communication skills, original problem solving, etc.). Moreover, innovative people tend to be intrinsically motivated and they are likely to opt for environments that provide opportunities for acquiring additional expertise and developing new ideas. SMEs should take this opportunity and develop recruitment and induction programmes that highlight learning and development opportunities, innovation, and diversity. The induction process should incorporate information about development and learning opportunities and it should convey the culture of the organisation. Induction can also facilitate the selection process, allowing individuals to decide whether they fit into the climate and culture of the organisation. Similarly, individuals who have innovative potential are more likely to be attracted by organisations that describe jobs in terms of broad job characteristics. To retain the best talent, SMEs must understand what is important to employees. An innovative employee's decision to stay or leave is likely to be related to opportunities for career and skill development, autonomy and participation, and support for innovation. Leaders of SMEs should regularly review employees' workload to ensure that employees have enough time to innovate.

Culture and Climate for Innovation

After analysing multiple cases of SMEs, Wan et al. (2005) concluded that 'what is ultimately of crucial importance to organisations is the nurture and development of an innovation supportive culture'. Innovation can be facilitated by improvements to the work environment, such as maximising opportunities for interaction and networking. Managers of SMEs should improve the perception of their firm as one that values innovative working.

It is important to conduct innovation audits, in order to find out whether the right skills, practices, and structures are in place to support the different phases of the innovation process. Climate surveys that assess the work environment for creativity are extremely helpful tools for evaluating shared perceptions of innovation. The Team Climate Inventory (TCI; Anderson & West, 1998) and the KEYS instrument for assessing the work environment for creativity (Amabile et al., 1996) are two robust instruments that have been validated in several studies. The TCI is designed to examine the shared perceptions of how things happen within a particular team, especially in supporting innovation. The TCI profile indicates how the team identifies problems, generates and implements solutions and has been shown to be predictive of teams' innovative performance (Agrell & Gustafson, 1994). The KEYS instrument, developed by Amabile (1995) covers the following dimensions: (a) Organisational encouragement – top management support for creativity, risk-taking and recognition of creative work; (b) Supervisory encouragement – setting clear expectations and goals, giving support to direct reports; (c) Work group support – mutual trust and support for and from colleagues, team work and skill diversity; (d) Sufficient resources – access to appropriate facilities, equipment, funds, and information; (e) Challenging work – combines the importance of motivation with difficulty in achieving goals; and (f) Freedom – the sense of control over work and ideas, and self-determination of how to accomplish tasks.

Developing Skills for Innovation

Enhanced *self-efficacy* via skills training allows employees to think more creatively (Cohen & Levinthal, 1990; Ashton & Felstead, 2001; Shipton et al., 2006). Several researchers argue that training in a variety of skills or jobs is likely to facilitate generative thinking through increased breadth of knowledge (Shipton et al., 2006; Bae & Lawler, 2000; Guthrie, 2001). Training and development interventions are most likely to enhance innovation if mapped to the characteristics of innovative people. For example, knowledge about innovative individuals' need for autonomy may inform the way team training is designed.

Moreover, by using appropriate feedback, leaders are able to create the conditions and context that motivate employees to be innovative (Zhou, 1998). Zhou (2008) recently provided a framework for examining the effects of feedback on creativity. The guidelines provided by Zhou are summarised in Table 11.1.

SUMMARY AND CONCLUSIONS

Innovation is a process with a variety of situational- and individual-level determinants. Innovative individuals have a creative cognitive style and are open to new experiences. Innovators are proactive, knowledgeable about the domain in which they are trying to implement their ideas, and persistent in the face of obstacles. We suggest that further research should focus on exploring more fully the higher order interactions between these domains, with the ultimate aim of understanding how best to design interventions to promote innovation in organisations. Here, multi-level analysis techniques could be used to define an evidence-based, integrative theoretical model to explain the casual associations between employee-level resources, work environment, organisational prac-

Table 11.1   How to use feedback to promote creativity and innovation

1. Whenever possible, provide positive feedback delivered in an informative style.
2. If negative feedback needs to be delivered, deliver it in an informative style.
3. Include a large amount of developmental information in the feedback.
4. Focus on task-focused rather than person-focused feedback.
5. Consider the characteristics of the feedback recipient, as they are likely to influence responses to the feedback provided. Employees with high levels of achievement motivation (i.e. striving to perform well against a standard of excellence) benefit from both positive and negative feedback, whilst employees with high levels of power motivation (i.e. need to exert influence on others) benefit only from positive feedback.
6. Employees with high levels of EI are likely to benefit more from creativity-related feedback than those with relatively lower levels of EI.
7. Employees are more likely to accept and respond to feedback provided by persons with more knowledge or expertise or more seniority and higher status. This in turn reinforces the importance of providing adequate and accurate feedback.
8. Employees must be aware of the fact that feedback coming from different sources may be inconsistent because of inaccurate feedback from some feedback providers and/or different viewpoints.
9. Providing feedback to promote creativity and innovation should be a long-term managerial strategy embedded in the organisational context.

Source: Adapted from Zhou, 2008.

tices and innovation in organisations. For example, when innovation is assessed at the individual level, it is inappropriate to analyse the data with simple multiple regression analysis, because an individual's contribution to outcomes is not statistically independent, but nested within teams (see Kenny et al., 2002). Instead, one should use multi-level techniques (see Snijders & Bosker, 1999), which are especially useful when several teams are investigated within one or more organisations.

Historically, there has been little research targeting group-level innovation, but this has expanded recently and there are now clear practical recommendations regarding enhancement of innovation in teams. A high level of diversity among employees enhances team innovation if there is integration of ideas among employees and team members. A positive team climate can have a significant influence on innovation and is characterised by participative safety, vision, support for innovation and task orientation. Future studies on innovation need to reflect the changing nature of work and the use of technology. Organisations wishing to create an innovative culture need to identify and develop people who are themselves innovative, and to ensure managers and leaders are equipped to support them by offering autonomy, resources, a shared vision, advice and feedback. Although most people tend to be naturally creative, in the past, workplaces have stifled creativity through command-and-control cultures, which consisted mainly of instructing and supervising employees to perform tasks. In such circumstances, there was little room to deviate from the norm. As well as recruiting potentially innovative people, developing the creative skills of employees is crucial for developing innovation – but only if people are given the freedom to use their capabilities. Support for innovation (particularly management support) and an infrastructure that enables creativity are important (Adobe, 2008). In order to show leaders' support for innovation, companies need to encourage employees to become more comfortable with both risk and change, and they need to allow room for failure.

Types or domains of innovation have been delineated within the innovation research literature (Jansen et al., 2006). The most widely discussed typology concerns explorative and exploitative innovation. There is a need to understand how such innovations work in SMEs because SMEs may have esoteric innovation strategies and responses, and a different level of susceptibility to external environment pressure from other organisations (Dean et al., 1998). Accordingly, SMEs face greater challenges than larger firms in managing tensions, contradictions, and trade-offs associated with explorative and exploitative innovations (Andriopoulos & Lewis, 2009; Bierly & Daly, 2007). Nevertheless, a few empirical studies have analysed how SMEs can achieve ambidexterity owing to the resource constraints associated with SMEs (Cao et al., 2009). Very recently, Chang et al. (2011) analysed internal and external antecedents of innovation ambidexterity outcomes in SMEs. They found that SMEs could achieve innovation ambidexterity through use of appropriate organisational structures. Also, highly dynamic and competitive environments are beneficial to innovation and business performance. However, Chang and colleagues' study does not address how the ability and willingness of top managers in SMEs influence the development of innovation ambidexterity. Future research should account for behavioural components of firms' internal environments along with typical, structural and contextual antecedents to examine the formation of innovation ambidexterity in SMEs. Furthermore, it would be useful to conduct both survey and case study research to understand more fully the relationships between individual characteristics and behaviours of top managers, and the appearance of innovation ambidexterity.

REFERENCES

Adobe (2008),'Unleashing innovation', *Loudhouse research commissioned by Adobe.*
Agrell, A. and Gustafson, R. (1994), 'The Team Climate Inventory (TCI) and group innovation: A psychometric test on a Swedish sample of work groups', *Journal of Occupational and Organizational Psychology*, **67**(2), 143–51.
Amabile, T.M. (1983), 'The social psychology of creativity: A componential conceptualization', *Journal of Personality and Social Psychology*, **45**(2), 357–76.
Amabile, T.M. (1988), 'A model of creativity and innovation in organizations', in B.M. Staw & L. L. Cummings (Eds.), *Research in Organizational Behavior*, vol 10. Greenwich, CT: JAI Press, 123–67.
Amabile, T.M. (1995), *KEYS: Assessing the Climate for Creativity*, Greensboro, NC:Center for Creative Leadership.
Amabile, T.M. (1996), *Creativity in Context: Update to the Social Psychology of Creativity*, New York: Westview Press.
Amabile, T.M., Conti, R., Coon,H., Lazenby, J. and Herron, M. (1996), 'Assessing the work environment for creativity', *Academy of Management Journal*, **39**(5), 1154–84.
Amabile, T.M., Barsade, S.G., Mueller, J.S. and Staw, B.M. (2005), 'Affect and creativity at work', *Administrative Science Quarterly*, **50**(3), 367–403.
Amabile, T.M., Schatzel, E.A., Moneta, G.B. and Kramer, S.J. (2004), 'Leader behaviors and the work environment for creativity: Perceived leader support', *Leadership Quarterly*, **15**, 5–32.
Anderson,N. and King, N. (1991), 'Managing innovation in organisations', *Leadership & Organization Development Journal*, **12**(4), 17–21.
Anderson, N. and West, M.A. (1998), 'Measuring climate for work group innovation: Development and validation of the team climate inventory', *Journal of Organizational Behavior*, **19**, 235–58.

Anderson, T.A. and Pratarelli, M.E. (1999), 'Affective information in videos: Effects on cognitive performance and gender', *North American Journal of Psychology*, **1**(1), 17–28.

Andrews, J. and Smith, D.C. (1996), 'In search of the marketing imagination: factors affecting the creativity of marketing programs for mature products', *Journal of Marketing Research*, **33**(2), 174–87.

Andriopoulos, C. and Lewis, M.W. (2009), 'Exploitation-exploration tensions and organizational ambidexterity: Managing paradoxes of innovation', *Organization Science*, **20**(4), 696–717.

Angle, H. (1989), 'Psychology and organizational innovation', in van de Van, A.H. Angle, H.L. & Poole, M.S., *Research on the Management of Innovation:The Minnesota Studies*, New York: Harper & Row.

Ashton, D. and Felstead, A. (2001), 'From training to lifelong learning: the birth of the knowledge society?', in Storey, J. (Ed.), *Human Resource Management: A Critical Text*, London: Thompson Learning.

Axtell, C.M., Holman, D.J., Unsworth, K.L., Wall, T.D., Waterson, P.E., and Harrington, E. (2000), 'Shopfloor innovation: Facilitating the suggestion and implementation of ideas', *Journal of Occupational and Organizational Psychology*, **73**(3), 265–85.

Baas, M., Dreu, C.K.W.de and Nijstad, B.A. (2008), 'A meta-analysis of 25 years of mood-creativity research: Hedonic tone, activation, or regulatory focus?', *Psychological Bulletin*, **134**(6), 779–806.

Bae, J. and Lawler, J. (2000), 'Organizational and HRM strategies in Korea: Impact on firm performance in an emerging economy', *Academy of Management Journal*, **43**(3), 502–17.

Baer, M. and Oldham, G.R. (2006), 'The curvilinear relation between experienced creative time pressure and creativity: Moderating effects of openness to experience and support for creativity', *Journal of Applied Psychology*, **91**(4), 963–70.

Barron, F. and Harrington, D.M. (1981), 'Creativity, intelligence,and personality', *Annual Review of Psychology*, **32**(1), 439–76.

Batey, M. and Furnham, A. (2006), 'Creativity, intelligence, and personality: A critical review of the scattered literature', *Genetic, Social, and General Psychology Monographs*, **132**(4), 355–429.

Bhaskaran, S. (2006), 'Incremental innovation and business performance: Small- and medium-size food enterprises in a concentrated industry environment', *Journal of Small Business Management*, **44**(1), 64–80.

Bhupatiraju, S., Nomaler, Ö, Triulzi, G. and Verspagen, B. (2012), 'Knowledge flows – Analyzing the core literature of innovation, entrepreneurship and science and technology studies', *Research Policy*, **41**, 1205–18.

Bierly, P.E. and Daly, P.S. (2007), 'Alternative knowledge strategies, competitive environment, and organizational performance in small manufacturing firms', *Entrepreneurship: Theory and Practice*, **31**(4), 493–516.

Burke, L. and Witt, L. (2002), 'Moderators of the openness to experience-performance relationship', *Journal of Managerial Psychology*, **17**(8), 712–21.

Cao, Q. Gedajlovic. E. and Zhang, H. (2009), 'Unpacking organizational ambidexterity: Dimensions, contingencies, and synergistic effects', *Organization Science*, **20**(4), 781–96.

Chang, Y.Y. and Hughes, M. (2012), 'Drivers of innovation ambidexterity in small- to medium-sized firms', *European Management Journal*, **30**(1), 1–17.

Chang, Y.Y., Hughes, M. and Hotho, S. (2011), 'Internal and external antecedents of SMEs' innovation ambidexterity outcomes', *Management Decision*, **49**(10), 1658–76.

Cohen, W.M. and Levinthal, D.A. (1990),' Absorptive capacity: A new perspective on learning and innovation', *Administrative Science Quarterly*, **35**(1), 128.

Csikszentmihalyi, M. and Csikszentmihalyi, I.S. (1988), *Optimal Experience: Psychological Studies of Flow in Consciousness(1st pbk)*.Cambridge, New York: Cambridge University Press.

Dean, T.J., Brown, R.L. and Bamford, C.E. (1998), 'Differences in large and small firm responses to environmental context: Strategic implications from a comparative analysis of business formations', *Strategic Management Journal*, **19**, 709–28.

Eisenberger, R. and Cameron, J. (1996), 'Detrimental effects of reward: Reality or myth?', *American Psychologist*, **51**(11), 1153–66.

Eysenck, H.J. (1994), 'Personality and intelligence: Psychometric and experimental approaches', in R.J. Sternberg and P.Ruzgis (Eds.), *Personality and Intelligence* (pp.3–31), Cambridge: Cambridge University Press.

Feist, G.J. (1998), 'A Meta-analysis of personality in scientific and artistic creativity', *Personality and Social Psychology Review*, **2**(4), 290–309.

Finke, R.A., Ward, T.B. and Smith, S.M. (1992), *Creative Cognition*. Cambridge, MA: MIT Press.

Frese, M. (2000), 'The changing nature of work', in L. Chmiel (Ed.), *Introduction to Work and Organizational Psychology* (pp.424–39), Oxford: Blackwell.

Frese, M. and Fay, D. (2001), '4. Personal initiative: An active performance concept for work in the 21st century', *Research in Organizational Behavior*, **23**, 133–87.

Frese, M., Teng, E. and Wijnen, C.J.D. (1999), 'Helping to improve suggestion systems: Predictors of making suggestions in companies', *Journal of Organizational Behavior*, **20**(7), 1139–55.

Furnham, A. (1999), 'Personality and creativity: Perceptual and motor skills', *Perceptual and Motor Skills*, **88**(2), 407–8.

Gelade, G.A. (1997), 'Creativity in conflict: The personality of the commercial creative', *The Journal of Genetic Psychology*, **158**(1), 67–78.

George, J.M. and Zhou, J. (2001), 'When openness to experience and conscientiousness are related to creative behavior: An interactional approach', *Journal of Applied Psychology*, **86**(3), 513–24.

George, J.M. and Zhou, J. (2002),'Understanding when bad moods foster creativity and good ones don't: The role of context and clarity of feelings', *Journal of Applied Psychology*, **87**(4), 687–97.

George, J.M. and Zhou, J. (2007), 'Dual tuning in a supportive context: Joint contributions of positive mood, negative mood, and supervisory behaviours to behaviors to employee creativity', *The Academy of Management Journal* L, **50**(3),605–22.

Gibson, C.B. and Birkinshaw, J. (2004), 'The antecedents, consequences, and mediating role of organizational ambidexterity', *Academy of Management Journal*, **47**(2), 209–26.

Grawitch, M.J., Munz, D.C., Elliott, E.K. and Mathis, A. (2003), 'Promoting creativity in temporary problem-solving groups: The effects of positive mood and autonomy in problem definition on idea-generating performance', *Group Dynamics: Theory, Research, and Practice*, **7**(3), 200–13.

Gumusluoglu, L. and Ilsev, A. (2009), 'Transformational leadership and organizational innovation: The roles of internal and external support for innovation', *Journal of Product Innovation Management*, **26**(3), 264–74.

Guthrie, J. (2001), 'High-involvement work practices, turnover, and productivity: Evidence from New Zealand', *The Academy of Management Journal*, **44**(1), 180–90.

Hale, A.and Cragg, P. (1996), 'Business process reengineering in the small firm: A case study', *Interntaional Small Business Journal*, **34**,15–29.

Harrison, M.M., Neff, N.L., Schwall, A.R. and Zhao, X. (2006), 'A meta-analytic investigation of individual creativity and innovation', Paper Presented at the 21st Annual Conference for the Society for Industrial and Organizational Psychology, Dallas,Texas.

Hartman, E.A., Tower, C.B. and Sebora, T.C. (1994),'Information sources and their relationship to organizational innovation in small business', *Journal of Small Business Management*, **32**(1), 36–48.

Hinterhuber, H.H. and Friedrich, S.A. (2002), 'The technology dimension of strategic leadership: The leadership challenge for production economists', *International Journal of Production Economics*, **77**, 191–203.

Hirt, E.R. (1999), 'Mood', in M.A. Runco and S.R. Pritzker (Eds.), *Encyclopedia of Creativity* (pp. 141–250), New York: Academic Press.

Hitt, M.A., Ireland, R.D., Sirmon, D.G. and Trahms, C.A. (2011), 'Strategic entrepreneurship: Creating value for individuals, organizations, and society', *Mays Business School Texas A&M University Research Paper*, **19**, 56–76.

Hotho, S. and Champion, K. (2011), 'Small businesses in the new creative industries: Innovation as a people management challenge', *Management Decision*, **49**(1), 29–54.

Hyland, P.and Beckett, R. (2005), 'Engendering an innovative culture and maintaining operational balance', *Journal of Small Business and Enterprise Development*, **12**(3), 336–52.

Ireland, R.D., Hitt, M.A., Camp, S.M. and Sexton, D.L. (2001), 'Integrating entrepreneurship and strategic management actions to create wealth', *Academy of Management Executive*, **15**(1), 49–63.

Isen, A.M. (1993), 'Positive affect and decision making', in M.Lewis and J.Haviland(Eds.), *Handbook of Emotions* (pp. 261–77), New York: Guilford.

Isen, A.M. (1999), 'On the relationship between affect and creative problem solving', in S.W. Russ (Ed.), *Affect, Creative Experience, and Psychological Adjustment* (pp. 3–17), Philadelphica:PA:Brunner/Mazel.

Jansen, J.J.P., George, G., van den Bosch, F.A.J. and Volberda, H.W. (2008), 'Senior team attributes and organizational ambidexterity: The moderating role of transformational leadership', *Journal of Management Studies*, **45**(5), 982–1007.

Jansen, J.J.P., van den Bosch, F.A.J. and Volberda, H.W. (2006), 'Exploratory innovation, exploitative innovation, and performance: Effects of organizational antecedents and environmental moderators', *Management Science*, **52**(11), 1661–74.

Janssen, O. (2005), 'The joint impact of perceived influence and supervisor supportiveness on employee innovative behaviour', *Journal of Occupational and Organizational Psychology*, **78**(4), 573–9.

Jones, O. and Tilley, F. (2003),*Creating and Sustaining Competitive Advantage in SMEs: Organising for Innovation*, Chichester:Wiley.

Kaufmann, G. and Vosburg, S.K. (1997), 'Paradoxical mood effects on creative problem solving', *Cognition and Emotion*, **11**, 151–70.

Kenny, D.A., Bolger,N. and Kashy, D.A. (2002), 'Traditional methods for estimating multilevel', in D.S. Moskowitz and S.L. Hershberger (Eds.), *Modeling Intraindividual Variability with Repeated Measures Data: Methods and Applications* (pp. 1–24), Mahwah, NJ: Lawrence Erlbaum.

Kerin, R.A. (1992), 'Marketing's contribution to the strategy dialogue revisited', *Journal of the Academy of Marketing Science*, **20**(4), 331–4.

Kickul, J. and Gundry, L. (2002), 'Prospecting for strategic advantage: The proactive entrepreneurial personality and small firm innovation', *Journal of Small Business Management*, **40**(2), 85–97.

King, L.A., Walker, L.M. and Broyles, S.J. (1996), 'Creativity and the five-factor model', *Journal of Research in Personality*, **30**(2), 189–203.

Lubart, T. (2003), *Psychologie de la créativité*, Paris: Armand Colin.

Macpherson, A., Jones, O. and Zhang, M. (2004), 'Evolution or revolution? Dynamic capabilities in a knowledge-dependent firm', *R and D Management*, **34**(2), 161–77.

Marcati, A., Guido, G. and Peluso, A.M. (2008), 'The role of SME entrepreneurs, innovativeness and personality in the adoption of innovativeness', *Research Policy*, **37**, 1579–90.

Mascitelli, R. (2000), 'From experience: Harnessing tacit knowledge to achieve breakthrough innovation', *Journal of Product Innovation Management*, **17**(3), 179–93.

Matzler, K., Schwarz, E., Deutinger, N. and Harms, R. (2008), 'The relationship between transformational leadership, product innovation, and performance in SMEs', *Journal of Small Business & Entrepreneurship*, **21**(2), 139–51.

Mayer, J.D. and Salovey, P. (1997), ' What is emotional intelligence?' in P.Salovey, and D. Sluyter (Eds.), *Emotional Development and Emotional Intelligence: Implications for Educators* (pp.3–31), New York: Basic Books.

McAdam, R., McConvery, T. and Armstrong, G.(2004), 'Barriers to innovation within small firms in a peripheral location', *International Journal of Entrepreneurial Behaviour & Research*, **10**(3), 206–21.

McAdam,R., Moffett, S., Hazlett, S.A. and Shevlin, M.(2010), 'Developing a model of innovation implementation for UK SMEs: A path analysis and explanatory case analysis', *International Small Business Journal*, **28**(3), 195–214.

McCrae, R.R. (1987), 'Creativity, divergent thinking, and openness to experience', *Journal of Personality and Social Psychology*, **52**(6), 1258–65.

McMeekin, A. and Coombs, R. (1999), 'Human resource sanagement and the motivation of technical professionals', *International Journal of Innovation Management*, **3**(1), 1–26.

Miles, M.P. (2005), 'Competitive advantage', in M. A. Hitt & R. D. Ireland (Eds.), *The Blackwell Encyclopedia of Management: Entrepreneurship* (pp. 36 –7). Oxford, UK: Blackwell Publishers.

Mumford, M. (2003), 'Where have we been, where are we going? Taking stock in creativity research', *Creativity Research Journal*, **15**(2), 107–20.

Mumford, M.D., Scott, G.M., Gaddis, B.H. and Strange, J.M. (2002), 'Leading creative people: Orchestrating expertise and relationships', *Leadership Quarterly*, **13**, 705–50.

North, D., Smallbone, D. and Vickers, I. (2001), 'Public sector support for innovating SMEs', *Small Business Economics*, **16**(4), 303–17.

O'Regan, N., Ghobadian, A. and Sims, M. (2005), 'Fast tracking innovation in manufacturing SMEs', *Technovation*, **26**(2), 251–61.

Parker, S.K., Williams, H.M. and Turner, N. (2006), 'Modeling the antecedents of proactive behavior at work', *Journal of Applied Psychology*, **91**(3), 636–52.

Patterson, F. (1999), *The Innovation Potential Indicato: Manual and User's Guide*. Oxford: OUP Ltd.

Patterson, F. (2002), 'Great minds don't think alike? Person-level predictors of innovation at work', in C.L. Cooper and I.T. Robertson (Eds.), *International Review of Industrial and Organizational Psychology 2002* (pp.115–144), West Sussex, England: John Wiley & Sons Ltd.

Patterson, F. (2004), 'Personal initiative and innovation at work', in C.Spielberger (Ed) *Encyclopaedia of Applied Psychology*, **2**, 843–55; Academic Press, USA.

Patterson, F., Kerrin, M. and Gatto-Roissard, G. (2009), *Characteristics and Behaviours of Innovative People in Organisations* (pp.1–54), London: NESTA Research Reports.

Pearce, C. and Ensley, M. (2004), 'A reciprocal and longitudinal investigation of the innovation process: The central role of shaded vision in product and process innovation teams (PPITs)', *Journal of Organisational Behaviour*, **25**, 259–78.

Port, R. and Patterson, F. (2006), *The role of managers in the innovation process*, proceeding from The BPS Annual Conference.

Rauch, A. and Frese, M. (2007), 'Let's put the person back into entrepreneurship research: A meta-analysis of the relationship between business owners' personality characteristics and business creation and success', *European Journal of Work and Organizational Psychology*, **16**(4), 353–85.

Runco, M.A. (2004), 'Creativity', *Annual Review of Psychology*, **55**,657–87.

Sauermann, H. and Cohen, W. (2008), *What makes them tick? Employee motives and firm innovation*. NBER Working Paper (14443).

Seibert, S.E., Kraimer, M.L. and Crant, J.M. (2001), 'What do proactive people do? A longitudinal model linking proactive personality and career success', *Personnel Psychology*, **54**(4), 845–74.

Shalley, C.E., Zhou, J. and Oldham, G.R. (2004), 'The effects of personal and contextual characteristics on creativity: Where should we go from here?', *Journal of Management*, **30**(6), 933–58.

Shane, S. and Venkataraman, S. (2000), 'The promise of entrepreneurship as a field of research', *Academy of Management Review*, **25**(1), 217–226.

Shin, S.J. and Zhou, J. (2003), 'Transformational leadership, connservational leadership, and creativity: Evidence from Korea', *Academy of Management Journal*, **46**(6), 703–14.

Shipton, H., West, M.A., Dawson, J.,Birdi, K. and Patterson, M. (2006),'HRM as a predictor of innovation', *Human Resource Management Journal*, **16**(1), 3–27.

Sirmon, D. G. and Hitt, M. A. (2003), 'Managing resources: Linking unique resources, management and wealth creation in family firms', *Entrepreneurship: Theory and Practice*, **27**(4), 339–58.

Snijders,T.A. and Bosker, R.J.(1999), *Multilevel Analysis: An Introduction to Basic and Advanced Multilevel Modeling*, London:Sage Publ.

Sosik, J.J., Kahai, S.S. and Avolio, B.J. (1999), 'Leadership style, anonymity, and creativity in group decision support systems: The mediating role of optimal flow', *The Journal of Creative Behavior*, **33**(4), 227–56.

Spearman, C.E. (1923), *The Nature of Intelligence and the Principles of Cognition*, London:Macmillan.

Sternberg, R.J. (1982), 'Nonentrenchment in the assessment of intellectual giftedness', *Gifted Child Quarterly*, **26**(2), 63–7.

Sternberg, R.J. and Lubart, T.I. (1999), 'The concept of creativity: Prospects and paradigms', in R.J. Sternberg (Ed.), *Handbook of Creativity* (pp.3–15), New York: Cambridge University Press.

Tidd, J., Bessant, J. and Pavitt, K. (2004), *Managing Innovation: Integrating Technological, Market and Organisational Change*, Chichester: Wiley.

Tierney, P. (1999), 'Work relations as a precursor to a psychological climate for change: The role of work group supervisors and peers', *Journal of Organizational Change Management*, **12**(2), 120–34.

Tierney, P. (2008), 'Leadership and employee creativity', in J. Zhou and C.E. Shalley (Eds.), *Handbook of Organizational Creativity* (pp.95–99), New York: Talylor & Francis Group.

Verbees, F.J.H.M. and Meulenberg, M.T.G. (2004), 'Market orientation, innovativeness, product innovation, and performance in small firms', *Journal of Small Business Management*, **42**(2), 134–54.

Verghaeghen, P., Joorman, J. and Kahn, R. (2005), 'Why we sing the blues: The relation between self-reflective rumination, mood, and creativity', *Emotion*, **5**, 226–32.

Voss, C. (1998), 'Made in Europe: Small companies', *Business Strategy Review*, **9**, 1–19.

Wan, D., Ong, C. and Lee, F. (2005), 'Determinants of firm innovation in Singapore', *Technovation*, **25**, 261–268.

West, M.A. (1987), 'Role innovation in the world of work', *British Journal of Social Psychology*, **26**(4), 305–15.

Wilson, N. and Stokes, D. (2006), 'Managing creativity and innovation', *Journal of Small Business and Enterprise Development*, **12**, 36678.

Wolfradt, U. and Pretz, J.E. (2001), 'Individual differences in creativity: Personality, story writing, and hobbies', *European Journal of Personality*, **15**(4), 297–310.

Zhou, J. (1998), 'Feedback valence, feedback style, task autonomy, and achievement orientation: Interactive effects on creative performance', *Journal of Applied Psychology*, **83**, 261–76.

Zhou, J. (2008),'Promoting creativity through feedback', in J. Zhou and C.E. Shalley (Eds.), *Handbook of Organizational Creativity* (pp.125–45). New York: Taylor & Francis.

Zhou, J. and George, J.M. (2003), 'Awakening employee creativity: The role of leader emotional intelligence', *The Leadership Quarterly*, **14**(4–5), 545–68.

12. Behavior of entrepreneurs – existing research and future directions
Barbara Bird, Leon Schjoedt and Ralph Hanke

INTRODUCTION

Three arguments are widely recognized as the foundation for considering entrepreneurship as a distinct field of inquiry (Shane & Venkataraman, 2000). The first argument is that entrepreneurship is a societal process that converts information and resources into new product and service offerings (Arrow, 1962). The second argument is entrepreneurship drives change in products and services (Schumpeter, 1934). The third argument is that entrepreneurship facilitates discovery and mitigation of economic inefficiencies, both temporally and spatially (Kirzner, 1997). All three arguments are grounded in economic thinking, not grounded in behavior.

The behavior of entrepreneurs is an important aspect of new venture creation because if entrepreneurs do not act, there will be no venture creation and, thus, no entrepreneurship. Because entrepreneurs' behavior is important to entrepreneurship, we would expect ample research on entrepreneurs' behavior. This, however, is not the case (Bird & Schjoedt, 2009; Bird, Schjoedt, & Baum, 2012). Thus, we lack understanding about what behaviors entrepreneurs engage in as part of the new venture creation process and whether entrepreneurs' behavior is distinguishable from that of other economic actors.

The purpose of this chapter is to encourage research on entrepreneurs' behavior. First, we clarify what constitutes entrepreneurs' behavior. Second, we distinguish behavior from other related concepts. Third, we also distinguish entrepreneurs' behaviors in terms of the role behaviors of entrepreneurs, managers, and leaders. Fourth, we connect entrepreneurs' behavior to three relevant constructs—cognition, motivation, and decision-making. Fifth, we review extant literature on entrepreneurs' behavior with a specific focus on research methodology. Sixth, we consider the specific behavior of selling, which has been neglected in the entrepreneurship literature, and we suggest how future research on entrepreneurs' selling behavior could proceed by the development of a measure for entrepreneurs' selling behavior.

BEHAVIOR, NOT BEHAVIORAL

Entrepreneurs' behavior is of interest to academics and practitioners because, it is worth repeating, without entrepreneurs' taking action there will not be a new venture. Many individuals come up with ideas and intentions for a new business, but few take the necessary action to create that business. Considering the outcomes of entrepreneurs' behavior—new ventures, job creation, innovations, new markets, new economic activity—and the major goals of research—to explain, predict, and control (shape and change) behavior of individuals or teams, research on entrepreneurs' behavior is important.

Academics and practitioners benefit from clarification of the term *entrepreneurs' behavior*. Behavior is human action that can be seen or heard; it is concrete, theoretically observable actions of individuals (either solo or in the context of a team). These behaviors are proximal outcomes of abilities, cognition, emotion, knowledge, motivation, personality, and skills. For example, decision-making (a topic we return to) is not behavior as it may be wholly cognitive, but announcing a decision or making the decision through a group process is behavior. Because we focus on the behavior of individuals (entrepreneurs) and not a type of behavior of other individuals or groups, we refrain from the adjective "entrepreneurial" when we refer to entrepreneurs' behavior.

We define entrepreneurs' behavior as the concrete enactment by individuals (solo or as part of a team) of tasks or activities required in some combination to start and grow new ventures. The tasks and activities we refer to in this definition include but are not limited to those named by Carter, Gartner and Reynolds (1996) [e.g., prepare a business plan, look for facilities, organize a team, hire employees, form a legal entity, or enter a market]. Also, as we will argue later, behaviors are best understood as discrete units of action that could be observed by others and that are "sized" to be meaningful to both actor and audience.

DISTINGUISHING BEHAVIOR

As noted earlier, entrepreneurs' behavior is individual-level behavior; it is *not* firm-level behavior such as entrepreneurial orientation (Lumpkin, Cogliser, & Schneider, 2009; Wiklund & Shepherd, 2003) and other firm-level constructs (Brown, Davidsson, & Wiklund, 2001). However, the behavior of entrepreneurs that involves strategic and operational choices for their venture (if observable) would constitute behavior for our arguments. At the individual level of analysis, there is often a failure to differentiate behavioral terms. *Behaviors*, *actions*, and *activities* are usually interchangeable terms. *Performance*, however, is usually a result achieved by actions and when measured is often a complex aggregation of many behaviors (the exception might be a specific task performance such as making an oral "pitch" to an investor). *Ability*, *skills*, and *competence* are generally enablers and precursors of behavior and each of these terms has nuanced differences from each other (see Bird et al., 2012 for details). *Processes* may, but do not necessarily, involve behavior. Business planning is a process that has cognitive and behavioral aspects and occurs over a long enough period of time that it cannot be coherently observed. The same cognitive/behavioral and observational problems apply to processes such as *creativity* and *searching for an opportunity*. We will later describe a conceptual and empirical way to parse at least some processes into behaviors that can be observed.

DISTINGUISHING ENTREPRENEURS' BEHAVIOR: A ROLE ANALYSIS

Entrepreneurs engage in a number of roles as they create and develop their ventures[1]. The classical view of the entrepreneur is based on economic thinking where the entrepreneur's role is to discover, create, and innovate (Arrow, 1962; Kirzner, 1997; Schumpeter, 1934). While these may be considered the hallmarks of entrepreneurs' behavior, for the entrepreneur to successfully create and develop a new venture, the entrepreneur will have to take on the roles of managers and leaders.

Penrose (1959) distinguished among the roles of entrepreneurs and managers. She noted that entrepreneurs carry out their ideas and plans, conduct marketing research and marketing activities, create the organization and its operations, motivate and build a management team, develop customer relationships, and acquire resources as part of the entrepreneurial role. She observed the entrepreneur in a managerial role when the entrepreneur reduces complexity and optimizes via planning, organizing, staffing, budgeting, and controlling activities to promote stability. In short, the entrepreneur's role is to discover, innovate, and create the new venture, while the manager's role is to stabilize the organization; and the entrepreneur has to engage, or hire someone to engage, in the behaviors inherent in the manager's role to develop the venture.

Schumpeter distinguished between entrepreneurs and managers while noting the entrepreneur is also a *leader in a special context* (Czarniawska-Joerges & Wolff, 1991; Vecchio, 2003). The entrepreneur creates goals for the new venture based on his/her personal goals and market opportunities. These goals motivate early resource providers to contribute financing, labor, information, etc. In contrast, many scholars of organizational leadership hold that the leader's role is to motivate, direct, and lead people towards achieving (personal or organizational) goals (Bass, 1990; Cogliser & Brigham, 2004; Kotter, 2001; Zaleznik, 1992). As a new venture forms an identity and establishes boundaries (Katz & Gartner, 1988), the entrepreneur hires employees, establishes work norms, and rewards performance (among other activities). When these activities occur the entrepreneur engages the leader role.

Collectively, these considerations show that entrepreneurs engage in distinct behaviors and also engage in the behaviors inherent in the roles of leaders and managers as they create and develop their new ventures. Thus, while the role behaviors of entrepreneurs, leaders, and managers are distinctive, the role behavior of managers and leaders complement those of entrepreneurs (Kotter, 2001) as illustrated in Table 12.1.

ENTREPRENEURS' BEHAVIOR: CONNECTIONS TO KEY CONSTRUCTS

As suggested earlier, behavior is often an outcome of key aspects in the entrepreneurial process. This section addresses three aspects[2]—cognition, motivation and decision-making, each of which has substantial theory and research pertaining to entrepreneurs. Our review is necessarily brief and aims only to connect these invisible processes to observable behavior.

Table 12.1   Distinguishing role behaviors

	Entrepreneur	Leader	Manager	Behavior Examples	
Discover	X			Conduct market research	Arrow (1962); Kirzner (1973);
Create	X			Create new ventures; build management team	Penrose (1959); Schumpeter (1934)
Innovate	X			Resource acquisition; set up operations	
Motivate, direct people, and lead towards goals	X	X		Hire employees; establish work norms; reward performance	Cogliser & Brigham (2004); Czarniawska-Joerges & Wolff (1991); Vecchio, (2003)
Reduce complexity	X		X	Budgeting; control activities; execute plans; staffing	Mintzberg (1973); Penrose (1959)

Cognition

In part because behavior is hard to measure (discussed later) and because early efforts to find distinguishable individual differences in personality and motivation failed to sufficiently predict entrepreneurs' performance, research has turned much attention to the cognitions of entrepreneurs. Cognition refers to an array of mental processes (both conscious and unconscious), which are often reflected in terms such as thought, intelligence, perception, belief, learning, and intention. The behavior of most interest to entrepreneurship is behavior that manifests the ideas and is strongly influenced by the (usually conscious) cognitions of entrepreneurs. Thus behavior follows from cognition. Even in the domain of creativity and opportunity identification, it is only behavior that one can observe, which has social, economic, political, aesthetic and other impacts. Cognitively recognizing, finding, or shaping an opportunity has no impact until that opportunity changes behavior (through communication, investing funds, etc.). The same applies to the broader process of creativity whether in opportunity shaping, problem solving, or operations. Behaviors can (but do not always) lead to creative cognitions (Tharp, 2003) and creative cognitions can (but do not always) lead to actions (and subsequent performances and artifacts) that may be judged as creative (Csikszentmihalyi, 1990; Gielnik, Frese, Graf, & Kampschulte, 2012).

Behavior is also the source of new cognition, especially learning, as the actor makes observations about his or her or others' actions and their outcomes, alters or reinforces his/her mental map (schemas, scripts, etc.), and makes similar or different behavioral choices in the future. This chapter cannot do service to this expanding array of research other than to point to the intersection of these mental processes and observable individual behavior.

While "thoughts of entrepreneurs" is not a specific research arena, the cognitive scripts or schemas that underlie the habits of thought have been proposed for study (e.g., Baron, 2004; Shook, Priem & McGee, 2003) but few studies have actually attempted to measure these structures (Mitchell, Smith, Seawright, & Morse, 2000). As measured by Mitchell et al. (2000) the closest script category to behavior is "arrangement" scripts (protecting an idea, having a network, having access to resources and having venture-specific skills) and these scripts were found to be positively predictive of new venture creation[3]. Schemas and scripts would be developed though one's experience and embodied in tacit and explicit knowledge and practical intelligence (Baum & B. Bird, 2010; Federici, Ferrante, & Vistocco, 2008). Among these cognitive structures are perceptual biases, such as overconfidence, representativeness, counterfactual thinking, affect, infusion (Baron, 1998; Baron, 2008; Busenitz & Barney, 1997), which for most individuals are not consciously monitored. Other more conscious cognitions might include the individuals' risk perception involved in a particular new venture (Forlani & Mullins, 2000; Simon, Houghton, & Aquino, 1999). These conscious and unconscious habits of thought and perceptions will influence the specific behaviors of entrepreneurs through the selection of behaviors from whatever repertoire the individual has of existing behavior.

Entrepreneurs' beliefs are also largely unexamined, with one important exception, the individuals' belief that they can successfully perform a specific behavior or complete a specific task (e.g., self-efficacy). Self-efficacy (Bandura, 1997; Chen, Greene, & Crick, 1998; Trevelyan, 2011) has been found to be closely associated with entrepreneurs' venture performance (Baum & B. Bird, 2010; Hmieleski & Corbett, 2008) and is a critical part of motivation (discussed below). Three belief-based research papers we found include examination of beliefs about market and industry (Cliff, Jennings, & Greenwood, 2006; Parker, 2006) and beliefs (perceptions) about oneself (McGrath & MacMillan, 1992).

Also closely aligned with work on entrepreneurs' motivation are the numerous efforts to theorize about (Bird, 1989; Katz & Gartner, 1988) and measure the impacts of an entrepreneur's intention to start and grow their venture (Dutta & Thornhill, 2008; Krueger, Reilly, & Carsrud, 2000; Nabi, Holden, & Walmsley, 2010; Sanchez, 2011; Shepherd & Krueger, 2002; Trevelyan, 2011). Theory and research across a large spectrum of behavior has shown that intention to behave in a certain way is a very good predictor of that behavior (Gollwitzer & Brandstätter, 1997; Krueger, 2010) especially as a component of the theory of planned behavior (Ajzen, 1991) which has been widely used in entrepreneurship research, e.g., Krueger (2010).

Finally, the cognitive process of learning is important to entrepreneurs' behavior since entrepreneurs can only choose from behaviors they have learned. Research addressing learning shows its importance in several contexts (Baum, Bird, & Singh, 2011; Corbett, 2007; Dimo, 2007). It is only through active learning (from experience and from observations of others) that new goal-oriented behaviors are learned and it is through experience again, that behavior choices are made in the future.

Motivation

The only behavior of real interest to entrepreneurship scholars is consciously motivated behavior[4] and motivation is what causes the entrepreneur to select this behavior over others, to apply effort, and to persist. Goals are consciously chosen and follow from cognitions. They are at the center of almost all motivation theories (Mitchell, 1997) including needs (Maslow, 1943; McClelland, 1965); expectancy and related self-efficacy (Bandura & Cervone, 1983; Klein, 1991); equity and justice (Greenberg, 1986); control (Klein, 1991) and more. The two key components of goal theory are goal setting and goal striving (Gollwitzer, 1990; James, 1890; Locke & Latham, 1990). Goals are thought to have hierarchical structure (Powers, 1973; Cropanzano, James, & Citera, 1993); when an individual is unsuccessful at achieving one goal, the person moves to the immediately next lower goal and if successful at attaining this goal moves to the immediate higher goal.

Despite the importance of goal setting and striving, these motivational factors have been examined in the entrepreneurship literature in a limited way, and mostly in an implicit manner. The research on career choice (e.g., Kolvereid, 1996) and pull-push hypothesis (Schjoedt & Shaver, 1997) are examples of studies that implicitly examine goal-based motivation theory. Based on a six-year review of the literature on entrepreneurs' behavior from 2004–2010 (Bird et al., 2012), we only identified one study that explicitly examined goals. Rauch, Frese, and Utsch (2005) examined how decision-making involvement by employees and goal communication to employees influenced employee growth in small businesses. Other works, not included in this review, have also addressed entrepreneurs' motivation. Naffziger, Hornsby, and Kuratko (1994) developed a conceptual model (with goals implied) of entrepreneurs' motivation in the start-up decision, start-up, and sustaining the entrepreneurial activities after start-up. Their empirical follow-up with 234 entrepreneurs found four kinds of goals (extrinsic rewards, independence/autonomy, intrinsic rewards, and family security) influenced entrepreneurs' sustained efforts in venture creation and management (Kuratko, Hornsby, & Naffziger, 1997). Other empirical studies addressing goals include a longitudinal study by Baum, Locke, and Kirkpatrick (1998), which found that when goals inherent in the company vision were explained or communicated in writing they impacted venture growth. While Baum et al. explained how goals influence firm-level performance (venture growth); Stewart, Carland, Carland, Watson, and Sweo (2003) examined how entrepreneurs' disposition (specifically achievement motivation, risk-taking propensity, and preference for innovation) influenced the entrepreneurs' goal setting for the venture (i.e., growth goals).

Decision-making

Decision-making is a process that involves choosing an idea, plan or course of action from an array of alternatives and is implicit in many entrepreneurship studies that link precursors such as individual differences, cognition, environmental characteristics, to the outcomes of venture creation (or venture growth). However, decision-making is examined explicitly in entrepreneurs' behavior to a very limited extent[5].

The over-arching models considered in the decision-making literature can be grouped in to outcome and process models both of which are grounded mostly in cognition, although consciously mediated decisions are also motivated. Decisions can (but do not necessarily) result in behavior.

Outcome models focus on probability and utility. These are normative in nature as they tend to explain how people *should* choose. The mathematical-decision model describes how to make decisions in terms of probabilities and utilities (Von Neumann & Morgenstern, 1947). Departures from normative decision theory are behavioral and psychological decision process models (e.g., subjective expected utility model, Edwards, 1954; prospect theory; Kahneman & Tversky, 1979), which focuses on *what* people do when making decisions. Social judgment theory describes how people adjust to a probabilistic ambiguous environment; thus, the model is focused on the interaction between a person and the environment when making decisions. Information integration approaches identify people's personal rules for making judgments. Examples include Simon's information model (Simon, 1947, 1957), the conflict model of decision-making (Janis & Mann, 1977), individual limitations in information processing (Tversky & Kahneman, (1974), groupthink (Janis, 1972), escalation of commitment (Staw, 1976), and attribution theory (Weiner, 1974). Other models include bounded rationality (March & Simon, 1958); meta-decision-making (Mintzberg, Raisinghani & Theoret, 1976); garbage-can model (Cohen, March, & Olsen, 1972); and more.

One recent study addressing entrepreneurs' decision-making process is provided by Sommer, Loch, and Dong (2009). These researchers examined complexity and unforeseeable uncertainty based on a sample of 58 start-ups in Shanghai. Based on their findings, these scholars note the best approach to decision making depends on the combination of complexity and unforeseeable uncertainty of the start-up. Another study, also using a process model (Talaulicar, Grundei, and Werder, 2005) examined how three different decision-making processes influenced decision speed and comprehensiveness in new German ventures. This limited consideration of the literature suggests that entrepreneurship scholars appear to focus on decision-making-process models in general but do not test decision models provided in the decision making literature per se.

METHODOLOGICAL ISSUES IN RESEARCH ON ENTREPRENEURS' BEHAVIOR

To appraise the quality of research on entrepreneurs' behavior, we reviewed articles in select top entrepreneurial and general management journals 2004–2010[6,7]. We noted methodological issues pertaining to the use of variables and measurement of entrepreneurs' behavior.

Our survey of the six years of literature showed that entrepreneurs' behavior was used as independent, dependent, control, and selection variables. Behaviors were used as an independent variable in little more than one-third of the studies whereas it was used as a dependent variable in about half of the empirical studies. Of the studies on behavior, seven percent used behavior as a control variable and about seven percent as a selection variable. It should be noted that some studies used behavior as two types of variable, e.g., independent and dependent variables. Among the variables measured were time spent on an activity or at work, involvement, communication intensity, receiving support, acquiring information, business plan writing, networking activities to mention a few. Studies based on the Panel Study of Entrepreneurial Dynamics (PSED) used behavior as a selection variable where samples that self-reported more than a certain number of activities were included in a sample and others with fewer activities were not (Reynolds, Carter,

Gartner, & Greene, 2004). This also pertained to studies based on similar data collection methdology, such as the Swedish PSED (e.g., Delmar & Shane, 2004) and the Global Entrepreneurship Monitor (Langowitz & Minniti, 2007). Other than these studies, our review showed there is a lack of consistency in conceptualization of behavior variables and in their measurement. Both of these issues contribute to fragmentation of the literature and inhibit advancement of our collective knowledge of entrepreneurs' behavior.

Inconsistent conceptualizations of behaviors or processes [e.g., in resource acquisition via the propensity to use ties in finding investors (Zhang, Souitaris, Soh, & Wong, 2008) and perceptions and behaviors in initiating investor relationships (Alsos, Isaksen, & Ljunggren, 2006)] makes it difficult to accumulate work into a coherent body of knowledge. It becomes even more difficult to build knowledge when there are operationalizations that lack measures of reliability and validity. Single-item measures (which may be binary or scaled) assess constructs globally but are affected by the respondents' interpretation and cannot be assessed for reliability; multi-item measures tend to mitigate these problems. However, even when summed across several items, binary responses have limited variance, are not interval (parametric) in nature, and do not submit to usual measures of reliability (leaving questions about validity and reducing the statistical tools that can be used).

Scaled multiple-response items are often presumed to approximate the interval data required for many parametric statistics. However, reliability estimates such as internal consistency while often provided, are insufficient to help build cumulative knowledge of entrepreneurs' behavior. Validity measures also needed are often not provided. To some degree validity concerns are mitigated by minimal face validity, assessed when item wording is provided. Future research will need more sophisticated measurement of construct validity to move the field forward.

Response biases also plague much of the research on entrepreneurs' behavior. This includes retrospective bias (when an entrepreneur is asked to recall the past when responding) and this bias increases over time (Schjoedt & Shaver, 2005). Many articles overcome this by asking for current information, attitudes, perceptions, and other self-reports. These snapshots lack outcome predictions that need longitudinal designs. A related yet separate issue is social desirability, the tendency to give desirable but possibly untrue responses, of critical importance in self-report measures which predominate the studies reviewed. This is routinely neglected in research on entrepreneurs' behavior and is a substantial threat to validity. Neither of these biases is adequately assessed through the more frequent use of common method variance estimates.

Even though measurement issues are pervasive in the reviewed studies, there are some examples of good methodological practices among the studies we reviewed. Dobrev and Barnett (2005) used a 14-item measure found in other published studies to assess perceived difficulty of organizational efforts. Forbes (2005) used principal component analysis on the two multi-item measures on decision comprehensiveness and use of information. Schjoedt and Shaver (2007) used post-stratification weights to make their sample nationally representative. Hanlon and Saunders (2007) used within-methods triangulation in their study on entrepreneurs' use of support. Lastly, Davidsson and Honig (2003) tested for common method variance and conducted a pre-test six months before collecting data for their study, allowing assessment of reliability (internal and across time) and validity of the measures. While these examples are present in the reviewed studies, they represent the minority of studies, Thus, it is critical for research on entrepreneurs' behavior, and for the field of entrepreneurship, to move forward that researchers use measures that are reliable and valid.

SELLING BEHAVIOR: AN EXAMPLE OF FUTURE RESEARCH ON ENTREPRENEURS' BEHAVIOR

While the first sale made by the entrepreneur is a critical benchmark (Carter et al., 1996), our review of the literature showed no attention to this set of fundamental behaviors necessary for entrepreneurship. We conducted a focused search with Scopus on "entrepreneur sales behavior" and found 19 academic articles none of which have anything to do directly with entrepreneurship sales let alone sales behaviors. A similar lack is found among entrepreneurship course offerings and textbooks. Although we did not comprehensively survey universities for courses on selling (c.f., sales management), there are a few in first- and second-tier universities that do (e.g., University of Chicago, Northwestern University, University of Missouri). Most of these are supported by trade books and how-to readings. In mainstream entrepreneurship texts, the topic is rarely covered. For example, one of the most widely used entrepreneurship textbooks (Barringer & Ireland, 2010) and one of the most respected entrepreneurship practitioner handbooks, *The Art of the Start* (Kawasaki, 2004), do not address any specifics of the sales process or entrepreneurs' sales behavior.

In fact, sales behaviors have been poorly identified and measured generally. Those behaviors that have been identified relate to account maintenance activities and working with established accounts. So there is very little to recommend them to specific entrepreneurs' selling behavior.

Any effort to address the selling behavior of entrepreneurs would need to account for at least two types of selling within an entrepreneurial context. The first relates to the selling of a new product or service and would have to describe the actions taken in order to sell a new product or service to the customer. The behavior of this type of selling would be most visible and important where personal selling is needed, for example by telephone, personal face-to-face calls, or a storefront. The more passive selling via internet and social media is another context of low behavioral visibility but behavioral measures are possible. The second relates to selling the entrepreneur's idea or concept to either investors or prospective partners. One study in this domain that is specifically behavior-centric is Pollack, Rutherford, & Nagy (2013). In this study the authors used an existing scale of preparedness (Chen, Yao, & Kotha, 2009) and using trained coders, scored the behavior of televised business pitches. Each of these selling domains would conceivably have different behaviors because the product, market, communication modalities, and customer are different. We turn our specific focus to selling to customers and arenas where personal selling of product or service is important to business success (e.g., real estate, insurance, elective/cosmetic survey, management consulting, auto dealerships, pharmaceutical representatives, accounting).

Research on Selling

Any review of the sales literature begins with the seven steps to selling, which are found in marketing textbooks and sales training books (Dubinsky, 1980; Hawes, Rich, & Widmier, 2004; Moncrief & Marshall, 2005). They are: prospecting, pre-approach, approach, presentation, overcoming objections, close, follow-up. "Canned" sales pitches, such as those used in direct door-to-door selling perhaps best exemplify the "steps" approach. Over time, however, effective selling methods have evolved from scripted, often forceful techniques to a relationship selling approach (Schurr, 1987) and so modifications have been made to the seven steps. For example, the original "approach step" was concerned with the first contact made with the customer and establishing a positive mood. Behaviors associated with that step included: shaking hands, small talk, strong eye contact, and creating a positive first impression. In the relationship approach, this step has the sales person focused on: providing information, creating solutions, and building relationships with the client (Moncrief & Marshall, 2005). One can see how this "approach step" would be configured very differently if sales were done exclusively through web-mediated interface. Some of these behaviors are more abstract and general (e.g., providing information which can be done in many different ways) and others much more specific parts of that (e.g., making eye contact).

Moncrief (1986) drawing from research and interviews with sales professionals identified 121 sales behaviors (e.g., prospects, selects the product to take on calls, writes up the order) that are midway in a hierarchy of specificity (Bird et al., 2012). Although well conceived, his approach proves problematic for identifying the sales behaviors of start-up entrepreneurs for at least two reasons. First, this scale anchors items in terms of frequency rather than importance. Given the limited resources and the urgent, fast-paced process of many start-ups, entrepreneurs who do early selling will likely choose behaviors based on perceived importance and may not have time to repeat behaviors frequently. Second, the scale items reflect sales into established accounts and account management techniques in mature industries, not developing new customers for new products and services, or creating a new industry. Nevertheless, this scale could be modified and used as a starting point for measurement of entrepreneurs' sales behavior; we encourage efforts in this direction.

If the venture enters a mature market and/or is founded by an entrepreneur with previous sales experience, it may begin with a mature sales strategy and the entrepreneur may engage relationship oriented sales behaviors. Here the sales literature shows two schools of thought: customer oriented selling and adaptive selling or smart selling. *Customer oriented selling* (Saxe & Weitz, 1982) focuses on customer satisfaction and assumes that a satisfied customer is inclined to buy more of the product. Saxe and Weitz created a scale that assesses customer oriented sales behavior (i.e., I try to get customers to discuss their needs with me). As this shows, however, the scale does not clearly tap into behavior and is used as a state-like, individual difference measure (Grizzle, Zablah, Brown, Mowen, & Lee, 2009). Weitz, Sujan & Sujan develop the construct of *adaptive selling* that addresses "the ability to adapt sales behaviors effectively to the demands of the sales situation" (1986, p. 174) and the construct is operationalised by Spiro and Weitz (1990) with the adaptive selling scale. However, this scale has only five items that claim to tap the behavioral "facet" (e.g., "I vary my sales style from situation to situation" and "I like to experiment with different sales approaches"). Thus even these five items have attitudinal items in the mix and all of the items are highly socially desirable. *Smart selling*, a variant of adaptive selling, adds knowledge (of sales situation) seeking behaviors and situational adaptation (Sujan, 1986) but by mixing traits into measures does not advance measurement of behavior.

Finally, literature on sales tactics, which lays some claim to identifying sales behaviors integrates the influence literature and methods into the selling context, reminding us that persuasion communication behavior is a critical selling behavior. Frazier and Summers (1984) developed what is considered the most widely used taxonomy of influence strategies in marketing (Boyle & Dwyer, 1995; Kim, 2000; McFarland, Challagalla, & Shervani, 2006). They proposed six tactics within distribution channel boundary spanners: information exchange, recommendations, requests, threats, promises, and legalistic pleas. McFarland et al. (2006) build on this work to identify tactics that are pertinent in personal selling. Items they used include: information exchange ("presented information related to your various purchase options"), promises ("offered to give special attention to your company if you would give him or her new business"), and ingratiation ("made you feel good about yourself before making his or her sales pitch"). Note that these items are perceptions of customers or sales targets, not perceptions of sales persons (avoiding self-response biases including social desirability).

We believe that more research into the personal selling behavior of entrepreneurs is warranted and that the sales literature noted above could be carefully modified and used to measure and assess entrepreneurs' sales behavior. We doubt that entrepreneurs' personal selling behavior is substantially different from personal selling in other contexts, other than that the seller is also the owner and has to enact a wide range of behaviors skillfully to achieve venture survival and growth with little, if any, training.

FUTURE THEORETICAL AND EMPIRICAL DIRECTIONS

Our intentions with this chapter are to stimulate research on entrepreneurs' behavior, both conceptual and empirical. While we encourage both types of research on entrepreneurs' behavior, we are especially interested in empirical research. We need to create reliable, valid measures of behavior that make sense, can inform us, and can be used by researchers. Empirical research based on such measures will assist us in advancing our understanding of the entrepreneurship phenomena and will help us assist entrepreneurs in what to do when starting a new venture.

NOTES

1. Roles are sets of appropriate "routine" actions taken by individuals in relation to others in the conduct of tasks or work (D. Katz & Kahn, 1978).
2. Other connections could be elaborated such as behavior as influencer of and influenced by social capital, venture strategy, and venture outcomes.
3. Mitchell et al. (2000) posited and found effects for scripts that were motivations (willingness) and ability which a correlate and precursor to behavior. Thus other scripts are not particularly useful for understanding behavior.
4. Unmotivated and/or unconscious behavior would include habitual behavior, instinctual and reflex behaviors.

5. Research on decision-making in the entrepreneurship literature has largely focused on venture capitalists (e.g., Zacharakis, & Shepherd, 2001) which is beyond the scope of this chapter.
6. For a more detailed description of the methodology employed in the review and for an overview of the findings please see Bird et al. (2012).
7. The journals surveyed were *Academy of Management Journal, Administrative Science Quarterly, Entrepreneurship and Regional Development, Entrepreneurship: Theory & Practice, Human Resource Management Review, Human Relations, Industrial and Labor Relations Review, Industrial Relations, Journal of Applied Behavioral Science, Journal of Applied Psychology, Journal of Business Venturing, Journal of Developmental Entrepreneurship, Journal of International Business Studies, Journal of Management, Journal of Management Studies, Journal of Occupational and Organizational Psychology, Journal of Organizational Behavior, Journal of Small Business Management, Journal of Vocational Behavior, Leadership Quarterly, Management Science, Organization Science, Organization Studies, Organizational Behavior and Human Decision Processes, Organizational Dynamics, Personnel Psychology, Psychological Bulletin, Small Business Economics, Strategic Entrepreneurship Journal,* and *Strategic Management Journal.*

REFERENCES

Amabile, T. M. (1996), *Creativity in Context*. Boulder, CO: Westview Press.
Ajzen, I. (1991), The theory of planned behavior, *Organizational Behavior and Human Decision Processes, 50*(2), 179.
Alsos, G., Isaksen, E., & Ljunggren, E. (2006), 'New venture financing and subsequent business growth in men- and women-Led businesses', *Entrepreneurship Theory and Practice, 30*(5), 667.
Arrow, K. (1962), 'Economic welfare and the allocation of resources for invention', in R. Nelson (Ed.), *The Rate Direction of Incentive Activity:Economic and Social Factors* (pp. 609–25). Princeton, NJ: Princeton University Press.
Bandura, A. (1997). *Self-efficacy: The Exercise of Control*. New York: Freeman.
Bandura, A., & Cervone, D. (1983), 'Self-evaluative and self-efficacy mechanisms governing the motivational effects of goal systems', *Journal of Personality and Social Psychology, 45*, 1017–28.
Baron, R. A. (1998), 'Cognitive mechanisms in entrepreneurship: why and when entrepreneurs think differently than other people', *Journal of Business Venturing, 13*, 275–94.
Baron, R. A. (2004), 'The cognitive perspective: A valuable tool for answering entrepreneurship's basic "why?" questions', *Journal of Business Venturing, 19*, 221–40.
Baron, R. A. (2008), 'The role of affect in the entrepreneurial process', *Academy of Management. The Academy of Management Review, 33*(2), 328.
Barringer, B. R., & Ireland, D. (2010), '*Entrepreneurship: Successfully Launching New Ventures', 3/E* Upper Saddle River, NJ, USA: Prentice Hall.
Bass, B. M. (1990), 'The work of leaders and managers', in B. M. Bass (ed.), *Bass & Stogdill's Handbook of Leadership* (pp. 383–414). New York: Free Press.
Baum, J., and Bird, B. (2010), 'The successful intelligence of high-growth entrepreneurs: Links to new venture growth', *Organization Science, 21*(2), 397–412.
Baum, J. R., Bird, B. J., and Singh, S. (2011), 'The practical intelligence of entrerpeneurs: Antecedents and a link with new venture growth', *Personnel Psychology, 64*, 397–425.
Baum, J.R., Locke, E.A., and Kirkpatrick, S.A. (1998), 'A longitudinal study of vision and vision communication to venture growth in entrepreneurial firms', *Journal of Applied Psychology, 83*, 43–54.
Bird, B. (1989), 'Implementing entrepreneurial ideas: The case for intention', *Academy of Management Review, 13*, 442–53.
Bird, B., and Schjoedt, L. (2009), 'Entrepreneurial behavior: Its nature, scope, recent research, and agenda for future research' in A. L. Carsrud & M. Brannback (Eds.), *Understanding the Entrepreneurial Mind* (pp. 327–58). New York: Springer.
Bird, B., Schjoedt, L., and Baum, J. R. (2012), 'Editors Introduction: Entrepreneurs' behavior: Elucidation and measurement', *EntrepreneurshipTheory and Practice, 36*, 889–913.
Boyle, B. A., and Dwyer, F. R. (1995), 'Power, bureaucracy, influence, and performance: Their relationships in industrial distribution channels', *Journal of Business Research, 32*(3), 189–200.
Brown, T. E., Davidsson, P. and Wiklund, J. (2001), 'An operationalization of Stevenson's conceptualization of entrepreneurship as opportunity-based firm behavior,' *Strategic Management Journal, 22*, 953–68.
Busenitz, L. W. and Barney, J. B. (1997), 'Differences between entrepreneurs and managers in large organizations: Biases and heuristics in strategic decision-making', *Journal of Business Venturing, 12*(1), 9.

Carter, N. M., Gartner, W. B., and Reynolds, P. D. (1996), 'Exploring start-up event sequences', *Journal of Business Venturing, 11*(3), 151.

Chen, G., Greene, P. and Crick, A. (1998), 'Does entrepreneurial self-efficacy distinguish entrepreneurs from managers?' *Journal of Business Venturing, 13*, 295–316.

Chen, X.-P., Yao, X. and Kotha, S. (2009), 'Entrepreneur passion and preparedness in business plan presentations: A persuasion analysis of venture captitalist funding decisions', *Academy of Management Journal, 52*(1), 199–214.

Cliff, J. E., Jennings, P. D. and Greenwood, R. (2006), 'New to the game and questioning the rules: The experiences and beliefs of founders who start imitative versus innovative firms', *Journal of Business Venturing, 21*(5), 633.

Cogliser, C. C., and Brigham, K. H. (2004), 'The intersection of leadership and entrepreneurship: Mutual lessons to be learned', *Leadership Quarterly, 15*, 771–99.

Cohen, M. D., March, J. G. and Olsen, J. P. (1972), 'A garbage can model of organizational choice', *Administrative Science Quarterly, 17*(1), 1–25.

Corbett, A. C. (2007), 'Learning asymmetries and the discovery of entrepreneurial opportunities', *Journal of Business Venturing, 22*(1), 97–118.

Cropanzano, R., James, K. and Citera, M. (1993), 'A goal hierarchy model of personality, motivation, and leadership', *Research in Organizational Behavior, 15*, 267–322.

Csikszentmihalyi, M. (1990), *Flow: The Psychology of Optimal Experience*. New York: Harper.

Czarniawska-Joerges, B. and Wolff, R. (1991), 'Leaders, managers, entrepreneurs on and off the organizational stage', *Organization Studies, 12*(4), 529–46.

Davidsson, P., and Honig, B. (2003), 'The role of social and human capital among nascent entrepreneurs,' *Journal of Business Venturing, 18*(3), 301–31.

Delmar, F., and Shane, S. (2004), 'Legitimating first: organizing activities and the survival of new ventures', *Journal of Business Venturing, 19*(3), 385–410.

Dimo, D. (2007), 'From opportunity insight to opportunity intention: The importance of person-situation learning match', *Entrepreneurship Theory and Practice, 31*(4), 561–83.

Dobrev, S. D., and Barnett, W. P. (2005), 'Organizational roles and transition to entrepreneurship.' *Academy of Management Journal, 48*(3), 433–49.

Dubinsky, A. J. (1980), 'A factor analytic study of the personal selling process', *Journal of Personal Selling & Sales Management, 1*(1), 26.

Dutta, D., and Thornhill, S. (2008), 'The evolution of growth intentions: Toward a cognition-based model', *Journal of Business Venturing, 23*(3), 307.

Edwards, W. (1954), 'The theory of decision-making', *Psychological Bulletin, 51*(4), 380–417.

Federici, D., Ferrante, F. and Vistocco, D. (2008), 'On the sources of entrepreneurial talent: Tacit vs. codified knowledge', *Journal of Knowledge Management, 6*(6), 7–27.

Forbes, D. (2005), 'The effects of strategic decision making on entrepreneurial self-efficacy,' *Entrepreneurship Theory and Practice, 29*(5), 599–624.

Forlani, D. and Mullins, J. W. (2000), 'Perceived risks and choices in entrepreneurs' new venture decisions', *Journal of Business Venturing, 15*(4), 305–22.

Frazier, G. L., and Summers, J. O. (1984), 'Interfirm influence strategies and their application within distribution channels', *Journal of Marketing, 48*(3), 43–55.

Gielnik, M. M., Frese, M., Graf, J. M. and Kampschulte, A. (2012), 'Creativity in the opportunity identification process and the moderating effect of diversity of information', *Journal of Business Venturing, 27*(5), 559–76.

Gollwitzer, P. M. (1990), 'Action phases and mind-sets', in E. T. Higgins & R. M. Sorrentino (Eds.), *The Handbook of Motivation and Cognition: Foundations of Social Behavior* (Vol. 2, pp. 53–92). New York: Guilford Press.

Gollwitzer, P. M., and Brandstätter, V. (1997), 'Implementation intentions and effective goal pursuit', *Journal of Personality and Social Psychology, 73*(1), 186.

Greenberg, J. (1986), 'Determinants of perceived fairness in performance evaluation', *Journal of Applied Psychology, 71*, 340–42.

Grizzle, J., Zablah, A., Brown, T., Mowen, J. and Lee, J. (2009), 'Employee customer orientation in context: How the environment moderates the influence of customer orientation on performance outcomes', *Journal of Applied Psychology, 94*(5), 1227–42.

Hanlon, D., and Saunders, C. (2007), 'Marshaling resources to form small new ventures: Toward a more holistic understanding of entrepreneurial support,' *Entrepreneurship Theory and Practice, 31*(4), 619–41.

Hawes, J. M., Rich, A. K. and Widmier, S. M. (2004), 'Assessing the development of the sales profession', *Journal of Personal Selling & Sales Management, 24*(1), 27–37.

Hmieleski, K., and Corbett, A. C. s.-e. (2008), 'The contrasting interaction effects of improvisational behavior with entrepreneurial self-efficacy on new venture performance and entrepreneur work satisfaction', *Journal of Business Venturing, 23*, 482–96.

James, W. (1890/1950), *The Principles of Psychology*. Vol. 2. New York: Dover.

Janis, I. L. (1972), *Victims of Groupthink*, New York: Houghton Mifflin.

Janis, I. L., and Mann. L. (1977), *Decision Making: A Psychological Analysis of Conflict, Choice, and Commitment*. New York: Free Press.

Kahneman, D. and Tversky, A. (1979), 'Prospect theory: An analysis of decision-making under risk', *Econometrica, 47*, 263–91.

Katz, D. and Kahn, R. L. (1978), *The Social Psychology of Organizations*, New York: John Wiley.

Katz, J. and Gartner, W. B. (1988), 'Properties of emerging organizations', *Academy of Management Review, 13*, 429–41.

Kawasaki, G. (2004), *The Art of the Start*. New York, New York, USA: Penguin Group.

Kim, K. (2000), 'On interfirm power, channel climate, and solidarity in industrial distributor-supplier dyads', *Journal of the Academy of Marketing Science, 28*(3), 388–405.

Kirzner, I. (1997), 'Entrepreneurial discovery and the competitive market process: An Austrian approach', *Journal of Economic Literature, 35*, 60–85.

Klein, H. J. (1991), 'Further evidence on the relationship between goal setting and expectancy theories', *Organizational Behavior and Human Decision Processes, 49*, 230–57.

Kolvereid, L. (1996), 'Organizational employment versus self-employment: Reasons for career choice intentions', *Entrepreneurship Theory and Practice, 21*, 23–31.

Kotter, J. P. (2001), 'What leaders really do', *Harvard Business Review, 79* (11), 85–96.

Krueger, N. (2010), 'Entrepreneurial intentions are dead: Long live entrepreneurial intentions', in A. L. Carsrud and M. Brännback (Eds.), *Understanding the Entrepreneurial Mind* (pp. 51–72). New York: Springer.

Krueger, N. F., Reilly, M. D. and Carsrud, A. L. (2000), 'Competing models of entrepreneurial intentions', *Journal of Business Venturing, 15*, 411–32.

Kuratko, D. F., Hornsby, J.S. and Naffziger, D.W. (1997), 'An examination of owner's goals in sustaining entrepreneurship', *Journal of Small Business Management, 35*, 24–33.

Langowitz, N., and Minniti, M. (2007), 'The entrepreneurial propensity of women', *Entrepreneurship Theory and Practice, 31*(3), 341–64.

Locke, E. A. and Latham, G. P. (1990), *Theory of Goal Setting and Task Performance*, Englewood Cliffs, N.J.: Prentice-Hall.

Lumpkin, G. T., Cogliser, C. C., and Schneider, D. R. (2009), 'Understanding and measuring autonomy: An entrepreneurial orientation perspective', *Entrepreneurship Theory and Practice, 33*(1), 47.

March, J.G. and Simon, H. A. (1958), *Organizations*. New York: John Wiley.

Maslow, A. H. (1943), 'A theory of human motivation', *Psychological Review, 50*, 370–96.

McClelland, D. C. (1965), 'N Achievement and entrepreneurship: A longitudinal study', *Journal of Personality and Social Psychology, 1*(4), 389–92.

McFarland, R. G., Challagalla, G. N. and Shervani, T. A. (2006), 'Influence tactics for effective adaptive selling', *Journal of Marketing, 70*(4), 103–17.

McGrath, R. G. and MacMillan, I. C. (1992), 'More like each other than anyone else? A cross-cultural study of entrepreneurial perceptions', *Journal of Business Venturing, 7*(5), 419–29.

Mintzberg, H., Raisinghani, D. and Theoret, A. (1976), 'The structure of "unstructured" decision processes', *Administrative Science Quarterly, 21*, 246–75.

Mitchell, R. K., Smith, B., Seawright, L. W., and Morse, E., A. (2000), 'Cross-cultural cognitions and the venture creation decision', *Academy of Management Journal, 43*(5), 974–93.

Mitchell, T. R. (1997), 'Matching motivational strategies with organizational contexts', *Research in Organizational Behavior, 19*, 57–94.

Moncrief, W. C. (1986), 'Selling activity and sale position taxonomies for industrial salesforces', *Journal of Marketing Research, 23*(3), 261–70.

Moncrief, W. C., and Marshall, G. W. (2005), 'The evolution of the seven steps of selling', *Industrial Marketing Management, 34*(1), 13–22.

Nabi, G., Holden, R., and Walmsley, A. (2010), 'Entrepreneurial intentions among students: Towards a re-focused research agenda', *Journal of Small Business and Enterprise Development, 17*(4), 537–51.

Naffziger, D. W., Hornsby, J. S., and Kuratko, D. F. (1994), 'A proposed research model of entrepreneurial motivation', *Entrepreneurship Theory and Practice, 18*, 29–42.

Parker, S. C. (2006), 'Learning about the unknown: How fast do entrepreneurs adjust their beliefs?' *Journal of Business Venturing, 21*(1), 1.

Penrose, E. E. (1959), *The Theory of the Growth of the Firm*. New York: Wiley.

Pollack, J. M., Rutherford, M. W., and Nagy, B. G. (2013), 'Preparedness and cognitive legitimacy as antecedents of new venture funding in televised business pitches', *Entrepreneurship Theory and Practice, 36*, 915–36.

Powers, W. T. (1973), 'Feedback: Beyond behaviorism', *Science, 179*, 351–6.

Rauch, A. M., Frese, M., and Utsch, A. (2005), 'Effects of human capital and long-term human resources development and utilization on employment growth of small-scale business: A causal analysis', *Entrepreneurship Theory and Practice, 20*, 681–98.

Reynolds, P. D., Carter, N., Gartner, W. B., and Greene, P. (2004), 'The prevalence of nascent entrepreneurs in the United States: Evidence from the panel study of entrepreneurial dynamics', *Small Business Economics, 23*(4), 263–84.

Sanchez, J. C. (2011), 'University training for entrepreneurial competencies: Its impact on intention of venture creation', *International Entrepreneurship and Management Journal, 7*(2), 239–54.

Saxe, R., and Weitz, B. A. (1982), 'The SOCO scale—A measure of the customer orientation of sales people', *Journal of Marketing Research, 19*(3), 343–51.

Schjoedt, L. and Shaver, K. G. (2005), '"I'll Happily Tell You What I Think (Now)": A Methodological Issue in Entrepreneurship Research', *Proceedings for the 2005 50th World Conference of International Council for Small Businesses (ICSB), Washington, D.C.*

Schumpeter, J. A. (1934), 'Fundamentals of economic development', *The Theory of Economic Development* (pp. 65–94). Cambridge, MA: Harvard University Press.

Schurr, P. H. (1987), 'Evolutionary approaches to effective selling', *Advances in Business Marketing 2*, 55–80.

Shane, S. and Venkataraman, S. (2000), 'The promise of entrepreneurship as a field of research', *Academy of Management Review, 25*(1), 217–26.

Shepherd, D. A. and Krueger, N. F. (2002), 'An intention-based model of entrepreneurial teams' social cognition', *Entrepreneurship: Theory and Practice, 27*(2), 167–85.

Shook, C., Priem, R. and McGee, J. (2003), 'Venture creation and the enterprising individual: A review and synthesis', *Journal of Management, 29*(3), 379–99.

Simon, H.A. (1947), *Administrative Behavior: A Study of Decision-Making Processes in Administrative Organization*, New York, NY: Free Press.

Simon. H. A. (1957). *Models of Man*. NY: Wiley.

Simon, M., Houghton, S., and Aquino, K. (1999), 'Cognitive biases, risk perception, and venture formation: How individuals decide to start companies', *Journal of Business Venturing, 15*, 113–34.

Sommer, S., Loch, C. and Dong, J. (2009), 'Managing complexity and unforeseeable uncertainty in startup companies: An empirical study', *Organization Science, 20*(1), 118–33.

Spiro, R. L., and Weitz, B. A. (1990), 'Adaptive selling: Conceptualization, measurement, and nomological validity', *Journal of Marketing Research, 27*(1), 61–9.

Staw, B. M. (1976), 'Knee-deep in the big muddy: A study of escalating commitment to a chosen course of action', *Organizational Behavior and Human Performance, 16*, 27–44.

Sujan, H. (1986), 'Smarter versus harder: An exploratory attributional analysis of salespeople's motivation', *JMR, Journal of Marketing Research, 23*(1), 41.

Stewart, W. H., Carland, J. C., Carland, J. W., Watson, W. E., and Sweo, R. (2003), 'Entrepreneurial dispositions and goal orientations: A comparative exploration of United States and Russian entrepreneurs', *Journal of Small Business Management, 41*(1), 27–46.

Talaulicar, T., Grundei, J. and Werder, A. (2005), 'Strategic decision making in start-ups: the effect of top management team organization and processes on speed and comprehensiveness', *Journal of Business Venturing, 20*(4), 519–41.

Tharp, T. (2003), *The Creative Habit*. New York: Simon & Schuster.

Trevelyan, R. (2011), 'Self-efficacy and effort in new venture development', *Journal of Management and Organization, 17*(1), 2–16.

Tversky, A. and Kahneman, D. (1974), 'Judgment under uncertainty: Heuristics and biases', *Science, 185*, 1124–31.

Vecchio, R. P. (2003), 'Entrepreneurship and leadership: common trends and common threads', *Human Resource Management Review, 13*, 303–27.

Von Neumann, J. and Morgenstern, O. (1947), *Theory of Games and Economic Behavior*. Princeton, N.J.: Princeton University Press.

Weiner, B. (1974), *Achievement Motivation and Attribution Theory*. Morristown, N.J.: General Learning Press.

Weitz, B. A., Sujan, H., and Sujan, M. (1986), 'Knowledge, motivation, and adaptive behavior: A framework for improving selling effectiveness', *Journal of Marketing, 50*(4), 174.

Wiklund, J., and Shepherd, D. (2003), 'Knowledge-based resources, entrepreneurial orientation, and the performance of small- and medium-sized businesses', *Strategic Management Journal, 24*(13), 1307.

Zacharakis, A. L. and Shepherd, D. A. (2001), 'The nature of information and overconfidence on venture capitalists' decision making', *Journal of Business Venturing, 16*(4), 311–332.

Zaleznik, A. (1992). 'Managers and leaders: Are they different?' *Harvard Business Review, 70*(2), 126–36.

Zhang, J., Souitaris, V., Soh, P., and Wong, P. (2008), 'A contingent model of network utilization in early financing of technology ventures', *Entrepreneurship Theory and Practice, 32*, 593–613.

13. Social embeddedness in entrepreneurship research: the importance of context and community
Edward McKeever, Alastair Anderson and Sarah Jack

INTRODUCTION

Since the mid 1980s there has been a noticeable increase in the number of studies focusing on the social structures, processes and mechanisms through which economic actions take place and entrepreneurial outcomes are achieved (Granovetter, 1985; Uzzi, 1997; Aldrich and Fiol, 1994). Within this growing body of research, the term social embeddedness has emerged and come to prominence (Granovetter, 1985), first as a metaphor relating to the influence of social and cultural factors on economic exchange, and more recently as an analytical concept in research interested in the role and importance of social networks for entrepreneurial action (Uzzi, 1997; Jack and Anderson, 2002). This growing recognition of entrepreneurs (both individually and collectively) as socialised actors is seen by many as a corrective adjustment based on mounting dissatisfaction with the simplicity and parsimony of neo-classical economic models (Hoang and Antoncic, 2003).

As a metaphor, theoretical lens and methodological tool, embeddedness has been described as an opportunity to form a deeper understanding of how membership of social groups at times facilitates, and at others constrains action (Portes and Sensenbrenner, 1993). Uzzi (1997: 22) has referred to embeddedness as a theoretical puzzle, that once understood will form the basis for making contextually informed sense of a whole range of complex social and economic situations. Yet despite this optimism and progress made, Block (2001) feels that while embeddedness represents a famous contribution to social thought, the concept remains a source of enormous confusion. This confusion Gemici (2008) feels is evident in the number of interpretations that the concept of embeddedness has drawn over the last quarter of a century (Reddy, 1984; Granovetter, 1985; Stanfield, 1986; Zukin and DiMaggio, 1990; Lie, 1991; Barber, 1995; Beckert, 1996; Krippner, 2001; Block, 2003; Krippner et al, 2004). However despite this variety, a key theme within all of these works is that embeddedness, identified broadly as the nature, depth and extent of an individual's ties into an environment, community or society, can be understood as a configurating element of general economic process, which indicates a direct link to entrepreneurship (Whittington, 1992; Uzzi, 1997; Anderson and Miller, 2003). From an entrepreneurship perspective, this conceptual vagueness we feel renders embeddedness theoretically problematic (Hirsch and Levin, 1999; Gemici, 2008). It also presents us with an opportunity in this chapter to make a contribution which starts to rectify this by exploring the emergence of social embeddedness theory in entrepreneurship and highlighting some of the insights gained to date. This provides the basis for then sketching what we see as a useful research agenda for the future.

We begin by looking at established social theory to identify and explore the foundations and emergence of the social embeddedness perspective. This allows us to look at the very roots of the concept. We then consider how this term has been imported, used and applied within the field of entrepreneurship. In doing so we demonstrate why social embeddedness is a particularly useful one to apply to the study of entrepreneurship and how it has been used to understand the entrepreneur and his/her relationship to the context and community in which he/she operates. Approaching the subject in this way provides us with the opportunity to demonstrate the work that has been done using the social embeddedness perspective but also how it might be used in future work to address certain gaps in knowledge and understanding about entrepreneurship.

THEORETICAL ORIGINS

It is difficult to definitively identify when the term social embeddedness was first adopted although Karl Polanyi (1944) is often cited as the first to explicitly use the phrase. However, when looked at more broadly, what seems to have occurred is that the term has emerged in a gradual manner based on a synthesis of contributions from across the social sciences. While sociology, anthropology and social psychology can be seen as the main schools of thought from which the concept of embeddedness has emerged, supporting contributions have also come from the disciplines of history (Thompson, 1971), political science (Scott, 1976), geography (Harvey, 1982) and mathematics (Harary, 1965).

In sociology, the roots of the social embeddedness concept can be traced back to Marx (1894 [1947]) and his ideas around group consciousness based on connected individuals experiencing common environmental realities. Park (1924; 1926) also argued that societies and their communal subgroups exist through interaction and by individuals communicating with others to whom they are connected. It is within these network interactions that experiences are shared and communal life is maintained (Park, 1926). The predominant theme to emerge in the early sociological literature is that connected individuals share a condition of community. This condition of affective belonging has been expressed by sociological scholars in terms of structural and moral congruence (Park, 1924), shared understandings of mutuality and insiderness (Weber, 1922, [1946]), sharing of group identities (Simmel, 1950), appreciation of within group rights and responsibilities (Homans, 1961), and adherence to protocols of behaviour and reciprocity. Simmel (1950) argued that interactions produce society and that by linking together, and interacting, people form group identities and boundaries. From this perspective, early sociological work retains a dual focus on the individual and at the same time paying attention to the influence of social relations on behaviour (Giddens, 1979).

Alternatively, others have emphasised the social nature of exchange, and the interrelationship between the social and economic spheres of life (Frazer, 1919; Malinowski, 1922; Lévi-Strauss, 1969; Bohannan, 1955; Ekeh, 1974). In his book *The Great Transformation*, Polanyi (1944) coined the word embeddedness to describe and interpret the influence of social structure on the functioning of exchange arrangements. Polanyi (2001 [1944]: 46) felt that "man's economy, as a rule, is submerged in his social relationships". He also argued that all observable economies are embedded, submerged and absorbed (terms he used interchangeably) in institutions, economic and non-economic, and that what is really important is that researchers capture the reality of society (as a connected body of people) in studying the process of economic life (Polanyi, 1968). In Polanyi's work, the notion of economic life is expanded to a societal level, i.e. the totality of relations and institutions, and which goes beyond the narrow transaction of goods and services (Gemici, 2008). In this holistic sense, writers like Polanyi (1968), Lévi-Strauss (1969) and Sahlins (1974) offered an expanded methodological principle for studying economic life in a way which contrasted with the atomistic individualism of economics. Anthropological interpretations of the empirical economy largely reject the formal notion of choice being solely induced by limited resources and insufficient means, while arguing that other motives including moral intent and historical association need to be accounted for (Sahlins, 1974).

Finally, the work of social psychologists can be related to the emergence of the embeddedness concept through a focus on the experiences and perceptions of group belonging. Lewin (1951) found through experiment that group members develop common perceptions of the world around them. Festinger (1954) also used the terms social comparison and cognitive dissonance to capture the dynamic attractions and repulsions between individuals and groups. The social psychology approach has mainly been used to explore the role and experience of individuals within organisations and institutions, seen by Katz and Khan (1966) as patterned acts of productive organising. Katz and Khan (1966) have shown how groups act to encourage or enforce certain behaviours while discouraging others. While commentators recognise the value of this work, they also recognise the limitations in dealing with intergroup relationships, a key aspect of entrepreneurial behaviour (Jack and Rose, 2010). Table 13.1 summarises what might be seen as the bibliographic foundations of the current social embeddedness perspective, and on which the rest of this chapter builds.

From the contributions outlined above, we developed an appreciation of the foundations on which more recent uses of the embeddedness concept have been built. The nature of the themes outlined have led some commentators to argue that ideas live in cycles, and that what we are seeing is a new flourishing or re-branding of old ideas which have never really gone away (Hirsch and Levin, 1999; Schuller et al, 2000; Kim and Aldrich, 2005). We would argue differently, and in this section show how scholars have imported and built upon these theoretical foundations and synergies to better explain and contextualise the activities and behaviour of entrepreneurs. To do this we begin by acknowledging Granovetter's (1973–92) work on the nature of social ties and the implications of embeddedness in modern societies. In many ways the timeliness of Granovetter's work created a paradigmatic shift and bridged the structural hole which previously existed between economic sociology and the emerging field of modern entrepreneurship research (Burt, 1992; Johannisson and Monsted, 1997; Uzzi, 1997).

GRANOVETTER'S SYNTHESIS

Theorising on what he called "a rough intuitive basis", Granovetter (1973: 1361) presented what he called the differing characteristics of strong, weak and non-existent ties. Through this typology he went on to focus on the strength of weak tie acquaintances, and

Table 13.1   Historical foundations of social embeddedness research

School of thought	Key theorists	Key emphasis/focus
Sociology	Marx (1894/1947) Simmel (1908/ 1950) Park (1924) Weber (1922/ 1978) Homans (1961) Giddens (1979)	– Group consciousness – Group dynamics – Societies based on interactive communication – Substantive rationality – The dynamics of the human group – The contradictions of individual actions

Anthropology	Malinowski (1922)
	Polanyi (1944)
	Polanyi, Arensberg
	  and Pearson (1957)
	Kapferer (1969)
	Sahlins (1972)
		– Economy submerged in social relationships
		– The evolution of ongoing exchange relationships
		– The relationships between groups and
		  environments
		– The significance of groups in complex societies
		– Multiplexity – the multiple contents of a
		  relationship
		– A critique of economically rational man

Social Psychology	Lewin (1951) Precker (1952) Festinger (1954) Heider (1958) Milgram (1967) Berscheid and Walster (1969)	– Group members develop common perceptions – The selection of peers and near authority figures – Social comparison and cognitive dissonance – The psychology of interpersonal relationships – The small world problem – Explores the nature of interpersonal attraction

their navigational role in enabling individuals realise job and other opportunities. Just over a decade later, Granovetter (1985) went on to provide a more sophisticated synthesis of previous work focusing on the ways individuals could actively use and manipulate their position within networks to access distant ideas, influences and information (Chell and Baines, 2000). In 'Economic action and social structure; the problem of embeddedness' (1985), Granovetter also alluded to embeddedness as a method for analysing this seemingly taken-for-granted behaviour. He argued that; "What looks to the analyst like non rational behaviour may be quite sensible when situational constraints, especially those of embeddedness, are fully appreciated" (506). He also felt that when social factors are fully analysed within context, behaviour looks less like the automatic application of cultural rules, and more like a reasonable response to the present situation. In a way which made current the earlier work of Polanyi (1944), Granovetter (1985) emphasised the natural and taken-for-granted ways in which practices are generated among people sharing a common context. For example, when focusing on dyadic business relationships and friendships, i.e. between salesmen and purchasing agents, Granovetter (1985: 496) made an explicit connection between social relations and modern business outcomes. In this setting he discusses contacts trading gossip, and news about upcoming events and opportunities. This led Granovetter (1992) to propose that all economic behaviour is embedded in networks and communities of interpersonal relationships; and that "economic action is affected by actor's dyadic relationships and by the structure of the overall network of relations" (33). In this sense Granovetter's work 1973–92 synthesised previous views and set the tone for much of the parallel debate about the costs and benefits of embeddedness among entrepreneurship scholars. It is to this debate which we now turn.

SOCIAL EMBEDDEDNESS AND ENTREPRENEURSHIP

Given that entrepreneurs are closely tied through a diversity of social relationships to a broader network of actors (Hoang and Antoncic, 2003), entrepreneurship has proved a fertile field in which the concept of embeddedness has taken hold and flourished. In the words of Polanyi (1944), it is now widely accepted that entrepreneurship is embedded, submerged and absorbed in ongoing networks of personal relationships, and that economic goals are typically accompanied by non-economic ones related to social context (Jones et al, 1997; Jack and Anderson, 2002; Sarasvathy and Venkataraman, 2011). Despite the impact and popularity of the embeddedness concept, Granovetter's (1985) ideas have not been received uncritically. For example, Uzzi (1997: 35) argued that Granovetter's work is "a potential theory for joining economic and sociological approaches to organisation theory", however his initial offering suffers from "a theoretical indefiniteness". This indefiniteness, he feels, stems from attempting to combine quite specific economic propositions with broad statements about how social ties influence entrepreneurial actions. Halinen and Tornross (1998) argued that while Granovetter's early work was important in moving social science forward, it made little attempt to explain the dynamic workings of embeddedness in entrepreneurship. Johannisson et al (2002) saw this as a challenge to the emerging field of entrepreneurship in terms of (1) moving the concept beyond a metaphor for social complexity, (2) capitalising on the possibilities of cross-disciplinary perspectives, and (3) moving beyond the individual firm to include the wider socio-economic context in which firms and entrepreneurs are embedded. Recognition of these challenges has led to the emergence of key research themes around the "structural contexts", "processes" and "performance implications" of embeddedness for entrepreneurs. While these themes retain the micro-macro link evident in the early sociological literature, they also represent an ambitious attempt to engage with key facets of the modern entrepreneurship phenomenon.

STRUCTURAL CONTEXTS

Building on the work of Burt (1992), Johannisson et al (2002) argued that entrepreneurs and their firms are anchored in larger structures, and within these structures, the economic and social spheres are largely inseparable, and are a rich source of motivations and opportunities to enact various realities (Johannisson and Monsted, 1997; Kloosterman, 2010). Within the entrepreneurial context, engaging with multiple and often competing realities points to the inherent pressures on entrepreneurs to simultaneously bring about change and maintain stability in existing structures. Uzzi (1997) argued that to capture this dynamism, entrepreneurship researchers needed to move beyond using embeddedness to merely represent the social complexity facing entrepreneurs, and instead focus on the development, use and operation of ties within a wider operating context (Johannisson and Landstrom, 1997; Uzzi, 1999). Jack and Anderson (2002) have also argued that when examining the entrepreneur (i.e. the individual/or "agent"), the context (i.e. "the structure") has to be taken into account, since the social whole is pre-eminent over its individual parts. Therefore the extent to which the entrepreneur is socially embedded and how he/she is embedded (their congruence with the structure) will affect their ability to draw on social and economic resources (Portes and Sensenbrenner, 1993). In this sense the process of embeddedness resembles individuals operating and behaving naturally as part of a larger structural whole (Johannisson et al, 2002).

Using the New York apparel industry (1997) and later the business banking sector (1999), Uzzi stressed the importance of contextualising individuals drawing upon their embeddedness for entrepreneurial purposes. This theme of affective belonging and drawing upon socialised resources has also appeared in the work of scholars exploring embeddedness through the lens of "family" (Aldrich and Cliff, 2003), "ethnicity" (Ram et al, 2002), "economic migration" (Kloosterman, 2010), "social class" (Anderson and Miller, 2003) and "gender" (Louch, 2000). The common message in all of these studies is that embeddedness in different types of social networks and contexts provides access to different types of resources and possibilities. This work has gone some way in starting to dissect the multiplex social and cultural settings from which entrepreneurs emerge and of which they are an integrated part (Aldrich and Kim, 2007). The contribution of work focusing on the contexts which influence entrepreneurship, while facilitating an analysis of the global network inhabited by entrepreneurs (Bourdieu, 1986), it has also led to increased focus on the actual processes and practices involved in becoming embedded in specific contexts and communities.

PROCESSES

Complimenting studies examining the structures where entrepreneurs are embedded, others have focused on the underlying processes through which business practices become embedded in social attachments, and which change the logic on which business is conducted (Jack and Anderson, 2002). Uzzi and Gillespie (2002) argued that this socialisation of economic activity effectively shifts the expectations associated with transactions away from economic maximisation towards a more socialised and personal view. Stressing the importance of interpersonal attraction and choice, Uzzi (1999) argued that not all weakly acquainted ties will become embedded, but that this loose-coupling provides an opportunity to begin offering and accepting symbolic acts of trust and mutuality development. Fukuyama (1995) explained this in terms of the development of social, cultural and cognitive commonalities (Nahapiet and Ghoshal, 1998). According to Jack and Anderson (2002), this implies developing and maintaining congruence with the surrounding community and society, and that this may play a role in the way in which value is extracted in terms of resource availability, opportunity perception and even the shape of the entrepreneurial event. This argument has gone some way in balancing Granovetter's (1973) earlier view.

From a behavioural and cognitive perspective, embeddedness then is a process of becoming part of the structure, for which Bourdieu (1977) used the term "genetic structuralism". However this structural integrity means more than just developing social networks in a mechanistic sense to access resources (Penrose, 1959). According to Jack and Anderson (2002) the embedding process consists of:

(1)   "Understanding" the nature of the structure,
(2)   "Enacting" the structure, and
(3)   "Maintaining" both the link and the structure.

In this sense community and societal structures provide the context, location and mechanism for becoming embedded (Slotte-Kock and Coviello, 2010; Elfring and Hulsink, 2003). Embedding is therefore a bilateral developmental process whereby mutuality, credibility, knowledge and experience are accumulated within a specific socio-spatial space (Zahra, 2007). The process of embedding is then about establishing and maintaining social relationships which enable the entrepreneur to become integral and maintain structural integrity. Littunen (2000) explains this in terms of the entrepreneur operationalising a context and its particular habitus – i.e. the values, attitudes and action rationales which are taken for granted by insiders, and which are largely incomprehensible to outsiders (Barth, 1967; Bourdieu, 1990). In Weick's (1969) terms, by understanding the logic of the structure, the entrepreneur enacts the environment. It is this growing appreciation of embeddedness as an affective condition between entrepreneurs and their networked environments, and recognition of the positive and negative effects which it can have, which has fuelled a research agenda linking embeddedness with venture performance and the nature of value creation (Uzzi and Gillespie, 2002).

PERFORMANCE IMPLICATIONS

While entrepreneurship has been described as the creation and extraction of value from an environment (Anderson, 2000), it has also been described as a process that draws from the social context, and which shapes and forms entrepreneurial outcomes (Jack and Anderson, 2002). Social embeddedness has been argued to be relevant for entrepreneurial performance because it is a mechanism that helps the entrepreneur identify resources through a socialised medium, an essential step to founding organisations and overcoming constraints (Hansen, 1995; Hite, 2005). Aldrich and Cliff (2003) have argued that this view of embeddedness shifts emphasis away from short-term profit maximisation towards a longer term group perspective where partners (and even competitors) share a perception that their relationship will continue into a relatively undefined future. According to Johannisson et al (2002), embeddedness provides a way of capturing the rich and complex medium of processes and practices through which performance outcomes are leveraged and achieved. Uzzi (1997) described this as an opportunity to more clearly specify "how" and "why" social ties affect entrepreneurial outcomes. Uzzi (1997) argued that embedded organisations and their entrepreneurs achieve certain competitive advantages over market arrangements, even in production markets with many substitutable sellers and low search and barriers to start up. This is through the formation of cliques and informal clusters, where patterns of behaviour emerge based on firms and entrepreneurs knowing and watching each other. Work of this type recognises that the social context, in which the entrepreneur is embedded, affects performance by providing a moral framework which largely determines what types of behaviour are socially appropriate (Aldrich and Waldinger, 1990; Aldrich and Kim, 2007; Kloosterman, 2010). Research adopting this socialised view of performance has found that being embedded within the social context means access to more support during the entrepreneurial process, and it may even increase the likelihood of entrepreneurial activity, including social entrepreneurship (Schell and Davig, 1981; Ostgaard and Birley, 1996; Anderson and Miller, 2003; Smith and Stevens, 2010). Lechner and Dowling (2003) found that embeddedness contributed to performance and growth based on the nature of the linkage to the local context, meaning privileged access to the benefits present in the structure.

However, it is also recognised that the benefits outlined above come at a cost, and that embeddedness can also act as a constraint, even a retardant to entrepreneurship (Gedajlovic et al, 2013). Uzzi (1997: 17) identified conditions when embeddedness can be turned into a liability, for example, the unforeseeable exit of a core network player; institutional forces rationalising markets; even over-embeddedness stifling economic action when social aspects of exchange, such as moral coercion, supersede economic imperatives. Grabher (1993) also argued that embeddedness creates and sustains a community where the welfare of actors is expected to be shared among that community. In many ways this begins to unearth some of the sub-optimality recognised by economists, but we currently know little about the complex nature of this typically assumed and almost unconscious redistribution of benefits (Starr and MacMillan, 1990). It has also been argued that these often deeply held understandings and reciprocities create the threat of lock-in, and generate tension between competition and co-operation within the organising context (Johannisson et al, 2002). Forbes et al (2006) highlighted the psychological pressure placed on embedded entrepreneurs to continue in established modes of operation despite the presence of non-local competitive pressures. These mental fences, Zerubavel (1991) found to be a source of behavioural constraint and reluctance to break with convention. Therefore the extent to which the entrepreneur is socially embedded, and how he/she is embedded, will affect their ability and willingness to draw on social and economic resources (Jack, 2005), impacting upon the nature of the entrepreneurial process and influencing the shape of ventures. Table 13.2 provides an abbreviated list of some of the key contributions outlined in the preceding section.

Table 13.2   Research on social embeddedness in entrepreneurship

Authors	Key findings
Granovetter (1985)	Embeddedness, social structure and economic action
Johannisson (1988)	Business formation as an embedded process
Burt (1992)	The structural embeddedness of competition
Powell, Koput and Smith-Doerr (1996)	Embeddedness, collaboration and innovation
Uzzi (1997)	Social structure, performance and embeddedness
Hite and Hesterly (2001)	Discuss embedded ties, sparse networks and firm success
Jack and Anderson (2002)	Embeddedness shapes opportunities and improves performance
Johannisson et al (2002)	Embeddedness as a lever for new business creation
Uzzi and Gillespie (2002)	Social embeddedness affects financial performance
Hite (2005)	Evolutionary processes and paths of embedded ties
Hagedoorn (2006)	The embeddedness of partnership formation
Smith and Stevens (2010)	Embeddedness and social value in social entrepreneurship
Kloosterman (2010)	The embeddedness of migrant entrepreneurship

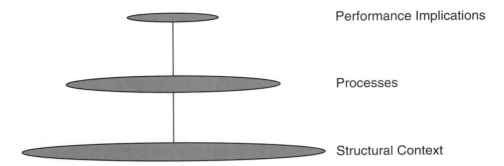

Figure 13.1   Key themes

DISCUSSION

Through historical overview, we have traced the development of social embeddedness from metaphor to scientific concept and methodological tool. From this platform we focused on how social embeddedness has been imported and applied in the field of entrepreneurship research. By emphasising "structural contexts", "processes" and "performance implications", our review builds into a framework through which embeddedness can be used as a tool to illuminate the dynamism and complexity of "entrepreneurial situations". By analysing entrepreneurship as a situated blend of social and economic goals and intentions – researchers can get close to the natural everyday settings in which entrepreneurship takes place. Figure 13.1 provides a tiered view through which this might be understood.

Figure 13.1 illustrates that the themes in our review should not be viewed in isolation, and that an important first step in employing an embeddedness perspective is to identify and structurally locate research subjects. In the tradition of Polanyi (1968), this bases research firmly in the reality of the entrepreneur, community and society, and immediately contextualises the actions and behaviour of those under investigation (see Uzzi, 1997; Coleman, 2000; Jack and Anderson, 2002 and Kloosterman, 2010). Thus situated, researchers can then begin building an insider view of how individuals interpret the structure and practice of entrepreneurship within it.

In the tradition of Park (1924), Homans (1961) and Uzzi (1997), the second stage of an embeddedness approach involves questioning the situated practices which constitute the entrepreneurial process in which individuals are engaged. Within this bounded complexity – steps can then be taken to more fully elaborate on the development; use and operation of embedded ties within particular operating contexts (see Jack, 2005). By engaging in field work – and interrogating the situated actions of entrepreneurs through an embeddedness lens – researchers are provided with intimate access to what is really going on. A good example of this is Kloosterman's (2010) contextual portrayal of a young Turkish immigrant building cargo bicycles in Amsterdam, and how embeddedness in family and community – including the time and place of the opportunity structure – made situated sense of his socialised economic actions. This illustrates how a social embeddedness perspective can begin adding depth and colour to work like Shane (2004) by including the social context in which opportunities are being constructed.

Building on the development and use of insider perspectives, embeddedness researchers are able to better interpret what "performance" means within a particular context. This situates performance in the world of the entrepreneur and creates links to the ambitions and abilities of individuals, but also the resource capabilities and constraints present in the surrounding environments (Ram et al, 2002). By getting close to the language and intentions of entrepreneurs (Parkinson and Howorth, 2008), a richer interpretation emerges which links the conditions and possibilities of the context, the intentions of the entrepreneur, and what success will ultimately look like. In the case of social entrepreneurship, it would seem that this is acutely appropriate (Smith and Stevens, 2010). In the language of Granovetter (1985: 506), the outcome of this cumulative process should hold no surprises, and with diligence and rigour should lead to "quite sensible" interpretations of entrepreneurial performance, framed against a backcloth of prevailing circumstances and situational constraints.

To date the majority of advocates of an embeddedness perspective have emphasised the usefulness of an inductive, interpretive focus on what people experience and how it is they experience what they experience (Bryman and Bell, 2003; Chell and Pittaway, 1998). Researchers adopting an interpretive philosophy are in the main predisposed to adopt qualitative methodological techniques (see for example Bouchikhi, 1993; Johannisson, 1995). However these can be used in conjunction with quantitative techniques (Birley et al, 1999). Work like Stewart (2003) demonstrates this underlying commitment to capturing a careful and authentic first-hand representation of ordinary conscious experience. Working within a context of discovery, Uzzi (1997) and Jack and Anderson (2002) demonstrate the use of in-depth interviews, situated observations and a range of secondary data to build a robust portrayal of entrepreneurs and entrepreneurship in context. Set against the stages of our model, embeddedness researchers have expressed a need to rigorously seek out illuminating cases which can add to and extend theory (Eisenhardt, 1989; Smith and Stevens, 2010). Researchers have made extensive use of theoretical sampling which has been argued to aid transparency, and support the validity of the interpretation being provided (Cronbach, 1982; Clarke, 2011). In the tradition of Glaser and Strauss (1967), work of this tradition emphasizes a need to clearly articulate the research process employed from philosophy through to empirical analysis (Cope, 2005).

A RESEARCH AGENDA

From the work explored in our review and discussion, it becomes clear that embeddedness is now a firmly established concept in the field of entrepreneurship. However, there are still areas where future research might further illuminate our understanding. For example, while researchers have recognised and stressed the importance of social context as an influencing factor on entrepreneurs (Uzzi, 1997), we feel that this is just the beginning. This leaves room for further contributions which explore unique entrepreneurial settings and situations where structure interacts with the ambitions and agency of individuals (Guba and Lincoln, 1994; Stewart, 2003). This is particularly poignant in places like Saudi Arabia, China, India and the former Soviet Union where structures differ greatly from those in the west. The family, community and political structures in these places provide interesting and varied contexts in which to use embeddedness to explain different manifestations of entrepreneurship.

By interpreting each context in terms of a tiered hierarchy – i.e. individual, family, firm, community, region and society, researchers are able to question and construct more complex contextual analyses. This would address the concerns of Slotte-Kock and Coviello (2010) with regard to the possibility of developing richer hybrid and multilevel perspectives on the social processes shaping entrepreneurial performance. This vein of work we see as an opportunity to further increase the definition which an interpretivist approach is already bringing to our understanding of entrepreneurship (Cope, 2005; Jack, 2005).

Appreciating the lineage to which present research is connected, this provides the next generation of researchers with an opportunity to generate new theoretical typologies which relate not only to embeddedness but also the nature of the structural environments in which entrepreneurship takes place (Borgatti and Foster, 2003). Within different types of structures and environments, there is also the opportunity to further unpack the very notion of social embeddedness. As outlined earlier, authors have viewed embeddedness through the lens of family, ethnicity, social class and gender. While this growing typology of identity-based themes is useful in itself, additional work could usefully look at a combinational approach to embeddedness, much in the same way Bourdieu (1986) approached the types of capital and their role in generating practice. This mixed approach is also of relevance as commentators become increasing dissatisfied with divisions which are currently institutionalised by the limitations of dichotomies like strong and weak ties (Granovetter, 1973; Jack, 2005).

These views point to opportunities which are currently being overlooked and it is through building upon established work and methodologies in other disciplines that new interpretations and recombinations can be generated. In agreement with Slotte-Kock and Coviello (2010) and Borgatti and Foster (2003) we would argue that interpretivist researchers are currently being presented with an opportunity to explore in a deeper and more complex way, the work begun by those now considered the founding fathers of the embeddedness and entrepreneurship disciplines. This then represents a period of deeper explanation and asking *why* are things as they are, and *why* are particular individuals and groups doing what they are doing? For example, it is all well and good to distinguish between strong and weak ties, close and loose coupling, and varying levels of embeddedness. The challenge now is to explain how and why the structure and processes of embeddedness affects entrepreneurs, and how this contributes to variations in the form of entrepreneurship generated. This will require fieldwork, and a sustained focus not just on the entrepreneur and structure, but both simultaneously in the tradition of Park (1924), Weber (1922) and Homans (1961). This provides both new and experienced researchers with the opportunity to build upon the foundations of the past, but also to develop new methods, techniques and theories which keep pace with the dynamic and changing face and tenor of modern entrepreneurship.

REFERENCES

Aldrich, H.E. and Cliff, J.E. (2003), 'The pervasive effects of family on entrepreneurship: towards a family embeddedness perspective', *Journal of Business Venturing*, 18(5), 573–96.
Aldrich, H. and Fiol, C. (1994), 'Fools rush in? The institutional context of industry creation', *Academy of Management Review*, 19(4), 645–70.
Aldrich, H. and Kim, P. (2007), 'Small worlds, infinite possibilities? How social networks affect entrepreneurial team formation and search', *Strategic Entrepreneurship Journal*, 1, 147–65.
Aldrich, H. and Waldinger, R. (1990), 'Ethnicity and Entrepreneurship', *Annual Review of Sociology*, 16, Annual Reviews, CA, 111–35.
Anderson, A.R. (2000), 'Paradox in the periphery: An entrepreneurial reconstruction', *Entrepreneurship and Regional Development*, 12, 91–109.
Anderson, A.R. and Miller, C. (2003), 'Class matters: Human and social capital in the entrepreneurial process', *Journal of Socio-Economics*, 32(1), 17–26.
Barber, B. (1995), 'All economies are "embedded": the career of a concept, and beyond', *Social Research*, 62, 387–413.
Barth, F. (1967), 'On the study of social change', *American Anthropologist*, 69(6), 661–9.
Beckert, J. (1996), 'What is sociological about economic sociology? Uncertainty and embeddedness of economic action', *Theory and Society*, 25, 803–40.
Berscheid, E. and Walster, E. (1969), *Interpersonal Attraction*, Reading, Mass: Addison-Wesley.
Block, F. (2001), 'Introduction', in Block, F. (Ed) *The Great Transformation: The Political and Economic Origins of our Time by Karl Polanyi*, Boston, Beacon Press, xviii–xxxviii.
Block, F. (2003), 'Karl Polanyi and the writing of The Great Transformation', *Theory and Society*, 32, 275–306.
Bohannan, P. (1955), 'Some principles of exchange and investment among the Tiv', *American Anthropologist*, 4, 56–73.
Borgatti, S.P. and Foster, P.C., (2003), 'The network paradigm in organizational research: a review and typology', *Journal of Management*, 29, 991–1013.
Bouchikhi, H. (1993), 'A constructivist framework for understanding entrepreneurial performance', *Organisational Studies*, 14(4), 551–69.
Bourdieu, P. (1977), *Outline of a Theory of Practice*, Cambridge University Press.
Bourdieu, P. (1986), 'The forms of capital', in *Handbook of Theory and Research for the Sociology of Education,* (Ed) J.G. Richardson, New York, Greenwood.
Bourdieu, P. (1990), *The Logic of Practice*, Cambridge, Polity Press.
Bryman, A. and Bell, E. (2004), *Business Research Methods*, Oxford University Press.
Burt, R. (1992), *Structural Holes*, Cambridge, MA, Harvard University Press.
Chell, E. and Baines, S. (2000), 'Networking, entrepreneurship and micro-business behaviour', *Entrepreneurship and Regional Development*, 12, 195–215.
Chell, E. and Pittaway, L. (1998), 'The Social Construction of Entrepreneurship', paper presented at the ISBA conference, Durham University.
Clarke, J. (2011), 'Revitalizing entrepreneurship: How visual symbols are used in entrepreneurial performances', *Journal of Management Studies*, 48, 1365–91.
Coleman, J. (2000), 'Social capital in the creation of human capital', in P. Dasgupta and J. Serageldin (Eds), *Social Capital: A Multifaceted Perspective*, Washington DC: World Bank, 13–39.
Cope, J. (2005), 'Toward a dynamic learning perspective of entrepreneurship', *Entrepreneurship: Theory and Practice*, 29, 373–97.
Cronbach, L. J. (1982), *Designing and Evaluation of Educational and Social Programs*, San Francisco, Jossey-Bass.
Eisenhardt, K. (1989), 'Building theories from case study research', *Academy of Management Review*, 14(4), 532–50.
Ekeh, P. (1974), *Social Exchange Theory: The Two Traditions*, Cambridge, MA, Harvard University Press.
Elfring, T. and Hulsink, W. (2003), 'Networks in entrepreneurship: the case of high-technology firms', *Small Business Economics*, 21, 409–22.
Festinger, L. (1954), 'A theory of social comparison processes', *Human Relations*, 7, 117–40.
Forbes, D.P. (2005), 'Managerial determinants of decision speed in new ventures', *Strategic Management Journal*, 26, 355–66.
Forbes, D.P., Barchert, P., Zellmer-Bruhn, M. and Sapienza, H. (2006), 'Entrepreneurial team formation: An exploration of new member addition', *Entrepreneurship: Theory and Practice*, 30(2): 225–478.
Frazer, J.G. (1919), *Folklore in the Old Testament*, Vol.2, London, Macmillan.
Fukuyama, F. (1995), *Trust*, New York: Free Press.

Gedajlovic, E., Honig, B., Moore, C. B., Payne, G. T. and Wright, M. (2013), 'Social capital and entrepreneurship: A schema and research agenda', *Entrepreneurship: Theory and Practice*, 37: 455–78.

Gemici, K. (2008), 'Karl Polanyi and the antinomies of embeddedness', *Socio-Economic Review*, 6, 5–33.

Giddens, A. (1979), *Central Problems in Social Theory: Action, Structure and Contradiction in Social Analysis*, University of California Press.

Glaser, B. and Strauss, A. (1967), *The Discovery of Grounded Theory: Strategies of Qualitative Research*, London, Wiedenfeld and Nicholson.

Grabher, G. (1993), 'Rediscovering the social in the economics of inter-firm relations', in Grabher, G. (Ed.), *The Embedded Firm: On the Socio-economics of Industrial Networks*, London and New York, Routledge, 1–31.

Granovetter, M. (1973), 'The strength of weak ties', *American Journal of Sociology*, 78(6), 1360–80.

Granovetter, M. (1985), 'Economic action and social structure: the problem of embeddedness', *American Journal of Sociology*, 91(3), 481–510.

Granovetter, M. (1992), *Problems and Explanation in Economic Sociology, Networks and Organisations*, Harvard Business School Press.

Guba, E.G. and Lincoln, Y.S. (1994), 'Competing paradigms in qualitative research', in N.K. Denzin and Y.S. Lincoln (Eds), *Handbook of Qualitative Research*, Thousand Oaks, CA: Sage, 105–17.

Hagedoorn, J. (2006), 'Understanding the cross-level embeddedness of interfirm partnership formation', *Academy of Management Review*, 31, 670–80.

Halinen, A. and Tornross, J. (1998), 'The role of embeddedness in the evolution of business networks', *Scandinavian Journal of Management*, 14(3): 187–205.

Hansen, E.L. (1995), 'Entrepreneurial networks and new organisation growth', *Entrepreneurship: Theory and Practice*, 19(4), 7–19.

Harary, F. (1965), 'Graph theory and group structure', in *Readings in Mathematical Psychology*, 2, R. Luce, R. Bush and E. Galanter, (eds), New York: Wiley.

Harvey, D. (1982), *Limits to Capital*, Chicago University Press.

Heider, F. (1958), *The Psychology of Interpersonal Relations*, New York: Wiley.

Hirsch, P. and Levin, D. (1999), 'Umbrella advocates versus validity police: A life cycle model', *Organisation Science*, 10(2), 199–212.

Hite, J.M. (2005), 'Evolutionary processes and paths of relationally embedded network ties in emerging entrepreneurial firms', *Entrepreneurship: Theory and Practice*, 29(1), 113–44.

Hite, J. M. and Hesterly, W. S. (2001), 'The evolution of firm networks: From emergence to early growth of the firm', *Strategic Management Journal*, 22, 275–86.

Hoang, H. and B. Antoncic (2003), 'Network-based research in entrepreneurship: a critical review', *Journal of Business Venturing*, 18(2), 495–527.

Homans, G.C. (1961), *Social Behaviour: Its Elementary Forms*, New York, Harcourt, Brace.

Hornby, A. (Ed) (1985), *Oxford Advanced Learner's Dictionary of Current English*, Oxford University Press.

Jack, S.L. (2005), 'The role, use and activation of strong and weak network ties: A qualitative analysis,' *Journal of Management Studies*, 42(6), 1233–59.

Jack, S.L. and Rose, M.B. (2010), 'The historical roots of socio network theory in entrepreneurship research', in *Historical Foundations of Entrepreneurial Research*, Hans Landstrom and Franz Lohrke, (Eds), Cheltenham, UK: Edward Elgar, 256–86.

Jack, S.L. and Anderson, S.L. (2002), 'The effects of embeddedness on the entrepreneurial process', *Journal of Business Venturing*, 17(5), 476–87.

Johannisson, B. (1988), 'Business formation: a network approach', *Scandinavian Journal of Management*, 4 (3/4), 83–99.

Johannisson, B. (1995), 'Paradigms and entrepreneurial networks – some methodological challenges', *Entrepreneurship and Regional Development*, 7(2), 215–31.

Johannisson, B. and Landstrom, H., (1997), 'Research in entrepreneurship and small business: State of the art in Sweden', In H. Landstrom, H. Frank, J.M. Veciana, (Eds), *Entrepreneurship and Small Business Research in Europe, An ECSB survey*, Aldershot, UK: Avebury.

Johannisson, B. and Monsted, M. (1997), 'Contextualizing entrepreneurial networking', *International Studies of Management and Organisation*, 27(3), 109–36.

Johannisson, B., Ramiirez-Pasillas and Karlsson, G. (2002), 'The institutional embeddedness of local inter-firm networks: a leverage for business creation', *Entrepreneurship and Regional Development*, 14, 297–315.

Jones, C., Hesterly, W. and Borgatti, S. (1997), 'A general theory of network governance: Exchange conditions and social mechanisms', *Academy of Management Review*, 22(4), 911–46.

Kapferer, B. (1969), 'Norms and the manipulation of relationships in a work context', in *Social Networks in Urban Situations*, (Ed) J.C. Mitchell, Manchester University Press.

Katz, D. and Khan, R. (1966), *The Social Psychology of Organisations*, New York: Wiley.

Kim, P. and Aldrich, H. (2005), *Social Capital and Entrepreneurship*, New York, Now Publishers Inc.

Kloosterman, R. (2010), 'Matching opportunities with resources: A framework for analysing (migrant) entrepreneurship from a mixed embeddedness perspective', *Entrepreneurship and Regional Development*, 22(1), 25–45.

Krippner, G. (2001), 'The elusive market: Embeddedness and the paradigm of economic Sociology', *Theory and Society*, 30, 775–810.

Krippner, G., Granovetter, M., Block, F., Biggart, N., Beamish, T., Hsing, Y., Hart, G., Arrighi, G., Mendell, M., Hall, J., Burawoy, M., Vogel, S. and O'Riain, S. (2004), 'Polanyi Symposium: A conversation on embeddedness', *Socio-Economic Review*, 2, 109–135.

Lechner, C. and Dowling, M. (2003), 'Firm networks: external relationships as sources for the growth and competitiveness of entrepreneurial firms', *Entrepreneurship and Regional Development*, 15, 1– 26.

Lévi-Strauss, C. (1969), *The Savage Mind*, Chicago, University of Chicago Press.

Lewin, K. (1951), *Field Theory in Social Science*, New York, Harper-Row.

Lie, J. (1991), 'Embedding Polanyi's market society', *Sociological Perspectives*, 34, 219–35.

Littunen, H. (2000), 'Networks and local environmental characteristics in the survival of new firms', *Small Business Economics*, 15(1), 59–71.

Louch, H. (2000), 'Personal network integration: transitivity and homophily in strong-tie relations', *Social Networks*, 22, 45–64.

Malinowski, B. (1922), *Argonauts of the Western Pacific*, New York: Dutton.

Marx, K. (1894), *Capital*, Vol III, New York: Vintage.

Milgram, S. (1967), 'The small world problem', *Psychology Today*, 1, 62–7.

Nahapiet, J. and Ghoshal, S. (1998), 'Social capital, intellectual capital and the organizational advantage', *Academy of Management Review*, 23, 242–66.

Ostgaard, T.A. and Birley, S. (1996), 'Personal networks and firm competitive strategy – A strategic or coincidental match', *Journal of Business Venturing*, 9, 281–305.

Park, R.E. (1924), 'The concept of social distance', *Journal of Applied Sociology*, 8, 339–44.

Park, R.E. (1926), 'The concept of position in sociology', papers and proceedings of the *American Sociological Society*, 20, 1–14.

Parkinson, C. and Howorth, C. (2008), 'The language of social entrepreneurs', *Entrepreneurship and Regional Development* 20(3), 285–309.

Penrose, E. T. (1959), *The Theory of the Growth of the Firm*, New York: John Wiley.

Polanyi, K. (2001[1944]), *The Great Transformation: The Political and Economic Origins of our Time*, with a foreword from Joseph Stiglitz and introduction from Fred Block, Boston MA, Beacon Press.

Polanyi, K. (1968), *Primitive, Archaic and Modern Economies: Essays of Karl Polanyi*, edited by Dalton, G. New York, Anchor Books.

Polanyi, K., Arensberg, C.M. and Pearson, H.W. (Eds), (1957*), Trade and Market in the Early Empires: Economies in History and Theory*, Glencoe Free Press.

Portes, A. and Sensenbrenner, J. (1993), 'Embeddedness and immigration: Notes on the social determinants of economic action', *American Journal of Sociology*, 98(6), 1320–50.

Powell, W., Koput, K. and Smith-Doerr, L. (1996), 'Interorganizational collaboration and the locus of innovation: Networks of learning in biotechnology', *Administrative Science Quarterly*, 41, 116–45.

Precker, J. (1952), 'Similarity of valuing as a factor in selection of peers and near-authority figures', *Journal of Abnormal and Social Psychology*, 47, 406–14.

Ram, M., Smallbone, D. and Deakins, D. (2002), *Access to Finance and Business Support by Ethnic Minority Firms in the UK*, London, British Bankers Association.

Reddy, W. (1984), *The Rise of Market Culture: The Textile Trade and French Society, 1750–1900*, Cambridge, Cambridge University Press.

Sahlins, M. (1974), *Stone Age Economics*, London: Tavistock Publications.

Sarasvathy, S. D. and Venkataraman, S. (2011), 'Entrepreneurship as method: Open questions for an entrepreneurial future', *Entrepreneurship: Theory and Practice*, 35: 113–135.

Schell, D. and Davig, W. (1981), 'The community structure of entrepreneurship: a socio-political analysis', in K.H. Vesper (ed), *Frontiers of Entrepreneurship Research*, Wellesley, MA, Babson College, 563–90.

Schuller, T., Baron, S. and Field, J. (2000), 'Social capital: A review and critiques', in S. Baron, J. Field and T. Schuller (Eds), *Social Capital: Critical Perspectives*, Oxford University Press.

Scott, J.C. (1976), *The Moral Economy of the Peasant: Rebellion and Subsistence in South East Asia*, New Haven, Yale University Press.

Shane, S. (2004), *Academic Entrepreneurship: University Spinoffs and Wealth Creation*, Northampton, Edward Elgar Publishing.

Simmel, G. (1908), *Exkurs uber den fremden, Sociologie*, Leipzig: Duncker and Humblot.

Simmel, G. (1950), *The Sociology of Georg Simmel*, Translated by K. Wolff, Glencoe Free Press.

Slotte-Kock, S. and Coviello, N. (2010), 'Entrepreneurship research on network processes: A review and ways forward', *Entrepreneurship: Theory and Practice*, 34, 31–57.

Smith, B. and Stevens C. (2010), 'Different types of social entrepreneurship: The role of geography on the measurement and scaling of social value', *Entrepreneurship and Regional Development*, 22(6): 575–98.

Stanfield, J. R. (1986), *The Economic Thought of Karl Polanyi*, London, Macmillan.

Starr, J. and MacMillan, I. (1990),' Resource cooptation via social contracting: Resource acquisition strategies for new ventures', *Strategic Management Journal*, 11, 79–92.

Stewart, A. (2003), 'Help one another, Use one another: Toward an anthropology of family business', *Entrepreneurship: Theory and Practice*, 27, 383–96.

Thompson, E.P. (1971), 'The moral economy of the English crowd in the 18th Century', *Past and Present*, 50, 76–136.

Uzzi, B. (1997), 'Social structure and competition: the paradox of embeddedness', *Administrative Science Quarterly*, 42, 35–67.

Uzzi, B. (1999), 'Embeddedness and the making of financial capital: how social relations and networks benefit firms seeking finance', *American Sociological Review*, 64(4), 481–505.

Uzzi, B. and Gillespie, J. (2002), 'Knowledge spill over in corporate financing networks: Embeddedness and the firm's debt performance', *Strategic Management Journal*, 23, 595–618.

Weber, M. [1922] (1946), 'Class status and party', in *From Max Weber: Essays in Sociology* (Eds) H.H. Gerth and C.W. Mills, Reprint, New York, Oxford University Press.

Weber, M., ([1922] 1978), *Economy and Society*, Berkeley, University of California Press.

Weick, K. (1969), *The Social Psychology of Organizing*, Reading, MA, Addison-Wesley.

Whittington, R. (1992), 'Putting Giddens into action: social systems and managerial agency', *Journal of Management Studies*, 29(6), 693–712.

Zahra, S. (2007), 'Contextualizing theory building in entrepreneurship research', *Journal of Business Venturing*, 22(3), 433–52.

Zerubavel, E. (1991), *The Fine Line*, New York, Free Press.

Zukin, S. and DiMaggio, P. (1990), 'Introduction', in S. Zukin and P. DiMaggio, (Eds), *Structures of Capital: The Social Organization of the Economy*, New York, NY, Cambridge University Press, 1–36.

14. Human resource management and entrepreneurship: building theory at the intersection

Susan Mayson and Rowena Barrett

AT THE INTERSECTION OF HRM AND ENTREPRENEURSHIP

In 2008 we brought together much work at the intersection of entrepreneurship and human resource management (HRM) (Barrett & Mayson, 2008), after calls for more research (Baron, 2003; Katz, Aldrich, Welbourne & Williams, 2000; Tansky & Heneman, 2003). More has been collated since (Soriano, Dobon & Tansky, 2010; Tansky, Soriano & Dobon, 2010). We think it is now time again to regroup, pull conversational threads together and have a critical look at recent research at the intersection of HRM and Entrepreneurship.

As editors of *International Handbook of Entrepreneurship and HRM* (Barrett & Mayson, 2008) we were privileged to collect 23 wonderfully diverse chapters from scholars around the globe addressing a range of issues at the intersection of the two pertinent disciplines or fields: HRM and entrepreneurship. This edition represented a coalescing of ideas that had been swirling about for some time. In three sections, the first dealt with theory and research methods, the second with the nature of HRM in small and entrepreneurial firms and the third with the functional aspects of HRM. At the time we were aware that the handbook did not cover the entire field and many topics were left unexplored. For example, the topic of regulation was generally absent while issues such as career advancement, performance management, organisational change and gender, diversity and ethnicity were also missing.

In essence, the majority of those contributions sought to develop an understanding of the context in which particular aspects of HRM can be played out. We acknowledged this in the Introduction, noting that contributions generally came from the HRM side of the ledger rather than the entrepreneurship side. The unbalanced ledger is also apparent in this review of recent publications and it suggests that while HRM researchers are interested (by exploring the HRM–Performance (HRM-P) link) in entrepreneurship, entrepreneurship people are not as keen to understand HRM. Indeed, one reviewer indicated that this chapter is very HRM-focused. True. Perhaps because we, the authors, are more "HRM" than "Entrepreneurship", however, we do think that the chapter reflects the focus of the literature collected for this review. We acknowledge that this is not an ideal situation and we hope that this chapter begins a conversation that seeks to balance the ledger.

We would welcome a greater balance because when we draw on ideas about theory building at the intersection of disciplines (Zahra & Newey, 2009) and Wiklund et al's (2011) identification of differences between focusing on entrepreneurial context and the phenomenon of entrepreneurship, a lack of balance is problematic. Zahra and Newey's

(2009) impact wheel of "theory building at the intersection" shows why when they identify three modes of theory building: Mode 1) borrowing and replicating; Mode 2) borrowing and extending; and Mode 3) transforming the core. Each mode has respectively low, medium and high impacts across the domains of theory, field, discipline, researcher and external stakeholder development. At the intersection of HRM and entrepreneurship we appear to be borrowing concepts, issues, questions from HRM, by and large, and extending our knowledge of HRM in the context of small and entrepreneurial firms. While our findings inform understanding about entrepreneurial processes, mechanisms and activities, we generally communicate findings back to HRM rather than to the entrepreneurship field, and this leaves gaps for the development of theory and practice.

Good theory needs well understood concepts. But concepts such as small, new, emergent, entrepreneurial, are not uniquely defined and without definitional clarity there is unlikely to be theoretical development. Moreover these concepts are often used as the context for a study rather than as the phenomenon – some aspect of effective resource (people) management – is the focus. This is perhaps why many studies at the intersection are of the Mode 2 type: borrowing and extending theory from one discipline to another. In all honesty HRM people are not all that interested in the context but in the phenomenon. In the entrepreneurship discipline there are pleas for researchers to go beyond context and consider the phenomenon of entrepreneurship, as the "emergence of new economic activity" (Wiklund et al, 2011: 5). They too are not all that interested in the context but it is the context that makes the phenomenon interesting.

In this chapter we pick up on these threads. We searched the key journals (see Table 14.1) likely to publish papers dealing with issues at the intersection of HRM and Entrepreneurship. We searched for articles available in these journals between the start of 2009 and the end of 2011 (whether these were in a volume published between this period or available on "early view") and our search yielded 39 articles. Interestingly in our Handbook the key concern was with individual HRM practices in the context of small and entrepreneurial firms, but now we are seeing a shift more broadly towards Strategic Human Resource Management (SHRM) or looking at the HRM-P relationship in the context of small and entrepreneurial firms. Discussion of the HRM-P link in our literature review reflects the interest of mainstream (read large firm) SHRM scholars but this needs to be tempered by the work of those who question whether large firm HRM models are applicable to small and entrepreneurial firms (Barrett & Mayson, 2006). This 'turn' of research, in the literature has important implications because it speaks to how HRM can contribute to effective entrepreneurial processes and outcomes. However we need to proceed with caution because HRM scholars point to a range of difficulties in demonstrating the HRM-P link (Guest, 2011; Paauwe, 2009). We discuss this in more detail below.

In this review we will not discuss all the papers we found, but instead we will survey those that exemplify the key issues in relation to the themes we discerned. The first theme we identify in the literature is concerned with explaining/exploring the HRM-P link through the presence and/or development of high performance/high commitment work systems (HPWS/HCWS). It is within this literature that we see much that can enter the conversation with entrepreneurship scholars, although only a few papers speak directly to the entrepreneurship field. The second theme focuses on the importance and development of human capital (HC) in entrepreneurial and small firms. This literature speaks

Table 14.1 HRM performance link: HPWS/contingency approach

Paper	Integration of HRM and Entrepreneurship	Implications for Policy and Practice
Fabi, Raymond & Lacoursiere (2009)	Small business focus, drawing on management and HRM literature. However in the adoption of Miles and Snow's adaptive cycle, the term 'entrepreneurial problem' is used to denote strategy of developing products and markets.	The studies summarised under this theme put HRM 'in the picture' for small, growing and entrepreneurial firms. For entrepreneurship studies, the explicit focus on aligning HRM systems, organisational culture (participative and team focused) and owner-manager values with firm strategy and performance offers a more differentiated examination of internal firm resources. From a practical viewpoint, entrepreneurial managers, depending on context and strategy, might consider how to best configure HRM systems to attract, retain, develop and make productive employees. From a policy perspective, the studies speak to the heterogeneity of small firms resulting in unique responses and adaption to complex contextual forces and owner-manager values. The evidence may inform policy development that moves away from a 'one size fits all' approach to a more context-specific understanding of small firms. Importantly, the evidence suggests that policy makers may contribute to improved outcomes for small firms by supporting the development of employment relations policy that facilitates employee participation and voice as well as support and education that encourages small firm owners-managers to adopt merit based and transparent HRM practices for example, performance and reward practices.
Messersmith & Wales (early view 16 Nov. 2011)	Contributes to the entrepreneurship literature by exploring the intersection of HRM and entrepreneurship and then testing links between HRM, firm performance and entrepreneurial processes.	
Messersmith & Guthrie (2010)	Integration with entrepreneurship implied with focus on emerging high-tech organisations. In this context, using the resource-based view (RBV) and dynamic capabilities theories to explore importance of internal resources (HRs) in the context of emerging firms.	
McClean & Collins (2011)	HRM focused, mostly drawing on mainstream HRM literature. No integration with entrepreneurship or small firm literature. However findings may speak to both areas in terms of the contribution of certain employee skills to competitive advantage.	
Patel & Cardon (2010)	HRM focus, integration with entrepreneurship literature not explicit but 'entrepreneurship' is included as a keyword so potentially the article speaks to the entrepreneurship field.	
Patel & Conklin (early view 2010)	Published in an entrepreneurship journal, the study is of interest to understanding entrepreneurial processes, most particularly the indirect role of HRM for enhancing firm performance through the development of internal HC by creating an employee focused organisational culture.	
Verreynne, Parker & Wilson (early view 2011)	Small business focus, drawing on the small firm and HRM literature. No integration with entrepreneurship literature, theory or concepts.	

239

Table 14.1 (continued)

Paper	Integration of HRM and Entrepreneurship	Implications for Policy and Practice
Human Capital Approaches		
Klaas, Klimchak, Semadeni & Holmes (2010)	Published in an entrepreneurship journal and speaks to entrepreneurship scholars with findings that HRM can contribute to small firm performance particularly larger small firms in the face of uncertainty and high product differentiation.	The practical relevance of the papers described within this theme is a more fine grained understanding of HC for those interested in effective entrepreneurial outcomes. For example many studies point to the importance of entrepreneurs' knowledge and experience and in particular managerial and/or HRM knowledge that can contribute to firm growth. Policy makers wanting to increase employment and entrepreneurial activities might look to educating proto-entrepreneurs as well as encouraging entrepreneurship through formal education such as university centres for entrepreneurship. However, policy makers might also suggest programs for encouraging entrepreneurial success that focus on helping entrepreneurs to gain skills, competences and knowledge related to entrepreneurial processes, including HRM issues such as attraction, retention and rewards.
Lafuente & Rabetino (2011)	Situated in the entrepreneurship literature. Focus on HC embedded in individual entrepreneurs as a valuable firm resource for employment growth. Link to HRM is implicit rather than explicit. HRM practices could be used to support and develop managerial capacities of entrepreneurs and entrepreneurial teams.	
Musteen & Ahsan (early view 2011)	Situated within the entrepreneurship literature. Integration with the HRM literature. By 'putting HRM in the picture' to strengthen and develop human and organizational capital may complement the theoretical framework.	
Schmelter, Mauer, Borsch & Brettel (2010)	HRM focused but paper contributes to HRM and Entrepreneurship literature by examining HRM factors that influence entrepreneurial behaviour within SMEs.	
Sullivan & Marvel (2011)	Situated in the entrepreneurship literature with focus on individual entrepreneur and his/her indicators of HC as measured by the entrepreneur's knowledge and extent of network ties. The study does not directly speak to the HRM literature but does so indirectly by recommending widening the knowledge base of entrepreneurs through business education.	
Tocher & Rutherford (2009)	Sits at the intersection of Entrepreneurship and HRM and advances knowledge using a novel two-level model of firm variables (size, age, growth rate, financial performance) and owner-manager variables (gender, experience, age, education) and impact of perception of HRM problems.	

Author	Description	
Unger, Rauch, Frese & Rosenbusch (2011)	Draws on studies of HC from an entrepreneurial perspective. There is little or no integration with HRM. This is evidenced by the coding and frequencies of HC variables relating to the entrepreneur's HC investments lists 'business'; 'management'; 'marketing'; 'international'; 'finance'; 'leadership' etc experience some of which could be a proxy for HRM experience. Similarly HC outcomes list managerial competencies and organisation skills (proxies for HRM) low down on the list of variables.	One size does not fit all and different kinds of formality have different firm impacts. That is some processes might be formalised and create benefits for the firms and others may remain less formal because the transaction cost of formalisation may be too high for internal employment practices that are not culturally accepted or appropriate. Importantly, in small workplaces, levels of formality/informality may be mobilised to improve job quality leading to improved performance. From a policy perspective, as Storey et al (2010: 321) suggest, policy makers might question the commonly accepted view that formalisation in small firms is universally beneficial and consider supporting certain kinds of formality eg, formal employee grievance and disciplinary procedures to ensure consistent treatment of staff and less formal HRM practices such as on the job training. Heterogeneity due to embeddedness and internal relations of the firm influences how employment relationship is negotiated which in turn affects the kinds interpersonal relations

Formality and Informality/Formality and Performance

Author	Description
De Grip & Sieven (2009)	HR focused. Looks at effects of different HRM systems on productivity and performance and outcomes of formalisation. Data collected from employers and employees.
Kim & Gao (2010)	HRM focuses. No integration with entrepreneurship. Examines the number and use of HRM practices in Chinese family firms.
Kirkwood (2009)	Draws on entrepreneurship literature to explore entrepreneurs' growth aspirations in small service firms. HRM issues impinge on growth realisation.
Marlow, Taylor & Thompson (2010)	SME and HRM focused. Dynamic and negotiated character of employment relations and embeddedness of SMEs in their economic, social and political networks. Analysis offers a situated and nuanced account of internal firm relations. Includes employees in the interview sample.
Richbell, Szerb & Vitai (2010)	No integration with entrepreneurship. Examines the number and use of HRM systems in micro, small and medium firms in Hungary.
Storey, Saridakis, Sen Gupta, Edwards & Blackburn (2010)	Located in the HRM literature with no integration with entrepreneurship. Draws on employee data to examine self-reported job quality. Points to the importance of context and the heterogeneity of small firms in that the relationship between job quality, size and formality is variable across the sample.

Table 14.1 (continued)

Paper	Integration of HRM and Entrepreneurship	Implications for Policy and Practice
Formality and Informality/Formality and Performance		
Thassanabanjong, Miller & Marchant (2009)	HRM and SME focused about investment in and approaches to training in Thai SMEs.	(formality/informality) that influence HR practices that can be implemented effectively.
Tsai (2010)	HRM and SME focused. Looks at formalisation and homogeneity of HRM practices within the semi-conductor industry in Taiwan.	
Employment Systems and Processes		
Edwards, Sen Gupta & Tsai (2010)	Small firm focused. Looks at the nature of the links between owners' networks and strategy in different sectors. Evidence suggests context is important. Findings could inform studies of entrepreneurs' network links.	Small firm needs and support is likely to be unique to their situation. Policy approaches underpinned by normative views about what small firms should do or be are unlikely to be effective. The focus of these papers takes us away from understanding the entrepreneur as an economic agent that makes rational decisions to an owner-manager whose working knowledge and decision making is socially, economically and politically shaped by context.
Jones & Ram (2010)	No integration with entrepreneurship. Draws on small firm industrial relations to examine labour processes in small ethnic firms. Points to the need to be sensitive to the 'mixed embeddedness' of small ethnic firms.	
Ram, Woldesenbet & Jones (2011)	Small ethnic firm focus. Links external context influences eg, supply chain relations on internal dynamics of these firms.	
Single HRM Activities		
Admiraal & Lockhorst (2009)	No integration with entrepreneurship. SME focus on owner-managers' attitudes to technology and learning and training. Found owners support and enthusiasm towards technology and training depended on size, sector and technology infrastructure.	These studies speak to the entrepreneurship field by situating owner-manager decision making, the organisation of internal firm resources and the acquisition of skills and knowledge are very much shaped by industry context.
Timming (2011)	HRM with a focus on recruitment and selection in a marginal industry, the body art sector where the nature of the industry and the context of body art studios impact on HRM practices.	
Wyatt, Pathak & Zibarras (2010)	SME focused that examines selection as a single HR practice and links use of best practice selection methods with employee performance.	

directly to entrepreneurship scholars, through the language of 'resources' required for entrepreneurial activity. The third theme is the frequently visited debate about the presence and benefits/costs of formality and informality in small and entrepreneurial firms and the effects of structure/lack of structure on firm performance. This literature retains a HRM and small firms focus, but is important in understanding HRM issues for entrepreneurial and growing firms. Finally, we look at single HRM practices and their contribution to small firm performance. This section includes our favourite paper of the whole review, an examination of HRM practices in UK body-art studios. This paper with its focus on context goes to the heart of why we are interested in small and entrepreneurial firms.

Turning to the review and our analysis of this body of literature. Following our discussion of the papers, we use what is known from this empirical description to discuss what it means for theory building at the intersection of entrepreneurship and HRM and where knowledge about HRM practice in small and entrepreneurial firms could head. The discussion has practical relevance for entrepreneurs and owner-managers of small and entrepreneurial firms because the literature puts HRM and/or HC theories "in the picture" in our understanding of management and entrepreneurial strategy, management practice and performance outcomes. From a policy perspective the evidence suggests that a focus on internal management processes, particularly, labour management and employment relations leads to improved firm performance, labour productivity and job quality.

REVIEW OF NEW RESEARCH: THE HRM-PERFORMANCE RELATIONSHIP

A number of articles in our review explore the link(s) between HRM systems (i.e. high performance work systems (HPWS)) or individual practices and firm performance. This interest reflects attempts to borrow from the large firm literature where the generally accepted view is that there is an association between HRM and firm performance (Guest, 2011; Wright and Gardner, 2003) to explore whether this relationship holds in the small firm context (see for example McClean & Collins, 2011; Patel & Conklin, 2010, discussed below). However, as Hesketh and Fleetwood (2006) and Fleetwood and Hesketh (2006) argue, while efforts (in the mainstream HRM literature) to empirically demonstrate the HRM-P link have occupied scholars since the mid 1990s, the evidence for the link is inconclusive. Scholars in the field point to a number of theoretical and methodological challenges that need to be addressed in order to move our understanding of the HRM-performance link beyond the "black box problem"– the inability of researchers to explain exactly how, in what direction, under what circumstances and to what extent, HRM contributes to individual and firm outcomes (Paauwe, 2009; Wright & Gardner, 2003).

This led Guest (2011: 3) to lament that after 20 years of extensive research "we are more knowledgeable but not much wiser" about the HRM-P link and we are still unable to convincingly explain either theoretically or empirically how the association works. Wright and Gardner (2003: 312) state that while there is evidence to support the view that HRM practices are weakly linked to firm performance, researchers must address significant methodological and theoretical issues to advance our knowledge about the HRM-P link(s). These include accounting for different levels of analysis (the individual, the group or firm/division), theoretical challenges such as reaching agreement on key relationships and clarifying concepts. Another important criticism is the managerialist perspective of the literature and the absence of employee voice in the research (Paauwe, 2009).

Since Huselid's (1995) seminal study that showed what HRM scholars were all hoping to find – an association between HRM practices and performance (measured as employee turnover and organisational performance) – empirical studies have continued to look for evidence to explain the HRM-P relationship in different contexts. Different combinations of HRM practices have been used and a diverse range of outcome variables have been drawn upon while ever more sophisticated research designs have been adopted (Paauwe, 2009). So while the articles in this review draw from mainstream HRM literature we must remind ourselves of these problems and challenges and examine whether the papers reviewed here offer us well theorised models, conceptual clarity, robust methodologies, appropriate research designs and inclusive samples (Guest, 2011; Hesketh & Fleetwood, 2006; Fleetwood & Hesketh, 2006; Paauwe, 2009; Wright & Gardner, 2003).

With these debates in mind, we note that the articles we review do offer complex analyses of the link between internal firm HRM processes and firm performance with researchers mindful of the theoretical and methodological pitfalls along the way (see for example Patel & Cardon, 2010: 283–5). Broadly sitting within the HRM subfield of SHRM (Lengnick-Hall et al, 2009), authors call on theories and concepts, mostly drawn from the mainstream HRM literature to understand firm performance in large organisations and contribute to our knowledge about the role that HRM or individual and firm level HC plays in the performance of small, new or emerging firms. But as noted earlier and as Table 14.1 indicates, many of the themes derived from this review come from the HRM side with some integration with the entrepreneurship literature. Generally the results are reported back to an HRM audience, which is problematic as the studies do speak to issues and problems of interest to the entrepreneurship field.

High Performance Work Systems (HPWS) and Configurational Approaches

High performance work systems (HPWS) or high commitment work systems (HCWS) feature strongly in the literature that seeks to demonstrate the HRM-P link. HPWS refer to bundles of interrelated and internally consistent HRM practices that are complementary to internal modes of production and which contribute to achieving a firm's strategy (MacDuffie, 1995: 197). MacDuffie argued that in situations where employee skill, motivation and commitment were central to the production process, innovative HRM practices to engender employee commitment and discretionary behaviour such as extensive off-the-job and on-the-job training, performance-related compensation and intrinsic rewards would lead to improved economic performance of the firm. For our purposes the importance of HPWS is that they are assumed to be most successful when aligned with the firm's culture and strategy. As such HPWS are considered useful and relevant to small and entrepreneurial firms where the management and control of the organisation is closely aligned to the owner-manager, and where organisational culture, values and employee commitment are salient for firm performance. As the next section of the review indicates, HPWSs are central to examining the HRM-P link.

Firmly located at the intersection of HRM and Entrepreneurship, Messersmith and Guthrie (2010) and Messersmith and Wales (2011) focused on internal firm factors and explored the HRM-P link in emerging firms. These articles bring together issues of entrepreneurial firm behaviour and the contribution of HPWS to firm sales performance and innovation in emergent (small and young) high-tech ventures. Data from a web-based survey of 119 emergent firms drawn from the National Establishment Time-Series (NETS) database in the US (n = approx. 2000; response rate = 10.7 per cent) was used. The median firm size in the study employed 25 people. The authors, drawing on "large firm" theories of the resource based view of the firm (RBV) and dynamic capability, hypothesised links between entrepreneurial orientation, the systematic take up of HPWS and management philosophy and firm performance (sales growth) and innovation.

Messersmith and Guthrie's (2010) article, published as part of the special issue of *Human Resource Management*, looked at the links between the implementation of HPWS and firm performance measured by sales growth and innovation. They considered the (partial) mediating role of employee turnover between the HPWS and sales growth but evidence of it was not found. They found merit-based compensation, information sharing, performance feedback and structured selection interviews to be the most extensively used. Training in company specific skills, compensation based on group performance and firm performance contingent pay were positively associated with sales growth and there was some evidence to support the link between HPWS and product and organisational innovation. They drew the conclusion that the effect of HPWS on firm performance found to exist in larger firms held for the smaller, emerging high-tech firms that participated in the study. But judgement was reserved on whether this was sufficient for sustainable competitive advantage. The authors noted that "neither sales growth nor innovation is enough to achieve sustainable competitive advantage. The results indicate that firm performance can be enhanced in developing firms by paying attention to employment practices. . ." (Messersmith & Guthrie, 2010: 256–7). So it seems that while there is some support for a HRM-P link the processes remain relatively opaque in the small firms studied.

Similar themes were explored in Messersmith and Wales' (2011) article. They hypothesised that a firm's entrepreneurial orientation (growth strategy), the systematic take up of HPWS and a management philosophy characterised by high trust, information sharing and profit sharing would contribute to firm performance (sales growth). Using the same data as Messersmith and Guthrie (2010) (see above), their analysis showed that entrepreneurial orientation did not have a significant effect on the firm's growth trajectory but rather, sales growth depended on the development of internal HC capabilities. Specifically, they identified the development of HRM practices and a management approach that enhanced trust, knowledge sharing and profit sharing were critical to firm performance. However the processes remain difficult to tie down and the authors acknowledge the causal ambiguity of link between HPWS and firm performance (Messersmith & Guthrie, 2010: 244).

Patel and Cardon (2010) and Patel and Conklin (2010) similarly explored the HRM-P relationship through the lens of HPWS. Although analysed differently, both articles drew on data from a sample of UK small firms (employing between ten and 100 employees) collected by Michie (2006). From a larger Dun and Bradstreet database, a response rate of approximately 5 per cent saw data gathered through a telephone survey of 172 firms located in six industry sectors: nursing homes, pharmaceutical/medical manufacturing, grocery stores, cleaning, textiles, and leisure (Patel & Cardon, 2010: 271–2; Patel & Conklin, 2010: 9). This data was supplemented with in-depth interviews with owner-managers of 145 firms.

Patel and Cardon (2010) looked at the effects of product market competition on the adoption and effectiveness of HRM practices and labour productivity in small firms. They hypothesised group culture and HRM intensity (measured by adoption of HRM practices) would mediate the relationship between product market competition and labour productivity. Their analysis found that higher levels of product market competition led to higher levels of labour productivity but returns from HRM practices were realised from positive levels of group culture. In other words, the link between HRM intensity and labour productivity was only indirect and through the effects of group culture. Reinforcing the Messersmith and Guthrie (2010) findings about trust, Patel and Cardon (2010) argued that the existence of a positive group culture assumed high levels of communication and trust which in turn was conducive to the implementation of HRM practices because of lower transaction costs and higher acceptance of the legitimacy of an HRM approach. Group culture played an important role in Patel and Conklin's (2010) analysis of whether employee retention mediated the effects of HPWS on perceived labour productivity. They found that as group cultures became more effective then employee retention was more likely to mediate the relationship between HWPS and labour productivity.

For practitioners clear guidelines emerge around the importance of building effective groups as they will impact on firm performance. But the studies discussed so far present a "chicken and egg" dilemma for understanding the HRM-P link. Is it an inclusive culture, characterised by group values that facilitates the introduction of HRM practices? Or is it the presence of HRM practices that reinforces a culture of trust?

In a study of semi-professional and clerical employees in small medical and legal service firms in the US (n = 180; median size = 41), McClean and Collins (2011: 363) explored high commitment HRM practices (training, formal selection, participation in decision-making, performance management linked to development opportunities and tenure) designed to enhance employee effort and firm performance. Drawing on social exchange theory they found that employees were more likely to engage in higher levels of discretionary behaviour under high commitment HRM practices. While the argument was generally that the use of high commitment HRM practices was contingent on the perceived value of employee groups to firm performance (suggesting an HRM architecture approach – Lepak & Snell, 2002), McClean and Collins (2011: 358) found that high commitment HRM practices tended to be more universally applied across employee categories.

In these papers the importance of HRM was affirmed, especially a systematic approach to developing appropriate HRM systems and practice appropriate to the firm. The findings indicate that these will contribute to firm performance in general and entrepreneurial performance in particular. Moreover, Messersmith and Wales (2011) noted that the development of internal HRM capabilities may well assist firms to better manage external relationships (with customers, suppliers, regulators) in different industry environments. With their focus on internal firm processes and entrepreneurial orientation the two Messersmith articles specifically contributed to knowledge at the intersection of HRM and Entrepreneurship. These studies also linked to Patel and Cardon's (2010: 15) concern with the effect of product market competition on internal firm processes.

Employer perspectives
Notably in these studies, if they are based on anyone's views, then it is the view of management. We can look for example at the finding that labour productivity is likely to increase with high levels of group culture (cohesion, communication and trust) and that trust and communications underpin the propensity of firms to adopt HRM practices by reducing costs of HRM implementation (Patel & Cardon, 2010; Messersmith & Guthrie, 2010). It could be questioned that if group culture was measured using responses from employees then a quite different assessment may emerge about its nature and strength and a different understanding of the role it plays in the HRM-P relationship. Studies by Marlow, Taylor and Thompson (2010) and Storey, Saridakis, Sen Gupta, Edwards and Blackburn (2010) discussed under the 'Formality/ Informality' theme below point to the negotiated nature of the employment relationship and the nature of interpersonal relationships that influences the degree and kinds of formality found within small firms.

Similarly, in the study by Verreynne, Parker and Wilson (2011) of the dynamics of firm success and the relationship between employment practices and firm performance, the "relatively neglected" (Edwards & Ram, 2010: 525) voice of employees was reported. Employees (n = 610) and CEOs from 50 small Australian firms responded to open and closed questions in a survey of strategy and HRM capabilities that facilitate success. Firms were categorised as either "higher" or "lower" performing and while there were no significant differences in terms of firm or CEO characteristics and their assessment of the employment system, employees were able to differentiate practices making up the employment system that lead to differential firm performance. Verreynne et al (2011) found that in high performing firms in their sample, employees identified practices commonly linked to HPWS, including participation and voice as key contributors to firm success. In the lower performing firms, these attributes were missing. CEOs were not able to do this, with one explanation being that employees were immersed in the informal systems and processes that enabled firms to succeed (or not) and CEOs were not. Asking CEOs or top managers for their perspective may miss some of the action taking place within firms and could lead to implementation of systems that may stifle the processes that lead to success.

Patel and Cardon (2010), Patel and Conklin (2011) and McClean and Collins (2011) remind us that we cannot always assume that small and entrepreneurial firms will respond to external environment pressures in the same ways as larger firms (see for example Arthur, 1994; Huselid, 1995; MacDuffie, 1995). Competitive and productivity pressures present small, new, emerging firms with particular challenges due to lack of resources and limited capabilities. While we might expect to see HRM adopted as a logical step in a firm's development (as we would in larger firms), perceived risks, costs or a firm's lack of legitimacy may not make this possible. However, it could be argued that external factors such as customer demands for higher quality products or price competition might simultaneously put pressure on particular firms to adopt bundles of high commitment HRM practices to increase productivity by engendering higher levels of employee discretionary behaviour.

The idea of *gestalts*, that the sum of the whole is greater than its constituent parts, can underpin the "black box" system effects noted in the debates about the HRM-P (Paauwe, 2009). Hence, research examining a broader spectrum of factors that might reveal competing and contradictory forces for internal change and adjustment to meet multiple demands seems relevant here. Fabi, Raymond and Lacoursiere (2009) looked at the firm's *gestalts* of strategic capabilities to understand whether these made a difference to SMEs' HRM practices. They found in their data from 176 Canadian SMEs that HRM practices did vary. They differentiated "local", "international" and "world class" SMEs based on the co-alignment of the strategic capabilities of network development, product development, market development and HRM. For example "world class" SMEs invested more in training and information practices, whereas international SMEs invested more in motivating practices. However world class SMEs outperformed on all performance measures except gross margin per employee where international SMEs outperformed all. The conclusion drawn was that HRM will enhance performance when the investment is coherent with the strategic capabilities of the firm.

The studies summarised under this theme put HRM "in the picture" for small, growing and entrepreneurial firms. However, we found with the exception of the Messersmith and Wales (2011) study examining entrepreneurial orientation, the majority of the studies outlined above come from the HRM side of the ledger and report back to this field. This means that while they have much to say to entrepreneurship, the conversation is muted. For entrepreneurship studies, the explicit focus on aligning HRM systems, organisational culture (participative and team focused) and owner-manager values with firm strategy and performance offers a more robust examination and differentiation between internal firm resources. Importantly the studies identify variables hypothesised to contribute to firm performance in the presence of HPWS/HCWS. In order to extend knowledge in the area, we suggest researchers recognise the importance of context and the limits of taking concepts and models from the mainstream HRM literature and applying them to small firms given their contextual embeddedness and heterogeneity. However the evidence of the effects (often indirect) of HRM on labour productivity and firm performance can inform future studies of small, growing and entrepreneurial firms. An important rider here is that in many of the studies described above, data were not collected from employees. However studies do point to greater interest in developing and testing sophisticated models that underline the contribution of HPWS/HCWS practices to developing internal capabilities, which in turn lead to improved performance.

From a practice and policy perspective, these studies speak to the heterogeneity of firms resulting in unique responses and adaption to complex contextual forces and owner-manager values. One size does not fit all and improvements to firm productivity and job quality could be encouraged (through education support and training) that focuses on the adoption of strategically aligned and organizationally appropriate HRM bundles in small, growing and entrepreneurial firms. Importantly, the evidence suggests that improved outcomes can emerge through employee participation and voice as well as merit based and transparent performance and reward practices. These practices could be encouraged in small, new and emerging firms.

Human Capital (HC)

In the SHRM literature there is an assumption that HRM delivers more than administrative contributions (Lengnick-Hall et al, 2009) while Wright and McMahan's (1992) redefinition of SHRM focused on the contribution of HC to firm performance. In small and entrepreneurial firms the entrepreneur's HC is critical. We see this for example in Lafuente and Rabetino's (2011) study of the contribution of HC to growth in Romanian entrepreneurial firms; Sullivan and Marvel's (2011) analysis of entrepreneurs' knowledge networks and employment growth in new SMEs; and Rauch & Rijsdijk's (2011) model developed from analysis of 201 firms' relationship between general and specific HC and growth and failure. A significant contribution was made by Unger et al's (2011) meta-analysis of 30 years of literature on the relationship between HC and entrepreneurial success. Their review yielded 70 independent samples (n = 24,733) and they found a significant but small relationship between HC and entrepreneurial success (measured as growth and profitability). The relationship was moderated by knowledge and skills as a characteristic of HC, high task relatedness (context), firm size and age (Unger et al, 2011: 341). The authors suggested that future research "should overcome a static view of HC [investment in HC c/f outcomes of investment in HC] and should. . .investigate the processes of learning, knowledge acquisition, and the transfer of knowledge to entrepreneurial tasks" (Unger et al, 2011: 341), as the application of contemporary knowledge through learning is more important than past experience in business success. The authors suggested that these findings were important for understanding the conditions for and type of HC in which entrepreneurs might invest.

Studies also considered HRM practices that build firm level HC more generally. For example, Schmelter et al (2010) considered how HRM practices boost corporate entrepreneurship in German SMEs, while Bryant and Allen (2009) theorised the conditions under which emerging firms required certain kinds of HC. Drawing on the concept of HR architecture (Lepak & Snell, 1999) and emerging organisation theory (Katz & Gartner, 1988), Bryant & Allen (2009: 347, 350) suggested a configurational model for employment modes in emerging organisations based on intentionality (strategy), available resources, boundary conditions and exchange. They argued that different stages of emerging firm development (child organisation, odyssey/emerging stage and adult/emerged organisation) required employment modes and HR configurations to ensure firm survival through the development of competitive advantage. Moreover the path dependent nature of HR architecture is such that getting it right early on is necessary for success in emergent firms. Like Unger et al (2011), Bryant and Allen (2009) point to viewing HRM in entrepreneurial and growing firms as contingent on both the internal resource limitations and the contexts in which firms operate.

While these studies show the importance of HC development for entrepreneurial firm success, others indicate this can be cost prohibitive for smaller firms (Klaas et al, 2005). Klass et al (2010) examined the adoption of HC services by SMEs. Using institutional theory and rational accounts theory explaining small firm behaviour in terms of innovation through adapting to environmental pressures and constraints, Klaas et al (2011) examined why and under what conditions some SMEs outsourced HC services and others did not. From their sample of 494 SME clients of Professional Employer Organisations, they found that when firms faced pressures from customers or they discerned the need to be more responsive to the market, they engaged in adaptive behaviour. However adaptive behaviour differed based on whether the SME was smaller or larger. Leaders of smaller SMEs reacted differently to those of larger SMEs: the former perceived they could take action or implement strategy to change employee behaviour or adjust work processes, whereas the latter saw HRM challenges and adjusted by outsourcing some HRM functions, particularly if they had observed others taking similar action (Klaas et al, 2010: 357). The study highlighted the heterogeneity of SME firm structures and behaviours and the ways in which owner-managers chose to adapt and develop HC in response to environmental challenges.

With a focus on SME owner-manager behaviour, Tocher and Rutherford (2009) attempted to identify the conditions under which HRM was perceived as an acute problem, and hence, we would assume, "something" would be "done" about it. They looked at the individual owner-manager (gender, age, education, experience) and organisational (based on organisational life cycle, size, age and growth) antecedents of the perception of acute HRM problems. In their logistic regression analysis they controlled for industry with five dummy variables. From their sample of 3561 US smaller firms (defined as employing less than 500 people) 21 per cent of respondents reported HRM as "the single most important problem facing your business today" (where "today" was a period from 1998–2000 when this National Survey of Small Business Finances was conducted). Their analysis showed that acute HRM problems were significantly more likely to be perceived by more experienced managers (not less as they hypothesised), younger managers, and those with college degrees (i.e. more education rather than less as they hypothesised). Acute HRM problems were more likely to be perceived in larger firms, and lower performing firms. Their hypotheses around gender, firm age and stage of growth were not supported. The framework they tested was aligned to the ways in which SME owner-managers perceived acute HRM problems and as they argued, by knowing who perceived HRM as an acute problem, we have a chance to target information and helping them successfully and positively resolve that problem.

The papers described under this theme use the lens of HC to examine entrepreneurship and entrepreneurial performance. Many of the studies point to the importance of entrepreneurs' knowledge and experience and in particular managerial and/or HRM knowledge to firm growth. Practitioners wanting to increase employment and entrepreneurial activities might look to educating proto-entrepreneurs as well as encouraging entrepreneurship through formal education such as university centres for entrepreneurship. Those interested in entrepreneurial success might offer programs to help entrepreneurs to gain skills, competences and knowledge related to HRM as a particular form of HC for both the entrepreneur and the need to develop internal HRM processes to contribute to entrepreneurial success.

SHRM or the HRM-P relationship is the theme uniting this group of studies – whether viewed through the lens of HPWS, or what and which type of HC makes a difference to entrepreneurial success or what the adaptive behaviours are within firms to develop HC or what the antecedents of HRM being perceived as a problem are and what this could mean in terms of understanding and supporting specific firms. HRM matters to smaller and entrepreneurial firms is what we can draw from these studies as well as what facilitates that relationship. In the next group of studies this is done more explicitly by focusing on the interplay between formal and informal HRM practices.

Formality and Informality

In terms of the informality-formality debate, the literature points to the view that internal firm relations are subject to negotiation and contestation in the context of adapting to internal and external forces for change. This leads to questioning the linearity of formalisation of HRM practices as firms grow.

Medium-sized firms were used to explore this question by Marlow et al (2010). They argued that processes for informality and formality operated in tension, particularly at times of change when existing power relations were exposed and challenged. For example, when firms grow, the recruitment of new staff or a more formal approach to managing staff, created tensions over proposed changes. Hence efforts to formalise HRM may or may not be successful resulting in degrees of formality and informality co-existing within firms (Marlow et al, 2010: 956). Their in-depth case studies of six firms, constructed from interviews with employers and employees, found clear evidence of formalisation through the professionalisation of the HR function in growing firms. However the shift to formal HRM practices was highly contested and formalisation was shaped through a complex web of power and influence within firms. A rich and complex account of employment relations in medium-sized firms was offered with pointers for how and why small firms behave the way they do without recourse to large firm frameworks and concepts.

In a similar vein, Storey et al (2010) compared small firms and large firms and examined the effects of HRM formalisation on self-reports of job quality (SRJQ). They found that in small firms and small workplaces (owned by small firms), employees' SRJQ was higher than in large firms and small workplaces owned by large firms. And while the results showed that in small firms SRJQ decreased as firm size grew, in large workplaces, SRJQ had a positive relationship with formalisation, for example the presence of a strategic plan (Storey et al, 2010: 305, 318). They found a negative relationship between having an HR manager and employees' SRJQ in small firms indicating that bureaucratic approaches may come with high transaction costs because they limit employee discretion, causing dissatisfaction (Storey et al, 2010: 316). However, other forms of formality had a positive relationship with SRJQ, for example, meetings between managers and employees and performance appraisal programs. Storey et al (2010) argued that the type of formal procedure was important and that highly rule-based and bureaucratic policies and procedures reduced SRJQ in small firms and workplaces because they impinged on employee autonomy and discretion. On the other hand, for employees in large firms, having a formal strategic plan may mean that employees were able to see a link between the work they did and the strategic vision of the firm.

Storey et al's (2010) findings pointed to the distinctive nature of HRM processes in small firms and the contingent and contextual nature of the HRM-P link in small firms. The study highlighted the importance of employee perceptions of the effects of particular HRM practices on existing employment relations in the firm. These findings have some resonance with those of Marlow et al's (2010), which showed that as firms grew internal structures adjusted and changed while power relations became transparent and/or began to be mobilised necessitating negotiation in the change process. In a similar vein, Verreynne et al (2011) were able to show that the way employees used informal practices contributed to firm success and again there were some connections with Marlow et al's (2010) findings of the synchronicity of formal and informal practices.

Overall the message from studies here is to focus on the differential impact of different kinds of formality that may create costs or benefits for the firm and its employees. Entrepreneurs or practitioners interested in improving job quality and firm performance, need to note that a "one size fits all" approach to formalisation of HRM practices may in fact reduce job quality and therefore impact negatively on firm performance. As Storey et al (2010: 321) suggest, policy makers might question a "one size fits all" approach to fomalisation in small firms and consider supporting certain kinds of formality that benefit organisational outcomes. For example, performance appraisal and formal employee grievance practices may increase employee satisfaction by enhancing employee voice and ensure consistent treatment of staff.

Formality and Performance

In the next group of studies, the exploration shifts to national contexts and industry sectors and we look at some not normally seen in the literature. To varying degrees these studies acknowledge the importance of size and context in understanding and examining the link between HRM formalisation and firm performance. This can be seen in De Grip and Sieven's (2009) study of HRM in small pharmacies in the Netherlands. They identified "thresholds of diffusion" for advanced HRM practices and argued that in smaller pharmacies formal HRM (both basic and advanced) are less important to firm performance than the informal and personal relationships between the employer and employees (De Grip & Sieven, 2009: 1914). A rider here would be the nature and outcome of the informal and personal relationships in the firm and whether these are beneficial or indicative of relations of control and autocratic behaviour by owner-managers (Rainnie, 1989) or more equitable relations where employees feel they have some voice in negotiating employment relations.

Richbell, Szerb and Vitai (2010) offer a picture of HRM practices across small firms in Hungary. They noted the heterogeneity of practices and the need for more detailed research. Kim and Gao (2010) explored small family firms in China and found, like many Western studies, a positive relationship between firm size and the presence of HRM practices but location, as a contextual factor, was not significant. The absence of HRM practices in small firms pointed to the flexibility needed to manage resource constraints while the lack of location effects was explained in terms of the wide diffusion of western HRM practices across China. Drawing on new institutionalisation theory and multiple case studies of Taiwanese semi-conductor design firms (12 SMEs, m = 109 and 12 large firms ranging in size from 48–695), Tsai (2010) found a high level of homogeneity of HRM. This rather contrary finding of HRM homogeneity was said to be due to industry (and perhaps national?) context factors such as competition for high skilled workers, values of professionalism in the industry and the characteristics of skilled workers (i.e. demand for financial and non-financial incentives). The larger size of the small firms (with only one firm employing fewer than 50 employees) may have also contributed to the findings. Similarly, Thassananbanjong, Miller and Marchant (2009) examined training in Thai SMEs (n = 438, mostly family owned) and found that formal training in Thai SMEs depended on industry sector such as IT and services and size, with more formal training happening in larger SMEs while smaller firms engage in informal, on the job training.

Employment Systems and Processes

Context is also important in some studies by UK scholars where the focus is on employment/industrial relations in small and entrepreneurial firms. This literature sees small and entrepreneurial firm behaviour as contingent on the social, economic and political relations in which they are embedded. Studies by Edwards, Sen Gupta and Tsai (2010), Ram, Woldesenbet and Jones (2011) and Jones and Ram (2010) play down the focus on owner-manager behaviour and smallness as a determinant of structure and action and argue that small and entrepreneurial firm behaviour (and that of the owner-manager) is contingent on the contexts in which they are located.

Edwards et al (2010: 543) examined the relationship between small firms' network links and their strategies and resources. The RBV was used as a starting point to understand the importance of actively developing internal firm resources, an examination of firm goals and attitudes to growth, and accounting for external contextual factors such as product and labour markets. In exploring how these factors interact, Edwards et al (2010: 546) argue, "We pursue a more contextualised approach, locating firms in their market context and addressing the ways in which the context imposes constraints on choice." Surveys (n = 413) and in-depth interviews (n = 43) with employers and employees were analysed to find that firms' external relationships were highly context specific and linked to the firms' strategic position. Importantly they concluded that future research should focus on relationships between internal structures and processes of firms (i.e. the mobilisation of resources) and external factors such as industry sector (i.e. ways in which certain industries impose operation requirements on firms) (Edwards et al, 2010: 561).

Taking a similar approach but this time to examine small ethnic firms, Ram et al (2011) examined the effects of supply chain relationships with large purchasing organisations (LPOs) on the internal structures and processes and the experience of employees in small ethnic firms. The LPO relationship was important and they found LPOs exerted pressure on internal firm structures and processes. This saw the tightening of control (formalisation) of HR practices such as recruitment, and processes such as work organisation and work hours (Ram et al, 2011: 309).

These studies have something to say to the entrepreneurship literature about resources. Specifically they deal with the role and importance of HC as context specific knowledge and networks and the capacity of entrepreneurs to mobilise such resources through internal structures and processes within the firm (see also Sullivan & Marvel, 2011).

Single HRM Activities

Finally, in our review we found a small number of papers focused on single HRM activities in small and entrepreneurial firms which could also be located in particular industry sectors or country locations. For example, there was Wyatt, Pathak and Zibarras (2010) on best practice selection methods; and Admiraal and Lockhorst (2009) on attitudes of owner-managers of European SMEs to e-learning, training and technology. In an interesting paper, and voted our favourite because of the unusual sample and clarity of findings, Timming (2011) constructed case studies of very small (and often marginal),

UK body-art studios (with 1–6 artists), to examine recruitment and selection practices. The informal practices he found could be understood not just because of the firm's size, but more importantly because of their context and embeddedness in marginal areas of the economy. As the author noted: "The results suggest recruitment and selection in the body art sector is characteristically informal [and] that the use of formal methods of recruitment and selection. . .appeared to enhance difficulties in attracting and retaining talent" (Timming, 2010: 570). Size was a "red herring" in understanding formalisation. Factors such as sectoral idiosyncrasies (use of word-of-mouth recruitment, lack of formal qualifications, tattoo artists' lifestyle and background), organisational culture, labour market factors, resource limitations and manager knowledge and experience all played a role in the nature of the specific practices.

DISCUSSION

A review of a discipline's progress, or the intersection of two disciplines, should occur regularly. In the entrepreneurship discipline there has been considerable reflection of late (for example, Low 2001; Wiklund et al, 2011; Zahra & Wright, 2011), while the HRM field is significantly larger, reflection has occurred (for example, Ferris et al, 2004; Martín-Alcázar et al, 2008) and particularly on the state of SHRM (Wright & McMahon, 1992; Lengnick-Hall et al, 2009) and more specifically the problems associated with the HRM-P link (Guest, 2011; Paauwe, 2009). We have collated and reviewed key papers published over a short period at the intersection of HRM and Entrepreneurship and can draw out some interesting points for research, policy and practice.

The first is that there is still only a limited literature at this intersection but more than there was before! It is the HRM literature that puts "HRM in the picture" for small, growing and entrepreneurial firms. However this literature mainly reports back to its own constituency. As a result of this, the entrepreneurship side, while concerned with entrepreneurial behaviour and outcomes, firm resources and outcomes, the link to HRM is implied rather than explicit. Hence we suggest that both sides need to continue to broach the divide through concerted efforts to maintain the conversation and it is heartening to see that there is not a reliance on a call for papers in special issues or Handbooks like ours to encourage researchers to take an interest in the topic. While we searched key journals (see Table 14.1) there were single papers published in other journals such as *International Journal of Manpower* and *Human Systems Management*. Papers published in a wide array of journals shows there has been some impact on developing the researcher community. Having a community of scholars is necessary because conversations cannot be had alone, and the more who are interested now are likely to attract more in the future.

The issues being researched largely emanate from the SHRM subfield of HRM. How HRM contributes to organisational performance (or even if it does) is the key question. It is the context of the exploration that makes a difference: small, new, growth, entrepreneurial firms. The question – how can entrepreneurial firms use the human resources they have available to gain better performance (or a similar question) – is not being asked. Does it matter? We think it does and it goes to who the conversation is between.

We are talking to other HRM scholars and this is evident in the journals where papers have predominantly been published, but we are also talking to those working on small firms, who may or may working on entrepreneurship. The conversation is unbalanced and so too is the ledger.

This review shows that the literature has moved beyond describing the situation, for example, what HRM practices exist, are they formal, how do they work, and into understanding whether they matter or not. Research shows that the linkages exist between HRM and organisational performance and increasingly studies are beginning to tell us more of how that happens. For example, this might occur through positive group culture (Patel & Cardon, 2010; Patel & Conklin, 2010) or informal processes such as voice (Verreynne et al, 2011) or through the organisation (horizontal alignment) of a particular set of HRM practices in bundles (McClean & Collins, 2011; Messersmith & Guthrie, 2010; Messersmith & Wales, 2011) or through congruency (vertical alignment) between goals of different internal processes (Fabi et al, 2009). There is some new and interesting theorising about small, new, growth, entrepreneurial firms using innovative models and concepts. For example the RBV (Messersmith & Guthrie, 2010; Messersmith & Wales, 2011; Edwards et al, 2010), social exchange theory (McClean & Collins, 2011; Zhang & Jia, 2010), HC theory (Bryant & Allen, 2009) and institutional theory (Klaas et al, 2010) amongst others have been used to frame the exploration.

Methodologically there is diversity, but sample sizes and response rates can be small while measurement issues need to be acknowledged. The HRM-P relationship can depend in proximity (Colakoglu et al, 2006) while other measurement errors in this type of research have been well rehearsed by Wall and Wood (2005). The ongoing issue of defining what a small firm is remains, with 'small firms' in some studies here defined as those firms with less than 500 employees. Smallness may be relative but this does make comparison easy. We see attempts to gather data from employees (Verreynne et al, 2011, Pajo et al, 2010) and this provides a more holistic view of managing people in small and entrepreneurial firms. Finally however, the problems of delimiting the fields (of HRM and Entrepreneurship) remain, as does how key concepts are defined: we will repeat, not all small, new or emerging firms are entrepreneurial and not all entrepreneurial firms are small, new or emerging!

CONCLUSION

In summary, we are excited by what we have read and are optimistic about the future of research at the intersection of HRM and Entrepreneurship, particularly as the conversation at the intersection of HRM and Entrepreneurship continues to grow. At the beginning of this chapter we drew attention to Zahra and Newey's (2009) impact wheel of "theory building at the intersection" where three modes of theory building at the intersection of fields or disciplines were identified. At the intersection of HRM and Entrepreneurship we appear to be borrowing concepts, issues, questions from HRM, and by and large, and extending our knowledge of HRM in the context of small and entrepreneurial firms. This is indicative of Mode 2 theorising where "researchers identify some salient but unique research issues and questions at the intersection and proceed to study them making use of imported theories. Such theorising assumes scholarly discourse across the two intersecting fields as well as at the point of intersection" (Zahra & Newey, 2009: 1067).

We need to move beyond Mode 2 if we are going to truly understand the multiple and complex ways the HRM and Entrepreneurship fields intersect and for us, the unique point of intersection is the recognition that people are a key resource in all firms, and more so in small, new or entrepreneurial ones. The core of the issue is resources – human resources. HRM scholars have a lot to say about processes to manage those resources but they appear to be less important than other resources to entrepreneurship scholars. We know human resources are difficult to manage but there is potential to affect firm performance. There is much to be won if we can engage those on the entrepreneurship side to look at those entrepreneurial processes, mechanisms and activities that will enable performance. But we need to continue to foster more communication between the two fields. As Lengnick-Hall et al (2009) have commented about the state of HRM theory building, "while it [Mode 2 or coupling] is potentially useful, it is not as likely to lead to breakthrough insights" (p. 80). The more we get the message out about the exciting opportunities that sit here, the more we will see others join the quest to make novel combinations of theories to understand the complex phenomena with which we are dealing.

REFERENCES

Admiraal, W., and Lockhorst, D. (2009), 'E-learning in small and medium-sized enterprises across Europe', *International Small Business Journal*, 27, 6, 743–67.

Arthur, J. (1994), 'Effects of human resource systems on manufacturing performance and turnover', *Academy of Management Journal*, 37, 3, 670–87.

Baron, R. A. (2003), 'Editorial. Human resource management and entrepreneurship: Some reciprocal benefits of closer links', *Human Resource Management Review*, 13, 253–6.

Barrett, R. & Mayson, S. (2006) 'The 'science' and 'practice' of HRM in small firms', *Human Resource Management Review*, 16 (4): 447–55.

Barrett, R. and Mayson, S. (2008), 'Introduction: At the intersection of entrepreneurship and human resource management' in R. Barrett and S. Mayson (Eds), *International Handbook of Entrepreneurship and HRM* (pp. 1–17), Cheltenham, Edward Elgar.

Bryant, P., and Allen D. (2009), 'Emerging organizations' characteristics as predictors of human capital employment mode: A theoretical perspective', *Human Resource Management Review*, 19, 347–55.

Colakoglu, S., Lepak, D., and Hong, Y. (2006), 'Measuring HRM effectiveness: Considering multiple stakeholders in a global context', *Human Resource Management Review*, 16, 2, 209–18.

De Grip, A., and Sieven, I. (2009), 'The effectiveness of more advanced human resource systems in small firms', *The International Journal of Human Resource Management*, 20, 9, 1914–28.

Edwards, P., and Ram, M. (2010), 'HRM in small firms: Respecting and regulating informality', in A. Wilkinson, N. Bacon, T. Redmond, and S. Snell (eds), *The Sage Handbook of Human Resource Management* (pp. 524–40). London: Sage.

Edwards, P., Sen Gupta, S., and Tsai, C. (2010), 'The context-dependent nature of small firms' relations with support agencies: A three-sector study', *International Small Business Journal*, 28, 6, 543–65.

Fabi, B., Raymond, L., and Lacoursiere, R. (2009), 'Strategic alignment of HRM practices in manufacturing SMES: A *gestalts* perspective', *Journal of Small Business and Enterprise Development*, 16, 1, 7–25.

Ferris, G. R., Hall, A. T., Royle, M. T., and Martocchio, J. J. (2004), 'Theoretical development in the field of human resources management: Issues and challenges for the future', *Organizational Analysis*, 12, 231–54.

Fleetwood, S. and Hesketh, A. (2006), 'HRM-performance research: under-theorized and lacking explanatory power', *International Journal of Human Resource Management*, 17, 12, 1977–93.

Guest, D. (2011), 'Human resource management and performance: still searching for some answers', *Human Resource Management Journal*, 21, 1, 3–13.

Hesketh, A., and Fleetwood, S. (2006), 'Beyond measuring the human resources management-organizational performance link: Applying critical realist meta-theory', *Organization*, 13, 5, 677–99.

Huselid, M. (1995), 'The impact of human resource management practices on turnover, productivity and corporate financial performance', *Academy of Management Journal*, 38, 635–72.

Jones, T., and Ram, M. (2010), 'Ethnic variations on the small firm labour process', *International Small Business Journal*, 28, 2, 163–73.

Katz, J., Aldrich, T., Welbourne, T. and Williams, P. (2000), 'Guest editors' comments. Special issue on human resource management and the SME: Towards a new synthesis', *Entrepreneurship: Theory and Practice*, 25, 710.

Katz, J., and Gartner, W.B. (1988), 'Properties of emerging organizations', *Academy of Management Review*, 13, 429–441.

Kim, Y., and Gao, F. (2010), 'An empirical study of human resource management practices in family firms in China', *International Journal of Human Resource Management*, 21, 12, 2095–119.

Kirkwood, J. (2009), 'To grow or not? Growing small service firms', *Journal of Small Business and Enterprise Development*, 16, 3, 485–503.

Klaas, B. S., Klimchak, M., Semadeni, M., and Holmes, J. (2010), 'The adoption of human capital services by small and medium enterprises: A diffusion of innovation perspective', *Journal of Business Venturing*, 25, 349–60.

Klaas, B. S., Yang, H., Gainey, T., and McClendon, J. (2005), 'HR in the small business enterprise: Assessing the impact of PEO utilization', *Human Resource Management*, 44, 433–48.

Lafuente, E., and Rabetino, R. (2011), 'Human capital and growth in Romanian small firms', *Journal of Small Business and Enterprise Development*, 18, 1, 74–96.

Lengnick-Hall, M. L., Lengnick-Hall, C. A., Andrade, L. S., and Drake, B. (2009), 'Strategic human resource management: The evolution of a field', *Human Resource Management Review*, 19, 64–85.

Lepak, D. P., and Snell, S. A. (2002), 'Examining the human resource architecture: The relationship among human capital, employment and human resource configurations', *Journal of Management*, 28, 4, 517–43.

Low, M. (2001), 'The adolescence of entrepreneurship research: Specification of purpose', *Entrepreneurship: Theory and Practice*, 25, 17–25.

McClean, E., and Collins, C. (2011), 'High-commitment HR practices, employee effort and firm performance: Investigating the effects of HR practices across employee groups within professional services firms', *Human Resource Management*, 50, 3, 341–63.

MacDuffie, J.P. (1995), 'Human resource bundles on manufacturing performance: Organisational logic and flexible production system in the world auto industry', *Industrial and Labour Relations Review*, 48,2, 197–221.

Marlow, S., Taylor, S., and Thompson, A. (2010), 'Informality and formality in medium-sized companies: Contestation and synchronization', *British Journal of Management*, 21, 4, 954–66.

Martín-Alcázar, F., Romero-Fernández, P.M., and Sánchez-Gardey, G. (2008), 'Human resource management as a field of research', *British Journal of Management*, 19, 103–19.

Messersmith, J., and Guthrie, J. (2010), 'High performance work systems in emergent organizations: Implications for firm performance', *Human Resource Management*, 49, 2, 241–64.

Messersmith, J., and Wales, W. (early view 2011), 'Entrepreneurial orientation and performance in young firms: The role of human resource management', *International Small Business Journal*, DOI:10.1177/0266242611416141, isb.sagepub.com.

Michie, J. (2006), 'Human resource management and performance in small and medium sized enterprises, 2004 – 2005' [Computer file]. From Colchester, Essex: UK Data Archive [distributor], July 2006. SN: 5382.

Musteen, M., and Ahsan, M. (early view May 2011), 'Beyond cost: The role of intellectual capital in offshoring and innovation in young firms', *Entrepreneurship: Theory and Practice*. DOI: 10.1111/j.1540-6520.2011.00477.x.

Paauwe, J. (2009), 'HRM and performance: Achievements, methodological issues and prospects', *Journal of Management Studies*, 46, 1, 131–42.

Pajo, K., Coetzer, A., and Guenole, N. (2010), 'Formal development opportunities and withdrawal behaviours by employees in small and medium-sized enterprise', *Journal of Small Business Management*, 48, 3, 281–301.

Patel, P. C., and Cardon, M. S. (2010), 'Adopting HRM practices and their effectiveness in small firms facing product-market competition', *Human Resource Management*, 49, 2, 265–90.

Patel, P. C., and Conklin, B. (early view 2010), 'Perceived labor productivity in small firms – The effects of high-performance work systems and group culture through employee retention', *Entrepreneurship: Theory and Practice*. DOI:10.1111/j.1540-6520.2010.00404.x.

Rainnie, A. (1989), *Industrial Relations in Small Firms*. London: Routledge.

Ram, M., Woldesenbet, K., and Jones, T. (2011), 'Raising the 'table stakes'? Ethnic minority businesses and supply chain relationships', *Work, Employment and Society*, 25, 2, 309–26.

Rauch, A., and Rijsdijk, S. A. (early view 2011), 'The effects of general and specific human capital on long-term growth and failure of newly founded businesses', *Entrepreneurship: Theory and Practice*.

Richbell, S., Szerb, L., and Vitai, Z. (2010), 'HRM in the Hungarian SME sector', *Employee Relations*, 32, 3, 262–80.

Schmelter, R., Mauer, R., Borsch, C., and Brettel, M. (2010), 'Boosting corporate entrepreneurship through HRM practices: Evidence from German SMEs', *Human Resource Management*, 49, 4, 715–41.

Soriano, D. R., Dobon, S. R., and Tansky, J. (2010), 'Guest editors' note: Linking entrepreneurship and human resources in globalization', *Human Resource Management*, 49, 2, 217–23.

Storey, D. J., Saridakis, G., Sen Gupta, S., Edwards, P. K., and Blackburn, R. A. (2010) 'Linking HR formality with employee job quality: The role of firm and workplace size', *Human Resource Management*, 49, 2, 305–29.

Sullivan, D., and Marvel, M. (2011), 'How entrepreneurs' knowledge and network ties relate to the number of employees in new SMEs', *Journal of Small Business Management*, 49, 2, 185–206.

Tansky, J., and Heneman, R. (2003), 'Guest editors' note: Introduction to the special issue on human resource management in SMEs: A call for more research', *Human Resource Management*, 42, 299–302.

Tansky, J., Soriano, D. R., and Dobon, S. R. (2010), 'Guest editors' note: What's next? Linking entrepreneurship and human resources in globalization', *Human Resource Management*, 49, 4, 689–92.

Thassanabanjong, K., Miller, P., and Marchant, T. (2009), 'Training in Thai SMEs', *Journal of Small Business and Enterprise Development*, 16, 4, 678–93.

Timming, A.R. (2011), 'What do tattoo artists know about HRM? Recruitment and selection in the body art sector', *Employee Relations*, 33, 5, 570–584.

Tocher, N., and Rutherford, M. (2009), 'Perceived acute human resource management problems in small and medium firms: An empirical examination' *Entrepreneurship: Theory and Practice*, 33, 2, 455–78.

Tsai, C. (2010), 'HRM in SMEs: homogeneity or heterogeneity? A study of Taiwanese high-tech firms', *International Journal of Human Resource Management*, 21, 10, 1689–711.

Unger, J. M., Rauch, A., Frese, M., and Rosenbusch, N. (2011), 'Human capital and entrepreneurial success: A meta-analytical review', *Journal of Business Venturing*, 26, 341–58.

Verreynne, M-L, Parker, P., and Wilson, M. (early view 2011), 'Employment systems in small firms: A multi-level analysis', *International Small Business Journal*.

Wall, T., and Wood, S. (2005), 'The romance of human resource management and business performance and the case for big science', *Human Relations*, 58, 4, 1–34.

Wiklund, J., Davidsson, P., Audretsch, D., and Karlsson, C. (2011), 'The future of entrepreneurship research', *Entrepreneurship: Theory and Practice*, 35, 1, 1–9.

Wright, P. M. and Gardner, T.M. (2003), 'The human resource-firm performance relationship: Methodological and theoretical challenges' in D. Holman, T. Wall, C. Clegg, P. Sparrow, and A. Howard (Eds), *The New Workplace: A Guide to the Human Impact of Modern Working Practices* (pp. 311–30), London, John Wiley and Sons.

Wright, P. M., and McMahan, G. (1992), 'Theoretical perspectives for strategic human resource management', *Journal of Management*, 18, 2, 295–320.

Wyatt, M., Pathak, S., and Zibarras, L. (2010), 'Advancing selection in an SME: Is best practice methodology applicable?' *International Small Business Journal*, 28, 3, 258–73.

Zahra, S.A., and Newey, L.R. (2009), 'Maximizing the impact of organizational science: Theory-building at the intersection of disciplines and/or fields', *Journal of Management Studies*, 46, 6, 1059–75.

Zahra, S.A., and Wright, M. (2011), 'Entrepreneurship's next act', *Academy of Management Perspectives*, 25, 4, 67–83.

Zhang, Z., and Jia, M. (2010), 'Using social exchange theory to predict the effects of high-performance human resource practices on corporate entrepreneurship: Evidence from China', *Human Resource Management*, 49, 4, 743–65.

PART IV

ENTREPRENEURSHIP, EDUCATION AND LEARNING

15. Entrepreneurship education: what we know and what we need to know
Janice Byrne, Alain Fayolle and Olivier Toutain

INTRODUCTION

Over the last few decades, entrepreneurship has become a global policy darling and has been promoted as a solution to a range of societal and economic ills. The first decade of the millennium has seen national governments, international organizations (i.e. UNESCO, OECD, the European Commission), civil society groups and others increasingly advocate the importance of entrepreneurship and the role that education plays in igniting it (World Economic Forum, 2009). This surge of support for entrepreneurship education and training has continued despite some researchers' reservations regarding the political promotion of entrepreneurship as an unequivocal source of economic and societal good (Shane, 2009; Jones and Spicer, 2009). Doubts have also been expressed as to the legitimacy and maturity of entrepreneurship education (Kuratko, 2005; Katz, 2008) and others have criticized the predominant approach to how we teach entrepreneurship (Honig, 2004; Neck and Greene, 2011). Governments investing in this area need to commit to research examining entrepreneurship education in order to improve the evidence base, to evaluate the impact of interventions and to gain a clearer idea of what policies might work more effectively in which contexts (Pittaway and Cope, 2007). Teachers and academics in the field of entrepreneurship would also benefit from re-thinking how they approach entrepreneurship education (Neck and Greene, 2011).

Entrepreneurship education is a troubled research object and theoretical field. The field has been found to suffer from an acute lack of theoretical grounding (Béchard and Grégoire, 2005). Unresolved disputes concerning the definition of both entrepreneur and entrepreneurship confuse our assessment of the current state of research in entrepreneurship education (Henry, Hill and Leitch, 2005a). Entrepreneurship education encompasses a large and varied subject matter and is built on numerous divergent theoretical assumptions. Ontological assumptions of what entrepreneurship 'is' impact on educational level questions of what, who, why and how to teach, as well as for which results (Fayolle and Gailly, 2008), thus when we talk about 'entrepreneurship education' we are often not all talking about the same thing. We believe that entrepreneurship education as a field suffers from a lack of clear theorizing and organizing taxonomies. This is perhaps due to its current status as a peripheral and less valued domain of contemporary entrepreneurship research. More analysis of and critical reflection on the existing research on entrepreneurship education would be useful to advance the body of knowledge. In this chapter, we elaborate on these propositions and present an overview of research on entrepreneurship education in the mainstream entrepreneurship and education journals.

This chapter is divided into three main sections. We begin by clarifying what we know. We outline some definitional issues and explain our terminology in the course of the chapter. We then present some specific entrepreneurship education and training (EET) 'audiences' and, in this context, discuss contextual factors which help explain EET's rising profile at an individual, societal, organisational, national and international level. We highlight some theoretical weaknesses and legitimacy issues in the current body of entrepreneurship education literature. In the second section, we present an overview of the entrepreneurship education literature published in seven key mainstream journals from the period 1984–2011 and identify five emergent themes in the literature. We then turn to addressing what we need to know. In the third and final section, we apply an entrepreneurship teaching model framework (Fayolle and Gailly, 2008) to our literature review findings to help frame our discussion and illuminate areas where future research is warranted.

WHAT DO WE KNOW? DEFINITIONAL ISSUES AND TARGETED AUDIENCES

Definitional Issues

Entrepreneurship education and training programmes can be classified in numerous ways. Jamieson (1984) proposed that entrepreneurship education programmes may be classified as one of three different types according to their general aims and objectives. The first, which he termed 'education about enterprise', groups those courses which aim to build awareness about entrepreneurship and business creation. Such programmes sensitize students to the issues involved in setting up and running a business from a mainly theoretical perspective. Another category, termed 'education for enterprise' is more specific and aims to help participants to set up their own business. Such courses emphasize practical skills and may, for example, provide instruction in preparing a business plan (Henry, Hill and Leitch, 2005a). The third category, 'education in enterprise' encompasses those courses which impart management training to established entrepreneurs and focuses on providing assistance in areas where they may need additional assistance (Jamieson, 1984). Education in enterprise type programmes also include courses which aim to help individuals and groups adopt an enterprising approach, regardless of the type of business they are involved in (Henry, Hill and Leitch, 2005a).

Classifications of EET can also be made on the basis of target audience. Gorman et al (1997) propose that different educational targets for entrepreneurship can be distinguished: formal education students, out of school individuals or existing owners and managers. These categories can be further classified, and we will return to this in the subsequent section. In another classification, Garavan and O'Cinneide (1994) divide entrepreneurship programmes into two broad categories: 'entrepreneurship education' and 'education and training for small business owners'. They treat 'entrepreneurship education' programmes as those which teach about favourable conditions for business start-up as well as the various types of characteristics required for successful entrepreneurship. This type of programme is generally theoretical in nature and is similar to Jamieson's 'education about enterprise' category. They then sub-classify 'education and training for small business' type programmes as being concerned with one of three goals: building awareness, helping employees make the transition to entrepreneurship or continuing small business training which helps (already existing) business owners update their skills. Kirby (2004) makes the distinction between educating 'about' entrepreneurship which he understands as teaching students about entrepreneurship practices and principles, and educating 'for entrepreneurship' which is all about equipping students with a set of personal skills, attributes and behaviours to allow them to succeed as entrepreneurs. A recent trend in the literature reveals a move away from teaching 'about' with more focus on teaching 'for' entrepreneurship (Fayolle, 2008).

In this chapter, we use the terms 'entrepreneurship education and training' and 'entrepreneurship teaching' interchangeably as catch-all terms to include both formal education and training. By 'formal' here, we mean organized and deliberate. Within this realm of formal or planned education an experiential approach may of course be adopted by the teacher/facilitator. We now look at the context for education and training in entrepreneurship and evoke recent trends in its provision. In doing so, we build on the above theorizing and illustrate the contemporary complexity of programme classification.

Context and Audience

Entrepreneurship is commonly acknowledged as a key driver of economic growth and job creation. Small- and medium-sized enterprises (SMEs) are 'the backbone of all economies and are a key source of economic growth, dynamism and flexibility in advanced industrialised countries, as well as in emerging and developing economies' (OECD, 2006). It is broadly acknowledged that public policy can play an important role in stimulating motivations and entrepreneurial attitudes and provide the right set of skills to start up and run a business (Hofer and Delaney, 2010). In the EU, the European Commission's 'Europe 2020 strategy' recognizes entrepreneurship and self-employment as key for achieving 'smart, sustainable and inclusive growth', and several flagship initiatives have been put in place across Europe to encourage entrepreneurship.

A qualification must be made, however, which acknowledges the varying penetration rates, form and type of EET that exist on a global basis. International, national, regional and local varieties of EET programmes exist depending on the economic, cultural, societal and political context in which they are embedded. A 2008 GEM report (Bosma et al, 2009) documented differences in training provision, uptake and quality across 39 of the 43 GEM country candidates. In factor-driven economies, the proportion of individuals who had received training in starting a business, either in school or after school varied from 40 per cent in Colombia to 8 per cent in Egypt. While in efficiency-driven countries, it varied from 43 per cent in Chile to 6 per cent in Turkey. Innovation driven countries varied from 48 per cent in Finland to 13 per cent in Israel (Bosma et al, 2008). The quality and level of EET may have different impacts on attitudes, aspirations, and activity in countries at different stages of economic development.

Entrepreneurship plays a social as well as an economic role. It is said to help society's disadvantaged persons 'break away from their unprivileged positions' (De Clercq and Honig, 2011). Entrepreneurship for social inclusion seeks growth by allowing more people – especially marginalized ones such as the very poor, women in many contexts, minorities, disabled and disadvantaged – to engage actively in productive economic activities (World Economic Forum, 2009).

Leveraging both economic and social justifications, public policy initiatives increasingly target specific populations. Entrepreneurship education and training programmes are becoming more and more diverse as governments and international bodies now pinpoint particular groups with specific objectives and varying instructional approaches. While disparities exist across the globe in terms of the form and scope of EET programmes, government initiatives often target the unemployed, youth, tertiary level students, women and immigrants.

- The unemployed: Several western economies have adopted programmes to foster and support small firm formation by unemployed workers (Evans and Leighton, 1990; Fairlie, 2005; Caliendo and Kritikos, 2010; Byrne and Fayolle, 2012). Entrepreneurship is promoted as a way out of poverty and an alternative to unemployment or discrimination in the labour market (Fairlie, 2005). As recent policy in the world's rich countries has swung towards encouraging self-employment among the unemployed (Block and Wagner, 2010; Fayolle, 2010), a large proportion of socially marginalized individuals choose self-employment as an alternative DIY route to economic and societal integration.
- Youth: Entrepreneurial activity is found to be lowest among young people under 25 (Harding and Bosma, 2006) and this group is viewed as a relatively 'untapped source of new business start-ups and economic growth' (Athayde, 2009). Governments are increasingly targeting enterprise policies at young people in order to unlock this potential resource (Hytti and O'Gorman, 2004). Youth entrepreneurship is an area of growing policy interest for OECD national and local governments (Hofer and Delaney, 2010).
- Tertiary level students: The number of relevant institutions and the amount of resources devoted to entrepreneurship education at tertiary level is growing rapidly (Katz, 2003; Vesper and Gartner, 1997; Kuratko, 2005; Meyer, 2011). The evolving dynamic between industry, government and the education sector, coupled with societal demands, increased globalization and changing knowledge structures explains the strong emphasis on entrepreneurship in tertiary education (Gibb et al, 2009; World Economic Forum, 2009). For entrepreneurship education, focusing on institutions of higher education offers the chance to develop knowledge-intensive, high-growth enterprises from multiple academic disciplines (World Economic Forum, 2009). Higher education institutions 'should create an environment that fosters entrepreneurial mind-sets, skills and behaviours across their organizations. Universities can teach students how to start and grow enterprises in ways that benefit society' (World Economic Forum, 2009; p 44).
- Women: In most industrialized nations around the world, women have a lower entrepreneurial propensity and the survival rate of women's businesses is lower in all countries and economic levels (Allen, Elam, Langowitz and Dean, 2008). Women have often been found to have lower financial capital (Hisrich, 1989) and more limited access to key social networks (Marlow and Patton, 2005). They are less likely to have an educational qualification in engineering and technology (Hisrich and Brush, 1984; Holmquist and Delmar, 2003) limiting their access to high growth entrepreneurship endeavours (Shane, 2009). Yet it is women who are more likely to work for, buy for, and share their economic and non-economic

rewards with other people. Hence, investment in women's entrepreneurship is an important way for countries to exponentially increase the impact of new venture creation (Allen et al., 2008).

- Immigrants: Immigrants are said to be more entrepreneurial and have a higher degree of self-employment and enterprise creation compared to the average population (Guzy, 2006). Over the past century, businesses set up by migrant communities have displayed a strong entrepreneurial capacity and potential and have made an increasingly substantial contribution to many national economies across Europe (European Commission, 2003). In the UK, for example, ethnic minorities are more likely to start their own business than the rest of the population and their businesses contribute approximately £15 billion to the British economy every year (Grove-White, 2010). In the US, immigrants have been found to play a particularly important role in high tech entrepreneurship (Hart, Acs and Tracy, 2009).

A combination of numerous developments – globalization; increased mobility and travel across borders; demographic change; social and cultural conventions; knowledge structure and technological change – have compounded the pervasive appeal of entrepreneurship. The economic downturn has also played its part. Decentralization, downsizing, strategic alliances, mergers and the increasing demand for a flexible workforce have all contributed to a more uncertain climate which favours entrepreneurship's ascent (Henry, Hill and Leitch, 2005a). Organizations that have not previously been recognized as behaving entrepreneurially begin to do so in order to survive and succeed in increasingly competitive and financially constrained environments (Phan, Wright, Ucbasaran and Tan, 2009). Human resource management practices are perhaps one of the best levers for organisations wishing to create more entrepreneurial employees and managers (Morris and Jones, 1993; Hayton, 2005). The role of training in creating and sustaining more entrepreneurial firms is increasingly recognized (Morris and Jones, 1993; Hayton and Kelley, 2006; Schmelter, Mauer, Börsch and Brettel, 2010). Thus many firms are looking at ways to develop and train more entrepreneurial employees and managers. Of all the previously mentioned classification systems, perhaps Gorman et al's (1997) classification of 'existing owners and managers' would cover this audience type.

At an individual level, today's young people are particularly familiar with the 'entrepreneur as hero' discourse. They are bombarded with media images of 'male entrepreneurs' as 'dynamic wolfish charmers, supernatural gurus, successful skyrockets or community saviors and corrupters' (Nicholson and Anderson, 2005). Indeed in western society today, it is difficult to avoid the 'phantasmic category' of the entrepreneur (Jones and Spicer, 2005). It is perhaps no wonder then that in today's ever changing and globalized environment, entrepreneurship education and training are considered 'incredibly important' (Neck and Greene, 2011). Clearly, there is a *push* effect, with entrepreneurship increasingly taught via education and training as a solution to social and economic ills. These education and training programmes may take numerous forms e.g. a degree course in entrepreneurship at university level, an enterprise awareness programme for young people, government sponsored business creation training for the unemployed, immigrants or women. There is also an increasing pull towards entrepreneurship education as individuals are enraptured by the hero/crusader image and organizations are seduced by the promise of improved performance for entrepreneurial and innovative firms.

Theoretical Gaps

Clearly, EET is an increasingly important issue for individuals, societies, governments and organizations. Yet despite this, we believe that the current typologies fall short of explaining the diversity and complexity of EET. To the best of our knowledge, no classification on the basis of how entrepreneurship programmes are delivered (i.e. teaching medium, approach and/or method) exists. The underpinning pedagogy that constitutes entrepreneurship education comes in a variety of forms and institutional approaches (Gibb, 1996; Neck and Green, 2011; Pittaway and Cope, 2007). There is a common recognition that entrepreneurs are action oriented and much of their learning is experientially based (Rae and Carswell, 2000, 2001; Cope, 2005; Tracey and Phillips, 2007). Thus many writers advocate for a combination of planned and experiential learning (Fayolle, 2008; Kuratko, 2005; Neck and Greene, 2011). Other modes of education and training other than face-to-face, in-class teaching are possible (and practised), such as distance learning and mentoring, but diverse modes of delivery are not often explored in the literature. We are also not familiar with any study which has effectively addressed the breadth of content which can be delivered in EET. What contents may make up an entrepreneurship curriculum or training programme? How do programme contents and course design vary according to local, regional, national and international contexts? Given the multidisciplinary field of entrepreneurship, the content covered in most entrepreneurship courses is far reaching (Neck and Greene, 2011). Various authors propose necessary, skill-based content. Developing students' communication, creativity, critical thinking, leadership, problem solving and social networking skills are essential elements of entrepreneurship education (Rae, 1997). Entrepreneurship educators may also teach 'the soft stuff' such as living with uncertainty, opportunity identification, decision making, work-life balance (Neck and Greene, 2011) as well as learning from failure (Shepherd, 2004; Minniti and Bygrave, 2001; Cope, 2011). Yet again a more comprehensive typology of EET would be helpful to capture the diversity of material which could be used as the basis for entrepreneurship teaching.

One explanation for this lack of sufficient theorizing and typologies of EET lies in the partially legitimate (Katz, 2008) and peripheral (dare we say inferior?) status of entrepreneurship education as a research object. Many entrepreneurship education researchers are drawn to publishing in mainstream 'parent' journals (i.e. Psychology related journals) as opposed to Entrepreneurship journals. Indeed publishing in education-based journals could be seen as a healthy indicator of the entrepreneurship scholar's engagement with the core underpinning theoretical body of the subject (Béchard and Grégoire, 2005). However, consistently publishing entrepreneurship education-related research in other disciplinary reviews and journals may be in fact damaging to the cognitive legitimacy of entrepreneurship education (Katz, 2008). Thus, Katz (2008) advocates the importance of contributing to one's own theoretical field and journal base. Yet we argue that entrepreneurship research is not always open to research on entrepreneurship education. Indeed at the time of writing, one highly-ranked entrepreneurship journal had a notice on its website alerting authors to the fact that the review was 'not currently accepting' manuscripts in entrepreneurship education. In the subsequent section, we engage in a closer examination of entrepreneurship education research published in the highest-ranking entrepreneurship and education journals. We believe that those researchers who do publish in entrepreneurship journals are not sufficiently addressing the theoretical gaps in entrepreneurship education outlined above but are rather pursuing other lines of inquiry. In the following section, we detail our literature review approach and methodology and present five 'themes' which published papers often adhere to.

A LITERATURE REVIEW OF MAINSTREAM JOURNALS

Previous literature reviews (Gorman et al, 1997; Garavan and O'Cinneide, 1994; Henry, Hill and Leitch, 2005a and b; Pittaway and Cope, 2007) have predominantly focused on lower-ranked journals where entrepreneurship education publications more often find an outlet. Most of these literature reviews involved a ten- to 15-year time frame. We engaged in a literature review of seven mainstream journals to explore the issues that have preoccupied researchers in the field of entrepreneurship education over the last 25 years. In this review, we look at published research on entrepreneurship education from high-impact factor entrepreneurship and education journals from the period 1984–2011. The application of this larger time frame allows us to identify theoretical clusters on entrepreneurship education in the mainstream literature. Because it operates at the interface of many fields and disciplines, the literature on entrepreneurship education may be found in a variety of journals, both in and outside the usual sources associated with the entrepreneurship and management domain (Béchard and Grégoire, 2005). Clearly, engaging in a comprehensive literature review of a topic which straddles numerous theoretical fields and varying publications is an arduous task. Thus, before presenting the predominant thematic clusters we identified, we will briefly outline the methodology involved in the literature review to clarify our research limitations.

Literature Review Methodology

In order to unearth the wealth of publications produced in the area of entrepreneurship education, our literature review began from a cross-disciplinary stance by exploring both entrepreneurship and education-based journals. We selected five leading entrepreneurship journals – *Entrepreneurship Theory and Practice* (ET&P); *Journal of Business Venturing* (JBV); *Journal of Small Business Management* (JSBM); *International Small Business Journal* (ISBJ); *Entrepreneurship and Regional Development* (ERD) and two high-impact education reviews – *Academy of Management Learning and Education* (AoMLE) and *Journal of Management Education* (JME). We searched the selected entrepreneurship journal indexes for articles that contained 'education' as well as 'learn' or 'learning' in the abstracts and author supplied keywords. In this way, research addressing entrepreneurship more generally but which contained recommendations or implications for entrepreneurship education were included. We searched the education-based journal indexes for articles that contained some variation of the word 'entrepreneurship' (searched using key word = 'entrep*'). Article citations were then reviewed and, once we confirmed that they were empirical, theoretical or essay-based articles dealing with issues of learning and entrepreneurship, we recorded them in the article database. Book reviews, letters from the editor and case studies were systematically excluded. The initial citation database consisted of 229 articles. Once the database was established, for the purposes of this chapter's focus, we further classified articles according to the level of analysis and the population being studied. For example, under the banner of 'learning', articles address both firm and individual level learning. Articles dealing with organizational learning and studies which adopted a firm level of analysis were excluded from the analysis as in line with our educational focus we were interested in articles dealing with individual (as opposed to organizational) learning.

The final database included 86 articles from six selected journals for the period 1984–2011. (The journal *Entrepreneurship and Regional Development* was excluded on the basis that only four relevant articles were found using the 'learn*' and 'educat*' search terms. Additionally these four articles did not sit easily within the five themes we had identified as emerging themes from the other journals.) The two highest impact journals in Entrepreneurship are the JBV and ET&P. We derived the research 'themes' by beginning with the highest-impact journal which had the broader scope in terms of types of manuscripts sought and accepted: ET&P. A total of 27 articles were published in this journal from 1984 to 2011 on entrepreneurship education (from the reduced total sample of 86 across the six journals). ET&P published more education related articles than JBV. Four broad clusters of articles were identified which were used as the basis to classify the articles in the four other entrepreneurship journals. These themes were: state of play (30 articles); specific audiences and special needs (25 articles); entrepreneurial learning (21 articles) and evaluation and measures (22 articles). Each article was read and re-read and key words were noted in each article, i.e. evolution, growth, development of entrepreneurship education (for the 'state of play' theme) and attitude, intention, efficacy, potential (for the 'measurement and evaluation' theme) to help classify the research preoccupation. The emerging theme clusters proved appropriate. However it was necessary to add a fifth theme 'teaching methods and mediums', especially after the inclusion of the education-based journals. A breakdown of the stages in the literature review is presented in Table 15.1 below.

Literature Review Findings: Emergent Themes

The literature review process led us to identify five clusters of themes in the entrepreneurship education literature, namely:

(i)   state of play
(ii)   specific audiences and special needs
(iii)   entrepreneurial learning
(iv)   measurement and evaluation
(v)   teaching methodology and mediums

While some articles clearly belonged to one thematic classification, others cut across one or more themes. For example, Athayde's (2009) ET&P article outlined the design of an 'enterprise potential' measure in young people using attitudes toward characteristics associated with entrepreneurship. This study found that young black students were more

Table 15.1   Literature review methodology

Stage	Description
Stage 1	The researchers selected six leading entrepreneurship journals and two leading management education journals using the British Association of Business Schools (ABS) Ranking 2010; the Financial Times 45 Ranking 2010 and the Centre National de la Recherche Scientifique 2011 to identify highly ranked journals.
Stage 2	The citation indexes of the six entrepreneurship journals from 1991–2011 were systematically searched using the root term 'learn*'. The citation indexes of the two management education journals from the period 1991–2011 were systematically searched using the root term 'entrepre*'.
Stage 3	The data were 'cleaned' as book reviews, interviews and editorial notes were excluded. As were other articles which were not relevant to the research, i.e. some abstracts contained the word 'learn' but did not look at learning per se. A total 229 articles were saved and filed according to the journal source on a shared platform which both researchers had access to.
Stage 4	A database of all relevant article abstracts was created and additional information such as the article title, its author(s) details, the journal and the year of publication were recorded.
Stage 5	Abstracts and articles were then read and analysed. Two additional columns were added to the database to further classify articles according to 1) their level of analysis (individual, firm, regional, national) and 2) their key concepts and theoretical grounding.
Stage 6	For the purpose of this research project, the researchers focused on those articles which were concerned with individual learning. A total of 86 articles dealing with learning and entrepreneurship on an individual level were identified.
Stage 7	Closer reading of the 86 articles was then carried out to identify themes. Two of the research team noted keywords and ideas which occured with high frequency. These keywords and ideas were then regrouped and merged to constitute five over-arching themes: state of play; specific audiences; measuring; entrepreneurial learning; methods. The keywords associated with each can be found in Table 2.

positive about self-employment and displayed greater enterprise potential than either white or Asian pupils (Athayde, 2009). Thus we classify this article as cutting across two thematics, that of the 'measuring and evaluation' grouping and also the 'specific audiences' thematic grouping. This notion of overlapping themes is illustrated in Figure 15.1. The composite articles and thematic descriptors are presented in Table 15.2 (see below).

1.   State of play

The first theme we identified encompasses articles which describe the field of entrepreneurship education, its scope, evolution and extent of institutionalization. Over one-third of the articles found in this review adhere to this thematic. Such papers outline emerging structures in entrepreneurship education (Plaschka and Welsch, 1990), describe the field's chronological and intellectual trajectory (McMullan and Long, 1987; Katz, 2003) as well as identify obstacles and challenges for the future (i.e. Kuratko, 2005; Katz, 2003; Meyer, 2011). Many publications within this theme undertake literature reviews and/ or critically evaluate research in the field of EET thus far. Hills (1988), McMullan and

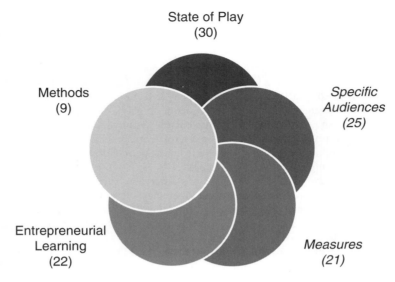

Figure 15.1   Five research themes

Long (1987) and Vesper (1982) for example have found that there is a lack of accepted paradigms or theories of EET. Numerous articles document the number, growth and types of courses, programme offerings, publications, endowed chairs, etc. (Vesper and McMullan, 1988; Katz, 1991; Kuratko, 2005) with some charting its development in specific geographical areas beyond the usual North American focus (i.e. Klandt, 2004). Extensive literature reviews have also been carried out resulting in elaborate thematic classifications (Pittaway and Cope, 2007; Béchard and Grégoire, 2005). Pittaway and Cope (2007) found a large majority of articles explore one of the following themes: the teaching of entrepreneurship, the role of management training for entrepreneurs, the role of the enterprising university and student entrepreneurship. They lament the lack of integration with theory from the fields of education, adult learning and management development. Interestingly, this is also the main crux of Béchard and Grégoire's (2005) article which groups the entrepreneurship education articles using theory from education science. Many authors concern themselves with the legitimacy and evolution of the field (Kuratko, 2005; Katz, 2003; Meyer, 2011) and are keen to set recommendations for how to proceed with entrepreneurship education in the 21st century. For some, it is the emphasis on theoretical development and institutional legitimacy that has relegated questions of knowledge transfer and education to a secondary place (Béchard and Grégoire, 2005) and prevents the advancement of entrepreneurship education as a field of teaching and research. Articles within this grouping are prescriptive in nature and address specific issues of course contents and curriculum design (Ray, 1990, Fiet, 2000b, Honig, 2004) as well as the role of academic centres and entrepreneurship faculty more generally (Zahra, Newey and Shaver, 2011). Johnson and Tilley (1999) take a pragmatic approach and discuss ways in which linkages between SMEs and higher educational institutions (HEIs) can be fostered to maximize learning and knowledge exchange. While higher-level educational institutions predominate the discussion, some articles (e.g. Anderson et al, 2009)

Table 15.2 Entrepreneurship education and training literature review, 1984–2011

Literature Theme	State of Play	Specific Audiences; Special Needs	Measurement and Evaluation	Entrepreneurial Learning	Methodology and Teaching Mediums
Theme Descriptor	Evolution and state of entrepreneurship education (EE); growth; issues of legitimacy and maturity; institutionalization of EE; curriculum design; prescriptions for programme contents and delivery	Audiences: ethnic minorities; females; corporate entrepreneurs; academic entrepreneurs and entrepreneurial universities; family businesses; social entrepreneurs; technology professionals Needs: emotion; growth; business planning; opportunity identification	Measuring entrepreneurial attitudes, skills and knowledge; self-efficacy; entrepreneurial potential; intention; programme effectiveness; impact of role models; opportunity identification	Defining and describing entrepreneurial learning (EL) – experiential learning; vicarious learning; transformative learning; critical events; cognitive scripts; heuristics; relational aspects; mobilizing and transforming symbolic, cultural, financial and human capital	Describing specific examples of ways of teaching entrepreneurship; games; simulations; commenting on mediums i.e. distance learning, IT
Journal Source (Entrepreneurship)	*Entrepreneurship Theory and Practice, Journal of Business Venturing, International Small Business Journal, Journal of Small Business Management*				
Representative Articles	Anderson et al (2009); Carsrud (1994); Curran and Stanworth (1989); Edelman and Yli-Renko (2010); Fiet (2000); Finkle and Deeds (2001); Gartner and Vesper (1994); Gorman,	Athayde (2009); Carsrud (1994); Hoy (2003); Jones, Macpherson and Woollard (2008); Honig (2001); Kaplan, George and Rimler (2000); Lee, Sohn and Ju (2010); Mann (1990); Menzies,	Athayde (2009); Curran and Stanworth (1989); Hindle and Cutting (2002); Hjorth (2011); Kaplan, George and Rimler (2000); Krueger, Reilly and Carsrud, (2000); McGee, Peterson,	Cope (2005); Corbett (2007) Corbett (2005); Corbett, Neck and DeTienne (2007); Cope (2011); DeClerc (2012); Dimov (2007); Edelman and Yli-Renko (2010); Groves, Vance and Choi (2011); Hjorth	Lee and Jones (2008); Pittaway, Rodriguez Falcon, Aiyegbayo and King (2011);

271

Table 15.2 (continued)

Literature Theme	State of Play	Specific Audiences; Special Needs	Measurement and Evaluation	Entrepreneurial Learning	Methodology and Teaching Mediums
Representative Articles	Hanlon and King (1997); Hills (1988); Hood and Young (1993); Johnston, Hamilton and Jing (2008); Katz (1991); Katz (2003); Kuratko (2005); Meyer (2011); McMullan and Long (1987); Neck and Greene (2011); Pittaway and Cope (2007); Plaschka and Welsch (1990); Ray (1990); Sexton and Bowman (1984); Sexton, Upton, Wacholtz and McDougall (1997); Vesper and McMullen (1988); Vesper and Gartner (1997)	Filion, Brenner and Elgie (2007); Mosey and Wright (2007); Sexton, Upton, Wacholtz and McDougall (1997); Shepherd, Covin and Kuratko (2009); Steier and Ward (2006); Thompson et al (2010); Walstad and Kourilsky (1998); Wilson, Kickul & Marlino (2007)	Mueller and Sequeira (2009); Mungai and Valamuri (2009); Peterman and Kennedy (2003); Scherer, Adams, Carley and Wiebe (1989); Sexton and Bowman (1984); Simon (2000); Souitaris, Zerbinati & Al-Laham (2007); Walstad and Kourilsky (1998); Wilson, Kickul and Marlino (2007); Thompson (2009)	(2011); Holcomb, Ireland, Holmes and Hitt (2009); Honig (2001); Levesque, Minniti and Shepherd (2009); Mann (1990); McGee, Peterson, Mueller and Sequeira (2009); Minniti and Bygrave (2001); Mosey and Wright (2007); Pittaway, Rodriguez Falcon, Aiyegbayo and King (2011); Politis (2005); Ravasi and Turati (2005); Karatas-Ozkan (2011); Karatas- Ozkan and Chell (2010)	

Journal Source (Education) *Academy of Management Learning and Education, Journal of Management Education*

Béchard and Grégoire (2005); Edelman, Manolova and Brush (2008); Hjorth (2003); Honig (2004); Klandt (2004); Zahra, Newey and Shaver (2011)	DeTienne and Chandler (2004); Honig (2004); Litzky, Godshalk and Walton-Bongers (2011); McCrea (2010); Mustar (2009); Shepherd (2004); Tracey and Phillips (2007); Thursby, Fuller and Thursby (2009); Munoz, Mosey and Binks (2011)	DeTienne and Chandler (2004); Florin, J., Karri, R. & Rossiter, N., (2007); Human, Clark and Baucus (2005); Shepherd (2004); Thursby, Fuller and Thursby (2009)	Kane (2011); Shepherd (2004)	DeTienne and Chandler (2004); Honig (2004); Shepherd (2004); Vega (2010); Wolfe (2004); Woods (2011); Munoz, Mosey and Binks (2011)
Total articles: 86				
30	25	21	22	9
% of total[1]				
35%	29%	24%	26%	10%

Note: [1] Some of the articles addressed more than one of the themes outlined i.e. some articles were counted more than once in the % of total column hence explaining why the five columns % total does not add up to 100%

address younger secondary (high school) populations. Interestingly, some of the older articles (such as Ray, 1990; Hills, 1988; Plaschka and Welsch, 1990) are still often cited in the more recent 'state of play' articles showing that concerns such as 'broadening student horizons' (Ray, 1990) remain a significant concern for contemporary entrepreneurship educators (Munoz et al., 2011; Neck and Greene, 2011).

Authors present varying entrepreneurial competencies, behaviours, attributes and skills which are an integral part of an entrepreneurship education and demonstrate how they can be fostered in the classroom. Much emphasis is placed on creativity and innovation (Plaschka and Welsch, 1990; Ray, 1990). Education for creativity should force students to deal with ambiguity and complexity (McMullan and Long, 1987). In the 1990s, the 'standard' entrepreneurship course included venture plan writing, speakers, readings, and cases (Gartner and Vesper, 1994). Despite significant continued usage of business planning in entrepreneurship courses (Solomon, 2007), change is called for and more representative contingent planning situations which account for the unpredictable aspect of entrepreneurship are advocated (Honig, 2004; Meyer, 2011; Neck and Greene, 2011). Experiential and self-directed approaches to competency development for adult entrepreneurs are strongly advocated (Bird, 2002). However, this emphasis on competency development and active learning should not mean the exclusion of theory (Fiet, 2000a). More recently, Neck and Greene (2011) call for a re-thinking of the way in which we teach entrepreneurship. Students should be given the opportunity to actively experience as well as 'practice' entrepreneurship. They should engage in serious games and simulations as well as design thinking and reflective practice (Neck and Greene, 2011).

2.   Specific audiences and special needs

Another prevalent thematic which we identified encompassed articles covering specific audiences of entrepreneurship education. In the sample, 29 per cent of the articles dealt with issues of particular interest to one particular group of entrepreneurs. These groups are based on ethnicity, gender, race and organization type (family, university or social). We also identified a small number of studies that address particular learning needs in entrepreneurship education and training, i.e. emotion; growth; business planning; and opportunity identification. As previously outlined, despite the significant tendency of policy makers to deliver EET on a tailored basis, research to date does not provide a classification of offerings based on 'who' the training and education is directed at. In light of this, we provide a breakdown here of the varying populations and to which extent they have been addressed. Family business, social enterprise training and specific learning needs (i.e. opportunity identification) emerge as those areas where policy makers do not offer specified training. Indeed setting aside their tertiary education focus, multilateral organizations such as the OECD, the EU and WEF all appear to target under-privileged sections of society in entrepreneurship training provision. Table 15.3 below presents a breakdown of these findings.

Researchers concerned with racial issues and ethnic minorities investigated the relationship between race and perceptions of entrepreneurship education programs. Differences were found to exist between Black and Asian students' perceptions of entrepreneurship training and entrepreneurial potential in both the US and the UK (Athayde, 2009; Walstad and Kourilsky, 1998). The issue of the different learning strategies adopted by managers and entrapreneurs was first tackled by Honig (2001). Shepherd,

Table 15.3   Special audiences

Focus	Research Studies	No. of Articles	Journal Source
Ethnic Minorities	Athayde (2009); Mann (1990); Menzies, Filion, Brenner and Elgie (2007); Thompson et al (2010); Walstad and Kourilsky (1998)	5	ET&P (2) JSBM (2) ISBJ (1)
Family Business	Carsrud (1994); Hoy (2003); Kaplan, George and Rimmler (2000); Steier and Ward (2006)	4	ET&P (4)
Corporate Entrepreneurship	Honig (2001); Howell, Shea and Higgins (2005); Shepherd, Covin and Kuratko (2009)	3	JBV (2) ET&P
Entrepreneurship in Universities	Jones, Macpherson and Woolard (2008); Mosey and Wright (2007)	2	ISBJ ET&P
Gender	Lee, Sohn and Ju (2010); Wilson, Kickul and Marlin(2007)	2	JSBM ET&P
Social Entrepreneurship	Litzky, Godstalk and Walton-Bongers (2011); McCrea (2010); Tracey and Phillips (2007)	3	JME (2) AoML&E
Technology Education	Mustar (2009); Thursby, Fuller and Thursby (2009)	2	AoML&E
Specific learning needs	DeTienne and Chandler (2004); Munoz, Mosey and Banks (2011); Sexton, Upton, Wacholtz and McDougall (1997); Shepherd (2004)	4	JBV (1) AoML&E (3)

Covin and Kuratko (2009) look at the issue of failure in corporate venturing and theorize as to how the organization can provide support for coping self-efficacy in managers. Howell, Shea and Higgins (2005) are more concerned with the validation of a scale of 'champion behaviors' which they feel can be used to help managers develop and nurture specific behaviours necessary for corporate entrepreneurship. The issue of gender and self-efficacy was tackled by Wilson et al (2007), with the effects of entrepreneurship education on entrepreneurial self-efficacy proving stronger for women than for men, pointing towards the importance of self-efficacy as a training objective for would-be women entrepreneurs. However, a recent article by Lee et al. (2010) found that Korean women entrepreneurs were indifferent to the scale of support, training and gender-sensitive policies currently employed in Korea.

Research articles dealing with the importance of entrepreneurship education in technical and engineering based education are also present. Two studies (Mustar, 2009; Thursby, Fuller and Thursby, (2009) present particular incidences of an approach to integrating entrepreneurial elements to engineering and technology-based curricula and cite the challenges and difficulties involved. Researchers also address some specific learning needs which they feel are lacking in curricula. Educators should not neglect the role that emotion plays in the entrepreneurial process and thus focus on how students 'feel' rather than on how, or what, they 'think' (Shepherd, 2004). Questions have also been posed regarding the over-usage of business planning in the entrepreneurship educa-tion domain (Honig, 2004; Meyer, 2011) as well as the neglect of the learning needs of growth-oriented entrepreneurs (Sexton et al, 1998).

3.   Entrepreneurial learning

One thematic which has arisen in the last decade is the notion of entrepreneurial learn-ing. According to Minniti and Bygrave (2001) 'a theory of entrepreneurship needs a theory of learning' (p. 7). While entrepreneurial learning articles are mostly concerned with how entrepreneurs learn, they also often contained suggestions for entrepreneur-ship educators dealing with both students in formal settings and training participants such as managers or would-be entrepreneurs. Just over a quarter of the articles that we found fell in to this thematic category. One common element in these studies is the importance attached to the notion of opportunity identification and development (Cope, 2005; Corbett, 2005; Corbett et al., 2007; Krueger et al., 2000; Dimov, 2005; Politis, 2005). Increasingly opportunity identification is viewed as a teachable facet of entrepre-neurship (Munoz, Mosey and Binks, 2011).

There is general consensus on the view that entrepreneurial learning is an experien-tial process (Politis, 2005; Corbett, 2005). Researchers call for more 'hands on experi-ence', 'active learning', 'learning by doing' and 'real world insights' (McMullan and Long, 1987; Gibb, 1993; Gartner and Vesper, 1994), and this remains very much in vogue. Essentially, learner-centred approaches should take precedence (Gibb, 1993). Entrepreneurial learning is also viewed as a dynamic process (Cope, 2005). Indeed the development of entrepreneurial knowledge in an individual is a slow and incremental process which takes place over an individual's lifetime (Politis, 2005). Entrepreneurial learning does not just occur at the venture creation stage, in fact it occurs before, after and during (Cope, 2005; Politis, 2005). It involves building different types of capital (symbolic, social, economic, and cultural) throughout the entrepreneurial process and the transformation of these capitals along the way (Karataş-Özkan and Chell, 2010). The very personal nature of this learning is also evident as individuals draw on varied life experiences, learning asymmetries and 'stocks of knowledge' as they engage in entrepreneurial acts (Corbett, 2005; Cope, 2005; Politis, 2005; Minniti and Bygrave, 2001). Recent work has pointed to the relational nature of entrepreneurial learning – entrepreneurs learn and evolve from individual, team, firm and network interaction and engagement (Karataş-Özkan, 2011).

4.   Measurement and evaluation

In this literature review 24 per cent of the articles which emerged deal with issues of measurement and evaluation. Given that there is an increase in the provision of entre-preneurship education, there is a need for investigation into the 'value-added' of train-ing and support structures for entrepreneurs (De Faoite et al, 2003). Entrepreneurship education programmes may positively influence students' attitudes towards entrepre-neurship and their career intentions (Souitaris et al, 2007; Krueger, Reilly and Carsrud, 2000; Thompson, 2009). EEP participation may also impact upon younger students' 'enterprise potential' (Athayde, 2009) and emotionally 'inspire' them (Souitaris et al, 2007). Entrepreneurship education and training programmes may change student per-ceptions of start-up feasibility or desirability (Peterman and Kennedy, 2003) as well as alter a student's entrepreneurial self-efficacy or their belief in their ability to be a successful entrepreneur (Wilson, Kickul and Marlino, 2007; McGee et al, 2009; Peterman and Kennedy, 2003). Recent work focuses largely on the pre-entrepreneurial event and integrates Ajzen's (1991) attitude and behavior theory, alongside Bandura's (1986) self-efficacy and social learning theory (Peterman and Kennedy, 2003). Many of the above take the individual as their targeted level of analysis. However these studies are often criticized for their lack of methodological rigour (Souitaris et al, 2007) and they predominantly sample third-level students in a university setting. Unanswered questions remain as how to effectively evaluate entrepreneurship education in a timely and robust fashion (Pittaway and Cope, 2007). Beyond entrepreneurial intentions, few empirical findings exist to assist in the pedagogical design of contemporary entrepreneurship education (Honig, 2004).

Some studies have addressed the broader macro-level effect of entrepreneurship training and support programmes and their impact on economic growth. Training and assistance has been found to improve ventures' expected rates of survival, growth, and innovation (Chrisman and McMullan, 2002; 2004) as well as general community development, knowledge and job creation (McMullan et al, 1986; McMullan and Long, 1987). According to McMullan and Long (1987), the success of entrepreneurship programmes should be measured by their economic impact. Evaluators need to consider questions like: How many companies were created? How many jobs were created? What kinds of companies emerged? What kinds of jobs? How fast do these companies grow? Do they compete internationally? Do they contribute to the local economy? Such practical questions which Long and McMullen posed in the late 1980s remain largely untackled by researchers in entrepreneurship education today. Essentially they view entrepreneurship in terms of the economic benefit it brings. Questions may also be posed regarding 'softer' or more human based outcomes.

5. Methodology and teaching mediums

Only 10 per cent of the articles from this literature review dealt with teaching methodologies or concrete strategies for educators in the entrepreneurship domain. Some researchers address the issue of information technology and how it can be used in entrepreneurship education and training while Pittaway et al (2011) look at how entrepreneurship clubs and societies can play a role in students' entrepreneurial learning. DeTienne and Chandler (2004) and Munoz et al. (2011) address opportunity development capabilities and promote the use of creativity exercises and integrative learning. Honig (2004) puts forward a notion of contingent planning as opposed to formal business planning which has become a staple feature of many entrepreneurship teaching efforts (Meyer, 2011; Solomon, 2007) and Shepherd (2004) draws on psychotherapy to illustrate the benefits of grief management. These studies remain sparse however and are generally applied in student settings. Existing theories from educational science could perhaps assist in the challenge to inform on the questions of 'what' to teach and 'how' to convey it. However, those articles that do attempt to integrate learning theories or work from the education sciences are few and far between (notable exceptions include Bird, 2002; Béchard and Grégoire, 2005). Kolb's (1984) experiential learning remains the most commonly incorporated theory but real 'how-to' theorizing is lacking. Indeed to find these types of articles, one needs to look beyond the journals searched in this literature review to more lower-ranked or practitioner-aimed articles. This perhaps perpetuates the claim that entrepreneurship education researchers are in danger of 'preaching to the converted' in the absence of reflecting upon why it all matters (Hindle, 2007).

DISCUSSION: WHAT WE NEED TO KNOW

The five themes evoked in the literature review – state of play; specific audiences and special needs; measurement and evaluation; entrepreneurial learning and teaching methodologies – are not discrete and independent conceptual areas. Many articles cut across more than one thematic. We will now take another look at these thematic groupings, and drawing on our precedent discussion, interrogate our findings to see what the implications are for future research. To help do so, we use an overarching unifying framework – a generic teaching model in entrepreneurship education (Fayolle and Gailly, 2008). The concept of 'teaching model' is well known in education science (see for instance Anderson, 1995 or Joyce and Weil, 1996) but rarely used in the entrepreneurship field, where there is no common framework or agreed good practices regarding how to teach or educate. Based on Legendre (1993) a teaching model is 'the representation of a certain type of setting designed to deal with a pedagogical situation in function of particular goals and objectives, which integrates a theoretical framework justifying this design and giving it an exemplary character'. This framework is helpful here in that the ontological and educational dimensions it outlines (see Figure 15.2) encompass the five themes that emerged throughout our data analysis. The ontological or philosophical level of the teaching model includes the 'state of the play' findings, but also touches on some key points which we identified in our 'Definitional issues' section. The five educational or didactical level dimensions of the teaching model correspond to the four other themes. The 'Why' didactic dimension does not correspond to a unique theme, but spans the 'Specific audiences and Special needs' and 'Measurement and evaluation' themes. The 'What' dimension corresponds with the 'Entrepreneurial learning' and the 'State of play' themes. We will now discuss both levels of the teaching model in more detail.

Ontological, Definitional and Methodological Issues in Entrepreneurship Education

As highlighted by a number of studies, there is a great level of variation in EET programme contents and teaching strategies (Gorman et al., 1997; Fiet, 2000a and b; Fayolle and Gailly, 2008). Also, operational definitions of enterprise and entrepreneurship vary considerably between higher education institutions (Pittaway and Cope, 2007). In our literature review, we show that some classifications of EET do exist (Jamieson, 1984 in Henry et al, Garavan and O'Cinneide, 1994; Gorman et al., 1997). But, these classifications are old and not the results of conceptual and empirical research aimed at producing robust typologies and taxonomies in the field of entrepreneurship education. The field of entrepreneurship is not homogeneous (Gartner, 1985) but rather context-based (Welter, 2010; Zahra and Wright, 2011) and this implies, among other things, this level of diversity within EET programmes and courses. In our first section, by drawing on the OECD, EU and GEM studies (among others), we demonstrated how current training

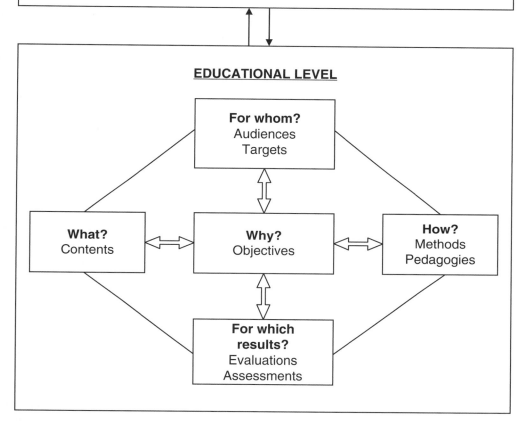

Figure 15.2   A generic teaching model in entrepreneurship education

programme audiences could be further broken down. By doing so, we highlighted how the existing classifications failed to account for the complexity of current educational offerings. We need, as researchers and educators, useful and relevant systems of classification, namely typologies or taxonomies to offer comprehensive views of such diversity in entrepreneurship education. From such typologies, it would be possible to design and experiment specific and properly contextualized teaching models (see, as an example, Béchard and Grégoire, 2007) which are well-adapted to the different types of EET identified from typological and/or taxonomical research. By doing so, we address part of a concern raised by, among others, Béchard and Grégoire (2005), Pittaway and Cope (2007) and Fayolle and Gailly (2008) who underline the lack of integration with theories, concepts and models from the field of education.

As stated by Pittaway and Cope (2007), there are various definitions of entrepreneurship that have been proposed in the context of entrepreneurship education, in various settings, used by various categories of actors. This is not per se an issue, as long as one of those definitions is explicitly selected and considered when designing an entrepreneurship education program. Hindle (2007), for example, proposes to articulate the definition of entrepreneurship education around that of the research object. In this light, if one defines the field of entrepreneurship as the 'examination of how, by whom, and with what effects, opportunities to create future goods and services are discovered, evaluated and exploited' (Shane and Venkataraman, 2000: 120) then entrepreneurship education should be defined as 'knowledge transfer regarding how, by whom, and with what effects, opportunities to create future goods and services are discovered, evaluated and exploited' (Hindle, 2007). A major concern is therefore more the absence of a precise definition of entrepreneurship as a teaching field than the significant number of existing definitions. Consequently, each entrepreneurship education program should be based on a clear conception of entrepreneurship leading to a non-ambiguous definition of entrepreneurship education.

Surprisingly enough, we did not find articles in our review, addressing issues in relation to the philosophical postures in EET. Even if numerous articles claim the importance of active, experiential, 'learning by doing', 'real-world', self-directed or reflective pedagogies (McMullan and Long, 1987; Gibb, 1993; Gartner and Vesper, 1994; Bird, 2002; Honig, 2004; Corbett, 2005; Politis, 2005; Meyer, 2011; Neck and Greene, 2011), there is no research focusing on ontological and epistemological issues in entrepreneurship education. What place and role for positivist, interpretivist and critical post-modern philosophical paradigms in EET? Understanding the educational consequences of such postures through research and clarifying their philosophical positions seems essential for entrepreneurship educators because as underlined by Merriam (1982: 90–91):

> Philosophy contributes to professionalism. Having a philosophic orientation separates the professional educator from the paraprofessional in that professionals are aware of what they are doing and why they are doing it. A philosophy offers goals, values and attitudes to strive for. It thus can be motivating, inspiring, energizing to the practitioner.

The philosophical paradigms which EET researchers adhere to have implications as to their choice of methodology. There are persistent calls for more rigorous evaluation of EET programmes (Meyer, 2011), reflecting a strong positivist leaning in entrepreneurship education research. Researchers have suggested that education and training for entrepreneurship should positively impact entrepreneurial activity by enhancing instrumental skills required to start-up and grow a business (Honig, 2004). Education and training in entrepreneurship should also enhance individual's cognitive ability to recognize and assess entrepreneurial opportunities (DeTienne and Chandler, 2004). It should also affect their cultural attitudes and behavioural dispositions (Peterman and Kennedy, 2003). However, demonstrating these effects is an oft-cited challenge (Bosma et al, 2009). In a thought-provoking article on opportunity identification, Munoz et al. (2011) observe how students find it difficult to articulate how their performance has changed (following an educational experience) but that radical shifts in their visual representations of entrepreneurship were evident by analysing students' causal maps. The qualitative study engaged in by these authors – consisting of semi-structured interviews,

Table 15.4   Teaching model framework and research themes

Questions:	Ontological	Educational:				
Themes:		What?	Why?	Who?	How?	Results?
State of Play	X	X				
Special Audiences			X	X		
Teaching Methods					X	
Measurement			X			X
E'prnl Learning		X			X	

an opportunity assessment and pictorial representations – marks a refreshing change from the standardized survey type instruments that predominate in evaluation research in entrepreneurship education.

Educational Level Questions in Entrepreneurship Education

Our findings reveal an interesting focus on specific audiences in EET. Research in entrepreneurship education has repeatedly tried to deal with issues in relation to particular groups of students and entrepreneurs based on field of study, ethnicity, gender, race and age. The variety of audiences of entrepreneurship education programmes includes students with various socio-demographic characteristics and various levels of involvement and aspirations in the entrepreneurial process. It represents incontestably a source of difficult questions and raises problems regarding the design and implementation of entrepreneurship education. Educators – particularly in the design phase – have to understand their audience and gather knowledge regarding the general psychological characteristics, the background and the social environment of the participants (Fayolle and Gailly, 2008). So research questions could turn around the ways by which, combining the objectives, contents and teaching methods, the needs and the specificities of each particular audience could be better addressed. Further research could probe the role and the impact of contextual and/or situational factors on the design and the teaching strategy of EET for disadvantaged or under-represented groups (e.g. unemployed, immigrants, seniors).

Our literature review reveals the growing importance (particularly in the last decade) of the notion of entrepreneurial learning – with an explicit emphasis on opportunity identification and development processes (Cope, 2005; Corbett, 2005: Corbett et al., 2007; Dimov, 2005; Politis, 2005). Interestingly this perspective doesn't leave much room for constructionist or views of opportunity (Dimov, 2007). The idea that individuals engage in a subjective perception of opportunities (Edelman and Yli-Renko (2010)) rather than search for existing opportunities that are already 'out there' is an area of increasing debate in the entrepreneurship literature as a whole (Alvarez and Barney, 2007) but does not yet seem to have found its way into entrepreneurship education research despite its strong implications for the learning process. The prevailing conception of entrepreneurial learning is not criticized or contrasted with others. Even if opportunity identification (or construction) is seen as a teachable facet of entrepreneurship (Munoz et al., 2011), we could argue that it alone does not define entrepreneurial learning. One interesting avenue for development could be centred on the relational aspects of entrepreneurial learning (Karataş-Özkan, 2011) and how (or if) they can be further developed and nurtured in the classroom.

Edelman, Manolova and Brush (2008) demonstrate the existing gap between the practices of nascent entrepreneurs and the textbook prescriptions for success. Additionally, Sarasvathy (2001), with her theory of effectuation, brings a totally different view on how entrepreneurs think and act entrepreneurially. Instead of thinking about pre-prepared shopping lists and recipes, we can also visualize contingency plans and impromptu meals based on what the kitchen cupboard holds. Finally, some of the particular learning needs which have been identified through our literature review, such as dealing with emotion or learning from failure, may not be compatible with a conception of entrepreneurial learning centred on opportunity identification and development processes. We feel that study is needed to further address the implications of research on entrepreneurial learning for entrepreneurship education. Further questioning is also needed concerning the notion of entrepreneurial competences (Man et al., 2002; Baron and Markman, 2003; Baron and Tang, 2009). How can research be more helpful in improving our understanding of the concepts of entrepreneurial learning and entrepreneurial competences? How can educators enable entrepreneurial learning and entrepreneurial competences in the classrooms and outside?

Borrowing ideas from Sarasvathy (2001) on the empirical study she did to elaborate the theory of effectuation, research issues could address key problems experienced by entrepreneurs in a range of situations and contexts in order to understand the ways, the strategies and the competences they are using to solve them. But this kind of research, based on experiential entrepreneurial learning, raises a new concern and so opens the door for new research about the pedagogical transferability of knowledge produced by studying true entrepreneurs in the real life, to the classroom and the students through educational processes.

Concerning the evaluation and measurement of EET, our findings clearly indicate that little research exists in this area. Several researchers have underlined a deep lack of studies and research regarding the outcomes and effectiveness of entrepreneurship education (Garavan and O'Cinneide, 1994; Hindle and Cutting, 2002; Honig, 2004; Souitaris et al., 2007). The issues and challenges regarding the assessment of entrepreneurship education programs relates on one hand to the selection of evaluation criteria and on the other hand to their effective measurement. We have here a very good example of the usefulness of education research for our field of entrepreneurship. We know from education sciences that at least six general approaches to educational evaluation can be identified: goal-based evaluation; goal-free evaluation; responsive evaluation: systems evaluation: professional review and quasi-legal (Eseryel, 2002). Among these six, goal-based and systems-based approaches are predominantly used in the evaluation of training (Phillips, 1991). For the former, the framework of Kirkpatrick (1959) remains the most influential and for the latter, several models can be used such as the Context, Input, Process, Product model (Worthen and Sanders, 1987), the Training Validation System model (Fitz-Enz, 1994) and the Input, Process, Output, Outcome model (Bushnell, 1990). Entrepreneurship education researchers could find in the field of education and training evaluation further inspiration, concepts and frameworks useful for their research. Other research could be aimed at throwing some light on why – among the little research on entrepreneurship education which uses as a dependant variable entrepreneurial intention or entrepreneurial motivation – we observe such contradictory results (Peterman and Kennedy, 2004; Souitaris et al., 2007; Oosterbeek et al., 2010). We also call for the innovative use of research methodologies which open up new possibilities and findings, such as that of Munoz et al (2011) and their 'pictorial representations' which provided a refreshing change to the dominant, survey-based research on entrepreneurship outcomes.

Finally, concerning the methods and pedagogies dimension, our findings show some interest by both researchers and educators. The focus is clearly on active pedagogies, but little evidence is brought on, for example, the adequacy between methods and audience specificities, between methods and the contents or on studies trying to compare the efficacy/efficiency of different teaching methods for the same group of students and participants or the same kind of objectives. Also, researchers could assess the appropriateness of using internet-based and computer-based technologies or using distance learning as a main vehicle to teach entrepreneurship. Other key challenges appear, in relation to the methods and pedagogies in entrepreneurship education. How should we teach softskills? How should we teach for an entrepreneurial mind or entrepreneurial thinking (Carsrud and Brännback, 2009)? How should we teach entrepreneurial action (Frese, 2010)? How should we teach entrepreneurial method or design thinking (Sarasvathy and Venkataraman, 2011; Neck and Greene, 2011)? How should we teach effectuation (Sarasvathy, 2001)?

CONCLUSION

Research in the area of entrepreneurship education lacks legitimacy and sufficient theorizing. There is a need for taxonomies or typologies of education and training in this area in order to help us more fully understand existing education and training offerings in entrepreneurship. In this research we have tried to make a first step toward a state of the art of knowledge in entrepreneurship education over a 25-year-period literature review based on the most influential scientific journals in the field of entrepreneurship and education. In a second step, by discussing our findings, we elaborated research issues and orientations about what we need to know to improve our practices. In doing so, we have developed a strong conviction for the need to create and develop a virtuous circle aimed at sharing knowledge and including all the different stakeholders in entrepreneurship education: researchers, educators, learners and policy makers. Researchers need to collaborate with educators and policy makers to identify the most useful research issues; educators need to strongly interact with learners to improve the design of their courses; and policy makers need to collaborate with researchers and educators to share and discuss to which extent their needs are achieved. We are fully convinced that counter to Edelman et al's (2004) findings (a huge gap between practice and research/education), the future of entrepreneurship education is strongly dependant on such collaborative partnerships.

REFERENCES

Ajzen, I. (1991), 'The theory of planned behaviour', *Organizational Behaviour and Human Decision Processes*, **50**, 179–211.

Allen, I.E., Elam, A. Langowitz, N & Dean, M. (2008). *Global Entrepreneurship Monitor*. 2007 Report on women and entrepreneurship. Babson College, Massachusetts.

Alvarez, S. A., and Barney, J. B. (2007), 'Discovery and creation: alternative theories of entrepreneurial action', *Strategic Entrepreneurship Journal*, **1**(1–2), 11–26.

Anderson, L. W. (1995), *International Encyclopaedia of Teaching and Teacher Education*, 2nd ed., Oxford, UK: Pergamon Press.

Anderson, A., Drakopoulou Dodd, S., and Jack, S. (2009), 'Aggressors; Winners; victims and outsiders', *International Small Business Journal*, **27**(1), 126–36.

Athayde, R. (2009), 'Measuring enterprise potential in young people', *Entrepreneurship: Theory and Practice*, **33**(2), 481–500.

Bandura, A. (1986), *Social Foundations of Thought and Action: A Social Cognitive Perspective*, Englewood Cliffs, NJ: Prentice Hall.

Baron A. R. and Markman G. D. (2003), 'Beyond social capital: The role of entrepreneurs' social competence in their financial success', *Journal of Business Venturing*, **18**, 41–60.

Baron A. R. and Tang J. (2009), 'Entrepreneurs' social skills and new venture performance: mediating mechanisms and cultural generality', *Journal of Management*, **35**, (2), 282–306.

Béchard, J. P. and Grégoire, D. (2005), 'Entrepreneurship education research revisited: The case of higher education', *Academy of Management Learning and Education*, **4**(1): 22–43.

Béchard, J. P., Grégoire, D. (2007), 'Archetypes of pedagogical innovation for entrepreneurship education: model and illustrations', in *Handbook of Research in Entrepreneurship Education*, vol. 1 (Fayolle, A., ed.), Cheltenham (UK): Edward Elgar Publishing.

Bird, B. (2002), 'Learning entrepreneurial competencies: The self-directed learning approach', *International Journal of Entrepreneurship Education*, **1**: 203–27.

Block J. and Wagner M. (2010). Necessity and Opportunity Entrepreneurs in Germany: Characteristics and Earnings Differentials. *Schmalenbach Business Review*, **62**:15474.

Bosma, N., Acs, Z., Autio, E., Coduras, A and Levie, J. (2009), *Global Entrepreneurship Monitor, 2008 Executive Report*, Global Entrepreneurship Research Consortium (GERA).

Bushnell, D. S. (1990), 'Input, process, output: a model for evaluating training', *Training and Development Journal*, **44**(7), 41–3.

Byrne J. and Fayolle A. (2012). 'Necessity Entrepreneurship and the Gender Dimension: Implications for Management and Entrepreneurship Educators'. Conference paper presented at Academy of Management Conference, Boston, USA, August 2012.

Caliendo, M. and Kritikos, A. S. (2010), 'Start-ups by the unemployed: characteristics, survival and direct employment effects', *Small Business Economics*, **35**:71–92.

Carsrud, A. L. (1994), 'Meanderings of a resurrected psychologist or, lessons learned in creating a family business program', *Entrepreneurship: Theory and Practice*, **19**(1), 44–67.

Carsrud, A. L. and Brännback M. (2009), *Understanding the Entrepreneurial Mind*, New York: Springer Science and Business Media.

Chrisman, J. J., and McMullan, W. E. (2004), 'Outsider assistance as a knowledge resource for new venture survival', *Journal of Small Business Management*, **4**(2), 229–44.

Chrisman, J. J., and McMullan, W. E. (2002), 'Some additional comments on the sources and measurement of the benefits of small business assistance programs', *Journal of Small Business Management*, **40**(1), 43–50.

Cope, J. (2005), 'Toward a dynamic learning perspective of entrepreneurship', *Entrepreneurship: Theory and Practice*, **29**(4), 373–97.

Cope, J. (2011), 'Entrepreneurial learning from failure: An interpretative phenomenological analysis'. *Journal of Business Venturing*, **26**(6): 604–23.

Corbett, A. C. (2005), 'Experiential learning within the process of opportunity identification and exploitation', *Entrepreneurship: Theory and Practice*, **29**(4), 473–91.

Corbett, A. C., Neck, H. M., and DeTienne, D. R. (2007), 'How corporate entrepreneurs learn from fledgling innovation initiatives: cognition and the development of a termination script', *Entrepreneurship: Theory and Practice*, **31**(6), 829–52.

Delmar F. and Homquist C. (2003), 'Women Entrepreneurship: Issues and Policies', Paper commissioned by OECD for the Budapest Workshop on Entrepreneurship in a Global Economy: Strategic Issues and Policies, 8–10 September 2003.

De Clercq, D and Honig, B. (2011), 'Entrepreneurship as an integrating mechanism for disadvantaged persons'. Entrepreneurship and Regional Development, **23**(5–6): 353–72.

De Faoite, D., Henry, C., Johnston, K., van der Sijde, P. (2004), 'Entrepreneurs' attitudes to training and support initiatives: Evidence from Ireland and the Netherlands', *Journal of Small Business and Enterprise Development*, **11**(4), 440–8.

DeTienne D. and Chandler G. (2004), 'Opportunity Identification and its role in the entrepreneurial classroom: A pedagogical approach and empirical test,' *Academy of Management Learning and Education*, **3**, 242–57.

Dimov, D. (2007), 'From opportunity insight to opportunity intention: The importance of person-situation learning match', *Entrepreneurship: Theory and Practice*, **31**(4), 561–83.

Edelman, L. and Yli-Renko, H. (2010), 'The impact of environment and entrepreneurial perceptions on venture-creation efforts: Bridging the discovery and creation views of entrepreneurship,' *Entrepreneurship: Theory and Practice*, **34** 833–56.

Edelman L., Manolova T. and Brush C., (2008), 'Entrepreneurship education: Correspondence between practices of nascent entrepreneurs and textbook prescriptions for success', *Academy of Management Learning and Education*, **7**(1), 56–70.

Eseryel, D., (2002), 'Approaches to evaluation of training: Theory and practice', *Educational Technology & Society*, **5**(2), 93–8.

Evans, D. and Leighton L., (1990), 'Small business formation by unemployed and employed workers', *Small Business Economics*, **2**(4), 319–30.

Fairlie, R. (2005), 'Entrepreneurship and earnings among young adults from disadvantaged families,' *Small Business Economics*, **25**, 223–36.

Fayolle Alain (2008). Entrepreneurship education at a crossroads: Towards a more mature teaching field. *Journal of Enterprising Culture*, 16 (4): 325–337.

Fayolle, A. (2010), 'Nécessité et opportunité: les 'attracteurs étranges' de l'entrepreneuriat,' *Revue Pour*, **20**(4), 33–38.

Fayolle, A. and Gailly B. (2008), 'From craft to science: Teaching models and learning processes in entrepreneurship education,' *Journal of European Industrial Training*, **32**(7), 569–93.

Fiet, J. O. (2000a), 'The theoretical side of teaching entrepreneurship', *Journal of Business Venturing*, **16** (1), 1–24.

Fiet, J. O. (2000b), 'The pedagogical side of entrepreneurship theory', *Journal of Business Venturing*, **16** (1), 101–17.

Fitz-Enz, J. (1994), 'Yes. . .you can weigh training's value', *Training*, **31**(70, 54–8.

Frese, M. (2010), 'Entrepreneurial actions: An action theory approach', in De Cremer D., van Dick R. and Murnighan J.K. (Eds.), *Social Psychology and Organizations*, Routledge.

Garavan, T. N. and O'Cinneide, B. (1994), 'Entrepreneurship education and training programmes: A review and evaluation – Part 1', *Journal of European Industrial Training*, **18**(8), 3–12.

Gartner, W. B. (1985), 'A conceptual framework for describing the phenomenon of new venture creation', *Academy of Management Review*, **10**(4), 696–706.

Gartner W.B. and Vesper K., (1994), 'Experiments in Entrepreneurship: Education Successes and Failures', *Journal of Business Venturing*, **9**: 179–87.

Gibb, A. A., (1993), 'The enterprise culture and education. Understanding enterprise education and its links with small business, entrepreneurship and wider educational goals', *International Small Business Journal*, **11**(30, 11–37.

Gibb, A. A., (1996), 'Entrepreneurship and small business management: can we afford to neglect them in the twenty-first century business school?' *British Journal of Management*, **7**(4), 309–24.

Gibb A., Haskins G. and Robertson I. (2009), 'Leading the Entrepreneurial University: Meeting the entrepreneurial development needs of higher education institutions', NGCE, Said Business School, Oxford, UK.

Gorman, G., Hanlon, D., and King W. (1997), 'Some research perspectives on entrepreneurial education, enterprise education, and education for small business management: A ten year review', *International Small Business Journal*, **15**(3), 56–77.

Grove-White, R. (2009). 'Moving Up: Immigrants into Entrepreneurship', Project e-zine Issue 1, September Available at http://eu-imminent.com/en/?page_id=46.

Guzy, M. (2006), *Nurturing Immigrant Entrepreneurship: A handbook for microcredit and business support*, European Microfinance Network, December 2006, Paris.

Harding, R. and Bosma, N. (2006). 'Global Entrepreneurship Monitor 2006 Results', Babson College and London Business School. GEM Executive Reports. Available at http://www.gemconsortium.org, accessed January, 2012.

Harrison, R. T. and Leitch, C. M. (2005), Entrepreneurial Learning: Researching the Interface Between Learning and the Entrepreneurial Context. *Entrepreneurship: Theory and Practice*, 29: 351–371.

Hart D., Acs Z. and Tracy, S. (2009), 'High-tech Immigrant Entrepreneurship in the United States', Report for SBA office of Advocacy, Washington, DC. Available at http://citeseerx.ist.psu.edu/viewdoc/download?do =10.1.1.186.7260&rep=rep1&type=pdf, accessed January 2012.

Hayton, J. C. (2005), 'Promoting corporate entrepreneurship through human resource management practices: A review of empirical research', *Human Resource Management Review*, **15**(1), 21–41.

Hayton, J. C., and Kelley, D. J. (2006), 'A competency-based framework for promoting corporate entrepreneurship', *Human Resource Management*, **45**(3), 407–27.

Henry, C., Hill, F. and Leitch, C. (2005a), 'Entrepreneurship education and training: Can entrepreneurship be taught? Part I', *Education + Training*, **47**(2), 98–111.

Henry, C., Hill, F. and Leitch, C., (2005b), 'Entrepreneurship education and training: Can entrepreneurship be taught? Part II', *Education + Training*, **47**(3), 158–69.

Hills, G. E. (1988), 'Variations in University Entrepreneurship Education: an Empirical Sudy of an Evolving Field'. *Journal of Business Venturing* **3**(1), 109–22.

Hindle, K. (2007), 'Teaching entrepreneurship at the university: from the wrong building to the right philosophy', in Fayolle, A. (Ed.) *Handbook of Research in Entrepreneurship Education*, vol 1, Cheltenham (UK): Edward Elgar Publishing.

Hindle, K. and Cutting, N. (2002), 'Can applied entrepreneurship education enhance job satisfaction and financial performance? An empirical investigation in the Australian pharmacy profession', *Journal of Small Business Management*, **40**(2), 162–7.

Hisrich, R.D. (1989). Women entrepreneurs: Problems and prescriptions for success in the Future, in

Hisrich, R. D. and Brush, C. (1984), 'The woman entrepreneur: Management skills and business problems'. *Journal of Small Business Management*, **22**(1), 30–37.

Hagan, O., Rivchin, C., Sexton, D. (Eds.), *Women-owned Businesses*, Praeger, New York, pp. 3–32.

Hofer, A. and Delaney, A. (2010), 'Shooting for the moon: Good practices in local youth entrepreneurship support', OECD Local Economic and Employment Development (LEED) Working Papers, 2010/11, OECD Publishing. doi: 10.1787/5km7rq0k8h9q-en.

Honig, B. (2001), 'Learning strategies and resources for entrepreneurs and intrapreneurs *Entrepreneurship: Theory and Practice*, **26**(1), 21–35.

Honig, B. (2004), 'Entrepreneurship education: Toward a model of contingency based business planning', *Academy of Management Learning and Education*, **3**(3), 258–73.

Howell, J., Shea, C. and Higgins, C. (2005), 'Champions of product innovations: defining, developing and validating a measure of champion behaviour', *Journal of Business Venturing*, **20**(5),: 641–61.

Hytti, U. and O'Gorman, C. (2004), 'What is "enterprise education"? An analysis of the objectives and methods of enterprise education programmes in four European countries', *Education + Training*. **46**(1), 11–23.

Jamieson, I. (1984), 'Education for Enterprise' in (Eds) TITLE Watts and Moran, CRAC, Ballinger: Cambridge: 19–27.

Johnson, and Tilley, (1999), 'HEI and SME linkages: Recommendations for the future'. *International Small Business Journal*, **17**(4), 66–81.

Jones, C., and Spicer, A. (2009). *Unmasking the entrepreneur*. Cheltenham: Edward Elgar.

Jones, C., and Spicer, A. (2005), 'Disidentifying the subject: Lacanian comments on subjectivity, resistance and enterprise', *Organization*, 12(2), 223–46.

Joyce, B.R.,and Weil, M., (1996), *Models of Teaching*, 5th ed., Boston, MA: Allyn and Bacon.

Karataş-Özkan, M. (2011), 'Understanding relational qualities of entrepreneurial learning: Towards a multi-layered approach', *Entrepreneurship and Regional Development*, **23**(9–10), 877–906.

Karataş-Özkan, M. and Chell, E. (2010), *Entrepreneurial Learning and Nascent Entrepreneurship*, Cheltenham, UK: Edward Elgar.

Katz, J. A. (1991), 'The institution and infrastructure of entrepreneurship', *Entrepreneurship: Theory and Practice*, **15**(3), 85–102.

Katz, J. A., (2003), 'The chronology and intellectual trajectory of American entrepreneurship Education', *Journal of Business Venturing*, **18**(3), 283–300.

Katz, J. A. (2008), 'Fully mature but not fully legitimate: A different perspective on the state of entrepreneurship education'. *Journal of Small Business Management*, 46: 550–66.

Kirby, D., (2004), 'Entrepreneurship education: Can business schools meet the challenge?' *Education + Training*, **46** (8/9), 510–19.

Kirkpatrick, D. L. (1959), 'Techniques for evaluating training programs', *Journal of the American Society of Training Directors*, **13**, 3–26.

Klandt, H. (2004), 'Entrepreneurship Education and Research in German-Speaking Europe'. *Academy of Management, Learning & Education*, 3 (3): 293–301.

Krueger, N. F., Reilly, M. D. and Carsrud, A. L. (2000), 'Competing models of entrepreneurial intentions', *Journal of Business Venturing*, **15**(5–6– 411–432.

Kolb, D. A. (1984), *Experiential Learning: Experience as the Source of Learning and Development*, New Jersey: Prentice Hall.

Kuratko, (2005), 'The emergence of entrepreneurship education: Development, trends, and challenges'. *Entrepreneurship: Theory and Practice*, 29: 577–98.

Lee, J. H., Sohn, S. Y. and Ju, Y. H. (2011), 'How effective Is government support for Korean women entrepreneurs in small and medium enterprises?' *Journal of Small Business Management*, 49: 599–616.

Legendre, R. (1993), *Dictionnaire Actuel de l'Education*, 2nd edition, Montréal: Guérin.

Man, T. W. Y., Lau, T. and Chan, K. F. (2002), 'The competitiveness of small and medium enterprises. A conceptualisation with focus on entrepreneurial competencies', *Journal of Business Venturing*, **17**(2), 123–42.

Marlow, S. and Patton, D. (2005), 'All credit to men? Entrepreneurship, finance, and gender'. *Entrepreneurship: Theory and Practice*, 29: 717–35.

McMullan W., Long W. and Wilson. A. (1985), 'MBA concentration on Entrepreneurship, *Journal of Small Business and Entrepreneur*ship, 3(1), 18–22.

McMullan W. and Long W. (1987), 'Entrepreneurship education in the nineties', *Journal of Business Venturing*, 2: 261–75.

McGee, J., Peterson, M., Mueller, S. and Sequeira, J. (2009), 'Entrepreneurial self-efficacy: Refining the measure', *Entrepreneurship: Theory and Practice*, **33**(4), 965–88.

Merriam, S. (1982), *Adult Education: Foundations of Practice*, Harper & Row: New York.

Meyer, D. (2011), 'The reinvention of academic entrepreneurship', *Journal of Small Business Management*, **49**(1), 1–8.

Minniti, M. and Bygrave, W. (2001), 'A dynamic model of entrepreneurial learning'. *Entrepreneurship: Theory and Practice*, 25(3), 5–16.

Morris, M. and Jones, F. (1993), 'Human resource management practices and corporate entrepreneurship: An empirical assessment from the USA', *The International Journal of Human Resource Management*, **4**(4), 873–96.

Munoz, C., Mosey, S., and Binks, M. (2011), 'The development of opportunity identification capabilities in the classroom: Evidence from visual representations', *Academy of Management Learning and Education*, **10**(2), 277–95.

Mustar, P. (2009), 'Technology Management Education: Innovation and Entrepreneurship at MINES ParisTech, a Leading French Engineering School. *Academy of Management Learning & Education*, 8(3), 418–25.

Neck, H. M. and Greene, P. G. (2011), 'Entrepreneurship education: Known worlds and new frontiers'. *Journal of Small Business Manag*ement, 49, 55–70.

Nicholson, L. and Anderson, A. R. (2005), 'News and nuances of the entrepreneurial myth and metaphor: Linguistic games in entrepreneurial sense-making and sense-giving'. *Entrepreneurship: Theory and Practice*, **29**, 153–72.

OECD, (2006), 'Financing SMEs and Entrepreneurs', Policy Brief, November 2006, OECD, Public Affairs Division, Public Affairs and Communications Directorate, Paris.

Oosterbeek, H., Van Praag, M. and Ijsselstein, A. (2010), 'The impact of entrepreneurship education on entrepreneurship skills and motivation', *European Economic Review*, **54**, 442–54.

Peterman, N. and Kennedy, J. (2003), 'Enterprise education: Influencing students' perceptions of entrepreneurship'. *Entrepreneurship: Theory and Practice*, **28**(2), 129–144.

Phan P. H., Wright M., Ucbasaran D. and Tan W. L., (2009). 'Corporate entrepreneurship: Current research and future directions, *Journal of Business Venturing*, **24**(3), 197–205.

Pittaway, L. and Cope, J. (2007), 'Entrepreneurship Education A Systematic Review of the Evidence', White Rose CETL Enterprise Working Paper 01/2007.

Pittaway, L. and Cope, J. (2007), 'Entrepreneurship education – a systematic review of the evidence', *International Small Business Journal*, 25(5), 477–506.

Pittaway, L., Rodriguez-Falcon, E., Aiyegbayo, O. and King, A. (2011), 'The role of entrepreneurship clubs and societies in entrepreneurial learning', *International Small Business Journal*,, **29**(1), 37–57.

Phillips, J. J. (1991), *Handbook of Training Evaluation and Measurement Methods*, 2nd edition, Houston, Texas: Gulf.

Plaschka, G. and Welsch, H. (1990), 'Emerging structures in entrepreneurship education: Curricular designs and strategies', *Entrepreneurship: Theory and Practice*, **14**(3), 56–71.

Politis, D, (2005), 'The process of entrepreneurial learning: A conceptual framework', *Entrepreneurship: Theory and Practice*, **29**(4), 399–424.

Rae, D. & Carswell, M. (2000), 'Using a life-story approach in researching entrepreneurial learning: The development of a conceptual model and its implications in the design of learning experiences'. *Education and Training*, **42**(4/5), 220–7.

Rae, D., Carswell, M. (2001), 'Towards a conceptual understanding of entrepreneurial learning', *Journal of Small Business & Enterprise Development*, **8** (2).

Rae, D.M. (1997), 'Teaching Entrepreneurship in Asia: Impact of a pedagogical innovation'. *Entrepreneurship, Innovation and Change*, **3**, 197–227.

Ray, D. (1990), 'Liberal arts for entrepreneurs', *Entrepreneurship: Theory and Practice*, **15**(2), 79–93.

Sarasvathy, S. D. (2001), 'Causation and effectuation: A theoretical shift from economic inevitability to entrepreneurial contingency', *Academy of Management Review*, **28**(2), 243–63.

Sarasvathy, S. D. and Venkataraman, S. (2011), 'Entrepreneurship as a method: Open questions for an entrepreneurial future', *Entrepreneurship: Theory and Practice*, **35**, 113–35.

Schmelter, R., Mauer, R., Börsch, C., & Brettel, M. (2010), 'Boosting corporate entrepreneurship through HRM practices: Evidence from German SMEs'. *Human Resource Management*, **49**(4), 715–41.

Sexton, D. L., Upton, N. B., Wacholtz, L. E. and McDougall, P. P. (1997), 'Learning needs of growth-oriented entrepreneurs', *Journal of Business Venturing*, ' **12**, 1–8.

Shane,S., (2009), 'Why encouraging more people to become entrepreneurs is a bad policy'. *Small Business Economics*, **33**, 141–9.

Shane, S. and Venkataraman, S. (2000), 'The promise of entrepreneurship as a field of research', *Academy of Management Review*, **25**(1), 217–26.

Shepherd, D, (2004), 'Educating entrepreneurship students about emotion and learning from failure', *Academy of Management Learning and Education*, **3**(3), 274–87.

Shepherd, D., Covin, J. and Kuratko, D. (2009), 'Project failure from corporate entrepreneurship: Managing the grief process', *Journal of Business Venturing*, **24**(6), 588–600.

Solomon, G., Duffy, S. and Tarabishy, A. (2007), 'The state of entrepreneurship education in the United States: A nationwide survey and analysis', *International Journal of Entrepreneurship Education* **1**(1), 65–86.

Souitaris, V., Zerbinati, S., Al-Laham, A. (2007), 'Do entrepreneurship programmes raise entrepreneurial intentions of science and engineering students? The effects of learning, inspiration and resources', *Journal of Business Venturing*, **22** (4): 566–91.

Thompson, E. (2009), 'Individual entrepreneurial intent: Construct clarification and development of an internationally reliable metric', *Entrepreneurship: Theory and Practice*, **33**(3), 669–94.

Thursby M., Fuller A. and Thursby J. (2009), 'An integrated approach to educating professionals for careers in innovation', *Academy of Management Learning and Education*,**8** (3): 389–405.

Tracey P. and Phillips N. (2007), 'The distinctive challenge of educating social entrepreneurs: A postscript and rejoinder to the special issue on Entrepreneurship Education', *Academy of Management Learning and Education*, **6** (2): 264–71.

Vesper, K. H., (1982), 'Research on education for entrepreneurship', in Kent, C. A. et al. (Eds), *Encyclopaedia of Entrepreneurship*, Englewood Cliffs, NJ: Prentice Hall.

Vesper, K. H. and Gartner, W. B. (1997), 'Measuring progress in entrepreneurship education', *Journal of Business Venturing*, **12**(5), 403–21.

Vesper, K. H. and McMullan, W. (1988), 'Entrepreneurship: Today courses, tomorrow degrees?' *Entrepreneurship: Theory and Practice*, **13**(1), 7–13.

Venkataraman, S. (1997), 'The distinctive domain of entrepreneurship research: An editor's perspective', in J. Katz and R. Brockhaus (Eds), *Advances in Entrepreneurship, firm, emergence, and growth*, vol 3, Greenwich, CT: JAI Press, pp. 119–38.

Walstad, W. and Kourilsky, M. (1998), 'Entrepreneurial attitudes and knowledge of black youth', *Entrepreneurship: Theory and Practice*, **23**(2), 5–18.

Welter F. (2010), Contextualizing Entrepreneurship – Conceptual Challenges and Ways Forward, *Entrepreneurship Theory and Practice*, 34, 165–184.

Wilson F., Kickul J. and Marlino, D. (2007), 'Gender, entrepreneurial self-efficacy, and entrepreneurial career intentions: Implications for entrepreneurship education', *Entrepreneurship: Theory and Practice*, **31**(3), 387–406.

World Economic Forum (2009), 'Educating the Next Wave of Entrepreneurs: Unlocking entrepreneurial capabilities to meet the global challenges of the 21st century', A Report of the Global Education Initiative, Switzerland.

Worthen, B. R. and Sanders, J. R. (1987), *Educational Evaluation*, New York: Longman.

Zahra, S. A. and Wright, M. (2011), 'Entrepreneurship's next act', *Academy of Management Perspectives*, **25**, 67–83.

Zahra S., Newey, L. and Shaver, J. (2011), 'Academic advisory boards' contributions to education and learning: Lessons from entrepreneurship centers', *Academy of Management Learning & Education*, **10**(1), 113–29.

16. Research perspectives on learning in small firms
Oswald Jones and Allan Macpherson

INTRODUCTION

Research perspectives on learning in small firms have evolved through a number of stages in the last 30 years (Breslin, 2008). This chapter examines work conducted through four stages of development by building on a number of themes related to theories of learning. Our intention is to examine critically various perspectives on learning in small firms as the field has evolved from early interest that followed publication of the Bolton Report (1971). We will demonstrate that researchers' understanding of learning in small firms has fundamentally changed over the last 30 years. The influence of the Bolton Committee meant that the focus was essentially management training and development rather than learning. Although, Burgoyne and Stuart (1977) claim that all management development programmes are underpinned by implicit learning theories. Gradually, a number of pioneering individuals stimulated interest in the topic of learning whether related to small firms (Gibb, 1997), to individual entrepreneurs (Deakins and Freel, 1998) or approaches to enterprise education (Caird, 1990).

Blackburn and Kovalainen (2009), in their review of the small firm literature, identify 'learning' as one of nine novel areas for future research in entrepreneurship studies. We suggest that in recent years learning has become one of the most important topics amongst the small firm research community. For example, there have been a number of special issues including the *International Journal of Entrepreneurial Behaviour and Research* (1999: issues 6:3 and 6:4); the *Journal of Small Business and Enterprise Development* (2010, issue 17:4; 2007, issue 14:2); and a particularly influential set of papers in *Entrepreneurship: Theory and Practice* (2005). In addition, a recent edited book brings together key contributors to the learning debate (Harrison and Leitch, 2008) as well as a monograph on entrepreneurial learning (Karataş-Özkan and Chell, 2010). There have been several systematic reviews on a number of related topics such as networking and innovation (Pittaway et al, 2004), knowledge (Macpherson and Holt, 2007; Thorpe et al, 2005), management development (Fuller-Love, 2006) and growth (Phelps et al, 2007; Levie and Lichtenstein, 2010). According to Wang and Chugh (2013) while there is a 'critical mass' of literature related to entrepreneurial learning it is highly diverse and lacks a coherent theoretical approach. Consequently, Wang and Chugh (2013) suggest there should be more focus on three research gaps: 1) individual and collective learning; 2) exploratory and exploitative learning; 3) intuitive and sensing learning. In Chapter 15 of this volume, Byrne et al. (2014) carry out a systematic literature review of the entrepreneurship education literature and identify 86 articles in the period 1984–2011. These authors also conclude that the learning literature lacks theoretical legitimacy and argue that there is 'a need for taxonomies or typologies of education and training in this area in order to help us more fully understand existing education and training offerings in entrepreneurship' (Byrne et al, 2014: 283). A rather different approach is adopted by Breslin and Jones (2012) who draw on evolutionary ideas to highlight the dynamic nature of variation, selection and retention in the process of entrepreneurial learning.

Our objective in this chapter is to engage in a 'sensemaking' process by which we provide a deeper understanding of how the learning literature has evolved over the last 30 years. At the same time, we hope to provide useful insight into the current state of knowledge related to learning in smaller firms. It is important to acknowledge that, as stated by Leitch and Harrison (2008: 3), links between learning and organizational effectiveness are 'far from proven, logically or empirically'. Patton et al. (2000) argue that the inability to establish a causal link between 'learning' and performance can be attributed to the wide range of research methods and variables adopted in studies of small firms. The authors recognize that the sheer heterogeneity of the sector also makes it difficult to establish a causal relationship (Patton et al. 2000). In this chapter, we intend to demonstrate that there is certainly convincing evidence of links between better performing small firms and effective learning. Perhaps more importantly, we argue that the nature of training designed to improve the leadership skills of owner-managers has become both more sophisticated and more appropriate for the complex role of managing a small business. For example, there has been a shift away from relatively straight-forward approaches based on specific 'recipes' or competences to the owner-manager as a situated learner or even part of a learning community (Figure 16.1).

It is our belief that improvements in understanding the nature of entrepreneurial learning can be attributed by the active engagement of UK university management/ business schools with the small business community. Much of this engagement has

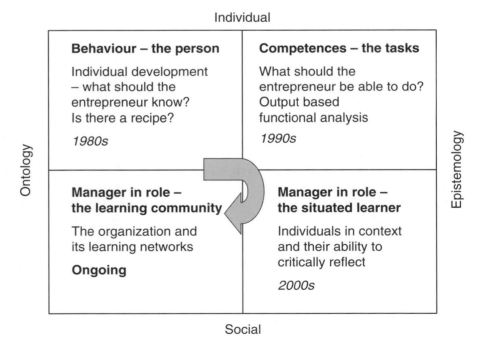

Figure 16.1 The evolution of learning in small firms

been facilitated by access to European structural funds (ERDF and ESF) as well as conventional research funding (Edwards et al., 2007; Kock et al., 2008; Thorpe et al., 2008). For example, Jones et al. (2008) describe the growth of Manchester Metropolitan University's *Centre for Enterprise* which was heavily dependent on structural funding to engage with smaller firms.

We acknowledge that learning may not necessarily lead to better performance although it is unlikely that in a changing context entrepreneurs and firms that do not learn will survive. Learning is required to deal with change, innovation, crises and new markets. The search for links to performance seems to be to be a particular economic obsession that has few implications for the practical problems associated with managing small businesses. We also consider that the four 'perspectives' discussed below contribute to a rounded approach to learning in small firms, which fits with the underlying philosophy of programmes such as LEAD [leadership, enterprise and development] developed by Lancaster University Management School (Smith and Robinson, 2007). Thus, we do not propose the figure as a 'true' representation of learning theory but as an organizing heuristic for the discussion which follows. It is difficult, if not impossible, to fit learning theory in to such a 2x2 matrix, but the intention is to show how the integration of learning theory with small firm development initiatives has progressed over time; hence we have included the arrow in Figure 16.1 that traces the temporal progression discussed below.

The chapter is structured in the following manner. We begin by discussing the way in which learning research has evolved over the last 25 years according to each of the four quadrants introduced in Figure 16.1, below. This is followed by a brief case study of the LEAD programme which brings together much of the recent knowledge about learning in small firms. We then set out the implications for policy and practice.

LEARNING PERSPECTIVES

Early perspectives on learning were concentrated on individual cognition (Ulrich and Cole, 1987). Over time this focus on individual entrepreneurs began to encompass perspectives that embraced the wider cultural and historical contexts in which small firms operate (Macpherson et al, 2010). We conceptualise the evolution of learning based on two dimensions: first, whether the learning focus is ontological or epistemological; second, whether learning is based on a cognitive or social approach (Figure 16.1). According to Burrell and Morgan (1979) ontological issues are concerned with the distinction between objective reality which is external to individual actors and a subjective reality, which is based on individual consciousness. In contrast, epistemological issues concern the nature and status of human knowledge: the extent to which knowledge can be transmitted in a codified form or whether it is based on personal experience and insight (Burrell and Morgan, 1979). According to Baker et al (2005) an ontological learning orientation draws on understanding and human experiences (Gadamer, 1984). Whereas, an epistemological learning approach places greater emphasis on the processes associated with the 'refining of knowledge'. Although many researchers use the terms interchangeably there is also a clear difference between conversation and dialogue (Baker et al, 2005: 414). 'Epistemologically oriented' critical theorists (Oswick et al,

2000) use the term dialogue in reference to an intellectual process of refining knowledge. The term conversation is used by 'ontologically oriented' writers (Gadamer, 1984) who are more concerned with human understanding and experience rather than 'abstract' knowledge. The distinction reflects differences in definitions of what it is 'to be' a successful owner-manager and how to become better at 'doing' small business management.

In our conceptual model, the vertical axis is related to the more familiar distinction between individual (cognitive and behavioural) learning and social learning (Figure 16.1). Behavioural learning theory is strongly associated with Skinner (1938) and Pavlov (1927). Behaviourism is based on the idea that an 'operant' is something that influences the environment or situation (hard work leads to additional pay). An operant response is influenced by either negative or positive reinforcement. Reinforcement is based on Thorndike's (1913) 'law of effect', which focuses on behavioural change. Behavioural theory has been widely used in education and training institutions via the application of positive feedback to enhance learning. In contrast, cognitive learning is based on the processes by which individuals perceive, store and apply new information. Two of the key figures in the emergence of a cognitive approach were child psychologist Jean Piaget (1929) and gestalt psychologist Wolfgang Köhler (1925). Piaget's stage model theory was regarded as crude by Köhler whose work with chimpanzees led to the concept of 'insightful learning' which indicates problem-solving occurs suddenly and understanding can be applied in new situations. Kolb's (1984) experiential learning model was influenced by the developmental psychology of Piaget. The action approach, developed by Lewin (1946), strongly influenced the work of Argyris and Schön (1978) and Argyris (1999). More recent approaches such as Senge (1990) are heavily cognitive in content (DeFillippi and Ornstein, 2003). Senge's (1990) approach [who was also significantly influenced by Lewin's work (Burns and Cooke, 2013)], specifically recognizes the cognitive limitations of one individual to be able to comprehend the complexity of the business environment in which they operate. Learning in such a difficult context means that 'mental models' within the business have to be constantly adapted to cope with changing contexts; deeper generative learning requires changes to underlying assumptions on which those mental models are based. When there is a tension between a vision for the future and current reality, then there is potential for learning to occur. Ultimately this requires translation of ideas into reality by implementing new processes, systems and strategies.

Social learning theorists see human development as something which occurs as a result of observation of those who are 'credible and knowledgeable' (Bandura, 1977). Observational learning occurs as a result of four interrelated processes: attention, memory, motor and motivation. Both cultural-historical theory (Vygotsky, 1978) and the communities of practice approach (Lave and Wenger, 1991) are based on social learning theory and are a reaction against the cognitive and behavioural approaches. Engeström's (1987) cultural-historical activity theory (CHAT) is concerned with the way in which 'artefacts' represent and mediate the socially situated nature of learning. The 'community of practice' approach is based on three key elements: a domain of knowledge, a community and their shared practices (Wenger, 2000). Situated learning, which can occur both formally and informally, stresses the importance of legitimate peripheral participation (Lave and Wenger, 1991). That is, the processes by which newcomers are able to join and engage in an established learning community. Thus, the primary sensemaking distinction concerns whether research is focused on developing individual knowledge and skills or recognition that learning is influenced by the context of experiences, problem-solving and networks in which owner-managers are embedded. Perhaps a 'cross-over' theoretical approach in this regard is Kolb's (1984) experiential learning theory. He has been criticized for being cognitive and technological in his approach (Holman et al, 1997). Others such as Kayes (2002) argue that critics of ELT have not paid enough attention to the influence of Vygotsky's (1978) social constructivist theory on Kolb's ideas about learning. This experiential approach has been highly influential in terms of action-centred solutions to learning support.

LEARNING IN SMALL FIRMS

We begin by exploring the evolution of learning research and understanding of management development in small firms as it has moved from a focus on individual know-how to owner-managers as part of a learning community. As shown in the four boxes in Figure 16.1, these perspectives have evolved sequentially (with continuing overlaps), as theoretical perspectives have enhanced understanding of individual and organizational learning. We suggest that all these perspectives are necessary to develop a fully rounded view of learning in small firms. In this chapter, we draw on our experience of undertaking an extensive study of small firms in the north-west of England (Thorpe et al, 2008) as well as our involvement with the LEAD programme (Cope et al., 2011; Gordon et al., 2011). Our intention is to demonstrate the way in which genuine *organizational learning* contributes to the long-term survival of small firms.

Individual Learning (Box 1: Behaviour – the Person)

Early approaches to learning in small firms concentrated on changing 'entrepreneurial behaviour' by focusing on what individuals should know to manage their businesses effectively (Bolton, 1971). In essence the approach reflected concerns with how 'to be' a successful owner of a small firm. As mentioned above, interventions at this stage were primarily concerned with management training and development (Lawlor, 1988; Watkins, 1983). It is important to acknowledge that conventional behavioural and cognitive approaches to learning were very influential on most of those who first promoted the development of owner-managers (Bolton, 1971; Curran, 1986; Stanworth and Curran, 1991). However, we suggest that these interventions were, at least implicitly, influenced by the idea of a 'recipe' for the management of smaller firms. The term recipe is most widely known through the work of Spender (1989) who suggested that there are particular 'guides to action' associated with specific industries or sectors. Hence, individual development concerns owner-managers applying 'generic' recipes in the context of their organizations (Sharifi and Zhang, 2009). This stresses an 'ontological' orientation in which individuals have to understand the nuances of a recipe rather than applying the ideas in a mechanical fashion.

Early small firm learning research focused on the person (owner-manager) and the development of their managerial knowledge (know-how). At this time, research concentrated on the key entrepreneurial attributes and traits, the managerial skills appropriate for running a successful business and, more importantly, how to develop functional and technical knowledge. According to the Bolton report there was a need for SME managers to have information and training in eight areas: raising and using finance; costing and control information; organization and delegation; marketing; information use and retrieval; personnel management; technological change; and production scheduling and purchase control (Bolton, 1971). It was suggested by Bolton that this training, and any such advisory services, could be provided through industry training boards on a 'pay-for-training' basis that should be self-sustaining. Basically it was concluded in the report that the provision of management training should be market-led, and the repertoire of management development was significantly influenced by the types of management techniques deployed in larger firms which were considered by Bolton to have made them more efficient. While Bolton acknowledged there was a 'need' for management training the recommendation controversially suggested this should be provided on a demand-led basis. What little provision and take up of management training existed was based on an assessment of lack of key management skills in SMEs – management development being a significant area in which the UK was seen to be lagging behind other nations. Small firm management training was quite extensive from a number of providers (private sector, FE, HE) and supported by local and national agencies, but it was piecemeal and inconsistent in approach.

A number of initiatives were developed through the 1970s and 1980s, delivered through Government Schemes, or private enterprise assisted schemes, that provided both training and advice designed to improve performance in marketing, design, quality management, manufacturing systems, business-planning and information systems (Stanworth and Curran, 1991). According to Stanworth and Curran (1991), however, there was little evidence relating to the effectiveness of training or its economic benefits. They also note that these conclusions were not surprising given the fragmented nature of training provision, the uncertain quality of delivery and the perceived lack of relevance given by owner-managers to such training. In reviewing the progress 20 years after the Bolton Report (1971) Stanworth and Curran (1991) concluded that small firms were reluctant to train and that 'training' delivery had to be more flexible and problem-oriented, focused on those specific needs most directly relevant to SMEs. They did not specify exactly what those needs were, but they did recommend the certification of management competence and company accreditation as an incentive to develop functional competences. Kirby (1990) confirmed that there was a considerable amount of scepticism among owner-managers about the value of investing in training.

Learning Key Competences (Box 2: Competences – the Tasks)

The competence movement was initiated by McClelland (1973) and initially focused on the values, traits and motives individuals need to enhance performance advantages when undertaking specific tasks or roles. Competences could be categorized into general areas that a person needed to be suitable for that role. However, the approach evolved and Dreyfus and Dreyfus (1980), through their research with military pilots introduced five distinct levels of competency progression from novice to expert which can still be seen in many competence frameworks.

The competency approach is strongly cognitive in orientation as the emphasis remains on individual learning (Council for Excellence in Management and Leadership, 2000).

However, in this case, the epistemological orientation indicates a strongly functional approach which stresses the refinement of management competences. Whereas Box 1 is concerned with what the owner should know, Box 2 concerns what the individual should be able to do (Boyzatzis, 1982). Hence, by the 1980s there was increasing interest in identifying specific managerial competences rather than inputs (in terms of what owner-managers were expected to know). The MCI (Management Charter Initiative) standards were re-written for small firm managers and the approach presumed a great deal about the universalist nature of small firms and of management (Martin and Staines, 1994; Mangham, 1985; Sadler-Smith et al., 2003). The competence and the managerial knowledge approaches are still evident in many small firm textbooks (Beaver, 2002; Stokes and Wilson, 2010) and in tools to support owner-managers develop their knowledge and competences (HMSO, 1990). Wider development of staff within small firms was also advocated through the competence-based National Vocational Qualification Systems in the UK (Matlay and Hyland, 1997; Matlay, 2000).

Given this preoccupation with management competences, research turned to a focus on either how to support the development of competences, or identifying the scope and nature of competences necessary. Stuart et al. (1995), for example, report on the outcomes of a project which was designed to develop a 'framework of managerial competence' that was generalizable for senior managers in SMEs (small- and medium-sized enterprises). A study of owner-managers in Scotland distinguished between specific and general competences (Martin and Staines, 1994). Such studies focused on identifying specific practices – strategic, functional and technical – that owner-managers should be able to perform in order to compete in changing contexts (Dodgson, 1991; Kock et al, 2008; Redmond and Walker, 2008). Bird (1995; 2002) developed both a theory and learning approach for entrepreneurial competences. There was also interest in how competence development might lead to improved performance (Man et al., 2002; Man and Lau, 2005). Man et al. (2002) draw on a wide range of literature associated with competiveness to identify factors which influence the performance of SMEs. In their conceptual model, the authors suggest that there are six entrepreneurial competences: opportunity, relational, conceptual, organizational, strategic and commitment. These competences enable owner-managers to develop organizational capabilities which are appropriate for the external environment in which the firm is operating (Jones, 2003). Other studies identified more intangible, relational competences (Hannon et al, 2000) that provided access to external knowledge from business and personal advice networks (Boussouara and Deakins, 2000; Macpherson et al, 2004; Moreira, 2009).

This preoccupation with competence informed the way enterprise education was initially conceived and evaluated (see for example, Chaston, 1992; Kirby, 1990) and still informs many small firm development programmes (see for example Redmond and Walker, 2008; Kock et al, 2008). However, despite work to identify lists of appropriate small firm competences evidence for direct links to improved performance was equivocal at best (Chaston et al, 1999; Patton and Marlow 2002; Storey 2004). Establishing a causal link between learning and performance is fraught with difficulties (Patton et al 2000). Learning (if that can be measured) does not necessarily mean that the firm will perform better within a competitive market (Storey, 2011) particularly if competitors are also learning. Nevertheless, given these unconvincing results, the reliance on competence maps came under increasing scrutiny with researchers suggesting that more attention should be paid to the contexts in which small firms operate (Banfield et al, 1996; Matlay and Addis, 2002; Smith et al, 1999; Loan-Clarke et al, 2000). It is not surprising, therefore, that the theory and research turned towards examining the lived experience of owner-managers to better understand their learning trajectories.

Experiential Learning (Box 3: Manager in Role – the Situated Learner)

Many scholars adopted the idea of 'critical learning events' to understand how owner-managers resolve day-to-day business problems (Deakins and Freel, 1998; Cope and Watts, 2000; Sullivan, 2000). This approach is influenced significantly by Chell's (1998; 2014) phenomenological-based critical incident technique developed from Flanagan's (1954) realist approach. This involves understanding how managers learn to solve the problems and learn from the day-to-day experiences they have. As such it deals with both their emotional responses and individual learning that they encounter as they deal with events. It also sets this discussion in context and considers the relations and contingencies the experience involves. Many critical incidents involve interaction with other actors, whether employees, customers or suppliers, as they attempt to refine knowledge (Baker et al, 2005). For example, applying quality management or FMEA (failure mode effects analysis) techniques to improve product or service quality involves discussions between owner-managers and employees (Macpherson and Jones, 2008).

Kolb's (1984) work on experiential learning has been extremely influential in this area of learning for entrepreneurship and small business. A range of writers identify various activities associated with 'learning-by-doing': trial and error (Young and Sexton, 1997); problem solving (Deakins, 1996); discovery (Deakins and Freel, 1998); experimentation and copying (Gibb, 1997); successes and setbacks (Reuber and Fischer, 1993); learning from crises (Macpherson, 2005; Herbane, 2010). While there is a focus on the functional elements of learning associated with this approach it has a far stronger social dimension than either Boxes 1 or 2. Studies on the internationalization of small firms emphasize that traditional educational approaches and large firm training strategies are not appropriate for small firms (Anderson and Boocock, 2002). Cope (2003; 2005) has been particularly influential in emphasizing that learning is strongly influenced by the context within which individuals work. There are also a number of studies which focus on understanding the 'lived experience' of owner-managers (Rae, 2000; 2004; Rae and Carswell, 2001). Such perspectives are linked to action learning (Revans, 1980) where owner-managers are encouraged to attend to those issues that they face in implementing practical solutions. Such an approach helps owner-managers help themselves to solve intractable problems with which they are faced (Lawlor, 1988).

While critical incidents and problem-focused reflection provides an impetus for learning and innovation (Macpherson, 2005; McAdam and Mitchell, 2010) it is the time spent in reflection and discussion that provides owner-managers with opportunities to attend to more strategic developments (Clarke et al, 2006). This can include learning from failure (Baker, 1995) as well as learning specific capabilities such as leadership (Kempster and Cope, 2010). Research from this perspective generally focuses on how to deliver problem-based action learning and critical refection skills to owner-managers (Chung et al, 2001; Coughlan et al, 2001; Clarke et al, 2006; Kelliher et al, 2009; Ram and Trehan, 2010); or, to a lesser extent, how owner-managers gain skills through their experience of crises and problem resolution to produce practical theories of action (Rae, 2002; Cope, 2003; Zhang et al, 2006; Sharifi and Zhang, 2009; Kempster and Cope, 2010; McAdam and Mitchell, 2010; Herbane, 2010). Although there is recognition that learning-in-action involves others there is still a significant focus on the outcome of individual owner-manager's learning. The consequence is that the importance of internal and external relationships and networks is largely ignored (Jones et al, 2010). The ideas underpinning Kolb's more recent work (Baker et al. 2005) explicitly reflect a similar shift in concerns from individual experiential learning to the social context of learning, which is discussed in the next section.

Learning in Social Context (Box 4: Manager in Role – the Learning Community)

Approaches associated with Box 4 focus on developing more interpretative and socially situated learning. There is also a switch from an epistemological orientation and the associated focus on refining knowledge to greater emphasis on broader human understanding. The entrepreneur becomes part of a learning community rather than an individualistic learner. Consequently, their conversations have relational and communal qualities which are important for increasing mutual understanding (Baker et al, 2005; Holman et al., 1997). In acknowledging that owner-managers learn 'by doing' researchers sought to examine the social dimensions of learning in small firms by focusing on the networks in which individuals are located (Perren and Grant, 2000; Devins and Gold, 2002; Gold et al., 2007; Macpherson et al., 2010).

Contributions to the fourth quadrant emanate independently of experientially based perspectives from a growing number of researchers working within the social constructivist paradigm (Karataş-Özkan, 2011). McHenry (2008), for example, suggests that the earlier focus on behavioural and cognitive learning has been superseded by 'interpretative, phenomenological, situated' approaches. Many critical incidents involve interaction with other actors, whether employees, customers or suppliers, as they attempt to refine knowledge (Baker et al, 2005). Recognition of the importance of experience-based knowledge and of the influence of social institutions (Dewey, 1916) promoted interest in the contextual factors that defined learning trajectories. Theoretical advancement in learning theories such as cultural historical activity theory (Engeström, 1987; 2000), communities of practice (Lave and Wenger, 1991), and situated learning (Gherardi, 2000), indicated that to focus on a senior manager led to an impoverished view of how firms develope (Thorpe et al, 2008). Wyer et al. (2000) also suggested that the concept of organizational learning could provide insight into how owner-managers influence collective learning (Chaston et al., 1999; Matlay, 2000). Jones and Macpherson (2006) also argue that there is a gap between individual learning and organizational learning (OL) which restricts the understanding of small firm development. It is important to pay attention to the particular institutional fields in which firms are embedded and the opportunities and barriers that these create (Jones, 2006; Jones and Craven, 2001). So, the owner-manager is not the only actor important for understanding learning trajectories within small firms. Genuine organizational learning requires that the learning of individual owner-managers is embedded within organizational routines which involves actors inside and outside the firm (Jones and Macpherson, 2006; Thorpe et al, 2008; Jones et al, 2010).

This shift in emphasis has led to the emergence of more in-depth, qualitative studies that have got much closer to the 'lived experience' of entrepreneurship (Rae, 2004). Researchers have sought to understand how individuals negotiate and embed new practices within a firm. Studies in this field are more concerned with how 'competent practice' is a negotiated activity. Approaches include how owner-managers engage in 'cultural entrepreneurship' (Lounsbury and Glynn, 2001) or adopt rhetorical strategies (Holt and Macpherson, 2010) to portray themselves as competent and convince others to engage with, or invest in, their enterprises. Thorpe et al. (2006) highlight a number of contextual factors that prevent entrepreneurs developing the capacity to embed their ideas within the wider economic and social activities of their firm. Other examples involving social and situated experiences include the influence of customer and supplier networks (Macpherson et al, 2004; Thakkar et al, 2011), innovation partnerships (Malik and Wei, 2011), top management teams (Breslin, 2010), organizational artefacts and the deployment of power (Macpherson and Jones, 2008; Macpherson et al, 2010), peer-based formal and informal networks (Bergh et al, 2011), decision making (Sharifi and Zhang, 2009), and regional clusters (Parrilli et al, 2010; Hervás-Oliver and Albors-Garrigós, 2008).

Zhang et al. (2006) argue that understanding how small firms embed new knowledge requires attention to a number of complex and interrelated factors such as: learning triggers (the nature of the learning event); learning modes (experiential based on active experimentation, information processing or dialogue and interaction); learning types (continuous adjustment of existing systems, changed behaviours and/or discourses, or continuous innovation through systems that encourage constant review and reflection); and finally learning scope (individual, group, intra-organizational, organizational, inter-organizational, or community of practice). Learning outcomes are evident in organizational change at a number of levels (actions, artefacts and discourses). However, while outcomes are negotiated and uncertain ultimately the goal is to embed knowledge, secure organizational longevity and establish competitive advantage (see Voudouris et al. 2011).

In summary, many of the early theories of learning (Box 1 and Box 2) assumed knowledge could be codified and easily transferred (Macpherson and Holt, 2007). The important thing was to identify the knowledge individuals needed to become successful owner-managers. In Box 3, there is increasing attention on the experiential nature of learning as owner-managers engage in day-to-day problem solving. In Box 4, we see a shift to socially situated views of learning that acknowledge a multitude of relationships and institutions that influence a firm's learning trajectories. We suggest that all of these perspectives are important in understanding how individuals and small firms learn. Man (2012) suggests a model in which learning behaviours are influenced by the entrepreneurs' tasks, experience, knowledge, skills and attributes as well as the learning context. We now provide an example of how theoretical knowledge is applied to practical problems by discussing development of a programme for owner-managers.

CASE STUDY: THE LEAD PROGRAMME

The Northwest Development Agency (NWDA) identified a £13 billion gross value added (GVA) gap compared to the average performance of other UK regions. According to the

Table 16.1   Forms of learning

Programme	Activities	Learning Theory
Experiential two days	Various	Social, experiential, behavioural and cognitive
Master-classes	Presentation by experts	Cognitive and experiential
Action learning	Identify problems and discuss options	Social and experiential
Coaching	Enhance decision-making	Behavioural and experiential
Shadowing	Feedback on leadership style	Behavioural and experiential
Reflection days	Sharing experiences	Experiential, social, cognitive and behavioural
On-line forum	Sharing knowledge and experiences	Cognitive and experiential

NWDA's (2006) strategy document £10 billion of the shortfall was due to a productivity gap in key business sectors and £3 billion was attributed to high levels of unemployment. One of the NWDA's strategies for dealing with the productivity gap was to instigate a programme that would enhance leadership skills in firms with less than 20 employees. LEAD (leadership, enterprise and development) was developed over a period of four years by Lancaster University Management School (Cope et al., 2011; Gordon et al., 2011; Gordon and Jack, 2010; Robinson, 2006). Initiated in 2003, LEAD was based on 'an integrated learning model' which combined a range of approaches to accommodate a variety of learning styles (Smith and Robinson, 2007: 9). The uniqueness of LEAD lies in the way in which various elements are blended into a coherent programme which requires participants to attend two days a month for 10 months. A range of interventions were used to deliver the programme outputs: master-classes, action learning, coaching, mentoring and peer-to-peer learning. A further crucial element of LEAD concerns encouraging participants to discuss informally the various interventions. Hence, a number of 'learning and reflection days' are included in the programme to help embed learning across the cohort of 25 participants (Table 16.1).

In 2009, the NWDA invited proposals for LEAD providers across the Northwest and eventually 13 organizations were selected. All 13 LEAD providers had to adopt the exact model pioneered by Lancaster University Management School. This model is highly structured and specifies exactly when each of the various interventions takes place. LEAD begins with a two-day experiential residential event which introduces the cohort to the principles of the course and also acts as a 'team-building' exercise. Other elements include: five three-hour master-classes, coaching, action learning sets, business shadowing, reflection days, and engagement with the LEAD forum (on-line knowledge-sharing).

LEAD has proved to be extremely successful both in terms of improving the performance of small firms as well as encouraging and embedding learning amongst the cohort. All elements of the LEAD programme are well established in training for entrepreneurs/owner-managers and are clearly influenced by experiential learning theory (Kolb, 1984). However, LEAD goes beyond experiential learning by encouraging group knowledge sharing and learning through a range of activities including regular action learning activities and 'reflection' days. The unique nature of LEAD concerns the way in which the various elements are combined into a programme which lasts for ten months. An independent evaluation of the Lancaster programme indicated that 90 percent of participants achieved an average increase in turnover of £200,000. Comments from LEAD participants at the University of Liverpool Management School emphasize the wide-ranging nature of their learning experiences (see Appendix 16.1). This group of owner-managers participated in LEAD during 2010 and 2011 and were all keenly aware of the difficult trading conditions associated with the post-2008 recession. We also acknowledge that participants were not necessarily representative of the wider group of owner-managers. All those who joined the LEAD programme knew that it was designed to encourage growth and, consequently, were certainly a self-selecting group. We are also willing to acknowledge that many of these firms may well have increased their turnover without joining LEAD. However, the point of using LEAD as a case study is to demonstrate the underlying theoretical sophistication of the programme which was delivered by a range of providers including small training organizations as well as university management schools including Lancaster and Liverpool.

DISCUSSION: IMPLICIT AND EXPLICIT THEORIES OF LEARNING

This overview of learning in small firms over the last 30 years describes a process whereby theory has become more explicitly linked to practice. Similarly, the LEAD case study demonstrates far greater sophistication in the delivery of training to entrepreneurs responsible for managing smaller firms. The LEAD programme incorporates experiential, cognitive, behavioural and social learning approaches. However, it is unlikely that many of the participants, nor most of those involved in the delivery, necessarily realized that that the programme was based on a range of learning theories (Burgoyne and Stuart, 1977). As mentioned above, it is suggested that the reason for this greater level of sophistication in utilizing learning theories can be attributed to the active engagement of management academics in the delivery of interventions designed to improve the performance of smaller firms. European structural funding has been widely used to fund interventions by 'new' universities as well as by 'research-led' institutions such as Birmingham, Lancaster, Liverpool, Leeds and Sheffield (Smith, 2008). This is not meant to belittle the contribution of the early pioneers such as Caird (1990), Gibb (1997) and Deakins and Freel (1998). Rather, entrepreneurship theory in general, and learning theory in particular, has become much more embedded in mainstream academic debates. This is signalled by the growing importance of entrepreneurship and small firm journals in the UK (*Entrepreneurship & Regional Development* and *International Small Business Journal*) and the US (*Entrepreneurship: Theory and Practice, Journal of Business Venturing, Journal of Small Business Management* and *Small Business Economics*) which are all rated 3* or 4* according to the ABS (Association of Business Schools). Equally significant is the fact that the entrepreneurship community now recognise the importance of publishing in mainstream business and management journals. Top-rated journals such as *British Journal of Management* (McKelvie and Davidsson, 2009), *Journal of Management Studies* (Clarke, 2011), *Organization Studies* (Elfring and Hulsink, 2007), *Academy of Management Journal* (Balagopal, 2011), *Academy of Management Review* (Cornelissen and Clarke, 2010), *Administrative Science* Quarterly (Zott and Huy, 2007) and *Organizational Science*

(Paul et al., 2011) have all published important contributions to entrepreneurship and small firm research in recent years.

Consequently, there has been a shift away from management development approaches which were strongly linked to cognitive and behavioural theories of learning. The emergence of social learning theories including communities of practice (Lave and Wenger, 1991) and cultural-historical activity theory (Engeström, 1987; 2000) have informed more recent work on learning in smaller firms. This change is manifest in a number of elements of the LEAD programme. On reflection days, for example, participants are encouraged to actively consider the impact of changes they have made in their leadership style. Hence, it is not simply a question of understanding differences between transactional and transformational leadership (Bass and Riggio, 2006). Rather, delegates have to reflect critically on how their staff responded to the changes and share that information with other members of their cohort. This is not always a comfortable process as inevitably there are failures as well as successes. All LEAD delegates have to commit to sharing their experiences and problems as openly as possible. As a consequence, there is a strong identification with problems that other people are having in managing their businesses. Reflection days help promote genuine social learning rather than the individual learning associated with personal reflection.

Links to ontological learning are demonstrated by the key principle of LEAD: *working on the business not in the business* (NWDA, 2009). So while some time is spent on specific problems such as dealing with difficult staff – the programme provides much greater encouragement for delegates to think about the 'bigger picture'. In other words, owner-managers need to consider the context of their business and what they are trying to achieve. The focus is very much on what the business could be with the appropriate leadership rather that concentrating on the micro aspects of small firm management.

IMPLICATIONS FOR POLICY, PRACTICE AND THEORY

In this section we highlight the implications of research on learning in small firms for both policy-makers and practitioners. There has been a long-standing and vigorous debate between those who subscribe to a 'free market' approach to the support of small firms (Storey, 1992; 2011; Westhead and Storey, 1996) and those of a more interventionist persuasion such as Gibb (1997; 2009). Our own view, based on a substantial number of projects designed to support entrepreneurs and small business owners is that it is possible to make a real difference to individuals and to their businesses (Jayawarna et al., 2011). However, proposing a holistic learning theory to explain the process of small firm learning is beyond the scope of this chapter even if it was desirable. What we have demonstrated, through our categorization of small firm learning research, is an evolution of understanding of the complexity of small firm learning.

Curran and Blackburn (2001) argued that more robust theoretical and methodological approaches were required when researching smaller firms. In particular, they noted that research on small firms lags behind developments in wider social science research. Small firm research is particularly challenging because the 'real life' of a small business inevitably crosses many boundaries both academic and social. In attempting to understand small firms, therefore, an approach that takes account of this complexity and allows researchers to draw on a variety of concepts from wider social science domains is necessary. Theoretical openness to new approaches can help researchers better understand learning in small firms. By opening up the review to consider the development of research on learning in small firms, this provides a robust grounding on which to base implications for both policy and practice. Table 16.2 summarises the policy and practice implications of the accumulated knowledge of research undertaken over the last 30 years.

Early approaches (behavioural and cognitive theories) remain complementary to situated and social learning theories and are still relevant today. There seems to be no doubt that the fundamental building block on which the firm operates is the human capital embedded in the entrepreneur, owner-manager or management team that runs the business. Thus, while early initiatives to develop management competences and knowledge are still relevant a range of other experiences and education programmes are also relevant. The crucial implication for practice, however, seems to be that the learning and knowledge gained need to be directed with energy, towards 'working on the business' (See Table 16.2). As research has evolved, the understanding of learning in small firms has become more sophisticated. This work has foregrounded the crisis driven and social experiences that underpin much of the learning in small firms. Hence, there is a need to consider small firm learning in context, which calls for a nuanced understanding of the experiences and problems faced by individual entrepreneurs.

The historical focus on individuals initially obscured learning as a collective, situated and transient accomplishment (Blackler, 1993). In understanding learning in small firms it is clear that we need to be more sensitive to the context in which knowledge is applied. Learning is an idiosyncratic, emergent and active process that must be investigated through the detailed ecology of each small firm (Watts et al, 2006; Perren and Grant, 2000; Baker et al, 2003; Rae, 2004; Jones et al, 2010). Hence, we need to consider the institutional forces that shape activity within a firm, the networks and markets as well as existing artefacts and routines that signal norms both inside and outside the firm. Issues of context – human capital, social capital, market conditions and institutional structures – mean that an infinite variety of social architectures are possible. Thus, if the learning processes of a particular firm are to be understood it is important to develop a deeper understanding of the specific arrangements that define that firm.

Given the shift in focus in this chapter from individual acquisition of knowledge to learning processes embedded in context there are a number of policy implications. While human capital can be developed through individual training and education the experiential and situated nature of learning also highlights other opportunities that can be grasped or developed. The owner-manager's leadership role, the influence of outside agencies and also the political nature of learning activity combine to create degrees of complexity not generally discussed in small firm policy. Nevertheless, these contingencies provide an opportunity to consider the status and role of networks within the learning process, and highlight the important role of softer relationship management skills for entrepreneurial learning (Clarke et al, 2006). Delivering generic 'enterprise education' or 'competence maps' still has a role to play but action-centred and context-sensitive solutions are clearly also indicated by the research.

A word of caution is probably necessary here. Given the context-dependent nature of learning simple or 'best practice' solutions in policy development are unlikely to succeed.

Table 16.2   Implications for policy and practice

Research Findings	Policy Implications	Practice Implications
It is important to continually develop human capital within the firm.	Providing training and education programmes, as well as a variety of experiences, all contribute to the development of human capital.	Practitioners must be prepared to devote time and energy to improving their skills/knowledge (working on the business not in the business – in LEAD terms).
Social and business networks provide sources of potentially useful knowledge.	Network development activities and skills are necessary to provide access to relevant knowledge and this resource can be enhanced by supporting and brokering new network connections.	Managing network relationships requires specific relational competences and social capital.
Learning is a situated and context-dependent process that means no individual is fully in control of their learning trajectory, or that of their firm.	It is important to understand the firm in its market and institutional context as well as the owner's ambitions and capabilities to deploy learning support appropriately.	If an intervention is going to be effective there needs to be a longitudinal element to the programme. One-off events or very short programmes do not work in terms of changing attitudes and behaviours.
Learning is not an individual activity. Genuine organizational learning requires others to engage in learning and for new practices to be embedded.	There should be a social element to the learning environment because most people learn most effectively when they are part of a community.	Achieving real organizational change means owner-managers must be willing to engage with their employees when adopting and implementing new practices (knowledge sharing).
Reflection on the suitability of existing practices requires problem-solving capacity and capabilities	Interventions should be action-oriented. New artefacts and tools can 'create crises' that provide the focus necessary to encourage reflection and reflexivity in small firms allowing individuals to create conversations within and across organizational boundaries.	Implementing new ways of working will inevitably lead to failures as well as successes. It is therefore important to continue the process of reflection and sharing experiences with others. Considering what is and what is not working is central to the learning process.
Not all owner-managers are ready, willing or able to learn.	Those delivering courses/ programmes for entrepreneurs/ owner-managers must be sympathetic to their approaches to 'learning' and whether they are ready to learn.	Improving business performance requires participants have openness (intellectual and emotional) to new ideas and a willingness to try new ways of working.

That is not to say that training in generic management techniques does not have value. Rather, a more targeted approach, addressing key problems faced by individual firms that encourage reflection on existing practices and that are more sensitive to context seems more likely to provide firms with sustainable benefits. Training undoubtedly improves the quality of available human capital (of all staff), but many other organizational conditions need to be met if the effects of this training are to be embedded and sustained. Moreover, learning is a long-term not short-term project and requires learning to be shared and embedded within the firm if it is to be sustained (Baker and Nelson, 2005; Jones et al, 2010). The benefits of social and action-orientated learning solutions are indicated by the research, but may involve engagement with employees if the outcomes are to gain long-term traction.

Creating situations in order to stretch existing human capital, or to enable access to new experiences, may encourage the reflection necessary to avoid rigidity and encourage innovation (Gibb, 2009). However, learning emerges through interaction (Gherhardi and Nicolini, 2002). Engaging with others and convincing them to embark on a particular course of action requires social and communication skills. Networking and institutionalizing new routines (genuine collective learning) requires that owner-managers have the ability to encourage others that a particular set of organizational relationships and activities are useful (Holt and Macpherson, 2010). Collective learning is only evident if new practices are embedded and sustained within the firm, and that means that knowledge sharing and institutionalization of new practices is essential (Jones and Macpherson, 2006).

It is perhaps important to end on a note of caution. Learning is not a magic bullet and much of the ambiguity of research results highlights the uncertain nature of learning outcomes. Learning often involves renewal, redesign or indeed complete replacement of existing activities with new ones. It is clearly possible that in doing so, the successful firm may destroy the basis on which their performance was built (Ambrosini and Bowman, 2009). Continual reflection on existing practices can help to reflect on what is working and what is not and allow corrective action to be taken.

CONCLUSIONS

In this chapter we have mapped the changes that have occurred in the field of 'learning in small firms' over the last 30 years. As we have demonstrated there has been a shift from the early, relatively straightforward focus on the individual entrepreneur/owner-manager. Gradually, there has been a shift to more sophisticated approaches in which the owner-manager is seen as a 'situated learner' who is part of a much broader learning community. Our argument is that this change has occurred as a result of two concurrent processes.

First, business school academics have had much greater engagement with smaller businesses as a result of various programmes associated with European Structural funding (Edwards et al, 2007; Kock et al, 2008) as well as other major initiatives such as the New Entrepreneur Scholarship (Jayawarna et al, 2011; Taylor et al, 2004). Much of the learning that has taken place as a result of this engagement has been shared with community at conferences such as the British Academy of Management and the Institute of Small

Business and Entrepreneurship as well as publications in many of the entrepreneurship and small business journals. As a consequence, awareness of approaches that are most effective in promoting entrepreneurial learning have been widely disseminated across the community.

The second reason is that the community has become much less insular in terms of intellectual influences. This may have contributed to the theoretical diversity that is criticized by the authors of recent systematic literature reviews on the topic of entre-preneurial learning (Byrne et al., 2014; Wang and Chugh, 2013). Our view is that this openness to new theoretical developments in social science and in 'mainstream' business and management studies provides a more sophisticated understanding of learning in small firms (Jones et al, 2010). The accumulation of this research provides a more com-prehensive understanding of the complex needs of the sector, resulting in more nuanced approaches to support development programmes as evident in the LEAD initiative. The challenge remains, however, in translating this research into policy and practice that can engage with the majority of small firms, since it is both difficult to overcome barriers to small firm engagement, and also to provide real and viable alternatives to the type of generic solutions favoured in policy instruments. In this case, research indicates that one size does not fit all. Despite these problems, we believe it is still possible, through policy development and sophisticated interventions, to make a real difference to entrepreneur-ial learning and the development of smaller firms.

REFERENCES

Ambrosini, V. and C. Bowman (2009) 'What are dynamic capabilities and are they a useful construct in strate-gic management?' *International Journal of Management Reviews*, **11** (1): 29–49.

Anderson, V. and Boocock, G. (2002) 'Small firms and internationalisation: Learning to manage and manag-ing to learn', *Human Resource Management Journal*, **12** (3), 5–24.

Argyris, C. (1999) *On Organizational Learning*, Oxford, Blackwell.

Argyris, C. and Schön, D. (1978) *Organizational Learning: A Theory of Action Perspective*, Reading, MA, Addison-Wesley.

Baker, H. (1995) 'The true value of failing', *Education & Training*, **37** (6), 27–32.

Baker, A., Jensen, P. and Kolb, D. (2005) 'Conversation as experiential learning', *Management Learning*, **36** (4), 411–27.

Baker, T., Miner, A. S. and Eesley, D. T. (2003) 'Improvising firms: Bricolage, account giving and improvisa-tional competencies in the founding process', *Research Policy*, **32** (2), 255–76.

Baker, T. and Nelson, R. E. (2005) 'Creating something from nothing: Resource construction through entre-preneurial bricolage', *Administrative Science Quarterly*, **50** (3), 329–66.

Balagopal, V. (2011) 'A matching theory of entrepreneurs' tie-formation intentions and initiation of economic exchange', *Academy of Management Journal*, **54** (1), 137–58.

Bandura, A. (1967) *Social Learning Theory*, Engleword Cliffs, NJ, Prentice-Hall.

Banfield, P., Jennings, P. L. and Beaver, G. (1996) 'Competence-based training for small firms: An expensive failure?' *Long Range Planning*, **29** (1), 94–102.

Bass, B. and Riggio, R. (2006) *Transformational Leadership (2ⁿᵈ Ed.)*, London, Erlbaum and Associates.

Beaver, G. (2002) *Small Business, Entrepreneurship and Enterprise Development*, Harlow, Financial Times Press.

Bergh, P., Thorgren, S. and Wincent, J. (2011) 'Entrepreneurs learning together: The importance of building trust for learning and exploiting business opportunities', *International Entrepreneurship and Management Journal*, **7** (1), 17–30.

Bird, B. (2002) 'Learning entrepreneurship competences: The self-directed learning approach', *International Journal of Entrepreneurship Education* 1: 203–27.

Bird, B. (1995) 'Toward a theory of entrepreneurial competency', in *Advances in Entrepreneurship, Firm Emergence and Growth*, J. A. Katz and R. H. Brockhaus (Eds). Greenwich, CT, JAI Press: 51–72.

Blackburn, R. and Kovalainen, A. (2009) 'Researching small firms and entrepreneurship: Past, present and future', *International Journal of Management Reviews*, **11** (2): 127–48.
Blackler, F. (1993) 'Knowledge and the theory of organizations: Organizations as activity systems and the reframing of management', *Journal of Management Studies*, **30** (6): 863–84.
Bolton, J.E. (1971) *Report of the Committee of Inquiry on Small Firms*, London, HMSO.
Boussouara, M. and Deakins, D. (2000) 'Trust and the acquisition of knowledge from non-executive directors by high technology entrepreneurs', *International Journal of Entrepreneurial Behaviour & Research*, **6** (4): 204.
Boyzatzis, R. E. (1982) *The Competent Manager: A Model for Effective Performance*, New York, Wiley.
Breslin, D. (2010) 'Broadening the management team: An evolutionary approach', *International Journal of Entrepreneurial Behaviour & Research*, **16** (2): 130–48.
Breslin, D. (2008) 'A review of the evolutionary approach to the study of entrepreneurship', *International Journal of Management Reviews*, **10** (4): 399–423.
Breslin, D. and Jones, C. (2012) 'The evolution of entrepreneurial learning', *International Journal of Organizational Analysis*, **20** (3): 294–308.
Burns, B. and Cooke, B. (2013) 'Kurt Lewin's field theory: A review and re-evaluation', *International Journal of Management Reviews*, **15** (4).
Burgoyne, J. and Stuart, R. (1977) 'Implicit learning theories as determinants of the effects of management development programmes', *Personnel Review*, **6** (2): 5–14.
Burrell, G. and Morgan, G. (1979) *Sociological Paradigms and Organizational Analysis*. London, Heinemann.
Byrne, J., Fayolle, A. and Toutain, O. (2014) 'Entrepreneurship education: What we know and what we need to know', in E. Chell and M. Karataş-Özkan (Eds), *Handbook of Research in Small Business and Entrepreneurship*. Cheltenham: Edward Elgar, Ch 15:261–88.
Caird, S. (1990) 'What does it mean to be enterprising?' *British Journal of Management*, **1** (1): 137–45.
Chaston, I. (1992) 'Supporting new small business start-ups', *Journal of European Industrial Training*, **16** (10): 3–8.
Chaston, I., Badger, B. and Sadler-Smith, E. (1999) 'Organisational learning: Research issues and application in SME sector firms', *International Journal of Entrepreneurial Behaviour & Research*, **5** (4): 106–29.
Chell, E. (2014) 'The critical incident technique', in E. Chell and M. Karataş-Özkan (Eds.). *Handbook of Research in Small Business & Entrepreneurship*. Cheltenham: Edward Elgar, Ch 7: 195–237.
Chell, E. (1998) 'Critical incident technique', in *Qualitative Methods and Analysis in Organizational Research: A Practical Guide*, G. Symon and C. Cassell, London, Sage: 51–72.
Chung, W. W. C., Pak, J. J. F. and Ng, C. H. (2001) 'Adaptation of quality function deployment for process reinvention in SMEs', *International Journal of Manufacturing Technology and Management*, **3** (4/5): 393–406.
Clarke, J. (2011) 'Revitalising entrepreneurship: How visual symbols are used in entrepreneurial performance', *Journal of Management Studies*, **48** (6): 1365–91.
Clarke, J., Thorpe, R., Anderson, L. and Gold, J. (2006) 'It's all action, it's all learning: Action learning in SMEs', *Journal of European Industrial Training*, **30** (6): 441–55.
Cope, J., (2005) 'Towards a dynamic learning perspective of entrepreneurship', *Entrepreneurship: Theory and Practice*, **29** (4): 373–97.
Cope, J. (2003) 'Entrepreneurial learning and critical reflection', *Management Learning*, **34** (4): 429–50.
Cope, J., Kempster, S. and Parry, K. (2011) 'Dimensions of distributed leadership in the SME context', *International Journal of Management Reviews*, **13** (3): 270–85.
Cope, J. and Watts, G. (2000) 'Learning by doing: An exploration of experience, critical incidents and reflection in entrepreneurial learning', *International Journal of Entrepreneurial Behaviour and Research*, **6** (3): 104–24.
Cornelissen, J. and Clarke, J. (2010) 'Imagining and rationalising opportunities: Inductive reasoning and the creation and justification of new ventures', *Academy of Management Review*, **35** (4): 539–57.
Coughlan, P., Harbison, A., Dromgoole, T. and Duff, D. (2001) 'Continuous improvement through collaborative action learning', *International Journal of Technology Management*, **22** (4): 285–302.
Council for Excellence in Management and Leadership (2000) *Joining Entrepreneurs in their World: Improving Entrepreneurship, Management and Leadership in UK SMEs*, London, CEML.
Curran, J. (1986) *Bolton 15 Years on: A Review and Analysis of Small Business Research in Britain, 1971–1986*, London, Small Business Research Trust.
Curran, J. and Blackburn, R. (2001) *Researching the Small Enterprise*, London, Sage.
Deakins, D. (1996) *Entrepreneurship and Small Firms*, London, McGraw-Hill.
Deakins, D. and Freel, M. (1998) 'Entrepreneurial learning and the growth process in SMEs', *The Learning Organization*, **5** (3): 144–55.
DeFillipi, R. and Ornstein, S. (2003) 'Psychological perspectives underlying theories of organizational learning', in *Handbook of Organizational Learning and Knowledge Management*, M. Easterby-Smith and M. A. Lyles (Eds), Oxford, Blackwell: 19–37.

Devins, D. and Gold, J. (2002) 'Social constructionism: A theoretical framework to underpin support for the development of managers in SMEs?', *Journal of Small Business and Enterprise Development*, **9** (2): 111–9.

Dewey, J. (1916) *Democracy and Education*, New York, Free Press.

Dreyfus, S. and Dreyfus, H. (1980) 'A Five-Stage Model of the Mental Activities Involved in Directed Skill Acquisition.' Operations Research Centre, University of Berkley.

Dodgson, M. (1991) 'Strategic alignment and organizational options in biotechnology firms', *Technology Analysis and Strategic Management*, **3** (2): 11–22.

Edwards, T. Delbridge, R. and Munday, M. (2007) 'A critical evaluation of EU interventions for innovation in the SME sector in Wales', *Urban Studies*, **44** (12): 2429–48.

Elfring, T. and Hulsink, W. (2007) 'Networking by entrepreneurs: Patterns of tie-formation in emerging organizations', *Organization Studies*, **28** (12): 1849–72.

Engeström, Y. (1987) *Learning by Expanding: An Activity-theoretical Approach to Developmental Research*, Helsinki:Orienta-Konsultit Oy.

Engeström, Y. (2000) 'Activity theory as a framework for analyzing and redesigning work', *Ergonomics*, **43** (7): 960–74.

Flanagan, J. C. (1954) 'Critical incident technique', *Psychological Bulletin*, **51** (4): 327–58.

Fuller-Love, N. (2006) 'Management development in smaller firms', *International Journal of Management Reviews*, **8** (3): 175–90.

Gadamer, H.G. (1994) *Truth and Method*, New York, Crossroad.

Gherardi, S. (2000) 'Practice-based theorizing on learning and knowing in organizations', *Organization*, **7** (2): 211–23.

Gherardi, S. and Nicolini, D. (2002) 'Learning in a constellation of interconnected practices: Cannon or dissonance?', *Journal of Management* Studies, **39** (4): 419–36.

Gibb, A. (2009) 'Meeting the development needs of owner managed small enterprise: A discussion on the centrality of action learning', *Action Learning: Research and Practice*, **6** (3), 209–27.

Gibb, A. (1997) 'Small firms' training and competitiveness: Building upon the small firm as a learning organisation', *International Small Business Journal*, **17** (1): 13–29.

Gold, J., Thorpe, R., Woodall, J. and Sadler-Smith, E. (2007) 'Continuing professional development in the legal profession', *Management Learning*, **38** (2): 235–50.

Gordon, I., Hamilton, E. and Jack, S. (2011) 'A study of a university-led entrepreneurship education programme for small business owner/managers', *Entrepreneurship & Regional Development*, 1–39 (i–first), http://dx.doi.org/10.1080/08985626.2011.566377.

Gordon, I. and Jack, S. (2010) 'HEI engagement with SMEs: Developing social capital', *International Journal of Entrepreneurial Behaviour and Research*, **16** (6): 517–39.

Hannon, P. D., Patton, D. and Marlow, S. (2000) 'Transactional learning relationships: Developing management competencies for effective small firm-stakeholder interactions', *Education & Training*, **42** (4/5): 237.

Harrison R. T. and Leitch, C. M. (2008) *Entrepreneurial Learning: Conceptual Frameworks and Applications*, London, Routledge.

Herbane, B. (2010) 'Small business research: Time for a crisis-based view', *International Small Business Journal*, **28** (1): 43–64.

Hervás-Oliver, J. and Albors-Garrigós, J. (2008) 'Local knowledge domains and the role of MNE affiliates in bridging and complementing a cluster's knowledge', *Entrepreneurship and Regional Development*, **20** (6): 581.

HMSO (1990) *Units of Competence for Setting up a Small Business*, London: Department of Employment Training Agency.

Holman, D., Pavlica, K. and Thorpe, R. (1997) 'Rethinking Kolb's theory of experiential learning in management education: The contribution of social constructionism and activity theory', *Management Learning*, **28** (2): 135–48.

Holt, R. and Macpherson, A. (2010) 'Sensemaking, rhetoric and the socially competent entrepreneur', *International Small Business Journal*, **28** (1), 20–42.

Jayawarna, D., Jones, O. and Macpherson, A. (2011) 'New business creation and regional development: Enhancing resource acquisition in areas of social deprivation', *Entrepreneurship & Regional Development*, **23** (9/10): 735–61.

Jones, O. (2006) 'Developing absorptive capacity in mature organizations: The change agent's role', *Management Learning*, **37** (3): 355–76.

Jones, O. (2003) 'Competitive advantage in SMEs: Towards a conceptual framework', in *Competitive Advantage in SMEs: Organizing for Innovation and Change*, O. Jones and F. Tilley (Eds),, Wiley, Chichester.

Jones, O. and Craven, M. (2001) 'Expanding capabilities in a mature manufacturing firm: Absorptive capacity and the TCS', *International Small Business Journal*, **19** (3): 39–55.

Jones, O., Macpherson, A. and Thorpe, R. (2010) 'Promoting learning in owner-managed small firms: Mediating artefacts and strategic space', *Entrepreneurship & Regional Development*, **22** (7/8): 649–73.

Jones, O., Macpherson, A. and Woollard, D. (2008) 'Entrepreneurial ventures in higher education: Analyzing organizational growth', *International Small Business Journal*, **26** (6): 683–708.

Jones, O and Macpherson, A. (2006) 'Inter-organizational learning and strategic renewal in SMEs: Extending the 4i framework', *Long Range Planning*, **39** (2): 155–75.

Karataş-Özkan, M. (2011) 'Understanding relational qualities of entrepreneurial learning: Towards a multi-layered approach', *Entrepreneurship & Regional Development*, 1–30 (i-first).

Karataş-Özkan, M. and Chell, E. (2010) *Nascent Entrepreneurship and Learning*, Edward Elgar, Cheltenham.

Kayes, D. C. (2002) 'Experiential learning and its critics: Preserving the role of experience in management education', *Academy of Management Learning and Education*, **1** (2): 137–49.

Kelliher, F., Foley, A. and Frampton, A. (2009) 'Facilitating small firm learning networks in the Irish tourism sector', *Tourism and Hospitality Research*, **9** (1): 80.

Kempster, S. and Cope, J. (2010) 'Learning to lead in the entrepreneurial context', *International Journal of Entrepreneurial Behaviour and Research*, **16** (1): 5–34.

Kirby, D. (1990) 'Management education and small business development: An exploratory study of small firms in the UK', *Journal of Small Business Management*, **28** (4): 78–87.

Kock, H., Gill, A. and Ellstrom, P. E. (2008) 'Why do small firms participate in a programme for competence development?' *Journal of Workplace Learning*, **20** (3): 181–94.

Köhler, W. (1925) *The Mentality of Apes*, New York, Harcourt Brace.

Kolb, D. (1984) *Experiential Learning: Experience as the Source of Learning and Development*, Englewood Cliffs, NJ, Prentice Hall.

Lave, J. and Wenger, E. (1991) *Situated Learning Legitimated Peripheral Participation*, Cambridge, Cambridge University Press.

Lawlor, A. (1988) 'Helping small companies to help themselves', *Industrial and Commercial Training*, **20** (3): 18–22.

Leitch, C. M. and Harrison, R. T. (2008) 'Entrepreneurial learning: A review and research agenda', in *Entrepreneurial Learning: Conceptual Frameworks and Applications*, R. T. Harrison and C. M. Leitch, London, Routledge.

Levie, J. and Lichtenstein, B. (2010) 'A terminal assessment of stages theory: Introducing a dynamic states approach to entrepreneurship', *Entrepreneurship: Theory and Practice*, **34** (2): 317–50.

Lewin, K. (1946) 'Action research and minority problems', *Journal of Social Issues*, **2** (4): 34–46.

Loan-Clarke, J., Boocock, G., Smith, A. and Whittaker, J. (2000) 'Competence-based management development in small and medium-sized firms: A multi-stakeholder analysis', *International Journal of Training & Development*, **4** (3): 176–95.

Lounsbury, M. and Glynn, M. (2001) 'Cultural entrepreneurship: Stories, legitimacy and the acquisition of resources', *Strategic Management Journal*, **22** (6/7): 545–64.

Macpherson, A. (2005) 'Learning to grow: Resolving the crisis of knowing', *Technovation*, **25** (10), 1129–40.

Macpherson, A. and Holt, R. (2007) 'Knowledge, learning and SME growth: A systematic review of the evidence', *Research Policy*, **36** (2): 172–92.

Macpherson, A. and Jones, O. (2008) 'Object-mediated learning and strategic renewal in a mature organization', *Management Learning*, **39** (2): 177–201.

Macpherson, A., Jones, O. and Zhang, M. (2004) 'Evolution or revolution? Dynamic capabilities in a knowledge-dependent firm', *R&D Management*, **34** (2): 161–77.

Macpherson, A., Kofinas, A., Jones, O. and Thorpe, R. (2010) 'Making sense of mediated learning: Cases from small firms', *Management Learning*, **41** (3): 303–24.

Malik, K. and Wei, J. (2011) 'How external partnering enhances innovation: Evidence from Chinese technology-based SMEs', *Technology Analysis & Strategic Management*, **23** (4): 401.

Man, T. W. Y. (2012) 'Developing a behaviour-centred model of entrepreneurial learning', *Journal of Small Business and Enterprise Development*, **19** (3): 549–66.

Man. T. W. Y., Lau, L. and Chan, T. (2002) 'The competitiveness of small and medium-sized enterprises: A conceptualization with focus on entrepreneurial competencies', *Journal of Business Venturing*, **17** (2): 123–42.

Man, T. W. Y. and Lau, T. (2005) 'The context of entrepreneurship in Hong Kong: An investigation through the patterns of entrepreneurial competencies in contrasting industrial environments', *Journal of Small Business and Enterprise Development*, **12** (4): 464.

Mangham, I. (1985) 'In search of competence', *Journal of General Management*, **12** (2): 5–12.

Martin, G. and Staines, H. (1994) 'Managerial competences in small firms', *Journal of Management Development*, **13** (7): 23–34.

Matlay, H. (2000) 'Organizational learning in small learning organizations: An empirical overview', *Education & Training*, **42** (4/5): 202–10.

Matlay, H. and Addis, M. (2002) 'Competence-based training, vocational qualifications and learning targets: Some lessons for the Learning and Skills Council', *Education & Training*, **44** (6): 25–60.

Matlay, H. and Hyland, T. (1997) 'NVQs in the small business sector: a critical overview', *Education + Training*, **39** (9): 325–32.

McAdam, R. and Mitchell, N. (2010) 'The influences of critical incidents and lifecycle dynamics on innovation implementation constructs in SMEs: a longitudinal study', *International Journal of Technology Management*, **52** (1/2): 189.

McClelland, D. C. (1973) 'Testing for competence rather than for "intelligence"', *American Psychologist*, **28** (1): 1–14.

McHenry, J. (2008) 'The role and management of learning from experience in an entrepreneurial context', in *Entrepreneurial Learning: Conceptual Frameworks and Applications*, R. T. Harrison and C. M. Leitch, London, Routledge.

McKelvie A. and Davidsson P. (2009) 'From resource base to dynamic capabilities: an investigation of new firms', *British Journal of Management*, **20** (SI): S63–S80.

Moreira, A. C. (2009) 'Knowledge capability flows in buyer-supplier relationships', *Journal of Small Business and Enterprise Development*, **16** (1): 93.

NWDA (2009) *Lead Provider Manual*, NWDA and Lancaster University.

Oswick, C., Anthony, P., Keenoy, T. and Mangham, I. (2000) 'A dialogic analysis of organizational learning', *Journal of Management Studies*, **37** (6): 887–901.

Parrilli, M., Aranguren, M. and Larrea, M. (2010) 'The role of onteractive learning to close the "innovation gap" in SME-based local economies: A furniture cluster in the Basque Country and its key policy implications', *European Planning Studies*, **18** (3): 351.

Patton, D., Marlow, S. and Hannon, P. (2000) 'The relationship between training and small firm performance: Research frameworks and lost quests', *International Small Business Journal*, **19** (1): 11–27.

Patton, D. and Marlow, S. (2002) 'The determinants of management training within smaller firms in the UK. What role does strategy play?', *Journal of Small Business and Enterprise Development*, **9** (3): 260–70.

Paul, T., Phillips, N. and Owen, J. (2011) 'Bridging institutional entrepreneurship and the creation of new organizational forms', *Organization Science*, **22** (1): 60–80.

Pavlov, I. (1927) *Conditioned Reflexes: An Investigation of the Physiological Activity of the Cerebral Cortex*, Oxford, Oxford University Press.

Perren, L. and Grant, P. (2000) 'The evolution of management accounting routines in small businesses: A social constructionist perspective', *Management Accounting Review*, **11** (4): 391–411.

Phelps, R., Adams, R. and Bessant, J. (2007) 'Life cycles of growing organizations: A review with implications for knowledge and learning', *International Journal of Management Reviews*, **9** (1): 1–30.

Piaget, J. (1929) *The Child's Conception of the World*, Paterson, NJ, Littlefield Adams.

Pittaway, L., Robertson, M., Munir, K., Denyer, D. and Neely, A. (2004) 'Networking and innovation: A systematic review of the evidence', *International Journal of Management Reviews*, **5/6** (3/4): 137–68.

Rae, D. (2004) 'Practical theories from entrepreneurs' stories: Discursive approaches to entrepreneurial learning', *Journal of Small Business and Enterprise Development*, **11** (2): 195–202.

Rae, D. (2002) 'Entrepreneurial emergence: A narrative study of entrepreneurial learning in independently owned media businesses', *The International Journal of Entrepreneurship and Innovation*, **3** (1): 53–9.

Rae, D. (2000) 'Understanding entrepreneurial learning: A question of how?', *International Journal of Entrepreneurial Behaviour & Research*, **6** (3): 145–59.

Rae, D. and Carswell, M. (2001) 'Towards a conceptual understanding of entrepreneurial learning', *Journal of Small Business and Enterprise Development*, **8** (2): 150–8.

Ram, M. and Trehan, K. (2010) 'Critical action learning, policy learning and small firms: An inquiry', *Management Learning*, **41** (4): 415.

Redmond, J. and Walker, E. A. (2008) 'A new approach to small business training: Community based education', *Education & Training*, **50** (8/9): 697.

Reuber, A. R. and Fischer, E. (1999) 'Understanding the consequences of founders' experience', *Journal of Small Business Management*, **37** (2): 30–45.

Revans, R. (1980) *Action Learning: New Techniques for Managers*, London, Blond and Briggs.

Robinson, S. (2006) 'Learning to lead: Developing SME leadership support for business development', *Institute of Small Business and Entrepreneurship Conference*, Cardiff (November).

Sadler-Smith, E., Hampson, Y., Chaston, I. and Badger, B. (2003) 'Managerial behaviour, entrepreneurial style and small firm performance', *Journal of Small Business Management*, **41** (1): 47–67.

Senge, P. M. (1990) *The Fifth Discipline: The Art and Practice of the Learning Organization*, New York, Bantam Doubleday.

Sharifi, S. and Zhang, M. (2009) 'Sense-making and recipes: Examples from selected small firms', *International Journal of Entrepreneurial Behaviour and Research*, **15** (6): 555–71.

Skinner, B. F. (1938) *The Behavior of Organisms: An Experiential Analysis*, New York, Appleton-Century-Crofts.

Smith, K. (2008) 'Embedding enterprise education into the curriculum at a research-led university', *Education & Training*, **50** (8/9): 713–24.

Smith, A., Whittaker, J., Loan-Clarke, J. and Boocock, G. (1999) 'Competence based management development to SMEs and the provider's perspective', *Journal of Management Development*, **18** (6): 557–72.

Smith, L. and Robinson, S. (2007) *Leading Enterprise Development: Report on the Design and Delivery of a Programme to Engage and Motivate Small Businesses in Leadership and Management Development*, Institute for Entrepreneurship and Enterprise Development, Lancaster University Management School, Lancaster.

Spender, J. C. (1989) *Industry Recipes: An Enquiry into the Nature and Sources of Managerial Judgement*, Blackwell, Oxford.

Stanworth, J. and Curran G. (1991) *Bolton 20 Years on: The Small Firm in the 1990s*, London, Paul Chapman.

Stanworth, M. and Curran, J. (1976) 'Growth and the small firm – an alternative view', *Journal of Management Studies*, **13** (2): 95–110.

Stokes, D. and Wilson, N. (2010) *Small Business Management and Entrepreneurship*, Andover, Cengage.

Storey, D. J. (2011) 'Optimism and chance: The elephants in the entrepreneurship room', *International Small Business Journal*, **29** (4): 303–21.

Storey, D. J. (2004) 'Exploring the link, among small firms, between management training and firm performance: A comparison between the UK and other OECD countries', *International Journal of Human Resource Management*, **15** (1): 112–30.

Storey, D. J. (1992), *Understanding the Small Business Sector*, London, Routledge.

Stuart, R., Thompson, J. and Harrison, J. (1995) 'Translation: From generalizable to organization-specific competence frameworks', *Journal of Management Development*, **14** (1): 67–80.

Sullivan, R. (2000) 'Entrepreneurial learning and mentoring', *International Journal of Entrepreneurial Behaviour and Research*, **6** (3): 160–75.

Taylor, D., Jones, O. and Boles, K. (2004) 'Building social capital through action learning: An insight into the entrepreneur', *Education + Training*, **46** (5): 226–35.

Thakkar, J., Kanda, A. and Deshmukh, S. G. (2011) 'Mapping of supply chain learning: a framework for SMEs', *The Learning Organization*, **18** (4): 313.

Thorpe, R., Holt, R., Macpherson, A. and Pittaway, L. (2005) 'Knowledge within small and medium-sized firms: A systematic review of the evidence'. *International Journal of Management Reviews*, **7** (4): 257–81.

Thorpe, R., Jones, O., Macpherson, A. and Holt, R. (2008) 'The evolution of business knowledge in smaller firms', in *The Evolution of Business Knowledge*, H. Scarbrough (Ed.), Oxford, Oxford University Press.

Thorndike, E. L. (1913) *The Psychology of Learning*, New York, Teacher's College.

Ulrich, T. and Cole, G. (1987) 'Towards more effective training of future entrepreneurs', *Journal of Small Business Management*, **25** (4): 32–39.

Voudouris, I., Dimitrator, P. and Salvaou, H. (2011) 'Entrepreneurial learning in new high technology ventures', *International Small Business Journal*, **29** (3): 238–58.

Vygotsky, L. S. (1978) *Mind in Society: The Development of Higher Sociological Processes*, Cambridge, MA, Harvard University Press.

Wang, C. and Chugh, H. (2013) 'Entrepreneurial learning: Past research and future trends', *International Journal of Management Reviews*, **16** (1), doi: 10.1111/ijmr.12007.

Watkins, D. S. (1983) 'Development, training and education for the small firm: A European perspective', *European Small Business Journal*, **1** (3): 29–44.

Watts, H. D., Wood, A. M. and Wardle, P. (2006) 'Owner-managers, clusters and local embeddedness: small firms in the Sheffield (UK) metal-working cluster', *Entrepreneurship and Regional Development*, **18** (3): 185–206.

Wenger, E. (2000) 'Communities of practice and social learning systems', *Organization*, **7** (2): 225–46.

Westhead, P. and Storey, D. (1996) 'Management training and small firm performance: Why is the link so weak?' *International Small Business Journal*, **14** (4): 13–24.

Wyer, P., Mason, J. and Theodorakopoulos, N. (2000), 'Small business development and the "learning organisation"', *International Journal of Entrepreneurial Behaviour & Research*, **6** (4): 239–59.

Young, J. E. and Sexton, D. L. (1997) 'Entrepreneurial learning: A conceptual framework', *Journal of Enterprising Culture*, **5** (2): 223–48.

Zhang, M., Macpherson, A. and Jones, O. (2006) 'Conceptualising the learning process in SMEs: Improving innovation through external orientation', *International Small Business Journal*, **24** (3): 299–321.

Zott, C. and Huy, Q. N. (2007) 'How entrepreneurs use symbolic management to acquire resources', *Administrative Science Quarterly*, **52** (1): 70–105.

APPENDIX 16.1   LEARNING FROM LEAD

Quotes from owner-managers attending their final learning and reflection day:

I have made more time to step back and have a clearer idea of difference between leadership and management.

I network more and am much more proactive with my collaborations. I have taken on board the lesson about social media and have set–up a Facebook and Linkedin account and revamped the website.

I now ensure that my staff are clear about their objectives and target and measure output rather than input. This has freed me up to do other things within the business.

I have learnt to give ownership of tasks to my staff, trust them and let them learn from their mistakes.

I now give myself time out to reflect. I am now not afraid to share my problems with staff and have become more positive. I have learnt to do the things I resist the most. . .first.

I use questions more in my approach to management. . .to get buy-in from staff.

LEAD has given me the confidence to put my case forward for change within the business.

I am a better reflector and now take time to think about what I want the business to look like. . . not how quickly I can get there.

I have learnt that it is counterproductive to spoon-feed staff – must delegate and let them use their own skills and abilities to complete the task.

I have learnt that people learn in different ways and that I can get them to develop more quickly if I identify their preferred learning style.

LEAD has helped me to support my staff better and has given me the confidence to validate my ideas.

The reflection day was a fantastic end to my learning and training experience. I will encourage business owners to go on the LEAD programme.

A great learning/training programme that has helped my personal development and character.

Increased confidence in my business ability.

Made me more focused and positive for my future ambitions personally and professionally.

Has made massive difference to my outlook.

Enabled me to develop greater insight into leadership skills to lead others in my team.

LEAD has given me the tools, techniques and insight to create a better business environment.

I feel like a new and improved person, ready to take on the world.

Extremely useful and very enjoyable.

A great way to build confidence and gain knowledge from like-minded people.

The course has been interesting/challenging and thought provoking but also a great experience.

Inspirational, challenging, informative, supporting – the best money I have spent on the business.

LEAD to me is not about golden nugget, it is about silver coins which add up, I can now take them out of the bag and start spending them.

PART V

APPLICATIONS OF ENTREPRENEURSHIP RESEARCH

17. Entrepreneurial innovation in science-based firms: the need for an ecosystem perspective

Sarah Lubik and Elizabeth Garnsey

INTRODUCTION

Influenced by Schumpeterian logic, policy makers and academics have long been intrigued and inspired by the promise of entrepreneurship as a source of economic regeneration. In recent years, there has been increasing focus on small businesses and entrepreneurship for job creation. Within the field of entrepreneurship, science-based entrepreneurship has been noted by academics and policy makers as particularly important, as the introduction of new innovations, such as materials, devices or biotech discoveries, often has a knock-on effect within the economy, requiring new value chains, infrastructure and complements, and thus providing new jobs and new opportunities (Pavitt et al., 1989). In the UK, entrepreneurship has been increasingly viewed as a way to capitalise on the UK's strengths in scientific knowledge creation and gain leadership in new and emerging markets (The Royal Society, 2010). In particular, university spin-out (USO) companies have been cast in a key role in the UK's shift from workshop-of-the-world to knowledge-based economy[1]. With lofty hopes pinned on a relatively small group of fledgling companies, a greater understanding of science-based entrepreneurship is needed.

In this chapter, we present an overview of the current state of knowledge regarding innovation by science-based ventures, with a focus on commercialising technologies stemming from universities[2]. Key findings, core concepts and possible avenues for future research are identified. While our concern is with science-based spin-out firms in the UK, these firms are a subset of new technology-based firms (NTBF) in general, which are again a subset of entrepreneurship and small businesses. Study of science-based ventures is also illuminating for other types of business, as these fledgling firms face many of the common start-up challenges alongside additional spin-out specific challenges such as technology development time lines and balancing multiple stakeholder objectives.

THEORETICAL PERSPECTIVES

USOs have been viewed through a variety of theoretical lenses, including business model, institutional link and, most often, by investigating resource endowments and the growth of the resource base (Mustar et al., 2006)[3]. Throughout this chapter, we take an ecosystem perspective because it aligns well with the analysis of value creation in new ventures which is often dependent on the venture's ability to attract external resources and persuade other players to do business with them. In addition, this perspective makes it clear value generation is a distributed process that involves co-innovation from other value-adding participants in the venture's environment. Moreover ecosystem analysis can accommodate the influence of policy makers, regulators and standards setters, who do not usually appear in standard value chain analysis nor in the industrial structure approach to the firm's business environment. This perspective also emphasises the importance of viewing the internal workings, resources and strategy of the firm in the context of its business (and often policy) environment, which is increasingly recommended by scholars in the area (Hofer and Bygrave, 1992; Venkataraman and Henderson, 1998). The ecosystem perspective has been revived and revised by Moore (1993) and Adner (2006), though the basic concept can be viewed earlier in one of the seminal works of Resource-Based Theory (RBT), *The Theory of the Growth of the Firm* (Penrose, 1959). The ecosystem perspective has been applied at various levels of specificity. Adner (2006) views the firm's ecosystem as the network of firms which contribute to the complete solution to the end customer, which can be complementary to the business model perspective as it also links the internal workings of the firm to its environment (Amit and Zott, 2010). In contrast, policy-oriented works often view the ecosystem in a much broader sense, to include networks, education institutions and financial structures (Sainsbury, 2007). The definition often depends on the objectives of the study. In the following, we also take a broader view of the firm's environment including policy development, market, partners and the national innovation system (NIS) as it influences these ventures.

THE PROMISE OF GROWTH FROM SCIENCE

The UK is at the forefront of scientific knowledge-creation[4], but this has not been translated into commensurate economic benefits as of yet. Recent changes in both the political climate and market dynamics have led to increasing importance being attributed to the role of entrepreneurship and a knowledge-based economy in wealth creation. In order to realise this hope, UK policy has evolved to support the commercialisation of scientific research and development (DTI, 1999; BERR, 2009), prompted by the promise of economic growth and leadership in new markets and industries (Mowery and Rosenberg, 1979; Freeman, 1982). From the early 1980s to the early 1990s, policy in the UK shifted from market-pull type initiatives favouring larger companies, toward a number of schemes intended to spark innovation and entrepreneurship, for example, offering innovation grants. In the late 1990s, UK policy began to recognise the potential of knowledge transfer from academia to industry, adding a "third strand" of activities to academia's traditional roles of research and teaching (Gill et al., 2007; Minshall, 2008).

Universities have adopted a variety of strategies for accomplishing knowledge transfer, some promoting spin-out formation, others strongly discouraging spin-out creation in favour of ongoing direct collaboration with large companies and others preferring licensing IP to established firms for further commercialisation (Druilhe and Garnsey, 2006; Livesey et al., 2008). The global success of high profile science-based and IT companies and increasing demand for their output has led to a significant increase in the overall number of spin-out firms, perhaps aided by tech transfer policies. However, these developments were not universally approved by those who look at the impact of spin-out activity. After a period where spin-outs were encouraged by most UK universities, the Lambert Review (2003, p50) concluded that there was "too little licensing and too many unsustainable spinouts", sparking a shift in policy preference back to licensing university technologies directly to large firms, on the assumption that corporate know-how and established commercial resources would result in faster time to market, lower costs and licensing revenues for universities. However, revenues from licensing remained relatively low overall and limited to a few universities (Minshall et al., 2008). Moreover, it has now been recognised that, although first-generation university spin-outs may not be particularly successful, over time firms spinning out from earlier spin-outs can create a technology cluster around the university that undoubtedly has considerable collective value (Garnsey and Heffernan, 2005).

However, in the case of science-based innovations, spin-outs remain important to bridge the gap between academic research and attractive market opportunity. These are those firms that are commercialising a product or process built on new or developing scientific principles; for example, new materials, biotech advances or photovoltaics. Generic technological innovations often have a number of divergent applications in a variety of markets but these may be too early stage to be attractive to established firms and often require costly further development (Tidd et al., 1998). Irrespective of policy decisions, it has been widely accepted among academics that in the very early stages of disruptive technologies, small firms are often the most appropriate commercial vehicles (Lieberman and Montgomery, 1988; Christensen, 1997). As they do not have existing products to cannibalise, markets to serve or capabilities to undermine, they can learn and adapt much faster than established firms in uncertain and emerging markets (Utterback, 1994; Christensen, 1997; Shane, 2004).

As economic conditions lead many large firms to re-evaluate in-house R&D and focus on their established customer bases, the composition of players in the arena of generic technological innovation has shifted to include higher education institutions (HEI) and small, science-based firms, often with university origins (Lubik, 2010; Pisano, 2010). These spin-outs take forward new ideas, providing proof of concept and demonstrating the innovation's potential for value creation (Pisano, 2006b; Rothaermel and Thursby, 2007). That does not mean that the role of large firms should be discounted. As the phenomenon of open-innovation[5] takes hold, many large corporations are opening their boundaries to work with ventures and spin-outs, supplying knowledge, direction, marketing, feedback, physical assets and, in some cases, investment, in order to keep abreast of the newest technologies for use and/or acquisition once they have been proven (Pisano, 1990; Chesbrough et al., 2006).

UNDERSTANDING SCIENCE-BASED VENTURES

A growing body of knowledge focuses on how best to move science-based innovations from the lab to the market through spin-outs (Christensen et al., 2004; Shane, 2004; Mustar et al., 2006; Minshall et al., 2008). A number of studies have investigated the key challenges that science-based ventures in particular face: business model development and evolution, market selection and partnerships.

Scholars investigating entrepreneurship have long recognised the importance of looking at entrepreneurship in context (Lockett and Wright, 2005; Djokovic and Souitaris, 2008). As such, business models are a useful starting point because they are a design embodying the logic that links technology to the realisation of economic value. They specify the firm's value proposition, market segment, value chain and structure (or value network), their cost structure/profit potential, and competitive strategy, as well as boundary spanning activities (Chesbrough and Rosenbloom, 2002; Zott and Amit, 2010). Despite a policy focus on bringing new technology to market, there has been little research focusing on the business models of science-based ventures, or how a successful science-based firm actually works.

Science-based Business Models

A small number of previous studies have shed light on different aspects of business models in science-based businesses, most often nanotechnology or biotech, including challenges (Bhat, 2005; Maine and Garnsey, 2006), location (Robinson et al., 2007; Maine et al., 2010) and organisational structure (Maine, 2008). Based on his study of the biotech industry from its emergence until the present, Pisano (2006a) has outlined the unique characteristics of such industries and suggests they require the development of new business models. He observes that firms being spawned at the intersection of academia and business have three disparate, and often conflicting, core objectives: to make use of existing science; to contribute to the advancement of scientific knowledge; and to turn a profit. By pursuing all three objectives simultaneously, these spin-outs create different types of value for parties who may not be in concert with each other, such as the parent university, investors, downstream partners, the scientific community and, not least of all, the focal firm.

Unlike ventures based on fairly accepted technical principles that do not require extensive further development, science-based firms must gain access to considerable resources in order to commercialise their products. They can rarely do this alone and instead seek these resources from a variety of sources (Maine and Garnsey, 2006; Rasmussen, 2007). In addition to any resources gained through a parent university, nearly all science-based ventures require the engagement of large firms and/or financiers. Rather than acting as a relatively passive customer, large firms who forge partnerships with science-based ventures are often highly interactive, acting as partner, customer and co-producer, especially in the early stages. Resources may also continue to flow from the parent university, investors, government or business support services. Therefore, the venture will have to create a business model that not only meets its own requirements for knowledge creation, growth and value creation but also balances the objectives of the other parties involved.

Thus, external parties are vital providers of complementary resources, including knowledge, manufacturing capabilities, influence, etc. How a firm structures itself to access these resources is a fundamental part of its business model. Creativity and how a company values and deploys different types of resources (such as financial, human or social) also makes entrepreneurial business models unique (Brush et al., 2001). For example some ventures are able to access resources or physical equipment through social connections rather than financial transactions. However, few studies provide evidence on how these ventures successfully structure and adapt themselves to accommodate the other parties in their environment. Since Matthew Bullock first defined the "soft" company model in 1982, studies have pointed out the importance of "soft start" models where companies fund their own growth through R&D projects and service models

(Minshall et al., 2008). However, it is difficult for young companies engaged in revenue generating services, such as contract R&D, to continue to focus on creating a market-ready product. The identification and evaluation of other novel business models and the circumstances under which they are effective, or ineffective, would be a useful contribution to this field. A core element of the business model is the selection of the appropriate market and the corresponding strategy.

Strategies for Market Selection and Entry

The choice of market often determines the appropriate value proposition, value chain position and, critically, the most appropriate alliances and partnerships. Market selection also plays a key role in the ability of these firms to secure finance. However, many of these technologies have possible applications across a number of markets; they may also be disruptive in nature, requiring the reconfiguration if not destruction of established value chains and capabilities of incumbent firms. A number of studies have put forward recommendations for the types of strategies that succeed in high-tech markets, though looking at a number of different sectors. Davidow (1986) proposed that high-tech firms should pursue a niche market strategy in order to capture a significant percentage of the market. A similar idea was put forward by Christensen (1997) and has received significant attention and citation from both academics and the investment community. Niche markets, those without large, dominant players, can provide a firm with a new technological offering a safe space in which to grow, prove its ability to satisfy customers and gain enough momentum, resources and credibility to then branch into larger markets. Teece (1986) proposed scenarios for these strategies, recommending that a small firm enter a market via a licensing strategy if it has strong IP, the use of which does not require specialised assets by the licensee. However, he also warned that when specialised assets are required, firms owning the resources required for manufacturing, usually a larger firm, would generally keep a higher percentage of the profits. Thus, a purely licensing strategy may lower a small firm's need for resources, but may also limit its ability to capture value from its innovation.

Christensen et al. (2004) recommend that firms undertake vertical integration to the "de-coupling point" of a value chain. They refer to the point beyond which the design and manufacturing interdependencies in an industry's value chain cease to be dependent on firm-specific assets. From this point, the firm is more likely to be able to sell a standardised product into multiple end markets. Particularly in emerging and changing markets, this point may shift over time, as standardised supplies and components become more widely available. This strategy implies that a new firm should choose a market, or markets, where it can access all the resources required to develop its technology to the point where the offering that embodies its technology (whether that is a material, a component, a product or a system) can be sold with minimal further modifications into the open market. However, vertical integration across many stages of the value chain may be unrealistic for resource-constrained USOs. A licensing strategy for firms with strong IP is recommended by Arora et al. (2001) who suggest that high-tech firms license to minimise the need for downstream assets such as production and distribution channels. This has implications for market as well as value chain selection. Specifically regarding advanced material ventures, Maine and Garnsey (2006) recommend that a firm limit the number of markets it pursues and choose near-term substitution markets in its early stages because these firms are unlikely to be able to secure sufficient resources to commercialise in all possible markets. Moreover, in areas such as materials with long development time lines, splitting the firm's focus can be detrimental to its overall progress.

The above shows a variety of market selection and entry options proposed for science-based ventures. While a number of different strategies have been favoured over time, there is an over-arching theme. Market selection involves many factors and to survive, the firm must align its strategy to its distinctive market and environment (Gans and Stern, 2003; Adner, 2006). This suggests that future studies focused on the distinctive market selection and entry requirements for specific science-based technologies are needed to provide guidance to these entrepreneurs and managers. The focus could be on the development of specific technologies for specific markets rather than the kind of generalist marketing advice that has been provided up to now. Partners and their availability can also be a significant factor in market choice.

In the literature on disruptive innovation, it is increasingly recognised that emerging markets with growing demand should be targeted in addition to established markets in advanced economies. These may require disruptive innovations (such as the reduced instruction chip developed by ARM and the e-commerce model of antibody distribution by Abcam). Disruptive innovations based on frugal engineering may provide affordable products attractive to customers in emerging markets. Thus, frugal design could be encouraged in place of the high end design education that is still predominant, with a view to producing products attractive to consumers on limited budgets, e.g. in the BRIC (Brazil, Russia, India and China) countries. This does not mean that standards of design should be lowered, but rather that design could pay more attention to resource economy and lower cost (Hang and Garnsey, 2011). It is also widely recognized that partnerships may play a significant role.

Partnership Strategies

There is a significant body of research regarding the range of reasons and options for strategic alliances amongst high-tech firms and their importance to the commercialisation of technology (Das and Teng, 2000; Minshall et al., 2008). Recent studies have tried to measure the success of these partnerships, with mixed conclusions. Hagedoorn and Schakenraad (1991) found that firms with technological partnerships were, for the most part, more successful than those without. Mitchell and Singh (1996) found a variety of effects and that the impact of partnerships appeared to depend on the state of the business environment and the closeness of the partnership. A small number of these studies specifically focused on alliances between ventures and incumbent partners (Hitt et al., 2000; Alvarez and Barney, 2001); an even smaller number investigate relationships between USOs and their partners (Minshall, 2003).

A number of studies also pointed out possible negative consequences of alliances to small firms, most notably the possibility of the larger firm appropriating most of the value created (Teece, 1986; Dodgson, 1992; Mitchell and Singh, 1996; Alvarez and Barney, 2001; Niosi, 2003). Pisano (2006a) warns that while alliances can lead to more rapid commercialisation, they may increase motivation to pursue short-term revenue at the expense of major scientific advance. Colombo et al. (2006) suggest that the transaction costs of alliances may be prohibitive for smaller NTBFs. However risky, alliances are also generally seen to be of crucial and growing importance to small high-tech firms (Bidault and Cummings, 1994; Stuart, 2000). Among other benefits, engaging in alliances allows firms to gain access to complementary knowledge and decrease their R&D costs. They can also aid in foreign expansion, give advantage over shared competitors, allow sharing of complementary expertise and increase speed to market (Dodgson, 1993).

In early-stage, science-based USOs, these alliances can be also be a vital source of development know-how, technological capabilities and scale-up facilities, in addition to complementary assets, such as market information or market access (Clarysee et al., 2005). Early development alliances can also provide contract income, and therefore a source of early revenue (Maine and Garnsey, 2006). Alliances can lend credibility and so provide, or assist access to, venture capital. The involvement of established firms can also provide access to some forms of government funding and support (Dodgson, 1992). In addition to these more tangible resources, alliances with corporate firms also convey credibility for start-ups (Maine and Ashby, 2002; Niosi, 2003). In return, corporate partners receive access to potentially lucrative innovations that can be used to improve their innovative capability and thus strengthen competitiveness in their core markets or ability to branch into new ones.

While the above literature examines venture-incumbent relationships, the literature on science-based business models points out that there are a number of other players involved, although few studies examine alliances by type of partner or type of partnership. Colombo et al. (2006) contribute to this discussion, emphasising the difference between a partnership that explores opportunities and one that exploits them. Belderbos et al. (2004) examine the variety of partnerships open to high-tech firms and find that large corporations tend to engage in the widest range of collaborations and benefit from academic relationships to a greater extent than do smaller firms; this may be because larger firms have the resources to manage these partnerships. In contrast, Lubik et al. (Lubik et al., forthcoming 2013) suggest that the most successful science-based USOs are those which make use of all available types of partner, and that the academic culture of information sharing may make these firms better at, or more comfortable with, alliances than those without academic roots. However, from the above discussion of collaborative strategies, it is also clear that strong and well-managed IP has a role to play in how well these alliances work, and who captures value from them (Ahuja, 2000a; Lockett and Wright, 2005).

An increasing number of studies also focus on the importance of networks and networking to spin-outs and other entrepreneurial ventures (Rothaermel et al., 2007). Like alliances, network membership offers credibility, access to resources and access to skills. Additionally, networks can be a major source of crucial information and technological diffusion in fast-moving fields (Peters et al., 1998; Ahuja, 2000b). Personnel with the appropriate skills, abilities and networks have been found to have a positive impact on ventures in terms of time to market, thus emphasising their importance. It has been suggested that if an academic founder does not have these network ties, finding a 'surrogate' or external person with industrial experience may be preferable to having the academic at the helm of the firm (Franklin et al., 2001). From an ecosystem perspective, this also emphasises the key role of network growth, facilitation and culture to commercialisation. This leads us to the need for an appropriate business environment for these firms.

BUILDING A SUPPORTIVE ECOSYSTEM

Significant policy attention has been directed at the resources and structures that must be in place for spin-outs and ventures to realise their potential. In particular, appropriate access to capital, realistic time horizons and a diverse ecosystem of players are critical.

Investment

Access to finance is a significant topic for spin-out formation and growth, although the amount of systematic research in the area is still small (Shane and Cable, 2002; Gill et al., 2007). In keeping with the belief that investment in the advance of science will yield economic results through translation into new products and processes, UK policy makers have increased the funding of university science[6] and put policies in place to encourage knowledge sharing and spin-out formation (The Royal Society, 2010). After the spin-out firm has been formed, there are a variety of funding options available to new technology-based firms; most notably, debt financing, public financing and equity financing (seed, angel, venture capital), the latter receiving the most attention from policy makers perhaps because it is somewhat better documented.

Traditionally, early-stage, high-tech ventures have faced constraints in obtaining debt finance because they are viewed as high risk, have a limited financial track record and lack collateral. While some UK banks claim that this view has changed, the high interest cost of debt financing often rules this out as a viable option. In Lubik's (2010) study of 67 material-based USOs in the UK, none were initially financed by debt.

An initial public offering (IPO) is one significant route to substantial funding for new firms, usually after private investment and venture capital. In 1995, the UK launched an alternative funding opportunity, the AiM stock exchange, in order to provide a mechanism for privately held ventures to raise early stage finance. This institutional innovation received praise and attention while the markets were doing well, but ran into problems in times of economic downturn. A study of environmental technology ventures by Mueller and Garnsey (2009), concluded that in the short term, price-driven objectives of shareholders were misaligned with the needs for strategic flexibility and long lead times of many of these ventures, lending further support to the earlier evidence from Pisano (2006a) and Maine and Garnsey (2006) with regard to the mismatch between the aims of these ventures and short-term shareholder objectives.

As relatively few young firms launch on the stock market, the most widely discussed form of non-debt financing is equity financing. However, in the UK, and to a similar extent elsewhere in Europe, venture capitalists tend to favour later stage companies (Mayer et al., 2005). A recent policy report suggested that efforts needed to be made to improve the flow of venture capital to early stage ventures (The Royal Society, 2010). Within the EU, public private partnership (PPP) funds are being encouraged to make this type of capital more readily available. However, merely increasingly the amount of capital available is unlikely to solve the long-term funding challenges these firms face. Recent evidence from an international study of the performance of firms funded by private vs. public venture capital suggests that a small amount of government funding, pooled with private funding, can lead to better venture performance, but ventures with significant government venture capital investment were less likely to perform well

(Brander, Du and Hellmann, 2010). A similar study, based in Canada, warned that subsidising private venture capital with government funds could lead to less rigorous selection by fund managers and therefore weaker portfolio performance (Brander, Egan and Hellmann, 2010).

As in the US and other European countries, UK equity funding is highly concentrated in a few geographical locations. The Cambridge region has drawn as much as around 25 per cent of all UK venture capital and 8 per cent of all European venture capital (Minola et al., 2008). In the US, investment pools around Silicon Valley, Cambridge (MA) and New York account for a significant percentage of all venture capital funds (Lerner et al., 2011). The US model, and Silicon Valley in particular, is often cited as an exemplar of how to generate the ideal environment for high-tech start-ups; however, there are a number of reasons why the US model is unlikely to translate directly. While the UK is one of the most active and established venture capital communities in Europe, it is still small and inexperienced in comparison to its US counterpart, with $1 billion under management in 2010 compared to the US's $20 billion (Minola et al., 2008; Lerner et al., 2011).

Venture capital investment is crucial to early-stage firms, not only for the funds they provide but because they can add significant value through assistance with management and strategic decisions, as well as introductions and relationship building for their portfolio ventures (Amit et al., 1998). In the US, funds tend to be more sector specific, for example, dedicated largely to nanotech or biotech (Lerner et al., 2011). Particularly in the early stages, evidence from US biotech clusters reinforces the importance of location for sector-specific investment in industries where scientific advancement and business intersect (Powell et al., 2002). However, the inexperience of its investment community means that UK ventures in emerging industries are unlikely to gain the benefits or even secure the investments available to such firms in a more established technology cluster. Their often long lead times to market and need for significant capital investment may also make science-based ventures less attractive to the comparatively smaller UK funds, because they are likely to require multiple rounds of financing over a period that can extend past the lifespan of such a fund. A recent report into the UK's success with venture funds for small businesses found that funds under a certain size were unlikely to generate a commercial return because they were too small to attract sufficient initial or follow-on investments (NAO, 2009).

Simply increasing the size of funds is not an economically viable option, and fostering an investment community with sector specific knowledge in science-based businesses is a solution which takes time. However, evidence from Germany and the US hints at one possible solution: the encouragement of relationships and co-operation between geographically distant venture funds (Sorenson and Stuart, 2001; Fritsch and Schilder, 2008). The critical mass of world class scientists and academics in the UK, many of whom have close relationships with companies who have commissioned research or in which former students are employed, may also offer an untapped resource to supplement the knowledge of the investment community. There is a need for further enquiry into possible solutions to both fund size and sector specific experience if the UK is to grow science-based spin-outs into internationally competitive firms. Creative solutions to these issues also provide a rich area for further academic exploration.

Evidence from Canada and elsewhere also points to further complications to using venture capital to fund emerging, science-based industries. In recent years the markets have not been favourable to IPOs by young companies in science-based industries, and there has been a strong downturn in IPO numbers since the economic boom (Amit et al., 1998). Venture capitalists are intermediaries answerable to their own investors, and to realise the value in their investee companies they promote the sale of the company if an IPO is not a viable option. Large corporate entities are on the lookout for innovative young firms to purchase in order to extend their innovation pipeline. Science-based spin-outs have a limited choice of acquirer, and the acquired unit may be steered toward short-term applications which curtail technical potential (although this can also occur in alliances). Moreover, in the absence of strong, domestic manufacturing firms to acquire these spin-outs, they will be acquired by foreign companies, as discussed further below.

A Longer Term Perspective

Despite the key role that spin-out companies clearly play, and the pivotal role that UK policy makers are assigning them in the nation's growth strategy, there appears to be a certain amount of myopia in the understanding of how these firms actually contribute to long-term economic growth. Do these firms generally grow to become the leading players in their markets, revive flagging economic areas and generate millions in tax dollars that will be reinvested in the domestic economy? A glance at the typical life cycle of a science-based spin-out suggests that long-term growth is much more complex than this.

In the case of biotech spin-outs, many are purchased by large global players when they have sufficiently demonstrated their technology and passed appropriate trials (Pisano, 2006b). When looking at UK advanced material ventures, there is also evidence of a trend toward partnerships focused around prospects for acquisition (Lubik, 2010). In recent years, many successful ventures in Cambridge have been acquired by incumbent firms from other countries; for example, Cambridge Display Technologies (P-OLEDs) was acquired by Sumitomo Chemical Group (Japan); and Orthomimetics (biological scaffolding) was acquired by TiGenix (Belgium). In cases where the companies are not immediately acquired, partners needed for access to, and funding for, manufacturing and scale-up have led companies like Plastic Logic (plastic electronics) and Q-Flo (carbon-nanotubes) to move their manufacturing to Russia and Israel respectively. Early work by Teece (1986) points out a significant issue with this pattern. He maintains that whoever controls the manufacturing of an innovation will generally capture the majority of the economic value from it. Similar observations were made by Hermann Hauser, one of the UK's most successful entrepreneurs, in the report *The Current and Future Role of Technology and Innovation Centres in the UK* (2011). He urged policy makers to increase the country's absorptive capacity and its ability to use its own technology. He specified a number of science-based sectors as being critical to the UK's successful translation of scientific achievements into economic growth, including plastic-electronics, renewable energy, fuel cells and composite materials. This is reminiscent of the SPRU researchers, who found that '"breakthrough innovations in science-based firms also induce clusters of technological opportunities upstream for suppliers, horizontally for partners, and downstream for users" (Pavitt et al., 1989, p81). Thus, science-based firms are symbiotic with others in a prosperous business ecosystem. A sparse domestic ecosystem will be able to make less use of their innovations.

The timeframes for the commercialisation of science-based innovations should be taken into consideration when suggesting further policy and research into the area, as should how we view success in the grander scheme. Many of the above studies have looked into the practices of successful firms. Evidence from the Cambridge cluster shows that building an ecosystem takes several generations of new firms. Even those ventures that are unsuccessful and are closed or taken over can make a significant contribution both to the knowledge base and the base of skilled personnel in a local economy (Garnsey and Heffernan, 2005). Cambridge is home to many serial entrepreneurs, known for their successes but also strengthened by their defeats. Companies fail for a variety of reasons including timing, lack of management skills and appropriate/ timely development of technology, but these failures often produce value in terms of IP developed and skilled personnel in the region. The US has taken additional steps to encourage the development of this resource-base, allowing academics a year to publish before filing a patent and basing some academic remuneration on commercial activities (MIT TLO, 2009). This is a stark contrast to the UK and most of Europe where academics are rarely rewarded for commercialisation of their research (Franklin et al., 2001). Assistance with commercialisation skills, and other resources, can also be gained through incubation, on which there is a growing debate that is beyond the scope of this chapter[7].

Second and third generation spin-outs also emerge from these skills, and the knowledge and IP produced by earlier attempts (Garnsey et al., 2008). Depending on how USOs are classified, this offspring of university spin-out companies may fall outside the definition of USO used in many studies, but are nonetheless valuable outcomes of the original commercialisation attempts. Acquired firms attract capital even when the acquired firm was ailing and often produce spin-outs by employees seeking autonomy. This may also shed light on the real return on investment from UK equity funds. We see these long-term developments as genealogical contributions of spin-out activity.

DISCUSSION AND CONCLUSIONS

UK policy reports declare that "we must build on [the UK's scientific strengths] and continue to aspire to be the best country in the world in which to do science" (The Royal Society, 2010, p8). But it is clear that encouraging technological discovery is only an initial (albeit critical) contribution to turning scientific advance into economic growth. Science-based USOs are key players in taking these discoveries and translating them into value-creating commercial applications on which so much hope is pinned. Our review points out the need for a holistic approach to further understanding of key challenges, both internal and external, faced by these USOs, which is further emphasised by the following implications which are rarely applicable to a single group of actors.

Implications for Theory

Research on academic entrepreneurship remains fragmented (Rothaermel et al., 2007), but several areas, both internal and external to the firm, have been identified as ripe for further theoretical enquiry. The business models of young firms operating at the intersection of research and business constitute an area that would benefit from further research. Identification and in-depth understanding of successful business models to serve as exemplars would be useful to both academics and academic entrepreneurs. Given the heterogeneity of spin-outs, further understanding as to which strategies work for which types of spin-outs would be a useful contribution. The study of partnerships for ventures in general is rapidly growing and some excellent work is being done in the area, particularly regarding corporate partnerships. As recent work suggests that NTBFs can benefit from a range of partnership opportunities, there is scope for significant work regarding partnerships with different types of organisations, including with other ventures, spin-outs and government agencies. A conceptual model for studying such partnerships is provided by the notion of the firm's transaction environment within its business ecosystem. Alliances with parent companies, suppliers, complementary innovators, distributors and competitors should be examined to gain a better understanding of the role of the ecosystem identified by Pavitt et al. (1989). While we note above that spin-out activities lead to the development of entrepreneurial skills, literature on successful (or unsuccessful) training and skill building for nascent entrepreneurs is still sparse. In practice, an ever-increasing number of universities are creating and promoting entrepreneurship courses for students, if not staff. Some extant literature, as well as university policy discussions, reflects on whether career academics should be encouraged to be entrepreneurs, hand over the commercial reins to more experienced personnel (Franklin et al., 2001), or more recently, turn responsibility for these activities over to commercially oriented students and post-docs (Fiske, 2012). This is an issue still ripe for discussion.

These findings also have a number of implications for research methodology in future studies. With regard to the creation and implementation of business models and strategies, detailed case study research on both successes and failures would provide practical insights for practitioners. Detailed accounts of missteps and failures are less often presented, but highly useful for practitioners and those seeking to support them. To understand the multi-generational developments of spin-outs and how they evolve, dyadic[8] cases also offer a useful perspective (Garnsey et al., 2008). An over-arching theme in this chapter has been the interconnectedness of the various contributions to spin-out research and the importance of viewing this area in context. There have been few studies that link phenomena on the firm, university, ecosystem and policy levels. This suggests that multi-level research could serve to view company case histories in the context of their environments and assist in the development of coherent strategies contributing to the entire system in complementary ways (Djokovic and Souitaris, 2008; Lubik, 2010). These recommendations are not meant to downplay the potential contributions that could be made by more quantitative or large-scale, survey-based studies. Surveys are very useful to give an overview of what is happening in large samples or which phenomena are most prevalent. Longitudinal data collection and analysis would also be highly useful to explore how these firms and the other organisations in their ecosystems evolve over time (Rothaermel et al., 2007). However, at the early stages of research, it is important to understand what variables to study, how they actually relate to each other and how to model them in order to properly setup rigorous studies and analyse results. Moreover, integrating broad surveys with more specific datasets and/or more detailed case studies carefully selected from the larger sample can give rich insight into the phenomena in question. Yin (2006) cites an example of examining a national organisation, then its regional entities, local entities and then supervisors and employees, to show how these levels of analysis and methods can be highly complementary.

Implications for Practice

A number of important recommendations for both practitioners and policy makers follow, such as the need to encourage both large firms and SMEs to participate in research consortia in emerging areas, to encourage financiers to build sector-specific expertise and to recognise the importance of larger innovative firms as resource providers, partners and potential exit strategies, even when focusing on new firms. Both future research and future policy could usefully take a more macro-level and holistic perspective toward profiting from technology, as well as a more long-term perspective toward establishing appropriate innovation ecosystems, an approach that could be termed genealogical in recognising the generations of spin-outs that populate a prosperous business ecosystem. Practitioners in particular are also advised to think creatively with regard to resource requirements and potentially early entry into emerging markets.

While there is a limited amount of literature available on appropriate training for new or possible academic entrepreneurs, there is clearly a movement in many universities to encourage and provide such training. Codifying and disseminating the results of these endeavours would be useful for both practitioners and researchers.

Implications for Policy and Research

Both policy and academia are taking steps toward understanding and encouraging science-based spin-outs, and more broadly, the commercialisation of scientific knowledge, but there is still much more work to be done to understand how to create the kind of ecosystems that can encourage, support and ultimately embed these spin-outs in a business environment conducive to growth. Access to appropriate and sufficient investment for these firms is critical, which may require new and creative initiatives. In particular, funds and fund managers are needed that can deal with sector specific challenges. Recent evidence also shows the importance of building ecosystems with sufficient variety of necessary players[9]. Table 17.1 summarises the above recommendations and selected references in current literature.

This chapter has reviewed the state of the literature regarding commercialisation by science-based university spin-out firms, arguing that researchers need to set these firms in their genealogical and ecosystem context in order to understand their challenges and prospects. It is clear from the above that science-based innovations, particularly from spin-out firms, do not happen in isolation, but within a complex network of other players and the exchange of their resources. We conclude that, in order to make good on the promise of scientific advance leading to economic growth, further research and policy could seek ways of achieving greater complementarity in the elements of the innovation ecosystem.

Table 17.1   Summary of recommended references and future work

Implications for		Selected References in Current Work	Recommendations for Future Work
Theory	Focus	– Business models (Chesbrough and Rosenbloom, 2002; Amit and Zott, 2010) – Strategies (Teece, 1986; Christensen et al., 2004; Maine and Garnsey, 2006) – General partnerships (Dodgson, 1992; Das and Teng, 2000) – Venture/Incumbent partnerships (Hitt et al., 2000; Alvarez and Barney, 2001) – Networking (Peters et al., 1998; Ahuja, 2000b) – Academic entrepreneurship (Rothaermel et al., 2007; Shane, 2004)	– Identification of sector specific business models – Alternative partnership options – Skill building and training for nascent entrepreneurs – Systematic and comparative views of funding alternatives and outcome
	Methodology	– Current perspectives (Mustar et al., 2006) – Common methodologies (Rothaermel et al., 2007)	– Dyadic cases (Garnsey et al., 2008) – Cases of unsuccessful companies – Ecosystems perspective (Adner, 2006) – Mixed method research (Yin, 2006) – Longitudinal studies (Rothaermel et al., 2007)
Practice		– Funding new ventures (Shane and Cable, 2002; Gill et al., 2007) – Entrepreneurship training programmes launched at universities	– Codification and publishing of successful and unsuccessful programmes/practices – Creative resource acquisition strategies by USOs – Attention to emerging markets (frugal design) by USOs – Participation in consortia (government, university and USO) – Build sector specific knowledge (financiers and government)
Policy		– Current UK policies (The Royal Society, 2010; Hauser, 2011)	– Holistic, long term perspective – Longer term perspective

NOTES

1. While the terms "spin-off" and "spin-out" both refer to a new entity with origins in a previous organisation, the term "spin-out" is sometimes used to refer to part of an existing organisation being demerged to form the kernel of a new venture, while "spin-off" often refers to employees leaving a former organisation to start a new venture, with or without endorsement (De Cleyn and Braet, 2009). The terms are often used interchangeably; however, we will be using the term "spin-out", referring to ventures formed to commercialise ideas generated within universities.
2. A comprehensive review of the foundations of literature in this and related areas, such as technology transfer and university policy, can be found in Rothaermel et al. (2007). Comparisons of various university policies can be found in Druilhe and Garnsey (2006) and Livesey et al. (2008).
3. For a thorough discussion of the perspectives used to investigate spin-offs, see Mustar et al. (2006).
4. In terms of publications, citations and high impact citations (The Royal Society, 2010).
5. We use Chesbrough et al.'s (2006, p1) definition of open innovation, i.e. "the use of purposive inflows and outflows of knowledge to accelerate internal innovations, and expand the markets for external use of innovation respectively".
6. It is important to note the investment in R&D alone is not a clear indicator of national innovation, which involves the use of that knowledge. For more information on that argument, see Baumol, W. (2002*). The Free Market Innovation Machine*.
7. Further information on incubation can be found in Dee et al., 2011.
8. Rarely found in literature, though highly useful, a dyadic case study contrasts the experiences of the parent to those of the progeny to determine key moments and how the new firm evolved over time.
9. On a European level, this would also involve a discussion of cluster policy, currently a key trend in policy around continental Europe, though not discussed as much in the UK.

REFERENCES

Adner, R., 2006. Match your innovation strategy to your innovation ecosystem. *Harvard Business Review* April, 98–107.

Ahuja, G., 2000a. The duality of collaboration: Inducements and opportunities in the formation of interfirm linkages. *Strategic Management Journal* 21,3, 317–43.

Ahuja, G., 2000b. Collaboration networks, structural holes, and innovation: A longitudinal study. *Administrative Science Quarterly* 45,3, 425–56.

Alvarez, S. and Barney, J., 2001. How entrepreneurial firms can benefit from alliances with large partners. *Academy of Management Review* 15,1, 139–48.

Amit, R., Brander, J. and Zott, C., 1998. Why do venture capital firms exist? Theory and Canadian evidence. *Journal of Business Venturing* 13,6, 441–66.

Amit, R. and Zott, C., 2010. Business model design: An activity system perspective. *Long Range Planning* 43,2–3, 216–26.

Arora, A., Fosfuri, A. and Gambardella, A., 2001. Markets for technology and their implications for corporate strategy. *Industrial and Corporate Change* 11,3, 419–51.

Baumol, W., 2002. *The Free Market Innovation Machine*. New Jersey, Princeton University Press.

Belderbos, R., Carree, M., Diederen, B., Lokshin, B. and Veugelers, R., 2004. Heterogeneity in R&D cooperation strategies. *International Journal of Industrial Organization* 22,8–9, 1237–63.

BERR, 2009. *New Industry, New Jobs*. April 2009.

Bhat, J., 2005. Concerns of new technology based industries-the case of nanotechnology. *Technovation* 25, 457–62.

Bidault, F. and Cummings, T., 1994. Innovating through alliances: experiences and limitation. *R&D Management* 24,1, 33–45.

Brander, J., Du, Q. and Hellmann, T., 2010. The effects of government-sponsored venture capital: International Evidence. *Sauder Business School Working Papers*. Vancouver, University of British Columbia.

Brander, J., Egan, E. and Hellmann, T., 2010. Government sponsored versus private venture capital: Canadian evidence. *International Differences in Entrepreneurship*. J. Lerner and A. Schoar. Chicaog, University of Chicago Press, 275–320.

Brush, C., Greene, P., Hart, M. and Haller, H., 2001. From initial idea to unique advantage: The entrepreneurial challenge of constructing a resource base. *The Academy of Management Executive* 15,1, 64–80.

Chesbrough, H. and Rosenbloom, R., 2002. The role of the business model in capturing value from innovation:

evidence from Xerox Corporation's technology spin-off companies. *Industrial and Corporate Change* 11,3, 529–55.

Chesbrough, H., Vanhaverbeke, W. and West, J., 2006. *Open Innovation: Researching a New Paradigm*. Oxford, Oxford University Press.

Christensen, C., 1997. *The Innovator's Dilemma*. Boston, Harvard Business School Press.

Christensen, C., Musso, C. and Anthony, S. D., 2004. Maximizing the returns from research. *Research Technology Management* 47,4, 12–18.

Clarysee, B., Wright, M., Lockett, A., Velde, E. and Vohora, A., 2005. Spinning out new ventures: a typology of incubation strategies from European research institutions. *Journal of Business Venturing* 20, 183–216.

Colombo, M., Grilli, L. and Piva, E., 2006. In search of complementary assets: The determinants of alliance formation of high-tech start-ups. *Research Policy* 35,8, 1166–99.

Das, T. and Teng, B., 2000. A resource-based view of strategic alliances. *Journal of Management* 26,1, 31–61.

Davidow, W., 1986. *Marketing High Technology: An Insider's View*. New York, Free Press.

De Cleyn, L. and Braet, J., 2009. Research valorisation through spin-off ventures: integration of existing concepts and typologies. *World Review of Entrepreneurship, Management and Sustainable Development* 5,4, 325–52.

Dee, N., Livesey, F., Gill, D. and Minshall, T., 2011. *Incubation for Growth*. London, NESTA.

Djokovic, D. and Souitaris, V., 2008. Spin-outs from academic institutions: a literature review with suggestions for further research. *Journal of Technology Transfer* 33, 225–47.

Dodgson, M., 1992. Technological Ccollaboration: Problems and pitfalls. *Technology Analysis & Strategic Management* 4,1, 83–8.

Dodgson, M., 1993. *Technological Collaboration in Industry: Strategy, policy and internationalization in innovation*. London, Routledge.

Druilhe, C. and Garnsey, E., 2006. Diversity in the Emergence and Development of Academic Spin-out Companies: A Resource-Opportunity Approach. In *High-tech Entrepreneurship*. M. Bernasconi, S. Harris and M. Moensted. London, Routledge.

DTI, 1999. Tomorrow's Materials. *Foresight*. Office of Science and Technology.

Fiske, P., 2012. Enterprising science. *Nature* 485, 269–70.

Franklin, S., Wright, M. and Lockett, A., 2001. Academic and surrogate entrepreneurs in university spin-out companies. *The Journal of Technology Transfer* 26,1–2, 127–41.

Freeman, C., 1982. *The Economics of Industrial Innovation*. Cambridge, Massachusetts, MIT Press.

Fritsch, M. and Schilder, D., 2008. Does venture capital investment really require spatial proximity? An empirical investigation. *Environment and Planning* 40, 2114–31.

Gans, J. and Stern, S., 2003. The product market and the market for "ideas": commercialization strategies for technology entrepreneurs. *Research Policy* 32,2, 333–50.

Garnsey, E. and Heffernan, P., 2005. High-technology clustering through spin-out and attraction: The Cambridge case. *Regional Studies* 39,8, 1127–44.

Garnsey, E., Lorenzoni, G. and Ferriani, S., 2008. Speciation through entrepreneurial spin-off: The Acorn-ARM story. *Research Policy* 37,2, 210–24.

Gill, D., Minshall, T., Pickering, C. and Rigby, M., 2007. *Funding Technology: Britian Forty Years On*. Cambridge, UK, University of Cambridge Institute for Manufacturing.

Hagedoorn, J. and Schakenraad, J., 1991. Inter-firm partnerships in generic technologies – The case of new materials. *Technovation* 11,7, 429–44.

Hang, C. and Garnsey, E., 2011. Opportunities and resources for disruptive technological innovation. *CTM Working Paper*. Cambridge, UK, University of Cambridge.

Hauser, H., 2011. *The Current and Future Role of Technology and Innovation Centres in the UK*. London, Department for Business Innovation and Skills.

Hitt, M., Dacin, M., Levitas, E., Arregle, J. and Borza, A., 2000. Partner selection in emerging and developed market contexts: Resource-based and organizational learning perspectives. *Academy of Management Journal* 43,3, 449–67.

Hofer, C. and Bygrave, W., 1992. Researching entrepreneurship. *Entrepreneurship: Theory and Practice* Spring, 91–100.

Lambert, R., 2003. Lambert review of business-university collaboration: Final report. *HM Treasury*. Norwich.

Lerner, J., Pierrakis, Y., Collins, L. and Biosca, A., 2011. *Atlantic Drift: Venture capital performance in the UK and the US*. London, NESTA.

Lieberman, N. and Montgomery, D., 1988. First mover advantage. *Strategic Management Journal* 9,5, 41–58.

Livesey, F., O'Sullivan, E., Hughes, J., Valli, R. and Minshall, T., 2008. A pilot study on the emergence of university-level innovation policy in the UK. *Centre for Economics and Policy Working Papers*. Cambridge, Institute for Manufacturing.

Lockett, A. and Wright, M., 2005. Resources, capabilities, risk capital and the creation of university spin-outs. *Research Policy* 34,7, 1043–57.

Lubik, S., 2010. Commercializing advanced materials research: A study of university spin-outs in the UK. *Centre for Technology Management*. Cambridge, University of Cambridge. PhD.

Lubik, S., Garnsey, E., Minshall, T. and Platts, K., forthcoming 2013. Value creation from the innovation environment: Partnership strategies from university spin-outs. *R&D Management*.

Maine, E., 2008. Radical innovation through internal corporate venturing: Degussa's commercialization of nanomaterials. *R&D Management* 38,4, 359–71.

Maine, E. and Ashby, M., 2002. An investment methodology for new materials. *Materials and Design* 23, 297–306.

Maine, E. and Garnsey, E., 2006. Commercializing generic technology: The case of advanced materials ventures. *Research Policy* 35, 375–93.

Maine, E., Shapiro, D. and Vining, A., 2010. The role of clustering in the growth of new technology-based firms. *Small Business Economics* 34,2, 127–46.

Mayer, C., Schoors, K. and Yafeh, Y., 2005. Sources of funds and investment activities of venture capital funds: evidence from Germany, Israel, Japan and the United Kingdom. *Journal of Corporate Finance* 11, 586–608.

Minola, T., Minshall, T. and Giorgino, M., 2008. Access to external capital for techno start-ups: evidence from the UK. *Investment Management and Financial Innovations* 5,4, 159–72.

Minshall, T., 2003. Alliance business models for university start-up technology ventures: A resource based perspective. *High Tech Small Firms Conference*. Manchester Business School.

Minshall, T., 2008. Evolution of UK Government Support for Innovation. In *Creating Wealth from Knowledge*. J. Bessant and T. Venables. Cheltenham, Edward Elgar.

Minshall, T., Wicksteed, B., Druilhe, C., Kells, A., Lynskey, M. and Siraliova, J., 2008. The role of spin-outs within university research commercialization activities: Case studies from 10 UK universities. In *New Technology-Based Firms in the New Millennium*. A. Groen, R. Oakey, P. Van der Sijde and G. Cook. Oxford, Emerald. VI, 185–201.

MIT TLO. 2009. *Preserving your patent rights*. Retrieved August 8, 2011, from http://web.mit.edu/tlo/www/community/preserving_patent_rights.html.

Mitchell, W. and Singh, K., 1996. Survival of businesses using collaborative relationships to commercialize complex goods. *Strategic Management Journal* 17,3, 169–95.

Moore, J. F., 1993. Predators and prey: A new ecology of competition. *Harvard Business Review* 71,3, 75–86.

Mowery, D. and Rosenberg, N., 1979. The influence of market demand upon innovation: A critical review of some recent empirical studies. *Research Policy* 8,1, 102–53.

Mueller, E. and Garnsey, E., 2009. Stockmarket Listing and Cleantech Business Development: Evidence from AiM. *CTM Working Papers*. Cambridge, University of Cambridge.

Mustar, P., Renault, M., Colombo, M., Piva, E., Fontes, M., Lockett, A., Wright, M., Clarysee, B. and Moray, N., 2006. Conceptualizing the heterogeneity of research-based spin-offs: A multi-dimensional taxonomy. *Research Policy* 35,2, 289–308.

NAO, 2009. *Venture Capital Support to Small Businesses*. London, National Audit Office.

Niosi, J., 2003. Alliances are not enough explain the rapid growth in biotechnology firms. *Research Policy* 32, 737–50.

Pavitt, K., Robson, M. and Townsend, J., 1989. Technological accumulation, diversification and organisation in UK companies, 1945–1983. *Management Science* 35,1, 81–99.

Penrose, E., 1959. *The Theory of the Growth of the Firm*. Oxford, Oxford University Press.

Peters, L., Groenewegen, P. and Fiebelkorn, N., 1998. A comparison of networks between industry and public sector research in materials technology and biotechnology. *Research Policy* 27, 255–71.

Pisano, G., 1990. The R&D boundaries of the firm: An empirical analysis. *Administrative Science Quarterly* 35, 153–76.

Pisano, G., 2006a. Can science be a business? Lessons from biotech. *Harvard Business Review* 84,10, 114–25.

Pisano, G., 2006b. *Science Business: the Promise, the Reality, and the Future of Biotech*. Boston, Harvard Business School Press.

Pisano, G., 2010. The evolution of science-based business: innovating how we innovate. *Industrial and Corporate Change* 19,2, 465–82.

Powell, W., Koput, K., Bowie, J. and Smith-Doerr, L., 2002. The spatial clustering of science and capital: Accounting for biotech firm-venture capital relationships. *Regional Studies* 36,3, 291–305.

Rasmussen, B., 2007. Is the commercialisation of nanotechnology different? A case study. *Innovation: Management, Policy and Practice* 9,1, 62–78.

Robinson, D., Rip, A. and Mangematin, V., 2007. Technological agglomeration and the emergence of clusters and networks in nanotechnology. *Research Policy* 36,6, 871–9.

Rothaermel, F., Shanti, D. and Jiang, L., 2007. University entrepreneurship: a taxonomy of the literature. *Industrial and Corporate Change* 16,4, 691–791.

Rothaermel, F. and Thursby, M., 2007. The nanotech versus the biotech revolution: Sources of productivity in incumbent firm research. *Research Policy* 36,6, 832–49.

Sainsbury, L., 2007. *The Race to the Top: A Review of Government's Science and Innovation Policies*. Norwich, HM Treasury.

Shane, S., 2004. *Academic Entrepreneurship: University Spinoffs and Wealth Creation*. Cheltenham, UK, Edward Elgar.

Shane, S. and Cable, D., 2002. Network ties, reputation, and the financing of new ventures. *Management Science* 48,3, 364–81.

Sorenson, O. and Stuart, T., 2001. Syndication networks and the spatial distribution of venture capital investments. *American Journal of Sociology* 106,6, 1546–88.

Stuart, T., 2000. Interorganizational alliances and the performance of firms: a study of growth and innovation rates in a high-technology industry. *Strategic Management Journal* 21,8, 791–811.

Teece, D. J., 1986. Profiting from technological innovation: Implications for integration, collaboration, licensing and public policy. *Research Policy* 15,6, 285–305.

The Royal Society, 2010. *The Scientific Century: Securing our future prosperity*. London.

Tidd, J., Pavitt, K. and Bessant, J., 1998. *Managing Innovation: Integrating technological, market and organization change*. Chichester, Wiley.

Utterback, J., 1994. *Mastering the Dynamics of Innovation*. Boston, Harvard Business School Press.

Venkataraman, S. and Henderson, J., 1998. Real strategies for virtual organizing. *Sloan Management Review* 40,1, 33–48.

Yin, R., 2006. Mixed methods research: Are the methods integrated or merely parallel? *Research in Schools* 13,1, 41–7.

Zott, C. and Amit, R., 2010. Business model design: An activity system perspective. *Long Range Planning* 43,2–3, 216–26.

18. Entrepreneurship in family businesses
Carole Howorth, Jacqueline Jackson and Allan Discua Cruz

INTRODUCTION: THE PREVALENCE AND RELEVANCE OF FAMILY BUSINESSES

This aim of this chapter is to provide a review of family business research focusing on studies that are related to entrepreneurship. This focus acknowledges key debates in the family business and entrepreneurship literature and highlights crucial links between these fields in terms of definitions, theories, methods and trends. The outcome is the identification of gaps in the overlap between family business and entrepreneurship literature which suggest future research paths.

There is growing recognition of the prevalence of family businesses and their importance to economies throughout the world. It is estimated that, in most countries, family businesses represent two-thirds or more of all businesses (Howorth, Rose and Hamilton, 2006). People are sometimes surprised to learn that some of the largest corporations are family-owned businesses, firms such as IKEA, Wal-Mart or Haribo. Other companies are more well known for being family businesses because they stress their family roots and use them as a marketing tool; UK readers will be familiar with the Warburton family who make a virtue of their familiness in promoting their products. For many though, family business is associated with SMEs (small- and medium-sized enterprises) and if you look around any town, you will discover a proliferation of family-owned SMEs.

The reality is that entrepreneurship is much less about the heroic individual seeking out opportunities that others cannot see (Ogbor, 2000) and more often about entrepreneurs founding and developing their enterprises along with other family members (Discua Cruz, Howorth and Hamilton, 2013). A high percentage of entrepreneurs found their businesses in the form of family firms, and, for many more, families are an important source of resources, especially human capital (Aldrich and Cliff, 2003). Many smaller firms find it difficult to disentangle the firm from the family and there is an intertwining of family and business motivations, resources and dreams (Hamilton, 2006). Families can be crucial breeding grounds for enterprise and new businesses, very much the "oxygen that feeds the fire of entrepreneurship" (Rogoff & Heck, 2003). Indeed, any study of small enterprises that ignores the influence of family can only ever be a partial representation of reality: family firms are so prevalent throughout the world.

And yet, despite them being the dominant business form, family firms are often overlooked in empirical studies and absent in theory development (Astrachan, 2010; La Porta, Lopez-de-Silanes & Shleifer, 1999). Family firms are especially interesting and possibly more complex than other types of firms because they are influenced by family, social and emotional factors, as well as economic ones (Craig & Moores, 2010). Gomez-Mejia, Takacs-Haynes, Nuñez-Nickel, Jacobson and Moyano-Fuentes (2007: 106) state "owners of family firms are concerned not only with financial returns but also with their socioemotional wealth through these firms." Socio-emotional wealth encapsulates the non-financial elements of the firm that meet affective needs and for some families it may dominate decision making (Gomez-Mejia et al., 2007).

It has sometimes been assumed that families overemphasise the social and emotional aspects of their businesses to the extent that established family businesses are traditional, stuck in the past and not entrepreneurial. There are many variants of the phrase "clogs to clogs in three generations" which represents the sweeping generalisation that succeeding generations do not have the entrepreneurial drive or skills of the business' founding fathers and therefore the family business can be expected to fail within three generations. In this chapter, we evaluate evidence on the performance of family businesses and show that many established family businesses are exceedingly entrepreneurial. Most importantly, researchers should understand that family businesses are not a homogeneous group. Recent studies have shown that different types of family firms can be identified. We highlight studies which show that some family firm owners and managers privilege family agendas and independence above entrepreneurship, profitability and competitive advantage (Howorth, Rose, Hamilton and Westhead, 2010); other family firm owners successfully balance family and business agendas to create high performing businesses (Westhead and Howorth, 2007); some families create large iconic businesses that last for generations with waves of innovation and entrepreneurial re-engagement (Roscoe, Discua Cruz and Howorth, 2012); others may change their path radically and exit the spheres of their original business (Salvato, Chirico and Sharma, 2010) and other families create teams of family members, which found and develop several businesses over time (Discua Cruz et al., 2013; Iacobucci and Rosa, 2010), an example of entrepreneurial teams that can be overlooked in research.

The key contribution of our chapter is to open up the world of families in business and explain the issues that are relevant to entrepreneurship researchers. By synthesising the key debates in extant literature we are able to identify gaps in knowledge and directions for future research. For those who are new to family businesses research we aim to provide an insight into the key theoretical, empirical and methodological issues that they should be aware of. We are especially keen to explore some of the myths and invalid assumptions that plague family businesses. For family business experts we hope that this chapter stimulates your thinking and suggests new ideas and approaches.

First, trends in the study of entrepreneurship in family businesses will be examined and we will discuss how studies have moved away from focusing on succession and governance issues to examine a diverse range of topics and different units of analysis. As with other developing research fields (including entrepreneurship), there has been debate about definitions, and so we will consider definitions of family business and their relevance for researchers and policy makers in particular. We will compare and contrast studies of family businesses across different parts of the world. Then we will examine the variety of methods and theories used to research family businesses and we will consider the implications for the building up of a body of knowledge and make recommendations for researchers who are new to studying family businesses. This broadening out of the family business entrepreneurship agenda leads us to suggest research topics which we believe deserve greater attention such as families as a source of habitual entrepreneurship, entrepreneurial cultures and leadership in family businesses. By underscoring the links between family business and entrepreneurship research and acknowledging key debates in the family business and entrepreneurship literature, we are able to provide some suggestions of where researchers could focus their efforts. We hope that our chapter also stimulates new ideas and approaches in what we consider to be a fascinating and important context for studying entrepreneurship.

FAMILY BUSINESSES

Family businesses dominate the business landscape around the world (IFERA, 2003). In the UK their importance in terms of numbers, contributions to employment and turnover in the private sector has been highlighted as significant (IFB, 2008). The family business model has been around probably longer than written records (Hoy & Verser, 1994). "One hundred years ago, 'business' meant 'family business' and thus the adjective 'family' was redundant" (Aldrich & Cliff, 2003: 575). Since its inception into academic research, the family business field has been associated with other academic arenas such as SMEs, owner-managed businesses and entrepreneurship (Neubauer and Lank, 1998). Understanding the small family business has become a relevant academic pursuit (Fletcher, 2002). The complex interplay between the family system and formal business activities fuelled the interest of scholars to study family businesses around the world (Colli, 2003; Colli et al., 2003).

When trying to define a family business the most noticeable aspect is the lack of consensus that exists (Howorth et al., 2010). Howorth et al. (2006) argue that definitions may vary because family businesses are not homogeneous. Many definitions have been utilised to serve different research purposes (Astrachan et al., 2002; Howorth et al., 2006). Broad, all-embracing family firm definitions focus on the degree to which the owners' family dynamics influence managerial behaviour, but they have been questioned on the grounds that they are too "inclusive" (Lansberg et al., 1988). Definitions which require that majority ownership or control of the business reside within a single family, and that at least two family members are involved in management of the business (Rosenblatt et al., 1985) may be too "restrictive" (Lansberg et al., 1988). Definitions have included aspects such as percentage of family ownership, percentage/number of family managers/employees, family controlling interest, multi-generation, family objectives and family intentions (e.g. succession to a family member) (Howorth et al., 2006: 228).

Studies in which the numerical dominance of family firms is greatest have used the broadest definitions, by asking respondents whether their business satisfied one specific criterion. Westhead and Cowling (1998) argued that two or more of the above elements in combination need to be considered when identifying family firms. They detected that the proportion of firms classified as "family firms" is highly sensitive to the definition utilised. Using the widest definition, they noted that 81 per cent of companies sampled could be viewed as "family firms". Using the narrowest definition, this fell to only 15 per cent. Recently, Mandl (2008) has proposed a family firm definition to the EU based on the family owning the majority of the decision-making rights and at least one family member being involved in management of the business.

Defining a family business should also consider context. In some contexts family influence can be strong without majority ownership. In Italy, for instance, family influence over large corporations has been maintained through the use of holding companies, agreements, cross-shareholdings and the issuing of stocks carrying multiple voting power. This allows the founders and their families to raise resources on financial markets, while also controlling the company with only a small proportion of the share capital. In other contexts, particularly developing countries, the concept of voting shares or owner-ship by stock is not recognised and has not been legally and economically developed and there is little separation of ownership and management (Discua Cruz & Howorth, 2008).

Family dynamics have been found to be a defining characteristic of the family firm as they influence business strategy over the life of the venture (Craig & Moores, 2006; Hall, 2001). Howorth, Rose and Hamilton (2006: 241) advocate that due to the absence of a definition that embraces the plethora of criteria there is a case for using a more general, less precise, definition as a starting point. They propose that a family business is: "one where a family owns enough of the equity to be able to exert control over strategy and is involved in top management positions".

The choice of family firm definition can have an impact on the scale of the "target group" for policy intervention (Westhead and Cowling, 1998). The lack of consensus relating to a universally respected family firm definition makes comparisons between countries and studies difficult. This has complicated the advance of the family business field and thus the development of theories that can help our understanding (Chrisman et al., 2005; Zahra et al., 2006).

ENTREPRENEURSHIP AND FAMILY BUSINESSES

Entrepreneurship is inextricably linked to family. While concepts differ, a wide consen-sus prevails that entrepreneurship deals with individuals and teams engaged in

> the discovery, evaluation and exploitation of opportunities to introduce new goods and serv-ices, ways of organizing, markets, processes and raw materials, through organizing efforts that previously had not existed. (Shane & Venkataraman, 2000: 218)

The family is considered crucial in this process (Rogoff & Heck, 2003). For many entrepreneurs the reason they found a business in the first place is influenced by family (Johannisson, 2003). Around the world entrepreneurs engage in the entrepre-neurial processes supported by (Morris et al., 2010; Steier, 2007) and in the company of family members (Kenyon-Rouvinez, 2001). Many businesses are founded, developed or acquired by families (Bertrand et al., 2008; Carney & Gedajlovic, 2002). Recent reviews suggest that the future of entrepreneurship research embraces wholeheartedly the study of family businesses (Wiklund et al., 2011).

The success of some family firms may be due to their focus on familial ties (Chrisman et al., 2003; Sirmon and Hitt, 2003). The positive relationships between family members can impact on the sustainability of any family business in the long term (Olson et al., 2003). Granovetter (1995) suggests that the comparative advantage of families in busi-ness rests on strong trust among members.

The traditional view is that entrepreneurial activities are mostly associated with founders and it has been questioned if succeeding generations can realistically have the entrepreneurial drive that existed in the founding generation (Westhead et al., 2001a). Intergenerational succession lies at the heart of family businesses and it is a process that is strongly linked to entrepreneurship (Howorth et al., 2006). Succession in family businesses is a process that reflects the intention, shared by most families involved in business, to transfer ownership, leadership and management of one business from one generation to the next (Davis & Harveston, 1998; Morris et al., 1996). It is known that entrepreneurial activities are often geared towards family business continuity (Naldi et al., 2007; Zahra, 2005). The changes in ownership and managerial structure that can occur as an outcome of succession (Gersick et al., 1999) offer potential for reinvigoration of entrepreneurial processes. Family businesses are unique in their potential to share knowledge, social capital, and a wide array of resources between generations. While some studies suggest that family firms can remain entrepreneurial throughout time (Koiranen, 2002; Littunen, 2003), others indicate that entrepreneurship may be hindered by the lack of the transmission of entrepreneurial values to potential successors by founders (Brockhaus, 2004). Dyer and Handler (1994) proposed the concept of "entrepreneurial succession" as an area for research and theory development. This area of research becomes relevant particularly as long-standing productive regions populated by SMEs are losing their competitive advantage (Johannisson et al., 2007). More recently this has been encapsulated in the study of "Transgenerational entrepreneurship" (Nordqvist and Zellweger, 2010) which has become an important topic of research in countries around the globe.

Researchers contend that despite the apparent overlap between entrepreneurship and family business, in practice they have remained independent arenas with separate research paths. In that sense, Anderson, Jack & Drakopoulou-Dodd (2005: 135) suggested that:

> entrepreneurship has focused on the pursuit of opportunities through the creation and growth of business organizations, paying special attention to the individuals and teams that undertake such activities, and the industrial, economic, and social environments in which they are located whereas family business scholarship has concentrated on the governance, management, development, and succession of the family business.

Aldrich and Cliff (2003) strongly contend that although research on entrepreneurship has gained importance, little attention has been given to the influence of family dynamics on fundamental entrepreneurial processes. Similarities in the research of entrepreneurship and family business fields are appreciated as scholars in both fields utilised and applied theories from mainstream management yet few contributions to those theories are often made (Bird et al., 2002; Zahra & Sharma, 2004). And yet, the incorporation of family into mainstream management theories has the potential to strengthen, test and/or extend traditional theoretical perspectives.

THEORETICAL PERSPECTIVES

The intertwining of relationships between family and business is a defining characteristic of family businesses (Astrachan, 2003; Sharma, 2006; Westhead et al., 2001b). A premise in small firms is that ownership and management overlap. If to this interrelation we add the family system we will be looking at what is known as one of the most popular representations of family businesses: the three circles model (Tagiuri & Davis, 1992). This model portrays the interrelationship between three systems: family, management and ownership. These systems form the basis for another influential model, the three dimensional developmental model, which incorporates the crucial aspect of time (Gersick et al., 1997). Models such as these are used by researchers and consultants to provide a "snapshot" of an individual family business and a starting point for identifying some of the issues they might face. Yet these models are often insufficient to understand fully the complexities of family businesses (Gimeno et al., 2010).

Jones (2005) argues that family businesses' isolation from management research is caused by a culture of abstinence from the dominant economic schema of public finance and capital markets, particularly in developed economies, and their resistance to participate in such arenas. Yet, a plethora of disciplines such as anthropology, economics, sociology, psychology, and management have strong interests in family businesses (Howorth et al., 2006). Many theories of management including agency; institutional; transaction cost economics and the resource based view are well used in organisational research, but are not often applied to the family firm. The inclusion of family may, as Miller and Le-Breton Miller (2005) comment, "surface weaknesses in the current theories and give rise to more relevant perspectives".

Family business research can be approached through different theoretical lenses (Howorth et al., 2006). While family business research is relatively young (Bird et al., 2002) it has reached a "tipping point" and is viewed as a legitimate field of study (Craig et al., 2009) with potential for significant progress to be made (Litz et al., 2011). Scholars argue that the inclusion of family businesses in management and entrepreneurship research will allow the strengthening of mainstream theories (Chrisman et al., 2003; Wright and Kellermanns, 2011). In the following paragraphs we concentrate on mainstream theories that have received greater attention in the overlap between entrepreneurship and family businesses and highlight limitations and consequent opportunities for research.

Resource Based View

The resource-based view (RBV) is a firm level theory that assumes that each organisation is a collection of idiosyncratic resources which are available for a period of time (Barney, 1991, 1996). Under this perspective, family provides uniqueness to the resources within the firm and some of those resources are embedded within family members involved in business (Sirmon and Hitt, 2003). Sirmon and Hitt argue that these unique resources include human capital, social capital, patient capital, survivability capital and governability structure and costs. Accordingly, the RBV is applied by those who emphasise the benefits of family involvement in business and has the potential to help us identify the resources and capabilities that distinguish family from nonfamily firms (Chrisman et al., 2003).

Scholars have used RBV to understand the strategic advantages of family businesses (Habbershon & Williams, 1999) and to understand further the process of succession (Cabrera-Suárez et al., 2001). It has been used to explore the dynamics of family business in different national contexts (Pistrui et al., 2000). Notions of "Familiness" by Habbershon and Williams (1999: 11) guided by the RBV highlight "the unique bundle of resources and capabilities resulting from the interaction of the family, its individual family members and the business with one another". These notions highlight the relevance of resources in the activities that family businesses carry on. The RBV has gained popularity in entrepreneurship studies within family businesses, as it allows further understanding of how resources, provided by family members and the firm they control, may enable further entrepreneurial engagement.

A particular strand, portfolio entrepreneurship, which deals with the establishment or acquisition of additional ventures by those who already own and control a venture (Rosa, 1998; Westhead & Wright, 1998) has been found to be influenced by resources emanating from existing family firms and family members. Resources such as the relationships developed by business founders (Chell & Baines, 2000) and their particular human capital (Ucbasaran et al., 2008) are influential in the re-engagement of fundamental entrepreneurial processes. Guided by the RBV and portfolio entrepreneurship perspectives, Discua Cruz (2010) provided empirical evidence that human and social capital provided access to a variety of resources that allowed a team of family members to engage in portfolio entrepreneurship leading to the development of small family business groups. However, RBV tends to view resources as assets to be employed and is limited in its ability to capture the affective bonds and relationships that underpin resources in family businesses.

Agency and Stewardship Theories

Agency theory (Eisenhardt, 1989; Jensen & Meckling, 1976) has been widely used in different studies in family firms (Chrisman, Chua, & Sharma, 2005, Corbetta & Salvato, 2004; Sharma, 2004). It seeks to explain organisational behaviour by focusing on the relationship between agents (managers) and principals (owners) of firms and where their interests diverge. Stewardship theory (Davis et al., 1997; Donaldson, 1990) has been presented as providing an understanding of behaviour when managers and owners' interests converge due to group-centred interest rather than self-interests. These theories have been employed in a complementary framework to identify typologies of family firms (Westhead & Howorth, 2007) and in untangling the complexity of family businesses in alternative cultural contexts (Discua-Cruz & Howorth, 2008).

Agency theory provides an understanding of the family firm when family and non-family managers base their decisions on individual goals rather than the good of the collective (e.g. family business and its stakeholders) and therefore rewards need to be structured to align the individual interests of owners and managers. This perspective "assumes self-interested, boundedly rational actors, information asymmetry and goal conflict to motivate principals (i.e. family firms owners) to devise mechanisms to monitor and control agents' actions (i.e. non-family managers)" (Sapienza et al., 2000: 336). Chrisman et al. (2005) state that agency studies of family business focus mainly on the interaction between ownership and management as drivers of competitive advantages or disadvantages. This perspective has been shown to be useful in understanding the interaction between family owners and non-family managers (Chua et al., 2003). Chua et al. (2003: 335) state that the application of agency theory to family firms has typically focused on the negative side of family involvement in business and "how the relationships among family members can lead to lower economic performance".

The stereotypical family firm is assumed to be owned and managed by a concentrated group of family members, where the firm's objectives are closely linked to family objectives (Zahra et al., 2004). In these circumstances, the traditional agency cost issue may not apply (Sapienza et al., 2000). Burkart et al. (2003) pose that family-based businesses with close ownership and control would minimise agency problems in countries where legal and judiciary systems, especially regarding shareholder protection, are not strong. This is especially the case where a primary capital market is not highly developed, such as in developing economies (Acemoglu et al., 2001). However, in order to grow and survive, some private family firms may no longer have aligned ownership and management in the same "family" hands, and this raises the potential for agency issues between separated family owners and non-family managers. Agency theory assumes a performance-based system with a focus on financial objectives, and individuals that are self-serving. If the objectives of owners and management differ there can be agency problems and agency costs (Schulze et al., 2001, Morck and Yeung, 2003). Owners seeking to minimise risks (Sapienza et al. 2000) when focusing on financial objectives (Smyrnios and Romano, 1994) may introduce agency control mechanisms such as performance related pay (Schulze et al., 2003) and non-executive directors (NEDs) (Westhead et al., 2001b) to enhance firm performance.

Where family firms are closely held, agency theory may be "silent" because there are no agency problems (Arthurs and Busenitz, 2003). Stewardship theory (Donaldson, 1990) could provide a useful counterpoint in these circumstances and has been used to suggest additional insights. The stewardship perspective suggests that motivation is based on intrinsic and intangible rewards and because individuals have high levels of organisational identification managers will not experience goal conflict (Lee & O'Neill, 2003: 214). Stewardship theory assumes a relationship-based system with a focus on non-financial objectives. When managers' and employees' motives are aligned to those of the organisation there are no agency costs (Davis et al., 1997) and they are organisation-serving (Randøy and Goel, 2003). Miller and Le Breton-Miller (2006: 74) argue that these attitudes are exhibited in family business when their leaders are either family members or emotionally linked to the family. Thus, family firm managers (either family members or not) would seek to protect the assets of the family firm rather than to pursue interests that maximise their own personal gain (Donaldson & Davis, 1991).

Within family business studies, stewardship theory has proved helpful in explaining motivations and strategies. A strong psychological ownership of the firm and a high occurrence of altruism are assumed. The latter traits are associated with the stereotypical family firm (Schulze et al., 2003), and a degree of overlap between the family, ownership and management sub-systems in terms of people and objectives is assumed (Chrisman et al., 2005). Reduced agency costs and stewardship attitudes may explain why some family businesses outperform their non-family counterparts (Le Breton-Miller & Miller, 2006). Stewardship theory is increasingly employed to explain family members' approaches to being in business together because it explains the bonds between individuals working together to serve the interests of an organisation (Davis et al., 1997; Schulze et al., 2003).

Stewardship perspectives have been particularly welcomed by scholars who question the dominance of an Anglo-American worldview (Bird et al., 2002). Table 18.1 shows that stewardship may be more common in collectivist cultures. Westhead et al. (2002) warn that the dominance of a particular view can limit the ability of studies to make

Table 18.1 Comparison of agency and stewardship theory

Theory /Implications	Agency Theory	Stewardship Theory
Model of man	Individualistic	Collectivistic
Behaviour observed	Opportunistic	Organisation oriented
	Self-serving	Group-benefit
Goals	Individualistic (Divergent)	Collective (Convergent)
Relationship	Principal-Agents	Principal-Stewards
	Based on performance, control and monitoring	Based on trust and loyalty
Cultural differences	Individualism	Collectivism
	High power distance	Low power distance

Source: Adapted from Davis et al., 1997.

inferences to other cultural and economic contexts. A growing body of research from countries with alternative cultures has highlighted limitations on theories and models developed in the Anglo-American context (Discua-Cruz & Howorth, 2008; Santiago, 2000).

FAMILY BUSINESS HETEROGENEITY

While family businesses are ubiquitous and may be defined through several criteria as presented earlier, every family business is unique. Researchers warn that family businesses are not a homogeneous group (Discua-Cruz & Howorth, 2008; Howorth et al., 2006). Family businesses differ tremendously in the variety of objectives and motives that drive them and many have multiple goals and objectives (Hall, 2001). In some family businesses, family objectives and goals are channelled through the business but, in others, business objectives are placed before family goals (Reid et al., 1999). Some family firm owners may trade firm profitability for other benefits (Feinberg, 1975). Further, they may neglect sustained entrepreneurship and professional management as the firm grows. However, while some family businesses may fit the stereotype of reluctance to change and bounded by family traditions, others are more prone to take risks, challenge the status quo and innovate and can thus be considered entrepreneurial (Westhead & Howorth, 2007).

The notion that family businesses remain the same in every place and over time is an incorrect generalisation (Colli, 2003: 74). The participation of family members in different stages of business development infuses greater heterogeneity in the way the family business operates (Gersick et al., 1997). Furthermore, family business heterogeneity is influenced by context, culture and temporal issues (Howorth et al., 2010). Family businesses survive and reshape their vision and adapt to particular markets or different contexts throughout time (Colli et al., 2003; Colli & Rose, 2006; Dyer & Mortensen, 2005).

In terms of context, a family's (and firm's) external environmental context (that is, cultural, demographic, economic, educational, legal and social) can shape family firm formation, diversity and development (Howorth et al., 2010). Each family firm is embedded in a society associated with a particular array of values, attitudes, laws and business practices. At the level of the individual firm, shared family experience can lead to shared understandings and perceptions, which can shape how the firm develops. Culture can shape the values reported by family firm owners, as well as the strategies and relationships within family firms (Howorth and Ali, 2001). Family culture can shape a family firm's ability to be strategically flexible (Zahra et al., 2004). Organisations associated with stronger family commitment are generally more flexible (Zahra et al., 2008). The values and attitudes of a locality can shape family firm development. In line with stewardship theory, some family firm owners select organizational cultures and structures that enhance employee commitment and organizational citizenship behaviour by employees (Zahra et al., 2008). A recent international family business compendium by Gupta et al (2008) examined family businesses in countries across the continents and supports the view that culture has a powerful influence in particular characteristics of family firms.

External environmental contexts change over time and, in part, shape variations in the formation, survival and development of private family firms (Winter et al., 2004). Family firms benefit from resource stocks generated by relationships with actors in the external environment (Chrisman et al., 2009). Colli et al. (2003) detected that distinctive national (and regional) family firm behaviour was shaped by the interplay between the cultural, economic, institutional and social environments over time. The evolution of firm behaviour shows strong evidence of path dependence, in that the causal links in the chain of past events, effects and states are evident (Rose, 2000). Temporal issues suggest that an understanding of family and firm history is required to explore variations between family firms with regard to resources, capabilities, behaviour and performance.

Typologies of Family Firms

The heterogeneity of family businesses is demonstrated by recent attempts to devise family business typologies. For instance, the Institute for Family Business (IFB) in the UK classifies family firms based on ownership as either owner-managed, owned by a single person who is also the managing director; family managed, where ownership is in the hands of at least two family members and family are involved in management; and family controlled, where the family takes a more hands-off approach and the management and/or ownership is shared with non-family members (IFB, 2008). This classification is a basic starting point but it is limited in revealing other areas that vary within the family firm.

Sharma (2004) conceptualised four "types" of family firms based on firm performance with regard to financial and emotional capital. The following four "types" of family firms were conceptualised: warm hearts–deep pockets, pained hearts–deep pockets, warm hearts–empty pockets and pained. This insightful conceptual framework is not theoretically grounded, nor empirically validated but indicates that a fruitful avenue for future studies is the exploration of whether variations in firm performance are shaped by family firm "type". The failure to recognise variations in the "types" of family firms could impact on the validity and generalisability of research findings. Further, assumptions regarding expectations about the stereotypical family firm (Zahra et al., 2004) may result in inappropriate assistance and recommendations being provided to family firms that belong to types that do not fit the stereotypical family firm profile.

Further studies by Westhead and Howorth (2007) conceptualised six "types' of family

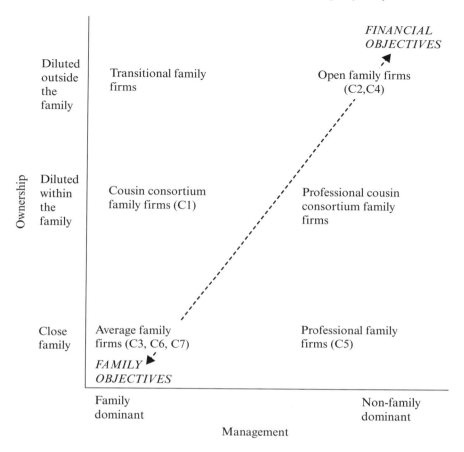

Notes: Empirical types of family firms are reported in brackets; C1 = 'cousin consortium family firms'; C2 = 'large open family firms'; C3 = 'entrenched average family firms'; C4 = 'multi-generational open family firms'; C5 = 'professional family firms'; C6 = 'average family firms'; C7 = 'multi-generational average family firms'.

Source: Westhead and Howorth (2007: Table 1).

Figure 18.1   Conceptualized 'types' of family firms

firms (Figure 18.1). A distinction is made between firms that have close family ownership, those that are diluted within the family, and those diluted outside the family (the vertical axis). A distinction is also made between firms that have family dominated management and those that have non-family dominated management (the horizontal axis). The cross-cutting theme of financial objectives (that is, agency theoretical assumptions of financial motivation and individuals who are self-serving) and family/non-financial objectives (that is, stewardship theoretical assumption that individuals put the organisation [either the family or the family firm] before their own interests [that is, altruism]) is represented by the arrow within Figure 18.1. The relative importance of financial or family objectives is represented by the distance in a straight line from the ends of the arrow.

Westhead and Howorth (2007) suggest that "average family firms" emphasise family objectives, and have closely held family ownership and family management. "Professional family firms" report a mix of family and non-family objectives, but emphasise family objectives. They have closely held family ownership and management dominated by non-family members. "Cousin consortium family firms" (Gersick et al., 1997) report a mix of family and non-family objectives. They have diluted ownership within the family and management dominated by family members. "Professional cousin consortium family firms" have diluted ownership within the family and management dominated by non-family members. Further, "professional cousin consortium family firms" place more emphasis on financial objectives than "cousin consortium family firms" and they place less emphasis on family objectives. "Transitional family firms" report both family and non-family objectives, but they place relatively more emphasis on financial objectives. They have diluted ownership outside the family but family members dominate management. These firms are transitional because the management is expected to move towards less family dominance. Finally, "open family firms" focus on financial objectives. They have diluted ownership outside the family and non-family management is dominant. Due to separated company ownership and control, the latter firms may report agency issues.

With reference to 17 variables relating to company objectives (that is, financial and family), ownership and management, Westhead and Howorth (2007) derived a theoretically grounded empirical taxonomy of family firm "types". The seven "types" of private family firms were as follows:

Cluster 1:   Cousin consortium family firms.
Cluster 2:   Large open family firms.
Cluster 3:   Entrenched average family firms.
Cluster 4:   Multi-generation open family firms.
Cluster 5:   Professional family firms.
Cluster 6:   Average family firms.
Cluster 7:   Multi-generation average family firms.

The "types" of family firms identified by Westhead and Howorth (2007) indicate the validity of employing agency and stewardship theories in a complementary framework in that, firms focusing more upon financial objectives generally reported organisational structures that suggest a self-serving culture and firms predominantly focusing upon non-financial objectives generally reported an organisation-serving culture.

This evidence casts some doubts (also see Rutherford et al., 2008) surrounding the wider validity and utility of a continuum or scale of "familiness" (Astrachan et al., 2002; Klein et al., 2005). Most notably, Westhead and Howorth (2007) illustrated that several distinct "types" of family firms can be conceptually and empirically identified. Differences in firm performance were also detected with regard to family firm "type" (Westhead and Howorth, 2006). The recognition and utilisation of "types" of family firms have the potential to provide fresh and contextualised insights into the multi-faceted family firm phenomenon.

METHODOLOGICAL IMPLICATIONS FOR FAMILY BUSINESS RESEARCHERS

The issues raised above have important implications for research methods. Clearly, methods that are based on blunt comparisons between family and non-family businesses do not allow for the heterogeneity that exists within family businesses. The intergenerational nature of family businesses indicates that multiple viewpoints are captured. And the longevity of families in business only serves to highlight the limitations of cross sectional studies.

Studying family businesses allows the deployment of various methods yet has often proved challenging for researchers. It is widely accepted that access to detailed information about family businesses is difficult to obtain (Handler, 1989). Scholars pose that family businesses are a rare population, difficult to identify, and hesitant to provide data (Winter et al., 1998). Indeed, reluctance by members of family businesses to provide information has proven a perennial issue for researchers (Karofsky et al., 2001; Neubauer & Lank, 1998). This is attributed to an "inward" orientation and potential distrust of researchers (Harris et al., 1994; Neubauer & Lank, 1998).

The relevance of a particular method to study family businesses and entrepreneurship depends primarily on the research question being asked. While some questions demand the use of statistical data, numerical datasets and statistical tools to derive factors and differences, other questions require a closer and prolonged interaction with families and businesses. There is a huge potential for ethnographic studies of family businesses that build up a trusted relationship and thus provide insights not available to other researchers. How and why questions are relevant when untangling the complexities of processes in family business research and entrepreneurship (Chrisman et al., 2005; Dyer, 2003). Qualitative methods can provide a fuller picture about how and why entrepreneurship in family businesses and by family members occurs (Carney & Gedajlovic, 2003; Carter & Ram, 2003; Iacobucci, 2002; Rosa, 1998). Researchers should be cautious about taking the view of an individual as representative when family businesses are such a collective arena. Qualitative methods may capture the perspectives of diverse stakeholders and provide a more valid explanation of the dynamics of entrepreneurship in family businesses (Carter & Ram, 2003; Ucbasaran et al., 2003).

Survey data and statistical methods have proved useful in comparing differences within family businesses and between family and non-family firms (Westhead & Cowling, 1998). For instance, differences in terms of small family businesses compared to small non-family firms have been found to have an impact on performance (Chrisman et al., 2009). However, recent reviews of the field suggest that there is a need for a fuller reporting of sample characteristics, descriptive statistics and more sophisticated and stringent statistical analysis techniques (Debicki et al., 2009). Furthermore Litz et al. (2011) suggest that researchers should aim to explore the "why" question behind quantitative results. Moreover, longitudinal studies are needed to provide reliable explanations of causality.

In a recent review of 217 articles focused on future research paths in family businesses Sharma (2006) highlighted the importance of considering different levels of analysis (Table 18.2). Table 18.2 indicates the importance of studying the range of people behind the establishment and development of the family business venture.

Table 18.2   Overview of family business research paths

Level	Items	Future paths
Individual	Founders	Understanding founding permutations
	Next generation members	Understanding transfer of knowledge between generations
	Women	Understanding the role of females in family businesses
	Non-family employees	Understanding the perspective of non-family employees
Interpersonal / group	Nature and type of contractual agreements	Understanding the dynastic family firm
	Sources of conflict and management strategies	Understanding of the root causes and temporal dimensions of conflict
	Intergenerational transitions	Understanding the extent of interest of new generations to get involved and the best mode for their involvement in the firm
Organisational	Identification and management of resources	Understand the mechanism to develop and reinforce vision and organisational culture throughout generations
	Strategic decision process	Understand the strategies used to maintain long-term relationships with external stakeholders and other organisations
Societal / environmental level	Sustainability of family business in different contexts	Understand the impact of context in family business and vice versa

Source: Sharma 2006.

A detailed understanding of the dynamics behind family businesses may imply the use of both quantitative and qualitative methodologies. Clearly there is the potential to be more creative in the actual methods employed and there is a huge opportunity for research to move on from cross sectional surveys and individual interviews. Family business researchers have started to take up this challenge and in doing so have developed interesting new trends in the approaches and also in the topics that are being studied.

TRENDS

Trends in the study of entrepreneurship in family businesses suggest that the field has moved away from focusing on succession and governance issues to examine a diverse range of topics and different units of analysis. Despite the dominance of the family firm form, few studies have explored family and firm interaction. Understanding private family firms requires the analysis of the complex interaction between family and firm, the forces underlying family values, and the way these shape the business culture as well as firm resources, capabilities, strategy and performance.

A recent study by Debicki et al. (2009) suggested that the most common themes are corporate governance, leadership and ownership succession, resources and competitive advantage, and behaviour and conflict. Wright and Kellermanns (2011) identify six elements to a future research agenda for family business and entrepreneurship: the type of family firm organisation; the types of family firm entrepreneurs; the processes in family firms; the environments in which entrepreneurship occurs; the intersections between these elements; and the outcome (Family Firm Performance). In the remainder of this chapter we focus on four areas that we believe could provide fruitful avenues for research in the overlap of family businesses and entrepreneurship: the unit of analysis, habitual entrepreneurship, entrepreneurial cultures and entrepreneurial leadership.

A Shift in the Unit of Analysis

Recent studies suggest that family business research has been anchored to the firm, often ignoring the relevance of family dynamics in management and entrepreneurship (Heck et al., 2006; Rogoff & Heck, 2003). Many earlier studies took the family business as the unquestioned unit of analysis and suggested that because an individual family business does not grow then succeeding generations are not entrepreneurial. Our understanding of businesses may be limited by our lack of research on family dynamics (Bertrand & Schoar, 2006; Dyer, 2003). Nordqvist and Melin (2010) suggest we should study the entrepreneurial family, as an institution or social structure that can both drive and constrain entrepreneurial activities.

The founding and development of businesses within a family context involves several family members in a diverse array of ways (Anderson et al., 2005; Iacobucci & Rosa, 2010). And yet, there is a tendency to atomise the entrepreneur and little is known about the dynamics of family members working together as entrepreneurs. Some family members' involvement in the entrepreneurial process may be overlooked because it is not always obvious at first glance; they may undertake invisible but nevertheless crucial roles (Hamilton, 2006). Hamilton (2006) shows that this is particularly the case for women involved in the founding and development of family businesses. Studies that focus on a single entrepreneur therefore provide a limited understanding of the entrepreneurial process in a family context.

The relevance of studying the family unit is that family is in essence the protagonist of family businesses. The genesis, development and continuity of a family business are influenced by family dynamics in management and ownership (Johannisson, 2003). Studying how family relationships impact on economic activities, such as setting up or acquiring one or more businesses, can prove more fruitful (Steier, 2007).

Discua Cruz (2010) homed in on family members who were actively engaged in entrepreneurship together, the family entrepreneurial team. A comprehensive review by Wright and Vanaelst (2009) argues that the identification and pursuit of opportunities is at the very heart of the concept of entrepreneurial teams. By concentrating on the family entrepreneurial team, Discua Cruz (2010) portrayed how different stages in the entrepreneurial process are impacted by a family's access to resources, such as human capital and social capital, leading to the creation of family business groups. Further studies by Discua Cruz et al. (2013) elucidate the formation and membership of family entrepreneurial teams and how further entrepreneurship engagement occurs through stewardship of a family's assets. The concept of "entrepreneurial stewardship" was posited in recognition that stewardship does not necessarily mean only maintenance of the status quo (Discua Cruz et al., 2013). Nevertheless, further empirical evidence is needed about the underlying patterns by which these teams operate (Discua Cruz et al., 2013; Wright and Vanaelst, 2009).

Habitual Entrepreneurship

In shifting the unit of analysis from one family business, we become more aware that many entrepreneurs engage in more than one entrepreneurial venture, either sequentially or consecutively (Rosa, 1998; Westhead & Wright, 1998). The rationale to engage in portfolio entrepreneurship revolves around a combination of family and business objectives (Carter & Ram, 2003). Family business founders may leverage firm-level and family resources (Sirmon & Hitt, 2003) to establish a portfolio of firms possibly challenging the traditional and historical roots of original family businesses (Plate et al., 2010). Yet most importantly habitual entrepreneurship revolves around fundamental entrepreneurial processes, namely opportunity identification and pursuit.

The importance of re-engaging in fundamental entrepreneurial processes has profound impact on the continuity or discontinuity of family firms (Salvato et al., 2010). Previous works argue that subsequent entrepreneurial efforts by those who already own and control a business are often visible in the re-engagement of entrepreneurial processes leading to additional business ventures being created or acquired (Westhead et al., 2005). This process may lead to establishing firms either related or unrelated to existing ones (Salvato et al., 2010). Recent studies highlight the importance of understanding how additional ventures are created or acquired in the context of family businesses (Discua Cruz, 2010; Plate et al., 2010). Family business founders might engage in the development of additional businesses with members of succeeding generations (e.g. children, or siblings) developing new businesses in an effort to enhance existing firms or provide opportunities for expanding families (Roscoe et al., 2012). This highlights that the approach to entrepreneurial processes in family firms may be more complex than originally perceived.

While family business founders are heralded in this process, researchers call for further understanding of the other family members involved in the creation or acquisition of additional ventures (Discua Cruz et al., 2013; Iacobucci & Rosa, 2010). Further studies are warranted to examine the extent and drivers of portfolio entrepreneurship in a variety of cultural contexts (Discua Cruz et al., 2012, Plate et al., 2010). For example, it could be argued that family portfolio entrepreneurship is more prevalent within developing economies (Rosa et al., 2013). Alternatively, portfolio entrepreneurship could be related to collectivist cultures. There is clearly a need to understand better the factors and processes involved in portfolio entrepreneurship within families (Johannisson, 2003; Ucbasaran et al., 2001).

Leadership in Family Firms

The significance of context cannot be underestimated in any field of research. And, depending on the context, those at the head of a family business may be considered entrepreneurs or they may be seen as leaders of the family business. Entrepreneurship

Table 18.3   Leadership heuristic model

Leadership as the 'person'.	Individual, person centred, who they are.
Leadership as the 'process'.	Style adopted or sense-making, how they get things done.
Leadership as the 'position'.	Considering what those in authority do and where they do it.
Leadership as the 'result'.	Achieving purpose through mobilisation, what leaders achieve.

Source: Adapted from Grint 2010.

can be stated as leadership in a different guise, (Czarniawska-Joerges and Wolff, 1991; Vecchio, 2003), the entrepreneur as the leader and entrepreneurship as the intersection of an enterprising person with potentially lucrative entrepreneurial opportunities (Shane and Venkataraman, 2000: 218). As far back as Schumpeter (1934), the belief was that entrepreneurship was a special case of leadership, distinguished by creating a company rather than managing one.

Society's interest in leadership has undoubtedly grown significantly, as evidenced by the rate of publications (a simple "Google" search reveals in excess of 2 million results). And yet, Grint (2010) states: "despite almost 3000 years of ponderings and over a century of academic research into leadership, we appear to be no closer to consensus as to its basic meaning, let alone whether it can be taught or its effects measured and predicted!" Grint provides a useful framework to break down the study of leadership into discernible chunks (Table 18.3): Leadership as the person; Leadership as the process; Leadership as the position; and Leadership as the result. Researchers could apply the same framework to the study of leadership in family businesses.

With the undoubted plethora of leadership theories: Great Man; Trait; Contingency; Situational; Behavioural; Participative and Relational and given the dominance of family-owned business within the commercial landscape of all free enterprise economies, it is surprising that very little is known about their leadership. Moores and Barrett (2010) commented: "these firms have, on occasion, attracted the attention of the popular press but it is invariably because of their "dark side": family feuds that escalate and affect the business operation, frequently ending up in the courts". And yet, there is evidence that the presence of a family CEO and increased homogeneity within the top management team, enhances business performance and family CEO-led firms seem to outperform non-family CEO-led firms regardless of setting (Minichilli et al., 2010). Moores and Barrett (2002) considered how successful firms engender learning in order to better anticipate need rather than react to crisis. They suggested that family business leaders learn their roles in four distinct phases: learning business; learning our business; learning to lead business and learning to let go, two of which are driven by individual need and two driven by the needs of the firm. A feature of all four learning phases is that each was characterised by a paradox and that the successful family firms found pathways through these paradoxes (Moores and Barrett, 2002). Greater understanding is required of how family business leaders negotiate their pathway, to what extent leadership learning processes are replicable or instinctive and the influence of culture in this process.

Many leadership theories involve a prediction model identifying traits, skills and behaviours which are then fitted into the leadership process. Yukl (2002) suggests that what are missing are the mediating variables necessary to explain leadership influence on individuals, group processes and organisational effectiveness. And yet, in terms of family firms, there is very little research on the intersection between family business leaders and entrepreneurship. Given the significance of the family business sector and the success of some family business leaders, further research in this area is one where scholars have potential to contribute to mainstream leadership and management theories (Bird et al., 2002; Zahra & Sharma, 2004).

Entrepreneurial Culture in Family Firms

Throughout this chapter we have highlighted the importance of recognising the influence that culture has on the family business. A fruitful avenue of research is to study the organisational culture within family businesses. For example, an entrepreneurial culture embodies beliefs, aspirations, histories and self-concepts that are likely to influence a firm's disposition to support and sustain entrepreneurship (Zahra et al., 2004: 364). Family initiative has been strongly related to entrepreneurship and the creation of a family business, which is clearly an entrepreneurial undertaking (Ucbasaran et al., 2001). An examination of the organisational culture may reveal insights into the commonly held view that while an entrepreneurial culture might prevail at the genesis and initial development of the family firm, over time conservative cultures stagnate entrepreneurial efforts (Zahra, 2005).

Family objectives and rationales may minimise risk-taking behaviour, innovation and entrepreneurial activity (Zahra, 2005). Moreover, as the business progresses, entrepreneurial efforts may be dominated by one or few family members (Kelly et al., 2000). Family embeddedness may neglect the transmission of entrepreneurial cultures to potential successors (Carr & Sequeira, 2007; Brockhaus, 2004). Alternatively, as the family business becomes more complex, entrepreneurship may develop through the interplay within and between generations (Bieto et al., 2010).

While some cultural patterns may tend to preserve traditional ways, others may support and entice entrepreneurship (Hall et al., 2001). A reduced dominance of any individual in entrepreneurial activities, increased reliance on information external to the family group, and a long-term orientation of strategic objectives are considered crucial aspects of an entrepreneurial culture (Zahra et al., 2004). The pursuit of opportunities can lead to several businesses being created or acquired (Johannisson, 2003) and the participation of family members from various generations (Carney & Gedajlovic, 2002; Zahra et al., 2008).

To gain further understanding of the way entrepreneurial practices become culturised we should be concerned with how and why values and beliefs come to be shared, taken for granted and how they get passed on to new members (Schein, 2004). Further studies by Discua Cruz et al. (2012) focusing on family entrepreneurial teams shows how entrepreneurship becomes part of the culture in family firms and how it can be sustained through succeeding generations. In that sense, studies that concentrate on the family unit behind entrepreneurial activities have huge potential, particularly in the study of different groups within a family business or family entrepreneurial teams involved in portfolio entrepreneurship.

International Comparisons of Family Business Research

The existence or not of an entrepreneurial culture is probably linked to the wider cultural context and there are many calls for further understanding of family firms located in different contexts (Gupta and Levenburg, 2010). We have already indicated that extant theoretical frameworks and many models utilised in family business (and management) research are premised on an Anglo-American worldview (Bird, Welsch, Astrachan, & Pistrui, 2002). This perspective focuses on the identification and pursuit of opportunities through individual action in an environment characterised by developed financial institutions, labour markets and legal frameworks. While in some contexts we may expect entrepreneurial activity to be conducted by one or few individuals, in others there is a more overt presence of, and reliance upon, family ties and relationships alongside collective approaches to the entrepreneurial process (Steier, 2009). The dominance of a particular view is dangerous as it can limit the validity of results when making inferences to other cultural and economic contexts (Westhead, Howorth, & Cowling, 2002). While some contexts highlight and herald the efficiency of institutions in the development of family businesses, other contexts highlight the historical existence of institutional voids, market imperfections, unreliable information flows and fragile legal and financial frameworks (Acemoglu, Johnson, & Robinson, 2001).

There is a growing interest in understanding further the differences in family business dynamics in diverse contexts and cultures. Using a culturally based framework Gupta et al. (2008) produced a compendium of studies that focus on cultural parameters in diverse clusters around the world. In devising their comparison they develop a heuristic understanding of the context within which most family businesses operate and how it influences aspects such as entrepreneurship behaviour and succession. The comparison highlights substantial variations across cultures and the need for further studies. Culturally sensitive lenses need to be employed when examining family firms around the world. Recent comparisons show further the nexus between family business and entrepreneurship. Research conducted through the Successful Trans-generational Entrepreneurship Practices (STEP) programme shows the importance of understanding entrepreneurship across generations of a family firm. Research conducted under STEP has increased understanding of factors associated with the geopolitical location and conditions of Europe, Latin America and Asia (Nordqvist & Zellweger, 2010, Nordqvist et al, 2011, Au et al., 2011). These studies serve to provide a deeper understanding of issues and challenges faced by family businesses and the families that engage in opportunity identification and pursuit.

CONCLUSIONS

This chapter provides a review of family business research as it relates to entrepreneurship. Key debates in the family business and entrepreneurship literature were discussed and links between these two fields highlighted. This allowed us to identify gaps in knowledge and suggest future research paths. Despite the importance of family businesses around the world, the association of family with business practices has sometimes caused controversy and concern among scholars (Jones, 2005) but more often the family influence has been ignored. Understanding the most pervasive form of organization in the world can represent a challenge for researchers (Handler, 1989). The applicability of mainstream theories needs to be carefully considered. Emerging research questions may be more appropriately explored with reference to conceptual platforms that draw upon complementary theories, rather than reliance on a single perspective such as agency theory (Eisenhardt, 1989, Sapienza et al., 2000).

Family dynamics can help us understand better the overlap between family businesses and entrepreneurship. Most importantly, this chapter highlights that family businesses are not a homogeneous group. Family firm diversity and development needs to be explored with regard to several theoretical and methodological lenses (Chua et al., 2003). Firm behaviour and performance studies that ignore the role played by families may lack validity. Additional research is required focusing upon the true complexities of entrepreneurial processes in the family firm (Ucbasaran et al., 2001). Furthermore, international comparisons tell us that we cannot separate the study of family businesses and entrepreneurship from the context and national culture in which they operate.

This chapter has highlighted that the majority of firms are family businesses and that entrepreneurship researchers should not ignore the influences of family dynamics. We have provided an agenda for further study on the overlap between family businesses and entrepreneurship. By opening up and questioning the concepts and principles that underpin the theories and models that we employ in family businesses and entrepreneurship research, we can address sceptics (Stewart, 2010) and improve the body of knowledge about family firms around the world.

REFERENCES

Acemoglu, D., Johnson, S., & Robinson, J. A. (2001). The colonial origins of comparative development: An empirical investigation. *The American Economic Review*, 91(5), 1369–1401.

Aldrich, H. E., & Cliff, J. E. (2003). The pervasive effects of family on entrepreneurship: toward a family embeddedness perspective. *Journal of Business Venturing*, 18(5), 573–96.

Anderson, A., Jack, S., & Drakopoulou-Dodd, S. (2005). The role of family members in entrepreneurial networks: Beyond the boundaries of the family firm. *Family Business Review*, 18(2), 135–54.

Arthurs, J. D., & Busenitz, L. W. (2003). The boundaries and limitations of agency theory and stewardship theory in the venture capitalist/entrepreneur relationship. *Entrepreneurship: Theory and Practice*, 28(2), 145–62.

Astrachan, J. (2003). Commentary on the special issue: The emergence of a field. *Journal of Business Venturing*, 28(5), 567–72.

Astrachan, J. (2010). Strategy in family business: Toward a multidimensional research agenda. *Journal of Family Business Strategy*, 1(1), 6–14.

Astrachan, J., Klein, S. B., & Smyrnios, K. X. (2002). The F-PEC Scale of family influence: A proposal for solving the family business definition problem. *Family Business Review*, 15(1), 45–58.

Au, K., Craig, J. B., & Ramachandran, K. (2011). *Family Enterprise in the Asia Pacific: Exploring Transgenerational Entrepreneurship in Family Firms*, Cheltenham: Edward Elgar.

Barney, J. B. (1991). Firm resources and sustained competitive advantage. *Journal of Management*, 17, 99–120.

Barney, J. B. (1996). The resource-based theory of the firm. *Organizational Science*, 7, 469.

Bertrand, M., Johnson, S., Samphantharak, K., & Schoar, A. (2008). Mixing family with business: A study of Thai business groups and the families behind them. *Journal of Financial Economics*, 88(3), 466–98.

Bertrand, M., & Schoar, A. (2006). The role of family in family firms. *Journal of Economic Perspectives*, 20(2), 73–96.

Bieto, E., Gimeno, A., & Parada, M. J. (2010). Dealing with increasing family complexity to achieve transgenerational potential in family firms. In M. Nordqvist & T. M. Zellweger (Eds.), *Transgenerational*

Entrepreneurship: Exploring Growth and Performance in Family Firms Across Generations (pp. 167–94). Cheltenham: Edward Elgar.

Bird, B., Welsch, H., Astrachan, J. H., & Pistrui, D. (2002). Family business research: The evolution of an academic field. *Family Business Review*, 15(4), 337–50.

Brockhaus, R. (2004). Family business succession: Suggestions for future research. *Family Business Review*, 17(2), 165–77.

Burkart, M., Panunzi, F., & Shleifer, A. (2003). Family firms. *The Journal of Finance*, 58(5), 2167–201.

Cabrera-Suárez, K., Saá-Pérez, P. D., & García-Almeida, D. (2001). The succession process from a resource- and knowledge-based view of the family firm. *Family Business Review*, 14(1), 37–48.

Carney, M., & Gedajlovic, E. (2002). The co-evolution of institutional environments and organizational strategies: The rise of family business groups in the ASEAN region. *Organization Studies*, 23(1), 1–29.

Carney, M., & Gedajlovic, E. (2003). Strategic innovation and the administrative heritage of East Asian family business groups. *Asia Pacific Journal of Management*, 20, 5–26.

Carr, J. C., & Sequeira, J. M. (2007). Prior family business exposure as intergenerational influence and entrepreneurial intent: A theory of planned behavior approach. *Journal of Business Research*, 60(10), 1090–98.

Carter, S., & Ram, M. (2003). Reassessing portfolio entrepreneurship. *Small Business Economics*, 21, 371–80.

Chell, E., & Baines, S. (2000). Networking entrepreneurship and microbusiness behaviour. *Entrepreneurship & Regional Development*, 12(3), 195–215.

Chrisman, J. J., Chua, J., & Steier, L. (2002). The influence of national culture and family involvement on entrepreneurial perceptions and performance at the state level. *Entrepreneurship: Theory and Practice*, 26(4), 113–30.

Chrisman, J. J., Chua, J. H., & Kellermanns, F. (2009). Priorities, resource stocks, and performance in family and nonfamily firms. *Entrepreneurship: Theory and Practice*, 33(3), 739–60.

Chrisman, J. J., Chua, J. H., & Sharma, P. (2005). Trends and directions in the development of a strategic management theory of the family firm. *Entrepreneurship: Theory and Practice*, 29(5), 555–75.

Chrisman, J. J., Chua, J. H., & Steier, L. P. (2003). An introduction to theories of family business. *Journal of Business Venturing*, 18(4), 441–8.

Chua, J., Chrisman, J. J., & Steier, L. P. (2003). Extending the theoretical horizons of family business research. *Entrepreneurship: Theory and Practice*, 27(4), 331–8.

Colli, A. (2003). *The History of Family Business: 1850–2000*: Cambridge University Press.

Colli, A., Fernandez, P., & Rose, M. (2003). National determinants of family firm development? Family firms in Britain, Spain and Italy in the nineteenth and twentieth centuries. *Enterprise and Society*, 4(1), 28–64.

Colli, A., & Rose, M. (2006). Family business. In *Oxford Handbook of Business History*. Oxford: Oxford University Press.

Corbetta, G., & Salvato, C. (2004). Self-serving or self-actualizing? Models of man and agency costs in different types of family firms: A commentary on "comparing the agency costs of family and non-family firms: Conceptual issues and exploratory evidence". *Entrepreneurship: Theory and Practice*, 28(4), 355–62.

Craig, J., & Moores, K. (2006). A 10-year longitudinal investigation of strategy, systems, and environment on innovation in family firms. *Family Business Review*, 19(1), 1–10.

Craig, J. B., & Moores, K. (2010). Championing family business issues to influence public policy: Evidence From Australia. *Family Business Review*, 23(2), 170–80.

Craig, J. B., Moores, K., Howorth, C., & Poutziouris, P. (2009). Family business research at a tipping point threshold. *Journal of Management and Organization*, 15(3), 282–93.

Czarniawska-Joerges B and Wolff R, (1991): Leaders, managers, entrepreneurs on and off the organisational stage. *Organisational Studies*, 12, 529–46.

Davis, J. H., Schoorman, F. D., & Donaldson, L. (1997). Toward a stewardship theory of management. *Academy of Management Review*, 22(1), 20–47.

Davis, P. S., & Harveston, P. D. (1998). The influence of family on the family business succession process: a multi-generational perspective. *Entrepreneurship: Theory and Practice*, 22(3), 31.

Debicki, B. J., Matherne, C. F., Kellermanns, F. W., & Chrisman, J. J. (2009). Family business research in the new millennium. *Family Business Review*, 22(2), 151–66.

Discua Cruz, A. F. (2010). Collective perspectives in portfolio entrepreneurship: A study of family business groups in Honduras. *EDAMBA Journal*, Thesis Competition, 8, 91–105.

Discua Cruz, A., Howorth, C., & Hamilton, E. (2013). Intrafamily entrepreneurship: The formation and membership of family entrepreneurial teams. *Entrepreneurship: Theory and Practice* 37(1), 17–46.

Discua Cruz, A., Hamilton, E., & Jack, S. L. (2012). Understanding entrepreneurial cultures in family businesses: A study of family entrepreneurial teams in Honduras. *Journal of Family Business Strategy*, http://dx.doi.org/10.1016/j.jfamily businesss.2012.05.002

Discua Cruz, A., & Howorth, C. (2008). Family business in Honduras: Applicability of agency and stewardship theories. In V. Gupta, N. Levenburg, L. Moore, J. Motwani & T. Schwarz (Eds.), *Culturally-Sensitive Models of Family Business in Latin America*. (pp. 222–43). Hyderabad: ICFAI University Press.

Donaldson, L., & Davis, J. H. (1991). Stewardship theory or agency theory: CEO governance and shareholder returns. *Australian Journal of Management*, 16(1), 49–64.

Donaldson, L. (1990). A rational basis for criticisms of organizational economics: a reply to Barney. *Academy of Management Review*, 15, 394–401.

Dyer, G. (2003). The family: The missing variable in organizational research. *Entrepreneurship: Theory and Practice*, 27(4), 401–16.

Dyer, G., & Handler, W. (1994). Entrepreneurship and family business: Exploring the connections. *Entrepreneurship: Theory and Practice*, 19(1), 71–83.

Dyer, G., & Mortensen, S. P. (2005). Entrepreneurship and family business in a hostile environment: The case of Lithuania. *Family Business Review*, 18(3), 247–58.

Eisenhardt, K. (1989). Agency theory: An assessment and review. *Academy of Management Review*, 14(1), 57–74.

Feinberg, R.M (1975) Profit maximization vs. utility maximization. *Southern Economic Journal*, 42(1), 130–1.

Fletcher, D. (2002). *Understanding the Small Family Business*. Oxon, UK: Routledge.

Gersick, K., Davis, J., Hampton, M. M., & Lansberg, I. (1997). *Generation to Generation: Life Cycles of the Family Business*. Boston, MA: Harvard Business School Press.

Gersick, K. E., Lansberg, I., Desjardins, M., & Dunn, B. (1999). Stages and transitions: Managing change in the family business. *Family Business Review*, 12(4), 287–97.

Gimeno, A., Baulenas, G., & Coma-Cros, J. (2010). *Family Business Models: Practical Solutions for the Family Business*. Basingstoke: Palgrave-Macmillan.

Gomez-Mejia, L. R., Haynes, K. T., Nuñez-Nickel, M., Jacobson, K. J. L., & Moyano-Fuentes, J. (2007). Socioemotional wealth and business risks in family-controlled firms: Evidence from Spanish olive oil mills. *Administrative Science Quarterly*, 52, 106–37.

Granovetter, M. (1995). Coase revisited: Business groups in the modern economy. *Industrial and Corporate Change*, 4(1), 93–130.

Grint, K. (2010). *Leadership: A Very Short Introduction* (pp.5,13, 15), Oxford University Press.

Gupta, V., Levenburg, N., Moore, L., Motwani, J., & Schwarz, T. (Eds.). (2008). *A Compendium on the Family Business Models Around the World* Hyderabad: ICFAI University Press.

Gupta, V., & Levenburg, N. (2010). A thematic analysis of cultural variations in family businesses: The CASE project. *Family Business Review*, 23(2), 155–69.

Habbershon, T. G., & Williams, M. (1999). A resource-based framework for assessing the strategic advantages of family firms. *Family Business Review*, 12, 1–25.

Hall, A. (2001). Towards an understanding of the strategy process in small family businesses: a multi-rational perspective. In D. Fletcher (Ed.), *Understanding the Small Family Business* (pp.32–45), Routledge.

Hall, A., Melin, L., & Nordqvist, M. (2001). Entrepreneurship as radical change in the family business: Exploring the role of cultural patterns. *Family Business Review*, 14(3), 193–208.

Hamilton, E. (2006). Whose story is it anyway? Narrative accounts of the role of women in founding and establishing family business. *International Small Business Journal*, 24(3), 1–17.

Handler, W. C. (1989). Methodological issues and considerations in studying family business. *Family Business Review*, 1(4), 257–76.

Harris, D., Martinez, J., & Ward, J. (1994). Is strategy different for the family-owned business? *Family Business Review*, 7(2), 159–74.

Heck, R., Danes, S., Fitzgerald, M. A., Haynes, G., Jasper, C., Schrank, H., et al. (2006). The family's dynamic role within family business entrepreneurship. In P. Poutziouris, K. Smyrnios & S. Klein (Eds.), *Handbook of Research on Family Business* (pp.80–124). Cheltenham, UK: Edward Elgar.

Howorth, C., & Ali, Z. A. (2001). Family business succession in Portugal: An examination of case studies in the furniture industry. *Family Business Review*, 14(3), 231–44.

Howorth, C., & Moro, A. (2006). Trust within entrepreneur bank relationships: Insights from Italy. *Entrepreneurship: Theory and Practice*, 30(4), 495–517.

Howorth, C., Rose, M., & Hamilton, E. (2006). Definitions, diversity and development: Key debates in family business research. In M. Casson, B. Yeung, A. Cassu & N. Wadeson (Eds.), *Oxford Handbook of Entrepreneurship* (pp.225–47): Oxford University Press.

Howorth, C., Rose, M., Hamilton, E., & Westhead, P. (2010). Family firm diversity and development: An introduction. *International Small Business Journal*, 28(5), 437–51.

Hoy, F., & Verser, T. G. (1994). Emerging business, emerging field: Entrepreneurship and the family firm. *Entrepreneurship: Theory and Practice*, 19(1), 9–23.

Iacobucci, D. (2002). Explaining business groups started by habitual entrepreneurs in the Italian manufacturing sector. *Entrepreneurship & Regional Development*, 14, 41–7.

Iacobucci, D., & Rosa, P. (2010). The growth of business groups by habitual entrepreneurs: The role of entrepreneurial teams. *Entrepreneurship: Theory and Practice*, 34(2), 351–77.

IFB, (2008): The UK family business sector, an Institute for Family Business Report by Capital Economics,

Accessed online: http:// www.ifamily business.org.uk/media/7404/uk_family business_sector_report.pdf, *last accessed: January 17th, 2012*

IFERA. (2003). Family businesses dominate: International Family Enterprise Research Academy (IFERA). *Family Business Review*, 16(4), 235–41.

Jensen, M. C., & Meckling, W. H. (1976). Theory of the firm: managerial behavior, agency costs, and ownership structure. *Journal of Financial Economics*, 3, 305–60.

Johannisson, B. (2003). Entrepreneurship as a collective phenomenon. In E. Genesca, D. Urbano, J. Cappelleras, C. Guallarte & J. Verges (Eds.), *Entrepreneurship* (pp. 87–109). Bellaterra: UAB publications.

Johannisson, B., Caffarena, L. C., Discua Cruz, A. F., Epure, M., Hormiga, M., Kapelko, M., Murdock, K., Nanka-Bruce, D., Olejarova, M., Sanchez Lopez, A., Sekki, A.,Stoian, M.,Totterman, H., Bisignano, A, (2007). Interstanding the industrial district: contrasting conceptual images as a road to insight. *Entrepreneurship & Regional Development*, 19(6), 527–54.

Jones, A. (2005). The elementary structures of the family firm: An anthropological perspective. *Human Organization.*, 64(3), 276–85.

Karofsky, P., Millen, R., Yilmaz, M. R., Smyrnios, K. X., Tanewski, G. A., & Romano, C. A. (2001). Work-family conflict and emotional well-being in American family businesses. *Family Business Review*, 14(4), 313–24.

Kelly, L. M., Athanassiou, N., & Crittenden, W. F. (2000). Founder centrality and strategic behavior in the family-owned firm. *Entrepreneurship: Theory and Practice*, 25(2), 27–42.

Kenyon-Rouvinez, D. (2001). Patterns in serial business families: Theory building through global case study research. *Family Business Review*, 14(3), 175–92.

Klein, S. B., Astrachan, J. H., & Smyrnios, K. X. (2005). The F-PEC scale of family influence: Construction, validation, and further implication for theory. *Entrepreneurship: Theory and Practice*, 29(3), 321–39.

Koiranen, M. (2002). Over 100 years of age but still entrepreneurially active in business: Exploring the values and family characteristics of old Finnish family firms. *Family Business Review*, 15(3), 175–88.

La Porta, R., Lopez-de-Silanes, F., & Shleifer, A. (1999). Corporate ownership around the world. *Journal of Finance*, 54(2), 471–517.

Lansberg, I. S., Perrow, E. L., & Rogolsky, S. (1988). Family business as an emerging field. *Family Business Review*, 1(1), 1–8.

Lee, P., & O'Neill, H. (2003). Ownership structures and R&D investments of U.S. and Japanese firms: agency and stewardship perspectives. *Academy of Management Journal*, 46(2), 212–25.

Le Breton-Miller, I., & Miller, D. (2006). Why do some family businesses out-compete? Governance, long-term orientations, and sustainable capability. *Entrepreneurship: Theory and Practice*, 30(6), 731–46.

Littunen, H. (2003). Management capabilities and environmental characteristics in the critical operational phase of entrepreneurship – a comparison of Finnish family and nonfamily firms. *Family Business Review*, 16(3), 183–97.

Litz, R. A., Pearson, A. W., & Litchfield, S. (2011). Charting the future of family business research: Perspectives from the field. *Family Business Review*. DOI: 10.1177/0894486511418489.

Mandl, I. (2008). Overview of Family Business Relevant Issues: Contract No. 30-CE-0164021/00–51 Final Report. Vienna: Austrian Institute for SME Research.

Miller, D., & Le Breton-Miller, I. L. (2006). Family governance and firm performance: agency, stewardship, and capabilities. *Family Business Review*, 19(1), 73–87.

Miller, D., & Le Breton-Miller, I. L. (2005). *Managing for the Long Run: Lessons in Competitive Advantage from Great Family Businesses*: Harvard Business School Press.

Minichilli, A., Corbetta, G., & MacMillan, I. C. (2010). Top management teams in family-controlled companies: 'familiness', 'faultlines', and their impact on financial performance. *Journal of Management Studies*, 47(2), 205–22.

Moores K., & Barrett M, (2002): *The Learning Family Business: Paradoxes and Pathways*. Bond University Press.

Moores K., & Barrett M. (2010): *The Learning Family Business: Paradoxes and Pathways*. Bond University Press.

Morck, R., & Yeung, B. (2003). Agency problems in large family business groups. *Entrepreneurship: Theory and Practice*, 27(4), 367–82.

Morris, M. H., Allen, J. A., Kuratko, D. F., & Brannon, D. (2010). Experiencing family business creation: differences between founders, nonfamily managers, and founders of nonfamily firms. *Entrepreneurship: Theory and Practice*, 34(6), 1057–84.

Morris, M. H., Williams, R. W., & Nel, D. (1996). Factors influencing family business succession. *International Journal of Entrepreneurial Behaviour & Research*, 2(3), 68–81.

Myers, M. D. (2009). *Qualitative Research in Business & Management*. London: Sage.

Naldi, L., Nordqvist, M., Sjöberg, K., & Wiklund., J. (2007). Entrepreneurial orientation, risk taking, and performance in family firms. *Family Business Review*, 20(1), 33–47.

Neubauer, F., & Lank, A. (1998). *The Family Business: Its Governance for Sustainability*. London: MacMillan Press.

Nordqvist, M., & Melin, L. (2010). Entrepreneurial families and family firms. *Entrepreneurship & Regional Development*, 22(3–4), 211–39.

Nordqvist, M., & Zellweger, T. (2010). *Transgenerational Entrepreneurship*. Cheltenham: Edward Elgar.

Nordqvist, M., Marzano, G., Brenes, E. R., Jimenez, G., & Fonseca-Paredes, M. (2011). *Understanding Entrepreneurial Family Businesses in Uncertain Environments: The Case of Latin America*. Cheltenham: Edward Elgar.

Ogbor, J. (2000). Mythicizing and reification in entreprenurial discourse: ideology critique of entreprenurial studies. *Journal of Management Studies*, 37, 605–35.

Olson, P. D., Zuiker, V. S., Danes, S. M., Stafford, K., Heck, R. K. Z., & Duncan, K. A. (2003). The impact of the family and the business on family business sustainability. *Journal of Business Venturing*, 18(5), 639–66.

Pistrui, D., Welsch, H. P., Wintermantel, O., Liao, J., & Pohl, H. J. (2000). Entrepreneurial orientation and family forces in the new Germany: Similarities and differences between East and West German entrepreneurs. *Family Business Review*, 13(3), 251–64.

Plate, M., Schiede, C., & Schlippe, A. v. (2010). Portfolio entrepreneurship in the context of family owned businesses. In M. Nordqvist & T. M. Zellweger (Eds.), *Transgenerational Entrepreneurship: Exploring Growth and Performance in Family Firms Across Generations* (pp. 96–122). Cheltenham: Edward Elgar.

Randøy, T., & Goel, S. (2003). Ownership structure, founder leadership, and performance in Norwegian SMEs: implications for financing entrepreneurial opportunities. *Journal of Business Venturing*, 18(5), 619–37.

Reid, R., Dunn, B., Cromie, S., & Adams, J. (1999). Family orientation in family firms: a model and some empirical evidence. *Journal of Small Business and Enterprise Development*, 6(1), 55–67.

Rogoff, E. G., & Heck, R. K. Z. (2003). Evolving research in entrepreneurship and family business: recognizing family as the oxygen that feeds the fire of entrepreneurship. *Journal of Business Venturing*, 18(5), 559–66.

Rosa, P. (1998). Entrepreneurial processes of business cluster formation and growth by 'habitual' entrepreneurs. *Entrepreneurship: Theory and Practice*, 22(4), 43–61.

Roscoe, P., Discua Cruz, A., & Howorth, C. (2012). How does an old firm learn new tricks? A material account of entrepreneurial opportunity. *Business History*, http://dx.doi.org/10.1080/00076791.2012.687540

Rose, M. B. (2000). *Firms Networks and Business Values: The British and American Cotton Industries since 1750*. Cambridge: Cambridge University Press.

Rosenblatt, P. C., de Mik, L., Anderson, R. M., & Johnson, P. A. (1985). *The Family in Business*. San Francisco: Jossey-Bass.

Rutherford, M. W., Kuratko, D. F., & Holt, D. T. (2008). Examining the link between "familiness" and performance: Can the F-PEC untangle the family business theory jungle? *Entrepreneurship: Theory and Practice*, 32(6), 1089–109.

Salvato, C., Chirico, F., & Sharma, P. (2010). A farewell to the business: Championing exit and continuity in entrepreneurial family firms. *Entrepreneurship & Regional Development*, 22(3–4), 321–48.

Santiago, A. L. (2000). Succession experiences in Philippine family businesses. *Family Business Review*, 13(1), 15–40.

Sapienza, H. J., Korsgaard, M. A., Goulet, P. K., & Hoogendam, J. P. (2000). Effects of agency risks and procedural justice on board processes in venture capital-backed firms. *Entrepreneurship & Regional Development*, 12(4), 331–51.

Schein, E. H. (2004). *Organizational Culture and Leadership*. San Francisco, Calif.; [London]: Jossey-Bass.

Schulze, W., Lubatkin, M., & Dino, R. (2003). Exploring the agency consequences of ownership dispersion among the directors of private family firms. *Administrative Science Quaterly*, 46(2), 179–94.

Schulze, W., Lubatkin, M., Dino, R., & Buchholtz, A. K. (2001). Agency relationships in family firms: Theory and evidence. *Organization Science*, 12(2), 99–116.

Schumpeter, J. (1934). *The Theory of Economic Development*. Cambridge, MA: Harvard University Press.

Shane, S., & Venkataraman, S. (2000). The promise of entrepreneurship as a field of research. *Academy of Management Review*, 25(1), 217–26.

Sharma, P. (2004). An overview of the field of family business studies: Current status and directions for the future. *Family Business Review*, 17(1), 1–36.

Sharma, P. (2006). An Overview of the field of family business: current status and directions for the future. In P. Poutziouris, K. Smyrnios & S. Klein (Eds.), *Handbook of Research on Family Business* (pp. 25–55), Cheltenham, UK and Northampton, MA, USA: Edward Elgar.

Sirmon, D. G., & Hitt, M. A. (2003). Managing resources: Linking unique resources, management, and wealth creation in family firms. *Entrepreneurship: Theory and Practice*, 27(4), 339–58.

Smyrnios, K., & Romano, C. (1994). The Price Waterhouse/Commonwealth Bank family business survey 1994. Sydney: Department of Accounting, Monash University.

Steier, L. (2007). New venture creation and organization: A familial sub-narrative. *Journal of Business Research*, 60(10), 1099–107.

Steier, L. (2009). Familial capitalism in global institutional contexts: Implications for corporate governance and entrepreneurship in East Asia. *Asia Pacific Journal of Management*, 26(3), 513–35.

Stewart, A. (2010). Skeptical about family businesses: advancing the field in its scholarship relevance, and academic role. In A. Stewart, G. T. Lumpkin & J. A. Katz (Eds.), *Advances in Entrepreneurshio, Firm Emergence and Growth* (Vol. 12, pp. 231–41): Emerald Group Publishing Ltd.

Tagiuri, R., & Davis, J. (1992). On the goals of successful family companies. *Family Business Review*, 5(1), 43–62.

Ucbasaran, D., Westhead, P., & Wright, M. (2001). The focus of entrepreneurial research: Contextual and process issues. *Entrepreneurship: Theory and Practice*, 25(4), 57–80.

Ucbasaran, D., Wright, M., & Westhead, P. (2003). A longitudinal study of habitual entrepreneurs: starters and acquirers. *Entrepreneurship & Regional Development*, 15(3), 207–28.

Ucbasaran, D., Westhead, P., & Wright, M. (2008). Opportunity identification and pursuit: Does an entrepreneur's human capital matter? *Small Business Economics*, 30(2), 153–73.

Vecchio, R. P. (2003): Entrepreneurship and leadership: Common trends and common threads. *Human Resource Management Review*, 13(2), 303–28.

Westhead, P., & Cowling, M. (1998). Family firm research: The need for a methodology rethink. *Entrepreneurship: Theory and Practice*, 23(1), 31–56.

Westhead, P., Cowling, M., & Howorth, C. (2001a). The development of family companies: Management and ownership imperatives. *Family Business Review*, 14(4), 369–85.

Westhead, P., Cowling, M., Storey, D., & Howorth, C. (2001b). The scale and nature of family business. In D. Fletcher (Ed.), *Understanding the Small Family Business* (pp. 19–31): Routledge.

Westhead, P., & Howorth, C. (2006). Identification of different types of private family firms. In P. Poutziouris, B. Klein & K. Smyrnios (Eds.), *Family Business Research Handbook*. Cheltenham, UK and Northampton, MA, USA: Edward Elgar.

Westhead, P., & Howorth, C. (2007). 'Types' of private family firms: an exploratory conceptual and empirical analysis. *Entrepreneurship & Regional Development*, 19(5), 405–31.

Westhead, P., Howorth, C., & Cowling, M. (2002). Ownership and management issues in first generation and multi-generation family firms. *Entrepreneurship & Regional Development*, 14(3), 247–69.

Westhead, P., Ucbasaran, D., & Wright, M. (2005). Decisions, actions, and performance: Do novice, serial, and portfolio entrepreneurs differ? *Journal of Small Business Management*, 43(4), 393–417.

Westhead, P., & Wright, M. (1998). Novice, portfolio and serial founders: are they different? *Journal of Business Venturing*, 13, 173–204.

Wiklund, J., Davidsson, P., Audretsch, D. B., & Karlsson, C. (2011). The future of entrepreneurship research. *Entrepreneurship: Theory and Practice*, 35(1), 1–9.

Winter, M., Danes, S. M., Sun-Kang Koha, Fredericks, K., & Paula, J. J. (2004). Tracking family businesses and their owners over time: Panel attrition, manager departure and business demise. *Journal of Business Venturing*, 19(4), 535–59.

Winter, M., Fitzgerald, R., Heck, R., Haynes, G., & Danes, S. (1998). Revisiting the study of family businesses: Methodological challenges, dilemmas, and alternative approaches. *Family Business Review*, 11(3), 239–52.

Wright, M., & Vanaelst, I. (2009). Introduction. In M. Wright & I. Vanaelst (Eds.), *Entrepreneurial Teams and New Business Creation* (Vol. 13, pp. iix–xli). Cheltenham, UK and Northampton, MA, USA: Edward Elgar.

Wright, M., & Kellermanns, F. W. (2011). Family firms: A research agenda and publication guide. *Journal of Family Business Strategy*, 2(4), 187–98.

Yukl, G. (2002). *Leadership in Organisations*, Fifth Edition, Prentice Hall: London

Zahra, S. A. (2003). International expansion of U.S. manufacturing family businesses: The effect of ownership and involvement. *Journal of Business Venturing*, 18(4), 495–512.

Zahra, S. A. (2005). Entrepreneurial risk taking in family firms. *Family Business Review*, 18(1), 23–40.

Zahra, S. A., Hayton, J. C., Neubaum, D. O., Dibrell, C., & Craig, J. (2008). Culture of family commitment and strategic flexibility: The moderating effect of stewardship. *Entrepreneurship: Theory and Practice*, 32(6), 1035–54.

Zahra, S. A., Hayton, J. C., & Salvato, C. (2004). Entrepreneurship in family vs. non-family firms: A resource-based analysis of the effect of organizational culture. *Entrepreneurship: Theory and Practice*, (28) 4, 363–81.

Zahra, S. A., Klein, S., & Astrachan, J. (2006). Epilogue: theory building and the survival of family firms – three promising research directions. In P. Poutziouris, K. Smyrnios & S. Klein (Eds.), *Handbook of Research on Family Business* (pp. 614–18), Cheltenham, UK and Northampton, MA, USA: Edward Elgar.

Zahra, S. A., & Sharma, P. (2004). Family business research: A strategic reflection. *Family Business Review*, 17(4), 331–46.

19. Developing entrepreneur networks in the creative industries – a case study of independent designer fashion in Manchester
Xin Gu

INTRODUCTION

Empirical research has so far emphasized the unique business behaviour of creative entrepreneurs, from the level of individual business up to industry sectors (i.e., both vertical and horizontal relationships). Some have suggested that creative businesses are not 'businesses' in conventional terms because they do not operate within a profit-seeking discipline. Others argue that if the creative industries are called industries, we should be able to evaluate them in the way we do conventional industries. This chapter evaluates and examines the two perspectives not as paradoxical, but as interrelated, using case studies of social networks in creative industries in Manchester, UK. In particular, I am concerned with how entrepreneurs in the independent designer fashion sector form and alter their social networks in relation to the nature of the specific industries they are in. As such, I explore to what extent the creative production is able to be assessed by sociological questions of culture and aesthetics, trust and identity, as much as by markets, risk management and innovation in economic terms.

This chapter uses a case study of independent fashion designers in Manchester in order to throw light on the role of networking in the creative industries and some of the methodological challenges this presents for researchers. While recognizing there is some controversy over the term 'creative industries', and that the terms cultural and creative industries are often used interchangeably, I settle on creative industries as the most frequently used in the academic and policy literature to which I refer. It is common to use the original definition of the creative industries as provided by the UK Government's Department of Culture, Media and Sport (DCMS), 'those activities which have their origin in individual creativity, skill and talent and which have a potential for wealth and job creation through the generation and exploitation of intellectual property' (DCMS, 1998: 3).

However, without wanting to engage directly with the creative/cultural debate, this definition has three problems. First, it overemphasizes the generation of intellectual property as a defining characteristic (not all products and services were organized in this way). Second, 'creativity' is notoriously wide (is science or management not also creative?) and although the subsequent list of sub-sectors are clearly involved in forms of 'cultural' or 'symbolic' or 'expressive' production, this continues to cause some confusion. Third, and the concern in this chapter, the emphasis on 'individual creativity, skill and talent' is often at the expense of the wider social, economic and cultural contexts that underpin the highly collaborative processes involved in the creative industries.

Research on the creative industries (which predates the actual term) has tended to focus on their local and regional contexts. In the UK, as in other developed economies, the majority of employment in the creative industries has been concentrated in metropolitan centres. More, the creative industries agenda emerged in close proximity to that of 'creative cities' (Landry, 2000) and culture-led urban regeneration (Bianchini, 1993) and was concerned with the linkages between the local socio-cultural context and the potential for creative industries growth. As such researchers drew on work in economic geography that stressed 'institutional thickness' (Amin and Thrift, 1995), socio-cultural 'embeddedness' (Park, 1996; see also McKeever et al., Chapter 13, this volume), and 'untraded interdependence' (Storper, 1995). These have been used extensively in cluster theory, where firm spin-off, inter-firm networks and local labour market characteristics provide the basis of local collective learning (Keeble et al., 1999) which is often tacit (O'Connor, 2004). Frequent interactions taking place in formal and informal networks between individuals within a cluster facilitate knowledge spillover, construction of mutual trust, social networking, and finally lead to a place-based identity (Amin and Thrift, 1995; Capello, 1999).

In adapting this literature creative industry researchers have pointed to three distinct characteristics. First, the specific nature of their products and services as 'symbolic', 'cultural' or 'expressive' suggests a range of different motivations for, or markers of, entrepreneurial success than that of profit. There are aesthetic and cultural aspects of their activities that are in play alongside their need to make a living and their aspirations to business growth. Second, their working patterns are strongly marked by a blurring of boundaries between work and 'play'; that is, their business and social networks exhibit strong overlap, giving a strong sense of informality to the former and elements of 'after-hours work' to the latter. Third, their strong reliance on the untraded interdependencies provided by cultural institutions, practices and knowledge and skills makes their embeddedness in local, mostly urban socio-cultural contexts particularly marked. These are not simple agglomeration economies but more like 'ecosystems' characterized by interdependence and mutual transformation (Pratt and Jeffcutt, 2009).

This chapter first expands in some detail on embedded networks in the creative industries (see also McKeever et al., Chapter 13, this volume for a discussion of embeddedness). It will emphasize the specific kind of sociality at play within these and how they come to be embedded in local contexts. Second, I will introduce a particular sub-sector – independent fashion design – from which I take my case study, and the specific locale – Manchester, UK – in which they operate. Third, I will then say something about the methods used to undertake such an investigation and some of the challenges these posed. Fourth, I outline the results of this case study in terms of the kinds of network sociality and entrepreneurial motivations and aspirations these involved. I suggest that these networks help sustain a particularly difficult 'business model' in which financial gain has to find its place alongside cultural and indeed ethical considerations. I suggest that this poses some specific challenges for these businesses and to those policy agencies that often seek to support and promote these sectors. Finally, in conclusion I suggest that these tensions are not due to an individual's fear or lack of understanding of 'proper' business practice, nor do they indicate a half-hearted entrepreneurialism. If we are to understand the creative industries we have to acknowledge that both 'cultural' and 'economic' aspects involve entrepreneurial spirit – the seeking of new markets and the establishment of new links between different actors (entrepreneur – 'to take between') – but that they may not sit comfortably together. This then might demand further conceptual and methodological work if we are to research this sector in more detail. (For a detailed discussion of the entrepreneurial personality research, see Rauch, Chapter 10, this volume.)

SOCIAL NETWORKS IN CREATIVE INDUSTRIES

Academics and policy makers have long identified the sociality of creative industries; in particular, the key role that informal networks of interpersonal relationships play within the creative industries sector. Granovetter's (1973) seminal work on 'weak ties' has been transposed with great effect to the fluid, urban, social milieu in which creative industries work (Scott, 2000; Currid, 2007). The blurring of work and life has become a major concern of those researching creative labour. They have asked if creative work represents a more liberating kind of work (Hartley, 2005) or a new form of self-exploitation (McRobbie, 1998, 2002) with serious consequences for personal and emotional life (Gill and Pratt, 2008). Similar concerns have emerged around networking. Andreas Wittel (2001), researching new media workers in London, saw social networking as about 'catch up' through rapid, informal information exchange. He raised the question whether such networking disrupts or cuts across other forms of social and communal life (cf. also Sennett, 2008). McRobbie (2002) too saw a 'commodification' of social relations in creative industry networking, suggesting it was a byproduct of an industry sector lacking protection against market turbulence. Others, such as Shorthose (2004) and Banks (2007) while not denying these negative tendencies, also point to the cultural and ethical dimension of these networks, highlighting those elements which might represent an extension or adaptation of more stable social and communal forms (e.g., Shorthose, 2004). Grabher (2001) describes these as 'narrative' based (building up over time) rather than the more instantaneous and transient 'informational' networks.

Networks are not just economic structures. They are also social and cultural processes for firms to integrate relationships of interdependence (Powell, 1990; Grabher, 1993). The informal practices, the shared identity and trust mechanisms are all important for the local agglomeration of businesses whose organizational relations are governed by 'reciprocity' underpinned by social norms rather than by written contract (Yeung, 1994; Crewe, 1996). Economic actors are also social actors situated within complex social networks; thus economic activities are embedded in the social networks of interpersonal relationships (Granovetter, 1985; 1991; Powell, 1990; Grabher, 1993). Behavioural rationality, contextuality, the strength of ties and power relations are socially and culturally constructed (Smelser and Swedberg, 2003; Grabher, 1993; Misztal, 1996; Amin and Hausner, 1997).

Networks are constitutions of cooperation, intelligence and trust mechanisms (c.f., Mulgan, 1989; Zukin and DiMaggio, 1990; Grabher, 1993; Morgan, 1997; Banks et al., 2000). A similar approach has been taken by some scholars suggesting that 'social capital' is just as important as other economic determinants in organizing economic activities (c.f., Putnam, 1993; Hansen, 1992; Saxenian, 1990). Maskell (2001), for instance, argued that social capital is a major factor for any economic community's long-term competitiveness.

Social networks in creative industries are seen to perform 'economic' functions; on the one hand, they sustain a pool of knowledge, skills and available personnel as 'untraded interdependencies' and on the other, they form the context of trust within which trading relationship they operate with confidence and predictability (c.f., Scott, 2000). At the same time these networks are seen to convey 'sociality', for example, high levels of personal investment, trust and support as the basis of these relationships, providing a sense of belonging and identity, and of creative or aesthetic validation (c.f., Banks et al., 2000). It is the high level of confluence of these two aspects – the 'economic' and the 'cultural' – in the practice of networking that has positioned creative work as a key site of contemporary debate.

The importance of the embeddedness notion in creative industries is that it offers ways of understanding the 'untraded interdependencies' (Storper, 1995) between creative firms. Particularly relevant here is that it acknowledges the importance of the informal practice of networking between firms in creative industries. These are social and cultural relations as well as economic ones. (Scott, 1986; 2004; Storper, 1995). Firms aren't just building relationships alongside their market relations; they are also looking for 'friends'.

Shorthose (2004), for example, identifies social networks in Nottingham's local independent sector as new forms of organization of work in creative industries. Coe (2000) suggests that economic activity is increasingly embedded in the networks that are 'socially constructed and culturally defined' (394). Pratt observes that networks among firms in new media industries are not strictly defined by industries or organizational boundaries but rather exist across organizations and amongst various projects (Pratt, 2000). This is confirmed by other literature in the field (Ross, 2003). What is crucial here is not simply the question of costs of transaction, but rather the social relationships developed alongside the economic relationship. These social relationships provide sustainability to firms by strengthening or intensifying their relationship with each other.

Spatial proximity is one way for firms to develop a social relationship. Bassett et al. (2002) observed the location-specific monopoly operated through firms in the film industry in Bristol. These alliances, they argue, create not only a concentration of industry-specific activities, such as recruitment, subcontracting and other service functions but also collective learning and transfer of knowledge among firms having indirect relations (c.f., Byrne et al., Chapter 15, this volume on learning). The coordination of economic activities in this sector is based mostly on tacit knowledge woven into the social interactions among individuals. Thus, it is suggested that the popularity of major cities in the film and other cultural industries involves not only the development of infrastructures but also 'atmosphere' – the concentration of relevant social and cultural activities of certain groups of individuals.

This notion of a metropolitan cluster has been argued most persuasively by Allen Scott (1999; 2000; 2004). Scott suggests that the concentration of creative communities in major cities represented the 'collective' interest of its members who were attracted by not only the economic infrastructure in these places but also their social and cultural infrastructure. These individuals form the 'cultural capital' of a local creative community within which critical cultural competencies are generated and circulated. The attraction of these communities are the 'repositories of an accumulated cultural capital' and institutional infrastructures that serve to sustain this cultural capital (Scott, 1999: 809).

Coe's (2000) research reflects a similar view. He argues that the materialization of making indigenous film and television in Vancouver is embedded in a small group of individual producers and their social and economic relationships with each other – and also with producers and investors at national and international levels. He observes that these localized relationships are more socially modified and thus beneficial in facilitating exchanges that are crucial for the actual needs – needs that are not straightforward – of local film making. By contrast, relationships at national and international level are less socially embedded and thus carry more instrumental functions such as fund-raising and rights distribution; e.g., it is more about making deals and negotiation. Moreover, relationships in the former setting cannot be replaced or reproduced elsewhere – unlike the latter ones.

The above theories on creative clusters are a far cry from the conventional cluster theory based on the idea of reducing the transaction cost or encouraging competition (c.f., Porter, 1998; 2000). As Shorthose pointed out, it is a 'hidden ecology' that orthodox economic statistics often fail to reflect and do not pick up on the real labour process and employment relations within it. As I will explain later in the case study, self-employment and freelance are the work norm in the creative industries. Moreover, this flexible labour is very mobile due to the lack of fixed 'contracts' and the dissolution of the 'workplace'. Work is organized via word of mouth and opportunities 'migrate' from one project to another. People with different skills and backgrounds are expected to cooperate in an informal manner rather than through formal organizational structures.

These remarks begin to reshape the relationship between culture and economy by going beyond the question of 'embeddedness' and asking to what extent cultural and social aspects influence the economic activities and choices. If, as Lash and Urry (1994) and many others have argued, economic and socio-cultural relations are more than ever interrelated, then we might assume a deepened relationship between community, place and creative work – a relation that is not about business as activities and culture as context, but rather both as activities and as providing conditions for the development of the other. But there is the worry of what might happen if the economic processes, needs, and principles are also increasingly in conflict with social and cultural needs. In the next section I examine how these debates work within a case study of one specific sub-sector – independent fashion designers – in Manchester.

THE INDEPENDENT FASHION DESIGNER SECTOR IN MANCHESTER

The 'independent designer fashion' sector in this research includes businesses that combine creativity and originality to produce a clothing collection with a specific or 'signature' identity, exemplified by, but not restricted to, the type of company that participates at international trade shows such as London Fashion Week and its equivalents. These independent businesses may produce diffusion lines in addition to their 'flagship' collections and range from established labels with an international 'brand' to cutting edge 'newcomers' (DTI and BFC, 2003: 5).

Post-Fordist production processes in the fashion industry have – despite predictions to the contrary – favoured big businesses. These are the businesses that are able to relocate manufacturing overseas, coping with the rising cost of marketing and the quickened pace in design. Post-Fordist flexible specialization in this case has not meant rewards for creative businesses; rather the opposite. Disintegrated production has translated into a harsh market form of economic governance that has left little space and time for creativity and innovation. The disintegration of small independent designer fashion businesses within this global network has tied these businesses to tiny local markets making up only a fraction of the global fashion industry.

In a report on the UK fashion industry prepared by Frontier Economics (FE), it was suggested that Designer Fashion is made up of 8,600 firms and has 22,000 employees and a turnover of £2.1 billion in 2008 (FE, 2008: 74). Within it, the 'creative core' – the layer that represents the most creative elements of the fashion industry and is at the top of the supply chain – only contributes 3 per cent of total turnover and employment. It is a fraction of the total sector. Even within this creative core, the picture is mixed:

> . . .the largest 24 per cent of firms (approximately 2,100 firms) account for 80 per cent of total [creative core] turnover. . .[T]he top 50 firms generate 28 per cent of total turnover. . . the top four firms generate 11 per cent and the top eight, 14per cent.' (FE, 2008: 75)

Small firms that employ fewer than nine people are 'very important' here. According to the same report, small firms contributed 68 per cent and 58 per cent to the total 'creative core' employment and turnover, respectively. In fact small firms are more important in this sector than any other in the creative industries (FE, 2008: 82). What this snapshot of designer fashion indicates is that we have a relatively small creative industry sector dominated numerically by small firms and economically by a small number of very successful firms. It thus exemplifies a common trait of creative industries, of a large number of 'struggling' individuals and firms and a small number of 'successes' at the top.

The UK national picture in the above study is replicated at local level, but with the notable absence of large successful firms, which tend to be based in London. Though regional centres such as Manchester and Glasgow have made great efforts to promote the creative industries in general and fashion in particular they find it hard to retain larger businesses in the face of the pull of London (much stronger, I suggest, than that of Amsterdam over Antwerp, a recent small city fashion success story).

Most of the independent designer fashion businesses in Manchester are small- to medium-sized businesses (see Table 19.1). This sector has also been identified as having a significant number of self-employed people. It was found that 67.3 per cent of the employment in this sector consisted of self-employed or sole traders (NWDA, 2003). The same study reports that the proportion of independents in this sector is the highest among the ten creative industries sub-sectors.

This gives a quite specific profile to these independent fashion businesses. They tend to be self-directed and disciplined in the face of global (which in this case can mean London-based) competitors. They cannot afford to outsource production resulting in extensive multi-tasking – not only designing but also sourcing fabrics, making and selling. 'Self-exploitation' has become a real issue for this sector (McRobbie, 1998: 70). While there are elements here that are shared across the spectrum of creative work, the independent designer fashion sector faces particular difficulties.

Though 'design' might indicate a purely immaterial input, in fact a range of material inputs is required. A musician might make a recording in her bedroom, or rent a studio for a day. Writers just need space and a computer. Visual artists might need materials in similar ways to fashion designers, but these materials are a relatively stable part of production – a constant need to update and extend textile sources and to check wider fashion trends is a central part of a designer's task. And reproduction, which is done digitally in other creative industries, here has to be done physically. On the other hand, film and TV makers, or games designers need high capital investment to move beyond a pure conceptualization of the end product. Given this their activities tend to be much more focused around the lead industry structures; they might live in Manchester or Glasgow (Turok, 2003) or Vancouver (Coe, 2000) but their networking is structured around the major clusters. They would only think of financing and organizing their own production at the very start of their careers. Fashion designers can produce high-quality garments, reproduce them in small numbers and distribute at local levels; but for this reason they can get locked into the materiality of the supply chain in a way that can undermine their specific design focus and ultimately their economic success.

The current designer fashion sector can be understood in terms of a traditional industrial sector in the sense that it is still represented by a 'material culture', by the organizational networks among design, machinery, suppliers, and retailers who are all operating in a pretty much price-based, competitive market economy. But to the independents, the materiality or physicality of this industrial sector has become their main disadvantage as a result of disintegration.

Finally, I need to say something about Manchester. Historically linked with the Lancashire cotton industry and 'shock city' (Briggs, 1965) of the industrial revolution, it was the mill towns around Manchester (Bolton, Bury, Rochdale and others) that were engaged in production with Manchester as their commercial centre. The built fabric of mills and warehouses still marks the city, and their re-use by creative industries is somewhat iconic of culture-led regeneration in the UK (O'Connor and Gu, 2010). However, despite this imaginative association independent fashion designers had very little relationship with this traditional sector. By the 1980s, when this independent sector emerged, Manchester's textile industry had either disappeared or gone relentlessly downmarket. The most important connection was the existence of strong fashion design and textiles departments at the local Manchester Polytechnic (after 1992 Manchester Metropolitan University) though, tellingly, these were separate departments on separate campuses. In addition fabric sourcing still benefited from a residue of a once thriving industry. In actual fact, independent fashion designers grew up in the wake of the resurgent music industry of the 1970s and the youth, street and club fashion markets this stimulated. In this sense, perhaps, although marked by the materiality of an older manufacturing sector, it had very few links with the manufacturing community and has never seen its particular businesses skills (as opposed to making skills) as relevant to its needs.

All these issues have important consequences for policy interventions, which I will discuss later in the chapter. They also make particular demands on researchers looking at their business and networking practices, whether for policy or academic purposes.

RESEARCHING CREATIVE INDUSTRIES

For this case study I chose a mixture of formal interviews and participant observation. There are other approaches to the study of creative industry networking, such as quantitative and qualitative mapping of connections – within and without the specific sector, and indicated as strong or weak. This has been used to affirm the interconnections within creative industries or cultural sector, or between policy makers and sector, or local and trans-local actors (c.f., Chaplain and Comunian, 2010 regional studies; 2011 urban studies). My purpose here is less to understand the extent of the network – which we already know is quite limited (see below), than the uses to which it was put and the range of meanings invested in it.

As we shall see in the case study that follows, socio-cultural relationships based on trust and identity are identified as a key feature of networking in this sector. Unlike conventional business networks, social networks observed among this group of creative entrepreneurs seem to be about longer term 'narrative relationships' of friendship and community. They have strong cultural and social dimensions that go beyond routine economic practices. As such, this research focuses on the independent sector and its social networks. I did not look at other related activities such as buyers or makers or material suppliers as these businesses operate on rather different models and principles.

The importance of networking in the creative industries suggested to me the following four aims. First, to understand the extent of the blurring or overlap of formal and informal networks, or 'work' and 'social life' (leisure, play, friends, etc.); second, how this was related to the specific working practices of independent fashion designers; third, what was being asked of these networks (information, trust, reputation, identity, etc.); and fourth, how did this impact on the specific shape or dynamics of the network.

Pursuit of these aims required a more ethnographic, qualitative approach. This research was part of a Doctorate sponsored in part by Manchester's City Council funded Creative Industries Development Service (CIDS). I will say more about the latter below (but note the potential influence of the institutional environment on the creative fashion industry and see Karataş-Özkan et al., Chapter 5, this volume). Here I note that one of its objectives was to promote sub-sectoral networking organizations that could provide a coherent voice by which the needs and aspirations of these sub-sectors could be represented at policy level. This research was charged with following this initiative and providing an assessment of its successes, problems and possibilities. In this way I had access to databases of independent fashion designers in Manchester and also to the early attempts by CIDS to set up a Manchester Fashion Network (MFN). (These initiatives will not be discussed in this chapter, except in a general way in the conclusion.) This enabled me to compile a list of potential interviewees and at the same time gain access to a number of events organized by the MFN and subsequently other formal and informal events by the fashion designers themselves.

The method consists of open-ended questionnaires aimed at getting a biographical account of the businesses – education, family background, why and how they got into the field, how their businesses had developed and so on. I then focused on how they balanced the 'cultural' and 'economic' elements of their business. In fact, although it seemed initially that these might be rather academic or abstract terms, this tension was broached almost immediately in every interview. They were doing this because of various aspirations related to cultural/aesthetic ambitions, and had to find ways in which this was negotiated with paying bills. However, at some point 'making it' would result in both objectives – but how they got there would be important. These findings are discussed below.

Second, and in parallel, I attended various formal and informal functions. Formal functions initially meant MFN meetings, and other events organized by CIDS and other cultural agencies in the city (such as the launch of Manchester Fashion Week). Informal functions initially included attending the independent fashion market – a group of designers taking over a large shopping mall floor on Saturdays – which, though clearly formal from a customer's point of view, provided me with much greater insight through elicited information and general gossip into their network. Eventually I was invited to the informal gatherings of the fashion scene in Manchester, which included publishers, music industry people and shop-owners.

These two methods provided different forms of information that could be checked against each other. Thus, interview-based accounts – with whom and on what basis networking was conducted – could be deepened (or contradicted) by observation of events. Particular actions or new people encountered (or gossip about people) picked up in events could then be explored in the interviews. In all I interviewed a total of 15 independent fashion designers – out of a total of 40 with creative businesses generally. I also interviewed 20 key policy makers at local and regional levels.

Though other actor-network methods for mapping networks are useful, as are more formal business questionnaires and statistical data-gathering, I suggest that this more in-depth ethnographic work can yield very useful results.

A DIFFICULT BUSINESS MODEL

When the creative industries' agendas began to gain policy traction from the late 1980s onwards, one of the most common policy recommendations was providing training and business support to the sector (O'Connor, 2007; Oakley, 2004; Oakley and Sperry, 2008). At first, these were undertaken by mainstream economic development agencies, with a view to adding business nous to cultural flair. But mainstream business support had very little knowledge of the sector; they tended to have a very different understanding of what 'doing businesses' actually meant, seeing creative businesses as 'risky' or 'flakey' businesses. In particular, the independent designer fashion sector tended to be labelled a 'cottage industry' or 'lifestyle industry' – hobbies, not serious businesses. There was always mistrust between the creative sector and mainstream business support agencies around the sector's 'problematic' business model. The mainstream support agencies frequently suggested a separation between 'lifestyle' and 'high growth' creative businesses, willing to help those who were serious about becoming 'proper' businesses.

On the face of it many fashion businesses seemed to be ignorant of their own markets. In Manchester, for instance, there is a high supply of casual urban wear for the youth market (see Table 19.1), yet they persist. They do not tend to follow seasonal fashion, thus forgoing the marketing rhythm of the high streets. Most of them sell small volumes of design-focused clothing through independent boutiques and private commissions, whereas 'street wear' is supposed to be high-volume, rapid-turnover and instantly accessible on the high street. Research on the independent sector in New York and London has indicated similar issues for this sector (Currid, 2007; McRobbie, 2002). However, whereas in global cultural capitals, small entrepreneurs could hope to 'make it' within

Table 19.1   Profile of independent designer fashion businesses in Manchester

Category	Characteristics	Estimated No. of Designers
Couture / Designer fashion	With in-house design team, outsource manufacturing overseas, with retail outlets or run concessions within department stores, license brands, trade internationally	5–10
Street wear (Directional)	With in-house design, manufacture in UK, wholesale, run concessions within department store, trade internationally	20–30+
Non-directional	Mainly independent or sole traders, self-manufacturing with the help of outworkers, mainly sell through independent boutiques, but also through private commissions	15–20
Accessories	Contemporary designer jewellery	10–15

the dense global networks, in Manchester the immersion in, and commitment to, the local scene was one that did not hold out such a glittering promise of material reward.

However, the lack of business 'common sense' need not be about levels of entrepreneurial commitment. According to this research, creative entrepreneurs do not reject the idea of commercial success – they just wanted to have it on their own terms. I noticed that the tension between culture and commerce can demand a choice – and commitment to aesthetic quality frequently won out (Gu, 2010). The creative entrepreneur's sense of what is aesthetically 'right', and their ability to have control over this, is crucial to their brand-building strategy. This commitment to 'aesthetics' is, in part, about producing something that is 'good' rather than perceived as shoddy and compromised. Creative entrepreneurs were as worried as much by shoddiness, the misuse of materials, the cutting of corners, and so on, as they were by the 'bad' aesthetics of 'High-Street' or the 'Corporates'. It is this commitment to a certain level of craft skill – embodied in the eye as well as the hand – as much as 'the artist starving in the garret', which gave a sense of purpose, a kind of justification, for their persisting in difficult circumstances. In other words, entrepreneurship building in creative industries includes both the creation of the products and the self – a sense of unique individuality that they project (Hearn and Bridgstock, 2010).

However, there is a price to pay for this choice. The creative entrepreneur's prospects, as the energy of youth declines, can look bleak. So how do they justify their 'odd' business practices, even in the face of those local economic development agencies seeking to offer them support?

Informal Business Networks

We may turn to the practice of social networking for an answer. The uncertainty associated with creative businesses seems to be the main reason leading creative entrepreneurs to look for affective bonds among themselves. Most of the initial social networks evolved around the idea of information exchange, they increasingly represent a space in which to identify with like-minded people. Social networks in general are organized on the principle of trust and reputation as I have shown above. But what is interesting here is that strategic business alliances are replaced by a notion of 'mates', who understand 'who you are' and 'how hard it is to be in this industry'.

Different to conventional business networks, such interpersonal relationships seem to be exclusive, less business-oriented and resistant to formalization and institutionalization. They appear to be influenced to a greater extent by shared interests, lifestyle and other social and cultural values; that is, interpersonal relationships rather than economic reciprocities (Powell and Smith-Doerr, 1994). Rather than 'informational' motives, where such networking provides the opportunity of 'catch-up' and information exchange (Grabher, 1993), these networks are also about constructing identity.

The source of 'self-exploitation' among these fashion entrepreneurs – the carrot of making it on their own terms – may be seen to lock them into a difficult situation and encourage them to ignore more 'reasonable' economic opportunities if only they would give up their artistic dream. The excitement and glamour of the 'creative field' play their part. There is the sense of remaining plugged into a 'scene', a world, in which their identities are very much invested. Though their ambitions might become scaled down they may still want to feel a participant on the wider creative scene. This cannot be overlooked as a key drive for creative entrepreneurship.

What unites these fashion entrepreneurs is their commitment to be creative, cutting edge and controversial. Social networks among these people are as much about creating a shared cultural understanding of particular moods, tastes and choices as about mutual support. These networks form part of a wider 'creative ecology' in which immediate personal networks become connected to a wider local socio-cultural identification.

This desire to be part of a wider set of networks and identities can be viewed as a solution to the conflicting values at play in creative businesses. These are social networks where work and play, business and shared values are deeply intertwined. This certainly produces tension between the aesthetic and business knowledge circulated. But what keeps the tensions of business and art in check is a sense of community, of shared aesthetic and ethical values. It does so by providing the support, the sense of meaning and validation needed to survive in a difficult economic context.

Formal Business Networks

Business networks among these fashion entrepreneurs were developed very much at the personal level, and communication was done mostly through informal socializing. In 2003, the local creative industries development agency (CIDS) initiated a formal network of industry professionals who would meet and work together to sustain and develop the fashion scene in Manchester. This became the Manchester fashion network (MFN). From the start, MFN's aim is to provide professional business development service to its members. It is to provide a point of contact for various industry professionals and encouraged communication and cooperation through events and exhibitions.

However, MFN was never going to be a standard business network. It formed to a large extent around personal relationship-building. The partnership was one formed out of an 'acquaintance' based on personality, style or shared background rather than economic reciprocity. This is exemplified in the constitution of the members. Most of them were local fashion entrepreneurs. The majority of them were from Manchester and had lived or worked in the area for many years. They associated themselves with the image of the city and stated that they would not have started their businesses elsewhere. Many of them had also attended arts and design courses at Manchester Metropolitan University, through which they established local know-how and contacts. Most of the members joined MFN via being introduced by their friends who were fellow fashion entrepreneurs. Such dependence on 'names' based on a strong personal connection indicates the specific form of trust operating within the sector.

The goals of the network, unlike those of a conventional business advisory agency, are therefore about facilitating rather than directing. MFN was publicly funded and supervised by an advisory panel consisting of independent fashion entrepreneurs and others in the local PR, retail and manufacturing sectors. Since the beginning, the independent fashion entrepreneurs wanted to promote the local fashion sector as part of the general 'cultural offer' of the city. The focus of MFN shifted therefore from developing collaboration between independent fashion and big manufacturers (as has been attempted by the local economic development agency), to that of how to give local independent fashion more publicity. In fact, independent fashion entrepreneurs have deliberately avoided high street retailers and manufacturing businesses. For these local fashion entrepreneurs, it is worth holding onto the 'independent' brand as it is about craftsmanship and unique creativity – values that are the essence of their business model comparing to businesses in 'fast fashion' whose success relies on economic scale and efficiency. These fashion entrepreneurs' preference for staying small rather than growing their business strategically suggests that social and cultural values were decisive in shaping their inter-firm relationships.

They were wary about too close an association with a commercial network not only because of their 'artistic value', but also because of long experience of 'hard knocks' from 'the industry'. These fashion entrepreneurs needed to keep close control over their reputation and image within an industrial context in which they were relatively powerless. It was not so much a reluctance to get involved in commerce per se, but a reluctance to risk their image and reputation, one of the few areas over which they did have some control. In these respects readers might be interested to consider Forson et al., Chapter 4, this volume, especially the reference to the theoretical framing work of Bourdieu.

The withdrawal from the more commercial orientation of the business practices may underline the lack of business ambition of these fashion entrepreneurs, their embracing of failure, or desire simply to run a 'lifestyle business'. But there were other factors at play as well. At a later date the MFN was taken over by a fashion business person and turned into a commercial organization. Many of the fashion designers left as this was seen as a privatization of their social relationships. This introduced a different atmosphere into the network as the local creative community could be seen to come under the control of one businessman. This exhibits a distinctive 'community sensitivity' which privileges 'culture values' rather than 'business values'. Alongside it, there is a shared interest in linking the collective identity of these independent businesses to a wider 'Manchester' brand because they believed the two to be mutually beneficial.

CONCLUSION

This chapter has suggested that social relationships and bonds of trust built within local cultures of production are part of a defensive reaction to the uncertainties of business, and that the over-institutionalization or formalization of these relationships carries the risk of eliminating the sense of aesthetic aspiration and identity that allow these entrepreneurs to survive in the city in the first place. It thus suggested that the socio-cultural embeddedness of the creative industries has implications for both business practices and the networks which sustain them. In particular these networks might work as compensation for an 'independent' sector, businesses that many see as losing out in a cultural economy characterized by growth.

The alternative value system within which the independent sector organized itself has resulted in seemingly paradoxical business behaviours among this group of cultural entrepreneurs. In fashion, it was observed that the networks were quite resistant to players who did not share the same lifestyle, cultural and aesthetic values. Practices of social networking among them illustrate the importance of friendship, acquaintances, formal and informal networks in developing cultural entrepreneurship. In fact, my case study shows that ties in each of these areas form an essential part of the cultural entrepreneurship building; each facilitated the success of the business, and each brought them into close connection with cultural and social capital active both locally, nationally and internationally.

Situating oneself among a group of people who have commitment to creativity and craftsmanship is critical for the development of an alternative support infrastructure. In the creative industries, knowing who your friends are and who you can go out with is as important a consideration as who the manufacturers are and who you might get business from. The difference is that the former relations are not replicable, or at least not easily cultivated, unlike the latter, which can be complemented through relocation for instance. This is the key to understanding, at least to some extent, the paradoxical business behavior creative entrepreneurs exhibited through their social networks.

Social networks in creative industries do not appear to be composed of ambitious artists/designers who mobilize their social connections instrumentally to forge business deals. Rather they seem to be the creation of a densely connected, self-conscious social group intensely unified by multiple ties in a wide range of social affiliations. This social group is integrated by variety of cultural interests and aesthetic judgments. I argue that seemingly 'anti-business' behaviour in the context of these networks can in fact be an essential survival strategy for SMEs in creative industries – overcoming high risks necessitates holding on to 'cultural/aesthetic values', to social norms within the group, and to the intrinsic value of cultural production when unpredictable economic conditions prevail.

This research shows that there is a strong sense of being 'plugged in' to a scene, the pleasure of being somehow 'part of something' which can persist even when the sense of unique individuality wanes. This is certainly related to the 'glamour' or 'intoxicating pleasure' of the art-fashion-music scene (c.f., Currid, 2007); but this pleasure is also a promise of being true to oneself and one's ambitions, of continuing to be an active player in a world one has made one's own.

The research also shows that there is an equally strong sense of doing something because it is 'good', it is worthwhile in itself. This 'romantic' view of the artist may have been sidelined in the era of 'creative industries', but it is still very powerful amongst many creatives and artists (Oakley and Sperry, 2008). The commitment of doing the job properly is rooted in social contexts that are quite complex and involve aesthetic and ethical judgements. The networks within which these aesthetical and ethical judgements are embedded cannot be reduced to 'business needs', and hence conventional business services struggle to cater to them.

When public agencies attempt in different ways to mediate between stakeholders with very different interests and priorities, they risk adopting values which might be in conflict with formal policy goals. The difficulties of policy intervention lie in the very nature of the creative industries – the ways in which creative entrepreneurs worked in this case study group was very much about establishing trust at the informal level of networking, rather than the formal institutional world of goals, pre-set agendas and outcomes which mark the policy world (especially economic development agencies).

However, there is a role for the public sector to play. The creation of MFN Manchester created a base through which the ideal of creative entrepreneurship could be given institutional flesh. The social and cultural aspects of these networks are important for the cohesion and sustainability of local cultures of production. In fashion, the designers' interpersonal relationships work as mutual support, protecting them from harsh competition, high street chains, and global manufacturers. MFN was important to designers who shared the same interests in developing high fashion in the city. Their aspirations could, under certain circumstances, be linked to the development of a wider brand for the city. A similar process can be seen with new media designers, who also trade in part of the wider brand of the city as a 'cool place' (Pratt, 2002). Many new media designers choose to stay in Manchester not only because of business reasons (London seems to hold more possibilities), but because they have personal and family connections with the place. They are also deeply 'embedded' in the city (c.f., McKeever et al., Chapter 13, this volume) in the sense of it providing a community within which to frame a narrative about what they do and what they aspire to be.

It could be said that cultural entrepreneurs were relying on this symbolic image of the city to support their activities. It was less to do with training and business support per se, than the symbolic representation of local creative industries and recognition of their key role in developing local identity. It was out of this context that various network development services were formed and given responsibility for developing local creative industries' networks based on the notion of 'commitment' or 'identification', rather than a market strategy.

Finally, this chapter has suggested the importance of qualitative, in-depth research that can complement the more standard business questionnaire approach or more formal and quantitative network mapping techniques (c.f., Chell, Chapter 7, this volume). This can yield insights into creative entrepreneurialism and their networks which can help extend our models to incorporate different motivations and standards of 'success'.

REFERENCES

Amin, A. (Ed.) (1994), *Post-Fordism: A Reader*, Oxford: Oxford University Press.
Amin, A. and Hausner, J. (1997), 'Interactive governance and social complexity', in Amin, A. and Hausner, J. (Eds), *Beyond Market and Hierarchy*, pp 1–31, Cheltenham: Edward Elgar.

Amin, A. and Thrift, N. (1995), Globalisation, institutional thickness and the local economy, in Healey Patsy et al. (Eds). *Managing Cities: The New Urban Context*, pp. 91–108, Chichester: John Wiley & Sons.

Banks, M. (2006), 'Moral economy and cultural work', *Sociology*, 40(3), 455–72.

Banks, M. (2007). *The Politics of Cultural Work*, Basingstoke: Palgrave.

Banks, M. et al (2000), 'Risk and trust in the cultural industries', *Geoforum*, 31, 453–64.

Bassett, K., Griffiths, R. and Smith, I. (2002), 'Cultural industries, cultural clusters and the city: the example of natural history film-making in Bristol', *Geoforum*, 33, 105–77.

Bianchini, F. (1993) 'Remaking European cities: the role of cultural policies', in Bianchini, F. and M. Parkinson (Eds), *Cultural Policy and Urban Regeneration*, pp. 1–20, Manchester University Press, Manchester.

Briggs, A. (1965), *Victorian Cities*. University of California Press.

Capello, R. (1999), 'Spatial transfer of knowledge in high technology milieu: Learning versus collective learning processes', *Regional Studies*, 33 (4), 353–65.

Chaplain, C. and Comunian, R. (2010), 'Enabling and inhibiting the creative economy: The role of the local and regional dimensions in England', *Regional Studies*, 44 (6) 171–34.

Coe, N. M. (2000), 'On Location: American capital and the local labour market in the Vancouver film industry', *International Journal of Urban and Regional Research*, 24, 74–94.

Crewe, L. (1996), 'Material culture: Embedded firms, organizational networks and the local economic development of a fashion quarter', *Regional Studies*, 30, 257–72.

Comunian, R. (2011), 'Rethinking the creative city: The role of complexity, networks and interactions in the urban creative economy', *Urban Studies*, 48 (6), 1157–79.

Currid, E. (2007), *The Warhol economy: how fashion, art, and music drive New York City*, Princeton: Princeton University Press.

DCMS (1998; 2000), *Creative Industries Mapping Document*, London: DCMS.

DTI and BFC (2003), *A Study of the UK Designer Fashion Sector*.

Frontier Economics (2008), *Creative Industry Performance: A Statistical Analysis for the DCMS*. London. http://www.cep.culture.gov.uk/index.cfm?fuseaction=main.viewBlogEntry&intMTEntryID=3104, accessed May 2012.

Garnham, N. (1990), *Capitalism and communication: global culture and the economics of information*, London: Sage.

Gill, R. and Pratt, A. (2008), 'The social factory: immaterial labour, precariousness and cultural work', *Theory, Culture and Society*, 25(7–8), 1–30.

Grabher, G. (1993), 'On the weakness of strong ties: the ambivalent role of interfirm cooperation in the decline and reorganization of the Ruhr', in Grabher, G. (Ed.). *The Embedded Firm: On the Socioeconomics of Industrial Networks*, pp. 255–77, London: Routledge.

Grabher, G. (2001), 'Ecologies of creativity: the village, the group, and the heterarchic organization of the British advertising industry', *Environment and Planning, A* 33, 351–74.

Granovetter, M. (1973), 'The strength of weak ties', *American Journal of Sociology*, 78 (6), 1360–80.

Granovetter, M. (1985), 'Economic action and social structure: the problem of embeddedness', *The American Journal of Sociology*, 91(3): 481–510.

Granovetter, M. (1991), 'The social construction of economic institutions', in Etzioni, A. and Lawrence, R. (eds). *Socio-Economics: Towards a New Synthesis*, pp. 75–81. New York: Armonk.

Gu, X. (2010), 'Social networks and aesthetic reflexivity in the creative industries', *Journal of International Communication*, 16(2), 55–66.

Hansen, N. (1992), 'Competition, Trust and Reciprocity in the Development of Innovative Regional Milieux', *Papers in Regional Science*, 71(2), 95–105.

Hartley, J. (ed.) (2005). *Creative Industries*, Oxford: Blackwell.

Hearn, G. and Bridgstock, R. (2010), 'Education for the creative economy: Innovation, transdisciplinarity and networks', in Michael Peters and Araya Daniel (Eds). *Education in the Creative Economy*, New York: Peter Lang.

Keeble, D. et al (1999), 'Collective learning processes, networking and 'institutional thickness' in the Cambridge region', *Regional Studies*, 33(4), 319–32.

Landry, Charles (2000). *The Creative City*, Comedia: London.

Lash, S. and Urry, J. (1994), *Economies of Signs and Space*, London: Sage.

Leadbeater, Charles (2012). *Its Co-operation, Stupid*, http://www.ippr.org/images/media/files/publication/2012/03/cooperation_leadbeater_Mar2012_8769.pdf, accessed 1st May 2012.

Maskell, P. (2001), 'Social capital and competitiveness', in Baron, S., Field, J. and Schuller, T. (eds.) *Social Capital. Critical Perspectives*. Oxford: Oxford University Press.

McRobbie, A. (1998), *British Fashion Design: Rag Trade or Image Industry?* London: Routledge.

McRobbie, A. (2002), 'Clubs to companies: notes on the decline of political culture in speeded up creative worlds', *Cultural Studies*, 16(4), 516–31.

Misztal, B. A. (1996), *Trust in Modern Societies*. Cambridge: Polity Press.

Morgan, K. (1997), 'The learning region: Institutions, innovation and regional renewal', *Regional Studies*, 31(5), 491–503.

Mulgan, G. (1989), *Communication and Control: Networks and the New Economics of Communication.* Cambridge: Polity.

NWDA (2003). *Benchmarking Employment in the Cultural Industries.* Manchester, UK: Regional Intelligence Unit.

Oakley, K. (2004), 'Not so cool Britannia – the role of the creative industries in economic development', *International Journal of Cultural Studies*, 7(1), 67–77.

Oakley, K. and Sperry, B. (2008), *Fine Artists and Innovation*, London: NESTA.

O'Connor, J. (1999), 'The definition of cultural industries', http://www.mipc.mmu.ac.uk/iciss/reports/defin. pdf, accessed 1st May, 2010.

O'Connor, J. (2004), '"A Special Kind of City Knowledge": Innovative clusters, tacit knowledge and the 'Creative City'', *Media International Australia*, 112, 131–49.

O'Connor, J. (2007), *Creative Partnerships Literature Review*, Arts Council England.

O'Connor, J. and Gu, X. (2010), 'Developing a creative cluster in a post-industrial city: CIDS and Manchester', *Information Society*, 26(2), 124–36.

Park, S. O. (1996), 'Networks and embeddedness in the dynamic types of new industrial districts', *Progress in Human Geography*, 20 (4), 476ç93.

Powell, W. (1990), 'Neither market nor hierarchy: Network forms of organization', *Research in Organizational Behavior*, 12, 295–336.

Powell, W. and Smith-Doerr, Laurel (1994), 'Networks and economic life', in Smelser, N. J. and Swedberg, R. (eds), *The Handbook of Economic Sociology*, pp 368–402, Princeton: Princeton University Press.

Porter, M. E. (2000), 'Location, competition and economic development: local clusters in a global economy', *Economic Development Quarterly*, 14(1), 15–34.

Pratt, A. C. (2002), 'Hot jobs in cool places: The material cultures of new media product spaces: the case of the south of market'. San Francisco. *Information, Communication and Society*, 5, 27–50.

Pratt, A. C. and Jeffcutt, P. (2009). *Creativity, Innovation and the Cultural Economy*, London: Taylor & Francis.

Porter, M. E. (1998), Clusters and the new economics of competition. *Harvard Business Review*, 76(6), 77–91.

Putnam, R. D. (1993), *Making Democracy Work: Civic Traditions in Modern Italy.* Princeton: Princeton University Press.

Ross, A. (2003), *No-Collar.* Philadelphia: Temple University Press.

Saxenian, A. (1990), 'Regional networks and the resurgence of Silicon Valley', *California Management Review* Fall, 89–112.

Scott, A. J. (1986), 'Industrial organisation and location: Division of labour, the firm and spatial process', *Economic Geography*, 62, 215–31.

Scott, A. J. (1999), 'The cultural economy: Geography and creative field', *Media, Culture and Society*, 21: 807C17.

Scott, A. J. (2000), *The Cultural Economy of Cities: Essays on the Geography of Image-Producing Industries*, London: Sage.

Scott, A. J. (2004), 'Cultural-products industries and urban economic development: prospects for growth and market contestation in global context', *Urban Affairs Review*, 39(4), 461–90.

Sennett, R. (2008), *The Craftsman.* London: Allen Lane.

Shorthose, J. (2004), 'Nottingham's de facto cultural quarter: the lace market, independents and a convivial ecology', in David Bell and Mark Jayne (Eds.) *City of Quarters: Urban Villages and the Contemporary City*, London: Ashgate.

Storper, M. (1995), 'The resurgence of regional economies, ten years later: The region as a nexus of untraded interdependencies', *European Urban and Regional Studies*, 2(3), 191–221.

Turok, I. (2003), 'Cities, clusters and creative industries: The case of film and television in Scotland', *European Urban Studies*, 11(5), 549–65.

Wittel, A. (2001), 'Towards a network sociality', *Theory, Culture & Society*, 18(6), 51–76.

Yeung, HO. W-C. (1994), 'Critical reviews of geographical perspectives on business organizations and the organization of production: Towards a network approach', *Progress in Human Geography*, 18: 460–90.

Zukin, S. and DiMaggio, P. (1990) *Structure of Capital: The Social Organisation of the Economy.* Cambridge: Cambridge University Press.

20. Business ethics and social responsibility in small firms
Laura J. Spence

INTRODUCTION

The complex role of business in society has never been purely commercial, and managing within business similarly has a social structure (Goss, 1990). With everything from familial obligation, community involvement and philanthropy to government policy enacted through the practices in small and large organizations alike, business is as much a part of society as any other organizational or institutional form, being an embedded 'interpenetrating system' (Muthuri, Moon & Idemudia, 2012). Despite small business being a technical and social activity (Kitching, 1994: 115), the social and ethical aspects of entrepreneurship and small firms are frequently overlooked, despite their importance (Fuller & Tian, 2006). Nevertheless, there is an emerging literature dispersed through a range of disciplines which addresses this perspective. These include perspectives from economics, sociology, management studies, applied moral philosophy, corporate social responsibility, entrepreneurship, geography, development studies and political science (see Table 20.1). In this chapter, a state of the art review of this literature is presented and two moral perspectives are discussed in detail as meaningful theoretical lenses through which to understand the social and ethical aspects of small business. The research presented contributes to the literature in two ways. First, it brings together the small business, entrepreneurship, business ethics and corporate social responsibility (CSR) literatures more even-handedly than other work has done, and secondly, it offers an original contribution by using the review to identify theoretical avenues for future size-sensitive, ethics and social responsibility studies.

Definitions of social responsibility and related topics are contested (Lockett, Moon and Visser, 2006) but in order to proceed with some clarity, broadly speaking, business ethics is understood as the everyday moral rules-in-use in organizations (Jackall, 1988), social responsibility is those expectations on business organizations beyond pecuniary ones (Carroll, 1999). Small business is considered to be in accordance with EU statistical definitions of the small firm, and entrepreneurship refers to "*sources* of opportunities; the *processes* of discovery, evaluation, and exploitation of opportunities; and the set of *individuals* who discover, evaluate, and exploit them." (Shane and Venkataraman, 2000: 218).

LITERATURE REVIEW: THE PUZZLE OF SMALL BUSINESS ETHICS

As an interdisciplinary topic, business ethics and small business is clearly at the intersection of two established areas of research. This, however, is just the start of the multiple

Table 20.1   *Literature overview: business ethics and social responsibility in small firms*

Topic (and disciplinary perspectives)	Authors (shown in chronological order)
The moral nature of entrepreneurship and entrepreneurs (business/ applied ethics; development, general management, geography, entrepreneurship, organization studies, political economy)	Baumol (1990); Dees & Starr (1992); Bucar & Hisrich (2001); Bucar, Glas & Hisrich (2003); Buchholz & Rosenthal (2005); Jones & Spicer (2005); Anderson & Smith (2007); Blackburn & McGhee (2007); Brenkert (2009); Godwyn (2009); Webb, Tihanyi, Ireland & Sirmon (2009); Dunham (2010)
Focused empirical evidence on the nature of ethics and social responsibility in small firms (business ethics, corporate governance; CSR; entrepreneurship, environmental management, innovation, public relations, regional general business; small business)	USA – Hornsby *et al* (1994); UK – Quinn (1997); Italy – Longo, Mura & Bonoli (2005); Ireland – Sweeney (2007); 39 countries – De Clercq & Dakhli (2009); Denmark – Nielsen & Thomsen (2009); Germany –Hammann, Habisch & Pechlaner (2009); Norway – Von Weltzien Høivik & Melè (2009); Sweden –Blombäck & Wigren (2009); China – Liu and Fong (2010); Bangladesh – Rahim & Wisuttisak (2012); India – Gupta & Kalra (2012); Malaysia –Nejati & Amran (2012); Medium firms – Preuss & Perschke (2010); Micro firms – Courrent & Gundolf (2009); Singapore – Lee & Pang (2012); Cameroon – Demuijnck & Ngnodjom (2013)
Ethnic minority and gender (business ethics, CSR)	Thompson and Hood (1993); Ede, Panigrahi, Stuart & Calcich (2000); Worthington, Ram and Jones (2006); Hazlina & Shen (2010)
Employees (business ethics, corporate governance, employee relations, health, sociology)	Eakin and MacEachen (1998); Christopher (2003); Massey (2003); Granerud (2011); Jones, Marshall and Mitchell (2007). In Fairtrade – Davies & Crane (2010)
Language and discourse (business ethics)	Spence & Lozano (2000); Lähdesmäki (2005); Murillo & Lozano (2006); Lähdesmäki (2012); Baden and Harwood (2013)
Theory development (business ethics, general management, small business)	Spence & Rutherfoord (2001); Jenkins (2004); Spence (2004); Udayasankar (2008); Blundel, Spence & Zerbinati (2010)
Philanthropy (business ethics, CSR, development, small business, strategy)	Acs & Phillips (2002); Brammer & Millington (2004); Schaper & Savery (2004); Amato & Amato (2007); Harvey, Maclean, Gordon & Shaw (2011); Lähdesmäki & Takala (2012)
Strategic aspects (business ethics, communications, CSR, entrepreneurship, technology management)	General – Sarbutts (2003); Graafland, van de Ven & Stoffele (2003); Castka, Balzarova, & Bamber (2004); Fassin (2008); Fenwick (2010); Schlierer et al. (2012) Innovation – Biondi, Iraldo & Meredith (2002); Anokhin & Schulze (2009) Performance – Tantalo, Caroli, & Vanevenhoven (2012); Torugsa, O'Donohue, & Hecker (2012);

Table 20.1   (continued)

Topic (and disciplinary perspectives)	Authors (shown in chronological order)
Supply chains, networks and social capital (business ethics, corporate governance, small business, supply chain management)	Spence, Schmidpeter & Habisch (2003); Fuller & Tian (2006); Murillo & Lozano (2009); Russo & Perrini (2009); Von Weltzien Høivik & Shankar (2011); Del Baldo (2012); Baden, Harwood & Woodward (2011); Lund-Thomsen, & Pillay (2012); Ciliberti, Baden & Harwood (2009); Rawlings (2012)
Development and developing countries (business ethics, CSR, economics, strategy)	Luetkenhorst (2004); Hamann, Abbazue, Kapelus & Hein (2005); Luken & Stares (2005); Vives (2006); Jamali, Zanhour and Keshishian (2009); Ahmad and Ramayah (2012)
Community (business ethics, CSR, entrepreneurship, socio-economics, voluntary sector)	Besser & Miller (2004); Besser, Miller & Perkins (2006); Fisher *et al.* (2009); Litz & Samu (2008); Besser (2012); Campin, Barraket, & Luke (2013); Koos (2012); Lähdesmäki & Suutari (2012)
Influence of religion (business ethics)	Islam – Graafland, Mazereeuw & Yahia (2009); Uygur (2009) Christianity – Werner (2008)
Decision-making/psychology of entrepreneurship (business ethics, entrepreneurship, small business)	Payne & Joyner (2006); McVea (2009); Rutherford, Buller & Stebbins (2009); Fassin, Van Rossem & Buelens (2011); D'Aprile & Mannarini (2012)
Social and Ethical Reporting & Communication (CSR, marketing, strategy)	Borga (2009); Gallo and Christensen (2011); Fraj-Andrés, López-Pérez, Melero-Polo, & Vázquez-Carrasco (2012)

Source: Author.

perspectives which the topic enjoys, as shown in Table 20.1, which gives an overview of some of the key disciplinary contributions. Each of these areas, in turn, is subject to a wide range of definitional issues[1]. Nevertheless, at this point in time the body of literature is sufficiently small as to make it possible to capture a flavour of the main extant relevant publications in this review[2].

Since the field is so diverse, collated in Table 20.2 is a comprehensive, interdisciplinary summation of the nature of responsibility and ethics in small firms. While there is an argument for cross-over between environmental and social issues, especially where sustainability is the over-riding theme, a distinction is made here. The reasoning for this is that environmental issues are primarily related to scientifically measured environmental damage, resource depletion and impact relating to climate change (usually greenhouse gas emissions [from energy use and transport] but increasingly also water use). These areas are increasingly legislated for within Europe at least, and pertain to future impacts. Social and ethical issues usually relate to contemporary challenges and – with the exception of labour standards – have tended to be voluntary rather than compulsory in nature. It should also be noted that the recent rise of social entrepreneurship has been considered elsewhere to be a continuum of social and ethical issues in small business and entrepreneurship (Blundel, Spence & Zerbinati, 2010). This claim is not disputed in this chapter,

Table 20.2   Summary of the nature of ethics and social responsibility in small firms

Description	Analysis
External influences	Community, networks and social capital. Supply chains, economic environment (e.g. developing country), cultural group, requirement to give report on social and ethical issues.
Key actor	Owner-manager as both principal and agent of the firm. Owner-manager as both responsible manager and responsible leader. Moral nature of the entrepreneur, decision-making and psychology perspective.
Internal organizational characteristics	Informal management; lack of codification; close communication; influential blue-print of the owner-manager; reputation and social capital dependent.
Organizational metaphor	The family. A team. Friends. Shared experience of work.
Key stakeholders	Workers. Followed by family, community members, customers and suppliers.
Main ethical concern	Health and welfare of workers.
Proposed most relevant moral perspectives	Moral proximity – physical and social. Linking responsibility to those closest to the owner-manager, i.e. the workers. The ethics of care – a context-respectful approach. Emphasis on relationships, shared experience and trust. Clear acknowledgment of power differential (between owner-manager and workers) and an embedded, interconnected network of needs.

Source: Author.

but the focus is on research on those organizations which do not have a social or ethical remit as their primary goal.

As Table 20.1 shows, the research reported on here covers a wide range of perspectives. The moral nature of entrepreneurship and entrepreneurs is the primary area where there are theoretical developments, for example in the application of utilitarianism, suggesting that consequences drive action (Ahmad and Ramayah, 2012), or egoism, suggesting that self-interest drives action (Besser and Miller, 2004) to seek to explain the behaviour of entrepreneurs (this is expanded upon in Table 20.3). Other theoretical developments focus on the difference between small and large firms in respect of corporate social responsibility (CSR) and business ethics, such as the work by Jenkins which develops a framework of key differences. The well-researched area of ethical decision-making is also represented in this literature, for example McVea (2009) links entrepreneurial decision-making to moral imagination. A further approach adopted, which is familiar from the large firm perspective, is quantitative research on philanthropic giving (e.g. Brammer & Millington, 2004). Some authors have tried to import strategic research perspectives to the small firm context (e.g. competition, innovation, strategy implementation), noting in some instances 'the fallacy' of formalizing CSR (Fassin, 2008). The study of communicating CSR through social and ethical reporting has also been attempted, though its applicability is debatable given that small firms are unlikely to provide financial, let alone social, reports. In this respect work on the language and discourses of CSR used by

Table 20.3   Summary of ethical theories used in business ethics research

Key theories, protagonists and seminal works*	Focal point for ethicality	Brief description
Kantianism Immanuel Kant –*Groundwork of the Metaphysics of Morals* (1785); *Critique of Pure Reason* (1788)	Do one's duty according to reasoned consideration (e.g. Anderson and Smith, 2007; Clarke and Holt, 2010)	Duty is defined by the Categorical Imperative: (1) Universal Law: Act only according to that maxim whereby you can at the same time will that it should become a universal law without contradiction. (2) Humanity: Act in such a way that you treat humanity, whether in your own person or in the person of any other, never merely as a means to an end, but always at the same time as an end. (3) Kingdom of Ends: Therefore, every rational being must so act as if he were through his maxim always a legislating member in the universal kingdom of ends. Commonly (though problematically) associated with the 'Golden Rule' – do unto others as you would be done by.
Utilitarianism (Act/Rule) Jeremy Bentham –*Introduction to Principles of Morals and Legislation* (1789) John Stuart Mill –*Utilitarianism* (1863)	Act according to consequences, the goal being to maximize utility/pleasure for all (e.g. Ahmad and Ramayah, 2012; Besser, Miller and Perkins, 2006)	Asks: "What maximizes the greatest good for the greatest number?" Act:Utilitarianism looks at the consequences of each individual act and calculates utility each time the act is performed. Rule:Utilitarianism looks at the consequences of having everyone follow a particular rule and calculates the overall utility of accepting or rejecting the rule.
Egoism Henry Sidgwick – *The Method of Ethics* (1874) Ayn Rand – *The Virtue of Selfishness* (1964)	Act according to one's own self-interest (e.g. Besser and Miller, 2004; Longenecker, McKinney and Moore, 1988)	Promotion of one's own interests is consistent with morality, assuming that each other person is also pursuing their own self-interest. Asks: "What benefits me?"
Social Contract Theory Thomas Hobbes –*The Leviathan* (1651) John Locke –*Two Treatises of Government* (1689) Jean-Jacques Rousseau –*The Social Contract* (1762) John Rawls –*Theory of Justice* (1971)	The set of rules governing behaviour (e.g. Bucar, Glas & Hisrich, 2003; Koos, 2012)	Moral obligations are considered to be dependent on agreements between people to determine the rules governing behaviour in the society in which they live. Asks: "What sort of society should we live in?" Closely relates to societal rules and laws, and conceptualizations of rights and justice.

Virtue Ethics Aristotle – *Nicomachean Ethics; Eudemian Ethics (Approx. 350 BC)* Alasdair MacIntyre – *After Virtue* (1981)	Judge the character of the individual (e.g. Blackburn & McGhee, 2007; Dunham, 2010)	Example of character-based ethical theory: To behave ethically, you need to be a virtuous person. Asks: "What sort of person should I be?" Aristotelian (cardinal) virtues –leaders only, courage, justice, wisdom, temperance. Modern day virtues – friendship, conscientiousness, faithfulness, kindness, co-operativeness, integrity, honesty, courage, loyalty, courteousness.
Discourse Ethics Jürgen Habermas – *Moral Consciousness and Communicative Action* (1983)	The process of decision-making (e.g. Lähdesmäki, 2012)	Asks: "By which process can this conflict be resolved peacefully?" Discourse ethics aims to solve ethical conflicts by providing a process of norm generation through rational reflection on the real-life experiences of all relevant participants. Requires that: Needs can be articulated; Power differences are suspended; Transparent process; Role empathy; All those affected are included.
Postmodern Ethics Emmanuel Levinas– *Totality and Infinity* (1961) Jean-François Lyotard – *The Post Modern Condition* (1979) Zygmunt Bauman – *Postmodern ethics* (1993)	Rejection of meta-narratives, ethics determined – morality without ethical codes, self-determined (Jones & Spicer, 2005)	The felt 'impulse' towards the Other and the Other's vulnerability, is the basis of ethics. It is the irrational nature of ethics that makes it ethics. Determined by the notion that "I act because I feel I must act". Ethics as characterized by uncertainty, doubt, and continual critique.
Ethic of Care Carol Gilligan – *In a Different Voice* (1982) Virginia Held – *The Ethic of Care* (2006)	Prioritize those with whom there is a relationship (e.g. Von Weltzien Høivik & Melé, 2009)	Acknowledge that: We have an emotional commitment and willingness to act on behalf of persons with whom one has a significant relationship. We are not autonomous with free choice and equal positions of power: We are bound by circumstance, relations and position; We have restricted information and choices; We are in positions of unequal power.

Note: * The works cited here are absolute classics and have been reprinted, translated and reproduced many times, lacking definitive versions. Therefore I have not included them in the bibliography. Works published since the beginning of the 20th century have however been included.

Source: Author.

379

owner-managers and entrepreneurs has proved highly relevant (e.g. Murillo & Lozano, 2006; Lähdesmäki, 2012).

It is qualitative empirical contributions, however, which dominate this sub-field. As is perhaps common in the early stages of research in a new area, there is an abundance of single country studies, seeking to explore small firm/entrepreneurship and ethics/social responsibility in particular settings (such as a Norwegian case study by Von Weltzien Høivik and Melé, 2009), or less commonly by comparing countries to try to establish the impact of political and cultural differences (De Clercq and Dakhli, 2009). Within this group of studies, a few have sought to differentiate according to size of SME, such as by looking at micro-enterprises in France (Courrent and Gundolf, 2009), or medium-sized UK firms (Preuss and Perschke, 2010). Some research has taken external factors into account, such as the influence of religion whereby Uygur (2009) compares 'secular' and 'pious' Islamic small business entrepreneurs in Turkey, or the influence of gender or ethnic minority run-businesses (respectively Ahmad and Seet, (2010); Ede, Panigrahi, Stuart and Calcich, (2000)). Small firm prosperity is regularly linked to development and the CSR field is no exception, reflecting closely on the contribution to social progress that business organizations can make (Luetkenhorst, 2004). Stakeholder perspectives are addressed through a group of research on employees, community, suppliers and networks. The work on employees is typified by a focus on health and safety (e.g. (Granerud, 2011). Besser and Miller lead the research on communities, employing sociological approaches in their studies (Besser and Miller, 2004; Besser, Miller and Perkins, 2006; Besser, 2012). Supply chains, networks and social capital are a fairly well developed theme, with several authors arguing for social capital perspectives as being valuable for small firms and CSR research (Russo and Perrini, 2009; Spence, Schmidpeter and Habisch, 2003).

Table 20.2 draws from the extant literature discussed above, extracting from it an overview of the most important aspects established in relation to ethical and social responsibility in small business. Having presented this overview, the remainder of this chapter focuses on an ethical analysis of the foregoing work, drawing in particular on the ethical lenses of moral proximity and the ethics of care.

MORAL LENSES FOR UNDERSTANDING ETHICS AND SOCIAL RESPONSIBILITY IN THE SMALL BUSINESS

As is clear from Tables 20.1 and 20.2, the majority of research on ethics and social responsibility to date has been *descriptive* in nature, with little progress in *explaining* behaviour in small firms. In this chapter the moral perspective of research in this area is given precedence since this is the implicit orientation when seeking to understand ethics and practice. Ethical theory is the primary source of explanatory concepts. The main ethical theories employed in the field are shown in Table 20.3 in order to give a context for the relatively new approaches identified here as being most relevant to small firms and entrepreneurship.

In the range of ethical theories each focuses on a different aspect to assess Ethics. Dominant in the field and somewhat oppositional in approach are the seminal works of Kant and duty based ethics, and Jeremy Bentham's consequentialist perspective of utilitarianism. Other common approaches are Aristotle's virtue theory, which looks at the character of the individual, social contract theory, discourse ethics and postmodern ethics. These key ethical theories are summarized in Table 20.3. Although the application of theory is underdeveloped in the field as has been shown, where authors have drawn on particular ethical perspectives, these are indicated in column two. So for example, Clarke and Holt (2010) have used the Kantian notion of reflective judgment to identify judgment in an entrepreneurial context as constituting social performance, public challenge and personal autonomy. Laura Dunham (2010), in contrast, argues that we should look beyond the perspective of rationality to consider entrepreneurship from a virtue perspective, in particular that of practical wisdom, highlighting personal character, values, and purpose of the entrepreneur. Taking an alternative postmodern approach, Jones and Spicer (2005) employ the work of Jacques Lacan and Slavoj Žižek to critique entrepreneurship.

There are ongoing debates in the ethics field about the most suitable theoretical perspectives from which to draw, and these tend to vary according to the empirical context. Providing moral perspectives is especially relevant for the small business and entrepreneurship fields since without them, normative judgments about behaviour are being made in a moral vacuum with only a popular, at worst journalistic, interpretation of ethics. Other moral perspectives which have dominated the field of business ethics more generally (and by implication large firm, multinational ethics) are Kantian ethics with its focus on rule-following and universal treatment, utilitarianism which is most useful at the level of large-scale, public decision-making, and virtue ethics with a focus on individual character. The latter has some resonance for small firms where the character in question is that of the owner-manager or entrepreneur, but this disregards the relevance of the small firm context and composition. The two perspectives drawn upon have been noted in some previous work as being of potential value, as will be shown, but they are developed further here. They are moral proximity which draws from the work on moral intensity, and the ethic of care. These theoretical perspectives have a presence in the mainstream business ethics field, but have not to date gained as much traction as the ethical perspectives previously mentioned.

Moral Proximity and Intensity

The notion of moral intensity was introduced by Thomas Jones in 1991 in the context of an issue-contingent model of ethical decision-making, and thus is of interest and relevance in the small business context since this has been a consistent theme in small business ethics and social research. In Jones' (1991) framework, which can be used to evaluate different ethical situations, the characteristics of the moral issue itself infuse every stage of decision-making and are determinants of ethical decision-making and behaviour. Six factors of moral intensity are identified by Jones (1991: 377) as follows:

- Proximity, the feeling of social nearness to the beneficiaries/victims of an act
- Magnitude of consequences (see Stein and Ahmad (2009) for further development of this component of Jones' framework)
- Social consensus that an act is moral
- Probability of an act occurring and associated effect/harm
- Temporal immediacy of an act and the effects being felt
- Concentration of effect is an inverse function of the number of people impacted by an act of a certain magnitude.

It is the first of Jones' components that is of immediate relevance in the small business case, proximity, along with the 'concentration of effect' element. Distance, he argues, affects the manner in which human beings view moral issues in respect of physical, psychological, cultural and social parameters. Nevertheless since these components are intertwined, they will all have an influence on the responsible management of the small firm. Social consensus is likely to be influenced by the norms and mores within the particular sector – whereby, for example, small mechanical engineers 'just don't poach' each other's clients (Spence, 2000). Indeed, Courrent and Gundolf (2009: 749) find that 'communities of ethics' have an important influence in micro-enterprises. Temporal immediacy may result in interesting tensions emerging, such as the need to enable firm survival in the short term and the desire to secure a respected legacy among peers, community and family (especially successors) in the long term. The importance of proximity also extends beyond the internal relationships of the firm. Lähdesmäki and Suutari (2012) have shown how proximity to the local community embeds the firm in a system of reciprocity with its neighbours.

Courrent and Gundolf (2009: 750) aver that proximity plays a determining role in very small organizational structures and for their entrepreneurial leaders. In particular, with workers being in close proximity, decision-making affecting them is immediately apparent. While virtual organizations may not be characterized by physical proximity, the research presented in Tables 20.1 and 20.2 suggests that owner-managers feel close to their employees, using metaphors and descriptors of friendship and family. Courrent and Gundolf (2009: 758) have found social proximity to be a more important factor in determining owner-manager decision-making than geographical proximity. Hence it is not sitting near each other which is important, but having a common purpose and perspective that one might expect to develop in the small firm, hence in this respect virtual firms are not excluded from the social aspect of proximity.

Moral proximity provides a space-based analysis of the ethical and social orientation of small firms. The next moral lens, the ethic of care, gives an explanation for the behaviours and practices resulting from proximity by drawing on the family metaphor noted in Table 20.2.

Ethic of Care and Responsibility

The relational nature of small business and entrepreneurial activity points to the need for deeper consideration of an ethic of care perspective (Spence, Schmidpeter and Habisch, 2003; Fuller and Tian, 2006; Russo and Perrini, 2009). Unlike the other theoretical approaches outlined in Table 20.3, an ethic of care does not focus on principles, outcomes or process, but on relationships. Borgerson (2007) noted that feminist ethics is underestimated in the business ethics field; moreover, it is a transforming perspective on moral concepts and theories (Held, 1990: 321; Kittay and Meyers, 1987). While there was some evidence of the ethic of care emerging as a business ethics perspective in the 1990s (see for example Liedtka, 1996), its popularity as an approach seems not to have lived up to its potential, with few publications in the business ethics literature of note. One exception in relation to large firms is Bauman's (2011) work on business ethics in crisis situations. He contrasts virtue ethics, an ethics of justice and an ethic of care, concluding that an ethic of care is the most effective approach to managing corporate crises particularly in relation to attending to stakeholder concerns. However, the ethic of care has failed to find an embedded voice in the business ethics field. It is argued here that the ethic of care offers a highly valuable lens for understanding the nature of responsibility in small firms.

Held (1990) argues, as demonstrated in Table 20.3, that the field of ethics has been dominated by perspectives which idolize a rational approach, in contrast to feminist ethics. She suggests that "a feminist ethic of care is more promising than Kantian ethics or utilitarianism for recommending social decisions concerning limits on markets" (Held, 2002: 19). Held also notes the problematic reliance on abstract rules rather than "context respectful" approaches to moral theory (1990: 330), and is critical of the distinction between the public and the private, which suggests an expected and acceptable separation between personal and private life (1990: 334). Von Weltzien Høivik and Melé (2009) propose that the ethic of care may reflect the empirically observable evidence of ethics and social responsibility in small firms and entrepreneurship effectively. Using a globally embedded SME as a case study, they observe that the organization engages as a partner in some voluntary labour initiatives promoted by the government, employs people in marginal situations, and exerts influence for the adoption of good working conditions in its supply chain. The authors identify the ethic of care and concern for specific aspects of the common good as important perspectives for global corporate citizenship in the smaller firm. Table 20.4 expands on the elements of an ethic of care in more detail, with illustrations relating to smaller firms.

An ethic of care by its nature focuses not on competing rights, but on competing responsibilities (Simola, 2007). Some, such as Nunner-Winkler (1993), talk not only of the ethic of care, but of an ethic of care and *responsibility*. The ethic of care builds on the work of Carol Gilligan and her book *In a Different Voice* (1982). Working from research findings she showed that female subjects tended to view morality in terms of relational responsibilities. She suggested that women would *tend* to embrace relationships, although contemporary analysis goes far beyond such simplistic perspectives (*cf* Borgerson, 2007). Nevertheless the depiction of employees as 'like a family', or 'like friends' (see Table 20.2) is consistent with an ethic of care approach. Certainly some kind of social bond between, for example, owner-manager and employees beyond a financial, contractual relationship is consistently indicated (Ciulla, 2009).

The ethic of care focuses on the interconnectedness of people and its social dimension, the self's connection to others, and the responsibility of the self in caring for the 'other' (Liedtka, 1996: 180). The rise of stakeholder theory (where a stakeholder is anyone who can influence or is influenced by the organization) in the business ethics literature is fundamentally based on relationships and interdependence and hence relates to the ethic of care (Wicks, Gilbert and Freeman, 1994). As highly networked and embedded organizations, characterized by informality and the importance of relationships, small firms are highly suitable terrain for the application of the ethic of care.

CONCLUSION

This chapter has sought to expand on the concept that business is a social and moral terrain (Jackall, 1988: 3–6) from a small firm and entrepreneurship perspective. The research presented contributes to the literature in two ways. First, it brings together

Table 20.4   Features of the ethic of care and responsibility in the smaller firm

Feature	Reasoning	Small firm example
Meeting the needs of others for whom we take responsibility	Caring for a child at the forefront of moral concerns. Recognition that human beings are dependent on others, especially as children, and for the vulnerable and elderly. The claims of particular others can be compelling regardless of universal principles.	Caring for dependents and employees at the forefront of moral concerns. Recognition that others are human beings dependent on the business, e.g. customers, suppliers, community members. (Spence, Schmidpeter & Habisch, 2003)
Valuing emotions	Sympathy, empathy, sensitivity, and responsiveness are seen as the kinds of moral emotions that are valuable for implementing reason and to ascertain what morality recommends.	The organization is run sensitive to human needs, not just as an economic production unit. Work as both a social and economic context. (Ciulla, 2009)
Accepts impartiality	The compelling moral claim of the particular other may be valid even when it conflicts with the requirement usually made by moral theories that moral judgments are universal.	Those most important to the owner-manager are bound to have a greater moral claim and emotional relationships formed outside of the business. This is especially pertinent in the family firm and where family members are employed (Churchill & Hatten, 1997).
Inclusion of the private sphere as territory for morality	Focus of dominant theories has been on public life while overlooking the private domains of family and friendship, where women are often economically dependent and subject to a highly inequitable division of labour.	Cross-over and sometimes conflation of family and business life, with e.g. relatives employed for non-economic reasons (Chrisman, Chua, Pearson & Barnett, 2012). The role of women as important but exploited and under-acknowledged labour resource (Janjuha-Jivraj, 2004)
People are relational and interdependent	People start out as morally and epistemologically relational and interdependent. This contrasts to traditional conceptualizations of fully autonomous and rational individual agents.	Small numbers of employees reduce the need for layers and bureaucracy, but the owner-manager is both principal and agent of the firm and therefore is bound to the organization and its goals both personally and professionally. (Lähdesmäki, 2012)

Source: Derived and developed from Held (2006:10–13).

the small business, entrepreneurship, business ethics and CSR literatures more even-handedly than other reviews have previously done. This has the advantage of breaking down the parallel silos of research in this area and enabling learning across disciplines. Second, in a field which has been relatively light on theory, it offers an original contribution by using the review to identify two theoretical avenues for future size-sensitive, ethics and social responsibility studies. Moral proximity, drawn from moral intensity theory and the ethic of care each offer explanatory frameworks for understanding ethics and social responsibility in the smaller organization and the entrepreneurial context.

Possible implications for future research and policy agendas are given here. While Tables 20.1 and 20.2 show that some clear progress has been made in research on ethics and social responsibility in small firms and entrepreneurship, considerable gaps remain.

One important research gap relates to the continuation of the theorization process to which this chapter contributes. Going beyond the empirical description of social and ethical issues in small firms it is important to explain rather than just describe the phenomena observed. In doing so, inspiration must be sought from the disciplines from which the field draws, ensuring its continued relevance and integration with the wider research arena. Ultimately, small business and entrepreneurship research should seek to influence the wider ethics and social responsibility fields, developing new theory where appropriate, and contribute new perspectives which may have wider resonance.

There remain some under-researched empirical perspectives including further exploration of the links to subjects alluded to at the beginning of this chapter, particularly environmental issues and social enterprise. Table 20.1 shows that the vast majority of empirical research has been in developed countries and particularly Europe, although this is gradually changing with more recent contributions from developing countries starting to open up the field. Given the imperative to enable social and economic development in developing countries, considerably more research in these contexts is still required. In particular, research which engages with the vagaries of the informal economy, where adherence to the law cannot be considered to be one of the most fundamental ethical obligations (see Carroll, 1999) offers an array of challenges to fundamental assumptions about what is ethical (see Spence and Painter-Morland, 2010).

A further related context to the small firm and entrepreneurial practice which has been mentioned in this chapter is the family firm. This is clearly a field of study in its own right, but where small firms are also family businesses (as is commonly the case) they are subject to issues relating to intensity and familial relationships which may indeed further the ethic of care and moral proximity lens developed here, but which are as yet under-researched. In similar ways the fledgling empirical work on ethnic minority firms and women-owned businesses in relation to ethics and responsibility warrant further study.

In addition to implications for research, this chapter leads to some clear policy and practice consequences. First, the evidence presented here may have wider relevance for organizational units other than the small firm. Large firm downsizing and decentralization result in emulation of a small firm context (Tsai, 2010). Smaller sub-units of a firm could potentially take on some of the characteristics of small organizations (Quinn, 1997), especially if the unit has a degree of autonomy from a parent organization. A future area of research is to investigate to what extent there is also evidence of an ethic of care in larger organizations. Furthermore, it is unclear where the tipping point is more generally for small firms to take on 'large firm' approaches, so further investigation of medium-sized organizations and study of the antecedents of a tipping point – from small firm characteristics to large firm ones – identified. Preuss and Perschke (2010), for example, find that medium-sized firms are already exhibiting primarily corporate social responsibility characteristics of large firms. At the other end of the size spectrum, the important fact that very many firms have *no employees* has been disregarded by this and every other paper on business ethics. This also needs addressing with some urgency.

Since policy-makers wish to promote ethical practice and social responsibility, they should take heed of the need to understand the ethical character of the small firm and avoid one-dimensional programmes relating social responsibility to profit-maximization. At the European level for example, small business has been recognized as the dominant business form and accordingly as highly relevant in the moves to promote Europe as leading in (Corporate) Social Responsibility initiatives (Commission of the European Communities, 2011). As this chapter shows, the ethical and social landscape for small firms and entrepreneurship is a complex and nuanced one which will require sensitive and informed policy-making initiatives to affect change.

Research on ethics and social responsibility in small- and medium-sized enterprises and in entrepreneurship is coming of age. Considerable research is still however needed to ensure that it comes to maturity, making a full contribution to business practice and policy as well as the constituent research fields from which it draws. Ultimately, small business and entrepreneurship are social and economic constructs and we must better understand the complex role they have in both respects.

NOTES

1. It is not the intention in this chapter to rehearse the definitional issues around the key concepts. Other publications have achieved this admirably, see for example on small business (Curran and Blackburn, 1994), corporate social responsibility (Carroll, 1999; Lockett, Moon & Visser, 2006), entrepreneurship (Veciana, 2007), and business ethics (Lewis, 1985).
2. Previous attempts to summarize the literature in this area have been completed by Thompson and Smith (1991), Spence (1999), Hannafey (2003), Lepoutre and Heene (2006), Spence (2007), Spence and Painter-Morland (2010), Kechiche and Soparnot (2012), Vázquez-Carrasco and López-Pérez (2012).

REFERENCES

Acs, Z. and R. Phillips (2002), 'Entrepreneurship and philanthropy in American capitalism', *Small Business Economics*, **19**(3), 189–204.
Ahmad, N. and P.-S.Seet (2010), 'Gender variations in ethical and socially responsible considerations among SME entrepreneurs in Malaysia', *International Journal of Business & Society*, **11**(1), 61–70.
Ahmad, N. and T. Ramayah (2012), 'Does the notion of 'doing well by doing good' prevail among entrepreneurial ventures in a developing nation?' *Journal of Business Ethics*, **106**(4), 479–90.
Amato, L. and C. Amato (2007), 'The effects of firm size and industry on corporate giving', *Journal of Business Ethics*, **72**(3), 229–41.
Anderson, A. and R. Smith (2007), 'The moral space in entrepreneurship: An exploration of ethical imperatives and the moral legitimacy of being enterprising', *Entrepreneurship and Regional Development*, **19**(6), 479–97.
Anokhin, S. and W. Schulze (2009), 'Entrepreneurship, innovation, and corruption', *Journal of Business Venturing*, **24**(5), 465–76.
Baden, D. and I. Harwood (2013), 'Terminology matters: A critical exploration of corporate social responsibility terms', *Journal of Business Ethics*, **116**, 615–627.
Baden, D., I. Harwood and D. Woodward (2011), 'The effects of procurement policies on 'downstream' corporate social responsibility activity: Content-analytic insights into the views and actions of SME owner-managers', *International Small Business Journal*, **29**(3), 259–77.
Bauman, D. (2011), 'Evaluating ethical approaches to crisis leadership: insights from unintentional harm research,' *Journal of Business Ethics*, **98**, 281–95.
Bauman, Z. (1993), *Postmodern Ethics*, Oxford: Blackwell Publishing.

Baumol, W. (1990), 'Entrepreneurship: productive, unproductive, and destructive', *Journal of Political Economy*, **98**(5), 893–921.

Besser, T. (2012), 'The consequences of social responsibility for small business owners in small towns,' *Business Ethics: A European Review*, **21**(2), 129–39.

Besser, T. and N. Miller. (2004), 'The risks of enlightened self-interest: Small businesses and support for community,' *Business & Society*, **43**(4), 398–425.

Besser, T., N. Miller and R. Perkins (2006), 'For the greater good: Business networks and business social responsibility to communities,' *Entrepreneurship & Regional Development*, **18**(4), 321–39.

Biondi, V., F. Iraldo, and S. Meredith (2002), 'Achieving sustainability through environmental innovation: The role of SMEs', *International Journal of Technology Management*, **24**(5/6), 612–26.

Blackburn, M. and P. McGhee (2007), 'The excellent entrepreneur: Old virtues for new ventures? *Australian Journal of Professional and Applied Ethics*, **9**(2), 46–55.

Blombäck, A. and C. Wigren (2009), 'Challenging the importance of size as determinant for CSR activities', *Management of Environmental Quality: An International Journal*, **20**(3), 255–70.

Blundel, R., L.J. Spence, and S. Zerbinati, (2010) 'Entrepreneurial social responsibility: Scoping the territory', in: L.J. Spence, and M. Painter-Morland, (eds) *Ethics in Small and Medium Sized Enterprises: A global commentary*, International Society For Business, Economics and Ethics Book Series, Volume 2, Dordrecht, NL: Springer, pp. 123–45.

Borga, F. (2009) 'Sustainability report in small enterprises: Case studies in Italian furniture companies', *Business Strategy and the Environment*, **18**(3), 162–76.

Borgerson, J. (2007), 'On the harmony of feminist ethics and business ethics', *Business and Society Review*, **112**(4), 477–509.

Brammer, S. and A. Millington (2004), 'Stakeholder pressure, organizational size and the allocation of departmental responsibility for the management of corporate charitable giving', *Business & Society*, **43**(3), 268–95.

Brenkert, G. (2009), 'Innovation, rule breaking and the ethics of entrepreneurship', *Journal of Business Venturing*, **24**(5), 448–64.

Bryant, P. (2009), 'Self-regulation and moral awareness among entrepreneurs', *Journal of Business Venturing*, **24**(5), 505–18.

Bucar, B. and R. Hisrich (2001), 'Ethics of business managers vs. entrepreneurs', *Journal of Developmental Entrepreneurship*, **6**(1), 59–82.

Bucar, B., M. Glas, and R. Hisrich (2003), 'Ethics and entrepreneurs: An international comparative study', *Journal of Business Venturing*, **18**(2), 261–81.

Buchholz, R. and S. Rosenthal (2005), 'The spirit of entrepreneurship and the qualities of moral decision making: Toward a unifying framework', *Journal of Business Ethics* **60**, 307–15.

Campin, S., J. Barraket, and B. Luke, (2013), 'Micro-business community responsibility in Australia: Approaches, motivations and barriers', *Journal of Business Ethics*, **115**: 489–513.

Carroll, A. (1999), 'Corporate social responsibility: Evolution of a definitional construct', *Business and Society*, **38**(3), 268–95.

Castka, P., M. Balzarova, and C. Bamber, (2004), 'How can SMEs effectively implement the CSR agenda? A UK case perspective', *CSR and Environmental Management*, **11**(3), 140–9.

Chrisman, J., J. Chua, A. Pearson and T. Barnett, (2012), 'Family involvement, family influence, and family-centered non-economic goals in small firms', *Entrepreneurship: Theory and Practice*, **36**(2), 267–93.

Christopher, D. (2003), 'Small business pilfering: the "trusted" employee(s)', *Business Ethics: A European Review*, **12**, 284–97.

Churchill, N. and K. Hatten (1997), 'Non-market-based transfers of wealth and power: A research framework for family business', *Family Business Review*, **10**(1), 53–67.

Ciliberti, F., D. Baden and I. Harwood (2009), 'Insights into supply chain pressure on CSR-practice: A multiple-case study of SMEs in the UK', *Operations and Supply Chain Management*, **2**(3), 154–66.

Ciulla, J. (2009) 'Leadership and the ethics of care' *Journal of Business Ethics*, **88**, 3–4.

Clarke, J. and R. Holt (2010), 'Reflective judgement: Understanding entrepreneurship as ethical practice', *Journal of Business Ethics*, **94**(3), 317–31.

Commission of the European Communities (2011) Communication from the Commission to the European Parliament, the Council, the European Economic and Social Committee of the Regions. *A renewed EU strategy 2011–14 for Corporate Social Responsibility*: Brussels, 25.10.2011 COM(2011) 681 final.

Courrent, J.-M. and K. Gundolf (2009), 'Proximity and micro-enterprise manager's ethics: a French empirical study of responsible business attitude', *Journal of Business Ethics*, **88**(4), 749–62.

Curran, J. and R. Blackburn (1994) *Small Firms and Local Economic Networks: the death of the local economy?* London, U.K.: Paul Chapman.

D'Aprile, G. and T. Mannarini (2012), 'Corporate social responsibility: A psychosocial multidimensional construct', *Journal of Global Responsibility*, **3**(1), 48–65.

Davies, I. and A. Crane (2010), 'CSR in SMEs: Investigating employee engagement in fair trade companies', *Business Ethics: A European Review*, **19**(2), 126–39.
De Clercq, D. and M. Dakhli (2009), 'Personal strain and ethical standards of the self-employed', *Journal of Business Venturing*, **24**(5), 477–90.
Dees, G. and J. Starr (1992), 'Entrepreneurship through an ethical lens: Dilemmas and issues for research and practice', in D.L. Sexton and J.D. Karsada (eds), *The State of the Art of Entrepreneurship*, Boston, MA, USA: PWS Kent Publishing Co, pp. 89–116.
Del Baldo, M. (2012), 'Corporate social responsibility and corporate governance in Italian SMEs: the experience of some "spirited businesses"', *Journal of Management and Governance*, **16**(1), 1–36.
Demuijnck, G. and H. Ngnodjom (2013), 'Responsibility and informal CSR in formal Cameroonian SMEs', *Journal of Business Ethics*, **112**: 653–665.
Dunham, L. (2010), 'From rational to wise action: Recasting our theories of entrepreneurship', *Journal of Business Ethics*, **92**(4), 513–30.
Eakin, J. and E. MacEachen (1998), 'Health and the social relations of work: a study of the health-related experiences of employees in small workplaces', *Sociology of Health and Illness*, **20**(6), 896–914.
Ede, F., B. Panigrahi, J. Stuart, and S. Calcich (2000), 'Ethics in small minority business', *Journal of Business Ethics*, **26**, 133–46.
Fassin, Y. (2008), 'SMEs and the fallacy of formalising CSR', *Business Ethics: A European Review*, **17**(4), 364–78.
Fassin, Y., A.Van Rossem and M. Buelens (2011), 'Small-business owner-managers' perceptions of business ethics and CSR-related concepts', *Journal of Business Ethics*, **98**(3), 425–53.
Fenwick, T. (2010), 'Learning to practice social responsibility in small business: challenges and conflicts', *Journal of Global Responsibility*, **1**(1), 149–69.
Fisher, K., J. Geenen, M. Jurcevic, K. McClintock and G. Davis (2009), 'Applying asset-based community development as a strategy for CSR: A Canadian perspective on a win–win for stakeholders and SMEs', *Business Ethics, A European Review* **18**(1), 66–82.
Fraj-Andrés, E., M. López-Pérez, I. Melero-Polo and R. Vázquez-Carrasco (2012), 'Company image and corporate social responsibility: reflecting with SMEs' managers', *Marketing Intelligence & Planning*, **30**(2), 266–80.
Fuller, T. and Y. Tian (2006), 'Social and symbolic capital and responsible entrepreneurship: An empirical investigation of SME narratives', *Journal of Business Ethics*, **67**(3), 287–304.
Gallo, P. and L. Jones Christensen (2011), 'Firm size matters: An empirical investigation of organizational size and ownership on sustainability-related behaviors', *Business & Society*, **50**, 315–49.
Gilligan, C. (1982) *In a Different Voice*. Massachusetts, USA: Harvard University Press.
Godwyn, M. (2009), 'Hugh Connerty and Hooters: What is successful entrepreneurship?' in E. Raufflet and A Mills (eds) *The Dark Side: Critical cases on the downside of business*. Sheffield, UK: Greenleaf publishing, pp. 36–51.
Goss, D. (1990) *Small Business and Society* London, UK: Thomson Learning.
Graafland, J., B. van de Ven and N. Stoffele (2003), 'Strategies and instruments for organising CSR by small and large businesses in the Netherlands', *Journal of Business Ethics*, **47**(1), 45–60
Graafland, J., C. Mazereeuw and A. Yahia (2006), 'Islam and socially responsible business conduct: An empirical study of Dutch entrepreneurs', *Business Ethics: A European Review*, **15**, 390–406.
Granerud, L. (2011), 'Social responsibility as an intermediary for health and safety in small firms', *International Journal of Workplace Health Management*, **4**(2), 109–22.
Gupta, S. and N. Kalra (2012), 'Impact of corporate social responsibility on SMEs in India' *Asia-Pacific Journal of Management Research and Innovation*, **8**(2), 133–43.
Habermas, J. (1983) *Moral Consciousness and Communicative Action*, Cambridge, USA: Massachusetts Institute of Technology.
Hamann, R., T. Abbazue, P. Kapelus and A. Hein (2005), 'Universalizing corporate social responsibility? South African challenges to the international organization for standardization's new social responsibility standard', *Business and Society Review*, **110**, 1–19.
Hammann, E.. A. Habisch, and H. Pechlaner (2009), 'Values that create value: socially responsible business practices in SMEs – empirical evidence from German companies', *Business Ethics: A European Review* **18**(1), 37–51.
Hannafey, F. (2003), 'Entrepreneurship and ethics: A literature review', *Journal of Business Ethics*, **46**, 99–110.
Harvey C., M. Maclean, J. Gordon and E. Shaw (2011), 'Andrew Carnegie and the foundations of contemporary entrepreneurial philanthropy', *Business History*, **53**(3), 425–50.
Hazlina, A. N. and P.-S. Shen (2010), 'Gender variations in ethical and socially responsible considerations among SME entrepreneurs in Malaysia', *International Journal of Business & Society*, **11**(1), 77–88.
Held, V. (1990), 'Feminist transformations of moral theory', *Philosophy and Phenomenological Research*, **50**, 321–344.

Held, V. (2002), 'Care and the extension of markets', *Hypatia*, **17**(2), 19–33.

Held, V. (2006), *The Ethics of Care: Personal, Political, and Global*, Oxford: Oxford University Press.

Hornsby, J.S., D.F. Kuratko, D.W. Naffiziger, W.R. LaFollette and R.M. Hodgetts (1994), 'The ethical perceptions of small business owners: A factor analytic study', *Journal of Small Business Management*, **32**(4), 9–16.

Jackall, R. (1988) *Moral Mazes: The World of Corporate Managers*, New York USA and Oxford, UK: Oxford University Press.

Jamali, D., M. Zanhour and T. Keshishian (2009), 'Peculiar strengths and relational attributes of SMEs in the context of CSR', *Journal of Business Ethics*, **87**(3), 355–77.

Janjuha-Jivraj, S. (2004), 'The impact of the mother during family business succession: Examples from the Asian business community', *Journal of Ethnic and Migration Studies*, **30**(4), 78–97.

Jenkins, H. (2004), 'A critique of conventional CSR theory: An SME perspective', *Journal of General Management*, **29**(4), 55–75.

Jones, C. and A. Spicer (2005), 'The sublime object of entrepreneurship', *Organization*, **12**(2), 223–46.

Jones, M., S. Marshall, and R. Mitchell (2007), 'CSR and the management of labour in two Australian mining industry companies', *Corporate Governance*, **15**(1), 57–67.

Jones, T. (1991), 'Ethical decision-making by individuals in organizations: An issue-contingent model', *Academy of Business Review*, **16**(2), 366–395.

Kechiche, A. and R. Soparnot (2012), 'CSR within SMEs: Literature Review', *International Business Research*, **5**(7), 97–104.

Kitching, J. (1994), 'Employer's work-force construction policies in the small service sector enterprise', in D. Storey, and J. Atkinson, (eds) *Employment, the Small Firm, and the Labour Market*, London, UK: Routledge, pp. 103–46.

Kittay, E. and D. Meyers (1987), *Women and Moral Theory*, New Jersey, USA: Rowmand and Littlefield.

Koos, S. (2012), 'The institutional embeddedness of social responsibility: A multilevel analysis of smaller firms' civic engagement in Western Europe', *Socio-Economic Review*, **10**(1), 135–62.

Lähdesmäki, M. (2012), 'Construction of owner–manager identity in corporate social responsibility discourse', *Business Ethics: A European Review*, **21**(2), 168–82.

Lähdesmäki, M., and T. Suutari (2012), 'Keeping at arm's length or searching for social proximity? Corporate social responsibility as a reciprocal process between small businesses and the local community', *Journal of Business Ethics*, **108**(4), 481–93.

Lähdesmäki, M. and T. Takala (2012), 'Altruism in business – An empirical study of philanthropy in the small business context', *Social Responsibility Journal*, **8**(3), 373–88.

Lee, M., A. Mak and A. Pang (2012), 'Bridging the gap: An exploratory study of corporate social responsibility among SMEs in Singapore', *Journal of Public Relations Research*, **24**(4), 299–317.

Lepoutre, J. and A. Heene (2006), 'Investigating the impact of firm size on small business social responsibility: A critical review', *Journal of Business Ethics*, **67**(3), 257–73.

Levinas, E. (1961) *Totality and Infinity: An Essay on Exteriority*, Pittsburgh, PA, USA: Duquesne University Press.

Lewis, P. (1985), 'Defining 'business ethics': Like nailing jello to a wall', *Journal of Business Ethics*, **4**(5), 377–83.

Liedtka, J. (1996), 'Feminist morality and competitive reality: A role for an ethic of care?' *Business Ethics Quarterly*, **6**(2), 179–200.

Litz, R. and S. Samu (2008), 'Altruistic by association, altruistic for advantage? Buying groups and small firm community involvement', *Nonprofit and Voluntary Sector Quarterly*, **37**, 646–67.

Liu, H., and M. Fong (2010), 'The corporate social responsibility orientation of Chinese small and medium enterprises', *Journal of Business Systems, Governance and Ethics*, **5**(3), 33–70.

Lockett, A., J. Moon, and W. Visser (2006), 'Corporate social responsibility in management research: Focus, nature, salience and sources of influence', *Journal of Management Studies*, **43**(1), 115–36.

Longenecker, J., J. McKinney and C. Moore (1988), 'Egoism and independence: Entrepreneurial ethics', *Organizational Dynamics*, **16**(3), 64–72.

Longo, M., M. Mura and A. Bonoli (2005), 'Corporate social responsibility and corporate performance: The case of Italian SMEs', *Corporate Governance*, **5**(4), 28–42.

Luetkenhorst, W. (2004), 'Corporate social responsibility and the development agenda – A case for actively involving small and medium enterprises', *Intereconomics*, **39**(3), 157–66.

Luken, R, and R. Stares (2005), 'Small business responsibility in developing countries: A threat or an opportunity?' *Business Strategy & the Environment*, **14**(1), 38–53.

Lund-Thomsen, P. and R. Pillay (2012), 'CSR in industrial clusters: An overview of the literature', *Corporate Governance*, **12**(4), 568–78.

Lyotard, J-F., (1979) *The Postmodern Condition: A Report on Knowledge*. Minneapolis, USA: University of Minnesota Press.

MacIntyre, A. (1981) *After Virtue: A Study in Moral Theory*, Notre Dame, Indiana, USA: University of Notre Dame Press.

Massey, C. (2003), 'Employee practices in New Zealand SMEs', *Employee Relations*, **26**(1), 94–105.

McVea, J. (2009), 'A field study of entrepreneurial decision-making and moral imagination', *Journal of Business Venturing*, **24**(5), 491–504.

Murillo, D. and J. Lozano (2006), 'CSR and SMEs: An approach to CSR in their own words', *Journal of Business Ethics*, **67**(3), 227–40.

Murillo, D. and J. Lozano (2009), 'Pushing forward SME CSR through a network: An account from the Catalan model', *Business Ethics: A European Review*, **18**(1), 7–20.

Muthuri, J., J. Moon and U. Idemudia (2012), 'Corporate innovation and sustainable community development in developing countries', *Business & Society*, **51**(3), 355–81.

Nejati, M. and A. Amran (2012), 'Does ownership type cause any difference in the perception of Malaysian SME owners/managers towards corporate social responsibility?' *International Journal of Business Governance and Ethics*, **7**(1), 63–81.

Nielsen, A. and C. Thomsen (2009), 'Investigating CSR communication in SMEs: A case study among Danish middle managers', *Business Ethics: A European Review*, **18**(1), 83–93.

Nunner-Winkler, G. (1993), 'Two moralities? A critical discussion of an ethics of care and responsibility versus an ethic of rights and justice', in *An Ethic of Care: Feminist and interdisciplinary perspectives*, New York, USA: Routledge, p.143–56.

Payne, D. and B. Joyner (2006) 'Successful U.S. entrepreneurs: Identifying ethical decision-making and social responsibility behaviors', *Journal of Business Ethics*, **65**, 203–17.

Preuss, L. and M.J. Perschke (2010) 'Slipstreaming the larger boats: Social responsibility in medium sized businesses', *Journal of Business Ethics*, **92**(4), 531–51.

Quinn, J.J. (1997), 'Personal ethics and business ethics: The ethical attitudes of owner/managers of small business', *Journal of Business Ethics*, **16**(2), 119–27.

Rahim, M. and P. Wisuttisak (2013), 'Corporate social responsibility–oriented compliances and SMEs access to global market: Evidence from Bangladesh, *Journal of Asia-Pacific Business*, **14**(1), 58–83.

Rand, A. (1964), *The Virtue of Selfishness: A New Concept of Egoism*, New York: New American Library.

Rawlings, G. (2012), 'Intangible nodes and networks of influence: The ethics of tax compliance in Australian small and medium-sized enterprises', *International Small Business Journal*, **30**(1), 84–95.

Rawls, J. (1971), *A Theory of Justice*, Cambridge, Massachusetts: Harvard University Press.

Russo, A. and F. Perrini, (2009), 'Investigating stakeholder theory and social capital: CSR in large firms and SMEs', *Journal of Business Ethics*, **91**(2), 207–21.

Rutherford, M., P. Buller, and J. Stebbins (2009), 'Ethical considerations of the legitimacy lie', *Entrepreneurship: Theory and Practice*, **33**(4), 949–64.

Sarbutts, N. (2003), 'Can SMEs 'do' CSR? A practitioner's view of the ways small- and medium-sized enterprises are able to manage reputation through corporate social responsibility', *Journal of Communication Management*, **7**(4), 340–7.

Schaper, M and L. Savery (2004), 'Entrepreneurship and philanthropy: The case of small Australian firms', *Journal of Developmental Entrepreneurship*, **9**(3), 239–50.

Schlierer, H., A. Werner, S. Signori, E. Garriga, H. von Weltzien Hoivik, A. Van Rossem and Y. Fassin (2012), 'How do European SME owner-managers make sense of 'Stakeholder Management'?: Insights from a Cross-National Study. *Journal of Business Ethics*, **109**(1), 39–51.

Shane, S. and S. Venkataraman, (2000), 'The promise of entrepreneurship as a field of research', *Academy of Management Review*, **25**, 217–26.

Simola, S. (2007), 'The pragmatics of care in sustainable global enterprise', *Journal of Business Ethics*, **74**, 131–47.

Spence, L.J. (1999), 'Does size matter?: The state of the art in small business ethics', *Business Ethics: A European Review*, **8**(3), 163–74.

Spence, L.J. (2000), *Practices, Priorities and Ethics in Small Firms*. London, UK: Institute of Business Ethics.

Spence, L.J. (2004), 'Small firm accountability and integrity', in G. Brenkert, *Corporate Integrity and Accountability*, (ed), London, UK: Sage, pp.115–28.

Spence, L.J. (2007), 'CSR and small business in a European policy context: The five 'C's of CSR and small business research agenda 2007', *Business and Society Review*, **112**(4), 533–52.

Spence, L.J., and J.F. Lozano (2000), 'Communicating about ethics with small firms: Experiences from the UK and Spain', *Journal of Business Ethics*, **27**(1–2), 43–53.

Spence, L.J. and M. Painter-Morland (eds) (2010), *Ethics in Small and Medium Sized Enterprises: A Global Commentary*, International Society For Business, Economics and Ethics Book Series, Volume 2, Dordrecht, NL: Springer.

Spence, L.J. and R. Rutherfoord, (2001), 'Social responsibility, profit maximisation and the small firm owner-manager', *Small Business and Enterprise Development*, Summer **8**(2), 126–39.

Spence, L.J., Schmidpeter, R. and Habisch, A. (2003), 'Assessing social capital: Small and medium sized enterprises in Germany and the UK', *Journal of Business Ethics* **47**(1), 17–29.

Stein, E. and N. Ahmad (2009) 'Using the Analytical Hierarchy Process (AHP) to construct a measure of the magnitude of consequences component of moral intensity', *Journal of Business Ethics*, **89**, 391–407.

Sweeney, L. (2007), 'Corporate social responsibility in Ireland: barriers and opportunities experienced by SMEs when undertaking CSR', *Corporate Governance*, **7**(4), 516–23.

Tantalo, C., M. Caroli and J. Vanevenhoven (2012), 'Corporate social responsibility and SME's competitiveness', *International Journal of Technology Management*, **58**(1), 129–51.

Thompson, J. and J. Hood (1993), 'The practice of corporate social performance in minority-versus nonminority-owned small businesses', *Journal of Business Ethics*, **12**, 197–206.

Thompson, J. and H. Smith (1991), 'Social responsibility and small business: Suggestions for research', *Journal of Small Business Management*, **29**(1), 30–44.

Torugsa, N., W. O'Donohue and R. Hecker (2012), 'Capabilities, proactive CSR and financial performance in SMEs: Empirical evidence from an Australian manufacturing industry sector', *Journal of Business Ethics*, **109**(4), 483–500.

Tsai, C.-J. (2010), 'HRM in SMEs: Homogeneity or heterogeneity? A study of Taiwanese high-tech firms', *International Journal of Human Resource Management*, **21**(10), 1689–711.

Udayasankar, K. (2008), 'CSR and firm size', *Journal of Business Ethics*, **83**(2), 167–75.

Uygur, S. (2009), 'The Islamic work ethic and the emergence of Turkish SME owner-managers', *Journal of Business Ethics*, **88**(1), 211–25.

Vázquez-Carrasco, R. and M. López-Pérez (2012), 'Small & medium-sized enterprises and corporate social responsibility: A systematic review of the literature', *Quality & Quantity*, 1–14.

Veciana, J-M. (2007), 'Entrepreneurship as a scientific research programme' in Á.G. Cuervo, D. Ribeiro and S. Roig (eds) *Entrepreneurship: Concepts, Theory and Perspective*, Heidelberg/Berlin, Germany and New York, USA: Springer-Verlag, pp. 23–72.

Vives, A. (2006), 'Social and environmental responsibility in small and medium enterprises in Latin America', *Journal of Corporate Citizenship*, **21**, 39–50.

Von Weltzien Høivik, H. and D. Melè, (2009), 'Can an SME become a global corporate citizen? Evidence from a case study', *Journal of Business Ethics*, **88**, 551–63.

Von Weltzien Høivik, H. and D. Shankar, (2011), 'How can SMEs in a cluster respond to global demands for Corporate Responsibility', *Journal of Business Ethics*, **101**(2/III), 175–95.

Webb, J., L. Tihanyi, R. Ireland and D. Sirmon (2009), '"You say illegal, I say legitimate": Entrepreneurship in the informal economy', *Academy of Management Review*, **34**, 492–510.

Werner, A. (2008), 'The influence of Christian identity on SME owner–managers' conceptualisations of business practice', *Journal of Business Ethics*, **82**(2), 449–62.

Wicks, A., D, Gilbert Jr, and R.E. Freeman, (1994), 'A feminist reinterpretation of the stakeholder concept', *Business Ethics Quarterly*, **4**(4), 475–97.

Worthington, I., M. Ram, and T. Jones (2006), Exploring corporate social responsibility in the UK Asian small business community, *Journal of Business Ethics*, **67**(2), 201–17.

21. Social entrepreneurship: looking back, moving ahead

Anne de Bruin, Eleanor Shaw and Dominic Chalmers

INTRODUCTION

While scholarly enquiries of social entrepreneurship (SE) and social innovation may be in their infancy, the practice of individuals, partnerships and community groups working together in innovative ways to identify and implement creative solutions to long-standing, complex social problems is not new. Growing research efforts to investigate the use of entrepreneurial activities for the pursuit of social gains is matched by increasing media and government interests in the capacity and potential for social entrepreneurs to identify innovative solutions, which address enduring social problems. A key driver of current government enthusiasm for social entrepreneurs, SE and social innovation are the increasingly liberal, arms-length ideologies underpinning recent policy platforms such as the *Big Society* in the UK and policy initiatives including Obama's *Social Innovation Fund*, which is designed to find and help 'scale' the best social innovations in the US. Combined with the imperative to address considerable holes in public finances, political leaders the world over are keen to understand the potential for social entrepreneurs and social innovation to help the global economy recover from the fall-out of the worst financial crisis experienced since the Great Depression.

This chapter critically considers growing research interest in activities and engagement in the entrepreneurial process for social and public rather than individual financial gains. Its overall contribution is the provision of a rigorous overview not only of the phenomenon of SE but also of the closely aligned topic of social innovation. It addresses an issue of growing importance in the field of entrepreneurship and social development, which is the accelerating movement away from 'state' responsibility to provide solutions to social problems. As such an important contribution is that the chapter serves to highlight that the process and enactment of SE and social innovation are inherently socio-political acts. Hence, following this introduction, the chapter opens by examining the evolution of the SE concept paying attention to historical background and evolving economic, social and political conditions and then considers SE within its contemporary settings. It is only after providing this essential contextual understanding, that identification and review of key themes in the research literature including definitions of SE and social enterprises takes place in the next section. Subsequently, sub-processes of SE: social opportunity and resources considerations are examined. A discussion of social innovation follows. The challenge of finding appropriate indicators of performance and impact of SE is then delineated. The chapter concludes by outlining a research agenda and recommending appropriate research methods to advance the field.

THE EVOLUTION OF SOCIAL ENTREPRENEURSHIP

Understanding the overarching context of SE cannot be divorced from historical and political economy considerations. As Roper and Cheney (2005: 95) emphasize, 'questions of who should and who can take responsibility for the needs of civil society' are crucial in any discussion of SE. Evolving political ideologies and contemporary socio-political perspectives on the nature and role of the welfare state therefore are important drivers which have encouraged both the rise of SE and growing media and research interests in social entrepreneurs, the process of social entrepreneurship and innovation for social purposes.

Importantly, while these growing interests might suggest that SE is a new phenomenon, economic, social and business history reveals that the existence of social and community enterprises is deeply rooted in many economies (Harvey et al., 2011). For example, in the UK, SE was the bedrock of Victorian private hospitals and is clearly evident in the contemporary hospice movement which employs innovative approaches to fundraising and financial management principles more commonly evident in the for-profit sector. Historically, SE has its origins in the nineteenth and twentieth centuries when philanthropic business owners and industrialists including Robert Owen, Andrew Carnegie (Harvey et al., 2011; Nasaw, 2006) and J.D. Rockefeller (Chernow, 1998) demonstrated concern for the welfare of employees by improving their working, education and cultural lives (Owen), promoting the belief that the wealthy had an obligation to give back to society by redistributing their money to good causes (Carnegie) and investing money in life-saving medical and scientific research (Rockefeller).

Set against this historical background it is useful to consider those social-economic and political conditions which, since World War Two, have combined to encourage the emergence of contemporary SE and the growing capacity of entrepreneurship for social, community and environmental purposes to become a dominant theme shaping the global economy in the twenty-first century. For developed, capitalist economies, the period post-World War Two through to the early 1970s was one of sustained prosperity and low unemployment. As government policy within these economies embraced Keynesian economics as the dominant economic paradigm, responsibility for providing social, educational, housing and health services lay firmly with the state which also, during this time had widespread ownership and responsibility for economic resources including, for example, transport, schools and defence. Throughout the 1970s a mix of unfavourable global conditions including oil price hikes following the 1973 'Oil Crisis', rising inflation and growing unemployment combined with emerging social trends such as single parent families witnessed the start of the erosion of the foundations of the welfare state. This continued into the 1980s as governments rejected Keynesian economics in favour of neo-liberal ideologies which, with respect to the welfare state, involved its radical restructuring as deregulation, privatization and reconfiguration of public services ensured the large-scale shift in ownership and control of resources from the state to private individuals and organizations.

Since the 1980s, increasingly liberal government policies have generated mixed results for the global economy. On the one hand, it has been argued that the socio-economic environment experienced globally throughout the end of the twentieth and the start of the twenty-first centuries created unique opportunities for individuals, typically entrepreneurs to amass significant personal wealth (Giddens, 2001; Handy, 2006). For example, the 2006 Forbes Billionaires List recorded 793 billionaires based in 49 countries, with an average net worth of US$3.3 billion, collectively totalling US$2.6 trillion. In tandem to the rising wealth of a tiny number of individuals, it is argued that those neo-liberalist ideologies which have dominated the socio-economic policies of most developed countries for the last 30–40 years, have significantly widened the gap between the world's richest and poorest (Harvey, 2010; Krugman, 2009). Specifically, these commentators argue that neo-liberal ideologies have created an unequal distribution of global income and wealth.

Set against this complex milieu of increasingly liberal government policies, shrinking welfare states, decentralization and reconfiguration of public services, divestment of enterprises and assets by central and local governments in developed economies and severe global problems like widespread poverty and increasing wealth inequalities; non-profit organizations, social entrepreneurs, social enterprises and SE have first intervened and more recently increased their efforts to plug gaps in social and welfare provision and mitigate global problems. Indeed, the opening decades of the twenty-first century have become known, at least socially and economically, for the unabated expansion of the third sector with names such as Nobel Prize winner Muhammad Yunus being cited as a leading example of a social entrepreneur motivated to mitigate pressing social problems in innovative ways and instigate far-reaching social change.

Heterogeneous geo-political and socio-cultural contexts underpin the development of the SE phenomenon. Thus in regions such as East Asia and Latin America and emerging dynamic market economies such as China and India, while there is a growing awareness of the notions of social entrepreneur and social enterprise, the underlying drivers of SE differ significantly from that of the developed market economies (Defourny and Kim, 2011; FYSE, 2012). In East Asia, a Confucian welfare state based on private welfare protection (Jones, 1993) and a hierarchical social structure resulted in a minimal role for civil society. The contemporary context of SE however, is a changing state of affairs and one of increasing awareness of the potential of SE to provide solutions to social problems and needs. Even in economies with more authoritarian political regimes like China, there is a growing realization that SE and social enterprises can have an important role to play in improving social cohesion and wellbeing (FYSE, 2012). In the next section therefore, we examine the current situation.

THE CONTEMPORARY CONTEXT OF SOCIAL ENTREPRENEURSHIP

Most recent interest and growth in SE has been encouraged by the wide-ranging effects of the hardest hitting economic crisis since the 1930s. It is widely accepted that the impact of the current global recession respects the boundaries of no country and its effect has drawn attention to the growing economic and social exclusion experienced by some of the world's most impoverished communities both in developed and developing countries (Chell et al., 2010; Mair, 2010). This, combined with the effects of neo-liberal policies has encouraged governments, the world over, to consider more seriously the potential of social entrepreneurs and social enterprises to address unmet social needs and help local economies recover from long term decline (Perrini et al., 2010).

For example, within the UK, the Coalition Government has introduced the idea of a Big Society in an attempt to encourage greater civic action on the parts of individuals, households, groups, non-profit organizations and social enterprises to address and meet growing social needs while maintaining a 'small' government and engaging in fiscal reduction involving the slashing of budgets including those used to provide and support social and community services. The Big Society rests on three core ideas: empowering communities; opening up public services and encouraging more individuals to become engaged in social action (HM Government, 2010; 2011a; 2011b). Conceived of in this way, Cameron (2010) has referred to the Big Society as 'the biggest, most dramatic transfer of power from elites in Whitehall to the man and woman in the street'. Despite these grand ambitions, analyses of the Big Society have been critical of the move from big government to big society with commentators typically arguing that in light of drastic reductions in government budgets, the Big Society discourse masks the Coalition Government's attempts to find alternative funding sources which will support the provision of public and social services.

As shown in Table 21.3 below, government interest in the potential for third sector organizations including social enterprises to tackle growing social problems and needs is not unique to the UK. Governments in several other countries are seeking to catalyze the development of social enterprises through support for the social impact investment market. The Australian Government for example introduced the Social Enterprise Development and Investment Funds (SEDIF) initiative in 2011 with grant funding to seed the establishment of two social impact investment funds (Commonwealth of Australia, 2011). In many economies, the transfer by local authorities of asset management and ownership or the transfer of asset management with retention of ownership to local community groups has given rise to new non-profit enterprises embedded within local communities. This indicates that changes to welfare state systems combined with liberal government policies and an on-going, far-reaching global economic recession are correlated with the rapid, global rise of social enterprises. Related to this, several researchers suggest that differences in welfare systems and political and institutional contexts also explain cross-country differences in responses to social needs (Amin, Cameron and Hudson, 2002; Mair, 2010). This is supported by research that indicates that while social enterprises are on the rise globally, this growth is not evenly distributed (Borzaga and Defourny, 2001). For example, Social Enterprise UK (2011) reports that 14 per cent of all UK social enterprises are start-ups of less than two years old which, significantly, is three times the proportion of start-ups amongst mainstream small businesses, and figures from the last UK Global Entrepreneurship Monitor (GEM) report on social entrepreneurship indicate that while the number of mainstream entrepreneurs had fallen, the volume of social entrepreneurs had increased (Harding, 2006). These figures contrast both with Italy, Sweden and Finland which boast considerable numbers of social enterprises and also with Greece and Denmark which, comparatively, have very few (Borzaga and Defourny, 2001).

It is not only in developed economies but also in emerging economies too that there is a new and growing awareness of SE. China is a noteworthy case. The seeds of SE were sown in the late 1970s when China launched market reform and commenced dismantling the rural commune system, the privatization and corporatization of state-owned enterprises and urban enterprise policy began an erosion of public services, e.g. education, health and housing; and welfare provision. Demographic and socio-economic change, including smaller families, population ageing and rapid rural-urban migration, also has eroded traditional family and kinship provision of welfare to vulnerable groups (Yu, 2011). Since 2004, the Chinese government and international agencies have actively culti-vated SE in China; and rising corporate social responsibility (CSR) and philanthropy has given strong support to the growth of social enterprises (Yu, 2011). Unlike democratic India, however, government relations and regulations are critical to advancing SE in the future (FYSE, 2012).

At an overarching level, a heightened responsiveness to SE and social innovation is supported by disenchantment with the existing form of capitalism. The sentiment of the Occupy Wall Street Movement signals popular disillusionment with the capitalist system that led to the Global Financial Crisis of 2007–8. Serious global problems like income inequality, poverty and environmental degradation continue unabated. For example, World Development Indicators (World Bank, 2012: 2) show that despite progress being made toward poverty reduction, hundreds of millions of people remain extremely poor, living on less than $1.25 a day and in sub-Saharan Africa, the number of extremely poor people even increased from 290 million in 1990 to 356 million in 2008. Similarly, income differentials are widening – the United Nations' Human Development Report (UNDP, 2010: 6) indicates that 'since the 1980s, income inequal-ity has risen in many more countries than it has fallen'. This has led to realization that there is an urgency to provide solutions to social and environmental problems and that the business sector too must play an important role in this. Business leaders like Sir Richard Branson are now pushing for transformation of capitalism. Most recently Branson has spearheaded a 'B Team' being put together with members championing a specific reform and working to produce solutions and action for implementation (The Economist, 2012). At the academic level, concepts like Michael Porter's 'shared value creation' (Porter and Kramer, 2011) also augurs well for SE partnerships across sectors.

THE SOCIAL ENTREPRENEUR, SOCIAL ENTREPRENEURSHIP AND SOCIAL ENTERPRISES

Social Entrepreneurs

Despite increases in the practice of SE and growing numbers of social enterprises, it is only more recently that social entrepreneurs, SE and social innovation have attracted the attention of the academic community. As a consequence, robust investigations of each of these are at an early, what Nicholls (2010) refers to as, a 'pre-paradigmatic stage' and there is widespread agreement that as an area of academic study social entrepreneur-ship lacks conceptual clarity, suffers from definitional fuzziness and is in need of robust theorization (Zahra et al., 2009). Despite this, a number of common themes can be found within the literature, which seeks to define what we mean by a social entrepreneur, SE and social enterprises (c.f. Mair, 2010).

Leadbeater (1997) suggests that social entrepreneurs can be characterized by three defining features: their ability to excel in spotting unmet needs and mobilizing under-utilized resources to meet these; their drive, determination and ambition; and their commitment to addressing an unmet social need rather than pursuing personal financial profit or shareholder wealth. It is recognized that of these, the last characteristic clearly distinguishes social from for-profit entrepreneurs and Dees (1998) has proposed that while social entrepreneurs may embrace both commercial and social aims, their primary objective is to have a 'mission-related impact'. Building on Leadbeater's work, other researchers have highlighted the relationship between social entrepreneurs and social innovation as a distinguishing feature (Friedman and Desivilya, 2010; Perrini et al., 2010; Zahra et al., 2009). For example, Shaw and Carter (2007: 418) suggest that social entrepreneurs 'tackle unmet socio-economic needs using innovative approaches'; Mair and Marti (2006: 37) agree that social entrepreneurs engage in 'the innovative use and combination of resources to pursue opportunities to catalyze social change' and Chell et al. (2010: 485) go so far as to argue that 'it is necessary for social enterprises to foster innovation'. Leadbeater too (1997: 8) has emphasized the innovative capacity of social entrepreneurs, arguing that:

> Social entrepreneurs will be one of the most important sources of innovation. Social entre-preneurs identify under-utilised resources – people, buildings, equipment – and find ways of putting them to use to satisfy unmet social (and community needs). They innovate new welfare services and new ways of delivering existing services. Social entrepreneurs who deploy entre-preneurial skills for social ends are at work in parts of the traditional public sector, some large private sector corporations and at the most innovative edge of the voluntary sector.

Drawing from their experiences of working with and representing social entrepreneurs, Ashoka (2012) has highlighted the innovative solutions which social entrepreneurs develop when addressing what they describe as some of society's most pressing prob-lems. Bill Drayton, founder of Ashoka, uses this example to capture the innovative capacity of social entrepreneurs, 'social entrepreneurs are not just content to give a fish or teach how to fish. They will not rest until they have revolutionalized the fishing industry'. The relationship between social entrepreneurship and social innovation can largely be explained by both the restricted resource base from which social entre-preneurs have been found to seek to address unmet social needs (Shaw and Carter, 2007) and their strong commitment to addressing unmet social needs and ultimately, to effect social change. Possessing few forms of capital, especially economic capital, social entrepreneurs have been found to be particularly adept at both the creative use of those scarce resources they do own and the use of these to leverage additional resources contained within the local environments and communities in which they are embedded (Shaw and Carter, 2007). In particular, as discussed below, social entre-preneurs have been found to make use of their social capital as a key entrepreneurial resource (Chell et al., 2010) and engage in bricolage to acquire the resources necessary to address unmet social needs. Evidence from a large-scale UK study of social entre-preneurs supports the suggestion social entrepreneurs are committed to addressing unmet social needs. The findings from Shaw et al.'s (2002) research found that 90 per cent of the social entrepreneurs in their sample reported that so motivated had they been to address an unmet social need in their local community that they had drawn upon their resources, specially their social capital, to establish a social enterprise for that purpose.

Writing on the ways in which social entrepreneurs have been presented in the literature, Nicholls (2010) observes two themes as dominating the discourse: the individual social entrepreneur as a hero whose successes and engagement in social innovation are widely documented (Shaw et al., 2002; Shaw and Carter, 2007) and social entrepreneurship as a process involving communities and action networks (Perrini et al., 2010; Tapsell and Woods, 2010). As mainstream entrepreneurship research has been dominated by Anglo-American discourse which emphasizes the prowess, power and success of individual entrepreneurs while masking the effect of their embeddedness, the involvement of others in the entrepreneurial process and the possibility that entrepreneurs can be motivated by both personal financial and societal benefits (c.f., Dodd-Drakopoulou and Anderson, 2007), it is unsurprising that Nicholls concluded that of these two perspectives, the social entrepreneur as hero is more common, even in a research base which he describes as pre-paradigmatic. Indeed in view of growing critique of the entrepreneur as hero metaphor, it might be argued that research interests in the SE phenomenon and social enterprses are part of an overarching move by researchers to give due recognition that entrepreneurship must encompass more than an economic efficiency driven value standpoint. Fayolle and Matlay (2010: 2) aptly point out that entrepreneurship is 'an evolving phenomenon that is heading towards . . . more social value added' and Steyaert and Katz (2004) make an eloquent plea for a socially and culturally aware engagement with entrepreneurship as a social force creating society as well as an economic force that creates businesses and consumer products and services. Hjorth (2010: 312) consolidates this train of thought by arguing for a shift in focus in the SE debate 'away from the entrepreneur as an instrument for solving societal problems with business skills . . . towards the social role of entrepreneurship as a sociality-creating force'.

Social Entrepreneurship and Social Enterprises

In common with studies of the social entrepreneur, a dominant theme within research on SE and social enterprises has been how to define and characterize features common to social enterprises, which help identify and distinguish them from their for-profit counterparts (c.f. Austin, Stevenson and Wei-Skillern, 2006, Chell, 2007). Defourny (2001) for example, suggests that social enterprises can be characterized by economic and entrepreneurial dimensions such as the provision of goods and services which can be traded for financial exchange and also social factors including objectives focused on realizing social and community benefits. Social enterprises are commonly distinguished from other entrepreneurial ventures because of their use of trading activities to achieve financial self-sufficiency including financial surpluses that can be used to address social goals. Conceived of in this way, social enterprises are often regarded as organizations, which combine the skills of the entrepreneur with a strong social mission and as such are often regarded as hybrid organizations, which straddle sectors with mixed motives of creating both social and economic value (c.f. Dees's 1998 'hybrid spectrum'; 'three-dimensional' hybrids – Evers et al. 2004).

Universal definitions of social enterprises are complicated by a number of factors including differing perspectives regarding why social enterprises emerge. For example, in the US social enterprises are viewed as an alternative to failing not-for-profit organizations such as charities while in the UK, social enterprises are regarded as mechanisms which emerge to tackle social exclusion and address community needs when market and public services fail to do so. Further hindering the likelihood of a one-size-fits-all approach to defining social enterprises are the broad spectrum of types of organizations and variable legal structures adopted by organizations that seek to combine financial with social objectives (Prabhu, 1999; Leadbeater, 1997). Over time, SE has become associated with community enterprises and community development, the public sector, education, churches, charities, the private sector and the not-for-profit sector or third sector. What is agreed upon is that social enterprises address a diverse range of social, community and environmental needs and rather than being restricted to the confines of the non-profit sector, now operate in all sectors of the economy (Austin, Stevenson and Wei-Skillern, 2006; Chell, 2007). It is also agreed that common to social enterprises is their position within complex multi-agency environments that require them to adopt an open and porous approach. Ultimately however, for social enterprises it is their financial motivation of sustainability and self-sufficiency through self-trading (Chell 2007) that distinguish them from their traditional not-for-profit organization counterparts. Unlike 'economic' enterprises, who focus on short-term profit maximization for shareholders, a multiple bottom line sees social enterprises motivated by economic surplus generation for sustainability and scaling up of their social value creation activities (Chell et al., 2010).

Mair's (2010: 2) review of attempts to conceptualize SE observes that as research interests in SE have grown, so too have the number of definitions used to describe the phenomenon. This leads her to suggest that as social entrepreneurship 'means different things to different people in different places', the phrase has become an umbrella term for a diverse range of activities which, while united in their desire to have social impact, can be distinguished 'substantially with respect to the actors, contexts and mechanisms at play' (p.2). Despite this Mair does seek to 'integrate and synthesize existing theoretical and practical perspectives on social entrepreneurship' indicating that some features and characteristics may be common across the variety of phenomena discussed under the umbrella construct of 'social entrepreneurship'. In particular Mair (p.3) draws attention to SE as a context-specific, local phenomenon. Specifically she argues that SE involves 'a process of catering to locally-existing basic needs that are not addressed by traditional organisations' (p.4). This line of thinking is not new but echoes earlier empirical studies of social entrepreneurship (Shaw et al., 2002; Shaw and Carter, 2007) and is supported by Leadbeater's (1997) proposal that rather than regarding the provision of specific services as their core aim, social enterprises view the formation of long-term relationships with their typically local client group as essential to their success. Shaw et al. (2002) too found that the needs which UK social entrepreneurs seek to address are typically local and also that 84 per cent of the social entrepreneurs in their sample lived in the same area as the need they were addressing, so reflecting the local embeddedness of social entrepreneurs and social enterprises. Mair (2010) proposes that as a consequence of differing government policies, social entrepreneurship and social enterprises will vary across countries. In particular she suggests that in liberal economies it is both more likely that social enterprises will emerge to address unmet social needs and also that such enterprises will be more likely to embrace market mechanisms to address these needs.

SOCIAL OPPORTUNITIES

Opportunity recognition, construction and development, lies at the heart of entrepreneurship (c.f. Short et al., 2010). Although the nature of opportunity is a much-debated concept in mainstream entrepreneurship literature, social needs and problems offer opportunities for entrepreneurial actions and processes (Steyaert and Katz, 2004; Zahra et al., 2009). Understanding the characteristics of social opportunities and their manifestation within a social context can be a useful starting point for coming to grips with the SE phenomenon (de Bruin and Kickul, 2011).

In common with their traditional counterparts research has found that for social entrepreneurs, the recognition of a gap in the provision of services or an unmet social need is the key driving force in their creation and development of community enterprises (Shaw et al., 2002; Shaw and Carter, 2007). Shaw et al. (2002) used interview data with UK social entrepreneurs to explore opportunity recognition within the context of social entrepreneurship. They found that like mainstream entrepreneurs, identifying and exploiting an unmet (social) need is *the* driving force. Their study also revealed the predominantly *localized* nature of the opportunities addressed by social entrepreneurs leading them to conclude that while mainstream small enterprises are often characterized by local and niche markets (c.f.: Curran and Blackburn, 1994) unlike social enterprises they are not restricted to primarily local markets. They support this suggestion with the following quote, 'I can see opportunities and facilitate developments for the community to take advantage of' (founder, regeneration initiative, Newcastle quoted in Shaw and Carter (2002: 427)).

Borrowing from the behavioural theory of the firm, Zahra et al. (2008) offer five criteria that are helpful to delineate viable social opportunities: 'Prevalence, relevance, urgency, accessibility, and radicalness.' Applying these criteria to determine if an organization fits a SE label can be useful. Noting that Zahra et al. (2008) emphasize that not all of the criteria have to be fulfilled for a social opportunity to exist, de Bruin et al. (2010) apply these criteria to determine if a locally embedded, non-profit organization qualifies by addressing a social opportunity. They examined the case of the Wellington Zoo in New Zealand to argue that the Zoo satisfies three of the five criteria – prevalence, relevance, and urgency, although the two remaining criteria – accessibility and radicalness – are not. By engaging in the conservation of endangered species and catering to the need for conservation education of largely urbanized populations increasingly disconnected from nature, Wellington Zoo confronts two *prevalent* and *urgent* social problems. *Relevance* 'denotes a match between the opportunity's salience to the entrepreneur and his/her background, values, talents, skills, and resources' (Zahra et al., 2008: 122). The Zoo's industry association and commitment to 'integrated conservation' as a member of the World Association of Zoos and Aquariums, is evidence of the relevance criteria being met. Zahra et al. (2008: 124) refer to *accessibility* as 'the level of perceived difficulty in addressing a social need through traditional welfare mechanisms, such as governments or charitable trusts', while *radicalness* involves major innovation or social change. Radicalness and inaccessibility of social opportunities usually goes hand-in-hand. The Zoo, as a local-government-supported charitable trust, is highly accessible but not radical. It engages a myriad of non-radical, incremental innovations and innovative practices, which aggregate to contribute to its success and viability. Given that

Zahra et al. (2008) developed their five criteria in relation to internationalization of SE activities, inaccessibility and radical innovation fit well with that context. However, as de Bruin et al. (2010) point out, for local community and regionally focused organizations that address the social needs and/or problems of their communities and which in many instances have an entrenched historic presence as for instance the Zoo, high accessibility can be an enabler of viability as funders and donors are also more likely to opt for such highly accessible opportunities. Similarly, radical innovation and change would rarely be associated with such organizations. Zahra et al. (2009: 519) maintain, SE encompasses opportunity discovery and development activities to enhance social wealth that could involve creating new ventures or 'managing existing organizations in an innovative manner'. The Wellington Zoo fits into the latter category, managing innovatively across its three prime stakeholder categories – visitors, animals and staff (de Bruin et al., 2010). In a similar vein to Zahra et al. (2008; 2009), other researchers too have argued that SE involves the development of opportunities for social value creation (Alvord et al., 2004).

RESOURCE CONSIDERATIONS

Drawing upon the resource-based perspective of the firm (Penrose, 1959; Barney, 1986; 1991), it is now recognized that entrepreneurial ventures are predicated on the availability of financial *and* non-financial resources. Supporting this, researchers have drawn from capital theory (Bourdieu, 1986) to develop the notion of 'entrepreneurial capital' as a theoretically robust means of conceptualizing and describing the various resources needed for venture creation (Morris, 1998; Erikson, 2002). Research on entrepreneurial capital suggests that in addition to financial capital, entrepreneurs make use of other forms of capital both possessed by them and accessed through their networks. While variously defined, there is agreement within the field that in addition to economic capital, entrepreneurs typically make use of human, social and symbolic or reputational capital (Boden and Nucci, 2000; Davidsson and Honig, 2003; Cope et al., 2007; Shaw et al., 2008) and that the variety and amount of capital possessed and available to entrepreneurs significantly impacts on their experiences of venture creation (Davidsson and Honig, 2003).

When considering the resources needed by social enterprises, entrepreneurial capital is also relevant. As mentioned, for social entrepreneurs, economic capital in the form of money is often very scarce (Shaw et al., 2002; Shaw and Carter, 2007). However this does not imply that social entrepreneurs possess scarce amounts of social, human and symbolic or reputational capital. Instead, research indicates that, given the locally embedded nature of most social enterprises, social entrepreneurs typically possess very strong social capital and reputation within their local communities (Chell et al., 2010; Shaw and Carter, 2007). For example, Shaw and Carter (2007) reported that the social entrepreneurs in their study identified their involvement in the local community as necessary for building credibility for their social enterprise. Building on discussion about the local focus of the opportunities addressed by social enterprises, this suggests that social and symbolic or reputational capital is an important SE resource. This is proposed by Shaw and Carter (2007) who comment that given the complex and challenging social needs addressed by social entrepreneurs, the social and symbolic capital they possess within local communities are essential for encouraging other local actors to trust and support their work.

Research also finds that social entrepreneurs are adept at leveraging by engaging in bricolage to acquire the resources necessary to address unmet social needs. Bricolage is a process of making do with resources at hand, improvising and refusing to be constrained by limitations including resource limitations (Baker and Nelson, 2005). Di Domenico, Haugh, and Tracey's (2010) investigation of the relevance of bricolage to social enterprises found three additional dimensions are important: *social value creation, stakeholder participation*, and *persuasion*. Active involvement of stakeholders to access resources and persuasion to convince stakeholders of usefulness of resources, assets and business case for social value creation was part and parcel of the tactics of social enterprises. Di Domenico et al. (2010: 698) therefore propose an extended theoretical framework and definition of social bricolage to include these dimensions: 'Social bricolage is a process that involves *making do, the refusal to be constrained by limitations, improvisation, social value creation, stakeholder participation*, and *persuasion*.' Kickul, Griffiths and Gundry (2010) too find bricolage is practised by social entrepreneurs who operate typically in resource-constrained environments. Importantly, they also show a link between catalytic innovation, bricolage and the growth rate of social impact.

Despite the field of SE being emergent, there is some agreement among scholars that innovation is closely associated with SE and innovation is a necessary activity for social enterprises and social entrepreneurs. Chell et al. (2010: 485) assert that: 'social enterprises seek business solutions to social problems and in order to do so . . . it is necessary for social enterprises to foster innovation'. Mair and Marti (2006) emphasize, social entrepreneurs engage in 'the innovative use and combination of resources to pursue opportunities to catalyze social change'. However, other scholars claim that the emphasis should be on innovation rather than on social enterprises or entrepreneurs. Phills et al. (2008: 37) highlight that 'enterprises are important because they deliver innovation. But ultimately, innovation is what creates social value'. In the next section therefore we critically examine the social innovation concept and discourse.

SOCIAL INNOVATION

The Grameen Bank example may be used to highlight the blurred boundaries and distinctions between SE, social enterprise and social innovation; terms often used interchangeably. Phills et al. (2008) use this case to forcefully illustrate their preference for a social innovation approach. For them it is the microfinance model associated with the Grameen Bank that should be in the spotlight and is the 'quintessential social innovation'. They fittingly point out that for those with SE leanings, the focus is on Yunus and how to foster more individuals like him, while for those who are more interested in social enterprises, the focus is on how social purpose organizations can walk in the footsteps of viable and effective ventures like the Grameen Bank to design and manage organizations so as to maintain their mission and be financially self-sustaining.

Social innovation scholars focus largely on the processes and outcomes of socially innovative behaviour rather than analysis of the individual social entrepreneur or social enterprise. Phills et al. (2008) argue that social innovation need not necessarily come from a social entrepreneur, and suggest that such innovation often emerges outside their scope. Similarly, Boschee and McClurg (2003) propose that while innovators are 'the dreamers' who create prototypes and work out kinks, entrepreneurs are 'the builders' who turn these into reality. Academic attention has overwhelmingly coalesced around the latter phenomenon of SE and less attention has been paid to the social innovation process (Mulgan et al., 2007). Although the term 'innovation' appears regularly in relation to conceptualizations of SE (Dees, 1998, Mort et al., 2003, Weerawardena and Mort, 2006), there is often only limited elaboration beyond describing it as a by-product of socially entrepreneurial behaviour. Pol and Ville (2009: 881) summarize this conceptual problem acutely with their observation that 'social innovation is a term that almost everyone likes, but nobody is quite sure of what it means'.

At the crux of the definitional issue lies an unsettled debate on the scope and boundaries of the concept. Leaving it wide open, as Pol and Ville (2009) acknowledge, risks including everything, yet narrowing down too much at this stage of the paradigm's development potentially hinders progress (Mulgan et al., 2007). Nicholls and Murdock (2012) also highlight the loaded nature of the terms 'social' and 'innovation'. To understand the dilemma faced by researchers, one need only consider recent high-profile innovations such as Twitter. Although developed for commercial, not social purposes, it has been cited as a key catalyst in the Arab Spring uprisings of 2011 – a movement generally viewed as a force for positive social change in the region. Categorizing this as a social innovation would seem appropriate under many current definitions. For example: 'social innovations are changes in the cultural, normative or regulative structures [or classes] of the society which enhance its collective power resources and improve its economic and social performance' (Heiscala, 2007: 59), or even that social innovations are 'new ideas that work' (Mulgan et al., 2007: 8). Yet, this notion becomes blurred when one considers that the same technology has been blamed for fanning violent riots after a recent ice hockey match in Canada (Dhillon, 2011) and for the central role it played in coordinating inner-city riots in the UK during the summer of 2011. To this end, scholars are beginning to acknowledge 'social innovation is not, in and of itself, a socially positive thing' (Nicholls and Murdock, 2012: 5).

The paradoxical nature of social innovation is not confined to Twitter. The iconic social innovation of microfinance was once regarded as *the* pioneering approach to providing small loans to individuals unable to obtain reasonable credit elsewhere. On the surface, there appears little to object to with this Nobel-endorsed innovation. Yet, when one fully examines the negative externalities associated with the service, a picture emerges in *some* instances of usury and exploitation by individuals who have easily corrupted the idea (ResponsAbility, 2011, Strangio, 2011). Even leaving aside issues of intention over implementation, it is notable that there has been only muted discussion as to whether introducing personal debt and pushing globalization and consumerism to countries such as Bangladesh is a socially positive innovation (see Bateman (2010) for a powerful critique of microfinance). This paradox is arguably a characteristic problem that hints at the 'dark side' of social innovation (Nicholls and Murdock, 2012: 5).

It is simultaneously recognized however, that a degree of courage is required to produce any kind of polemic against a form of innovation almost universally perceived as being a positive force. Reflective of this, the field of social innovation remains dominated by 'feel good' cases that create an idealized vision of what the phenomenon is and can be. This however has the effect of limiting any critical analysis of the construct that may help tease out some conceptual boundaries. This dilemma also reinforces the inherent and inescapable subjectivity over what constitutes 'positive social innovation', and which, coupled with a general lack of debate into the philosophical and ontological basis of social innovation (with the exception of Mulgan's (2012) promising attempt at articulating the epistemological and theoretical foundations of social innovation), continues to hamper understanding and development of this value-laden, culturally contingent (Nicholls and Murdock, 2012) construct.

Perhaps inevitably, those involved in the grassroots practice of what is generally considered to be social innovation have overlooked these esoteric definitional considerations. Most individuals and organisations have taken a pragmatic approach, normally arriving at some variation of The Skoll Centre's definition of social innovation as 'innovative activities and services that are motivated by the goal of meeting a social need and that are predominantly developed and diffused through organisations whose primary purposes are social' (Mulgan et al., 2007: 8).

Social Innovation in Practice

Part of the perceived strength of the social innovation paradigm is the agnostic attitude it takes to the locus of social innovation, in particular that it need not necessarily emerge from the social economy (Murray et al., 2010). A notable high-profile example of social innovation in the UK involves celebrity chef, Jamie Oliver, who has successfully campaigned against the poor nutritional content of school meals. Addressing the escalating problem of childhood obesity, Oliver's multifaceted campaign and practical advice for school cooks had more impact in a short space of time than 'a corduroy army of health promotion workers or a £100m Saatchi & Saatchi campaign' according to one British GP (Spence, 2005: 678). Contrast this with another recent success story, the Violence Reduction Unit (VRU) in Glasgow (www.actiononviolence.com), set up by former nurse and forensic psychologist Karen McCluskey, who now works for the Strathclyde Police Force. Originally created to tackle Glasgow's then unenviable reputation as the Murder Capital of Europe, the VRU has succeeded where other approaches have largely failed. This has been achieved by: adopting a new philosophical stance towards tackling gang violence; developing multi-agency partnerships with groups such as medics and the judiciary; and recruiting ex-gang members to work with at-risk youths. The scheme has delivered an average 45 per cent reduction in violent offending among participants (Glasgow Community to Reduce Violence, 2011) and the potential of scaling out the model to other areas in light of the English inner-city riots of 2011 is being explored at cabinet level (Carrell, 2011).

What is initially striking about these examples, both from academic and practical perspectives, is their diversity and commonality. Both innovators are operating within distinctive environments across contrasting institutional milieus and each have uniquely different resource endowments. Uniting the cases however are the key tenets of social innovation, namely: the creation and leveraging of new cross-functional relationships (Mulgan et al., 2007; Murray et al., 2010); individuals and groups working together to overcome institutional barriers to address a social or environmental problem (Kuznets, 1974; Hamalainen and Heiskala, 2007); the creation of new multifunctional institutions (for example the Open University) and individuals and groups adopting a proactive risk-taking approach to address social or environmental problems (Goldsmith et al., 2010).

Drivers of Social Innovation

An understanding of the underlying forces that create the need for social innovations in the first place is necessary to piece together the social innovation puzzle. The most compelling of these explanations emerges from analysing the architecture of the economic system. Market failures, especially in the form of positive and negative externalities where pricing mechanisms do not account for the full social costs and benefits of production and consumption, are addressed by the state through traditional methods like taxes, surcharges and legislation. Yet these traditional approaches often fail to address these market failures effectively (Santos, 2009). Many organizations now operate transnationally and can quickly move operations (and jobs) out of a country should regulation or taxation become too onerous.

Leading economists and commentators including Krugman (2009) and Klein (2002; 2008) too have offered powerful critiques of the dominant neo-liberal economic orthodoxy and there has been widespread criticism of laissez-faire approaches to both financial and industrial regulation. In response to the failure of traditional approaches, social innovators have emerged to fill the void by devising creative solutions to overcome market failure. Echoing the Kirznerian interpretation of the entrepreneur as an individual restoring equilibrium to the economy, the social innovator can be seen as driven to restore social equilibrium where either the market or state has failed to do so. Market and state failures are system-based inertias that can springboard social innovation. Nicholls and Murdock (2012) conceptualize social innovation as a force that disrupts and reconfigures systems to overcome inertia, reshaping institutions, norms and traditions to meet changing social and environmental needs.

It has been well documented that individuals and organizations have been developing social innovations from as early as the first industrial revolution (Banks, 1972). However, only over the past 20 years or so, formal institutions have emerged to catalyze and diffuse the practice more widely. These institutions have taken on many varied shapes and forms ranging from offices of state in the USA (The Office of Social Innovation and Civic Participation), independent research and knowledge exchange institutes (e.g. NESTA and the Young Foundation in the UK), university based academic groups and centres to hybrid public-private sector organizations in India (e.g. Srishti Labs, Bangalore). Although most organizations work along many different frontiers, often overlapping in their activities, it is important at this juncture to review how each organization is uniquely contributing to the development of the field which, in line with Nicholls (2010), remains in a pre-paradigmatic stage.

For this purpose, after reviewing[1] a non-exhaustive selection of the key institutions involved in promoting social innovation values globally, a typology is proposed to both appreciate and differentiate the contributions being made. Organizations and institutions can be loosely typified as: (1) Social Innovation Hubs, (2) Applied Social Innovation Laboratories, (3) Social Innovation Research Centres, and (4) Social Innovation Public Policy Initiatives (i.e., offices of state or policies aimed at encouraging social innovation).

Table 21.1   Social innovation hubs

Name	Location	Mission/approach	Activities
The Melting Pot	Edinburgh, UK	The Melting Pot aims to stimulate and support social innovation – helping people realize their ideas for a better world.	Meeting space, peer-to-peer learning, event space and hosting, networking.
Centre for Social Innovation	Toronto, Canada	'. . . to catalyze social innovation in Toronto and around the world. We believe that society is facing unprecedented economic, environmental, social and cultural challenges. We also believe that new innovations are the key to turning these challenges into opportunities to improve our communities and our planet'.	Meeting space, social innovation incubator, education and research.
The Hub (Westminster)	UK and branches throughout the world	'The Hub aims to provide access to investment, space, programmes and a global peer network hosted to foster collaborative practices and learning opportunities.'	Meeting place, office facilities and support for social innovators.

Social innovation hubs

Social innovation hubs are growing rapidly in number and can now be found in most large cosmopolitan cities. This 'Hub' network, now numbering 30, covers diverse geographical areas, from Tel Aviv in Israel to Oaxaca in Mexico. Hubs provide similar services including hot-desking office space, the opportunity to network with fellow social innovators, incubation support and educational events. Unlike other social innovation centres that focus to a greater extent on research, social innovation hubs concentrate on creating innovative spaces for members of the public to meet, collaborate and work. As such, these hubs provide a valuable role as a central node in local social innovation networks and are important in spreading best practice, new ideas and advice. Their emergence supports Murray et al.'s (2010) and Mulgan's (2012) characterization of social innovation as a practice that is social both in its ends and its means, and that creates and sustains new social relationships.

Applied social innovation centres

Applied Social Innovation Centres are an interesting and important development within the social innovation field. It is widely acknowledged that innovation requires failure (Mulgan, 2006), yet those funding the development of social innovations tend to be naturally risk-averse (Antadze and Westley, 2010). This is quite understandable when one considers that any radical innovation may have an equally positive or negative effect on user wellbeing unless tested adequately. Applied Social Innovation Centres appear to be imitating commercial R&D departments by developing (albeit unconventional) laboratories that allow ideas to be tested, simulated and piloted before being diffused widely. In doing so, these Centres are bringing much-needed rigour to the process of social inno-

Table 21.2   Applied social innovation centres

Name	Location	Mission/approach	Activities
Mindlab	Copenhagen, Denmark	'MindLab is a cross-ministerial innovation unit which involves citizens and businesses in creating new solutions for society. We are also a physical space – a neutral zone for inspiring creativity, innovation and collaboration . . . . MindLab is instrumental in helping the ministry's key decision-makers and employees view their efforts from the outside-in, to see them from a citizen's perspective. We use this approach as a platform for co-creating better ideas.'	Public service redesign, service user engagement, piloting and assessing new approaches, private sector engagement, meeting/collaboration space for government workers.
Srishti Labs	Bangalore, India	'Through strategic design services, its mission is to dramatically increase the success rate of new products and services developed by early phase innovators for emerging markets.'	Design thinking approach to innovation, tailoring innovation to the needs of rapidly growing Indian consumer population, user-engagement and education.
BRAC Social Innovation Lab	Bangladesh (and beyond)	'The Social Innovation Lab seeks to institutionalize innovation at BRAC and create an accessible space for all where ideas are shared, generated and nurtured. It supports programs in identifying existing innovations, running pilot programs, and facilitating dissemination of experiences, as well as seeking new partners with promising solutions to work with BRAC in tackling complex issues.'	Capacity building, idea piloting and facilitating cross-organizational collaboration.

vation, and are providing a critically important bridge between cutting edge commercial knowhow and problems faced within communities.

Social innovation research centres
Heightened awareness of the importance of social innovation especially in academic circles has seen a corresponding rise in the number of social innovation research and consultancy centres (Howaldt and Schwarz, 2011). These include the Stanford Center in Palo Alto, US, INSEAD Social Innovation Centre in Fontainebleau, France and the Centre for Social Innovation (ZSI) in Vienna, Austria. Collaboration between institutes is also growing as evidenced by the new European School of Social Innovation which is

Table 21.3   Social innovation public policy initiatives

Name	Location	Mission/approach	Activities
Office of Social Innovation and Civic Participation	USA	'The Office of Social Innovation and Civic Participation is focused on doing business differently by: • promoting service as a solution and a way to develop community leadership; • increasing investment in innovative community solutions that demonstrate results; and • developing new models of partnership. These three mission areas together comprise the community solutions agenda.'	Funding innovative projects, developing and diffusing new social business models, recapitalizing fractured communities.
The Big Society	UK	'The Big Society is about shifting the culture – from government action to local action. This is not about encouraging volunteering for the sake of it. This is about equipping people and organizations with the power and resources they need to make a real difference in their communities.'	Dispersing power to communities, reducing regulatory burden on social organizations, implementing policies in support of the Big Society philosophy.
Social Innovation Europe (European Commission)	Europe	'The Social Innovation Europe initiative (SIE) represents a major effort to build and streamline the social innovation field in Europe.'	Raising awareness of social innovation in EU policy circles, facilitating learning between Member States.

an initiative between the Centre for Social Innovation (ZSI) and the Central Scientific Institute (sfs) of the Dortmund University of Technology, Germany. It is envisaged as an 'international competence network' that will reach out to European and global scholars and institutions involved in social innovation research, education and training. This philosophy resonates with the objective of many other social innovation centres, which seek to stimulate cross-pollination of ideas across research clusters. For example, the well-established Stanford Center for Social Innovation and the Stanford Center on Philanthropy and Civil Society have done much to promote social innovation through their quarterly journal *The Stanford Social Innovation Review* along with educational programs targeted at developing future social innovators.

Social innovation public policy initiatives
Social innovation has gained sufficient traction to penetrate senior government policy-making circles, and it can no longer be considered a 'fringe curiosity'. This interest has

manifested itself in several tangible ways; from the establishment of a dedicated office of state in the USA to an explicit mention of 'social innovation' by European Commission President José Manuel Durão Barosso in the recent Europe 2020 strategy document (European Commission, 2010: 19). The concept of social innovation has not however always been universally well received by the public. The 'Big Society' policy, introduced in the UK by the Conservative government, shares many common objectives and characteristics with social innovation. However, perhaps owing to the manner in which it was sold and packaged, there remains suspicion and cynicism amongst members of the public who view it as an abdication of traditional governance and public service provision.

From the brief evaluation of organizations and institutions involved in promoting social innovation practices across the world, of particular interest is the breadth and scope of activity. On reflection, what appears to be building resilience within the movement is that it is has avoided co-option by any one particular interest group or narrow section of the political spectrum. The exponential rise in social innovation hubs can be interpreted as evidence of a burgeoning grassroots participation in the development of social innovations, while the growing prominence of academic centres indicates an acceptance within the 'establishment'. Governments, on the whole, have been slower to harness the potential of social innovation, however fiscal constraints following the global recession have led to politicians seeking creative new approaches to persistent old problems. Social innovation's eventual arrival on the 'main stage' has come via the establishment of the American Office of Social Innovation and Civic Participation, and in Europe, the Social Innovation Europe initiative, which is currently helping shape policy and practice across the continent. So, to answer the question posed by Pol and Ville (2009) in their paper: social innovation: buzz word or enduring term? The evidence increasingly points to the latter.

MEASURING IMPACT OF SOCIAL ENTREPRENEURSHIP AND SOCIAL INNOVATION

As the outcome of social ventures cannot be expressed in purely financial terms, measurement of impact and performance is complex. Social mission imperatives of social entrepreneurs when coupled with the forces of market competition and the demands of diverse stakeholders produce tensions that can be difficult to reconcile. For example, this can make it difficult to get others to 'buy in' to proposed social ventures. Also, because rewards are not always financial, this has implications for the 'Risk: Reward Ratio': at start-up, entrepreneurs often calculate this ratio using financial indicators and as this is not always possible for social ventures, making the decision to become involved is less clear cut.

Some researchers such as Paton argue that social impact and performance measurement is socially constructed: Paton (2003: 5) eloquently expresses this sentiment:

> For social enterprises (particularly) performance is not some underlying attribute that exists and can be known independently of the people centrally involved in and concerned about that organization. Performance is what those people more or less agree, implicitly or explicitly, to be performance, what they have in mind when they use the term.

Nevertheless, despite this sort of normative and subjective dominance in relation to measurement, there are some metrics that are already being used.

Social return on investment (SROI) is a simple metric that is popular with organizations that wish to monetize the value of their social impact (REDF, 2000). Frumkin (2011) maintains, however, that we should give up on SROI and other simplistic approaches; accept the complexity of the measurement challenge and embrace multi-dimensionality. He extols the benefits of a dashboard approach and derives a universal dashboard with three main clusters of indicators: finance, social impact, and people (board, workers and stakeholders), with four to five essential and universal indicators in each cluster. He admits that while there is a time and money commitment to collecting data, dashboards can improve management and accountability of social enterprises. He recommends starting with a base model dashboard and regular measurement.

'Blended Value Accounting' is the construct Nicholls (2009) puts forward to capture the spectrum of disclosure and reporting practices used by social entrepreneurs to access resources and fulfil mission objectives with primary stakeholders. Nicholls however warns of 'a dark side to these reporting innovations' especially when social enterprises might be coerced by external power imbalance forces, into using conventional business models 'rather than develop their own unique forms' (2009: 766). More internally driven but multifaceted measures like Frumkin's 'universal performance dashboard' might therefore be an answer (Frumkin, 2011). Further development of appropriate social impact metrics remains a challenge for the field and there is also a need to ensure that impact measurement becomes a means to an end rather than an end in itself.

SIGNPOSTS FOR FUTURE RESEARCH AND CONCLUDING COMMENT

Despite growing academic interest in SE and social innovation, as with any emergent pre-paradigm field, there remains a large theory development gap to be filled, presenting plenty of future research scope. Nicholls (2010: 626) advocates taking a social innovation perspective as this 'offers scholars an opportunity to enact their own reflexive isomorphism based on the legitimacy of impartial research . . . a space in which scholars can reconcile competing legitimating discourses around social entrepreneurship to build a new paradigm'. We too believe that a greater focus on social innovation is a way forward for advancing theoretical and empirical understandings of SE. Despite the compelling evidence we have presented in this chapter to illustrate that social innovation is gaining legitimacy as a field of enquiry, conceptual difficulties continue to pervade academic discussion and there remains a dearth of empirical research or meaningful datasets (Murray et al., 2010, Mulgan et al., 2007). Rather than 'reinvent the wheel' by treating social innovation as *sui generis*, we suggest that scholars make use (where appropriate) of theories from the well-established technological innovation paradigm to gain insight into the process of innovation within a social context.

First, social innovation is widely perceived as a means of achieving societal change through altering the institutional environment of a particular geographical location. It is proposed therefore, that the systems of innovation framework developed by Freeman (1995) and Lundvall (1995) among others, be adapted to analyse *systems of social innova-*

tion. There has, thus far, been no systemic mapping of the various actors and interrelations between actors seeking to introduce social innovations into society, leaving social innovation something of a conceptual 'black box'. Uncovering this, in theory, could prove a very fruitful means of understanding where the 'bottlenecks' are in the system, and could therefore explain why so many social innovations are "stillborn" (Mulgan et al., 2007: 35). It would further allow for comparison of countries with very different socio-political arrangements and could provide insights into why some nations are more able to socially innovate than others. Within this systemic approach, institutional theory (Hollingsworth, 2000, North, 1991) can be used to examine the 'rules of the game' social innovators must navigate to implement ideas, and the closely related construct of institutional entrepreneurship (Tracey et al., 2011; Pacheco et al., 2010; Di Maggio, 1988) can be examined to provide insight into processes of social innovation. Secondly, a more recent strand of research has emerged (Goldsmith et al., 2010; Moore and Westley, 2011) examining the systemic nature of social innovation using complexity and resilience theories. These approaches are valuable in order to understand and counter the 'silo' thinking that leads innovators to address only symptoms of social problems rather than the complex and multifaceted causes (Jankel, 2011). Additionally, it can assist in identifying the problem 'traps' caused by rigid social structures that prevent complex and messy problems from being properly solved (Moore and Westley, 2011).

At a micro-level of analysis, much can be gained from examining theories of embeddedness and agency within a social innovation context. As many social innovations offer localized solutions to localized problems, it is important to consider how the innovator's milieu influences processes of innovation. These processes are traditionally understood within a formal setting such as an R&D department or innovative company, yet when the literature on social entrepreneurship and social innovation is reviewed, innovation is found to take place in informal, often makeshift and resource-constrained environments (Di Domenico et al., 2010). This is the antithesis of the dominant logic found in the innovation management literature, and as such, offers an exciting avenue for social innovators to explore by revisiting established theories such absorptive capacity (Zahra and George, 2002; Cohen and Levinthal, 1990) and open innovation (Chesbrough, 2003) in search of new insights.

In addition to our suggestions for social innovation research, we draw attention to other fruitful possibilities for developing the field. First, on the basis of contributions to a recent special issue on SE in *Entrepreneurship & Regional Development*, Chell, Nicolopoulou and Karataş-Özkan (2010: 491) highlight the need for studying 'in-depth, a cross-country, comparative dimension of social entrepreneurship, thereby "operationalizing" the notion of different "spaces", contexts and situations in which it might flourish; and moreover, to turn to social, anthropological and cultural studies to further understand and explore its nature and variety of forms'. We endorse this call and add that there is also a need for comparative studies of support environments, including enabling legal forms, which can foster SE and social innovation and enhance the capacity of each to maximize their contribution to addressing and catalyzing social change. Second, we alert researchers to the relevance of a stakeholder approach for SE research (Matlay and Fayolle, 2010). As discussed, social entrepreneurship is typically locally embedded and social entrepreneurs rely on their social and reputational capital as they engage in bricolage to leverage the resources needed to address unmet social needs. As such our understanding of the SE phenomena can be improved by considering not just social entrepreneurs but also local stakeholders with whom they interact; echoing Hjorth (2010), we support the recommendation that relational studies of SE will prove fruitful.

We also identify a number of emerging and under-researched topics within the field of SE, which merit further study. Included within these are studies of eco-entrepreneurship which is typically motivated by environmental and social objectives and also the role of technology in providing opportunities to connect people and so help them overcome resource constraints in a cost effective manner with crowd sourcing for social objectives being a case in point. GEM data on social entrepreneurship (Harding, 2007) also suggests the involvement of young people and women in SE are relevant research topics, which we argue will be important to consider in order to ensure that SE research avoids the masculinized characterisation of entrepreneurship which the dominant Anglo-American discourse has encouraged within studies of mainstream entrepreneurship. Nicholls and Murdock (2012) have initiated more critical discussion of the SE phenomenon and we suggest that going forward studies which consider both the positive and negative dimensions of SE including its impact within local communties will be beneficial.

Methodologically, it has been suggested that while theoretical foundations for SE are slowly developing there is a need for less description and more empirical evidence from which generalizations can be drawn. Specifically Short et al. (2009) argue for more quantitative studies. We adopt a more balanced approach and recommend that going forward there is a need for mixed methods to both enhance theory and contribute to a growing base of empirical evidence from which generalizations might be suggested. In particular there is a need for cross-country studies to reveal the impact which differing political ideologies (macro factors) and local context (micro environments) have on SE responses to unmet social needs. Further studies of social enterprise models in East Asia (Defourny and Kim, 2011) and also of social innovation in countries like China are also warranted.

In summary, this chapter makes several noteworthy contributions. First, it provides a critical review of the state of SE research. Second, it examines social innovation, not merely as a corollary of the SE discourse, but as a dedicated evaluation of this concept, highlighting also the potential it offers for theoretically advancing the field of SE. Third, by examining the evolution and contemporary context of both SE and social innovation it sheds light on the inherent socio-political nature of these phenomena. Thus this chapter emphasizes that both SE and social innovation are social constructions that have serious economic, social and political consequences. Fourth, in terms of resolution of an important issue, we draw attention to the difficulties of performance measurement in the SE field and the need for finding appropriate measures that reflect the complex nature of the social problems being addressed. Fifth, it delineates our novel suggestions to advance research in social innovation and supplement these with insights from other scholars on opportunities for moving forward both fields of SE and social innovation.

Finally, to conclude, we raise the issue of 'responsible reciprocity', and higher obligations of the SE researcher (de Bruin and Kickul, 2011). We too agree that the SE researcher and the research process should contribute through feedback of findings to the development of organizations and social enterprises that are studied. It is our role as SE and social innovation researchers to develop practical and meaningful implications through our work and assessment that can assist social entrepreneurs and innovators in driving change for broader social, environmental and economic wellbeing. Above all SE researchers have a responsibility in helping hitherto relatively marginalized actors 'in the processes of legitimation at the discourse level' – 'social entrepreneurs, their peers and beneficiaries' (Nicholls 2010: 626), find a greater voice and influence.

NOTE

1. All information in this section is drawn from the official website of each institution.

REFERENCES

Alvord, S., Brown, L. and Letts, C. (2004). Social entrepreneurship and societal transformation. *Journal of Applied Behavioural Science, 40*(3), 260–82.
Amin, A., Cameron, A. and Hudson, R. (2002). *Placing the Social Economy*. London: Routledge.
Antadze, N. and Westley, F. (2010). Funding social innovation: How do we know what to grow? *The Philanthropist*, 23.
Ashoka (2012), Ashoka, available at: www.ashoka.org.
Austin, J., Stevenson, H. and Wei-Skillern, J. (2006). Social and commercial entrepreneurship: Same, different or both? *Entrepreneurship: Theory and Practice 30*(1), 1–22.
Baker, T., and Nelson, R. E. (2005). Creating something from nothing: Resource construction through entrepreneurial bricolage. *Administrative Science Quarterly, 50*(3), 329–66.
Banks, J. (1972). *The Sociology of Social Movements*. London, MacMillan.
Barney, J. B. (1986) Organization culture: Can it be a source of sustained competitive advantage. *Academy of Management Review 11*: 656–65.
Barney, J. B. (1991). Firm resources and sustained competitive advantage, *Journal of Management* 17, 99–120.
Bateman, M. (2010). *Why Doesn't Microfinance Work?: The Destructive Rise of Local Neoliberalism*, Zed Books.
Boden, R.J. and Nucci, A.R. (2000). On the survival prospects of men's and women's new business ventures. *Journal of Business Venturing, 15*(4), 347–62.
Borzaga, C. and Defourny, J. (Eds.) (2001). *The Emergence of Social Enterprise*. London: Routledge.
Boschee, J. and McClurg, J. (2003). *Towards a Better Understanding of Social Entrepreneurship: Some Important Distinctions*. Social Enterprise Alliance.
Bourdieu, P. (1986). The forms of capital. In J. Richardson (Ed.). *The Handbook of Theory and Research for the Sociology of Education*, NY, Greenwood Press, 241–58.
Cameron, D. (2010) Big Society Speech, Liverpool, 19 July, accessed at www.number10.gov.uk/news/big-society-speech 02 December 2011.
Carrell, S. (2011). Glasgow gangs chose route to peace in face of tough crackdown. *The Guardian* 11 August 2011.
Chell, E. (2007). Social enterprise and social entrepreneurship. *International Small Business Journal, 25*(1), 5–26.
Chell, E., Nicolopoulou, K. and Karataş-Özkan, M. (2010) Social entrepreneurship and enterprise: International and innovations perspectives. *Entrepreneurship & Regional Development*, 22(6), 485–93.
Chernow, R. (1998). *Titan: The Life of John D. Rockefeller*. New York: Random House.
Chesbrough, H. (2003). *Open Innovation: The New Imperative for Creating and Profiting from Technology*. Boston, Harvard Business School Press.
Cohen, W. M. and Levinthal, D. A. (1990). Absorptive capacity: A new perspective on learning and innovation. *Administrative Science Quarterly*, 35, 128–52.
Commonwealth of Australia (2011). Social Innovation: The Social Enterprise Development and Investment Funds (SEDIF) Available: http://www.deewr.gov.au/Employment/Programs/SocialInnovation/Social Enterprise/Pages/SEDIF.aspx
Cope, J., Jack, S. and Rose, M. B. (2007). Social capital and entrepreneurship: an introduction, *International Small Business Journal, 25*(3, 213–9.
Curran, J. and Blackburn, R. (1994). *Small Firms and Local Economic Networks: The Death of the Local Economy?* London, U.K., Paul Chapman.
Davidsson, P. and Honig, B. (2003) The role of social and human capital among nascent entrepreneurs, *Journal of Business Venturing*, 18, 301–31.

de Bruin, A., Fabrizi, S., Lee, L., Lippert, S. (2010) Not for loss: Insights on building a community asset, The 7th Annual Satter Conference of Social Entrepreneurs, New York, November 3 – 5. Available as Massey University, College of Business Research Paper No. 28, Downloadable in SSRN at http://ssrn.com/abstract=1934278.

de Bruin, A. and Kickul, J. (2011). Conducting social entrepreneurship research: Beginning, middle, end? In de Bruin, A., and Stangl, L. (Eds). (2011). *Proceedings of the Massey University Social Innovation and Entrepreneurship Conference: Extending Theory, Integrating Practice*, 70–72. Available: http://sierc.massey.ac.nz/conference/proceedings/.

Dees, J. G. (1998). 'The Meaning of 'Social Entrepreneurship''. Stanford University: Draft Report for the Kauffman Center for Entrepreneurial Leadership, 6pp.

Defourny, J. (2001). From third sector to social enterprise. In Borzaga, C. and Defourny, J. (Eds). *The Emergence of Social Enterprise*, London, New York, Routledge, 1–18.

Defourny, J., and Kim, S. (2011) Emerging models of social enterprise in Eastern Asia: A cross-country analysis, *Social Enterprise Journal*, 7(1), 86–111.

Dhillon, S. (2011). When rioters trashed Vancouver, Twitter fanned the flames – and gathered the evidence. *The Globe and Mail*, Dec. 21, 2011.

DiMaggio, P. (1988) Interest and agency in institutional theory, in L. G. Zucker (ed.), *Institutional Patterns and Organizations: Culture and Environment*. Cambridge, MA, Ballinger. 3–22.

Di Domenico, M., Haugh, H. & Tracey, P. (2010). Social bricolage: Theorizing social value creation in social enterprises. *Entrepreneurship: Theory and Practice*, 34(4), 681–703.

Dodd-Drakopoulou, S. and Anderson, A. R. (2007). Mumpsimus and the mything of the individualistic entrepreneur. *International Small Business Journal*, 25(4), 341–60.

Erikson, T. (2002). Entrepreneurial capital: the emerging venture's most important asset and competitive advantage. *Journal of Business Venturing*, 17, 3, 275–90.

European Commission (2010). EUROPE 2020: A strategy for smart, sustainable and inclusive growth. Brussels: European Commission.

Evers, A., Laveille, J., Borgaza, C. Defourny, J., Lewis, J., Nyssens, M. and Pestoff, V. (2004). Defining the third sector in Europe, in Evers, A., and Laveille, J. (Eds). *The Third Sector in Europe*. London, Edward Elgar.

Fayolle, A. and Matlay, H. (2010). Social entrepreneurship: A multicultural and multidimensional perspective. In Fayolle, A. and Matlay, H. eds. (2010). *Handbook of Research on Social Entrepreneurship*. Cheltenham, UK. And Northampton, MA, USA, Edward Elgar, 1–11.

Forbes.com (2006). Billionaires List, http://www.forbes.com/free_forbes/2006/0327/111.html.

Freeman, C. (1995). The 'National System of Innovation' in historical perspective. *Camb. J. Econ.*, 19, 5–24.

Friedman, V. J. and Desivilya, H. (2010). Integrating social entrepreneurship and conflict engagement for regional development in divided societies. *Entrepreneurship & Regional Development*, 22(6): 495–514.

Frumkin, P. (2011). In de Bruin, A., and Stangl, L. (Eds). *Proceedings of the Massey University Social Innovation and Entrepreneurship Conference: Extending Theory, Integrating Practice*, http://sierc.massey.ac.nz/conference/proceedings/, pp. 34–46.

FYSE, (2012). *China Social Enterprise Report* www.fyse.org.

Giddens, A. (Ed.) (2001). *The Global Third Way Debate*. Cambridge: Polity Press.

Giddens, A. (1998). *The Third Way: The Renewal of Social Democracy*, Cambridge, Polity Press.

Glasgow Community To Reduce Violence (2011). The Violence Must Stop – Second Year Report. Glasgow: Violence Reduction Unit.

Goldsmith, S., Georges, G., Burke, T. G. and Bloomberg, M. R. (2010). *The Power of Social Innovation: How Civic Entrepreneurs Ignite Community Networks for Good*. San Francisco, Jossey Bass.

Handy, C. (2006). The *New Philanthropists: The New Generosity*. London, William Heinemann.

Hamalainen, T. J. and Heiskala, R. (2007). *Social Innovations, Institutional Change, and Economic Performance: Making Sense of Structural Adjustment Processes in Industrial Sectors, Regions, and Societies*, Cheltenham, UK. and Northampton, MA, USA, Edward Elgar.

Harding, R. (2006). *Social Entrepreneurs Specialist Summary*, Global Entrepreneurship *Monitor*. London, London Business School.

Harvey, C., Maclean, M., Gordon, J. and Shaw, E. (2011). Andrew Carnegie and the foundations of contemporary entrepreneurial philanthropy. *Business History*, 53(3), 425–50.

Harvey, D. (2010). *The Enigma of Capital and the Crisis of Capitalism*. London, Profile Books.

Heiscala, R. (2007). Social innovations: structural and power perspectives. In Hamalainen, T. J. and Heiskala, R. (Eds). *Social Innovations, Institutional Change and Economic Performance*. Cheltenham,: Edward Elgar.

Hjorth, D. (2010). Ending essay: Sociality and economy in social entrepreneurship. In Fayolle, A. and Matlay, H. (Eds). *Handbook of Research on Social Entrepreneurship*. Cheltenham: Edward Elgar, 306–17.

Hjorth, D. and Bjerke, B. (2006). Public entrepreneurship: Moving from social/consumer to public/citizen. In

Steyaert, C. and Hjorth, D. (Eds). *Entrepreneurship as Social Change*. Cheltenham, UK. and Northampton, MA, USA, Edward Elgar, 97–120.

HM Government (2010) Giving Green Paper, London: The Stationery Office. www.cabinetoffice.gov.uk/sites/default/files/resources/Giving-Green-Paper.pdf

HM Government (2011a) Localism Act (2011a), London: The Stationery Office. www.legislation.gov.uk/ukpga/2011/20/contents/enacted

HM Government (2011b) Giving White Paper, London: The Stationery Office.www.cabinetoffice.gov.uk/sites/default/files/resources/giving-white-paper2.pdf.

Hollingsworth, J. R. (2000). Doing institutional analysis: Implications for the studiy of innovations. *Review of International Political Economy*, 7(4), 595–644.

Howaldt, J. and Schwarz, M. (2011). 'Social innovation – social challenges and future research fields', in:Jeschke, S., Isenhardt, I., Hees, F. and Trantow, S. (eds), *Enabling Innovation*, Springer Berlin Heidelberg, 203–23.

Jankel, N. (2011). Radical (re)invention. http://radicalreinvention.org/.

Jones, C. (1993). The pacific challenges: Confucian welfare state. In Jones, C. (Ed.), *New Perspectives on the Welfare State in Europe*, Routledge, London and New York, NY, 198–219.

Kickul, J., Griffiths, M. and Gundry, L. (2010). Innovating for social impact: Is bricolage the catalyst for change? In A. Fayolle and H. Matlay (Eds). *Handbook of Research on Social Entrepreneurship*, Edward Elgar: Cheltenham, Chapter 12, 232–51.

Klein, N. (2002). *No Space, No Choice, No Jobs, No Logo*, Picador.

Klein, N. (2008). *The Shock Doctrine: The Rise of Disaster Capitalism*, Picador.

Krugman, P. (2009). *The Conscience of a Liberal: Reclaiming America from the Right*, London: Penguin.

Kuznets, S. (1974). *Population Capital and Growth: Selected Essays*, Norton.

Leadbeater, C. (1997). *The Rise of the Social Entrepreneur*, Demos, London.

Lundvall, B.-A. K. (1995). *National Systems of Innovation: Towards a Theory of Innovation and Interactive Learning*, London; New York, London; New York: Pinter.

Mair, J., (2010). Social entrepreneurship: Taking stock and looking ahead. In A. Fayolle and H. Matlay (Eds). *Handbook of Research on Social Entrepreneurship*, Edward Elgar: Cheltenham, Chapter 2, 15–28.

Mair, J., and Marti, I. (2006). Social entrepreneurship research: a source of explanation, prediction, and delight. *Journal of World Business*, 41(1), 36–44.

Margolis, J. and Walsh, J. (2003). Misery loves companies: Rethinking social initiatives by business. *Administrative Science Quarterly*, 48(2), 268–305.

Matlay, H. and Fayolle, A. (2010). Conclusions, recommendations and an agenda for future research in social entrepreneurship. In A. Fayolle, and H. Matlay (Eds). *Handbook of Research on Social Entrepreneurship* (ch. 17). Cheltenham: Edward Elgar Publishing.

Moore, M. & Westley, F. (2011). Surmountable chasms: Networks and social innovation for resilient systems. *Ecology and Society*, 16(1).

Morris, M. (1998), *Entrepreneurial Intensity: Sustainable Advantages for Individuals, Organisations, and Societies*, 1st ed., Westport, CT, Quorum Books,.

Mort, G. S., Weerawardena, J. and Carnegie, K. (2003). Social entrepreneurship: Towards conceptualisation. *International Journal of Nonprofit and Voluntary Sector Marketing*, 8(1), 76–88.

Mulgan, G. (2006). The process of social innovation. *Innovations: Technology, Governance, Globalization*, 1(2), 145–62.

Mulgan, G. (2012). The theoretical foundations of social innovation. In Nicholls, A. and Murdock, A. (Eds). *Social Innovation: Blurring Boundaries to Reconfigure Markets*. Hampshire: Palgrave MacMillan.

Mulgan, G., Tucker, S., Ali, R. & Sanders, B. (2007). *Social Innovation: What it is, Why it Matters, How it can be Accelerated*. Oxford: Skoll Centre for Social Entrepreneurship.

Murray, R., Caulier-Grice, J. and Mulgan, G. (2010). *The Open Book of Social Innovation*, London, NESTA.

Nasaw, D. (2006). *Andrew Carnegie*. New York: Penguin.

Nicholls, A. (2009). 'We do good things, don't we?': 'Blended Value Accounting' in social entrepreneurship *Accounting, Organizations and Society 34*, 755–69.

Nicholls, A. (2010). The legitimacy of social entrepreneurship: Reflexive isomorphism in a pre-paradigmatic field. *Entrepreneurship: Theory and Practice*, 34(4), 611–33.

Nicholls, A. and Murdock, A. (2012). The nature of social innovation. In Nicholls, A. and Murdock, A. (eds.) *Social Innovation: Blurring Boundaries to Reconfigure Markets*. Hampshire: Palgrave MacMillan.

North, D. C. (1991). *Institutions, Institutional Change and Economic Performance*, Cambridge, Cambridge University Press.

Pacheco, D. F., York, J. G., Dean, T. J. & Sarasvathy, S. D. (2010). The coevolution of institutional entrepreneurship: A tale of two theories, *Journal of Management*, 36(4), 974–1010.

Paton, R. (2003). *Managing and Measuring Social Enterprises*. London: Sage.

Penrose, E. T. (1959). *The Theory of the Growth of the Firm*, New York: Wiley.

Perrini F., Vurro C. and Constanzo L.A. (2010). A process-based view of social entrepreneurship: From opportunity identification to scaling-up social change in the case of San Patrignano. *Entrepreneurship & Regional Development 22*(6), 515–34.

Phills, J., Deiglmeier, K. and Miller, D. (2008). Rediscovering Social Innovation. *Stanford Social Innovation Review*, (Fall).

Pol, E. and Ville, S. (2009). Social innovation: Buzz word or enduring term? *Journal of Socio-Economics, 38*(6), 878–85.

Porter, M. and Kramer, M. (2011). Creating shared value. *Harvard Business Review, 89*(1/2), 62–77.

Prabhu, G. N. (1999). Social entrepreneurship leadership. *Career Development International, 4*(3), 140–5.

ResponsAbility (2011). Corruption and financial crime – an issue in microfinance? *In:* Responsabiltiy (Ed.). http://www.responsability.com/domains/responsability_ch/data/free_docs/disscussion_paper_04_en.pdf.

Roper, J. and Cheney, G. (2005). The meanings of social entrepreneurship today, *Corporate Governance, 5*(3), 95–104.

Santos, F. (2009). A Positive Theory of Social Entrepreneurship. *Faculty & Research Working Paper*. INSEAD Social Innovation Centre: INSEAD.

Shaw, E. and Carter, S. (2007). Social entrepreneurship: Theoretical antecedents and empirical analysis of entrepreneurial processes and outcomes. *Journal of Small Business and Enterprise Development, 14*(3): 418–34.

Shaw, E., Lam, W. and Carter, S. (2008). The role of entrepreneurial capital in building service reputation. *Service Industries Journal, 28*(7), 899–917 (special issue on Entrepreneurship in services).

Shaw, E., Shaw, J. and Wilson, M. (2002), *Unsung Entrepreneurs: Entrepreneurship for Social Gain*, Durham: Barclays Centre for Entrepreneurship Research Report, 53pp.

Short, J. D., Ketchen, D., Shook, C., Ireland, D. (2010). The concept of "opportunity" in entrepreneurship research: Past accomplishments and future challenges. *Journal of Management*, 36, 40–65.

Short, J., Moss, T., and Lumpkin, G. (2009). Research in social entrepreneurship: Past contributions and future opportunities. *Strategic Entrepreneurship Journal*, 3, 161–194.

Social Enterprise UK (2011). *Fightback Britain Findings from the Social Enterprise Survey 2011*, London: Social Enterprise UK.

Spence, D. (2005). TV: Jamie's School Dinners. *BMJ: British Medical Journal, 330* (7492), 678.

Steyaert, C. and Katz, J. (2004). Reclaiming the space of entrepreneurship in society: Geographic, discursive and social dimension. *Entrepreneurship and Regional Development, 16*(3), 179–96.

Strangio, S. (2011). Is Microfinance Pushing the World's Poorest Even Deeper Into Poverty? *The New Republic*. http://www.tnr.com/article/world/98499/microfinance-drive-poverty.

Tapsell, P. and Woods, C. (2010). Social entrepreneurship and innovation: Self organization in an indigenous context. *Entrepreneurship & Regional Development 22*(6), 535–56.

The Economist (2012). Call in the B Team: Richard Branson's big idea for building a better version of capitalism, October 6th.

Tracey, P., Phillips, N. and Jarvis, O. (2011). Bridging institutional entrepreneurship and the creation of new organizational forms: A multilevel model. *Organization Science, 22*(1), 60–80.

UNDP – United Nations Development Programme (2010). *Human Development Report 2010*. UNDP.

Weerawardena, J. and Mort, G. S. (2006). Investigating social entrepreneurship: A multidimensional model. *Journal of World Business, 41*(1), 21–35.

World Bank (2012) *World Development Indicators*. The World Bank.

Yu, X. (2011). Social enterprise in China: driving forces, development patterns and legal framework. *Social Enterprise Journal, 7*(1), 9–32.

Zahra, S. and George, G. (2002). Absorptive capacity: A review, reconceptualization, and extension. *The Academy of Management Review, 27*(2), 185–203.

Zahra, S., Gedajlovic, E., Neubaum, D. and Shulman, J. A. (2009). Typology of social entrepreneurs: motives, search processes and ethical challenges. *Journal of Business Venturing, 24*(5), 519–32.

Zahra, S., Rawhouser, H., Nachiket, B., Neubaum, D. and Hayton, J. (2008). Globalization of social entrepreneurship opportunities. *Strategic Entrepreneurship Journal, 2*(2), 117–31.

Index